Nicholas Darnell

The Gentile and the Jew in the courts of the Temple of Christ

Volume II

Nicholas Darnell

The Gentile and the Jew in the courts of the Temple of Christ
Volume II

ISBN/EAN: 9783337017873

Printed in Europe, USA, Canada, Australia, Japan

Cover: Foto ©ninafisch / pixelio.de

More available books at **www.hansebooks.com**

THE
GENTILE AND THE JEW

IN THE

COURTS OF THE TEMPLE OF CHRIST:

AN

Introduction to the History of Christianity.

FROM THE GERMAN OF
JOHN J. I. DÖLLINGER,
PROFESSOR OF ECCLESIASTICAL HISTORY TO THE UNIVERSITY OF MUNICH.

BY

N. DARNELL, M.A.
LATE FELLOW OF NEW COLLEGE, OXFORD.

IN TWO VOLUMES.

VOL. II.

LONDON:
LONGMAN, GREEN, LONGMAN, ROBERTS, AND GREEN.
1862.

LONDON:
PRINTED BY ROBSON, LEVEY, AND FRANKLYN,
Great New Street and Fetter Lane.

CONTENTS OF VOLUME II.

BOOK VII.

THE RELIGIONS OF THE WEST: ETRURIA—ROME—GAUL—GERMANY.

I. *The Religion of the Etruscans.*

	PAGE
Connexion of the Etruscan religion with the Greek	1
Etruscan deities	2
Doctrine of lightning; importance of lightning	5

II. *The Religious System of the Romans.*

1. *Historical Development.*

Elements of Roman existence as a people and a religion	7
Religious distinction between patricians and plebeians	9
Agrarian ingredients in the Roman religion	10
Influence of Greek mythology	12
Dissection of the idea of God	13
Laboriousness of the ceremonial	15
The Regia, the centre of the worship	16
The Capitoline temple	19
Expulsion of the kings; the priesthood passes into the patrician families	20
Admission of the plebs to priestly functions	23
Religion as a political instrument	23
Hellenising of the gods	25
Numa's books	28
Introduction of foreign worships	29
Signs of decay in religion	31
Apotheosis	31
Varro's attempt at a restoration	34

2. *The Roman Gods.*

Service of Janus	35
Faunus Lupercus	37
Saturn	38

		PAGE
Jupiter, and his cultus	. . . .	39
Sol, Apollo .	. . . .	41
Mars .	. . . .	41
Other gods .	. . . .	42
Female deities: Ceres	. . . .	43
,,	Vesta	45
,,	Minerva	46
,,	Fortuna	47
,,	Juno	48
,,	Diana	49
,,	Venus	50
Liber and Libera	. . . .	51
The vast numbers of inferior deities	. . . . .	53
The Penates	. . . .	59
The Lares .	. . . .	60

3. *The Roman Priesthood.*

Rise of colleges of priests	63
The pontiffs: derivation of their name	64
,, their occupations	65
The king of sacrifice and the flamens . . .	66
The Salii, priests of Mars	67
The Luperci, the oldest of the Roman priests .	68
Epulones, Curiones, Augustales . . .	69
Vestal virgins: their origin and number	69
,, ,, privileges . .	70
,, ,, duties . . .	71
Augurs	72
,, their power and privileges . . .	73

4. *Roman Forms of Cultus. Prayers, Vows, Sacrifice, Ritual, and Festivals.*

Magical and formal character of prayer . .	75
Formulæ and essential contents of prayers . . .	76
Number and subject-matter of vows	77
Sacrifice	78
Choice of victims according to the peculiarities of the gods . .	79
Number of sacrifices	79
Expiatory sacrifices	81
Quality of the animal sacrificed	81
Purity required in the sacrificers	82
Rite of sacrifice	82
Lectisternia, or banquets of the gods . . .	84
Human sacrifice	85
Expiations and purifications, lustrations . . .	88
Festivals of the dead	89
,, ,, gods, feriæ	92

5. *Investigation of the Will of the Gods.*

	PAGE
Etruscan origin of Haruspicinium	99
Prodigies, how averted	99
Inspection of victims	100
Fulguratores	102
Augury from flight of birds	102
Soothsaying through the Sibylline books	106

III. *The Religions of the Gauls and the Germans.*

Druidism in Gaul	108
Great numbers of human sacrifices among the Gauls	111
Gaulish deities	112
The German religion according to Cæsar and Tacitus	113
German deities	114
Priests and sacrifice	116

BOOK VIII.

PHILOSOPHY AND RELIGION IN THE ROMAN EMPIRE FROM THE END OF THE REPUBLIC TO THE ANTONINES.

I. *Philosophy and Literature in their relations to Religion.*

1. *Philosophy in Rome: Lucretius, Cicero. The Roman Stoic School: Seneca, Epictetus. Platonico-Pythagorean Philosophy: Plutarch.*

The Greek philosophy penetrates into Rome	118
Didactic poem of Lucretius, the first fruit of Epicurean teaching	119
Cicero and his philosophy, sceptical eclecticism	119
,, his doctrine concerning God	121
,, his ethics	122
Partiality to Stoicism in Rome	124
Teaching of Seneca	125
Cornutus, Musonius	127
Epictetus	128
Marcus Aurelius	129
The Platonics, and their position in regard to the other schools	129
Plutarch the platonic and eclectic	131

2. *Literature: Diodorus, Strabo. The Poets of the Augustan age. Pliny, Tacitus.*

Religious creed of Polybius, Diodorus, and Strabo	135
,, the poet Manilius	136
,, Virgil and Ovid	137
Religious sentiments of Horace	138
,, ,, the elder Pliny and Tacitus	138

3. *Notions of a Future State.*

	PAGE
Uncertainty of these notions	139
Views of the older and new Stoics	140
Cicero on immortality	141
Doubts cast on immortality; their cause	143
Their connexion with the views entertained concerning the origin of the human race	144
The later Greek notions thereon, according to Plutarch and Lucian	145
Despondency	146

4. *The later Platonists and New-Pythagoreans.*

Return to a more believing mind	148
Platonists	148
New-Pythagoreans	148
Their interpretation of the popular gods	152

5. *Duration and Influence of the Schools of Philosophers; their Dissolution.*

Repute of the different schools, particularly those of the Stoics and Platonists	155
Degeneracy and decrease of their repute	156
Decay and dissolution	159

II. *State of Religion.*

1. *Idea of an Imperial Religion. Religious Tolerance and Persecution.*

Identification of foreign deities with the Roman	160
Realisation of an empire-religion thereby attained	161
Tolerance and intolerance of foreign worships	162

2. *Apotheosis.*

Deification of the emperors	165
,, female members of the imperial family	167
Private apotheosis	169

3. *The Element of Superstition.*

Blending of superstition with religious spirit	170
Examples: Sylla, Augustus, Alexander, &c.	172

4. *Fall of the old Roman Religion. Strange Gods and their Cultus. Female piety. Taurobolia. Inclination to Judaism. Theolepsy. Theopæa and Image-worship. Intercourse of Man with the Deity. Prayer.*

Decay of the old Roman religion	173
Reliance on foreign worships	174
Success of the cultus of Isis	176
,, ,, Serapis	178
Worship of the Idean Mother of the gods	178
Taurobolia and Criobolia connected with it	179

	PAGE
Judaism among the heathen	181
Theoleptics and Fanatics, possessed people	182
Theopæa, the science of inducting gods into their statues	184
Idolatry in its proper and narrowest sense	185
Ideas of a providence	186
Prayers, their material, nay immoral, objects	188

5. *Decay of Morality and Religion on the increase.*

The old believing sense still dominant	190
Impure worship of Aphrodite	192
Demoralisation through myths in themselves	193
,, intensified by the representations of them in mimes	194
,, by spectacles and gladiatorial combats	195
,, by impure paintings in houses and temples	196
Impurity in temples	197
Alexander the wizard	198
Religious juggleries and impostures	199

6. *The Oracles. Media of Divination. Dreams. Astrology.*

Renewed life in several of the oracles	202
Explanation of their extinction	204
Generality of belief in divination and dreams	206
Astrology penetrates into Rome	208

7. *Magic, Necromancy, and Theurgy.*

Close connexion between magic and the pagan religious system	210
Magic favoured by philosophy	211
Necromancy and oracles of the dead	213
Human sacrifice for magical purposes	214
Theurgy, the highest form of magic	215

BOOK IX.

THE SOCIAL AND MORAL STATE OF GREECE AND ROME, AND OF THE ROMAN EMPIRE.

I. *The Greeks.*

1. *Citizenship: Greek versus Barbarian. Political Freedom. Idleness and Industry. Position of the Rich. Slavery. Education.*

The personality of the Greek disappearing in the state	217
Opposition of Greek and Barbarian	218
Contempt of international law: the law of the stronger	219
Idea of freedom	220
Dependence of the individual on the state	222
Domination of poor over rich	223

	PAGE
Dislike of labour among the Greeks	224
Slavery: Aristotle's theory thereon	226
Number of slaves	226
Their treatment	228
Moral prejudice of slavery to slaves and masters	231
Education, and school instruction	231

2. *Women among the Greeks. Marriage. Hetairai. Paiderastia. Exposition of Children. Depopulation.*

Monogamy an advantage of the Greeks over the Orientals	233
Women nevertheless thought light of	233
Marriage a duty	234
Spartan legislation on marriage	235
Hetairai, and their relation to married women	237
Paiderastia, the Greek national vice	238
Socrates' and Plato's views upon it	240
Philosophers addicted to it	243
Its causes and effects	244
Exposition of children as good as allowed	246
Moral depravity of the later Greeks	247

II. *The Social and Moral Condition of the Romans.*

1. *Character of Roman Nationality. Roman jus privatum. Strangers. Power of the father of the Family.*

Roman national character: energy and egotism	248
Their jus privatum, a work of enduring value and effect	249
Freedom of citizens	250
Strangers out of the pale of the law	251
Household law	252

2. *Women in Rome: Marriage, Aversion to, and Divorce from, it.*

Women in Rome: forms of marriage	253
Marriage-contract by confarreation; divorce	254
Prevalence of divorces	256
Augustus, marriage-law of	257
Advantages of the unmarried state	258

3. *Slavery in Rome.*

Cruel treatment of slaves	259
Their numbers	262
Slaves and gladiators	265
Number of slaves in relation to that of freemen	266

4. *Effects of Slavery on the Free Population. Poverty. Exposition of Children. Small Number of Children. Paiderastia. Courtesans. Female Depravity.*

Slavery a principal cause of the corruption of morals	267
,, a cause of poverty	269

	PAGE
The exposition of new-born children an every-day affair	271
Practice of abortion	272
Paiderastia among the Romans	273
Women of pleasure	275
Infrequency of marriage	276
Female debauchery	277

5. *Treatment of the Poor. Education. Public Spectacles.*

The number of poor and of beggars	277
Hardheartedness of the rich towards them	278
Method of education: no public instruction	279
Slavery the principal source of the corruption of youth	281
Passion for public spectacles, particularly gladiatorial games	282
Contempt of life; suicide	283

6. *General Survey. Auguries of the Future.*

Spread of corruption of morals from Rome into the provinces	284
Impotence of Stoicism to stem the tide of ruin	285
,, philosophy generally	286
,, the worship of the gods	287
Objectlessness of life	288
Longings and hopes	289
The Capitol in Rome, and the Temple in Jerusalem	289

BOOK X.

I. *Historical Development of Judaism.*

1. *Until the Elevation of the Asmonean Dynasty.*

Beginning of the Jewish state	291
Its heyday under David and Solomon	292
Division into two kingdoms: Israel and Juda	293
The Captivity	293
,, return from	294
The Samaritans enemies of the Jews	295
Fusion of Jews with heathens	296
Their hellenising in foreign countries	297
The great Synagogue, and the teachers of the law	298
Persecution under Antiochus: rise of the Asmoneans	300

2. *The Chasidim. Sadducees, Pharisees, Essenes, Therapeutæ.*

The Chasidim or the pious	301
Their antipodes, the Sadducees	302
The Pharisees no sect, but representatives of the whole nation	305
,, the national teachers	307
Pharisaic expansion of the law	308

	PAGE
The Essenes: time of their rise	310
,, ascetical mode of life; akin to Pythagoreans	311
,, strict observance of the sabbath, and purity	312
,, cultus of the sun among	313
,, community of goods ,,	314
,, their position towards the dominant Judaism	316
The Therapeutæ, and their contemplative mode of life	316

3. *The Times of the Asmoneans and Family of Herod. The Roman Government.*

The Asmonee, John Hyrcanus; splendour of his reign	317
Crimes committed in the Asmonean family	318
Its overthrow	319
Pompey conquers Jerusalem	319
The Jews under the double yoke of Herod and the Romans	320
Heathenism, inclination of Herod to	321
His building of the Temple; his cruelties	322
The Jews under the immediate supremacy of Rome	323
The zealots against foreign rule	325
Increasing exasperation	326
Degradation of the office of high-priest	327
Expectation of the Messias	328
Philo's expectation of the same	331
Spirit of legal observance: its prejudicial effect	332
The schools of Hillel and Schammai	334

II. *The Law.*

1. *The Moral and Social Condition of the Jewish People according to the Law.*

Holiness the object of the law	335
Principle of love contained in the law	335
Contents of the law	336
Constitution	337
The Sanhedrim at Jerusalem	337
Marriage legislation	338
Polygamy tolerated	339
Position of the female sex	341
Ordinances regarding sexual relations	342
Slaves and their treatment	343
Law of love of neighbour	344
Care for the poor	344
Law of protection for the stranger and for animals	346
Kinds of punishment	347
Vengeance for blood limited	347

2. *The Religious Life.*

Circumcision	348
The Sabbath	349

	PAGE
Sabbatical and jubilee year	350
The Levites	351
The priesthood	352
Its service	353
Maintenance	354
The high-priest, his duties, and his vestments	355
His position in regard to the king	358
The Nazarite, the monk of the Old Testament	358
The prophets, and schools of the prophets	359
The Temple, its objects and its parts	362
Law forbidding images: its principle; its extent	363
Severity against every thing heathen	365
The proselytes, and their baptism	366
Sacrifice: its importance; materials of sacrifice	366
Different kinds of sacrifice	367
Burnt-sacrifice	368
Trespass-offering	368
Sin-offering	369
Peace- or thank-offering	371
Meat- and drink-offering	371
Prayer, not contained in law, but in tradition	372
Vows	372
Festivals	373
Day of atonement	375
Fasting-days	376
Synagogues	376
The clean and unclean	376

III. *The Religious Doctrines of the Jewish People.*

1. *Scripture and Tradition.*

Holy Scripture: its contents	377
Tradition	378

2. *God and the Angels.*

God: His incomprehensibility, and two chief names	380
His transcendance and other qualities	381
Anthropomorphism of holy Scripture	382
The doctrine of the Divine Wisdom	383
,, the angels	384
,, their fall; Satan	385

3. *Creation. Man and his Fall. God's Requirements of him. Penance. Death and the Future State.*

Creation of the world and of man	386
Fall; original sin; demands and mercy of God	387
Repentance and remission of sins	388
Notions concerning Sheol	389
Belief in the resurrection, and prayers for the dead	390

4. *Prophecies of the Messias.*

	PAGE
Importance of the prophecies of the Messias to the Jews	391
The older prophecies	392
The Son of David	392
The suffering Messias	393
Isaias, Daniel, and Zacharias touching the Messias	393

5. *Alexandrine Judaism: Philo's Doctrines.*

The temple of Onias	396
Aristobulus	397
Philo: his relation to the Greek philosophy	398
,, derives the Greek wisdom from Moses	400
Philo's teaching: the Deity	401
Matter: dualism	401
Mediate beings	402
The Logos	404
Angels and human souls	405
State after death	405
Composition of the human soul	406
The Fall: innate sinfulness	407
Philo's ethics; doctrine of grace	408
Ecstasy	408
Chiliastic notions of the Messias	408

6. *The last Days of the Jewish State, and Church Polity.*

The tyranny of the governors of the country	409
Hatred of the heathen	409
Corruption of the people	410
False prophets	411
The Zealots: their rule of terror	412
The eighteen resolves of the assembly in the house of Eleazar	412
Factions in Jerusalem, and their combats	413
Fate of captives after the taking of the city	414
Consequences of the destruction of the Temple	415
Impossibility of sacrificial worship	415
Hope in the restoration of the Temple	415
Sanhedrim and school at Jamnia	416
Rabbinism	416
Insurrections under Trajan and Hadrian	417
Bar Cochba	418
Ælia Capitolina	419

ERRATA IN VOL. II.

p. 3 l. 12 *for* Vidius   *read* Vedius
,, 205 ter   ,, Ænomaus ,, Œnomaus
,, 267 l. 31 ,, novetius ,, novitius
,, 290 ,, 20 ,, ago   ,, before

PART I.

THE GENTILE.

BOOKS VII. TO IX.

Encore que les philosophes soient les protecteurs de l'erreur, toutefois ils ont frappé à la porte de la Vérité (*Veritatis fores pulsant.* Tertullian). S'ils ne sont pas entrés dans son sanctuaire, s'ils non pas eu le bonheur de le voir et de l'adorer dans son temple, ils se sont quelquefois présentés à ses portiques, et lui ont rendu de loin quelque hommage.

BOSSUET, *Panég. de Ste. Cathérine.*

BOOK VII.

THE RELIGIONS OF THE WEST.
Etruria — Rome — Gaul — Germany.

I. The Religion of the Etruscans.

The Etruscan state in Central Italy comprised the Rasena, who had probably immigrated as conquerors from the north; the old subjugated population of the Umbrians, who were of kindred race with the Latins, and were anciently called Tusci, dwelling particularly in the southern parts of Etruria, between Tarquinii and Rome: and the people of the coast, of Greek origin, with the cities of Pisæ, Alsium, Agylla, and Pyrgi, names which sufficiently indicate they were Hellenic settlements. The Etruscans had received art and the commencement of a literature from Greece; the connexion of Corinth with Tarquinii is well attested. The Greek element, indeed, must have been lost in the cities of the coast, which declined so early as hardly to be mentioned again after the third century B.C.; but Greek influence is nevertheless unmistakable in the Etruscan religious system; and as the Rasena brought their own gods and notions of religion with them from the north, and adopted others from the conquered Tusci, the Etruscan religion is to be viewed as composed of three elements. The Tusci had certain Latin and Sabine deities, either in common with these kindred tribes from the first, or receiving them afterwards at their hands.

A purely Etruscan doctrine, and strange to Roman and Greek, was that of the " veiled deities,"[1] who were above even

[1] " Diis quos superiores et involutos vocant." Seneca, Quæst. Nat. ii. 41 (from Cæcina).

Jupiter, and yet were not objects of regular worship, but only resorted to by suppliants in certain cases, as supreme powers of destiny, from whom a respite from an impending calamity might be obtained.[1] The Consentes and Complices must have been distinct from these veiled deities. There were twelve of them, six of either sex, with names unknown, because kept secret, forming a council of gods, who stood at the side of Jupiter, but were inferior to him. Their name was given them, according to Varro, because they were born together and were to die together[2]—an idea reminding one of the mortal "Asen" of the north. Besides these were nine Novensiles, nine deities to dart the lightning, to whom alone Jupiter conceded the power of hurling his missiles; they included Juno, Minerva, Vejovis, Summanus, Vulcanus, Saturnus, and Mars.[3] Of the Tuscan penates there were by rights four species or classes—penates of Jupiter, of the sea, of the lower world, and of mortal men.[4]

Three supreme gods, Jupiter, Juno, and Minerva, necessarily had their temples in every city of Etruria that would pass for a city in the full sense of the term.[5] Jupiter, sometimes represented as seated and with a beard, sometimes standing and beardless, was called Tinia or Tina. A sun-god Usil, a god Aplu, corresponding to Apollo, Vulcan under the name of Sethlans, and a Bacchic Phuphluns, with Turms or Mercury, are known through works of Etruscan art. Varro calls the changeful god of the seasons Vertumnus, whom the Volsinian settlement had brought with them to Rome, a chief god of Etruria,[6] in spite of his Latin name. Juno Regina, as city goddess of Veii, was introduced into Rome by Camillus.[7] Juno Curitis (Juno of the lance), in the border town Falerii, by her Sabine surname made it known that even where a language, differing in dialect from the Etruscan, was spoken, a blending of races as well as of worship had taken place. In the older times, young maidens were actually sacrificed to the goddess, whose rite resembled that of the

---

[1] Serv. Æn. viii. 398, where, with O. Müller, Etr. ii. 108, we must read "postea a fatis."

[2] Arnob. iii. 40; Varro, R. R. i. 1; Mart. Capell. i. 41, p. 88, ed. Kopp.

[3] Arnob. iii. 8.

[4] Nigidius, in Arnob. iii. 40, says "Neptuni;" but Neptune appears not to have been an Etruscan god. The context shows that penates maris—"permarini," as they are styled in Livy, xl. 52—must have been meant.

[5] Serv. Æn. i. 422. [6] Varro, v. 14. [7] Livy, v. 21.

Argive Hera.¹ Cupra was the name of this Etruscan Juno, pointing to the circumstance that she had combined in herself the properties of Aphrodite and Hera; but on works of art there is also found an Aphrodite with the name Turan. The Volsinian head-goddess Nortia must have been a goddess of fortune or fate, for she is compared with Tyché and Nemesis.² The Romans probably imported from Etruria the worship of Minerva, who was also the patroness of flute-music there. Janus, represented in Falerii with four faces, was by Varro's account the all-seeing god of heaven there. Mantus, from whom the city of Mantua took its name, was the ruler of the lower world,³ and Vidius judge of the dead.⁴

Charun, a conductor of the dead, appears on Etruscan sepulchral monuments, deformed and with distorted countenance. This Etruscan Charon was distinct from the Greek one. He was an active demon of the dead and of hell, and not only conducted the shades into the nether world, but also murdered men, and tormented the souls of the wicked. He is delineated as an ugly, lean, gray-headed old man, frequently with the tusks and features of a beast of prey, armed with a hammer, sometimes also with a sword, and not seldom accompanied by other demons with serpents. He is also found represented as the messenger of death, leading or driving a horse on which the soul is sitting.⁵ The torments of departed souls in Orcus were not unfrequently represented by the Etruscans in their sepulchral chambers. In one of such, for instance, three souls are figured as naked men suspended to the ceiling by the hands, and demons with instruments of torture standing before them.⁶

The Etruscans shared the doctrine of Genii with the Romans. The wondrous boy Tages, who in the fields of Tarquinii sprang out of the soil opened by the plough, and communicated to the Lucumones the doctrines of divination by sacrifice, by the flight of birds, and by observation of the lightning, was the son of a Genius, and grandson of Jupiter.⁷ The Lares are in name Etruscan; and it seems Lar was the Tuscan name for all beings called by the Romans Genii, Penates, or Demons.⁸

[1] Plut. Parall. xxxv.
[2] Mart. Cap. i. 18, 9.
[3] Serv. Æn. x. 199.
[4] Mart. Cap. ii. 9, 3.
[5] Dennis, Cities and Cemeteries of Etruria, ii. 206 et sqq.
[6] Dennis, i. 318.
[7] Fest. s. v. "Tages;" Cic. de Divin. ii. 23.
[8] Gerhard, Gottheiten der Etrusker, in the Berl. Univ. Abhdl. 1845, p. 531.

The worship of the gods was worked up by the Etruscans into a regular science, which was pursued with a zeal and carefulness unequalled by almost any other people.[1] Hence, in the judgment of antiquity, the Etruscans had the credit of being the most religious nation of the whole West. This science was hereditary in the family of the Lucumones, a race of priestly nobles. Tages had chanted them his lessons of lore, and the Etruscans were admonished, once from Rome even, that at least six sons of distinguished families should be trained in this holy discipline, in order that a science, indispensable to the state, might not be degraded to a trade, when practised by persons of the lower ranks;[2] for the Romans themselves could never thoroughly master this science, and therefore made Etrurian haruspices come to Rome from time to time. The books of Tages, from which, besides the living tradition, the religious teaching and ordinances were drawn, were cast in a rhythmical mould. One part of them was the Acherontica, in which the double art was taught, one of converting souls into gods by means of the blood of certain beasts sacrificed to certain gods; and the other of averting, by similar means, a fatality which threatened human life, and of effecting a respite of the same; yet, according to Tuscan teaching, this delay could not be asked to extend beyond the eightieth year, for there were no means of obtaining such a favour from the gods; in general, however, it was inculcated in the Tagetic discipline that, by having recourse to the right method, an event decreed by destiny might be retarded for ten years.[3]

Besides the Acherontic books, there were also books ritual, fulgural, and augural, books of ostenta, and collections of old prodigies and oracles belonging to the sacred writings of the Etruscans. A work of equal reputation with the Tagetic writings, and ascribed to the Tuscan nymph Begoë, was the science of the fulgurita, or of reconciling places struck by lightning, and it was even preserved at Rome, along with the Sibylline books, in the temple of the Palatine Apollo.[4] These documents were con-

[1] Liv. v. 1.

[2] Cic. de Divin. i. 41. 92; comp. O. Müller's Etrusker, ii. 5, as to the right reading here.

[3] Arnob. ii. 62; Serv. Æn. viii. 399; Censorinus de Die Fat. c. xiv. p. 66, ed. Havere.

[4] Serv. Æn. vi. 72.

sulted by Tuscan interpreters of signs on emergencies. Learned Romans, such as the Pythagorean Nigidius Figulus, a friend of Cicero, studied them carefully, and used them in faith. Cornelius Labeo, at a still later date (the second century after Christ, or perhaps later) wrote a work in fifteen books upon the Etruscan discipline of Tages and Begoë. Umbricius, the haruspex of the Emperor Galba, was the author of an earlier treatise. But in Etruria, naturally the sacred science and art was acquired not only in books, but by colleges and schools for the purpose, at the head of which an old haruspex of tried sagacity was usually placed. The essential contents of this doctrine or discipline were formed of a doctrine drawn out into an artificial system, upon the means and the ceremonies necessary to investigate the will of the gods, and, when ascertained, to appease them and avert the evil, should it signify misfortune or threaten harm.

No people in the world have attributed so great importance to thunder and lightning as the Etrurians did. Lightning was to them the most distinguished instrument of divine manifestation, the surest source from which the knowledge of the divine will was to be drawn, the language in which Tinia conversed with them; it was the one irrevocable presage; its errand could not be rendered futile or be changed by any other sign; but it had the essential power of blotting out all other signs and communications of knowledge,[1] descending, as it did, immediately and instantaneously upon earth, from the hands of God, its ruler. The prognostics of evil afforded by the entrails of the victim, or the flight and notes of birds, were looked upon as set aside so soon as a flash of good promise had ensued. Even Pliny thought it not to be doubted but that the Tuscan science had advanced so far in the interpretation of the lightning as to predict with accuracy, if, on a particular day, other lightnings would take place, nay, if a flash was meant to avert a doom, or to indicate another and hidden doom.[2]

It was one of the first tasks devolving upon the Tuscan science of fulguration to decide what god it was who had hurled the lightning; for there were nine gods who performed that feat.

---

[1] So the Etruscan Cæcina, in Seneca, Qu. Nat. ii. 34; comp. Micali, Storia degli ant. Pop. Ital. ii. 156.

[2] Plin. H. N. ii. 53.

Jupiter had three manubiæ, or kinds of lightning. That which he sent according to his own good pleasure showed him to be well-inclined and placable, and was a mere reminder; that, on the contrary, which he threw with the advice of the twelve gods, called Consentes, was an indication at times of something good, but always involving a punishment or damage; while the lightning, hurled only after he had taken the veiled gods into his counsels, announced a change of the whole present situation, to individuals, as well as to the state.[1] These distinctions were recognised in the colour and effects, in the quarter of heaven the lightning came from, and other circumstances. The Etruscans had divided the heaven into sixteen regions, and distributed the gods amongst them. The author and the import of the lightning were decided according to the quarter from which it issued, and still more by that to which it returned. Lightnings which apparently came from the earth were held to be particularly baneful.[2] As, moreover, they were not taken in a passive sense, simply as unexpected signs of the divine will, but as formally demanded, and calculated beforehand, the Tuscan haruspices had divided them into three classes. If the lightning happened after the resolution and before the execution of a purpose, it was a counselling flash, and showed if the matter was to be executed or to be given up; if the flash followed after the act was already completed, it was one of "authorisation," and prognosticated whether good or evil was to come of it; in fine, if the lightning appeared at a time when any thing was going on in a general way, in that case it was a "reminder," threatening or calling to action. According to the duration of their import, there were lightnings indicating—some, an influence to extend over a whole life, or a determinate time only; others prorogative, the operation of which might be delayed. There were also "domestic lightnings," appearing at birth, or marriage, or succession to an inheritance.[3]

All places where lightning struck were holy, and required a particular consecration and atonement, in accordance with the Tuscan rite, adopted even in Rome. The spot had to be converted into a templum, *i. e.* a place consecrated by auspices, and to be enclosed. The lightning was buried—that is, the earth.

---

[1] Seneca, Qu. Nat. ii. 41.
[2] Pliny, H. N. ii. 53; Seneca, Qu. Nat. ii. 49.
[3] Pliny, H. N. ii. 53; Seneca, Qu. Nat. ii. 39-41.

thrown up by it, or other matters struck by it, were put into the ground at the very spot, and the place consecrated by the sacrifice of a two-year-old sheep, therefore called bidental. Such a place was not to be touched, or even looked at. Whoever destroyed it was punished by the gods with loss of reason.[1] There were formulæ, besides, belonging to the Tuscan secret discipline, by which lightning could be drawn down from heaven, partly by way of entreaty, partly, too, by compulsion; and as late as the fifth century after Christ the Tuscan haruspices thought it was they who had protected the town of Narnia by these means from Attila, and offered to protect Rome too by "the arms of Jupiter."

THE RELIGIOUS SYSTEM OF THE ROMANS.

I. Historical Development.

A Latin settlement on the Palatine hill by the Ramnes formed the groundwork of the Roman state. These were joined by the Sabine community of the Tities on the Quirinal. The united community bore the name of Quirites, and were at first under a double kingdom, which soon passed into an elective monarchy, with a senate and a popular assembly. The Latin element was, and continued to be, the predominant one; and the Ramnes retained, on the whole, the same gods and forms of worship as the Latins generally had in their old towns of Laurentum, Lavinium, Alba, Ardea, &c. But the Latins, as well as the Umbrian Sabines, were a race of the same stock as the Hellenes, being descended, like them, from a common aboriginal people; and the elements of the old Italic religions that are of kin to the Greek system of worship are partly to be explained by these relations of race, partly by intercourse with the Greek commercial marts and colonies in central and lower Italy. It was specially Cyme (Cumæ), the oldest of the Greek colonies on the western coast of Italy, which exercised an important influence, even in religious matters, on Latium as well as Rome.

The Sabines or Tities had, above all, the Vesta worship, in common with the Latin Ramnes; for this worship of the hearth-

---

[1] Varro, v. 42; Pers. ii. 27. cum schol.; Amm. Marc. xxiii. 5; Hor. Ars Poet. 471.

goddess was universal in families of the Hellenic Italian race. Quirinus, on the other hand, and Sancus, the mythical ancestor and king of the Sabine people, with his sanctuary on the Quirinal, and Sun-god, were the deities whose worship was at first peculiar to the Sabine settlement.[1] The primeval sanctuary of the three associate deities, Jupiter, Juno, and Minerva (the last probably a stranger to the Latins originally), which stood upon the old Capitoline, *i.e.* Quirinal, prior to the Capitoline temple, was of Sabine origin. So strong was this distinction between the Sabine and the Latin form of religion felt in Rome, that a particular association was formed expressly for the purpose of preserving the Sabine rite.

In process of time, a third element, a tribus or tribe, composed of Roman population, that of the Luceres, was annexed to the Ramnes and Tities, the origin of which was obscure even to the ancients. Yet it may be recognised as having been composed of Alban Latins, who came and settled at Rome after the destruction of their city. This third race, receiving constant reinforcements from Latin settlers, attained an equality of rights with the two first, under the Tarquinii. An Etruscan immigration, according to the saga, under Cœles Vibenna, is likewise mentioned; and from him the Tuscan quarter in Rome derived its name. Thus Rome acquired a mixed population of Latins, Sabines, and Etruscans, as the towns of Fidenæ and Crustumerium had, except that the Etruscans fell short of the other two in numbers, importance, and political rights. The Roman religion was also formed, in essentials, of two very different and peculiar, though indeed kindred, national worships—the Latin and the Sabine. From Alba and Lavinium came the primeval rite of Vesta, with its priesthood; Janus, Jupiter, and Juno, Saturn and Ops, Diana and Mars, with the Salian institute, and that of the Arvalian brothers;—this and more all formed part of the Latin religious system; and that this was for a length of time independent of the Sabine, in Rome, is proved by the feast of the Septimontium, during which sacrifice was offered in seven different places in Rome, none of which were in the Sabine settlements. Nevertheless a later saga made the Sabino-Roman king Numa into the real founder of religion, and legislator of

[1] Comp. Ambrosch, Studien, pp. 160-172; Preller, Röm. Mythol. pp. 633-637, and notes.

the divine ritual in the Roman state. Regulations have been ascribed to him, while master of a petty state, still in its infancy, and confined within a very limited jurisdiction, which in part are clearly antique and pre-Roman, and in part exhibit a more matured political development. It was he, they said, who introduced the Vesta worship, the Salii, the Pontifices, and Flamines, the Augurs, Feciales and Curiones; and established the cultus of Quirinus to the honour of Romulus, and those of Terminus, the Manes and Libitina; and his intercourse with the nymph Egeria was to impress the seal of a higher and divine revelation upon these institutions, in order to free them from the suspicion of being the arbitrary production of mere political wisdom in a legislator. Now, though it quite contradicts every law of history to discern in any one individual the creator of the complete Roman cultus, which so clearly shows itself to be the product of a longer development, and on the whole to be the organic creation of the Roman people, the saga, nevertheless, by a violent anachronism, converted Numa into a Pythagorean philosopher, and there was discovered a striking resemblance between his religious directions and their maxims. Accordingly Castor the Rhodian, a contemporary of Cicero, instituted a comparison between the Roman institutes and Pythagorean precepts. The fact of the Roman people having for one hundred and seventy years worshiped their gods without statues, was interpreted as a law of Numa, which, in keeping with the Pythagorean creed, forbade the Romans to set up human or animal representations of the gods.[1] With the like object, he was supposed to have instituted unbloody sacrifices chiefly, consisting merely of coarse sacrificial cakes and other inconsiderable things—a presumption not borne out by history, and only invented to bear out a theory; the plain truth being, that such Roman rites as bear the stamp of a higher antiquity were, for the most part, connected with the sacrifice of animals.

In the older times of the republic the plebs formed a portion of Rome, quite distinct in a religious point of view. Having had its origin in the Latin country-folk who had settled in the city, and in the citizens of petty towns dismantled, who had been attracted thither, and consisting of peasants and husbandmen in a preponderating degree, it took its place, like a distinct

[1] Clem. Alex. Strom. i. p. 358. Pott.

but subject people, by the side of the old patrician burghers. The plebeians had no portion in the worship and religious functions of the old citizenship. The patricians, being alone qualified for them by descent and purity of blood, remained in exclusive possession of the priesthood and of the religious tradition transmitted in their families, thus forming, in contrast to the plebeians, a close priest-caste, to each member of which, by right of birth, one sacerdotal function belonged, that of taking auspices to ascertain the divine will; and as the application of these was indispensable in an officer of the state, therefore no plebeian could enter upon office. On the same principle of religious separation, no connubium could take place between patrician and plebeian. Accordingly, as often as the plebeians made an effort to obtain office, the cry was, that divine and human things were being confounded, and the sacred ceremonies profaned; and that the gods regarded the attempt as a sin, and their anger threatened the republic with calamity.[1]

Such a state of things could not continue: in spite of the patrician notion that the deity itself had established such distinctions between men for ever, the plebeians won their way, step by step, to access to the different offices of state, and, as is at the same time self-evident, to the right of the auspices of the office, though still not without a certain dependence upon the patrician augurs and pontiffs. But they remained further excluded from sacerdotal functions proper till the Ogulnian law, in the year 452 A.U.C. Thus, up to that time, they could offer no more than a private worship to the public gods of Rome, and be present as spectators of the sacrificial actions, and not all of them; and yet they retained their own worship and their own sanctuaries, which they had brought with them from their earlier homes.

The oldest elements of the Roman religion pointed to agriculture, and indeed to the pastoral life, in some of its features. The old Latin god Saturn owed his name to sowing. After the beasts of the flock, the commonest offering was toasted flour, from which the most solemn of the forms of marriage had its name of *confarreatio*. The oldest Latin deities, Picus and Faunus, were patron gods of agriculture; the first, Picus, or Picumnus, was the inventor of manure, as his brother Pilumnus of grinding;[2] Faunus, himself a husbandman, but seer and soothsayer

[1] Liv. i. 11; iv. 2; v. 14; vi. 41; x. 6.   [2] Serv. Æn. ix. 4.

besides, had a son Stercutius, also honoured as inventor of manure.[1] Mars even, though otherwise god of death, and in his principal aspect a deity of ruin and destruction, was at the same time an agrarian divinity, invoked to avert blight and mildew from the standing corn; to keep the flocks and herds in health; and having vows made to him for the well-being of the cattle.[2] There were soon special gods for all the occupations of agriculture, for sowing, ploughing, harrowing, and grafting. The very day the manure was carried from the temple of Vesta was a half-festival day; and to kill a plough-ox was as great a transgression as killing a man.[3] The offering of milk on the Palilia betrayed the pastoral origin of the feast, which was a principal one till the latest times of the empire; and Pales, in fact, was a goddess of herbage.[4] So too with the service of Rumina, a shepherd-goddess of suckling and rearing, to whom offerings of milk were made even after the Christian period.[5] The institution of the Fratres Arvales, on whom lay the performance of sacrifice for the fertility of the fields, and the conducting of the victims about the newly ploughed land, was referred to Romulus himself, and he was fabled to have been the first of these priests, who was decked out in a crown of ears of corn, tied round with a white fillet.[6]

A mythology such as the Grecian is quite foreign to the Roman system. The Romans troubled themselves not with the origin of things, nor how the human race arose: they took the world as they found it to hand. It was no anxiety to them how it came into existence; myths, cosmogonic and theogonic, had no interest for, nor place with, them. There are indeed indications of this disposition. Particular gods have wives. Picus is son of Saturn, and is himself the father of Faunus;[7] but these gods do not, like the Homeric deities, form a great family: the Romans knew nothing of successive dynasties of gods, or of their warfare. These gods have no history, generally speaking; and if Augustin called attention to the fact that it was entirely of the greater gods, the 'Selecti' of Varro, that such scandalous things and impurities were told, while nothing of the kind was mentioned of the minor deities,[8]

---

[1] Plin. H. N. xvii. 6.   [2] Cato, R. R. lxxxiii.
[3] Colum. R. R. vi. pr. "tam capitale."   [4] Serv. in Georg. iii. 1.
[5] Aug. C. D. vii. 11.   [6] Plin. H. N. xviii. 2; Gell. vi. 7.
[7] Aug. C. D. xviii. 15.   [8] Ibid. vii. 1.

the ground of his assertion was this, that when the fusion of Roman and Greek deities took place, the Hellenic myths were also transferred to the Roman deities. It was also on this account that the genuine Italic Janus, though one of the greater gods, formed an exception: of him there were no myths, as he could not be blended with any Greek deity. Hero-worship, too, was strange to the Romans. Romulus even was not worshiped as a hero properly speaking, but as a god, after he had been identified with the great Sabine god Quirinus: and Numa was never worshiped in Rome, though, as creator and arranger of the Roman religious system, as favourite of Egeria, and conciliator of Jupiter,[1] furnished with magical powers, he had, agreeably to Greek notions, appropriated the character of hero to himself before all others, and had earned a full title to an heroic cultus. It is true that single sons of gods make their appearance, here and there, in the old Latin and Roman sagas; but their birth was explained in a different way from that of the Greek myths; the god had appeared as a phallus in the ashes of the hearth, or as a spark had shot from out the hearth into the woman's womb.

The chief deities of the Romans, before they had been coloured by Greek inspiration, were general nature-powers, or mere abstractions of the human state; they advanced to no real personality, but, on the contrary, remained far behind the plastic individualisation of the Hellenic deity-world. The Romans had no religious poetry, no Homer or Hesiod to give their gods a form, and breathe life into them. Their sacerdotal books, besides being inaccessible to the people, contained only dry registers of the names of gods, with a short account of their sphere of action, and the peculiarities of their rites. This was all changed when the Roman circle of gods was enlarged by numerous accessions from without, and many of their forms were humanised by being blended together with corresponding Greek deities; but under the influence of Greek mythology, and, somewhat later, of Greek philosophy, the old reverence for the gods died away; the firm belief in the universality and comprehensiveness of their power was shaken; and the downfall of the state-religon, like a severe internal and incurable malady, began with attacking the upper ranks, and so infected the whole body of the state.

[1] See Preller, Römische Mythol. p. 170; Ovid. Fasti, iii. 267 et sqq., and other passages there cited.

The importance of Greek mythology to the Roman religious system must not, however, be estimated by the position which it occupied in Roman literature. The poets made many myths and mythical ideas their own, as poetical matter, which never passed into the religious creed of the Roman people. Among the Romans there never could arise the case of such personal relations to particular gods as we find drawn in the most glowing colours in Greek poetry, and as was not unfrequently met with in actual life. Even in the zenith of his state and of his religion, the Roman did, without preference for this or that god, just as much as law and custom demanded of him, not more, and not less. It never occurred to him to draw closer to one god or the other, or to attach himself particularly to the service of one. But in this way the Roman system of gods, quite differently from the Greek, was the most faithful of mirrors, in which every act and constituent portion of public as well as private life was accurately reflected. The world of a Roman's gods was, so to say, the "double" of his daily doings and movements; whatever he undertook, a special deity was sure to be at hand; whatever happened in nature among the beasts, in vegetable or human life, the intervention of a god had wrought it; and the immediate practical requirements of life were the soul and generating principle of this religious system.

The Roman religion, as regards the nature of the deity, presents two peculiarities, which at first sight completely contradict one another. On one side there is a bias to monotheism running through it; there must have been one single nameless god in existence at its mysteriously veiled commencement, who, in the event, turned into a Jupiter Optimus Maximus, but was never entirely lost to the conscience of the Romans, therefore they continued, even till late times, to invoke him in the most violent and irresistible of natural phenomena, such as the earthquake. Rightly does Augustin assert that all the manifold gods and goddesses were, in the end, but the one Jupiter,[1] for these gods melt away into each other on nearer inspection. So near they are of kin, and so closely do they run into one another, that at last one is driven to a single god, comprising in his one self all the powers of nature in undistinguishable unity and totality; to a god, who, by the dissection of his essence into the various aspects of his operations,

[1] Aug. C. D. iv. 11.

and by the personising of his individual powers and properties, has been resolved into a multiplicity of gods.

Now the Romans went further than any other people of antiquity in this breaking-up of the idea of God, in the hypostasising of particular powers, modes of operation, physical functions and properties. From the earliest times they were in the habit also of personifying human qualities and actions, whilst making them into expressions of a divine being. In this way they swelled the number of gods so incalculably, that the generality of Romans were far from being acquainted with the names even of all their deities, and we, too, remain in ignorance of many of them, including such as had a worship of their own. A single human action, for example, the conclusion or consummation of a marriage, was actually split up into a number of moments, each of which was shaped into a deity of its own. Once on this road, there was no resting-place; the god-casting business could never be wound up. In proportion as the customs and fashions of life changed, and assumed richer and more copious forms, new requirements came in, new institutions arose, and new deities had necessarily to be formed, or, in reality, coined for the emergency; and it is one of the strange things in the Roman religious system, that one can get a peep, so to say, of the workshop where the process went on. It lay within the sphere of a pontiff's vocation. The pontifices had to take care that each new want and new element in political life received its god, either by enlargement of the occupations of a god who had already become an object of worship, or by the introduction of the service of a new one. Thus the Romans had a goddess Pecunia, who may have belonged quite to the early times, when buying or bartering took place through the exchange of cattle, instead of coined money. But when, after the time of Servius Tullius, the use of copper money became common in Rome, there arose a god Æsculanus; and when, about the year 485 A.U.C., silver money also came to be coined, a god Argentarius had to be intercalated, who, of course, was a son of this Æsculanus.

In the fourth century of the same era, when a voice, heard down from the Palatine, was said to have announced the approach of the Gauls, the Greeks, in such a case, would have discerned to a nicety which of their known gods or heroes such voice belonged to; the Romans, on the contrary, were equally ready with a new deity for the occasion: he was styled Aius Locutius, and had a sacellum built for him on the spot from which the voice proceeded.[1]

As the number of deities increased from within, by new creations of numina and by the progressive dismemberment and hypostasising of particular properties in the gods already known, so it waxed in proportion, from without, by the violent naturalisation of foreign and conquered gods. In old times, so often as a hostile city was besieged and taken by storm, the custom was, after a certain preliminary ceremonial, to invite the gods of it to leave and settle away at Rome. They were promised in their new domicile the same service, and still more zealous worship than they had hitherto enjoyed; and as it was hardly possible to extend a becoming public cultus to all, they were in part distributed amongst Roman families, where they were treated with a private one.[2] Now this worship must have been the same as that practised at their homes; for every god was jealous about the maintenance of the original form of his worship, as established in accordance with his own will. Hence the Romans were careful that images, ritual books, and every thing pertaining to the cultus, should be brought from the conquered city to Rome, and the pontiffs saw to the proper application of these things.[3]

As, in this manner, whole troops of gods and an unmanageable amount of the most various forms of worship, ceremonial, and sacrifice, came to be crowded into a single city, the priests required special books of their own, in which to record the names of the gods and the rites of their worship. These 'indigitamenta' must have been, in part, of great antiquity, and in their first rough form have descended from the regal period; for they were afterwards appealed to, in order, from the omission of a god's name in them, as for instance of Apollo, to infer his introduction at a later time.[4] But the worship, as indicated in these indigitamenta, and other old records or traditions, was in reality not expensive; for all that was requisite was to be taken from the most obvious necessaries of life, and could easily

[1] Liv. v. 32-52; Cic. de Div. i. 45.
[2] Arnob. iii. 38; Prudent. contra Symm. ii. 346; Macrob. Sat. iii. 9; Serv. Æn. ii. 351.
[3] Liv. i. 38; v. 22; xxvi. 34. [4] Arnob. ii. 73; cf. Macrob. Sat. ii. 12.

be procured; but was none the less tiresome, wasteful of time, and imperative on the whole man; so much so, that Tertullian compares Roman religious discipline with the burdensome yoke of the Mosaic law; and the ancients were of opinion that Numa —for to him the entire religious legislation was ascribed—intended, by the imposition of this galling yoke, to soften and tame a people still wild.[1] For here even, the least thing was of the greatest importance, and had to be looked to with a painful accuracy and anxious vigilance, and to be executed strictly according to rule. As the Romans believed in, and were convinced of, the omnipotence of formula and ceremony, and that the gods were thereby compelled to lend themselves to the will of man,— for instance, to desert a city they had inhabited hitherto and leave it a prize to the besiegers,—so they were fully impressed with the belief that all the virtue and activity of the formula depended on the most liberal and punctual fulfilment possible of the solemn words and actions. A single omission or word out of place attracted a guilt that required a special expiation, or made the repetition of the whole act inevitable. It sometimes happened that a sacrifice had to be repeated thirty times, because a mistake had been made every time, or an unlucky circumstance had occurred. In the sacred games and chariot-races of the gods, if an actor came to a dead stop, or a flute-player paused suddenly, or a driver let the reins fall,—here was a mischance foreboding evil, and requiring an instant atonement. Cornelius Cethegus and Quintus Sulpicius were both removed from the sacerdotal dignity at the same time, because the first had not laid the entrails of the victim upon the altar quietly, according to rule; the other because his priest's cap had fallen off his head. If, at a festival where images of the gods or other sacred objects were being carried about on litters, a horse became tired or stopped, or one of the conductors took the reins in his left hand, so surely it was at once determined to celebrate the desecrated feast again.[2]

The centre of Roman cultus in the older times was the Regia in the Forum, formerly Numa's house, partly used as a residence for the Pontifex, and partly as a sanctuary, in which the sacred spears of Mars were kept. Here the supreme gods

[1] Tertull. Præser. xl.; Cicero de Rep. ii 14; Liv. i. 21.
[2] Arnob. iv. 31.

of old Rome, Janus, Jupiter and Juno, Mars and Ops, were adored: the service was conducted by the king in person, and afterwards by the sacerdotal dignitaries who supplied for him, the sacrificial king (rex sacrorum), the two Flamines, the Dialis and Martialis, and the Pontifex Maximus. Close at hand stood the Vesta-temple. Next to the Regia, the Palatine was reckoned the seat of the genuine Roman gods, whilst the Sabine deities were seated on the Quirinal. On this hill stood the old Capitol, with the sanctuary dedicated to the three deities, Jupiter, Juno, and Minerva. Seven objects of veneration,—the conical stone, the earthen chariot of Jupiter from Veii, the ashes of Orestes, the sceptre of Priam, the veil of Helena, the ancile thrown down from heaven by Jupiter, and the Palladium,—were most carefully preserved as protectors of and securities for the eternal duration of the city. And yet, the whole of the hallowed objects and rites indispensable to the Romans were not to be found in Rome. The city had no Penates of its own, for they belonged to and remained at Lavinium, the old metropolis of the Latin confederation, whose daughter Rome was, and the "first city of the Roman line," as Varro styled her.[1] There were kept Trojan images of the gods, in clay; and in the very times of the highest power and pride of the state, none of the higher officers entered office, none laid it down, nor did a proconsul leave Italy, without having first sacrificed in Lavinium to Vesta and the Penates, guardian-gods of Rome.[2] Every year, there the Roman flamines and augurs offered sacrifice in the name of the Roman people.[3] It was from thence, also, the legend of the Trojan settlement in Latium had come to Rome, and of Æneas, after his disappearance from the battle-field on the bank of the Numicius, exalted to the rank of Jupiter Indiges,—for such were called Indigetes, or indigenous deities, as had first dwelt in Latium in human form, and were deified after their death.[4] Æneas, in his sanctuary on the Numicius, received every year from the Roman authorities a worship, of the antiquity of which, however, no account can be rendered.

In the time of the Tarquins, Etruscan, and, in a still higher

---

[1] Varro, v. c. 32; Dionys. viii. 21.
[2] Macrob. Sat. iii. 4; Serv. Æn. ii. 296; Val. Max. i. 6, 7.
[3] Ascon. in Cic. Scaur. p. 21; Serv. Æn. viii. 664; comp. Zumpt de Lavinio, p. 21. [4] Macrob. in Somn. Scip. c. ix.

degree, Greek influence worked upon the religious sense of the Romans, modifying their system of gods and their forms of worship. It was in particular Cumæ, in the neighbouring Campania, a colony of the Æolian town Cyme, and the oldest of all the Hellenic settlements in Italy, which was the medium of this influence; and from there the form of written letters and the Sibylline books found their way to Rome. By the same way probably some knowledge of the Homeric poems, or at least of the Homeric cycle of legends, reached Rome; for Octavius Mamilius, son-in-law of Tarquin, traced his pedigree from Ulysses and Circe; and a temple of Circe and a cup of Ulysses were to be found in the town of Circeii, a foundation of the older Tarquin. The Latin federal sanctuary of Diana, on the Aventine, was built under Servius Tullius, on the model of the Ephesian Artemis-temple, and the wooden idol of the goddess resembled that of the Phocæans of Massilia (with whom the Romans had at that time concluded an alliance), and, therefore, resembled the one at Ephesus also.[1] We must not omit to add to the above instances the religious intercourse between Rome and the Phocæan colonial town Velia, as also with the Tuscan one of Cære, which was so closely connected with Greece as to have a treasury of its own at Delphi.

It was, then, owing to Greek influence that the important transition from the hitherto imageless worship to the use and worship of wooden and clay idols now came in. Until Tarquin's time, the Romans had only used holy symbols or fetishes, such as those already mentioned, and the stone worshiped as Jupiter; so that, quite at a late date, the most solemn oaths sworn were by Jupiter the Stone.[2] Now and henceforth images of the gods were prepared for the new temples in Rome by Etruscan artists, whose craft had already been developed under Greek influences. Through the Sibylline books the Greek gods and their cultus came into Rome; the worship of Apollo, to whom the first temple was vowed in the year 351 A.U.C., in consequence of the great epidemic, thirty-four years later, and, on the same authority and for the same reason, a lectisternium was prepared for Latona, along with Apollo, Artemis, and other Grecian deities.[3] In the year 463, in order to guard

---

[1] Strabo, p. 180; Dionys. ii. 22, iv. 25; Liv. i. 45.
[2] Polyb. iii. 25; Cic. ad Fam. vii. 12; Gell. i. 21. 4.   [3] Liv. v. 13.

against a lingering pestilential sickness, the cultus of Æsculapius was introduced from Epidaurus into Rome;[1] and finally, in 549, Cybele, the Idæan mother, was brought from Pessinus in Phrygia, in the shape of a black stone, and her worship naturalised in Rome by order of the Sibylline books.[2] The Decemviri or Quindecemviri, too, to whom the consulting of the Sibylline books was intrusted, had to perform their religious functions, not according to the Roman, but the Greek, ritual; particular decrees of the senate, made on the spur of occasions, directed them to that most distinctly.[3] "It was not an insignificant brooklet," said Cicero, "but a rich and copious stream of Hellenic discipline that here poured into the city."[4] By frequent embassies to Delphi to consult the oracle, this fusion of Roman and Greek gods and rites acquired a new impetus.

Another event, and one fraught with important consequences in the province of religion, was the building of the Capitoline temple, and the founding of the worship there. Hitherto the Sabine Romans had been in possession of the old Capitol on the Quirinal, with a sacellum of three deities; but now the religious blending of the three races was to be attained through a new and common sanctuary, and the political and national unity of the Romans thereby strengthened. This requirement seemed to be all the more pressing, as the Luceres up to this time had retained their own rites, while the Plebs, in a complete religious isolation, had never been admitted to a share of those of either of the two first races. The new national sanctuary was to be built on the Tarpeian rock; but as this was already occupied by the altars and chapels of the old Quirinic gods, the process of evocation had to be resorted to. By sacrifice and promises of other temples, they were accordingly enticed from the spot; but as Terminus, Juventas, and Mars, refused to budge, they were therefore included in the circuit of the temple. This Terminus, a mere shapeless stone, which was afterwards taken for a boundary-stone and converted into the god Terminus,[5] was probably no other than the old Jupiter Lapis. Of the three cells of the new Capitoline temple, the central one was set apart for Jupiter, the two side ones for Juno and Minerva; gods, that is, who belonged

---

[1] Liv. x. 47. epit. 11; Val. Max. xviii. 1, 2.
[2] Liv. xxix. 10; Varr. vi. 15; Strabo, p. 567; Ovid. Fast. iv. 257.
[3] Varr. vii. 88; Liv. xxv. 12.   [4] De Rep. ii. 19.   [5] Lact. i. 20-37.

of old to all the races represented at Rome—Latins, Sabines, and Etruscans.

By this time the Roman state had acquired a territory of considerable extent in the heart of Italy. Several nations recognised her supremacy. The new Capitol became the religious centre of this empire, and there was no lack of portents and predictions to the effect that the will of the gods had assigned the sovereignty of the wide world to this state, and attached it to this particular spot for all time.[1] Images of all the gods were by degrees set up in the Capitol.[2] All presents which the state and its allies devoted to Jupiter were deposited here; all religious acts connected with the welfare of the entire community were here performed, and done in honour of the Capitoline deities. On the other hand, the old worship of the gods in the Regia now lost somewhat of its earlier importance; it was, at least in later times, exercised by priests of the older establishment, but without the people, or any class of them, having a share in it.

The Hellenisation of Rome was in full career when the downfall of the sovereign power, and with it the circumscription of the kingdom founded in Middle Italy by the last kings, took place. By this event a stop was put for a length of time to Roman familiarity with the seats of Greek worship and civilisation. The whole movement was, at the same time, one of complete reaction against the in-coming tide of exotic Greek elements, or, at any rate, its working was such; and it strengthened the exclusive sacerdotal supremacy of the old citizen or patrician families. Hitherto the king had been supreme head of the priesthood, and of the cultus as a whole, and a priest himself, in the proper sense of the word. This high-priesthood now was transferred to the gentes, who, without it, already enjoyed the privilege of filling up vacancies in all the sacerdotal dignities from their own body. For, according to old Roman notions, the genuine rite, and the only one acceptable to the gods and effective, was a something propagated in gentes attaching to birth, and not transferable to others of alien blood; it was, at the same time, a secret, on the observance of which the whole welfare of the state hung; and if strangers and foes succeeded in

---

[1] Liv. i. 55; Dionys. iv. 61; Flor. i. 7.
[2] Serv. Æn. ii. 319; Tertull. de Spectac. xii.

furtively obtaining and appropriating to themselves a Roman rite, or in learning the hallowed and secret names of deities, and therefore resorted to the practice of evocation, what mischief might not result therefrom to the republic! Thus, then, the entire state-worship was exclusively in patrician hands until the Ogulnian law (452 A.U.C.). The plebeians had only the private worship of the Roman gods allowed them. It is true they might have continued to practise the worship of their ancestral gods, but even so only in private.[1] Yet they celebrated in common the ancient feast of the Septimontium, national to the Plebs, divided into seven hill-circuits; and the solemnity of the Compitalia, introduced by Servius Tullius, had the like object of plebeian worship; the whole city was divided into compita of the Lares (of which, in Pliny's time, there were 265),[2] resembling parishes, and at the corner of every street in Rome stood the sacella of the compitales, like the Hermæ at Athens. Here to the Lares of each vicus offerings were presented, and sacrifices performed by the families included within the district.[3]

The religious functions which the kings had discharged passed after the fall of the kingdom to the sacerdotal office of the rex sacrorum, or sacrificial king, created for the purpose; he was, however, stripped of all political importance, excluded from all offices of state, and chosen by the colleges of pontiffs and augurs. He was himself under the authority of the Pontifex maximus, though in reality he had precedence of him in his religious character, and therefore also ranked before him at the banquets of the gods. This dignity was of course only accessible to patricians; and they also succeeded in maintaining an exclusive possession of these priestly offices from the beginning of the republic, for the space of 209 years, in spite of all the pressure from the plebs. Besides this, many patrician families had their own private worship of gods, and priests of their own, such privileges being founded in part on a fabulous pedigree, and in part on special historical grounds. Thus the Nautii derived the service kept up within their family to Minerva, from a certain Nautes who had accompanied Æneas to Italy, and had brought the image of the goddess with him.[4] The Aurelii had a worship

---

[1] Liv. i. 31. [2] Plin. H. N. iii. 5; Serv. Æn. xi. 836.
[3] Dionys. iv. 14; Cato de R. R. v.; Varro, vi. 25; Macrob. Sat. i. 7.
[4] Dionys. vi. 69; Serv. Æn. ii. 166, v. 704.

of the sun-god peculiar to themselves; from him they claimed to descend, and the state had actually appointed them a place of their own on which to offer their sacrifice. The Julian family always conducted the service of Vejovis at Bovillæ, and it was only when the Julii acquired sovereign power that the cultus became a public one. The Fabii had a sacrifice to Hercules on the Quirinal; the Horatii certain expiatory rites to direct; the Servilii, Æmilii, and Cornelii had also similar family obligations.[1] The duties of a priesthood of this kind were always to be executed by a male of the family, but beside him the greater solemnities also required the presence of three or four more only of the Gentiles.[2] Still these duties were burdensome; for a general was often obliged to leave his army in the middle of warlike operations, and to hurry to Rome to take part in a sacrifice of his gens.[3]

The long succession of victories, and the conquests, but seldom interrupted by discomfitures, which the Romans made from the beginning of the republic to the end of the second Punic war, fed and cherished, during these three centuries, belief in, and attachment to, the gods of Rome. Such a course of victories was to them the most striking proof that their gods were the mightiest, and the devotion of the Romans the best and most pleasing in their eyes. It was the gods who made Rome great, Rome's arm invincible; and they could not do otherwise, for, by their zealous exactness in the auspices, sacrifices, and ritual, their clients had, as it were, constrained them to give them victory and dominion over the other nations. If a Roman army or fleet met with a misfortune, that was a punishment for an error occurring in their cultus, or a sin committed against the gods. Thus the Roman fleet at Drepanum had to do penance for the sacrilege of Claudius, who ordered the sacred pullets to be thrown into the sea for not eating; so, too, Flaminius was punished with his own and his army's destruction at the lake Thrasymene for daringly and contemptuously acting against the divine portents. But, on the whole, " is it a marvel that the uninterrupted favour of the gods should have watched over the extension and maintenance of a kingdom which seems, with a superfluity of carefulness, to submit the most insignificant religious relations to trial? for

[1] Macrob. Sat. i. 16. [2] Dionys. ix. 19. [3] Liv. v. 6 and lii. 41, 15, &c.

never has our citizen community turned away its eyes from the most scrupulous observance of the worship of the gods."¹ Thus a Roman both thought and spoke.

The first blow of consequence which the existing state of religion in its exclusive patrician character received was inflicted by the Licinian law, in the year 367 B.C. Hitherto the custody of the Sibylline books had been committed to two priests of patrician blood; now a college of ten men, afterwards increased to fifteen, was formed, half of which number was to be made up of plebeians. They were "interpreters of the destiny of the Roman people;"² on their judgment any foreign worship was introduced (the cultus of Apollo may be specified), and the holding of the Apollinarian games was a duty of theirs. (These games, at first only vowed casually, were repeated every year from 210 B.C., and Apollo was added to the number of the guardian gods of Rome, though he still had his sanctuary outside the city.) After this, in the year 300 B.C., the Ogulnian law laid open even the pontificate and the augurate to the plebeians, who were now on terms of complete political equality with the patricians, and through this the old order of things received a tremendous shake. In the year 253, for the first time, a plebeian, Titus Coruncanius, became Pontifex maximus, and in 210 another was Curio maximus.

Greeks, like Polybius, who saw the whole edifice of the Roman state-religion already in the first stage of its downward progress (about 140 B.C.), admired it still as a masterpiece of human prudence and of political calculation, holding, in accordance with the notions of their day, the natural growth—the produce of ages—to have been a systematic erection. "It is my opinion," said Scipio's friend and counsellor, "that the Roman constitution deserves the preference in its comprehension of divine things, and just that which is blamed by others is to my mind the mainstay of the Roman state, viz. a superstitious fear (*deisidaimonia*) of the gods. For with them their religious system is so surrounded with terror, and so woven into all the relations of social and political life, that nothing can surpass it. This they seem to me to have done for the sake of the many; for as these are thoughtless, full of irregular desires, of blind anger and hot passions, there is nothing left but to tame that multitude by

---

¹ Val. Max. i. 1, 8; cf. Plut. Marcell. iv. 5.   ² Liv. x. 8.

such jugglery as will work on their fears."¹ This judgment of one who lived seventeen years in Rome, and of whom it has been said with justice that he was more an intelligent and politically wise Roman than a Greek, assuredly was the view of not a few Romans of the day.

The fact is, that the Roman religion, and, above all, the wide field of auspices and other means of ascertaining the divine will in it, was perfectly adapted to be a master-key to domination in the hands of a priestly class of aristocrats. As all political transactions were united with a host of religious formalities and external tokens of divine assent, so long as the patricians were in exclusive possession of the state-auspices, the temptation was always a proximate one to them to make use of these means to throw obstacles in the way of all popular decrees that were displeasing to them. One sees this clearly in the case of the laws Ælia and Fufia, 156 B.C. These, in the first place, inculcated generally the necessity of taking auspices in the popular assemblies, and then further decreed that it was open to all the officers of state to observe the heavens when they chose; and that, when this happened, no assembly of the people could be held. For it was, in fact, quite possible that any one of the public officials, during his observation, might notice an unfavourable appearance, lightning or such like, sufficient to say that the gods forbade the assembly and its decree. Later on, Bibulus (59 B.C.) employed this weapon in order to impede the new Agrarian law of Cæsar, giving notice of his intention to observe the heavens every comitial day;² and, two years after, Milo resorted to the same expedient.³ The Sibylline books, which were said by Cicero to be so equivocal in their composition that any event could be predicted from them, were similarly abused to the service of factions or influential persons, as, for instance, when the banished Egyptian king Auletes repaired to Rome for assistance, they were made to say that danger threatened Rome in case she replaced an expelled Egyptian king on the throne by force of arms.⁴ These examples are from the last times of the republic; but it cannot be doubted that the same thing happened frequently

---

¹ τῇ τοιαύτῃ τραγῳδίᾳ. Polybius says, vi. 56.

² Dio. Cass. xxxviii. 6; Suet. Cæs. 20; Cic. pro Domo suâ, 15; de Harusp. resp. 23.   ³ Cic. ad Att. iv. 3.

⁴ Dio. Cass. xxxix. 15; Cic. ad Fam. i. 7, 3; Appian. Mithr. p. 251.

before. Fabius Cunctator, himself an augur, veiling his want of faith under a mask of patriotism, had before this time declared that whatever was for the interests of the republic took place under good auspices, whatever to its detriment under bad.[1]

Greek influence became eminently decisive of the existence of the old Roman religion. Beginning with the middle of the third century B.C., after the second Punic war, it penetrated with irresistible force into Roman life, Roman ways of thought, and religious views. The subjection of the Greek cities in lower Italy, which took place at that time, had first the effect of opening a way for the Greek tongue, and then for fragments of Greek literature. The Romans next carried the war into the soil of Greece proper, and, from the year 146 B.C. till the Christian era, the whole of the Greek-speaking world became, directly or indirectly, tributaries to Rome. From the year 167, thousands of Achæans, who had been carried into Italy, the most cultivated minds of their nation, carried Greek civilisation over the whole peninsula; and the philosophers, who came to Rome as ambassadors from Athens in the year 155 B.C., awakened in the Roman youth, whom they instructed, an entirely new enthusiasm for Greek rhetoric and wisdom.

From this period there runs through Roman history a struggle between two tendencies, extremely opposite, yet of very unequally matched powers. On the one side, the patriotic-minded amongst the Romans were desirous of having the primitive worship of the gods of their fatherland preserved in as undisturbed a purity as possible, and of excluding the insinuation of foreign ideas and usages, especially Greek. But, on the other, the poverty and want of ideas in this religious system and service pressed for the introduction of new types of gods and forms of worship, with a richer garniture of mythology, and promising a speedier contentment of the greatly changed requirements of the Roman; and called also for an assimilation of the old Latin and Sabine gods, by blending them together with the Greek. To these points the educated already felt themselves drawn through the acquaintance they had formed with Greek literature. Only by hellenising their own deities could they, on their side, delight themselves in the poetic glory with which the Greek invested his gods, and converted them into objects, if not of reverential devo-

[1] Cic. de Senect. 4.

tion, at least of æsthetical pleasure, and cheerful and intimate relations. At bottom, the Roman religion was based only on two ideas,—the might of the gods who were friendly to Rome, and the power of the ceremonies over the gods. How could a religion, so poverty-stricken of thought, with its troops of phantom gods, beingless shadows and deified abstractions, remain unscathed and unaltered when it came in contact with the profusion of the Greek religion, with its circle of gods, so full of life, so thoroughly anthropomorphised, so deeply interwoven into every thing human? Those primitive agrarian deities and ceremonies, those sacrifices and rude rites of fratres Arvales, Salii, and Luperci, must have struck the eye of the Roman of Greek education, like the boyish sports of his people's youth, which the mature manhood of a state, advancing with firm stride to a world's dominion, had long outgrown.

Up to this time Rome had produced no literature. Documents about public contracts, a dry city-chronicle, ritual and calendar notices of the pontiffs, which were for long inaccessible to the plebeians, augural books, genealogical records of particular families and panegyrics of their more distinguished members,—to such reading, and no better, Rome was limited. After the year 250, Livius Andronicus and Nævius began to domesticate in Rome the Greek legends of god and hero; the first in tragedy, the latter principally in comedy. From the year 200, a still more powerful impression was produced by Ennius, the real creator of Roman poetry and poetical language, who, in his poetical version of Euhemerus, made the Romans acquainted with the theory that the gods were but deified men, whose death and places of burial were known to people; and, in his Epicharmus, published the Pythagorean doctrine of the Sicilian comic writer about God, nature, and the soul; and actually wove into his Roman annals long episodes of Pythagorean philosophy. From him the Romans learned to consider as the kernel of old Italic wisdom the doctrine that, fundamentally, there was but one god, Jupiter, and that he was naught else but the sun-fire, which, as the world's soul, is the source of all that is living and spiritual, pervading corporeal nature.[1] An expression of his had been already welcomed in Rome with tumultuous applause, to this effect: "I have ever

---

[1] The passages in Varro, v. 64, 65.

said, and will say still, there is a race of celestial gods; but I believe they do not trouble themselves about the doings of men."[1]

Meanwhile the number of Greek slaves increased at Rome; amongst them were rhetoricians, grammarians, and partisans of one or other of the schools of philosophy; and the Romans began to intrust the education of their sons to these men, in whose eyes the old Roman rite was, certainly in many cases, nothing but a rude and barbarian superstition. The experience was soon acquired, which Cicero's grandfather gave expression to: "A Roman's wickedness increases in proportion to his acquaintance with Greek authors."[2] The conquests in Greece and the East, particularly the capture of Syracuse and Corinth, brought together at Rome images of gods, the *chefs-d'œuvre* of the best sculptors, in ever-increasing quantities: the patriots took alarm; they feared, and rightly, the effects of these statues on their religious system; they heard many ridicule the simplicity and deformity of the old clay gods of Rome, which now first struck all eyes when compared with the Hellenic statues.[3] But while the works of Grecian art were now powerfully abetting the hellenising of the Roman gods, the forms and rites of divine worship haughtily withdrew from any more attractive transformation through the æsthetic Greek ritual. The awe of the unassailable holiness of ritual was too deeply rooted in a Roman's soul, and there were far too great results from the punctual fulfilment of each particular, for people to have ventured on meddling with it or introducing novelties. Meanwhile the meaning of these antique usages had been lost in many cases, with the thorough change of manners: a strange sense was often imputed to them, as to the deities themselves; and the elder Cato already complained that many of the auguries and auspices had become entirely obsolete through the negligence of the college.[4]

In proportion as contact and intercourse with other nations increased, the longing for strange gods also grew. Where a few supreme gods do not absorb the complete and unconditional confidence of their worshipers, as in the case of Syrians and Phœnicians, polytheism is insatiable; even the hosts of untold gods, such as Rome possessed, could not satisfy them. There is

---

[1] Cic. de Div. ii. 50.   [2] Cic. de Orat. 6.
[3] Liv. xxxiv. 4, xlv. 39.   [4] Cic. de Div. i. 15.

always a suspicion that this or that god may have been forgotten, and perhaps one of the most important; that if this much-esteemed stranger-god and his worship could be introduced, people would soon have satisfactory proof of the advantage of doing so. And then such new gods take precedence of the old native ones; they have not been so used up; they have still more of the mysterious about them; there are not so many instances of prayers and vows left unheard.[1] As often as Rome was visited with heavy distress, dangers, or misfortunes, this desire was roused, and the people were not contented with the deities brought in on this or that occasion, by advice of the Sibylline books. When a pestilence lasted, shrines were raised of exotic and barbarian gods, and, in private houses, new and extraordinary ceremonies and expiations were resorted to; this had been experienced as early as the year 428 B.C., during a lingering drought and plague. The Ædiles had been directed by the senate to take steps against new and foreign ceremonies; and to provide that no other but Roman gods should be worshiped, and these only after the fashion of their fathers. So again in the year 215, after the overthrow at Cannæ, the urban Prætor, besides interdicting foreign rites, made proclamation "that every one who had in his possession books of divination, prayers, or instructions upon the service of the gods, should deliver them up to him." These regulations had scarcely even a transitory effect.

The discovery of the abominations practised in the Bacchanalia must have increased the repugnance in all Roman-minded people to foreign religions. In Rome alone as many as seven thousand men had joined these nocturnal orgies, which had been brought by Greeks to Etruria, and from thence into Rome and the rest of Italy, and in which unchastity, murder, or human sacrifice, and poisoning were rife. Executions *en masse* followed their discovery, in the year 186. The celebration of the Bacchanalia was prohibited to all Romans and their allies; and it is only casually mentioned, that a few years afterwards a Prætor condemned in one year three thousand men for poisoning, so frightful a hold had this union of crime and religious worship taken.[2]

Shortly afterwards, in the year 181, the far-famed finding of the books of king Numa took place. Two stone coffins were

---

[1] Comp. Lucian, Icaromenipp.   [2] Liv. xxxi. 8-19; Val. Max. vi. 3 7.

dug up in the field of a scribe, Petillius, one of which, according to the inscription, professed to contain the corpse of the king, and the other his writings. The first was empty, but the writings discovered in the second had quite a fresh appearance; the Latin, treating of pontifical law, regarded the principles of divine rites and ordinances, and the Greek contained philosophy. It was found that the tendency of the greater part of these writings was to the destruction of religion, and they were therefore burnt by decree of the senate.[1] Every circumstance here points to a forgery: whilst the bones of the king had quite disappeared, from the length of time, in one of the coffins, the books in the other seemed quite fresh; moreover, these books were written on paper, which only came into use centuries after; and, besides, were partly in the Greek tongue, and that at a time when as yet no writings in prose had issued in Greece itself. All these facts taken in connexion with the facility of reading the documents, where and when the language had undergone a thorough change, raise the suspicion of imposture almost to a certainty. Many contemporary events point to a religious fermentation and movement going on at the time; the occurrences in the Bacchanalia, the translation of Euhemerus by Ennius, the expulsion of two Epicureans, Alcæus and Philiscus,[2] a few years afterwards, and the decree of the senate of the year 161, that philosophers and rhetoricians could not be tolerated in Rome.[3] The writings were certainly an attempt to interpret the Roman gods and religious usages in the sense of a philosophical system, probably that of Epicurus, and thereby to pave the way to insure it a position in Rome.[4]

It cannot be affirmed that the Romans of the later times of the free commonwealth were discontented with their state-gods in a political point of view—gods who had granted their republic to the full all they had in early times promised them, victory, power, and dominion: and if a great calamity befell the state in battle with a foreign people, like the loss of Crassus and his army, most people were even ready to believe that the fault was imput-

---

[1] Liv. xl. 29; Plin. H. N. xiii. 27; Plut. Num. c. xxii.
[2] Athen. xii 68. p. 547; Ælian. V. H. ix. 12.
[3] Gell. xv. 11; Suet. de Clar. Rhet. c. i.
[4] For what can be said as to the authenticity of the books, see Lasaulx, Studien des Klass. Alterth. pp. 99-105.

able to the generals having obstinately despised all warnings from the gods.¹ But in matters of private interest the old native gods no longer satisfied the people. In sickness, love-affairs, gains and losses, and the like, the foreign deities rendered, as they thought, better service. In the last times of the republic it was no longer in the power of the state-officers to check the current of this deisidaimonia; and yet, as a rule, it was only a foreigner who could minister as a priest to a foreign god; no born Roman was allowed to give himself such an office. Accordingly the Idæan Mother in Rome had a priest and a priestess, but both were Phrygians; and Dionysius was particularly struck with this forbearance from strange priesthoods on the part of the Romans, though indeed this became different in the times of the Cæsars. The senate continued the war against the strange worships, such as the people preferred; but its powers of resistance were constantly being more and more crippled. It had the images of Serapis, Isis, Harpocrates, and Anubis overthrown; but the people set them up again by force.² It decreed that the temples erected to Isis and Serapis should be destroyed, but not a workman would lay hand upon them; the consul Æmilius Paulus himself seized an axe and broke-in the doors of the temple;³ but not long after, the Isis-cultus was again in full swing at Rome. In Sylla's time there even existed a college of Pastophori at Rome. In the year 48 B.C. the haruspices again had all the temples of Isis and Serapis destroyed; but shortly afterwards the number of the priests of Isis was so increased that Volusius, when exiled by the Triumvirs, chose their dress in order to slip unobserved into the camp of Brutus.⁴ In the year 43, the Triumvirs, Antony, Lepidus, and Octavian, even decreed the erection of an Isis-temple.⁵

Dionysius was struck with admiration of this also in the Romans, that while they revelled in riches and luxury, they still preserved the ancient simplicity and poverty of worship, and went on setting before their gods cakes of barley-meal, toasted wheat, and a few fruits upon the antique wooden tables in earthen pots and dishes, and poured their libations from wooden cups and beakers.⁶ It struck him how every thing that concerned the

---

¹ Dionys. ii. 6. ² Tertull. ad Nat. i. 14.
³ Val. Max. i. 3. ⁴ Val. Max. vii. 3-8; Dio. Cass. xlii. 26.
⁵ Dio. Cass. i. 7-15. ⁶ Dionys. ii. 23.

gods was undertaken with prudence and reverence, quite different from the ways of Greeks and barbarians. Nevertheless, the long period of the civil wars, during which the republic was languishing and dying out, was, on the whole, also a period of religious decay; and indeed it could not be otherwise, apart from all the influence of Epicurean philosophy, in a religion so closely blended with the being of the state, and only valued in proportion to the successes it brought. A priesthood of such importance as that of the Flamen Dialis remained vacant for the space of seventy-six years, till Augustus at last, in the year 743, again appointed to it.[1] The auspices—what scores of times they had deceived during this last period!—were either quite given up, especially in war, or were used as empty formalities to make a show, or they were publicly treated as a mere political tool with which to hamper an adversary in his undertakings. On the other hand, there were undoubtedly religious solemnities of which a more extensive use was now made than formerly. The supplications—those solemn prayer-meetings or processions in which all ranks took part, and, with garlands on their heads, marched to the temples of the chief gods—used only to last a single day at first; then, on the suppression of the Catilinarian conspiracy, and afterwards in thanksgiving for Cæsar's victories, a solemnity of the kind was ordained for fifteen days; and they were further prolonged to twenty, forty, and even fifty days.[2] This, however, took place more with a view of doing homage to great statesmen or conquerors than to the gods. There was also now no longer any hesitation about adopting the oriental custom of apotheosis in Rome. At first it was simply unapproved that Greek cities should institute festivals, priests, and sacrifices to Roman generals or consuls; and in this way the inhabitants of Syracuse had already kept a feast in honour of Marcellus. In Asia Minor the same devotion had been shown to Mucius Scævola and Lucullus; Titus Flamininus, in Plutarch's time, still retained priests and sacrifice in the town of Chalcis, which he had saved. Public buildings there were dedicated to him and Apollo. The cities of the province of Asia offered to erect a temple to Cicero, but he

---

[1] Dio. Cass. liv. 36; Suet. Octav. 31; Tac. Ann. iii. 58 (where the time is incorrectly stated at seventy-two years).

[2] Cæs. B. G. ii. 35, iv. 38; Cic. de Prov. Cons. 10; Phil. xiv. 11; Suet. Cæs. 24.

declined the honour.[1] It happened, too, that states impeached of extortion at Rome the very men to whom they had previously erected temples at home, as was the case with Appius Clodius and the Cilicians. The building of temples in honour of the Roman proconsuls became a regular custom in the provinces, though many of them were more like evil demons than philanthropic beings.[2] This practice seems to have been favoured at Rome; for, in a law which forbade the governors of provinces laying on arbitrary taxes, the case of an impost in aid of a building of the kind was expressly excepted.[3]

Though Cicero's opinion of the Asiatics was, that, through long slavery, they had become inured to excessive adulation, yet the Romans soon chimed in with the conviction that they were allowed to do for their new lords what the other cities of the empire had long done for the officers of the republic who were liable to be called and recalled. The senate exalted Cæsar, the descendant of Venus, to a seat among the gods. His house had a pediment like a temple; and games were to be celebrated every lustrum in his honour. His image was carried round in procession with those of the other gods in the circus, and in the lectisternia it was laid upon the cushions in the same company. He was called Jupiter, and a temple in common was decreed to him and Clementia, on account of his mildness, and in it the two deities extended hands one to the other. Antony esteemed it an honour to become the Flamen of the new Jupiter.[4] And yet no temple of his own was built to the new deity during his lifetime; and instead of this he was made temple-associate of Quirinus, where his statue was erected with the inscription "To the invincible god."

Octavian, more moderate than Cæsar, did not tolerate divine honours being paid him in Rome itself; temples, at least, were not allowed to be erected to him in Italy, though he winked at that being done in the provinces. Immediately after his death, however, his cultus was set up on the largest scale. Twenty-one senators, chosen by lot, Tiberius himself being one of them, undertook the priesthood of the new god, and his widow Livia in like manner became his priestess.[5] In a very short time every

---

[1] Cic. ad Attic. v. 21.   [2] Suet. Oct. 52.   [3] Cic. ad Quint. fratrem, ep. i. 1.
[4] Cic. Phil. ii. 42; Suet. Cæs. 81; Flor. iv. 2; Dio. xliv. 6; Appian, ii. 404, 519; Plut. Cæs. 57.   [5] Tac. Ann. i. 54.

one of the more distinguished houses in Rome had its own college of worshipers of Augustus.[1]

When Octavian, now absolute sovereign, added to his other dignities and powers the supreme priesthood as the keystone of his princedom, he did not neglect to invest himself with the conduct of the whole system of religion. All the colleges of priests were put under him. He filled the vacated benefices, he himself named the vestal virgins, and decided upon the authority of books containing soothsayings and interpretations of prodigies, as well as upon the consultation and exposition of the Sibylline ones. In all religious cases, or such as were in any way connected with religion, and over all crimes having the character of religious offences, he constituted himself supreme judge.[2] If, in many instances, the colleges of priests still passed sentence, yet there were others settled by a simple decree of the Cæsar as high-priest. The power of the pontifex maximus had previously been confined to the city of Rome and its liberties, but under the Cæsars it was extended even to the provinces. There is an instance on record of Pliny consulting Trajan whether an ancient shrine of the Mother of the gods in Bithynia might be pulled down.[3]

Octavian laid considerable stress upon the revival of this office, partly to satisfy the obligations of his sacerdotal dignity, and partly because of the almost universal conviction, even including those Roman statesmen who were privately the most unbelieving, that the religious system formed an indispensable basis of empire. He himself, it is true, by his union with Livia, had thrown ridicule upon religion and the college of pontiffs; but now he restored many religious customs that had fallen into oblivion;[4] he increased the number of patricians, who during the civil war had been so sadly reduced, in order that the rites and sacerdotal offices of patrician families might not be extinguished.[5] Meanwhile, though he was so strongly averse to foreign religious practices, as a noxious parasitical growth sapping the tree of the state, he was unable to curtail the extent of its grasp, and to loosen its increasing tenacity in Rome, for a length of time. The numbers of peregrini in Rome had been swelled

---

[1] Tac. loc. cit. i. 73.
[2] Dio. Cass. liii. 7; liv. 17; Gell. i. 12; Tac. Ann. iii. 59.
[3] Plin. Epist. x. 73, 74.   [4] Suet. Oct. xxxi.   [5] Dio. Cass. lii. 42.

enormously since the opening of his reign; and they could not be prevented practising their native worship, at least in private houses without temples. Rome became more and more a Pantheon of the gods and religions of the whole empire.

Terentius Varro, the most learned Roman of his time, had shortly before attempted to come to the assistance of these religious exigencies by another way, that of learned investigation and compilations. His undertaking to revive and bring nearer to the people the old religion, partly gone to decay and forgotten, and partly obscured by mistakes and rude mechanical treatment, evidently betrayed how desperate such a task was. Many temples, sanctuaries, and old images of the gods had already disappeared, or had been destroyed, or become private property.[1] Many a rite that had been long in use was lost for want of place to practise it, or from a family dying out. Varro, with his industry in compilation and his knowledge of Roman antiquities, intended to put together again the, as it were, scattered limbs, to replace what was lost, and to reinfuse life into the whole. Addicted himself, at least in an eclectic way, to the Stoic philosophy, he caught at an idea, first broached by the Stoics, and then developed by the famous pontifex maximus Mucius Scævola, namely, that one must distinguish a triple religion and divine teaching,—the mythical system belonging to poets, a religion peculiar to philosophers, and the municipal one of cultus in the cities. Varro certainly thought the latter had taken up the first, the poetico-fabulous, and that these legends, unworthy as they were of the gods, were represented in the theatrical games instituted by the state, as a component part of the worship of the gods, and unfortunately found an easy entrance into the popular creed. At this point philosophy was to come in to aid the state-religion by symbolic explanation of the myths. Varro used the Stoic teaching for this purpose, starting with the dogma of an ether-god, or divine world-soul. To him the primary Roman gods are symbols of a mundus consisting of ether and body, the two parts of which, Cœlus and Tellus, were at the head of two series of gods, a male and female, whilst the demons (Lares, Penates, and Genii) dwelt in the lower region of the air. He explained the immense number of Roman deities simply by the multiplication of names that were given one god according

---

[1] Cic. N. D. i. 29; St. Aug. Civ. Dei, iii. 17.

to his different functions; thus, on one side, comparing Jupiter (his ether) with the God of the Jews,[1] on the other, enumerating 300 different Jupiters. And, as the soul of man is an emanation from the world-soul, it was easy for him to adopt an order of gods who had become so, namely, by being exalted through consecration from men to gods, and in this way to justify the cultus of the Lares. But, since his explanations, as he probably himself felt, by no means squared with the real historical sense of the system of gods and usages, again he maintained there was much that was true in religion which it was not beneficial for the people to know; nay, even that it was often of advantage to the community that the people should hold what was false to be true.[2]

II. The Roman Gods.

The worship of Janus must have been as old in Italy as it was widely spread. Both Etruscans and Latins had it; and though, according to one account, the god came from Perrhœbia, in the north of Greece, to Italy, yet he was such a strange being, and so different from the known Grecian gods, that neither Dionysius nor Ovid was able to identify him with any single one of the latter.[3] By origin he was a sun-god, or the power of nature working through the sun,—an inference deducible from the antique Jana, who was a goddess of the moon. He was represented either with two heads, as surveying east and west, or as the rising and setting sun, or with four heads in Falerii, as looking to the four quarters of the heavens. In all he was a natural and elemental god in the most general sense of the term; hence Varro interpreted him to be the world, *i. e.* the heaven; or he was made a son of Cœlus and Hecate (the primeval mother Night), and people hesitated between this interpretation and the other, which took him to be a sun-god.[4] But as in the Roman system of gods the elemental and astral deities generally retired into the background, or were metamorphosed into beings more personal and of greater freedom in action, it is also impossible now to discern the ancient meaning involved in the Roman Janus.

---

[1] St. Aug. de Cons. Evang. i. 22, 41.   [2] Tertull. Apol. xiv.
[3] Dionys. iii. 32; Ovid. Fasti, i. 89, 90.   [4] Arnob. iii. 9.

He continued throughout one of the supreme gods, and was eulogised in the Salian hymns as god of gods. The sacrificial king continued to offer him the significant sacrifice of a ram in the Regia; but the Capitoline Jupiter had ousted him from his earlier high position. As the saga, giving elsewhere expression to a definite stage of reflection in the popular mind, represents the gods as earthly monarchs and fathers of races, so in the Italic saga Janus also was converted into the oldest of the native kings of Italy, who taught the inhabitants their customs and how to worship the gods. It was he who hospitably welcomed the stranger Saturn on his arrival, and, when he became the inventor of agriculture, associated him with himself as co-regent.

As to cultus, Janus was the guardian of the gates of heaven, the opener and shutter of heaven, the land, and the sea: the mover of "the hinges of the universe," the bearer of the symbolical key, and alternately invoked by the priests in the sacrifice, under the titles of Clusius and Patulcius, and in prayers which related to propagation of the human species, as Consivius. His power was of unlimited extent, for as vouchsafing a beginning, and granting a blessing, it related to all states and operations of nature, as well as of human life. He was, as St. Augustine styles him,[1] the Jupiter Initiator, who, from the commencement, sent down blessing and increase on the whole work. So, on every solemnity, he was the first to be prayed and sacrificed to, in order, as Macrobius says, to open communications with the god whom a man intended to worship, just as if he passed the prayer on through his doors to the other deities.[2] In the myth of his having with Juturna begotten Fontus, the god of springs, and therefore the parent-source of water, a trace is discoverable of his antique elemental signification. It was only at a much later period he became a god of time, though he early had the beginning of the year dedicated to him; and one of the principal feasts, that of the first of January, celebrated with the offering to him of the Janual, a sacrifice of cake. His image—it was only afterwards and in exceptional cases that he came to be delineated in human form complete—represented with its fingers the number 365. It was the business of twelve Salii, one for each of the months, to sing his praises; and twelve altars were dedicated to him. Perhaps, as a consequence of his

[1] Civ. Dei, iv. 11. [2] Macrob. Sat. i. 9.

attribute of a key, he also became a god of the thoroughfare, of the city gates, which had formerly two arches in Rome, and of the house-doors; and thus his power or action extended to all in-comers and out-goers, and his two heads or faces pointed to the exit or entrance through such gates or doors. A gated hall in Rome was called Janus Bifrons, or Geminus; and, as the image of the god with its double face was placed in it, it was afterwards also called a temple. This was the sanctuary which, by a regulation dating back to Numa, was shut every time peace was concluded, and opened on the outbreak of war. In fine, Janus also stood in immediate relations to the Roman citizenship. His titles were Quirinus, as protector of the Quirites; Curiatius, in respect of the assembly of the Curia:[1] and, besides the gated hall just mentioned, he had also another temple restored by Augustus, and dedicated by Tiberius.[2]

Whether Faunus be one with the phantom wood-god Silvanus, or distinct from him, what his relation was to the Fauns, and whether he were god or demon, are questions easier asked than solved. His worship was pre-Roman, and Latin. The Romans, says Dionysius, ascribe to this demon all panic-striking and ghostly appearances, and all strange cries and sounds that alarm the ear.[3] It was, therefore, natural that he should afterwards have been put on a par with the Greek Pan, whom in fact he strongly resembles. Like him, he was a god of flocks and herds, a provoking demon of the forest; and as Pan was also a god of oracles, there was, in a precinct at Tibur, an oracle of Faunus, under the designation of the soothsaying god Fatuus, the consulters of which slept upon the fleeces of sheep, slain by the priests, in order to learn the god's answer in dreams. He was called Lupercus, as guardian and preserver of the flocks from wolves, and in old times human sacrifices were offered to him, as is indicated in the saga, that he sacrificed all the strangers coming into Latium. In Rome, on the feast of the Lupercalia, goats were sacrificed, but at the same time, two youths, led up to the altar, had their foreheads marked with the bloody knives of sacrifice, the blood-mark being immediately rubbed off with milk, upon which they were to laugh, as expressing their joy that the goats had been slain instead of them-

---

[1] Varro, v. 165, vi. 34, vii. 85; Serv. Æn. vii. 608; Joh. Lyd. de Mens. p. 56.
[2] Tac. Ann. ii. 49.   [3] Dionys. Hal. v. 16.

selves. The skins of the slaughtered he- or she-goats were cut into pieces and strips after the sacrificial banquet, and then the Lupercus-priests, naked, except so far as the pieces covered, and with the strips in hand, ran from the place of sacrifice through the city, and struck with the strips all the maidens and women they met, or who put themselves in their way in the hope of being purified by the blows and becoming fruitful mothers.[1]

Saturn was one of the old Latin deities, who, at a very early period, came to be identified with the Greek Cronos, and thus also with the Phœnician. He and Janus, with whose worship his own was intimately connected, belong to the oldest of the Italian deities. The Saturnii, probably before the Trojan war, were sacrificing to him upon the Capitol, and the sagas make him into a primitive sovereign who came from the East into Italy, and, by the introduction of agriculture, tamed and humanised the aborigines. The sickle and pruning-knife were his emblems. He blest the harvest, and, as Stercutius, was also a manure-god.[2] To him was attached the memory of a golden age and a peaceful kingdom. On his feast, which was celebrated with banquets, slaves enjoyed a transitory freedom and equality with their masters, and offenders a remission of punishment. His images were hollow, and filled with oil, the head covered, the feet swathed in a woollen fillet, removed on feast-days; and to him alone sacrifice was offered with bare head and lighted tapers.[3] The same confusion of deity, which frequently makes the real nature of the Roman gods so enigmatical and uncertain, is exhibited in his being also a god of the lower world, and in the old rite, which, however, was soon mitigated, requiring an atonement of human life to be made him;[4] so that it was said of him he had ruled with great cruelty in Italy, Sicily, and the larger portion of Libya.[5] With this double aspect of the god appears to be connected the attribution of two different consorts; the one, Lua, to whom after battle the captured arms were burnt in expiation for the blood shed; the other Ops, like himself, a goddess of fruitfulness and protectress of agriculture,

---

[1] Varro, v. 60; Ov. Fasti, ii. 265 sqq.; Serv. Æn. viii. 343; Justin. xliii. 1.
[2] Macrob. Sat. i. 7; St. Aug. Civ. Dei, xviii. 15; Lact. i. 20, 36.
[3] Macrob. Sat. i. 7; Fest. p. 184, v. "Saturno;" Serv. Æn. iii. 407.
[4] Plut. Quæst. Rom. 11-34.
[5] Lyd. de Mens. iv. 48; Macrob. Sat. i. 7; Arnob. ii. 68.

thence called Consiva, the plantress; but also a Chthonic deity like Demeter; and therefore, whoever invoked her, did not omit touching the ground.[1]

Jupiter, like the Grecian Zeus, was preëminently the Roman god of the heaven and the weather. As lord and giver of the light, he was styled Lucetius; and his power over the phenomena of the atmosphere, rain and storm, thunder and lightning, was indicated by the Romans in his titles of Pluvius, Fulgurator, Tonans, and Serenator. His surname of Elicius, under which invocation he had an altar on the Aventine, bore reference to the saga that there was a secret means of drawing down lightning, and even the god in person, from heaven; and that Numa, who succeeded in this practice with the aid of the other gods, had obliged the god, demanding human sacrifices, to content himself with a promise of substitutive symbols.[2] As an emblem of the lightning, he carried a flint-stone in his hand, from which sparks could be elicited.

The worship of Jupiter Latiaris, who, as patron-god of the old Latin confederation, had his annual festival with sacrifices of bulls on the Alban Mount, passed into Roman hands. They observed it with the greatest solemnity, but also with the addition of a human sacrifice, for which purpose a criminal was chosen in later times.[3] But the real Roman state-god and supreme protector of Rome was Jupiter, "the highest and best," whose worship was already established on the Capitol by the Tarquins. There stood his colossal bronze image, cast from the armour of vanquished enemies; there were deposited all the presents that Rome or her allies appointed to be made him; and thither the new consuls resorted to offer their vows for the welfare of the republic, and the victorious generals to present their thank-offerings. The warlike signification was the prevalent one in him, in accordance with the tendency of the state, and the designations under which he held particular sanctuaries or images related to battle and victory. He was called Imperator, Stator (the stayer of flight), Feretrius (or the smiter of the flying foe), &c.

---

[1] Varro, vi. 21; Macrob. Sat. i. 10.

[2] Ov. Fasti, iii. 285 sqq.; Arnob. v. i.

[3] Minuc. Octav. 30; Lact. i. 21; Prudent. adv. Symmach. i. 397. It is not gladiatorial combats that are meant, as Hartung and Schwenck say: Minucius expressly contradicts that view.

The Romans were cognisant of no mythical sagas of their Jupiter; with them, who in general were averse to making their gods genealogically related, he had neither parents nor sons. In fact, so little was there of the concrete or personal about him, that most of the other male deities were all but identical with him, and had their rise in the idea of him. Thus one of the old Latin gods was Vejovis or Vedius, an idol with arrows and hunting spears in its hands.[1] When invoked by Lucius Furius in the battle of Cremona, it was he who brought the rescue; and in urban devotions he was named along with Dis and the Manes. Still it was not known whether he was an Apollo or a younger Jupiter, or a panic-god of the nether world who had immigrated from Etruria. Then, further, there was a lightning-god, Summanus, whose image was on the pediment of the Capitoline temple of Jupiter, though after the war with Pyrrhus he also had a temple of his own dedicated to him in the Circus Maximus. The Arval brothers sacrificed black lambs to appease him when trees were struck by lightning; and he was also propitiated by dogs crucified alive on elder-trees;[2] and in inscriptions he is styled Pluto, and associated with other Stygian gods. Since, however, even Ovid could not tell who this Summanus really was, and the lightning was exclusively Jupiter's prerogative, we are compelled to assume him to be a Jupiter of the night.

When once the solar signification of Janus had fallen into the back-ground or been forgotten, the sun-god in the Roman system had very little prominence, notwithstanding his decided bearing on agriculture; indeed, he came to be yet more neglected by the Romans than the Greeks. Sol, though a Sabine deity, and, according to St. Augustine, a "deus selectus," was long without any temple in Rome; people were satisfied with erecting some altars to him in the open air. The reason given for this, at a later period, that no one ventured to shut up in a building him who is always visible in heaven, is certainly not the original one. Only the single Sabine family of the Aurelii kept up his cultus. At a later date, we find a sanctuary of his near the temple of Quirinus;[3] and Augustus erected him an obelisk on the Campus Martius. At a later date again, Sol is mentioned as

---

[1] Ovid. Fasti, iii. 429 sqq.; Gell. v. 12, 11; Serv. Æn. ii. 761.
[2] Plin. H. N. xxix. 4; Marini. Frat. Arv. pp. 686 sqq.
[3] Quintil. i. 7, 12; Varro, v. 52; Tertull. de Spectac. viii.

the genius imparting the breath of life to the newly born, for it is the way of genii to enter by solar atoms into man, and thus unite themselves with his soul.¹ Luna, likewise a Sabine goddess, had betimes a temple dedicated to her by Servius Tullius on the Aventine, and another on the Palatine.

Apollo, in whom the early Romans saw as little of the sun-god as the Greeks, always continued in Rome to be a foreign god in reality, though in high repute on account of his much-consulted Delphic oracle. In the times of the Republic he had no public sanctuary at all within Rome; though he was known from the Tarquinian era through the influence of the Phocæans and of Cumæ, and the Sibylline books, composed under his inspiration, made him into a being of very great importance to the Roman state. Accordingly it was to a Sibylline injunction that the erection of the first Apollo-temple on the Flaminian meadow in the year 323 was owing, for the averting of an epidemic disease.² Henceforth he was adopted into the state-worship proper, and then principally as a god of healing; pestilences every now and then afforded occasions for recourse to him with vows and offerings. The Apollinarian games were established to his honour at the close of the second Punic war, in gratitude for the victory, predicted by an oracle;³ and the sacrifices for the purpose had to be conducted according to the Greek rite. It was Augustus who first built this god the beautiful marble temple on the Palatine.

Mars, however, or, in Sabine dialect, Mamers, was an aboriginal god of the Latin races, who had nothing, properly speaking, in common with the Greek Ares, but rather was a god of soothsaying, and had an ancient oracle in the Sabine territory, which was given by a woodpecker (the bird sacred to the god), perched on a pillar of wood.⁴ Besides, he was agricultural in character, inasmuch as that up to a late date sacrifices were offered him for the increase of the fruits of the earth and the flocks, and the Arvalian fraternity kept a festival in his honour with particular solemnities as a guardian of the fields.⁵ But since Numa's times he had already become a war-god, and as he was at the same

---

[1] Orelli, Inscr. 324, 1928; Serv. Æn. xi, 57; Macrob. Somn. Scip. i, 19, 12.
[2] Liv. iii. 63; iv. 24; Ascon. Or. in tog. cand. p. 90.
[3] Liv. xxv. 12.   [4] Dionys. Hal. i. 14.
[5] Marini, Fr. Arv. p. 660; Cato de R. R. lxxxiii. 141.

time the reputed father of the ancestral hero of the Romans, there was no god, after Jupiter, held in such veneration at Rome as Mars. In him, too, the deities of different races appear to have been eventually blended in one, for Mars is to be found in three different aspects at Rome: as Mars Gradivus, the war-god proper; the agrarian Mars, or Silvanus; and a Mars Quirinus. This last name indicated originally a peculiar (Sabine) deity, who with Jupiter and Mars was one of the gods-protectors of Rome, and each one of these three had his own flamen and a particular sacrifice. Servius, too, contrasts Quirinus as a god of repose with Gradivus as war-god.[1] But as Quirinus himself was converted gradually into a war-god, he came also to coincide with Mars.[2]

Lances and shields were the symbols of the god Mars, and the pledges of his presence. The shield had fallen from heaven, and, in order that it might not be stolen, it was counterfeited by eleven other exact copies. These sacred shields (ancilia) and spears, carefully preserved in the Regia, were a palladium of the empire. Before an expedition, the general shook them with the words, "Wake, Mars;" but if they moved of themselves, it was a sign betokening disaster, and expiatory rites had to be performed. On the Campus Martius, which was consecrated to the god for martial exercises, contests, and reviews, the October horse was annually sacrificed, and its amputated tail carried in such haste to the Regia that the drops of blood might still fall on the hearth, and be used, with the ashes of a calf taken from the carcass of a cow that had been sacrificed, for the purification of the Roman territory, on the Palilia. The head of the horse of sacrifice was hung round with bread, as with a garland, and suspended on some public building.[3]

Vulcan, or Mulciber, *i. e.* the smelter, corresponded perfectly with the Greek Hephæstos, and his workshops in Italy, too, were all the volcanic mountains. He was god of the fires of the stove and the hearth, and his image of clay was placed on the domestic hearth. Originally he was a god worshiped by plebeians only, and specially invoked by such craftsmen as were workers by fire; and he, too, seems to have received human sacrifice in the oldest times; for on his feast, the Vulcanalia, live fishes were thrown into

---

[1] Ad Æn. i. 296. [2] Ovid, Met. xiv. 828; xv. 862.
[3] Plut. Quæst. Rom. 97; Festus, pp. 111, 186, 120; Ov. Fasti, iv. 733.

the flames to him, evidently a substitute for the human lives which were his due.[1] Mercury and Neptune enjoyed still less importance and consideration in Rome than Vulcan. Mercury claimed to be Hermes, appropriating but one of the many properties of that god, namely that of patron of business and gain. It was not till the expulsion of the kings, 495 B.C., that a temple was built to him, when a merchant-guild (Mercuriales) was set up and placed under his protection. On his festival (May 15), the tradespeople offered incense and prayed to him for success in business; at the same time they drew water from a spring sacred to him, with which they sprinkled their hair and their wares, and supplicated him, as Ovid says, to assist them in cheating, and to pardon previous false oaths and affirmations in his name.[2] Afterwards, indeed, when Greek literature had gained a wider influence, other attributes of Hermes were transferred to Mercury, and so he passed for a god of the lower world also, for Psychopompos, and hence as father of two Lares. The name of the sea-god Neptune was still less frequently in use, though he had a temple on the Campus Martius, and a festival, the Neptunalia, kept merrily under arbours.[3]

Of the female deities, the Romans worshiped, as earth-goddesses, besides Ops, already mentioned, first, Tellus, Ceres, Bona Dea, and Maia. According to Ovid,[4] Tellus and Ceres were distinct, as the soil of the earth and her productive power, and both were propitiated with sacrificial cakes and the sacrifice of a sow in young. The solemn oblation of the Hordicidia was considered as proper to Tellus alone, during which a cow in calf was sacrificed in each of the thirty curiæ, and the calves taken from their several mothers were consumed by fire. Devotions were paid to Tellus as a deity of the lower world.[5]

Though a stranger and immigrant deity, Ceres, the goddess of the corn and of the tilled soil, attained to an importance in the Roman republic which appears to have obscured the cultus of older and analogous goddesses. In the 258th year A.U.C. a temple and service were appointed her by the consul Aurelius Postumius, to avert a famine imminent from a failure in the crops. She came from the Grecian lower Italy, and therefore was the Demeter whose renowned cultus at Enna in Sicily re-

---

[1] Varro, vi. 20, 57; Fest. p. 208. [2] Ov. Fast. v. 663 sqq.
[3] Liv. xxviii. 11; Fest. p. 161. [4] Fasti, i. 674. [5] Liv. x. 29, 8, 9.

acted on the Roman. The whole rite was Greek from the commencement, and Greek priestesses were ordered to Rome for the purpose, chiefly from Naples and Velia.[1] A sow was sacrificed to her before the harvest. On her feast-day, the 12th of April, all were clad in white; and therefore the feast was omitted after the defeat of Cannæ, because all the matrons were then in mourning. Races in the circus, the throwing of nuts and flowers amongst the people, the oblation of meal, salt, incense, and swine, formed the ingredients of a festival which was principally a plebeian one. Its connexion with the Thesmophoria is shown by the continence and fasting imposed on matrons, which fast was first enjoined in the year 191 B.C., after consulting the Sibylline books, as a religious ordinance to be observed once every five years.[2] Fasting was, otherwise, a thing strange to Roman notions and habits. On the last day of the feast, which was to be observed an entire week, foxes were let loose with burning torches tied to their tails.[3]

Ceres had no special mystery-rite of her own in Rome. There was nothing corresponding to the Thesmophoria and Eleusinia in this particular. The Bacchanalia were hastily and bloodily suppressed when on the point of becoming domesticated, and the emperor Claudius was the first to undertake the transference of the Eleusinian mysteries from Attica to Rome.[4] But Rome had a mystery-rite consecrated to one of the other goddesses, the Bona Dea, who was called the good, kind goddess, for her proper name was not to be spoken, as was the case with the Greek Despoina.[5] Her nature was so many-sided, or rather so little concrete, and therefore capable of so many interpretations, that she seems to be akin to or identical with a number of Greek or Italian deities. She passed for an earth-goddess, Maia, but in the pontifical books was also designated as Fauna, Ops, and Fatua; again she was taken for a Juno, or a goddess invested with Juno's powers, and hence she carried the sceptre in her left hand; or she might be a Proserpine by reason of the sacrifice of swine to her; or as goddess of death, the Hecate of the lower world. The Bœotians took her to be Semele. The Greeks distinguished her generally as the deity of women, and even a Cybele was detected in her. Varro

---

[1] Cic. pro Balbo, c. 24.   [2] Liv. xxxvi. 37.   [3] Ov. Fasti, iv. 683.
[4] Suet. Claud. 25.   [5] Paus. viii. 37.

knew her to be the chaste daughter of Faunus, who had never passed out of the women's apartments, nor ever seen a man, nor been looked upon by one. Yet another saga told of her being killed with myrtle-branches by her husband Faunus, who had found her intoxicated, and, when he rued the deed afterwards, honoured her as a goddess.[1] She had a temple erected to her by the famous vestal virgin Claudia who, when her chastity was suspected, proved its integrity by the ship, which carried the mother of the gods from Pessinus, allowing her to tow it; but her festival, as being of the utmost importance for the welfare of the state, was kept in the house of the consul or prætor. Women only could take part in this solemnity, which was intrusted to the vestal virgins: every thing male, down to the very animals, was excluded, and the statues of males at least covered. The myrtle too, the plant of the goddess of love, was in like manner prohibited; an amphora of wine was at hand and broached, but the wine was to be called milk, and the vessel mellarium. Tame serpents were used in the rite, and the house and image of the goddess bedecked with vine-leaves. Women were obliged to prepare themselves by a previous abstinence of several days from intercourse with men, after which the nightly worship was celebrated in an excited and unrestrained manner: the music of the orgies and the wine bred a fanatic madness and wild desires, which in the times of the Empire broke out into the most hideous excesses.[2]

The worship of Vesta was of great antiquity in Rome, and a main feature of its religion. The goddess was the fire of the house-hearth, conceived to be a deity, just like the Greek Hestia, each house thus becoming, in fact, a temple of Vesta. Her public sanctuary, where the inextinguishable fire was tended by the vestal virgins, was connected with the Regia, in which the pontifex maximus dwelt. But when this dignity fell into the hands of Augustus, he had the sacred fire brought into his house on the Palatine, and thus the palace of the Cæsar became the religious centre of the state. To let the fire out from neglect was visited on the culpable priestess with stripes, and a feast of expiation resorted to with extraordinary sacrifices, to propitiate the anger of the goddess. It was the duty of the Pontifex maximus to kindle the fire anew by a kind of burning-glass, or by pure fire

---

[1] Varro. ap. Lact. i. 22. 9.   [2] Juven. Sat. vi. 314 sqq.

produced by rubbing pieces of wood together.[1] It was regularly renewed on the first of March, the ancient new year. Vesta, too, seems to have had some relation to water, for in her shrine, which had to be daily sprinkled with it, and for the libations on her feasts, only water from a particular spring, or from the brook Numicius, could be used.[2] For long the goddess was worshiped without an image, and it is still doubtful whether there even was an idol of her in her sanctuary, the inner room of which was inaccessible to man, even the high priest; and there stood the vessels with the holy brine.[3] Heifers of a year old were sacrificed to her as a maiden goddess; grasses, and the first-fruits, and afterwards incense, were thrown into her fire, and water, oil, and wine served as drink-offerings.

Minerva, a deity worshiped already by the Italic aborigines, and specially a Sabine goddess, was a member of the supreme triad of gods in the Capitoline temple. Varro believed he recognised in her the personification of those Platonic "ideas" or eternal archetypes after which Jupiter as Demiurge, or heaven, had fashioned matter, which is Juno, into the world.[4] Like the Pallas Athene of the Greeks, she was a maiden goddess, to whom accordingly none but intact heifers could be sacrificed. Her prominent signification was that of a goddess putting into active motion or stirring up: she inclined children to learn, men to agriculture, the chase, and war; hence the wakening cock was sacred to her in the towns of the Aurunci, and in Rome the trumpet sounding the reveillé; and on the Tubilustria, the last day of her feast of the Quinquatria (observed every five years with gladiatorial fights), the trumpets sacred to her were purified by the sacrifice of a lamb.[5] The domestic spinning of wool by the female portion of the family was also under her special patronage.

Minerva's character in Rome, as a protectress of the state, had reference chiefly to the palladium, kept in the shrine of Vesta, the possession of which was thought to afford a divine voucher for the welfare of the empire. It was kept with such secrecy, that for a long time the people did not know whether there really was an image of Minerva in the building; and many

---

[1] Plut. Num. 9. [2] Liv. i. 11; Plut. Num. 13; Tac. Hist. iv. 53.
[3] Serv. Georg. i. 498; Macrob. iii. 9. [4] Ap. Aug. de C. D. vii. 28.
[5] Fest. p. 269; Varro, vi. 14; Ov. Fasti, iii. 849.

thought nothing else holy was there but the fire of Vesta; others that Samothracian symbols which Æneas had brought with him were preserved there; it was, however, really on the spot, only male eyes were not allowed to look at it, probably because undressed, and the pontifex maximus Metellus, who saved it from burning, was struck with blindness for doing so; at last, a second fire, under Commodus, brought it fairly to light.[1] The family of the Nautii were the guardians of another image of Minerva, with a secret service, known only to themselves; and this idol, too, had the reputation of being the very palladium stolen from Troy, and given by Diomede to Nautes, the hero-progenitor of the line.[2]

The worship of Fortuna was more in favour, and took a deeper hold on life in Rome, than that of Minerva. To the Romans she was not the mere personification of an idea, but a divine form, replete with life, conducting and swaying the destinies of individuals, filling all with hope, and imposing the duty of gratitude on them; and indeed the Roman state itself, raised from its petty beginnings to the world's sovereignty, was the bosom-child of the goddess, whose cultus was, in fact, first introduced into Rome by that Servius Tullius who, as a special favourite of the goddess, had been exalted from the condition of a slave's son to kingly dignity. There are many ancient temples of Fortune, says Plutarch, and there are glorious ones too, in all quarters and places of the city.[3] The Fortuna Primigenia from Præneste was in particular esteem, and was there a goddess of fate, at whose breasts Jupiter himself had sucked, and to her the consul Sempronius vowed a temple, dedicated 214 B.C., in the struggle with Hannibal. The plebeians made merry on the feast of Fors Fortuna, goddess of luck, when they had a water expedition in garlanded boats, in which they ate and drank sumptuously. The image of Fortuna Muliebris was forbidden to be touched by a woman who had been twice married;[4] and the women stripped themselves at a hot spring, and with offerings of incense besought Fortuna Virilis to conceal their personal blemishes from their husbands, and to maintain their affection towards them.[5] But there were temples, chapels, images, and altars besides, of

---

[1] Cic. Scaur. ii. 48; Plin. H. N. vii. 43, 45; Herodian. i. 14.
[2] Serv. Æn. ii. 166; iii. 407; Dionys. vi. 69.
[3] Plut. Fort. Rom. x.   [4] Serv. Æn. iv. 19.   [5] Ov. Fasti, iv. 145.

the darling goddess of the Romans, under the most different invocations, many of which were raised in fulfilment of a vow, and a victory in consequence. Even the bad one, Fortuna Mala, had an altar dedicated to her on the Esquiline.[1] The universal worship of Fortuna, invoked and lauded in all places, and at all hours, to whom people attributed, and of whom they asked, every thing, appeared to the elder Pliny to be one of the strongest proofs of the joint prevalence of irreligiousness and superstition.[2]

In Juno we have a goddess whose worship, on one side extending over the whole of central Italy, passed from Latins, Sabines, and Etruscans to Rome; but, on the other, was so little certain and concrete, that it assumed numberless forms, in each of which it seemed again to dissolve. In her particularly we may discern the colourless, shadowy nature of Italic deities, unable, from the defect of creative imagination peculiar to that people, to develop into the form of mythic personalities, and who consequently remained at a stand-still, almost on the level of ghosts, until their outline received a firmer shape, through the influx of Greek gods and myths. Originally Juno was the female deity of nature in its widest extent, the deification of womanhood, woman in the sphere of the divine, and therefore also her name of Juno was the appellative designation of a female genius or guardian spirit. Every wife had her own Juno, and the female slaves in Rome swore by the Juno of their mistresses; and as the genius of a man could be propitiated, so could also the Juno of a woman. The whole of a woman's life, in all its moments, from the cradle to the grave, was thus under the conduct and protection of this goddess, but especially her two chief destinations, marriage and maternity. Accordingly the Roman women sacrificed to Juno Natalis on their birth-day, and observed in a similar manner the Matronalia in the temple of Juno Lucina, in commemoration of the institution of marriage by Romulus, and the fidelity of the ravished Sabine women. The goddess, as Fluonia, in common with Mena, presided over the purification of women, and was worshiped as Juga, Curitis, Domiduca, Unxia, Pronuba, or Cinxia, according to the several usages immediately concerning the bride, in the solemnisation of marriage. As Ossipaga she compacted the bones of the child in its mother's womb; as Opigena she assisted mothers in labour; and as Lucina

[1] Cic. N. D. iii. 25.   [2] Plin. H. N. ii. 5, 7.

she brought the child into the light of day: and therefore when the time of birth approached, Lucina and Diana were invoked, and a table was spread with viands for the former.[1] As Conciliatrix and Viriplaca, she softened the wrath of a husband towards his wife; and as Sororia, sustained harmony between brothers and sisters.

The Romans, however, were also acquainted with Juno as queen of heaven,—Juno Regina, in which character she had her place in the Capitol, and on the Aventine as well, when translated from Veii after its fall. Juno Covella, a title which had reference to the vault of heaven, was invoked by the pontiff in the calculation and announcement of the days of the month. Under the name of Populonia, she stood in the relation of increaser of population to the whole people. She was called Moneta, as presiding over mintage; and the first silver money in Rome was coined in her temple.[2] Besides this, the worship of Juno Sospita and Caprotina had been introduced into Rome from Lanuvium, where she was worshiped as a goddess of defence, clad in a goat-skin, while in honour of the latter the Poplifugia were celebrated,—a festival of merry-making for women, in which also the female slaves took part, and were allowed to place themselves on terms of equality with their mistresses.[3]

Diana was a deity common to the Latin races. Servius Tullius attached the league of the Latin people with Rome to her cultus on the Aventine; her name Dia Jana was old Latin. Her festival in August was celebrated particularly by slaves, whose patroness she was. If she was really identical, as Livy thought, with the Ephesian Artemis, her statue must also have been like the Ephesian one, and Rome have become acquainted with her through the medium of the Phocæans of Marseilles.[4] No man was admitted into the temple which she had in the Patrician street. On the whole, her worship in Rome, when compared with that of the other goddesses, stood somewhat in the background. It was of more importance and more frequented at Aricia, one of the oldest towns of Latium. There she was said

---

[1] Tertull. de Anim, 39.

[2] Livy, vi. 20. Cicero, on the contrary, deriving the appellation from *monere*, mentions a miraculous hint she once gave, about the sacrifice of a swine to her. De Divin. i. 45.

[3] Plut. Camill. 33; Macrob. Sat. i. 11.

[4] Dionys. Hal. iv. 26; Liv. i. 45; Strabo, iv. 180.

to be the Artemis Taurica, and Orestes to have carried off her image from Tauris and brought it. Thither, then, the Roman women repaired with garlands on their heads and lighted torches in hand, to suspend their votive tablets within the precincts of the goddess. The manner in which the priesthood there was obtained points undoubtedly to human sacrifice at an earlier date. The priest, or king of the grove, Rex Nemorensis as he was called, was always a runaway slave, who fought and obtained his office by the sword, but had in turn to be ready either to master any claimant ambitious of the post, or to fall by his hand.[1] It is told of Caligula that he named a stronger man to fight with the priest of the day, because he had been long in the possession of his office.[2] Diana, however, was nowhere a goddess of the moon; for there was a special one, Luna, having a temple on the Aventine, and another on the Palatine: but Greek influence came into operation here too, later on; for Horace, in his Carmen Sæculare, addressed as Sun and Moon Apollo and Diana, of whose relationship as brother and sister the Romans had no conception previously.

The worship of Venus came to Rome from Alba with the Julian family, originally of that place, and in the early times of the state was kept up in part by the family, and in part by the plebs; she did not appear in the hymns of the Salii.[3] She was an old Latin goddess of the garden, so that Nævius still used the term "venus" for garden-produce; and she was also convertible with Flora. Then, in Rome, Venus came to be identified with Aphrodité, it is not clear why; and as the Romans traced their descent from Ascanius, the son of Æneas, she became, in consequence, the ancestral mother of the Roman people. It frequently happens in the Roman system that the older and inferior deities, by losing their independence, are merged in a kindred one of higher distinction, and become mere attributes of theirs; and this was the case with Cloacina, Murcia, Calva, and Libentia, who were now combined with Venus. To this we may add that, in the second Punic war, the Erycinian Venus, in reality a Phœnician Astarte, and there honoured with an impure rite, was transferred to Rome by the building of a temple to her.[4] She got this first temple in the year 215 upon the Capitoline; and in

---

[1] Ov. Fasti, iii. 271 sq.   [2] Suet. Calig. 35.
[3] Varro, i. 1; Plin. H. N. xix. 4, 19.   [4] Cic. Verr. ii. 8; Hor. Od. i. 2, 33.

183, a second at the Colline gate, again in consequence of a vow made in war. Here the courtesans celebrated a feast of their profession, and presented their goddess with incense, cresses, and chaplets of myrtle and roses, to obtain a good harvest from her favour. Before these two, however, Fabius Gurges, about the year 297, had already built a Venus-temple out of the fines of matrons convicted of adultery.[1] Another was erected to Venus Verticordia in 114, when three vestal virgins at a time had been convicted of unchastity.[2] Besides these there were the later-built temples of Venus Genitrix, or ancestral mother of the Romans, and of Venus Victrix. Still, upon the whole, the worship of this goddess was more a matter of private devotion than a state affair. There were no public festivals and sacrifices consecrated to her.

It is not easy to decide who Liber and Libera actually were. That an old Latin country god was called Liber, is certain. People thought he was styled "free" because of the looseness of speech exercised on his festivals; but when he was identified in Rome with the Greek Bacchus, he was supposed to be so called because, as god of wine, he freed the soul from care.[3] Yet the usages of his festivals show that he was not a wine-god proper, but a god of blessing to the fruits of the country in general. In the country a huge phallus was carried about on a wagon, then set up at the crossways, and last of all in the town. In Lavinium his festival was kept for a whole month, impure language being bandied about on each day whilst the phallus was carried in procession, and the lengthy feast concluded with the crowning of the phallus by the most respectable matron to be found.[4] On the Liberalia, hot cakes, dipped in honey, were offered to Liber, as discoverer of honey; women, crowned with ivy, sat in the streets to sell these cakes, and burned them as an offering for the buyer upon a small hearth kept ready at hand.[5] The ceremony of giving young men the toga virilis on this feast probably implied that the power of generation and manhood was of the essence of this god. Libera, of whom one has but little to say, seems to have been taken for the wife of Liber, and therefore Ovid calls her Ariadne;[6]

---

[1] Liv. x. 31. [2] Val. Max. viii. 15, 12; Jul. Obsequens. 97.
[3] Sen. de Tranq. Animae. xv. 15.
[4] Varro, ap. Aug. C. D. vii. 21. [5] Varro, L. L. vi. 14.
[6] Ov. Fasti, iii. 512.

but she was also identified with the Proserpina Cora, and even the Roman Libitina.

The Romans had a god of the lower world, Dis, or "the rich" (because of the treasures to be found in the interior of the earth), whom they compared to Pluto, but of whom nothing more precise is to be said. The god Consus, who was invoked at a subterranean altar in the great games of the circus, was perhaps one with Dis. By the altar of Saturn, too, Dis had a shrine, to which earthen puppets were brought as offerings of atonement for the offerer and his family, for it was said Hercules had taught the Pelasgi to present such oscilla instead of human sacrifices.[1] Dis too, like Consus, was not without a subterranean altar, shared with Proserpine, and standing in Terentum, a part of the Campus Martius, which was uncovered for the purposes of his feast, and then covered with earth again. Here secular games were celebrated at long intervals, afterwards at the distance of a century. They were properly a commemoration of the dead, but when Augustus had them held again, in the year 14 B.C., they had already lost this signification. In the Comitium there was a pit, sacred to Dis and Proserpina, and called Mundus, *i. e.* Orcus, said to have been dug out by Etruscans at the command of Romulus, into which were thrown first-fruits of all the necessaries of life, and clods of earth from all the different territories in the neighbourhood from which the followers of Romulus had come. This hole was closed up with the Manes-stone (Lapis Manalis), and taken off three days in the year, in August, October, and November, and with it the doors of the realm of shadows being, as it were, opened, people were afraid of undertaking any thing of importance during the three dismal days.[2]

Proserpina (a name coined by the Romans in imitation of the Greek "Persephone") was not properly queen of the kingdom of the shades, for she had no independent worship; it was rather Libitina, whom Roman scholars, on etymological grounds probably, converted into an Aphrodité, for which reason Plutarch compared her with the Aphrodité "of the tomb" at Delphi.[3] All that was required for the burial of the dead was deposited in her temple, and was sold or let out to hire; and, according to a law originating with Servius Tullius, a piece of money was to be paid

---

[1] Macrob. Sat. i. 11. [2] Macrob. Sat. i. 16; Varro, 16.
[3] Plut. Quæst. Rom. 23.

there for every dead person. The bier, or death-bed, too, on which the corpse was burnt, used to be called Libitina,[1] and so the poets termed death itself.

In the time of the kings, boys had been sacrificed to Mania, a goddess of death, for the well-being of families, "head having to be atoned for by head," in obedience to an oracle of Apollo; under the republic, heads of poppy and garlic were offered for the purpose, and the hanging up of images of Mania at the house-doors was a sufficient propitiation against a danger imminent on a family.[2] Lastly, to this circle of deities also belonged Nænia, the personified death-wail, and Viduus, the god who deprived the body of its soul.

The Romans, with their dry and practical understanding, went far farther than the imaginative Greeks in god-making, and gradually invented gods for every relation and action of life. To the principal deities, who had a distinct sphere of life assigned them,—birth, for instance, marriage, and agriculture,—they added a host of single subordinate gods, who sometimes were not even representatives of an action, but only of a circumstance, purely accidental and insignificant, accompanying an action. Many may have grown into independent gods out of a title assigned to a deity. The numbers were swelled by a troop of allegorical beings, who had temples and chapels erected to them.

The boundary-god, Terminus, had his stone in the Jupiter temple on the Capitol, and the feast of the Terminalia, with its unbloody offerings, consecrated to neighbourly concord. The wood-god, Silvanus, was at once a guardian of bounds, a keeper-off of wolves, and a goblin, the terror of lying-in women; while against his pranks women who had given birth to a child required no less than three protecting deites, Intercidona, Pilumnus, and Deverra, and for them a couch was prepared in the atrium, where the woman in labour lay.[3] Vaticanus attended to the first cry of the newly-born child, which, when laid upon the ground according to Roman custom, the father took up; if he omitted to do so, the omission was equivalent to a repudiation, and the child was killed or exposed. Hence there was a goddess of this taking-up, a Levana.[4] A cradle-goddess, Cunina, a Statilinus, an Edusa and Potnia, a Paventia, Fabelinus, and Catius, were all called

---

[1] Plin. H. N. xxxvii. 3, 11. [2] Macrob. Sat. i. 7.
[3] Varro, ap. Aug. C. D. vi. 9. [4] Gell. xvi. 17; Aug. C. D. iv. 8.

into play in the first period of the child's life, of his nourishment, and speech. Juventas, a goddess of youth, had a temple, and a lectisternium was dressed up for her when the portents were threatening. Orbona also, the goddess of orphan age, had her sanctuary. Two temples were erected to the goddess of fever, who was invoked in precaution against this sickness. Pietas, Pax, Bonus Eventus, Spes, Quies, Pudicitia, Honos, Virtus, and Fides, had their temples or chapels. Concordia was particularly rich in sanctuaries.

Over and above these, Rome abounded in deities whose original value had been obscured or blotted out in the course of time, or who, with all the importance of a worship, were wanting in the plastic and mythical capacity for refinement, or of such again as, with little importance in themselves, were but rarely mentioned. Thus, on the banks of the Tiber, on the fifteenth of March, the festival of Anna Perenna was observed, who also had a sacred grove. In the open air, under arbours or tents, people surrendered themselves to unrestricted mirth and sumptuous feasting, accompanied with obscene songs and jokes, and sacrifices were offered her to obtain a successful year;[1] but of her antecedents so little was known, that she was actually converted into a sister of the Carthaginian Dido. The fable of Leucothea had been laid in Rome upon Mater Matuta, a Latin goddess of the dawn of day and of voyaging, to whom the Matralia, or mothering feast, was celebrated by the Roman women; female slaves were forbidden entrance into her temple, only one was introduced in allusion to the legend of Ino, scourged, and thrust out again. The correction of maid-servants seems to have been put under her superintendence.[2] Of the Stata Mater, whose image was in the Forum, and to whom fire was lighted at night under the open heaven, no one in Ovid's time seems to have had any accurate knowledge.[3] The case was no better with the goddess Vacuna, of great repute among the Sabines, and of whom Ovid only mentions that on her festival people either stood or sat before the Vacunalian hearth.[4] The goddess Laverna, on the contrary, who had both altar and grove in Rome, was well known to thieves

---

[1] Ov. Fast. iii. 523 sq., 651 sq.; Macrob. Sat. i. 12.
[2] Plut. Quaest. Rom. 17, Camil. 5; Ov. Fast. vi. 469 sq.
[3] Hor. Ep. ii. 2, 186; Colum. xxii. p. 57.
[4] Fast. vi. 305.

and impostors, who were her supplicants for protection in their pursuits. Horace makes one of the class pray: "Beauteous Laverna, grant me to deceive, to be fair and pure to the eye; throw night round my misdeeds, and a cloud over my frauds."[1]

The Roman religion was exceedingly well stocked with deities of flocks and of gardens. To the Dea Dia, not farther known, and who had an altar and precinct in the neighbourhood of Rome, the Arval brothers offered a worship, which proves her to have been protectress of the fruits of the field. Pales, god of shepherds, deriving his name from straw, whose sex, nevertheless, the Romans could not certify, was honoured by the important festival of the Palilia on the twenty-first of April.[2] Protection and increase was implored of the deity on the flocks and domestic animals; and therefore the sacrifices had to be unbloody; to put beasts to death, while asking for their preservation, would have seemed a contradiction. At the same time a great ceremonial of purification was gone through; flocks and cattle leaped over kindled hay and straw, they were asperged with water, and, in the city, the reserved blood of the October-horse, and the ashes of the calf that had been taken from the carcass of its mother and consumed by fire on the feast of the Fordicidia, were used in the purification of the people.

The service of Flora was of great antiquity in Rome: Tatius was said to have vowed her an altar, and Numa to have instituted a flamen for her, and in 239 B.C. a temple was built out of pecuniary fines, and annual games appointed her in consequence of a failure in the harvest. The solemnities now reached the highest degree of license and offensiveness; it was customary for prostitutes, who presented themselves at them as actresses, to throw aside their clothes, and play naked, sometimes chasing hares and roe-deer, at others fighting like gladiators.[3] The legend probably arose from this,—Flora had been a courtesan who had earned a large fortune, made the people her heirs, and appointed a certain sum for keeping up the games called, after her, Floralia; but the senate, to palliate the scandal, gave out

---

[1] Ep. i. 16, 60.
[2] Ov. Fasti, iv. 721 sq; Serv. Æn. ii. 325; Georg. iii. 1.
[3] Ov. Fast. v. 184-375; Plin. H. N. xviii. 29, lix. 3; Juvenal, vi. 249, and the Schol.

Flora to be a goddess, who presided over the flowers.¹ A tradition, quite similar, attached to Acca Larentia; while some explained the mortuary solemnity which took place yearly at her grave, by her having been the nurse of Romulus, others preferred to assert she was a rich courtesan, who made a present of the Campus Martius to the Roman people at her death, and had hence acquired the worship paid her in Rome.²

The old Latin Vertumnus, original representative of the changes of the seasons, became, by degrees, a god of sowing, corn-fields, and fruit-gardens, receiving their first-fruits from gardeners, and having in Rome the feast of Vertumnalia in October, with temple and statue. His female aspect, Pomona, made by the myth into his wife, had a flamen of her own, the lowest of the fifteen flamines.³ In every field, garden, and vineyard, a Priapus, daubed red with vermillion, and with an immense phallus, was set up as guardian-god. Milk, honey, cakes, and even he-goats and asses, were sacrificed to him.⁴ The Romans received him first from Greece; but there was a very similar old Roman phallus-god, Mutinus-Tutunus, or Fascinus, and, as the belief in the protecting and averting power of the phallus was deep-rooted among the Romans, his image, or at least the simple phallus (fascinum), was set up every where, and his worship carefully tended. People believed he had the power of putting a whole army to flight by a sudden panic-fear; for instance, he had made Hannibal's force retire from Rome;⁵ and he was considered specially effective against wicked enchanters and the magical operations of envy and jealousy. Hence a colossal phallus of Tutunus was set up in the courts, or even over the hearths of private dwellings, and on it a newly-married bride had to take her seat on her entrance into her husband's house.⁶ Even the vestal virgins were obliged to the worship of this god, as belonging to the protecting deities of Rome. His phallus was

---

¹ Lact. i. 20; Arnob. iii. 23, where "meretrix" clearly ought to be read, and not "genetrix;" Minuc. Fel. 25.

² Varr. vi. 23; Macrob. Sat. i. 10; Ov. Fasti, iii. 57; Gell. vi. 7.

³ Ovid. Met. xiv. 641; Propert. iv. 2; Varro, v. 46, 74.

⁴ Ov. Fast. i. 391, 415; Serv. Georg. ii. 84.

⁵ Varro, ap. Nonium, p. 47.

⁶ Aug. C. D. vi. 9; Arnob. 417; Lact. i. 20. Comp. Pitture d'Ercolano, pl. 26, p. 178 sq.; Antiq. Hercul. (bronzi), ii. p. 372, pl. 94. Panofka, Terracotte, pp. 67, 106.

set upon the car of the "triumphator," and people used it for the protection of small children, and at Rome matrons sacrificed in his sanctuary, though with veils on.[1]

Deities of fate, on whom birth and death particularly depended, were also known in Rome; but the belief of the Romans, during their religious time, was not generally fatalistic, as in fact planet-worship, which elsewhere generally led to fatalism, was well-nigh excluded from their system. Nevertheless, on the seventh day after the birth of a child, the Fata Scribunda were invoked, *i. e.* the nameless deities who marked out beforehand his future destiny for the child. The Parca—for the Romans of old knew probably but one—received her name, according to Varro's assumption,[2] from birth, and was originally an assistant at births; and there was also a Morta in opposition to her. Then, in order to put together three Parcae, after the Greek pattern, Nona and Decima were counted as such, goddesses of birth, so called after the number of the months of pregnancy, and Morta, the Death-Parca. The names of the Greek Moirai, Clotho, Lachesis, and Atropos, were also made use of.[3] The place of deities of fate was really occupied amongst the Romans by Fortuna, changeable and capricious, but still accessible to prayer, and adhering to the everlasting city in other respects with a fidelity unheard of elsewhere.

Further, there was a Mana-Geneta, or "kind birth-goddess," to whom young dogs were sacrificed,[4] with the prayer that no one in the house might become a Mané. Carmenta seems to have been of a like signification, but not capable of more accurate definition, into whose sanctuary nothing of leather was allowed to be brought. On occasion of a dispute of the senate with the women, two sacrifices were appointed her, one for boys, and the other for maidens. But altars had also been erected to two Carmentas for the prevention of unhappy births, who were styled Antevorta or Prorsa, and Postvorta, with relation to the position of the child in the maternal womb.[5] Egeria too, Numa's counselling nymph, and worshiped at Rome on the Aventine, was invoked by pregnant women to help them in labour.

[1] Plin. H. N. xxviii. 4, 7 ; Fest. pp. 103, 172.
[2] Varr. ap. Gell. iii. 16.   [3] Cassell. Vindex, ap. Gell. iii. 16.
[4] Plin. H. N. xxix. 4; Plut. Quæst. Rom. 52.
[5] Ov. Fast. i. 199 sq.; Gell. xvi. 16 ; Serv. Æn. viii. 339.

The Roman Hercules enjoyed a higher reputation in Rome than in Greece, being in Rome more god than hero, which was caused partly by the immigrant Heracles from Sicily and lower Italy having combined with the Sabine god Sancus-Fidius. This Sancus, who retained, however, his own worship on the island of the Tiber, and in a temple on the Quirinal, was the ancestral god of the Sabine people, and was therefore also conceived to be their first king. Oaths were sworn in his name, and the records of treaties deposited in his temple.[1] He was, in a general way, the Sabine Jupiter, and his name of Deus Fidius was also repeated in that of Zeus Pistios. This same god may be detected in Hercules; people swore by him, and his name was the ordinary formula of asseveration; and just as the person swearing by Sancus-Fidius betook himself out of the house into the open air, so also boys, when they intended to swear by Hercules, were taught to leave the room and to go outside the house.[2] The special place of his worship was the famous Ara maxima, at the foot of Mount Aventine, erected by himself to Jupiter, in memorial of his combat with the giant Cacus, who had stolen his cattle. Here tithes of booty and spoil acquired in war, or of profit made, were dedicated to him, an oblation not omitted by wealthy Romans of so late a date as Lucullus, Sylla, and Crassus.[3] By Tertullian's time, indeed, it was hardly a third of the tithe that was laid on the altar of Hercules.[4] Sacrifice was offered to Hercules or Sancus on setting out for a journey. A great number of victims and popular banquets were generally offered to Hercules, as the "mighty protector" or "victor," in which characters he had two temples at Rome; from these festivities, however, women, slaves, and freedmen were excluded.[5] At the same time the ordinance, that in the prayers for the occasion no other god but he should be named, proves that, in fact, and in spite of all the transfer from the Greek of the Heracles legends, and in spite of a great deal of the Greek rite being ingrafted on his worship, the old god Sancus-Fidius preponderated in him. When, in the year 310 B.C., at the instigation of the censor, Appius Claudius, the Potitii, who had had the care of the worship of the god from time immemorial, sold their priesthood to public slaves, the whole family died

---

[1] Dionys. iv. 58; Hor. Ep. ii. 1, 25.
[2] Varr. v. 66; Plut. Quaest. Rom. 28.
[3] Diod. iv. 21.
[4] Tertull. Apol. 14.
[5] Plut. Q. R. lx. 90.

out within a short time, and Appius fell blind,[1]—events which confirmed the Romans in their conception of the greatness and power of the god.

Every Roman family had its particular guardian-gods presiding in the interior of the house; the gods and guardians of the penus, or domestic store and household provisions, whose numbers, names, and race were unknown. They were invoked under the common designation of Penates. In the atrium, the interior and partly unceiled space of the house, where the community life of the family was spent, their images were placed near the hearth, on which offerings were made them, the never-extinguished flames of the hearth-fire always burning in their honour,[2] and the family table being always spread and furnished for them, with a salt-cellar and some viands. In general the kitchen was dedicated to them. The son took his father's place at the head of the household, under the protection of the Penates, who were handed down with the succession from generation to generation. They had the care of the welfare and honour of the family, and were also the patrons of the domestics and of the laws of hospitality, and whoever could embrace their images was in safety.

There were also Penates of the Roman state, having their own temple on the Velia, a piazza on the Palatine hill. No one could give any accurate account of who these Penates were. In the eyes of the Romans those were the true and genuine Penates of the state which were worshiped in the old Latin metropolis at Lanuvium, whither the Roman consuls, prætors, and dictators betook themselves on entering into office, in order to sacrifice to them and Vesta.[3] In the two temples both at Rome and Lanuvium, the Dii Penates were kept from the sight of the people, and could only be seen by the priests.[4] The historian Timæus only heard that in the innermost shrine at Lanuvium iron and copper heraldic staves and earthen vessels, inherited from Troy, were to be found.[5] Amid the contradictions met with in the Roman accounts of the nature of the Penates, the assertion of Varro, supported by the pontifical books, continues to have the greatest weight, viz. that the Penates of the state were the great gods, who had their

---

[1] Liv. ix. 29, 34.   [2] Virg. Æn. i. 707; Serv. Æn. ii. 469.
[3] Varro, v. 144; Macrob. Sat. ii. 4.   [4] Serv. Æn. ii. 296; iii. 12.
[5] Ap. Dionys. i. 67.

dwelling-place in the penetralia of the heavens; and he designates them in an abstract manner as "Heaven and Earth," the two principles of all that exists (in the books they are styled Saturn and Ops). Symbols of these for the popular belief were the two little male images which, after being carried by Dardanus, first to Samothrace and then to Troy, and from thence by Æneas to Latium, ended with being honoured there as powerful guardian deities; these were two youths seated with spears in their hands in the temple on the Velia, which were also taken to be the Dioscuri, Castor and Pollux.

The Romans had received the worship and name of Lares, or "lords," from Etruria. They were not of the number of great gods, like the Penates, with whom, nevertheless, they were often interchanged, but were gods who had become so, souls of men of earlier times exalted to the dignity of god or hero. In the houses where, like the Penates, they were set up as images in the atrium (or sometimes in a lararium of their own), and had their own cultus on the hearth, they were the guardian spirits of families, over whose continuance they watched. They belonged, as a species, to the genus Manes, these not being honoured, but only the lares; and amongst the lares of the house there was one, the Lar familiaris, who was oftenest named, and also most distinguished in worship: he was master of the family, its divine head, though one did not attach to him the idea of a distinct individual, bearing a name and belonging to the ancestors, as for instance first father of a line. "It is now many years since I came into possession of this house," says the Lar familiaris in Plautus.[1] This Lar seems rather to have been a personification of the vital and procreative powers, assuring the duration of a family; bound up as he was with the family, he changed houses along with it. As the Romans, up to the time of the laws of the twelve tables, kept the remains of their dead relatives in ashes in their own houses, the veneration for the departed, then turned into family gods and guardian spirits, with whose remains or "deposits" a man shared the same roof, was all the more natural. But as to the question which of the members of a family belonged decidedly to the Lares, and which not, whether women for instance, and maidens as well as others, it was probably never raised; it is only mentioned that the re-

[1] Prolog. Aulular.

mains of children dying before the fortieth day, and which were kept under the roof, were called the Lares grundiles.¹ At meal-times the Lares received libations and first-fruits; on domestic festivals they were crowned, and the bride, on entering into the house, made her offering to the Lares first of all.

But as there were two kinds of Penates, domestic and public, so there was also, besides the family Lares, others to which a public service was rendered. Of this number were the Præstites, the patron spirits of the town, and the Compitales, to whom Servius Tullius ordered wooden chapels to be erected at the cross-ways intersecting the quarters of the city. In the temple proper of the Lares, restored by Augustus, together with their public worship, then fallen into disuse, two figures were to be found, probably Romulus and Remus; before them a dog, their ordinary sacrifice, for "god and dog love the 'compita,'" as Ovid says.²

But what was the relation of the Genius to the Lares? This was a difficult and obscure question even for a Roman, and in answering it people seem to have been satisfied, for the most part, with very vague notions. Into the idea of a "genius," Etruscan, Greek, and peculiar Roman conceptions entered. In many of the authorities the genius appears as the guardian spirit imparted to man at his birth, inseparable from him indeed, but still essentially distinct;³ in other expressions, it is not possible to distinguish the genius of a man from himself: he seems to be but the habitual bias or direction of a man's own will, objectively conceived; and where, as with Varro, a philosophical system comes in, there the genius is that divine ingredient of the spirit dwelling in each man, that portion of the divine world-soul, which, thinking and willing in man, returns to it after death; and as the world-soul is termed god, so the genius also is god. But the genius again was conceived as a being of generative power, deciding the position and distinctive properties of a man from his first origin.⁴ The idea of a man having two genii, one good and exhorting to good, the other evil,⁵ is more rarely met with; yet it is well known that shortly before his death his evil genius was reputed to have

---

¹ Voss. in Etymol. "subgrundaria."

² Tac. Ann. xii. 24; Ov. Fasti, v. 129 sq.; Propert. iii. 22, 22 (Paley); Arnob. iii. 41; Serv. Æn. v. 64.

³ Censorin. de Die Nat. c. iii. 5; Amm. Marc. xxi. 4.

⁴ Paul. Diac. p. 71; Hor. Ep. ii. 2, 183 sq.

⁵ Serv. Æn. vi. 743.

appeared to Brutus.[1] As a rule mention is made but of one, who is called Juno in the case of women; and Pliny saw, in the whole of this belief and worship, a formal self-deification, proceeding upon the view that the genius or Juno was nothing else but the spiritual element of individual men.[2] In life, people's behaviour was in accordance with this view: what the Roman did for the enjoyment of life, he therewith enlivened his genius; his self-imposed privations did detriment to his genius. The birthday was the annual festival of this genius: he was then treated with wine and flowers, sacrificial cakes, honey, and incense, and the offerer alone tasted of the offerings.

Not only the individual, but each and every place also, had its genius. There were countless genii of places. "Why talk to me," says Prudentius, "of the genius of Rome, when your wont is to ascribe a genius of their own to doors, houses, baths, and stables; and in every quarter of the town, and all places, you feign thousands of genii as existing, so that no corner is without its own ghost?"[3] "No place," says Servius, "is without a genius, generally manifesting itself in a serpent." The people, the Curiæ, the centuries, the senate, the army, the different burgher companies, each and all had their genius. There were even genii of particular deities. Amongst the twenty gods whom Varro enumerates as the select, we find, besides Jupiter, the "Genius;"[4] a Genius Jovialis was counted among the public Penates of Rome,[5] and the Etruscan Tages was a son of the genius, and grandson of Jupiter. The Genius Jovialis was therefore an emanation of Jupiter, the generator generated by him. Only in a religion such as the Roman, one must not expect an idea of the kind to be in any way firmly grasped or developed; so then there is no further mention of this Genius Jovialis.

---

[1] Val. Max. i. 7, 7; Plut. Brut. 36.   [2] Plin. H. N. ii. 5-7.
[3] Prud. adv. Symmach. ii. 444.   [4] Ap. Aug. C. D. vii. 2.
[5] Cæsius, ap. Arnob. iii. 40.

The Roman Priesthood.

The Roman state-worship originated in those of single families and gentes; and when these rites came to be public, or common to the whole state, the gens, which had hitherto kept the cultus to itself, formed a college of priests. The priesthoods for the most part were already in existence in the time of the kings: on the rise of the republic the sacrificial king took the place of the king, and in 196 B.C. the triumviri Epulones, the last independent creation were added. In proportion as the plebeians aimed at obtaining their share in the sacerdotal offices, hitherto absorbed by the patricians, such offices were enlarged in many ways, doubled, or otherwise altered. Thus, by the Licinian law first, the Sibylline decemviri were increased, for the sake of the plebs, to the number of ten. About the same time, too, that the pontificate and augurate, and the community of vestals were thrown open to the plebs (159 B.C.), a plebeian also obtained the dignity of Flamen Carmentalis, who had a sacrifice to offer to the soothsaying goddess Carmenta.

The ministers of religion in Rome were partly individual priests, such as the Flamines, the king of sacrifice, and the Curiones, though these latter had a superior in the Curio Maximus, yet without forming a college in reality, and were partly independent communities, such as the Pontiffs, the Salii, Luperci, and Arval-brothers, filled up by election (coöptation) from their own body. At no time was there in Rome one organised association of the priests comprising every member of the sacerdotal class, to present the appearance of a whole and powerful corporate body. The separate sacerdotal ones were tolerably independent of one another; their members could not be deprived, and kept their office for life; yet a flamen would lose his dignity by a small oversight committed in ritual; and a Salian on becoming consul or prætor had to resign. They were not, however, civil authorities, responsible either to senate or people: they might fill the political and military posts at the same time, and it was not uncommon for an individual to be in possession of several priesthoods at once. This, however, does not seem to have taken place in earlier times. The first of whom history makes mention is Otacilius Crassus, pontifex and augur together, after the second Punic war.[1] The emperors not only invested themselves with the high-priesthood, but also belonged to a number of the colleges of priests, sometimes to all.[2]

The holiness and importance of the ceremonial required a special and unvarying tradition, and a careful training of the postulant for the duties of a religious office. This double requirement could only be satisfied by close corporations. Such colleges as those of the pontiffs and augurs filled up the vacancies in their numbers, caused by death, by a free choice (coöptatio), and thus preserved the peculiar spirit of their order, and the tradition which they received and handed on. By a law of Domitius Ahenobarbus, tribune of the people, in the year 104, the right of election to these colleges was first made over to the popular comitia tributa. These named an individual, who was then received by coöptation (now become an empty form) and was inaugurated into the society. After many changes of the law on this head, these appointments fell at last into the hands of Augustus and his successors.

The Pontifices appear to have derived their name from the Pons Sublicius, which they had built and kept in repair in order to be able to sacrifice on either bank of the Tiber, and celebrate the Argean rite on the bridge itself. According, however, to a later opinion, the name was deducible from the knowledge of numbers and arithmetic, which was a requisite accomplishment, for calculating the festal calendar was one of the occupations of this college.[3] In any case, their employment in the historical times was not sacrificial service principally, but general superintendence of the whole religious system, and their place, within the sphere of their own operations, resembled that of the senate in the civil life. Still they certainly had a succession of religious duties, vows, and sacrifices to fulfil in the name of the Roman people and state. The kings were at first presidents of their college; whence too, at the beginning of the commonwealth, certain regal rights passed to the new head, the Pontifex maximus. The society first consisted of four members, two for

---

[1] Liv. xxvii. 6.

[2] Dio. Cass. liv. 19; Eckhel, D. Num. xvii. 102; Marini, Atti dei Fr. Arv. p. 153; Lamprid. Commod. 12.

[3] L. Lange, Röm. Alterthümer, Berlin, 1856, p. 267.

each of the races, the Rhamnes and Tities. The supreme pontiff was chosen out of the college itself. Their number was doubled by the Ogulnian law.

The supervision of the pontiffs extended therefore to all public and private worships; they were the guardians of the old tradition, propagated in part by oral communication and practice, and partly stereotyped in their written documents, or Indigitamenta; and as the civil law was originally most closely connected with the religious, they had also to keep up an acquaintance with law, and had juridical decisions to give. Their decisions concerned the law of marriage and inheritance, public games, the consecration of a temple, the form of a ceremony to be performed, or the validity of one that had been, and the like. All priests and their ministers were their subjects; and as they settled the calendar, they had scope for a powerful and frequently a decisive influence on the whole of the public and civil life of the people. They could not only inflict pecuniary punishment, but even pass sentence of death; for instance, in case of incest, *i. e.* a crime consisting in the profanation of a sanctuary or a religious function by unchastity, as when a vestal virgin allowed herself to be seduced, or Clodius in woman's attire stole into Cæsar's house at the celebration of the rite of the Bona Dea; though in this latter case, by an exceptional decree of the people, a mixed judicial board of fifty-six persons was specially instituted to try the offender.

Ordinarily, in republican times, it was only an elderly man, who had already discharged curule offices, who attained to the dignity of pontifex maximus. He conducted the business and voting of the college, promulgated and executed its decrees, and in matters of any consequence dared not act lightly in opposition to it. Yet he acted on the plenitude of his own power where the application of an existing law, or of a custom that had acquired the force of a right, was indubitable. His office was held in such high veneration, that when attacked on the score of the use of his power, he almost always got the best of it, and he could make any one, even against his will, Flamen Dialis, a dignity encumbered with great and burdensome personal restrictions.[1] This sacerdotal chief was elected from the college by the people in the Comitia Tributa. It was only late, in the times of the

[1] Val. Max. ix. 3; Liv. xxvii. 8.

downfall of the religion, that he was allowed to exercise secular functions; thus Licinius Crassus, in 131 B.C., as pontifex maximus, became consul also, and went in person to command in Asia, breaking through the custom of no bearer of that dignity leaving Italy.[1] The Regia, in the Via Sacra, that place of old sanctuaries of the state, was also the official residence of the pontifex maximus and of the king of sacrifice; but Augustus converted a portion of his own house into state buildings in order to have a separate sacerdotal residence, without being obliged to live in the Regia.[2]

The priest who had to perform the sacred duties, formerly proper to the kings, had the title of "king," in other respects so grating to Roman ears; for people in Rome generally went upon the axiom, that religious relations ought to be immutable; care was taken, however, that, in despite of his high rank and title, he should be without the reality of power, even in the religious department. Named by the pontifex maximus (but not till he had advised with the pontiffs and augurs), he was also dependent on him, could never assume a secular office, but was always chosen from the patricians only, and at banquets enjoyed precedence of all the other priests. The wife of the king of sacrifice was styled "queen," and had to assist him in certain sacrifices. The Comitium in the forum, the place appointed for the assembly of the people to deliberate on political and legal objects, was only frequented by the sacrificial king for the purpose of offering the monthly sacrifice, after which he hurried away, so that he might not by tarrying longer be led through his lofty title into the temptation of ambitiously mixing himself up with public proceedings; and this was called the Regifugium.[3]

The fifteen Flamines, who, without composing a college, were consecrated to the service of separate deities, had their name either from the woollen bands wound round their sacerdotal caps,[4] or from lightning. The three flamines majores, of Jupiter, Mars, and Quirinus, were priests held in the highest esteem, who appeared always together, and were at all times to be chosen from patrician families, whereas the plebeians too could become flamines minores. The people chose them, and the pontifex maximus received and initiated them with the assistance of the augurs. The regulations by which the life of the Flamen Dialis had to be

[1] Liv. Epit. 59; Dio. Cass. fragm. 62.   [2] Dio. Cass. liv. 27.
[3] Plut. Quaest. Rom. I. 63.   [4] Varro, iv. 15; Festus, s. v.

guided are surprising; they give the impression of a kind of foreign, non-Roman institution, in no way connected with the other religious ideas of the Romans, and seeming to present the appearance of ruins of an older and more comprehensive system of ceremonial ordinances more detailed. Ovid calls the Flamen Dialis a Pelasgic priest,[1] and by this designation, as well as by the prescriptions alluded to above, one's suspicions are aroused that the priesthood of the Flamen Dialis, in any case primitive and pre-Roman, might have been somehow or other connected with the equally Pelasgic institute of the Selli in the Dodonean sanctuary of Zeus, whom Homer describes as a body of priests living under a distinct and austere rule.[2] The flamen also was not allowed to take an oath, to ride, or have any thing knotted about him, or to look at bodies of armed men. The sight of a prisoner in chains, or criminal taken to be scourged, made him unclean. If any such met him, his fetters were taken off, or the chastisement deferred till another day. If a man in chains took refuge in his house, his chains were thrown over the wall into the street. On festivals he was defiled by the sight of a man occupied in work, and if one so employed put his work purposely within sight of the flamen, he was punished. For fear of becoming unclean, the flamen also could not touch a goat, or dog, or raw flesh, beans, or leaven. He could not bathe under the open heaven, lest Jupiter should see his nakedness, nor could he spend a night outside of the city. No slave could cut his hair, while his cut-off hair and the parings of his nails had to be buried under a fruit-bearing tree. His wife took her part in his ministry, and was in great measure subject to the same regulations; he was obliged to live united with her in the marriage which had received the sacerdotal benediction of confarreatio, and ought himself to have been born in the same. If the flaminica died, he had to resign his office.[3] He enjoyed still higher honours. No oath could be exacted of him when acting as witness; the sella curulis, the apex of Roman ambition, belonged to him, as well as a place in the senate.

The priesthood of the Salii, who danced in armour, is in like manner of pre-Roman and Pelasgic origin. It was to be found in the oldest Latin towns, and ancient records point to Mantinea

---

[1] Fast. ii. 282.
[2] Iliad, xvi. 233 sqq., where they are called ἀνιπτόποδες, χαμαιεῦναι.
[3] Gell. x. 15; Plut. Quæst. Rom. 100 sqq.; Liv. v. 52.

and Samothrace as places from which, in the Pelasgic period, this rite was introduced into central Italy.¹ As priests of Mars, and divided into two colleges, always consisting of twelve young men, they went about in March in embroidered garments fitting the body, with brazen cuirass, sword, spear, and shield, and, accompanied by flute-players and singers, danced through the city, on the Forum, and in the Capitol; at their head they had a magister, a dancer before them (præsul), and a precentor. In their antique Saliaric hymn, besides Mars, Jupiter, Juno, Minerva, Hercules, Mania, and Volumnia, were introduced, and, as a rare distinction, also the praises of individuals of eminence, as, for example, Octavian during his life, and Germanicus after his death, by a special decree of the senate; and, later still, Marcus Aurelius caused the name of Verus to be inserted.² As the procession through the city, with the sacrifices in different places, lasted a number of days, the Salii had their stations accordingly, where they passed the night, after a sumptuous repast. On the fourteenth of March, the last day of the procession, called the Mamuralia, a man went with them, wrapped in thick skins, who quietly submitted to be beaten with long sticks. He was the representative of the Mamurius, celebrated in the hymn,—probably Mars himself in his Sabine name,—who, according to the later sagas, was the maker of the sacred shields.³ Of the two colleges, that of the Palatine Salii was the older and the more respectable; the second and younger, the Colline or Agonensic Salii, were established by Tullius Hostilius to honour the sons or comrades of Mars, Quirinus, Pavor, and Pallor: with them the warlike signification of the god and the rite seems to have been the prevalent one, while the ancient Salii of the Palatine, at least according to the old view, afterwards confessedly obscured, celebrated a feast of the new year, for the year formerly began in March, thus worshiping Mars as the conductor of the year and god of the month of spring; the number twelve of the Salii also had relation to that of the twelve months.

The Luperci too, the oldest priests in Rome, the institution of whom was therefore put as far back as the Arcadian Evander, were divided into two colleges of Fabii and Quintilii, to whom

---

[1] Serv. An. viii. 285, ii. 375; Fest. s. v. Salios.
[2] Hor. Carm. iv. 5, 31; Tac. Ann. ii. 83; Capitol. Ant. 21.
[3] Lyd. iii. 29, iv. 36; Fest. s. v. Mamurii.

Cæsar afterwards added a third of Julii. It was thus a priesthood of families, but in the later period of the republic was no longer in esteem, because of the strangeness and indecency of its rite. Cicero reproached Antony with having become a Lupercus, and spoke of the college as a boorish institution, begun previous to all civilisation, and to any thing like law;[1] and yet they kept their ground till the fall of the Empire. The equally primitive Arvalian fraternity of twelve were in higher repute. Their office was for life, and was not even forfeited by exile. They filled up their numbers by coöptation, until the emperors at length appointed them, and they had a magister at their head.

In order to relieve the pontiffs of the number of sacrifices which they had to perform, the Epulones were instituted in the year 196 B.C. They were at first three, then seven, and under Cæsar ten, and had the charge of the sacrificial banquets, the luxury of which gradually became proverbial.[2] The Curiones were spiritual ministers of the curiæ, thirty in number, each selected by his own curia, and then instituted by the augurs; they too were, as might be supposed, of patrician rank only.[3] Nevertheless, plebeians too were afterwards admitted, when the divisions of the curiæ had lost their importance, and the office had become a mere sacerdotal one.[4] How long the Tities continued to be the special ministers of the Sabine cultus is not known. In the year 14 after Christ the Sodales Augustales, a congregation of priests, consisting of twenty-five, taken from the highest ranks, were appointed.[5] Similar colleges were afterwards erected, in succession, for the deceased emperors become gods; and we meet with Claudiales, Titiales, Flaviales, Hadrianales, and so on, and from time to time a single Flamen Augustalis makes his appearance.[6]

Apart from the foreign female ministers of Ceres, the Romans had but one kind of priestess, the vestal virgin. To them was intrusted the custody of the holiest securities, on which the welfare of the state depended, and their institution originated in Alba Longa, according to the legend. At the first there were four, two each, that is, of the two oldest races; by the addition of the Luceres they became six, which number remained un-

[1] Cic. pro Cælio, c. 2. [2] Liv. xxxiii. 42. [3] Dionys. ii. 21, 64.
[4] Liv. xxvii. 8, xxxiii. 42. [5] Tac. Ann. i. 54.
[6] Tac. Ann. iii. 64; Suet. Claud. 6; Galb. 8.

changed till the very last times of the state. The right of choosing them passed from the kings to the pontifex maximus; but afterwards the Papian law decreed he should look out for twenty maidens, and that one of them should be chosen by lot; still, by a provision of the Papilian law, a father could offer his daughter to the pontifex as a vestal virgin. In order to be perfectly sure of their maidenhood, they were chosen while still children, between the ages of six and ten years. According to the legal expression, the pontifex was to possess himself of the maiden, and to carry her off like a booty; whereupon she was inaugurated, but did not incur any obligation for life; she might leave and marry after a service of thirty years, and this sometimes took place through a kind of formal exauguration; but the gods, it was thought, were not favourable to such a step. Evil befell the married pair, and the recusant came to an unhappy end.[1] Ten of a vestal's thirty years were spent in learning the sacred usages, ten in their practice, and the last ten were devoted to giving instructions.

Only a maiden both of whose parents were still living could become a vestal. Patrician birth was required at first, but afterwards plebeians were admitted. Augustus even gave permission for the choice of freed women (libertinæ), but it never took place. Families often tried to evade the choice of one of their daughters, so that Tiberius publicly thanked Fonteius Agrippa and Domitius Pollio for the offer of theirs; by so doing they had laid the state under an obligation. And yet, putting aside the loss of marriage, their lot was as brilliant as the state could make it. They received the highest honours; whoever attacked them had death to expect in requital.[2] To meet them accidentally saved a criminal who was being led out to die; consuls even, and prætors, had to give way to them in the streets, or, if that were impossible, had to lower their fasces to them.[3] Contracts and wills were deposited with them. In the enjoyment of ample revenues, they led a very independent life, assisted at all public entertainments, not only in the circus and the theatres, but even in the amphitheatre at the contests of gladiators, and Augustus appointed them a special seat there, over against the prætor's. Attended by a numerous retinue, and carried on litters (even to the Capitol), they visited their relations, were invited to dinner by them, and

[1] Dionys. ii. 67.   [2] Plut. Num. 10.   [3] Sen. Excerpt. Controv. vi. 8.

received the visits even of men in the daytime, and of women at night, at their dwelling in the Regia. Their intercession could not lightly be passed unheeded,[1] as in the case of Caesar, when proscribed by Sulla, who was spared accordingly. Their mere presence protected from violence; on which account the daughter of Appius Claudius Pulcher, a vestal, took her place in the triumphal car beside her father, in order to prevent the tribune of the people tearing her father down from it. With the right to give evidence in court, they could not be compelled to take any oath.

Besides the daily ministrations in the temple and sacrifice of Vesta, and care of the sacred fire, the vestals were charged with the preparation of the casta mola and the sacrificial cakes of meal from the ears of corn and of brine, articles necessary for every sacrifice. They took part in many sacrifices, namely, those of the Bona Dea, Ops Consivia, the Fordicidia, and of the Argei. On certain occasions they were intrusted with extraordinary sacrifices and prayers, expiatory actions and lustrations, by the senate or pontiffs. Their prayers and rites were reckoned to be particularly efficacious; amongst other things, it was commonly believed that they could, by a formula, infallibly detain runaway slaves who had not yet left the city.[2] On an appointed day they repaired to the sacrificial king to invite him to vigilance. It has been scarcely noticed, but is nevertheless well accredited, that the vestal virgins were also intrusted with the attendance on a holy serpent, who, it is highly probable, was worshiped as the genius of the city of Rome. They had to supply his table with meats on all the Kalends, and every five years to furnish a more sumptuous banquet.[3] All the vestal virgins, even the maxima, who, as the eldest, had precedence, were under the pontifex maximus, who exercised a very strict superintendence over them, actually chastising them with blows for any grievous negligence in their duties, as for letting the sacred fire go out, an event of the most sinister foreboding.[4] A vestal virgin convicted of incontinence was buried alive, to prevent the executioner laying

---

[1] Tac. Ann. ii, 32; Hist. iii. 81; Cic. pro Font. 17.

[2] Plin. H. N. xxviii. 3.

[3] Paulin. adv. Pagan. i. 143; Tertull. ad Uxor. i. 6. Compare the passage from the apocryphal acts of St. Sylvester, in Lips. de Vestâ, Opp. iii. 1097.

[4] Val. Max. i. 1, 6; Plut. Numa. 10; Dionys. ii. 67; Liv. xxviii. 11.

hand on her, and that her death might ensue without having recourse to violence, and every year expiatory rites were performed over her burial-place. In the later Roman history the number of trials and condemnations of vestal virgins for violation of chastity appears very frequent in proportion. If the fire under their charge was extinguished, or they happened to attire themselves with too great nicety, great suspicion was awakened, an investigation followed, and sometimes they were admonished and absolved by the pontiff.[1]

The augurs did not belong, strictly speaking, to the Roman priesthood, but their proper concern was with the inquiring into and communication of the divine will; and yet mention of sacrificial acts of theirs does occur, though not frequently. To help decision by a plurality of votes, their college was generally composed of an uneven number of members, at first but three, and then four or five. Vacancies were filled by coöptation. An augur was never displaced or degraded: he was for good and all a seer, initiated in science which was always receiving a new lustre and perfection from time, and could only be accurately understood by one who had long pursued it as a vocation; and hence the augurs were in high estimation, and their influence on state occasions was often decisive. By their obnuntiatio, or declaration that the signs were unfavourable, they could compel the authorities to break up a popular assembly leaving business undone, and dismiss an assembly or session already opened, or render the decrees of one already held invalid. A single augur standing out was sufficient to interrupt at once the prosecution of a matter in hand; their decision bound even the consuls to lay down their office, and it was in their hands to grant or to deny permission to deliberate with the assembled people.[2] Besides this, the higher curule magistrates, after their election, further required inauguration from an augur, for it was only by that they were put into a position to make use of the auspices in official business.

In the earliest times, there does not seem to have been an augurate apart from the magistracy, and so the kings themselves practised augury, as a gift imparted to them from the gods; and Romulus, in the legend, has the character of being the best augur.[3] The fact of the legend attributing to him or

---

[1] Liv. iv. 44; Plut. de Inim. Util. 6.   [2] Cic. de Legg. ii. 12.
[3] Cic. de Div. i. 2.

Numa the first appointment of augurs proper, speaks certainly for the high antiquity of the institution, *i.e.* the business became soon so difficult, and, in proportion as it became more artificial, demanded so much time, care, and observation, that it seemed matter of necessity to have in the state competent persons to choose this science as their profession; and at last the system of taking auspices became a kind of *disciplina arcani*, the principles of which were understood only by the augurs themselves.[1]

It is true particular auspicia still continued to be taken and decided upon by the officers of the state, without the assistance of an augur, as, for instance, on the naming of a dictator, or in a campaign; it is also true, when the auspices were taken by the augur, the magistrate continued to be the commander, the augur the executive;[2] but if the magistrates once called in an augur, they were obliged to obey his nuntiatio or obnuntiatio. There was therefore a mutual interdependence between magistrate and augur. The augur could not *proprio motu* and at his own pleasure consult the auspices (whether lightning or birds) in regard to the transaction of a matter of state; he required an authorisation from the magistrate for the purpose, and only when he had given the commission was he obliged to act upon the report of the augur. The augurs, however, had important privileges on their side too, for they had the power, without their being commissioned, if, without their seeking, the auspices appeared unfavourable, of interrupting the comitia by simply reporting the fact; and they could also investigate how a state officer had conducted the auspices, even when no augur had been called in to assist, and, after inquiry made according to the rules of their art, could pronounce upon the admissibility or validity of the acts of state in respect of which the auspices had been taken in the first instance.[3] The college of augurs also decided doubts arising on the validity of an act, and thus it happened not unfrequently that magistrates were obliged to resign, because, in the judgment of the college, a vitium, that is, any unfavourable portent, had occurred in their election. Still more frequently laws and judicial proceedings were annulled on the same ground or pretext.[4]

[1] Liv. viii. 23, ix. 38.   [2] Cic. de Div. ii. 34.
[3] Cic. Phil. ii. 33; De Legg. ii. 12; Dio. Cass. xxxviii. 13.
[4] Cic. de Div. ii. 35; de N. D. ii. 4.

By the Ogulnian law, five plebeian augurs, chosen by the people, were added to the hitherto patrician ones. Sylla increased their number to fifteen, and Cæsar added a sixteenth. The emperors named augurs at will, and in excess, too, of the legal number. The slippery art which they practised required a close combination amongst them, and hence provision was made that no one living in enmity with any of the members of the college should be chosen augur,[1] and further, that the younger augur should honour as a father the elder one who had admitted him. Even after the time of the Ogulnian law, the augurate was still predominantly the organ of the aristocracy, and its influence was often employed as a counterpoise to the power of the tribunes of the people.

The keepers and expounders of the Sibylline books were originally but two; they could not undertake any political office or military service. After the plebs had acquired their share in these sacerdotal dignities, there were ten of them, five patricians and five plebeians, and in Sylla's time fifteen. The Haruspices, whose duties included the inspection of the entrails of beasts, and the interpretation of prodigies, were established in Rome first after the expulsion of the kings, and were as exotic as their art; in fact, they always came from Etruria, and therefore enjoyed no personal esteem, and formed no college, but were frequently consulted by decree of the senate. Lastly, the Feciales were a half-sacerdotal, half-political society, consisting of patricians, and coeval with the state itself. Their functions regarded the foreign relations of Rome, negotiations with other people, embassies, conclusions of peace, and declarations of war, and they had to look after the fulfilment of treaties that had been made. In such occurrences many ceremonies of a religious nature had to be observed, the exact performance of which was either matter of personal obligation to themselves, or had to be superintended in others. In earlier times it had been their task to pass sentence upon the justice of a war; but after that this right had passed into the hands of senate and people, they had only formalities to decide.[2]

---

[1] Cic. ad Fam. iii. 10.   [2] Liv. xxxi. 8, xxxvi. 3.

IV. Roman Forms of Worship.

Prayers, Vows, Sacrifices, Ritual, and Feasts.

The magic and thoroughly formal character of the Roman religion, in no way concerned as it was with the instruction, elevation, or purifying of man, but only with the most effectual means of making the gods subservient to its own designs, is discerned principally in the employment of prayer, and in the contents of the Roman formulæ of prayer. Every thing here depended on the words used,—a mistake might render the whole prayer inoperative; but if the formula was pronounced correctly, without a wrong word, an omission or addition, all disturbing causes and things of evil import being kept at a distance the while, then was success assured, independently of the intention of the person praying. Hence, as Pliny tells us,[1] the highest officers of state, during religious acts, had the formula read before them from a ritual, one priest being obliged to follow attentively each word as it was pronounced, and another to keep silence among the assistants; moreover, the flutes were played to prevent another word besides being heard. For experience, he thought, had proved that, as often as a noise or word of bad omen was heard during the time, or any error committed in the prayer, a defect portending calamity, or a monstrosity of some kind, was sure to be discovered in the entrails of the victim.

The Romans when at prayer were in the habit of covering the head, or, properly speaking, the ears, so that no word or sound of evil augury might be heard at the time.[2] One of the acts to be performed by a suppliant praying was to kiss his right hand, and then turn round in a circle by the right, and seat himself upon the ground.[3] This was supposed to be a direction of Numa. The turning round in a circle signified, so subtle criticism made out, the circular movement of the world; the sitting posture and repose indicating confidence that the prayer would be heard. If a man found himself near an altar of the deity to whom his prayer was to be addressed, it was necessary to touch the altar, as the only way of softening the deity.[4] Also

---

[1] H. N. 28; cf. Cic. de Div. i. 29.   [2] Plut. Quæst. Rom. 10.
[3] Suet. Vitell. 2; Plut. Numa, 4; Plin. H. N. xxviii. 2.   [4] Macrob. Sat. iii. 2.

to touch or embrace the feet of images was considered peculiarly efficacious. In temples where the images were enclosed, people had recourse to the door-keepers, and begged to be admitted to the image, to pray to it on the spot.[1] In crises of great importance, or danger impending, the Roman women would throw themselves on the pavement, and rub the slabs clean with their hair.[2] But if prayer and other means of appeasing the deity proved ineffectual, then it came to pass, as when the death of Germanicus ensued in spite of all the prayers and sacrifices offered, that the temples were pelted with stones, and the altars overthrown, and many went so far as to cast the idols of their family Lares out of the house.[3]

A certain selection and order of precedence had, as was natural, to be observed in the prayers. Janus, as the god of all good beginnings, was frequently first named. In prayers of more general importance, particularly those offered on behalf of the state, Jupiter Capitolinus ordinarily assumed the first place, as was his due. If there were many gods to be invoked, Vesta usually formed the conclusion. It is not clear by what rule on special occasions, at Rome, sometimes only single gods, at others many of them together, had "supplications" presented to them. At times also general prayer-feasts were appointed to all the gods together. As it was often not known exactly whether it were god or goddess to whom the prayer or the sacrifice should be directed, or how the deity was to be addressed, people expressed themselves cautiously, using the proviso, " Be thou god or goddess." Sometimes, too, the name of the deity was omitted, for fear of substituting a wrong one. Indeed, the Romans could not be surpassed by any other people in the number and constant repetition of formulæ, and in crowding together invocations of gods, and expiatory and purifying rites, into every nook and cranny of life. If it was but the most trifling action, toll of prayers and homage had to be paid to a whole series of gods; and it was a critical matter to pass over but one of the persons or things having claims or weight in the matter.

It was an indispensable condition of success that an appointed form of prayer should be repeated three times, in some instances nine.[4] As often as he mounted his chariot even, Cæsar usually

---

[1] Sen. Ep. 41.   [2] Liv. iii. 7, xxvi. 9; Lucan. ii. 30.
[3] Suet. Calig. 5.   [4] Marini, Atti dei Fr. Arv. p. 604.

repeated three times a formula to avert dangers; a custom generally in vogue in the time of Pliny. Of Marcus Aurelius it was observed that, as master and president of the Salii, he required no one to repeat before him the forms at his inaugurations and exaugurations, because he knew them by heart.[1] The Emperor Claudius also repeated the words of prayers before the people himself. In all the formulæ, no instance is to be found of any thing else ever being asked for, but prosperity and health for individuals, and victory and power for the state, nor of prayer being offered for moral good; and, indeed, it was not to be expected from the character of the Roman religious system. Many prayers and hymns were taken up with the praise of the gods, and salutations to them; for some people had the habit of making early morning visits, the first hour of the day, to particular gods. Arnobius speaks of morning serenades sung with an accompaniment of fifes, as a kind of reveille to the sleeping gods, and of an evening salutation, in which leave was taken of the deity with the wishing him a good night's rest.[2] Prayer was also addressed to the gods at meals, and while, at the end of the first course, a second was being set on the table, crowded with dishes, that which had been selected from the repast, and consecrated to the gods, was taken to the "focus," and was thrown into the fire, amid the solemn silence of the company, the slave crying out, "The gods be gracious!"[3]

If the Romans laid claim to be the most pious of all people, it was partly because they dwelt, in mind, upon the great number of their vows, and their care and conscientiousness in the fulfilment of them; for to vow the dedication of a temple, or altar, or public games to a deity for the welfare of the state generally, or the obtaining of any particular favour, a victory or the taking of a city, was one of the most frequent resources of Roman statesmen and generals; the latter particularly thought to increase at once the spirit of their troops and their certainty of victory by vows pronounced aloud immediately before the beginning of a battle. At home an epidemic was the most common motive of vows; and in the uncertainty as to which deity sent the calamity, and which was the fittest to remove it, many gods were included in one and the same vow. Thereupon special decrees of the senate

---

[1] Capitolin. M. Aur. c. 4.   [2] Arnob. vii. 32.
[3] Marini, Atti dei Fr. Arv. p. 536.

were made, and the vow then was executed with particular solemnity, according to a formula first enunciated by a priest, often the pontifex maximus himself. The promise was inscribed on a tablet, and hung up on the walls or pillars of the temple.

Most of the temples, and a great number of altars, were erected in Rome in fulfilment of vows; not unfrequently too it was great sacrifices, share in spoils, or the best of the armour captured, golden crowns, festal games, and libations, that were vowed; and to these sometimes lectisternia were added, or, when there was a long drought, Nudipedalia, *i.e.* pilgrimages of Roman matrons barefoot and with dishevelled hair.[1]

Towards the end of the republic began the custom of making public vows for the safety of persons in authority. This first took place when Pompey fell ill, and next for Cæsar, and for the latter, indeed, annually. This led on, by a natural progress, to their being renewed for all the emperors yearly, then for the happy return of an emperor from a journey or campaign, for the happy delivery of the empress, and the like. Countless were the votive offerings to conciliate a god promised by individuals in illness, at the outset of a journey, in undertakings, in storms, and other dangers; these always consisted of victims or hallowed presents; they were specially made to a man's genius and to Juno Lucina on his birthday. The most peculiar one was that of a "sacred spring," in accordance with which all cattle born between the first of March and the last of April were dedicated to Jupiter. This Ver sacrum was promised in the second Punic War, after the overthrow and death of Flaminius, and the promise afterwards performed. With the Italic races, Samnites, Sabines, and others, the Ver sacrum included still more, embracing the whole generation of a spring; man and beast were offered alike, boys and girls were allowed their lives, but sent out as colonists when grown up, being carried over the borders with their faces veiled.[2]

The sacrificial rites of the Romans coincided for the most part with the Greek, still having much that was peculiar to themselves. On the whole, sacrifices were very frequent among the Romans, more so than the Greeks, Athens excepted. Thanksgiving for benefits received, the fulfilment of vows made, and

---

[1] Tert. de Jejun. 16; Apol. 40; Petron. Sat. 44.
[2] Paul. Diac. p. 379; Fest. v. Mamertini; Liv. xxii. 10; Justin. xxiv. 4; Plin. H. N. iii. 18.

propitiation of the gods, were the objects and occasions of extraordinary sacrifices, which were performed in addition to the standing one, regularly recurring; in particular, sacrifices of atonement were more common among the Romans than the Greeks. There were, besides, sacrifices of consultation, the principal object of which was inspection of entrails, to inquire into the will of the gods, or get counsel from them; in these the surrender of the life of the animal to the deity was a secondary matter, while it was a primary one with the others, which were therefore called "animal."[1]

In the laws of the twelve tables it was said "such beasts should be used for victims as were becoming and agreeable to each deity;" the animal therefore stood in some peculiar relation or other to a characteristic of the god. White cattle with gilded horns were sacrificed to Jupiter Capitolinus, but no bull or ram.[2] A bull could only be sacrificed to Apollo, Neptune, or Mars. Asses, cocks, and horses were sacrificed to Mars; a white cow, because of her moon-shaped horns, to Juno Calendaris; an intact heifer to the virgin Minerva; a sow in young to the great Mother; doves and sparrows, as wanton animals, with the loins of numberless other beasts, to Venus. Swine were the due of almost all agrarian deities; and to Mars, Ceres, and Tellus, they were also used for sacrifice in imprecations and on the conclusion of treaties. Female deities ordinarily had female animals sacrificed to them. Unweaned puppies were offered as victims of expiation to Robigus, the Lares, and Proserpine. To the gods of the infernal regions black animals were slaughtered, with their necks bowed downwards, and the blood poured into a hole dug for its reception. Sheep and swine were the animals in most frequent use for sacrifice.

The expenses incurred by the state in the sacrifices which it appointed were paid out of pecuniary penalties or the forfeited goods of condemned criminals;[3] but as these sources were not adequate, they became by degrees such a burden on the state-finances that the Emperor Nerva did away with many of them for this reason.[4] Indeed, Servius says: "One must know

---

[1] Macrob. Sat. iii. 5.   [2] Serv. Æn. ix. 628; Macr. Sat. iii. 10.
[3] Fest. v. Sacramentum et Supplicia.
[4] Dio. Cass. lxviii. p. 770; Æn. ii. 116.

that, in sacrificing, the appearance is taken for the reality; accordingly, when animals difficult to be got are required for the purpose, representations are made of them in bread or wax, and are offered as substitutes." But this took place in the public sacrifices only on very unusual occasions, as when it happened that the demand for the sacrifice of such uncommon animals originated with the Sibylline books. The number of beasts consumed in a single sacrifice was often very great: thus, after the defeat at lake Thrasymene three hundred bulls were sacrificed to Jupiter, white cattle to many other gods of the first rank, and to the rest victims of less value. Hecatombs do not seem to have been frequent, though Marius vowed one in the Cimbric war; Æmilius Paulus, too, vowed and slaughtered a hundred oxen in the Macedonian. At this kind of sacrifice, the Romans commonly erected a hundred altars of turf close by one another, and then sacrificed on them one hundred sheep or swine, and so on. If it were an imperial sacrifice, even lions, eagles, and such-like animals were used.[1] It is calculated that on the death of Tiberius, and on Caligula's mounting the throne, upwards of one hundred and sixty thousand victims, principally, perhaps, oxen and calves, were slaughtered throughout the Roman empire in testimony of the universal joy.[2] Augustus and Marcus Aurelius required so great a number of beasts for their sacrifices, that it was said of them, " All oxen and calves hoped and prayed they might never return from their journeys or campaigns, as otherwise they were infallibly lost."[3]

In private and family life, too, important events were solemnised by sacrificing—above all, marriage. The nuptial sacrifice admitted the bride to a participation in the " sacra" of her spouse. In earlier times no marriage was concluded without sacrifice, as an essential ingredient of the religious ceremony;[4] but later on, when bare consent rendered a contract of the kind valid, sacrifice came to be considered as no longer necessary, though still it was in frequent use. In those ancient days the bridegroom offered the sacrifice (a swine) in person, with the aid of the bride; but afterwards competent people, popæ or victimarii, assisted in that duty.

---

[1] Capitol. in Max. et Balb. c. 11.   [2] Suet. Calig. 14.
[3] Sen. de Benef. iii. 27; Amm. Marc. xxii. 14, xxv. 4.
[4] Serv. Æn. 136.

Sacrifices of expiation must have been of very common occurrence among Romans who were at all punctilious in the observance of their religion; for the faults, negligences, and evil prognostications, which had to be atoned for or averted by them, were of the greatest variety, and in numberless instances unavoidable. If a sacrifice was interrupted by a sudden attack of illness, a new one was required as an atonement. If any one washed animals, or watered the fields, on a festival, or if the vestal virgins placed their holy-water vessels on the ground,—these were transgressions that had to be expiated by a sacrifice. A common sacrifice of this kind, and almost always resorted to in all lustrations, was the Suovetaurilia,[1] in which the animals to be slaughtered—a swine, sheep, and bull—were conducted three times in procession round the object to be purified, *i.e.* the whole people, and were then sacrificed to Mars. By the state of the entrails it was known whether the deity was really appeased and propitiated: if they presented unfavourable signs, the sacrifice required repetition as long and as often as the state of the entrails did not pronounce the god to be reconciled. Cato himself supplies the formula that was to be used in the Suovetaurilia, in case of repetition: "Father Mars, if any thing has been not to your mind in the previous sacrifice, so now do I propitiate thee by this new sacrifice."[2] Symmachus, writing in the latest period of decaying paganism, says it caused him much anxiety that there was so great difficulty in making expiation for the prodigy at Spoletum, though the sacrifice was so often repeated, and Jupiter hardly contented the eighth time.[3] On the day of his assassination Cæsar, though he slaughtered one hundred victims one after the other, could not arrive at a litamen, or true atonement and its proof in the favourable appearance of the entrails.[4] Paulus Æmilius succeeded in this object at the twentieth time.

The choice of the victims from the flocks and herds demanded great attention: for there was much that entered into consideration, down to the length of the tail. A calf was only fit for sacrifice when its tail reached the joint of the leg. In a sheep the points to be looked to were, that the tail was not

---

[1] Dionys. ii. 22. [2] Cato de R. R. c. 141.
[3] Symmach. Epist. i. 49; Plaut. Pœn. act. ii. sc. 5.
[4] Flor. iv. 2.

pointed, the tongue not cloven, and the ear not black.¹ An ox, to be available for sacrifice, ought to be white; and if with spots, they had to be rubbed white with chalk.² Then, in the action of the sacrifice itself, there were many bad signs, rendering it dubious whether the god had really accepted it or not; as when the beast bellowed on arriving at the altar, or even after receiving its death-wound, or did not keep quiet at the altar, or ran away;³ for all the fillets it was tied with were taken off it at the altar, as any thing fastened on the beast was of bad import,⁴ and therefore a popa held the creature by one of its horns. It was also an unfavourable omen if the beast sprinkled the assistants with its blood,⁵ and if it did not bleed copiously, or fell to the ground not in the right position,⁶ or if the portion thrown on the pan of live coals would not burn properly,⁷ or, in fine, if the flames of the altar did not mount up to heaven straight and pure.

After bathing in spring-water, the sacrificer should appear in fresh white garments for the sacred action, and wash his hands again before beginning. In many sacrifices abstinence from sexual intercourse was required the night before, sometimes for many days previously. It was not on the strength of any ideas of morality attaching to this abstinence, but because such abstaining, like the fresh-washed garments and hands, &c. were calculated to produce that physical purity with which a person ought to present himself before the deity, and enter into the communion of sacrifice with him: hence the poetical dictum, "The pure is pleasing to the celestial;" and Cicero's prescription, "One should approach the gods in purity."⁸

It was usual for a man to veil himself during the action of the sacrifice, except in sacrifices to Saturn and Hercules. The animal was first tried by a libation of wine or water upon the

---

¹ Plin. H. N. viii. 70.
² Juv. x. 66.
³ Sil. Ital. v. 65; Lucan. i. 611; Flor. iv. 1; Suet. Ital. 10; Lucan. vii. 165.
⁴ Serv. Æn. ii. 134.
⁵ Liv. xxi. 63.
⁶ Fest. v. piacularia; Senec. Œdip. ii. 2. 51. ⁷ Virg. Georg. iii. 486.
⁸ This Zumpt translates, and rightly, "Ad Divos adeunto castè" (De Legg. ii. 8), not as Lasaulx (Studien, p. 153) translates it, "A man must approach the gods with a pure heart," adding besides that this prescription was the ordinary one in antiquity, whereas all the Roman authorities adduced by him merely speak of the physical purity of the body, of washing of hands, &c., indicating this by the term "castus," the idea of which does not approximate to the modern one of purity. Purity of heart might well consist with what was here directly forbidden;

head; if it moved or trembled during that, it was considered qualified.[1] "Far" too, that is meal and salt mixed, was crumbled upon each victim (immolatio), and the same was done to the knives used and to the altar. Next, the priest cut off the animal's forelock and threw it into the fire, as a symbol of the consecration of the whole victim, together with incense and a little wine. The success of the sacrifice with the deity was gathered from the smoke and the crackling; and then the victimarius slaughtered the victim at the priest's bidding with axe or knife: if for a deity of the super-terrestrial world, the knife was thrust from below upwards into the neck, if to an infernal deity, in the contrary direction. The blood was poured on and about the altar, but the beast was sprinkled on the sacrificial table with wine and incensed, and then disjointed.[2] The entrails were not to be touched, but taken out with knives. In case the haruspex found them favourable, the second principal act of the sacrifice began with a libation, for which the sacrificulus presented a flagon with wine to the assistants round. Upon this the priest, having first sprinkled the entrails with wine, meal, and incense, set them upon the altar and burnt them; holocausts seem to have been very infrequent among the Romans, except when the sacrifice was intended for an infernal god. In earlier times the flesh of the victim was carried to the questors of the public treasury, who sold it for the advantage of the state. It sometimes happened that contagious diseases arose from the quantity of accumulated flesh of the sacrifices becoming suddenly corrupt; to avert these, games of a peculiar kind (ludi taurii)[3] were once held. Later on, the priests, popae, and victimarii divided among themselves what was over of the sacrifice, the flesh-meat or cakes; if the sacrifice was offered by private individuals, these took home what remained (the polluctum), and made a meal upon it.[4] The poorer class availed themselves of the offering of an animal

on the other hand, as the expressions of the poets prove, such as offered sacrifice and invoked the gods to obtain the satisfaction of impure lust, were in the habit of submitting punctiliously to the required abstinence one or more nights. Vico and Bayle had already hit off the meaning of Cicero's expression when they asserted there was no idea of chastity involved in it. The first (Scienza Nuova, xi. 14, Opere, v. 278) translates it, "Let him who goes to sacrifice first make the sacred ablutions." What Bayle says is to be found in his Œuvres, iii. 256.

[1] Serv. Æn. vi. 244.   [2] Ovid. Fasti, iv. 934 sq.; Hor. Od. i. 19, 14.
[3] Festus, s. v. Taurii.   [4] Plautus, Rud. v. 3, 63; Mil. Glor. iii. 1, 117.

victim, the cost of which was defrayed by several contributing, or they brought baked images of animals from the bakers of such sacred articles,[1] instead of real ones, or lastly, contented themselves with the simple offerings of milk, meal, and salt.

Sacrificial cakes were also baked of " far," without which no sacrifice could be made, according to a provision of Numa; and these appeared under a great variety of forms and names. Such liba were sacrificed, *i. e.* thrown into the fire and burnt, to many gods by preference, as to Tellus, Ceres, Janus, Priapus, and Terminus.[2] "The cakes are ready, the sacrifice prepared; come and sacrifice," cries the freedman in Varro.[3] Besides this, the priests had composed a peculiar religious art of cookery of their own, and method of killing and cutting up, with a number of technical terms not in use in ordinary conversation; the most varied dishes, especially sausages, cakes, and buns, were made out of numerous ingredients, and of the different parts of the victim, and were again offered to the gods, and consumed on the altar. A late authority says: "People seem to have strange notions of the daintiness of the gods, since they invent innumerable meats to set before them, sometimes roast, sometimes still dripping with blood, at others half boiled and almost raw; and they must needs think the favour of the gods is to be purchased by the testicles and windpipes of beasts, and preparation of tripe and pieces of tails."[4]

The banquets prepared for the gods in Rome, and to which they were formally invited, are likewise to be considered as sacrifices, but in a wider sense of the word. Thus there was yearly in the Capitol, at the Roman and plebeian games, an epulum of Jove furnished, in which Juno and Minerva took part.[5] The supreme god lay at it, on a pillow, while the two goddesses were set upon chairs. Lectisternia of the kind took place in most of the temples throughout the whole year, and therefore almost daily;[6] and on extraordinary occasions, feasts of thanksgiving, or "supplications," particularly when it was a matter of danger threatening, or the expiation of prodigies, they were prepared for a number of gods together, whose images were laid in

---

[1] Fictores a fingendis libis,—Varr. vii. 44.
[2] Virg. Eclog. vii. 33; Dionys. ii. 74; Ovid. Fast. iv. 743.
[3] Varro de R. R. ii. 8.   [4] Arnob. vii. 24, 25.
[5] Val. Max. ii. 1. 1, 2; Arnob. vii. 32; Liv. v. 52, 31. 4, 33. 42.
[6] Liv. xlii. 30.

pairs on cushions beside the table, or set up at them; these lasted several days. The oldest lectisternium was held in the year 355 A.U.C. Once, Livy tells us, the gods turned on their cushions away from the table, upon which the mice came and devoured the meats.[1] As in the epulum of Jove the epulones and senators dined with the god at the Capitol, so, on the other hand, the lectisternia were popular feasts of harmony and union, in which hospitality was practised in the widest sense, with open doors; so at least, with a touch of poetical colouring, Livy describes the celebration of the first lectisternia: but afterwards there is no more mention of such general good-will and hospitality. We also find that the company of the gods to dinner was formally asked. Thus it is said on an old tablet, that on the birthday-feast of the emperors Augustus and Tiberius, before the decuriones sat down to table, the genii of the Cæsars were to be invited to dine by incense and libations of wine at the altar of Augustus.[2] Hence a serpent frequently appears on the monuments representing the genius as fed by the libations. The meaning was the same when little images of the gods were placed upon the dinner-table. The notion of the gods enjoying the odour and steam of the meats appears to have been at the bottom of this practice.

Innumerable indications, preserved both in rites and in the sagas, bear abundant testimony to the fact of human sacrifices having been offered by the Romans, and races kindred to them, in prehistoric times. Every year, on the ides of May, twenty-four shapes of men, made out of rushes, were thrown by the vestal virgins from the Sublician bridge into the Tiber. They were substitutes for the human victims once thrown into the stream, bound hand and foot, to Saturn.[3] In like manner, on the feast of Mania and of the Lares Compitales, at the crossways and before the house-doors, woollen puppets (oscilla) were hung up, to the number of persons of both sexes in a family, these also supplying the place of the earlier human sacrifice:[4] Mania and the Lares, it was expected, would be contented with these puppets, and spare the living. A custom the oldest Romans had of casting gray-headed men of sixty from the Pons Sublicius

---

[1] Liv. xl. 59.   [2] Marini, Atti dei Frat. Arvali, p. 91.
[3] Ov. Fasti, v. 621; Plut. Quæst. Rom. 32; Fest. p. 32; Varro, vii. 44.
[4] Macrob. Sat. i. 7. 34, 35.

into the Tiber, must have been retained up to historical times, and probably the rush figures were substituted instead of them.¹

But it was not always that human sacrifice was supplied for by these unbloody representatives. In spite of the disinclination manifested by the Romans to such victims, and the dislike with which they observed the use of them among other nations, they themselves had frequent enough recourse to the same means of propitiation. In the year 227 B.C., it was discovered from the Sibylline books that Gauls and Greeks were to make themselves masters of the city. To ward off this danger, a decree was passed that a man and woman of each of those two nations should be buried alive in the forum, and so should fulfil the prediction by being allowed to take that kind of possession of the city.² It was done; and though Livy speaks of it as a thoroughly un-Roman sacrifice, yet it was often repeated. Plutarch mentions a similar one of Greeks and Gauls, on the occasion of two vestal virgins being deflowered, and a third struck with lightning, which was regarded as a prodigy portentous of evil.³ In the year 95 B.C., indeed, all human sacrifices were interdicted by decree of the senate; up to that time, as Pliny says, they had been performed in public; but on extraordinary occasions it was thought admissible to set aside this prohibition: and the same Pliny observes that instances of it had occurred in his time.⁴ There was a particular form of prayer for this kind of sacrifice, when carried into effect by burying alive, which the master of the college of the Quindecemviri had to repeat first, the peculiar force of which, Pliny remarks, made itself felt by every one who read it.

In times of violence and disturbance, the idea of a strange effectiveness in human sacrifice always returned upon the people. Once, when a tumult was raised by Cæsar's soldiers in Rome, two of them were sacrificed to Mars by the pontiffs and the flamen martialis in the Campus Martius, and their heads were fixed upon the Regia, the same as in the sacrifice of the October horse.⁵ Besides this, the Romans were familiar with the notion of offering human lives as victims of atonement for the dead; this was the object with which gladiatorial games had

---

¹ Ov. Fast. v. 623; Fest. p. 334; Varr. ap. Non. pp. 86, 523, 214.
² Liv. xxii. 57.   ³ Plut. Marcell. 3; Oros. iv. 13.
⁴ Plin. H. N. xxxviii. 2.   ⁵ Dio. Cass. xliii. 24.

begun.¹ In the slave war, Spartacus took a heavy revenge when he dedicated to his fallen comrade Crixus a mortuary offering of three hundred Roman prisoners, whom he made to fight around the funeral-pile.² The triumvir Octavian afterwards competed with the slave-general, when he caused three hundred prisoners to be put to death, as an offering of expiation, at the altar of Divus Julius, on the surrender of Perugia.³ The fact has been doubted on the ground that the times and manners of the age would not have suffered it :⁴ but the evidence is far too strong. The previously mentioned example of a sacrificial murder committed by the most distinguished Roman priests, in the heart of Rome, on Roman soldiers, shows how little custom was a restraint: and the time was that of the proscriptions, and of promiscuous butchery, in which citizen-blood was poured out like water. Sextus Pompeius, too, had men thrown alive into the sea along with horses, as an oblation to Neptune, at the time when his enemies' fleet was destroyed by a great storm.⁵ Caligula's having innocent men dressed out as victims, and then thrown down precipices, as an atonement for his life, was indeed the act of a bloodthirsty tyrant; but it shows what ideas were abroad.⁶ In the year 270 A.D., further proof was given that, in spite of the late decree issued by Hadrian, recourse was still had, from time to time, to this means of appeasing the angry gods in dangers threatening the state, when, on an irruption of the Marcomanni, the emperor Aurelian offered the senate to furnish it with prisoners of all nations for certain expiatory sacrifices to be performed.⁷

But there was also a standing sacrifice of the kind. The image of Jupiter Latiaris was annually sprinkled with human blood; that shed by the gladiators in the public games was used for the purpose. A priest caught the blood in a cup from the body of one who was just wounded, and threw it when still warm at the face of the image of the god. This was of regular occurrence still in the second and third centuries after Christ: Tatian, amongst many others, speaks of it as an eye-witness.⁸

---

¹ Val. Max. ii. 4. 7.   ² App. Bell. Civ. i. 124; Flor. iii. 20; Oros. v. 24.
³ Dio. Cass. xlviii. 14; Suet. Octav. 15; Senec. de Clem. i. 11; Zonar. x. 21.
⁴ Drumann, Gesch. Roms, i. 412.   ⁵ Dio. Cass. xlviii. 48.
⁶ Suet. Calig. 27.   ⁷ Vopisc. Aurel.
⁸ Auctor Libri de Spectac. post Cypriani. opp. p. 3; Minuc. Octav. xxi. 30; Tertull. adv. Gnost. 7; Apol. 11; De Spect. 6; Just. Mart. Apol. ii. 12; Lact. i. 21; Tatian, c. 46; Athan. adv. Gr. c. 25; Firmic. Mat. 26.

The more external and mechanical the relation was in which the Roman stood to his gods, the more they appeared to him as beings who, in the closest connection with nature, were perpetually being injured by nature, and by natural things without free will. There was a number of purely physical acts and accidents through which a deity might be so wounded, and for which its vengeance had to be averted by an atonement. This did not depend on the mind or the purpose of the author of the act: it was not a question merely of doing adequate penance for sin incurred in unthought-of ways; on the contrary, a man might undertake, with full prevision, any thing that involved an offence against the deity, provided only he took care the expiation or piaculum followed immediately thereon, or indeed even preceded the act.[1] Thus, for example, the holy groves consecrated to a god had to be kept in good condition, cleared from time to time, and rotten branches cut away from the trees; but, as contact with iron polluted and profaned the trees, it was necessary, as often as any thing of the kind took place in a precinct, to have a piaculum made by the sacrifice of a swine. It was just the same if digging took place in the grove, or in the field adjoining: even the simple act of carrying an iron tool through the grove required an expiation. Thus, again, the Arval brothers had, in the grove of their goddess Dia, a temple, and in it marble tablets on which their several religious acts were recorded: and as often as the stylus or graver was taken in or out again, a sacrifice of atonement was requisite on each several occasion.[2] If a fig-tree in the grove was rooted up, or the temple of Dia repaired, or the grove cleared of trees struck by lightning, the greater atonement of the Suovetaurilia was necessary. In like manner every little offence, though quite unintentional, against a prescription of the ritual, or against custom, was to be atoned for by an expiation of its own.

Grand acts of atonement and purification (lustrationes) were celebrated on certain occasions on behalf of the state. One of the kind was held in the Campus Martius for the people collectively who were present at the closing of the census, or taking the estimate of the number and property of citizens, and consisted in the sacrifice of a swine, a ram, and a bull, which were first led three times round the entire people in procession. In like

---

[1] Comp. Cato de R. R. c. 140.
[2] Marini, Atti dei Frat. Arv. pp. 218, 309, 339, 363; Cato, l. c.

manner an army was lustrated before a campaign, as also before and after battle. The lustration of a fleet was in this wise: on the extreme edge of the shore, where the waves dashed up, an altar was erected; the ships, with their crews complete, lay at anchor before it. The priests went quite into the water and sacrificed the victims, with which they then proceeded round the whole fleet in small boats; afterwards the victims were divided, and the one half consumed by fire, the other thrown into the sea.[1]

All sacrifices of animals were performed, of course, in the open air, and not in the temple. The altar of sacrifice stood before the principal entrance, and was usually adorned with a triple fillet of wool, garlands of verbena and flowers.[2] These altars were very unequal in height; those of Jupiter and the heavenly gods were to be very high, while those of Vesta and Tellus were low.[3] On the altars in the interior of the temple incense was burnt before the images of the gods; a custom which, according to the observation of Arnobius, took its rise only in later times, and was practised neither by Latins nor Etruscans.[4] The Christians afterwards, speaking of the sacrificial altars proper, said they were but places for the burning of animals by fire; and that it was not supposable that the smoke and stench of hides, bones, bristles, fleeces, and feathers, a smell intolerable to the sacrificers themselves, could excite an agreeable sensation in the nostrils of the gods.[5] Where the images of the gods were placed in the open air, they were frequently blackened by the smoke of the sacrifices.

Though they had very imperfect notions about the state of souls after death, the Romans nevertheless took a deal of trouble about them, and their festivals of the dead were most strictly observed. So soon as the bones showed in the burning of the body, the nearest relations cried out that the dead was now a god,[6] and collected in their garments whatever remained unconsumed, sprinkled them with wine and milk, and enclosed them in an urn, after mixing spices and aromatic waters with them. These urns were then deposited in the dead-chamber. Nine days after this deposition, the novemdialia were cele-

---

[1] App. B. C. v. 96.
[2] Propert. iv. 6, 6; Virg. Ecl. viii. 64; Hor. Carm. iv. 11, 6.
[3] Vitruv. iv. 8. [4] Arnob. vii. 26.
[5] Arnob. vii. 16; Tertull. Apol. [6] Plut. Quaest. Rom. p. 267.

brated in memorial of the departed, during which the funeral feast (silicernium), generally a very luxurious banquet, took place. Solemn games and contests of gladiators were also held on occasion of the death of rich and distinguished Romans. A swine or a sheep was sacrificed to Ceres on behalf of the dead, a libation of wine poured out to him in his funeral chamber, and a limb severed from the corpse; a finger or bone remaining after the funeral pile was then first buried, *i. e.* covered with earth; or if this was not done, earth was still sprinkled on the grave, one or other being absolutely necessary to save the family from being unclean.[1] Next, a peculiar rite of purification, the Denicalia, had to be performed; for the idea that every touching of a corpse, as well as of a woman in childbed, was an abomination and defilement, and only removable by careful purifications, before any kind of religious act could be gone on with, was as prevalent among the Romans as the Greeks. If a man died at sea and was thrown overboard, the family, according to the decision of Mucius, the pontifex maximus, were to be considered clean, because not a bone of the dead was visible upon the earth; and yet the heir had to observe three days as feriæ, and to sacrifice a swine in expiation.[2]

Every year a public general festival of the dead (Feralia or Parentalia) was solemnised on the nineteenth of February, when meats were offered at their sepulchres. Generally speaking, the Roman service for the departed was a strange combination of erroneous and contradictory notions. People gave out their dead relations for gods, if they had owed duties of affection and reverence to them when living. "When once I am dead," wrote Cornelia to her son Gracchus, "then wilt thou sacrifice to me, and invoke thy goddess-mother. Wilt not thou then be ashamed to ask the intercession of a divine being, whom living, and present to thee, thou hast not cared for, but despised?"[3] But there is no instance of such thing as a father invoking his dead son as a god; nor did it ever occur to any one to look upon a member of another family as god, and to honour him accordingly. On the whole, the endeavour to satisfy the spirit of the departed with sacrifices and dainties, to appease him and to keep him at a distance, was the prevailing one. And there

---

[1] Varr. v. 23; Fest. s. v. membrum abscindi; Cic. de Legg. ii. 24.
[2] Cic. de Legg. ii. 22.
[3] Corn. Nep. Fragm.

could be no certainty whether this or that departed spirit belonged to the good and guardian Lares, or to the Lemures and Larvæ; for it was thought that the souls of such as had been evildoers in life were turned into night-errant spectres after death.[1] And yet this can only have been a partially received notion, disseminated in a kind of way in some few countries, otherwise there would have been more general evidence of it. For this reason the houses were lustrated with sulphur, resin, and torches, sulphur being held to be particularly operative against spirits;[2] and in May again, for three whole nights, the Lemuria, or ceremonies of atonement and expulsion, were celebrated. The father of the family proceeded at midnight, barefoot, to the front doors, driving the spirits from before him by waving his hand, which he then washed three times in running water. He then turned round, putting black beans into his mouth, which he went on to throw behind him with the words, "These I give unto you; with these beans I purchase me and mine." This form had to be repeated nine times, after which he washed again, made a din with vessels of brass, and cried nine times, "Out with you, ye paternal Manes!"[3] The redemption with beans, which were a dead-offering, and must have had a particular relation to the dead, resembles that other practice appointed for the Lares Compitales, and their mother Mania, of presenting dolls of wool to them, in the stead of the members of a family.

There can be no mistake about the fact of human sacrifices having been offered to the dead, when one considers the real signification and intention of the gladiatorial combats.[4] This kind of sacrifice was held in the higher esteem for the dead because of the uncertainty who was to fall in the contest, and of the appearance of a voluntary renouncement of life. In the year 217 B.C. the three sons of Emilius Lepidus made twenty-two pairs of gladiators fight for three days at the funeral-games of their father.[5] Somewhat later, Titus Flaminius held for three days a combat of seventy-four men in honour of his father.[6]

After that the Romans changed from a small agricultural people into a martial and victorious one, and the bearing of arms

---

[1] Apul. de Deo Socrat. p. 152 f. Oud.
[2] Ov. Fasti, ii. 35 sq.; Juvenal, ii. 156; Plin. H. N. xxxv. 15.
[3] Ov. Fasti, v. 419 sq.; Varro, ap. Nonium, p. 135.
[4] Serv. Æn. iii. 67.   [5] Liv. xxiii. 30.   [6] Ib. xli. 33.

had become their chief occupation, their festivals of the gods also assumed a different character. Labour was no longer their employment, but rather was unbecoming in a Roman citizen. In the intervals of his campaigns, he would take his repose, and his victories supplied him the means, in booty, and slaves to work for him. Thus the popular assemblies in part, and in part the festivals, became the leading duties of his city-life. About fifty of such feasts composed his calendar, most of them embracing several days, and so filling up a third of his year. The old country and agricultural festivals were kept up indeed, but under entirely different relations, with a change of signification, or without any at all but that of serving as days of enjoyment for an idle town population.

Festival-time received its name (Feriæ[1]) from sacrifice, the essential act of the religious life. The day on which sacrifice was offered for the people was equivalent to a "festus dies," a day which could only be employed in religious acts, or was exempt from work. When we add thereto banquets, games, and various enjoyments, the idea of the Roman feast-day is complete. There were also feriæ not feast-days, *i.e.* on which sacrifice only was offered, as was the case with the Nundinæ, on which the sacrificial king finished the Nonalia at the citadel (the Regia of Numa). When the state became more wealthy, that is, after the fall of Carthage, and rivalry arose between corporations and state officers as to which should celebrate the services of the gods with the greatest possible splendour, and to the greatest satisfaction of the popular taste, lectisternia were multiplied, and contests and games in theatre, amphitheatre, and circus were introduced.

Accordingly there grew up amongst the Romans a peculiar law of festivals, on which a complete literature was expended. Days were fasti or nefasti, on the former of which only the transaction of legal business was allowed; further, there were days called "black;" on such public business was unhallowed, nor could a battle be fought, nor any action of divine service or political necessity be undertaken. Great calamities had befallen the state for not regarding this distinction: for instance, the defeats on the Allia and Cremera were entirely owing to sacrifice having been offered on a dies nefastus,[2]—so the haruspex

---

[1] Fest. s. vv. feriæ, and feriendis victimis.   [2] Macrob. Sat. i. 16.

assured the senate ; and hence all days after the calends, nones, and ides in each month, as well as those following a feast-day, were interpreted to be black days; this would give about eighty-six of such.

The pontiffs had declared it to be sin against religion to take in hand any ordinary business on a holy day, and the transgressor of the prohibition had a fine imposed upon him, and to make an offering of a swine as an atonement ; but works of necessity, the omission of which would have been detrimental, were allowed ; and this also held good of a feria suddenly proclaimed, because of a prodigy, or on an extraordinary occasion. Lamentations too, and brawling and scolding, were to be avoided on feast-days.[1] When once, on a day of the plebeian games, a Roman had chastised his slave in the morning upon the arena, Jupiter communicated to another citizen that the leader of the dance in those games had displeased him, and that the whole must be begun over again.[2]

Taking a glance at the more important festivals, as they follow in succession throughout the year, we find the more recondite meaning of the Janus-feast of the Agonalia, on the ninth of January, and two days in May and December, to have been lost amongst the Romans themselves. And they seem to have had as little knowledge of the women's festival of the Carmentalia on the eleventh of January; yet there was an opinion that it was held to commemorate a reconciliation between the Roman husbands and their wives, who were exasperated by an attempt to forbid them the use of chariots. The thirteenth of January was a festival in honour of Octavian's receiving the surname of Augustus on that day. It was followed on the sixteenth by a feast of the dedication of a temple of Concord, on a reconciliation effected between the plebeians and patricians, and of the institution of the palatine games by Augustus in honour of Cæsar, and the completion of the Venus temple. Sementina and Ambarvalia, feasts of sowing and of the fields, were celebrated by the country-folk before the termination of January. A special peace-festival had been established by Augustus in memorial of the closing by him of the gates of Janus. The month concluded with the feast of the penates, on whose day an ox was sacrificed.

The first of February was sacred to Juno Sospita, the saviour,

---

[1] Ovid Fast. i. 71 sq.   [2] Plut. Fab. Max. 18 (? *Tr.*).

the old goddess of Lanuvium, and on it the consuls had to offer a sacrifice of she-goats to her. We have already mentioned how on the feast of the Lupercalia the Roman women let themselves be struck by the naked Luperci, as they ran about, in order to become mothers of a numerous family. The feast of the Fornacalia, the next in succession, retained the old agrarian character, and was to the honour of an oven-goddess Fornax, that she might make the drying of the corn succeed, and prevent its burning.[1] Next came, for eleven days, from the eighteenth to the twenty-eighth of February, the Februatio, from which the month had its name, a general festival of purification and atonement, united with the mortuary feast of the Feralia,[2] both being connected together through Februus, an old Etrurian god of the lower regions. Between the two the Charistia were also kept, a family festival for the adjusting of quarrels amongst relations, by their joining in a banquet in common. The Terminalia, observed on the twenty-third of February, the last of the year, old style, belonged to the more important feasts; and as the Greeks placed their boundaries under the protection of Zeus Horios, so in Italy the sacredness and irremovability of the boundary-stones were secured by the cultus of the god Terminus, who had also his place in the Capitol, in the shape of a parallelogram of stone. On the Terminalia the boundary-stones were anointed and crowned as the protecting genii of places and ways, the god receiving offerings of milk, cakes, wine, and fruits, which were thrown from an altar of turf three times into a fire brought from the house; the bloody sacrifices of sheep and lambs were a later addition.[3]

In March fell the feasts of the Liberalia, kept by the country people with uproarious mirth : and in Rome young men were solemnly invested with the toga libera, or virilis, the only way of accounting for which seems to be the similarity of the words, Liber and toga libera.[4] Five days after these were occupied by the Minerva feast of the Quinquatria. The first day was treated as the birthday of the goddess; and as she was goddess of wisdom, arts, and trades, unbloody offerings were made to her, at which all who pursued any calling that required technical skill or intellectual qualifications, astronomers, shoemakers,

[1] Ov. Fasti, ii. 525 sq.   [2] Lyd. de Mens. p. 68; Isidor. Orig. v. 33.
[3] Dionys. iii. 69.   [4] Ovid. Fasti, iii. 771.

poets, dyers, sculptors, turners, medical men, and so on, crowded into the temple to invoke the goddess: and, in particular, troops of young scholars took part in the festival. On the following days, the warlike aspect of the goddess came out in the gladiatorial contests held in her honour. The feast concluded with the Tubilustria, on which flutes and trumpets used in the service of the gods were purified by the sacrifice of a lamb, and dedicated to sacred worship.[1]

April opened with the Megalesian festival, and games in honour of the mother of the gods and her Attys. They lasted six days. The bringing-in of the pine-tree into the temple, the search for, the emasculation, the finding and resurrection of Attys, &c., and on the last day the solemn ablution of the sacred stone representing the goddess, constituted the acts of the feast. Begging, and carrying before them the curved knife, the instrument of their mutilation, the emasculate Galli went about the streets of the city in white dresses;[2] and the Quindecemviri, the guardians of the Sibylline books, were not ashamed to join the procession.[3] On the twelfth of April followed the Cerealia, dignified by the Circensian games, and a great festal procession after the circus. There was a kind of offering to the goddess in the shape of foxes, which were tied together in pairs, with a lighted torch fastened between them, and so were thrown into the circus.[4] After this came, on the fifteenth of April, the feast of the Fordicidia, with the sacrifice of the thirty cows in calf for the thirty curiæ of the people; and, on the twenty-first, the country one of the Palilia, when the country people leaped through fires of burning straw;[5] but in Rome the day of the foundation of the city was celebrated. The Romans procured from the altar in the temple of Vesta the means of purification, namely horse's blood, the ashes of the calves that were burnt on the Fordicidia, and bean-straw; these were cast on live coals, and the persons to be purified were at the same time sprinkled with lustral water. The first Vinalia were next celebrated on the twenty-third. In them an oblation of new wine was made to Jupiter by opening a cask; and then the Robigalia, to obtain of the demon of blight, Robigus, that he would spare the Roman corn-fields. The sacrifice consisted of red dogs and swine, whose

---

[1] Ov. Fasti, iii. 813 sq.   [2] Lucr. ii. 621.   [3] Lucan, i. 600.
[4] Ov. Fasti, iv. 682.   [5] Ibid. iv. 721 sq.

colour is said to have had reference to the dog-star rising on the twenty-fifth of April, and who is pernicious to the harvest.[1] The month terminated with the Floralia, beginning on the twenty-eighth, and famous for their licentiousness. It is also remarkable that no sacrifices were offered to the goddess Flora, but only the games were dedicated to her.

In May the secret sacrifice of the women to the Bona Dea took place. There were games, instituted by Augustus, in honour of Mars, that were held in the circus: a second Tubilustrium followed for the consecration and purifying of the trumpets of sacrifice and funeral-fifes. In June, first of all, an oblation of lard and bean-meal was made to the goddess Carna, under the notion of her being the president or protectress of the inner parts of the human body. After that, seven days, from the seventh to the fifteenth, were devoted to Vesta, during which the purification of the entire sanctuary of the goddess was undertaken; and as a sign of mourning, the flaminica, the wife of the flamen dialis, would not comb her hair, or pare her nails, or allow her husband to touch her. The proper feast of the Vestalia was solemnised on the ninth of this month, and, in remembrance of the preparation of bread which once took place in the Vesta temple, was at the same time a special feast for bakers and millers, who led asses through the city, bedecked with collars of little loaves strung on ribbons.[2] It was said an ass had waked Vesta when lying asleep and intoxicated in the grass, and so saved her from the snares of Priapus.[3] The Roman ladies made pilgrimages barefoot on the day to the shrine of the goddess. The Matralia, kept on the tenth of June in honour of Matuta, were one of the feasts only celebrated by women.

On the seventh of July the so-called Populifugium, in memorial of an occasion, that was forgotten afterwards, in which the people had taken to flight, concurred with a merry-making festival of women and female slaves, called the Nonæ Caprotinæ, when Juno was presented with the sap of the wild fig-tree instead of milk.[4] In obedience to an announcement of a seer called Marcius, the games of Apollo were celebrated with dramatic and gymnastic representations from the year 214 B.C. A

---

[1] Aug. C. D. iv. 21; Fest. s. v. catularia.
[2] Ovid. Fasti, vi. 311 sq.; Lyd. de Mens. iv. 59.　　[3] Ovid. Fasti, vi. 319-346.
[4] Macrob. Sat. i. 11; Varro, vi. 18; Plut. Romul. 29.

festival, the Lucaria, on the nineteenth and twenty-first, also combined with games, is said to refer merely to some Romans having hidden in a wood, who had been defeated by the Gauls.[1] Of the August festivals we are for the most part deficient in accurate knowledge. A feast of slaves, in which the women washed their heads, the Portunalia and the Consualia, a second Vinalia, solemnised to Jupiter to implore a blessing on the vintage; and then the Vulcanalia, on the twenty-third, celebrated by throwing animals into the fire, by fireworks, and torch-races; finally, the Opeconsivia, kept in a secret apartment of the Regia, in the presence of the vestal virgins and the sacrificial king only. These were the religious solemnities of August. September was poor in feasts, with the single exception of the Ludi Romani, dedicated to Jupiter, Juno, and Minerva, with scenic entertainments, which fell within it.

In October the Meditrinalia occurred, a wine-festival, in which the new wine was broached. The late-established Augustalia, in commemoration of the victorious return of Augustus to the Capitol, were celebrated with such a pomp and lavish expenditure on games as to throw most of the older feasts into the shade. On the fifteenth the October horse was sacrificed to Mars, and its head attached to a wall: and on the nineteenth the Armilustrium took place, a martial feast of sacrifice, celebrated by consecration of armour and blowing of trumpets.[2] On November, which was without feasts, followed December, with its Saturnalia, which lasted at first but one day, but was extended under Augustus to three, and under Caligula to five. The shrines of Saturn were then illuminated with wax-lights, and the woollen fillets bound about his feet were loosened. The original meaning of the feast was one of thanksgiving for the harvest, with which was inwoven a memorial of that primitive Saturnian age when as yet master and slave were not. In Rome the festival-days were spent in unbridled merriment, with feasting and drinking-bouts, dice-playing, and interchange of presents. The richer people kept open table. To the slaves especially it was an interruption of their misery, like a kind of armistice in the perpetual war with their masters.[3] Released from all their toils, they wore the toga and the hat, tokens of freedom, might indulge in sportive jests, and dine with their masters, who some-

[1] Fest. s. v. [2] Ibid. s. v.; Varro, vi. 22. [3] Arrian. Epist. iv. 1, 58.

times even served them at table.¹ To the Saturnalia were annexed the Opalia, a feast of the earth-goddess Ops, and the Sigillaria: the latter, a festival of images and puppets, derived its name from the little clay figures, offered to Saturn instead of living children, as it was said, by Numa; afterwards it was little images of the gods which were made presents of to children.² Last of all came the Compitalia and Larentalia, festivals of the Lares and deities of the crossways, which were also counted in as belonging to the Saturnalian holiday-tide.

V. Investigation of the Will of the Gods.

NATURE and deity are so inseparably connected and identical in the Roman religious system, that people conceived themselves obliged to consider directly as a manifestation of deity what the other said to him, or what he drew from her. The gods, who fill nature in all her departments, animating and moving her, make known to men, partly through the animal world, partly through the other provinces of creation, their will, and the future in store for them, by certain signs, by phenomena, and antecedents: and all depends only on the accurate observation and right interpreting of this language of signals. Such was the ruling idea of the Roman in this matter. Not in the state only, but even in private life, nothing took place without the auspices having been previously taken.³ " If there be gods,"—this was even the Stoic's conclusion,—" they must care for man; and if they care for him, then also must they necessarily supply him with tokens of their will and of the future."⁴ But here a certain selection was unavoidable: for it could not be the ordinary and perfectly regular every-day incidents in the natural life that might be indifferently consulted regarding the will of the higher powers; nor could every beast pass as the organ of the divine revelations. There were of necessity certain species of beasts— some extraordinary phenomena not explainable by the intel-

---

¹ Macrob. Sat. i. 7; Dio. Cass. lx. 19; Hor. Sat. ii. 7, 4.
² Arrian. Epict. i. 29; Mart. xiv. 70.   ³ Val. Max. ii. 1, 1; Liv. vi. 41.
⁴ Cic. de Div. i. 38, ii. 49.

ligible catena of causes—which were subservient to man's use therein: the physical circumstances of the country, and ancient tradition, determined this point. In those early times one cannot think of conscious imposition and prudential views of state as having turned the error of the greater number into a political tool; though, indeed, in later times, many Romans and Greeks did think that such calculation might have been at the bottom of the whole system from the beginning. If Eastern people attempted to read the decrees of the deity and the destiny of man in the stars, it was a science that was strange to the Romans, and excited their suspicions; it was long before they would tolerate the Chaldeans and astrologers, and repeated sentences of banishment were issued against them and other strange artists in soothsaying. There was no such thing as a Roman oracle, though the Delphic one was consulted, from time to time, for state purposes. Soothsayers and prophets—the declarations, for instance, of a certain Marcius, and of a Cornelius Culleotus in the Octavian war—were exceptionally reverenced during times of heavy trial and great danger, and adopted as canons.[1]

The Romans had naturalised among themselves the institute of the haruspices, which they had translated from Etruria, and that in both its branches, of divination from the entrails of animal victims, and of the interpretation and careful observing of lightning and prodigies, yet so as always to procure a succession of their haruspices from Etruria, thereby contriving to remain in such a state of dependence on that country, before it was subjugated, as frequently proved burdensome. The energies of these seers, indispensable as they were to the state, were directed principally towards the wide field of prodigies. A want of acquaintance with nature, an eager desire and readiness to find something of the wonderful in things the most insignificant, and a boundless credulity, multiplied these signs of warning to such a degree, that we can only dwell with astonishment on the indefatigable anxiety of the senate in taking them all into account. Not only eclipses of sun and moon, but other phenomena of both these heavenly bodies, rainbows of unusual colours, shooting stars, and abortions of man and beast, entered into the list of these prodigies. Then there were showers of stones, earth, chalk,

[1] Cic. de Div. i. 2, 40.

and ashes; idols shed tears or sweated blood, oxen spoke, men were changed into women, cocks into hens, lakes or brooks ran with blood or milk, mice nibbled at the golden vessels of the temples, a swarm of bees lighted on a temple or in a public place, or lightning struck a temple or other public building, an occurrence especially alarming. For all these prodigies, which terrified senate and people, a procuration was necessary, that is, they had to be averted by prayer and expiatory rites, for the favour of the threatening or angry deity had to be reconquered. A shower of stones, under king Tullius, already gave ground for a public sacrificial solemnity of nine days, and thenceforward supplications of the same length and costliness were frequently ordained on similar occasions. Ordinarily it was a sacrifice of beasts by which a procuratio was fulfilled, either in obedience to the Sibylline books, consulted thereupon, or to the behests of haruspices or augurs.

The inspection of the entrails of victims too, or extispicium, was a Tuscan science: and still, in the times of the empire, it was Etruscans born who had the best understanding of the art. Hence Tuscan haruspices accompanied the armies; and powerful Romans, such as afterwards the emperors, kept their own inspector of the sacrifice. Tongue, lungs, heart, liver, gall-bladder, spleen, kidneys, and caul, were the parts which they made the closest inspection of, with a small knife or a needle. According to the division of the sacrifice of beasts into animal and consulting, this investigation of the state of the entrails, to ascertain the will of the gods therefrom, was the chief object of the latter. Accordingly there were in the organs enumerated supposed favourable and inimical parts. If the adverse side was particularly strong, and had largely-developed veins, that was a signification of misfortune. There were fissures or indentations appearing in the examined parts, some of which portended danger, some advantage; sometimes there were defects in them, at other times they were in excess. It was an eminently disastrous token when the head or protuberance in the right lobe of the liver was wanting.[1] As the liver was taken out and boiled with other entrails, if it shrunk together, the sign was of the very worst import.[2] The Romans, however, were far removed from the weakness of allow-

---

[1] Cic. de Div. ii. 12, 15; Lucan. i. 617, 628; Senec. Œdip. 362 sq.
[2] Liv. xli. 15; Fest. s. v. Monstrum.

ing themselves to be deterred from carrying out an undertaking that had been resolved upon, because of a bad presage in the entrails: they determined to be successful in the sacrifice (litare), *i.e.* the sacrifice ought and must exhibit favourable signs, and in this they commonly obtained their object; for either sacrifices were offered to many gods at once, and then it hardly ever happened, if one victim showed unfavourable signs, that there were not favourable ones from another; or the sacrifice was repeated over and over again, with new victims, till the desired result was attained: and it frequently occurred, as Cicero tells us, that while the victim but just now exhibited the most terrifying of all phenomena, the want of a head to the entrails, the very next gave all the tokens that could be desired.[1]

There was no want of cases in which the truth of the haruspicini was strikingly confirmed by the result. When Cæsar was sacrificing shortly before his death, the day on which he first took his seat in the golden chair, and went into public in the purple robe, there was no heart in the bull: and on the following day the liver of another victim had no head. By this time Spurinna, the haruspex, had intimated that danger threatened the life of the dictator. On the morning of the day of his death the sacrifices again gave unfavourable signs as often as they were repeated.[2] With such examples, they who were inclined to disbelieve silenced their doubts, whilst they only awoke those of others. The question was asked, What explanation could be given of the strange changes of mind in the gods, often threatening evil on the first inspection of the victim, and at the second promising good? How did it happen that a sacrifice to Apollo gave favourable, and one to Diana unfavourable signs? Why did the Etruscan, the Elean, the Egyptian, and the Punic inspectors of sacrifice interpret the entrails in an entirely different manner? Again, what connection in nature was there between a fissure in the liver of a lamb and a trifling advantage to a man, an inheritance to be expected, or the like?[3] And on a man's intending to sacrifice, did a change, corresponding to his circumstances, take place in the entrails of the beast; so that, supposing another person had selected the same victim, he would have found the

---

[1] Cic. de Div. ii. 15.
[2] Ibid. i. 52; Plut. Cæs. 63; App. ii. 500; Hor. iv. 2.
[3] Cic. de Div. ii. 12, 14, 15.

liver in quite a different condition? And yet, while the genuine Roman augury from the flight of birds had fallen into disesteem and disuse, the extispicium maintained a certain reputation, and in the last times of the republic was resorted to, where in earlier ones auspicia had been employed.[1] Cato, indeed, who probably disliked the foreign and un-Roman character of the inspection of the victim, declared he wondered how an haruspex did not laugh when he met another of the craft: and the responses and promises made during the civil wars deceived people numbers of times, above all Pompey, who held much to them.[2] The science, however, still kept its ground; a single striking example of a fulfilment, such as happened on the occasion of Cæsar's death, had more weight than twenty deceptions, for which people were always ready with apologetic explanations.

For a long time in Rome the haruspices were not employed as fulguratores, or observers of lightning, which was reckoned among the prodigies, and, as such, in certain cases, required procuratio (an expiation) and burial; for example, if lightning was seen in a clear sky, which was considered exceedingly ominous, and then the services of the haruspices were required. The question, of much importance with the Etruscans, as to which of the nine lightning-gods had thrown this or that flash, did not trouble a Roman, who attributed all the day-lightning to Jupiter, and all the night-lightning to Summanus.[3] But, in the time of Diodorus, lightning-observers were already spread over the face of the earth,[4] and, later on, they often appear in attendance on the Roman armies, and on the emperors, when taking the field.[5] The haruspices, too, found a zealous patron in the emperor Claudius, who was particularly well versed in Etruscan matters; and it seems that, in his reign first, a regular college of haruspices, numbering as many as sixty members, was founded,[6] and ranked along with the other sacerdotal guilds. In the rest of the imperial period, they had dangerous rivals in the Chaldeans, towards whom the favour and confidence of the people was, on the whole, more strongly evinced.

There was a division of views among the Romans themselves on the point whether the system of augury of old time was really

---

[1] Cic. de Div. i. 12. [2] Ibid. ii. 24. [3] Plin. H. N. ii. 53.
[4] Diodor. v. 40. [5] Suet. Dom. 16; Amm. Marc. xxv. 2, xxii. 12, xxiii. 5.
[6] Suet. Claud. xxii. 25; Tac. Ann. xi. 15.

based on a conviction of its being possible to ascertain the will of the gods through it, or was merely introduced on political speculation as a well-contrived engine of state. Two clever augurs, Marcellus and Appius, as we are told by Cicero,[1] favoured, the one the first, the other the latter opinion. But the fact, already established by Cicero himself elsewhere,[2] that in the earlier times of the Roman state the use of auspices was general even in domestic life, and that scarcely any thing of any importance was undertaken without their intervention, is decisive that this was no matter of politic invention, but a something rooted in the prevailing error. In truth, the augural system, as practised in Rome, was a combination of the Tuscan, Latin, and Sabine systems.

The kinds of birds appropriated to divination were divided into Oscines, or such as had significant voices or notes, and Alites, in which the quickness or slowness of flight, and the flap of the wings, was the decisive point. If their flight was from the left of the augur to his right, that was a favourable sign; if in the contrary direction, the matter had to be given up or deferred. Eagles, vultures, and some other species of birds gave augury by flight; while ravens, crows, woodpeckers, screech-owls, and cocks announced by note, good or evil, the approval or disapproval of the gods. Besides, the side from which the voice came had to be considered; a raven's croak from the right, or a crow's from the left, was an augury of assent; the cry of a screech-owl, on the contrary, was always of evil import. And if all the birds of augury kept silence, that too was in like manner a bad sign.[3] Moreover, auspices were divided again into great and small, according to the size and importance of the bird; so that when, for instance, a crow gave a sign, and thereupon an eagle gave an opposite one, the auspicium of the latter, as the greater, made that of the former of no effect;[4] but even when the auspices were most favourable, the squeak of a mouse was sufficient to render them entirely inoperative.

If the augur, or the state official with him, intended to observe the auspices, the latter with his lituus quartered off on the right and left from a fixed point (tabernaculum), chosen according to

---

[1] De Legg. ii. 13.   [2] De Div. i. 16.
[3] Cic. de Div. i. 39; Plaut. Asin. ii, 1, 111; Hor. Carm. iii. 27, 10; Lucan. v. 396.   [4] Serv. Æn. v. 374.

rule, the space in the heavens and on the earth (templum) within which he resolved to reckon as an augury whatever he observed during a given time; and he prayed Jupiter to send an indication of his will.[1] If twenty-four hours elapsed without any sign being given, the consulter returned back into the city, in order to renew the attempt on the following day, but not from the same spot. Altogether, in the whole business, there was a good deal to observe, and nothing was easier than to discover a mistake or omission afterwards that made every thing connected with the auspices go for nothing. No temporal or spiritual officer could be elected or nominated, or any senate or popular assembly be held, without the auspices having preceded: hence the obnuntiatio of the augurs, *i.e.* the announcement of unfavourable auspices, dissolved every assembly, and barred all transaction of business. When Tiberius Gracchus held the comitia for the election of new consuls, one of the rogatores (the holders of the election) dropped down dead suddenly. The haruspices, on being consulted by the senate on the point, replied that Gracchus was disqualified from holding the comitia. Gracchus answered angrily, in refutation of the haruspices as Tuscans and foreigners, who had nothing to say in a question of Roman divining by the auspices, that he had, as augur, correctly observed the flight of the birds. Afterwards, however, he discovered that he had really committed a clear error in doing so, having neglected, when he passed the pomœrium of the city to betake himself a second time to his tabernaculum for the purpose of observing the auspicia, to wait for the proper sign warranting his again passing the city boundary: and by virtue of a decree of the senate, the consuls, whose election was vitiated by this oversight of Gracchus, had to lay down their office.[2] And so Antony could threaten, that as augur he had power to prevent or invalidate the election of Dolabella to the consulship by the auspices in any case; and he carried his threat into execution by falsifying them, as Cicero says.[3] One can understand how an art of soothsaying like this, that had been trained up into a formalism, so pedantic and insignificant, and that allowed an augur at once the most boundless caprice and the grossest abuse, fell into contempt and decay still earlier than other modes of inquiring of the gods; so that

---

[1] Cic. de Div. ii. 35; Varro, i. 51; Liv. i. 18
[2] Cic. N. D. ii. 4.   [3] Cic. 2 Philipp. 33, 35.

in spite of its pure old Roman character, it was obliged to yield precedence to the Tuscan estispicia in Cicero's time; and Cicero himself was of opinion that the office of augur had only been allowed to exist for political considerations a long time past.[1] Meanwhile people were still appealing, on behalf of the credit of the augural system, to the old augur Attus Navius, who had demonstrated the truth of his art to king Priscus by cutting through a whetstone with a razor.[2]

Less troublesome for investigating the will of the gods, less insecure and exposed to the caprice of the augur, was the divining from the eating of fowls, which was resorted to before comitia, but especially on a campaign. Young chickens for the purpose were kept by the pullarius shut up in a cage, and starved intentionally; when the birds pounced voraciously on the food presented to them, and that some of it fell from their beaks on the ground (which was called a tripudium), this was a happy omen. Cicero describes how the art was practised in his time, before which an experienced person had to be called in by the general; in his time, the best person within reach was invited, who responded at once to the question, if there were silence, without looking round, "There seems to be silence," *i. e.* nothing observable in the heaven to render the augury defective.[3] Here, too, the result had strikingly confirmed the divining power of the chickens. Claudius, who had ordered them to be thrown into the sea, when they did not eat, was, with his fleet, beaten in a naval engagement; and Flaminius, besides being defeated, lost his life, when, instead of putting off the battle for a day according to the counsel of his pullarius, he ridiculed people's acting only when the chickens were hungry, and doing nothing when they were full.[4]

Besides the flight and notes of birds, and the feasting of the chickens, thunder and lightning played an important part in the Roman system of augury. It was a rule, when Jupiter thundered or lightened, that no comitia should be held;[5] and thus Marcellus was compelled to lay down the consulate because it thundered on his accession to office. Otherwise, lightning was a favourable sign, in particular demand on such occasions. But

---

[1] Cic. de Div. ii. 12; but see de Leg. ii. 13.
[2] Ibid. i. 17.
[3] Ibid. ii. 34.
[4] Ibid. ii. 35.
[5] Ibid. ii. 18, 35; Tac. Hist. i. 18.

as lightning was not so easy to be had, nor always at the right time, people arranged the matter conveniently for themselves at a later period. On the occasion of an officer of state entering on his duties, he arose before sunrise, and went into the open air accompanied by an augur, where he prayed; then the augur said he had seen lightning, though he had seen no such thing; and that was enough.[1]

The Sibylline books presented another means of inquiring into the divine will, though less usual and ordinary, and one only resorted to when prodigies were very threatening and gloomy. The saga pointed out by name several women in Greece, and Lower Italy with its Greek population, who had prophesied coming events under the inspiration of Apollo, and collections of whose prophetical announcements were in circulation. The generality of these were rough-cast, obscure, and enigmatical in sound, and left a wide margin for interpretation. The collection preserved in Rome, which had found its way there under the last Tarquin, from the Græco-Campanian city of Cumæ, perhaps in consequence of his connection with Aristodemus of that place, seems to have travelled thither from Hellas, nay, from Gergis in Troas, through Erythræ and Cyme, the parent city of Cumæ. The Erythrean collection of Sibylline oracles was the most famous, and probably the most copious. When the Apollo-temple at Rome was burnt, the Sibylline books preserved there also fell a prey to the flames; and therefore the Romans sent in the year 670 A.U.C. to Samos, Ilium, Africa, Sicily, and the cities of Magna Græcia, and even to Erythræ, in order to collect oracles; and on that occasion it was discovered that the collection of the last-mentioned city was identical with the lost Roman one.[2] The Romans brought back from thence about a thousand verses transcribed, and others were added from other places. Thus, neither the elder nor the latter Sibylline oracles originated in Cumæ, but in the Ionian and Asiatic state of Erythræ; and so the Cumæans had not a single oracle of their Sibyl to show, as Pausanias observes.[3] Apollo-worship came along with the Sibylline books to Rome, for these prophecies

---

[1] Dionys. ii. 6.

[2] So I understand the words of Servius (Æn. vi. 36) in Varro, "Apud Erythræam ipsa inventa sunt carmina." Comp. Lact. i. 6. 11, 14; Dionys. iv. 62.

[3] Paus. x. 12, 8.

were given by Apollo; and thus people learned to refer all powers of divination to him. The Sibyl in her oracular sentences asserted of herself that her body after death would indeed become dust, but dust which would feed plants and vegetables, and these would render beasts that fed on them fit for extispicia; while her spirit would mingle with the air, and communicate to that element prophetic voices and sounds.[1]

Augustus and Tiberius ordered a fresh revision of the Sibylline books, and had the spurious parts cut out; the numerous unauthentic collections in private hands were all ordered to be destroyed, and thus as many as two thousand books in roll were then burnt. Such as were acknowledged genuine were composed in Greek acrostic verse, so that the first letters of the verses, when read together, expressed the idea of a whole piece. This acrostic form served as well in the elimination for a criterion, as, in consultation, for a means whereby to find the right oracle. For example, supposing the books to be consulted on account of an epidemic breaking out in Rome, the six verses would be arranged whose first letters in succession formed the word "Loimos," and in them would be found, certainly not without laborious interpretative skill in many cases, what was understood to be the prescribed expiatory remedy.[2] Only the decemviri, afterwards the quindecemviri, assisted, however, by two Greek interpreters, were allowed to read these books,[3] and their contents were not to be communicated to the people without express authority from the senate.[4] The answers usually discovered were to the effect that, in order to obtain the favour of the deity, or to appease an angry one, a new festival should be established, new ceremonies be added to old ones, or this or that sacrifice should be offered; for consultation was mostly resorted to when it was a case of calming spirits agitated by an alarming prodigy, or danger, or when there was any serious cause to fear for the well-being, or perhaps existence, of the state.[5] It is self-evident that very much in this depended on, and resulted from, the interpretation preferred by decemviri or quindecemviri, and hence it was that so much stress was laid by plebeians on obtaining seats in that college. For the pro-

---

[1] Plut. de Pyth. Orac. p. 398. [2] Cic. de Div. ii. 54; Dionys. iv. 62.
[3] Zonar. vii. 11. [4] Dio. Cass. xxxix. 15.
[5] Liv. xxii. 9; Varro de R. R. 1.

phecies were so contrived as to fit all possible cases, or, as Cicero says, so that whatever took place might seem to have been predicted, inasmuch as all accurate definition of persons and times was wanting. The composer, he adds, took shelter in obscurity, so as that the same verses might be accommodated to a variety of periods and a variety of objects;[1] or, as Boethius expresses himself, commenting on Plutarch, "the authors had poured out words and phrases combined at hazard into the sea of undefined time in such way that their fulfilment was pure accident." As, however, the Sibylline books of the Romans were of Greek origin, the worship of Greek divinities was naturally preferred and recommended throughout them. The cultus of Apollo and of his mother Latona, with which the Romans first became acquainted in this way, were followed by those of Æsculapius, Dis, Ceres, and Cybele. It is remarkable, too, that human sacrifices were found to be prescribed therein.[2]

III. THE RELIGIONS OF THE GAULS AND THE GERMANS.

THE Gauls had a body of priests, the Druids, who occupied among them a position similar to that of the same body in Egypt. Without forming a regular caste, for their dignity was not of hereditary right, they were nevertheless an exclusive corporation, in possession of a secret doctrine, which was only presented under the veil of symbol. Although they kept the disciples who solicited reception into their order sometimes as many as twenty years under training and probation, yet the sons even of their most distinguished families eagerly strove for admission.[3] The Druids, indeed, were alone possessed of intellectual civilisation; and their course of instruction included not merely the department of religion, but those of mathematics, astronomy, natural science and ethics, imparted, however, without writing, and only by oral tradition, so that their lore might more easily be kept secret. At the head of the whole order, itself in the enjoyment of the unlimited confidence of the peo-

---

[1] De Div. ii. 54.   [2] Plut. Marc. 3; Quæst. Rom. 83.
[3] Cæs. B. G. vi. 13, 14; Mela, iii. 2.

ple, and probably divided into grades, stood a high-priest, whose election was sometimes decided by wager of battle, the dignity lasting his lifetime. His power was supreme in the nation; for the Druids, at whose head he was, themselves composed the dominant class in the collective social or political life of the Gauls. The entire power of judging and punishing was in their hands. Amongst the Ædui they elected the president of state for the year, the Vergobret.[1] The yearly convention of their council of state was held in the district of Chartres, in the heart of Gaul; and the contending factions of the whole country appeared there to adjust their differences. Whoever they banned, or excluded from the sacrifices, was avoided by all, and was stripped of his rights and honour. In Cæsar's times the power of the Druids was already on the wane, in face of the nobiliary influence of the clans; but the hypothesis of Amédée Thierry[2] is not probable, that, according to the Cymric tradition, the entire Druidical system, with its religious teaching and composition, had been introduced amongst the Gauls, till then addicted to a rude religious rite of nature, through a victorious invasion of the Cymri under their afterwards deified leader, Hesus. Nothing appears in Gaul proper of such a dualism of a stranger conquering race and a subject Celtic one,—the necessary consequence of an event of the kind supposed. True, Thierry thought Druidism had become the prevalent worship in Southern and Eastern Gaul without force of arms; but still the difficulty remains, how a foreign institution, not the growth of the nation, should have attained to so complete an authority, and one that dominated the whole life of the Gauls.

It seems that the Bards, the religious minstrels, and the Eubagæ, engaged in the functions of religion,[3] both belonged to the Druid order in a wider signification. The real Druids led a retired life, devoted to intellectual pursuits. The Druidesses, too, had a very considerable influence; for instance, there were sacrifices which could only be performed by priestesses, and sanctuaries open only to them. These priestesses must some of them have been married, and others have abstained from wed-

---

[1] Cæs. i. 16, comp. vii. 32, 33.

[2] Histoire des Gaulois, Brux. 1842, ii. 128.

[3] Amm. Marc. xv. 9 [? Perhaps the reference is to Strabo, iv. p. 276 (Oxf.), ἱεροποιοὶ καὶ φυσιολόγοι. *Tr.*]

lock either temporarily or for life. On the island of Sena, off the western promontory of Armorica, there was a community of nine maidens, who gave oracular responses, and to whom an extraordinary power over nature was ascribed.[1] Another college of priestesses of the tribe of the Nannetes[2] inhabited a little island at the mouth of the Loire, which the foot of no male could approach. They were obliged to take the roof off their temple once a year, and then replace it in the space of one night. If one of these lady-priests allowed any of the building-material to drop in so doing, she was straightway torn to pieces by the rest.[3]

The teaching of the Druids concerning the state after death is generally understood as adopting a kind of Pythagorean migration of souls. Diodorus says this in terms, and Cæsar seems to say it;[4] but on weighing his words more accurately, when taken together with the distinct testimonies of Mela[5] and Lucan,[6] and the funeral usages of the Gauls, it is clear that it was not the Pythagorean metempsychosis the Gauls believed in, but a life after death, in another world of the departed: death, according to Lucan's expression, would only be the mid-entrance into a long life, transferred to a world beyond the grave, dividing the two halves of life,—the earthly and unearthly. This also explains the Gaulish custom of burning every thing with the dead, whatever belonged to or served them, and all that they particularly cherished,—utensils, arms, animals, and even slaves,—and also the throwing into the flames of letters for delivery by them to other deceased, their predecessors. Mela, who wrote in the year 44 A.D., mentions accounts and bills of debt incurred by the deceased being, formerly at least, burnt along with them, and sometimes that their friends shared their funeral pile in order to live in their society in another world; but that in his time—and Cæsar, too, had found it so before him—people were content with committing to the flames along with him what a man had made use of in his life.

Human sacrifices, wherever the influence of the Druidical religion extended, were exceedingly numerous; and the Romans looked upon the Gauls as a people who distinguished themselves

---

[1] Mela, iii. 6, 23.   [2] B. G. iii. 9.   [3] Strabo, p. 498 (277, Oxf.).
[4] B. G. vi. 14, "Animas or . . . . ab aliis post mortem transire ad alios."
[5] Mela, iii. 2.   [6] Lucan, i. 155 sq.

above all others by its devotion to the service of the gods, and that a very bloody and cruel service. The priest administered the death-stroke from behind to the victim appointed for sacrifice, with the sword, on the diaphragm; and the will of the deity, or the future, was read in the manner of his falling headlong, the convulsions of his limbs, and the colour and gushing of his blood. Ordinarily, grown men, and not cattle, were sacrificed. According to Druid doctrine, the deity would not be satisfied for the life of one man without the death of another, and preferred a human sacrifice to every thing else, because humanity was the best of all seeds.[1]

The victim was not always struck down by the sword; sometimes the man was bound to a stake in the middle of the temple, and there put to death by arrows and javelins. It happened still more frequently that a gigantic basket of wicker-work, in human form, was filled with men and beasts, and then kindled.[2] Sacrifices of this kind were particularly set up, in consequence of a vow; for before a battle the presentation of warlike trophies, and amongst them of prisoners also, was the subject of vow, or at other times, in extremity of illness, a man would promise the sacrifice of the life of slaves and clients. If it were a state sacrifice, the criminals were produced who would otherwise have been executed, and they were often kept many years for this purpose. If there were none such, men were bought and fed, and taken in procession round the city on the day of the solemnity, and at last crucified outside of it, or put to death in some other way. There were volunteers besides, prepared either to share the pile with an honoured person deceased, or to sacrifice their own life for that of a sick person. When the Romans rigorously suppressed these human sacrifices, the custom still continued of scratching the skin of the person devoted, and offering the deity the blood so obtained.[3]

The Druids held the mistletoe, the parasitic plant growing on oaks and other trees, to be quite a remarkable boon from the deity, a kind of panacea, a remedy for barrenness and against poison. The gathering of this plant was conducted with great solemnity; a golden sickle was used, and a couple of white

[1] Varro, ap. Aug. C. D. vii. 19.   [2] B. G. vi. 16; Strabo, p. 198 (277, Oxf.).
[3] Mela, iii. 2.

cattle sacrificed on the occasion.¹ No less effect, in other respects, was claimed for a certain pretended egg of a snake, of the origin of which strange histories were told by the Druids; but which, from Pliny's account, seems to have been a petrifaction, an echinite.² It was a sure way of winning a cause or trial; and a Roman knight from the territory of the Gallic Vocontii, who carried one about his person with that object, was executed for so doing by the emperor Claudius, the enemy and persecutor of the Druids and their religion.

Of the Celtic deities there is little certain to be advanced. Romans, such as Cæsar, gave those that struck them most, from some incidental resemblance, the names of Roman deities of the first class. Accordingly, Cæsar styles the six most prominent Gallic gods, Mercury, Apollo, Mars, Jupiter, Minerva, and Dis. Lucan alone mentions the native designations of the three principal gods, Hesus, Taranis, and Teutates,³ males only, while a female is found in Cæsar's list. Probably the Gauls had but this one chief-goddess; and yet we meet with a goddess Belisana on an inscription, supposed to be the Minerva of Cæsar,⁴ and an Arduinna, who would be Diana. One of their most general worships was that of the Matronæ, a name appearing often on inscriptions, who may have been female genii, guardian spirits, and goddesses of destiny; generally there were but three of them, sometimes more; afterwards, in consequence of their romanising, the Gauls seem to have substituted on their monuments Junos, Parcæ, and Nymphæ. The Apollo of Cæsar, a god of healing, was called, in Celtic, Belenus; their war-god appears under the name of Camulus; Taranis, the thunder-god, was confounded with the Roman Jupiter: Teutates-Mercury had, according to the same author, the most extensive cultus, and the greatest number of idols; in him was honoured the inventor of all arts, the god of gain and trade, and the patron deity of roads, and conductor on journeys.⁵ Regarding the god Esus, or Hesus, who is represented on a monument at Paris as cutting branches from a tree, there is nothing more to be said.

All the images of gods found in Gaul belong to the period after the Roman conquest. And yet it is likely that the Gauls

¹ Plin. H. N. xvi. 44.   ² H. N. xxix. 3.
³ Cæs. B. G. vi. 17; Lucan, i. 445 sq.   ⁴ Martin, Relig. des Gaulois, i. 504.
⁵ Cæs. vi. 17.

had such images already before their romanising, for it is certain they had temples;[1] though thick groves, such as Lucan poetically describes, were their favourite haunts for worship, and were the most frequent witnesses of the flow of human blood. But all the more important temples were erections of the Roman period; and the Roman titles of gods either expelled the Celtic ones, or were coupled with them.

From their organisation and influence on the people, the Druids were far too powerful a corporate body to be endured by the emperors. They composed the core and the connecting link of Gallic nationality; this was to be crushed and broken, and the people were to become romanised in manners, language, and religion. This fusion was in general effected through the aid of numerous Italian colonies, and of the elastic Græco-Roman system of deities, which was able to assimilate and absorb rude coarse worships such as the Gallic. And this fusion was the easier, as, in the thorough victory of the Romans, the Roman gods had proved themselves the true potentates and wielders of earthly destinies, while those of the Gauls had surrendered their worshipers, or proved too weak to protect them. The Druid hierarchy had, however, to be broken up. Tiberius early began the task of the suppression of the institute; and Claudius took a still more decided step by forbidding the entire Druid worship under pain of death.[2] Whether that interdict led to formal persecutions or not, we do not know; at least there is no mention made in the later insurrections of the Gauls of the suppression of their religion having been the pretext for their taking up arms.

Regarding the nature of the German gods, we are reduced to accounts of Cæsar and Tacitus, and particularly the latter, for Cæsar seems to have contented himself with a very general and superficial impression. "The Germans," he says, "have no Druids who superintend in divine things, and they are not zealous in sacrificing. They acknowledge those only as gods whom they see with their eyes, and by whose power they feel themselves unmistakably supported,—the sun, Vulcan, and the moon; the rest are not even known to them by report." According to this, the German religion had become a mere worship of the element and stars, from which, it is obvious, there was but one

---

[1] Suet. Cæsar, v. 4; Plut. Cæsar, 26. [2] Plin. H. N. xxx. 1; Suet. Claud. 25.

element—that of fire—deified by the Germans. The addition, that no other god was known to the Germans but these three, can only be defended if understood of the Roman gods, or such, at least, as easily admitted of being blended with them. Long before Cæsar, as early as the time of Pytheas of Massilia, the Germans were in possession of gods other than those named by Cæsar, two brothers of immortal youth, in whom the Greeks, as the Romans after them, recognised the Dioscuri.

The statements of Tacitus, made one hundred and fifty years later, are more accurate, and to be depended upon, though still not without Roman admixture. While, however, he advanced that the Germans had no images of the gods, or temples, as deeming it unworthy of gods that they should be shut up within walls, or that images of them should be made, he was probably lending his own Stoic-philosophy views to the Germans. They had no temples while and where they had no towns, when they were often changing their settlements, and when artistic skill was wanting to them for the construction of temples and idols in human form. The rule was not without exceptions, and Tacitus himself speaks of a temple of Tanfana, and tells how the goddess Nerthus was carried about on a wagon, and bathed in a lake, which would suppose an image of her.[1] Like the Greeks and Romans, the Germans too, in their earliest times, had honoured sanctuaries, half fetishes, half symbols, stakes or pillars, or even figures of beasts; and where they afterwards settled down for good, there also temples were raised.

Tacitus mentions three gods by name, as distinguished by preference in the worship of the Germans,—Mercury, Hercules, and Mars. The testimony of Paul the Deacon leaves it undoubted that by the first named, Wuotan, or Wodan, the supreme god common to all the Germans, is meant, though it is difficult to say on which of his attributes the Romans relied to assign him a position so subordinate as that occupied by Mercury. The god of the sun, mentioned by Cæsar, is probably none other than Wodan. Though the growth of the corn and the abundance of harvest was ascribed to him, still his nature was to the Germans predominantly gloomy and terrible. He appears at the same time as god of the infernal world and of death; and on appointed days human sacrifices were allotted him, consisting

---

[1] Germ. 40.

most frequently, it may be supposed, of prisoners of war. It is to this god that the holy grove, the common sanctuary of the Semnones, must have been consecrated, to which all people of that name, at fixed times, forwarded delegates to arrange a solemn human sacrifice. People only ventured to visit the sanctuary in chains; and whoever fell in it, could not rise again, but was obliged to be rolled out of it on the pavement.[1]

We may conjecture, though not assert, that the Hercules and Mars of Tacitus correspond to the two old German deities, Thunaer, or Donar, and Ziu. In any case, they were both warlike gods, who were invoked at battles. Songs of battle were current, addressed to Hercules before all the other gods. As god of lightning and fire, Donar was, without doubt, the Vulcan whom Cæsar found amongst the Germans. Particular German tribes, the Suevi, for instance, had their particular cultus. Tacitus speaks of three female deities: Isis, whose worship he believed he discovered in existence among a portion of the Suevi, they having, as a symbol of the goddess, a ship of the build of a Liburnian galley;[2] and centuries after, a custom is met with of dragging about with festal pomp a ship of the kind. The mother of the gods was worshiped among the Œstyi; she was symbolically represented by figures of boars, which, when carried into battle, afforded security to the bearers.[3] The mother-earth, Nerthus, who was worshiped by seven of the Suevic clans on the Baltic, and on an adjacent island, was assuredly the same goddess. Every year she was jaunted about on a car, harnessed with cows, and covered with a white cloth, and every where received with demonstrations of joy, and then bathed in a lake by slaves,[4] who were drowned after the ceremonies were concluded. Among the Naharvali a priest in woman's apparel ministered in the rites of the two brothers "Alcis," whom the Greeks and Romans took to be Castor and Pollux.[5]

We learn further through Tacitus that the divine progenitor of the German races was the god Tuisco, a son of the earth, and that from his son Mannus, and his three sons, the three principal branches of the nation descended.[6] On this statement, and on the nature of the gods of the Germans generally, a light would be thrown only by the introduction of Scandinavian

[1] Germ. 39.   [2] Ibid. 9.   [3] Ibid. 45.
[4] Ibid. 40.   [5] Ibid. 43.   [6] Ibid. 2.

mythology into the question; but as to the extent to which such a process would be admissible as a complement to these obscure and very unsatisfactory Roman notices, there are the widest differences of view; in any case, it is no longer possible, in consequence of the community of fundamental principles, to determine how much is to be put down to Scandinavian influence lasting eight hundred years. The Anglo-Saxons traced their origin back to Woden himself. But following the formation of words, it is certainly probable that by Tuixo, or Tuisco, a son of the war-god Tiu, or Ziu, is to be understood.

Cæsar's account of the Germans not being much addicted to sacrificing must be understood as spoken in a comparative sense: they were not so zealous in that duty as the Gauls, that is, they did not suffer human blood to flow in streams, as the others did, on merely private occasions. Human sacrifice, it seems, was offered to Wodan only; Hercules and Mars received that of certain beasts dedicated to them.[1] The priest performed all religious actions for the community, the father of the family in it and for it. The priests, reverenced and invested with great authority, and in war with the exclusive power of punishment, formed no hereditary or close caste with a compact hierarchy, like the Druids. On them it lay on public occasions to investigate the will of the gods, and to execute the sentence of death on malefactors and traitors, which was considered a religious act, an atonement made to the gods; and having also the conduct of the popular assemblies, they appear as the first and most powerful class. The Germans had no priestesses,— they are only spoken of among the Cimbri, who were probably not a pure German tribe; but they had prophetesses, who were reverenced as holy women,—Velleda, for instance, among the Bructeri in the time of Vespasian, or Aurinia, and Ganna. The Germans, who generally ranked women high, and honoured them, were so far carried away with the notion of their being organs of the deity, speaking through them, that they actually worshiped particular women as goddesses, if the expression of Tacitus be not too strong.[2]

As with the Gauls, so with the Germans, groves were their favourite places of worship: here were to be found residences of priests and altars; here were their national objects of venera-

---

[1] Germ. 9.   [2] Hist. iv. 61.

tion, and here their military ensigns and implements of sacrifice were deposited. Some trees were invested with a special sanctity, such as the thunder-oak at Geismar in Hesse, connected with the cultus of Thor or Donar; and the preachers of the gospel had often in later times to inveigh against tree-worship, as well as the reverence for springs and streams. That there were holy pillars in existence, is clear, from the mention of pillars of Hercules in North Germany; as also of the Irmen-pillar, destroyed by Charlemagne, an upright trunk of enormous size, the name of which signified "the all-supporting world-pillar." There is no appearance of the worship of particular animals in Egyptian fashion among the Germans; yet they had sacred beasts,—the white horses, for instance, which were kept in holy groves at public expense, and had to draw the holy chariot, and whose prophetic neighings priests and kings interpreted.[1] Divination was also practised from the flight and notes of birds.

[1] Germ. 10.

BOOK VIII.

PHILOSOPHY AND RELIGION IN THE ROMAN EMPIRE

FROM THE END OF THE REPUBLIC TO THE ANTONINES.

I. PHILOSOPHY AND LITERATURE IN THEIR RELATIONS TO RELIGION.

1. PHILOSOPHY IN ROME: LUCRETIUS, CICERO—THE ROMAN-STOIC SCHOOL: SENECA, EPICTETUS—PLATONICO-PYTHAGOREAN PHILOSOPHY—PLUTARCH.

WHEN the Greek philosophy first made its way into Rome, it appeared to Roman statesmen like a foreign element, of suspicious aspect, threatening the religion of the state and the whole Roman system, the extent of the bearings of which it was impossible to calculate. But the attempt to prevent it spreading early betrayed its own fruitlessness; and the zeal of Porcius Cato, which effected the speedy dismissal of Greek philosophers from Rome, was soon ridiculed by the Romans themselves as narrow-minded and short-sighted. Scipio Africanus and his friend Lælius were already in confidential intercourse with the famous teachers of Stoic doctrine, Panetius and Diogenes of Babylon. If in this way a Stoic school was soon formed among the Romans, the doctrines of Epicurus also found an early entrance, and—we are at the last days of the expiring republic—from the general tendency to a voluptuous sensuality, met with greater applause from numbers than any of the other systems; though, indeed, Cicero still asserted, that no Epicurean dared to make open acknowledgment of his creed before the people, and that such a confession would disgrace him even in the senate.[1] And yet the new Academy was then planted in Rome by Philo of Larissa and Antiochus.

The first fruit of importance was the doctrinal poem of Lucretius, consecrated to the glorification of the Epicurean teaching. This poet died by his own hand when only forty-four years old; but the end of all his efforts, the glory which he claimed, was this, that following in the wake of the great teacher and benefactor of mankind, he had rendered powerless the curse which pressed heavily on the human race, viz. the horrors of religious illusion, and had emancipated spirits from the oppressive thraldom of god-worship. No doubt, no scruple restrained him from holding out the popular belief as equally unworthy of the gods as it was deserving of the contempt of man. The heroine of his poem is in reality Nature, whom he personifies as creative power, all-ruling, for whose freedom he contends, while he refutes the error of a divine domination. Man, on the contrary, is not free, in his view; for our will is dependent on the conceptions of the soul, and these are determined by the impressions of sense received from without.[2] But the soul itself (composed of heat, air, breath, and a fourth, the subtlest material, the seat of perception) is dissolved as soon as she is despoiled of the protecting shell of the body; and thus immortality is a silly delusion. That Lucretius approved and recommended a man's blunting the edge of sensual lust through the satisfactions obtained by indiscriminate indulgence, we cannot contemplate for a moment as any peculiarity of himself or his school, when we regard the ordinary views that were current in his day.

In naming his contemporary, Marcus Tullius Cicero, the most important and influential of the Roman friends of philosophy, we must, at the same time, remember that he did not approach philosophy with the profound earnestness and speculative endowments of the great Greek thinkers, and that he was far removed from considering such investigations as the highest object of his life. He had indeed received in his earliest youth the instructions of Phædrus the Epicurean, and was afterwards the pupil at Athens of the Academicians, Philo of Larissa, and

---

[1] De Fin. ii. 22.   [2] Lucr. iv. 887 sqq.

Antiochus; and of the Stoics, Diodotus, who lived and died in his house, Posidonius at Rhodes, and Antiochus of Askalon: and yet philosophy was to him but the complement of his more vacant hours and an employment of compulsory leisure. Without being an independent thinker, his only aim was to make the Romans acquainted with the results of the Greek systems in an agreeable and generally intelligible form. Far removed too was he, as all the Romans, from the thought that religion could be a guide to morality and virtue. Only philosophy, he deemed, could bar the frightfully increasing degeneracy; either she or nothing led to virtue.[1] Cicero possessed in the highest degree the faculty of assimilating the ideas of others, provided only they did not approach that higher level of speculation in which he was unable to breathe. With his elastic and richly-imaginative spirit, he also expanded much of what he drew from his Greek sources, though there was often also a failing in acuteness of comprehension. Whether from design, or unintentionally, he broke off the points of many of the Greek philosophical apothegms, or softened away accidental asperities. His point of view was that of half sceptical eclecticism; he felt himself most drawn to the new Academy. In morals he was more of a follower of the Stoic school. No one view, however, really satisfied him: in each he met with hesitation or defect; and therefore also he preferred throwing the *pro* and the *contra* of conflicting systems into the form of a dialogue, without adding any conclusion of his own at the end. For in all, even the highest and weightiest questions, man can only bring it to a matter of probabilities; real knowledge for man there is none; all truth has an element of the false in its composition, with so strong a resemblance to the true, that no safe criterion is discernible to form a judgment or found an assent upon.[2] By these means, nevertheless, he preserved a greater liberty of spirit than the Romans and Greeks, his philosophical contemporaries, who for the most part gave themselves up as unconditional tributaries to a single school, while he carried his detachment to such an extent, that he could say of himself, that he lived on, in regard to philosophy, from day to day, and gave utterance to whatever just recommended itself to his intellect from its probability.[3]

[1] De Off. ii. 2; de Fin. i. 4.   [2] N. D. i. 5.   [3] Tusc. v. 11; de Off. i. 2.

Cicero preferred the Socratic philosophy in so far as it had betaken itself to the province of the moral and practical, and had set physical speculations aside; though he himself again was of opinion that a knowledge of nature and of science was the true bliss, in the enjoyment of which even the gods were blest.[1] But to him, to know was but a means to an end, to action. With him knowledge was always as it were the lower, and action the higher; and when he renounced certainty in accordance with his sceptical bias, in which the contradictions of the philosophical schools hardened him, he thought even the probable was adequate for his object, practical action.

In the highest problems, to which Cicero turned with predilection, he himself felt the meagre and unsatisfactory nature of his theory of probability, and sought to fill it in by the adoption of innate ideas. The germ of morality, he asserted, the seed-corn of the virtues, the first comprehensions of right, the ideas of the deity and immortality, are already lying within us from the first, and develop themselves in our intellect necessarily, and independently of all experience.[2] On the strength of the divine origin of our soul, we have a natural knowledge of the existence of God, consequently one common to all people, even the most barbarous; but that is confined to the existence only,[3] for the most contradictory notions are current among men as to what God is; and his own opinion was that nothing certain could be predicated of the nature of the deity.[4] He is, indeed, for having God conceived to be a sort of simple free spirit, unmixed with aught that is transitory, cognizing and moving all, and itself endowed with eternal power of motion;[5] and yet he could imagine this spirit only as material, as fire, air, or like the fifth primal substance of Aristotle, ether;[6] and at another time he inclined to the view that God was the extreme sphere of the universe, embracing within itself and dominating all the others.[7]

In speaking of the existence and nature of the deity, Cicero uses the expressions "god" and "gods" indifferently, more frequently the latter, more perhaps out of regard to the state religion and universally received ideas. He felt himself obliged

---

[1] Hortens, ap. Aug. de Trin. xiv. 9 (Cic. ed. Gronov. not.).
[2] Tusc. iii. 1; Fin. v. 21; Legg. i. 8.   [3] Tusc. i. 13; Legg. i. 8.
[4] N. D. i. 21, iii. 40.   [5] Tusc. i. 27.
[6] Ibid. i. 26.   [7] De Rep. vi. 17.

to the conception of a supreme God and ruler of the universe; but has not spoken out precisely what he held concerning the popular deities. In his work on "Laws," he nowhere speaks of the service of the one supreme deity; only the worship of the gods as a body is enjoined, and that in three classes, of those who had always been held celestials, of heroes and semi-gods, and of personified virtues.[1] His notion that even the gods of the first class were deified men,[2] did not prevent his accepting their worship. It seemed to him perfectly right, that men should be regarded as gods after death. "Know that thou art a god;" so he represented the glorified Scipio addressing himself in a dream.[3] Then he also accepted a divine providence having sway over the whole world, only he could not be clear as to its limits; the saying of the Stoics, "the gods care only for great things, and neglect small," seems to have met his approbation.[4]

Now it is striking that Cicero had no understanding how to make any use of his knowledge of the deity in the whole department of ethics. In his work, "De Officiis," he slurs over the duties of man to the deity with a short notice, though he accords them a precedence over all others; one gets no information as to what they consist in. Nowhere is the doctrine of the gods brought into close relation with moral doctrine; nor are moral precepts and obligations based on the authority, the will, or the pattern of the deity; his motives spring always and only from the beauty and excellence of the "honestum," and the evil and disgracefulness of vice. If, in speaking of testimony to be given on oath, he bids us think that man has called god to witness, the next thing is, we find this god none other than our own soul, as the divinest gift man has received from god.[5] The idea of a retribution after death was not only strange to him, as to so many of his contemporaries; but he openly declared it in one of his speeches to be an absurd fable, and that, he added, was the general opinion:[6] "Do you take me to be so crazy as that I should believe such things?" is the exclamation he puts in the mouth of a hearer on the mention of a judgment in the lower world after death. And as regards the state after death, he knew no other alternative than either a cessation of existence or a state of bliss. In taking an oath, it should not be the fear of

---

[1] Legg. ii. 8.   [2] Tusc. i. 13.   [3] De Rep. vi. 24.
[4] N. D. ii. 66.   [5] De Off. iii. 10.   [6] Or. pro Cluent. c. 61.

the anger of the gods that restrained people from perjury, for the gods have no such feeling as anger, but simple regard to rectitude and truth.[1]

As a statesman, and under the conviction that without religious institutions the Roman commonwealth could not be sustained, Cicero expressed himself strongly conservative of the existing system of religions. As he generally took it for lawful that the magistrate should impose on the people, so religion appeared to him to offer the most appropriate means of deception; and though he gave vent to a sweeping critique upon the whole system of divination in his work on that subject, yet he laid stress on the point that all magistrates should have the right of auspices, so as "to be supplied with available pretexts for stopping detrimental assemblages of the people."[2] He required, indeed, that superstition should be eradicated,[3] but with the saving clause that it became a wise man to maintain the ordinances of his ancestors by the observance of holy rites and ceremonies; and thus, in fine, all must prove to be superstition that is strange and foreign, and not instituted by the state, in religious matters, and the investigation of the future. Every thing, on the other hand, should be externally observed and treated with extreme respect that rested upon the practice of forefathers, on law or on custom, however corrupt and full of imposture it might be; and this was the ordinary view of the statesmen of antiquity.

No attempt was made by any Roman towards a new creation, or any thing peculiarly Roman, in the department of philosophy. If any one of them occupied himself entirely with that study, he was either content to attach himself unconditionally to one system, or to put together eclectically or syncretically portions of various systems. This last course Quintus Sextius took, in the time of the transition of the republic into a monarchy, and so became the founder of an ephemeral school, to which Sotion, Seneca's tutor, belonged, whose lectures contained a practical morality, partly Stoic, and partly Pythagorean. In particular, abstinence from flesh-meat, and animal food generally, was required in it, with reference to the migration of souls;[4] and that the wise man was just as powerful as Jupiter

---

[1] De Off. iii. 29.   [2] Legg. iii. 12.   [3] De Divin. ii. 72.
[4] Sen. Ep. 59; Quæst. Nat. vii. 32; Sotion, ap. Stob. Serm. xiv. 10; lxxxiv. 6-8.

himself, was the doctrine of Sextius in common with the Stoics.[1]

In Rome the Stoic doctrine alone met with enduring applause and adherents, alongside of the more transitory success of Epicureanism. Yet not only in Rome, but in all other parts of the empire, the schools of philosophy became extinct after the rise of the imperial power; and they only held their ground whose tendency was predominantly practical, and directed to the department of ethics. In Seneca's time the old and new Academies had already died out, and the school of Pyrrho was silent.[2] The prevalent bias of the age was to acknowledge nothing real but what was corporeal, nothing to exist beyond nature, and to turn all science into mere physics. Metaphysics seemed like an empty phantom; for all incorporeal intelligible beings passed for mere abstractions of thought, sensation for the single source of our knowledge. Thus philosophy, especially in Stoicism, had become much simpler, more superficial, and accommodating. Plato's ideas, "the pure intelligence" of Aristotle, were shelved; the sensualistic dogmatism of the Stoical physics, with a palpable solution in readiness for all questions, suited the Romans. In this system God and the world are only logically distinct; man, as the crown of, and most perfect element in, nature, is God's equal, nay, stands higher than God; the divine nature really reaches perfection in man only. Such a creed as this flattered the pride of the Romans; but it was also in a better position than any other system of Greek speculation to justify the whole system of religion and of the gods, so important and indispensable to the statesman; and to represent participation in it as a something beseeming even a philosopher, and which did not entangle him in any contradiction with his principles. For the material pantheism of the Stoic admitted of worshiping, in each natural product or fragment of the same, in every manifestation of a physical power, the all-pervading and all-moving divine power; and eight thousand gods, or personifications of physical matter and powers, had just as much of truth and authority for themselves to plead as one or two. And then the better kind of Roman also felt himself attracted by the ideal of the Stoic wise man, which streamed upon him, in all the more brilliant colours, when con-

[1] Sen. Ep. 73.   [2] Sen. Quest. Nat. vii. 32.

trasted with the general corruption. The doctrine probed him to the heart, which promised to make its followers invulnerable to the destroying might of an inimical destiny; and in a period of forced subjection to a despotic dynasty, Stoic apathy, calm acquiescence in all the decrees of fate, cold resignation and constant readiness for a self-chosen death, seemed the disposition that best became a Roman.

Meanwhile, in its Roman school, the Stoic system was ever dwarfing and shrinking into narrower dimensions. If metaphysics had already become mere physics, Seneca was by this time maintaining that it was only the intemperance of man which had allowed philosophy to extravagate so widely; that she must be simplified, and limited to what was immediately of advantage for life and conduct.[1] Though this famous philosopher,—who in fact was far more of a brilliant rhetorician, delighting in antithesis and nervous epigrammatic sententiousness, than of a calm inquirer,—desired rather to be taken for an eclectic than for an affiliated Stoic, yet he never in reality travelled beyond the boundaries of the Stoic system. The pride, which lies at the heart of Stoicism, not unfrequently cropped out in his writings without disguise. The wise man, he says, lives on a footing of equality with the gods, for he is really God himself, or bears within him a portion of the deity.[2] We are at the same time God's companions and his members. The good man differs from God only by duration; and God, though surpassing man in duration of time, yet, as concerns bliss, has no advantage of him;[3] nay, in one point, the wise man has even the better of God, insomuch as God is of his own nature wise already, while the wise man owes his wisdom to no one but himself. And who could possibly be afraid of the gods? no one in his sound senses is so.[4] The gods neither can nor will injure any one;[5] and they are as little capable of receiving as inflicting harm; and thus it is utterly impossible for man ever to offend the deity.[6] Even prayer is of no use. Why lift up the hands to heaven? Why trouble the gods, when you are able to make yourself happy? It is in your own hand, to be company on even terms for the gods, instead of appearing before them as their suppliant.[7] The everlasting succession of destiny unfolds events

[1] Ep. lxxxix. 106. [2] Ep. 59. [3] De Provid. 1. [4] De Benef. iv. 19.
[5] De Irâ, ii. 27. [6] Ep. 95. [7] Ep. 41.

in an unalterable order, just as in the huddling brook of the wood the preceding wave of water is ever pressed upon by its successor; its first law is to stand firm to its decrees, and therefore expiations, ceremonies, and prayers are of no avail, and serve only as consolations for a sick spirit.[1]

If, according to Seneca's notion, we speak of nature as having given us any thing, that is but another name for the deity, who is interwoven with the whole of the world and its parts, and whom we may distinguish by a variety of names. We call him Jupiter, or even destiny, for that is nothing else but the chain of causes holding together; God being the first link of that chain, and the one from which the rest depend. But we also style him Father Liber, or Hercules, or Mercury, each one being a distinct name of the very same deity, exercising his power now in one way, now in another.[2]

The intrinsic contradiction in the anthropology of the Stoics comes out clearly to light in Seneca. Every man carries God about with him in his bosom: in one aspect of his being he is God; accordingly, nothing further is required for virtue than that we should follow our nature, the easiest thing in the world at bottom.[3] But now, consistently with all experience, men are vicious; they have been so, and will be so in future. Dominant vices may change, but vice itself will never cease to prevail;[4] and we all have erred. Whence, then, this universality of sin? Seneca can account for it in no other way than a general madness among men. And so little did he cherish the hope of an amelioration, that he thought, after the destruction and reconstruction of the world, the new race and innocent, who inhabited the new world, would soon forfeit their innocence again;[5] we are provided with no explanation how the gods, in human form, come to this common madness. Seneca, indeed, had much that was beautiful to say about divine providence; for God—the world-directing power or world-soul—is intelligent, but is limited by matter that is in no way to be entirely kept under; and the immutability of this matter bears the brunt of the charge of God's being so far from upright in the appointments of fortune, and of his sending poverty and suffering upon the good.[6]

[1] Quæst. Nat. ii. 35.   [2] De Benef. iv. 7, 8.   [3] Ep. 41.
[4] De Benef. i. 10.   [5] Quæst. Nat. iii. 30.   [6] De Provid. 5.

Unlike those earlier Stoics in the time of Cicero, who defended the entire system of augury, Seneca handled the religion of his day with severity, in his work "Against Superstitions." He rejected the whole sacrificial system, for God could not take delight in the butchery of innocent creatures.[1] The entire of the pagan worship of images was folly to him; they dressed the gods in human forms, or in those of beasts and fishes, or even in a compound of these,—calling a creature divine, that would appear a monster to us were it ever to come into existence and before our eyes. The old Romans had even converted Pavor and Pallor, fear and anguish, into gods. It were madness, beyond that of any tyrant, to think of appeasing the gods by mutilation and wounding of self. While ridiculing the marriages of the gods, and the common herd of deities whom superstition had amassed together in the course of time, he concluded, nevertheless, with the advice, that one might even adore this rabble rout of gods, provided one remembered such act of adoration was a mere matter of custom.[2]

Seneca, however, appears to have stood alone among the Stoics with his trenchant views on the popular and state religion. Two contemporaries of the same school, Cornutus and Musonius, struck out in another direction. The first, in his work upon "The Nature of the Gods," put forth a physico-allegorical interpretation of the Greek and Roman gods in the Stoic manner. The latter would not allow philosophy any other object at all than the department of practical ethics, or confess it of other importance than as a theory of virtue, and a guide to conduct; and on this very account he would require all, even women, to study philosophy;[3] for philosophy, as he naïvely expressed it (meaning, of course, his own), was the remedy for that thorough corruption of society in his day that filled every reflecting mind with the gloomiest perplexity. Moreover, on questions concerning the deity and the soul of man, he was an unconditional believer in his school, speaking without suspicion of the nourishment which the gods attract to themselves from the exhalations of earth and water; and of the human soul, cognate to the gods, as a material substance, composed of warm exhalations, and sustained by vaporous secretions from the

---

[1] Ap. Lact. vi. 25. [2] Ap. Aug. Civ. D. vi. 10.
[3] Ap. Stob. Serm. App. pp. 415, 425.

blood, and which is liable, as other bodies are, to be spoilt, dirtied, and wetted by bodily influences.[1] This does not prevent his asserting that the wise man despises exile, as he bears the universe about with him.[2] With him, as with the rest of the school, who have much that is very beautiful to say of the respect and imitation of the deity which beseems man, the imitating of God turns out to be but the following one's own nature and light, allowing the divine substance which each one carries within him its play; and Proteus is the closest symbolical representation of the god of the Stoics,—a substance in itself formless, but clothing itself in every possible variety of form in the world.

The far-famed Stoic moralist, Epictetus, a scholar of Musonius, displays a clearer insight into the inner life of the soul than his predecessors of the same school, and, with the exception perhaps of Aristotle, has exercised a wider influence than any other thinker of ancient times upon succeeding generations, the Christian period inclusive. Philosophy to him begins in the consciousness of our own weakness and impotence. In order to be good, we must first come to the understanding that we are bad.[3] Philosophy, above all, must clear away the darkness caused by our erroneous belief that we are lacking in naught, as well as from mistrust in our own strength. Epictetus then directs man to God. In God man has to seek for what is wanting to him, moral help;[4] and never was there a system of morality which found so many and such striking echoes in Christianity as his does. Still, the God to whom we must betake ourselves is the God in us, for God has stripped himself of part of his own being and assigned it to us.[5] This demon in us,[6]—*i.e.* our own intelligence, and our own will, as emanating originally from God, and conceived in its ideal purity,—that is the higher power, in whose aid we must confide, and which we must invoke.

The doctrine of Epictetus bears throughout a deep impress of egoism. Freedom from desires and passions, an undisturbed tranquillity of spirit, carried out into impassibility, are objects of attainment at any cost. We ought not to trouble ourselves about externals at all, parents or brothers, children or fatherland; nay, we are instructed to refrain from sympathy for the

---

[1] Ap. Stob. Serm. xvii. 43.   [2] Τὸ πᾶν, ap. Stob. xl. 9.   [3] Diss. ii. 11.
[4] Ibid. ii. 18.   [5] Ibid. i. 14.   [6] Ibid. i. 15.

misfortunes of others; at times perhaps we may assume the semblance of such compassion, but we must never really indulge the feeling. The man of perfect wisdom will also abjure marriage.

The succession of Stoic moral philosophers closes with one of the noblest and grandest forms of antiquity, the emperor Marcus Aurelius. Still it is as if he were filled with the presentiment that all about him, the very school and doctrine he was so closely bound up with, would come to an end. The uncertainty and nothingness of all human things, the resistless stream of life, in whose vortex all being, and every struggle after a frail and fleeting existence, are sucked up and disappear, form the ever-recurring burden of his thoughts. A sentiment of sorrow and a deep disheartenment cast as it were a black veil of mourning over the whole of his system of contemplation, and almost every one of his reflections. "Farewell all hope to you who enter here," was the inscription upon the gates leading into the sanctuary of the Stoa.

Towards the close of the first century a school was growing up by the side of the Stoic philosophy, and gradually absorbing it, in which the Platonic and Pythagorean doctrines were blended, and a third and new form, the last birth of Græco-pagan philosophy, issued; not, however, without some of the characteristics of the Aristotelian and Stoic creeds. Stoic naturalism, with its comfortless fatalism, and the contradictions between its theory and its moral precepts, no longer gave satisfaction to minds. Even Platonism in its original form, and after the defects which Aristotle had laid bare in its doctrine of ideas, could not now again be raised into new life. There still, however, predominated among the later Platonicians for a considerable time the notion of a substance existing external to God, and independent of him, eternal and material, thrown into wild and irregular motion by a soul of its own. A division, however, already existed on the question whether this soul of matter, passive and impotent in itself, had been subjected from eternity to the will and law of God (which Alcinous, about 150 A.D., represented as the doctrine of Plato[1]), or whether a living active principle of evil, resisting the divine activity, were to be adopted as the only possible explanation of evil in the world. The latter was the

[1] Alcin. Introd. in Plat. Dogm. 12-14.

view taken by Plutarch,[1] Atticus,[2] and Numenius, all Platonists, who, at the same time, discovered in their master the doctrine of a primal chaos, overpowered and fashioned by God, and yet without his being able to annihilate or transform the evil principle therein inherent.

The Aristotelian doctrine had allowed the divine intelligence on the one side, and the world containing the human soul on the other, to stand in immediate opposition to, and severed from one another in such a way, in fact, that the world itself seemed to be defective in a principle of unity. Stoicism, on the contrary, had attained a unity on the principle that the whole of nature was contained in God as the universal soul, thereby making God (the intelligent primal fire) rise in nature, and fall with it. The Platonists recognised the necessity, and felt the desire, of a living God, really supernatural and external to the world, at once intelligent and willing; they wanted to make nature more dependent on God than she was in the Peripatetic system, and the human soul at the same time more independent of matter. But on them too Stoic ideas worked strongly; and while they clung to this universal soul of the Stoics, they sought to ally it, though without confounding it with God, to a higher principle, to a God beyond nature, but they failed in getting beyond a second material principle, not depending on God for its existence; at the same time they could not free themselves from the thraldom of Stoic views, and they transferred the laws of the material world, eternal motion, to the soul and to God himself. Thus, about the middle of the second century, Numenius assumed three divine hypostases, the Supreme Being or the good, the father, according to him, of the second hypostasis or God the world-creator, the third being the world; at the same time he described the repose of the first as the eternal motion implanted in it by nature.[3] And as the Demiurge, the creator of the world, thus also becomes the world-soul, and is therefore identical with the third hypostasis, while the first is the essential equivalent of the second, the result is that the whole of nature was again thrust back into the essence of God.

In the Syrian Numenius we already discover traces of Jewish and Christian, or at least Gnostic, influences; while,

---

[1] Plut. de an. procr. vi. p. 1015. [2] Jambl. ap. Stob. Ecl. i. 894.
[3] Ap. Euseb. Praep. Ev. xi. 18.

on the other hand, the Pythagorean Apollonius, somewhat his senior, takes his stand still upon the ground of pure Grecian speculation. In the letters bearing his name, which if not really composed by him, at any rate are exponents of the views of the Neo-Pythagoreans,[1] he is represented as teaching that all coming into and going out of being, birth and death, were but apparent, and had no existence in fact; that birth was the transition from the state of substance to that of nature; death, the return of nature into substance: what takes place in them was but a mere appearance and disappearance of matter, according as it was condensed or rarefied, or alternated between emptying and filling. If matter fills the being, it becomes visible, and that is what is ordinarily termed birth; if it withdraws from the being, that is termed death. The substance of things remains always the same: there is but the change from motion to rest. It is an illusion in parents to suppose they generate the child, whereas they are but purely passive instruments. Man, however, by death becomes God, inasmuch as it is not his nature which is changed, but only the form of his being. Such is this theory of a general metamorphosis effected through the modifications of the one substance; the same as Ovid[2] had previously put into the mouth of Pythagoras himself, and was probably at that time taught by his followers.

Plutarch, the contemporary of Apollonius, takes a higher rank than he, and unquestionably the highest among the Greeks of this later period. He was born A.D. 50, and died at a great age under Hadrian. Though addicted to Platonism more than any other doctrine, yet he was, on the whole, an eclectic, and frequently came into contact with Stoicism, which he combated with spirit. No one, to our knowledge, has, in those times, shown so warm a love for the religion of his people as he. His earnest endeavour is to contrive to keep the sinking creed above water, and yet at the same time to purge religious ideas and rites, and to make them accord as nearly as possible with his own view of the just medium between superstition and unbelief.

According to Plutarch, the authorities one has to hold with in a knowledge of the gods and of religion are the poets, the old lawgivers, and the philosophers; but the reliance to be placed on the poets and lawgivers is again so circumscribed as to

---

[1] Apoll. Tyan. Ep. lviii. s. 25, 26.   [2] Metam. 15.

leave the ultimate decision upon divine things to philosophers alone. These, however, should not be either Epicureans or Stoics; Plato was principally to be followed. The special province assigned to philosophy was that of putting a right construction on the rites and the festivals established by law;[1] in other words, to prop up ceremonies by a substructure of ideas, that were to be borrowed chiefly from the circle of the Platonic. Plutarch himself supplies a copious illustration of the caprice and violence pursued in this matter of philosophical interpretation. He lays it down as a canon: "In the poets, and especially in the myths, should any thing unworthy be attributed to the gods, if Mars be spoken of, we must imagine it as said of war; if Hephæstos, as of fire; if Zeus, as of fate; but if any thing honourable, then as of the real gods." He explains the adultery of Ares and Aphrodite as if Homer intended to convey through it the lesson that bad music and bad language generated effeminate manners.[2] One fruit of his philosophy besides is the assertion that the different nations of the world always worshiped the same gods at bottom, the one God namely, and the ministering powers by him placed over people.[3] He himself took Isis and Osiris to be really deities, whom the Greek did well to honour, though they were strangers.

Plutarch was, in reality, a monotheist, in so far as he accepted a one personal supreme god, Zeus, to whom he attributed every imaginable perfection, moral and spiritual, making his blessedness consist in his knowledge. Far too high and distant though he be to stand in any relation whatever with the world, nevertheless the universe is sustained by his will and his thought. There are also intermediate beings who occupy themselves with the world, nature, and man, or even appertain to nature, yet are subordinated to the supreme God: these are the gods of the Greeks. Plutarch reckons, as belonging to them, the Sun and Moon, beings with souls, whom, as he says, all men pray to as gods.[4] Further, Apollo is, he thinks, the god of nature, who takes pleasure in his own transformations, so far as he is changed into fire; and Dionysos the same, so far as he is turned into wind, water, earth, stars, plants, and beasts.[5] In justification of polytheism, Plutarch appeals to the fact that there were divine

---

[1] De Isid. 68. [2] De Aud. Poet. 4. [3] De Isid. 67.
[4] Adv. Colot. xxvii. p. 1123. [5] De Ei. ap. Delph. 9.

properties which would undeniably remain at once objectless and inoperative in God, and could be turned to no account, were there not other godlike beings in existence by the side of the one supreme God;[1] meaning, that in God there was a justice and a love which would be without object, unless there were other gods.

Plutarch is a dualist, in so far as he adopted a principle of evil (Typhon, Ahriman, Ares, and Hades) confronting the perfect God from all eternity. But in reality he has three principles, God, Hyle, and the evil unintelligent world-soul, which, even after the complete organisation of matter by God, still lords it over its lower parts, and is the ever-active source and cause of all that is evil and counter to God, as well as of all the irregular and wicked impulses stirring the human soul.[2] With Plutarch, therefore, it is not matter itself which is the seat of evil; rather, matter in its higher elements is of kin to the divine nature, and longs for its formative influence; but that evil soul has coöperated with God in the creation of the world. One might accordingly have expected Plutarch to hold two world-souls,—one good, the other evil; and yet he speaks but of one, and one only, composed of two absolutely inimical elements, one of which is the divine intelligence, pouring itself out on matter, the divine principle of life implanted in matter at the creation of the world, which, while a portion of God himself, is at the same time detached from the divine being;[3] the other portion is that old and evil soul, originally inherent in matter, which can never be wholly brought into subjection by the good and divine, but is every where setting evil at the side of good, and is also at work in the human soul, producing sensual desires and uncontrolled passions.[4] Hence Plutarch enters into conflict with the doctrine of other schools concerning a primitive matter without properties; for then the existence of evil in the world would be unexplained, as God would have fashioned such matter into something perfectly good, having no one able to resist him. In order, therefore, not to be untrue to his Platonism, Plutarch essays to fasten this doctrine of a double world-soul, the one tending to good, and the other eternally bad, upon certain passages of Plato.[5]

Plutarch's whole cosmical theory, and particularly his way of

---

[1] De Orac. Def. xxiv. p. 423. [2] De Isid. 46-49. [3] Quæst. Plat. ii. 1, 2.
[4] De Isid. 49; de an. procr. 24. [5] De an. procr. 8, 9; de Isid. 48.

looking at the religion of his fathers, which seemed to him to stand in urgent need of a purgation, forced him into laying greater stress upon a species of intermediate demonic beings, holding a position half way between God and man. These beings, souls clothed with an aerial form, are of a changeable nature, weak and imperfect, and partially subject to the conditions of mortality;[1] and from the frequent confusion of the demonic with the divine, a thorough misunderstanding has arisen.[2] Deny the existence of demons, and you destroy all communion between the gods and man. To do that would be to set aside all intermediate natures, obeying and interpreting the will of the gods.[3] These demons are the vehicles of the different kinds of divination; they are invisible assistants at worship, and at secret rites of initiation, and are, so to say, servants and secretaries of the gods. Many of them traverse the earth as avengers of impieties committed. Such demons Plutarch required for his Theodicea, for the special purpose of laying on their shoulders whatever he deemed unworthy of the gods. Accordingly he lets the evil world-soul appear and energise in them, yet so as that a slight residuum of evil exhibits itself in one, while in another it is much stronger and more difficult to annihilate. As to marked division or insurmountable barrier between men, demons, and gods, there is none such. The souls of men can become heroes and then demons, and these again gods. There are but few demons that are able to arrive at a perfect participation of the divine nature, and that only by a long process of purification in virtue; others, in whom the evil was strongly predominant, are obliged to enter again into mortal bodies, and to lead a sad and gloomy existence.[4] To evil demons of this class Plutarch ascribes the introduction of human sacrifice. Every feast and sacrifice, he thinks, in which raw flesh was consumed, people gashed themselves, fasted and lamented, uttered words of shame, or accompanied distortions of the body with shrieks, were modes of appeasing and keeping off evil spirits.[5]

Plutarch believed that divine revelations were vouchsafed to man. It was the gods themselves who allowed him a certain knowledge of divine things; but the instruments of these revelations, which generally relate to the future, were, he thought,

---

[1] De Def. Orac. 12. [2] De Ei. ap. Delph. 21. [3] De Def. Orac. 13.
[4] Ibid. x. 12. [5] Ibid. 14.

partly demons, and partly vapours arising from the earth, as in the oracles—Delphi, for instance. Now as the character of the demon imparting the revelation is itself obscure, and one might be easily deceived by mistaking an evil demon for a good, the chances of the truth of such a manifestation must have been but problematical in Plutarch's eyes. As for other things, he thought people ought to worship God and demon according to the popular tradition to which he belonged.[1] Besides, he was well furnished with resources for removing what was corrupt or offensive to the eyes of others in myths and ritual ceremonies; in each of which he discovered either a religious idea, or a physical relation, or a moral precept and practical rule of life, symbolically expressed, or a record of an event in the life of a demon. His treatise on Isis and Osiris shows particularly how cleverly he could make his way out of every difficulty arising in this department, and sometimes, too, by very forced and far-fetched interpretations. This notwithstanding, Plutarch is the last of the really religious-minded Greeks, who were devoted to their hereditary religion in its entirety. After him there was no one to take up the cause of the Greek religion with the like warmth, or at the same time with such cultivated philosophical abilities. The religious zeal and conservative opinions of the Neo-Platonists, of whom Plutarch was in some degree a precursor, took an essentially different direction.

---

2. LITERATURE: DIODORUS, STRABO. THE POETS OF THE AUGUSTAN AGE. PLINY, TACITUS.

IF we may judge of the prevailing tone of an age from the leading names in the literature surviving to us from it, the educated classes during the last times of the Roman republic, and the first of the empire, among the Greek-speaking portion of the world, as in Rome, were infected with an unbelieving spirit, either hostile or indifferent to the gods. There was a change in it, however, towards the close of the first, and the beginning of the second century A.D., when religious paganism made a new and a last effort.

An undisguised contempt for the Hellenic worship pervades

[1] De Def. Orac. 12.

the judgments of a Polybius and Dionysius on Roman religion. The political point of view which they both occupy in passing them, shows strikingly how religious grounds were wanting. The historian Diodorus, of Agyrium in Sicily, a contemporary of Cæsar and Octavian, gives us in his first six books the mythical and primitive history of Asiatics and Greeks; but in vain does one look for a single positive evidence of his religious creed throughout his work. Sometimes, indeed, he speaks as if belief in mythical history still existed, but not a word ever of a divine, world-creative intelligence. He usually explains the origin of things from physical causes, from the relations between the different elements of matter alternately uniting together by virtue of their specific gravity, or repelling one another in consequence of their opposite essences. His gods are but stars or deified men. In his preface he speaks once of the divine providence which brought the stars and natures of man into combination and harmony, and thus had formed for all time a circle within which it stores all that destiny has marked out for every individual.[1] The same providence, then, has so interwoven the course of the stars and the events of man's life, that, as regards men, it has no other part to play than that of executioner of astrological destiny.

Strabo, who lived some thirty years later than Diodorus, displays a kindred spirit to that of Polybius and Dionysius of Halicarnassus,[2] so far as concerns the myths of the gods, and their political use for the guidance of the multitude. He thinks the commoner sort of people and women are not to be led by the understanding, but by the fear of the gods, which cannot be aroused without fabulous and marvellous tales. Founders of states employed stories of the avenging power of the arms of the gods as bugbears for the simple. He, too, makes mention once of a "providence" as having decided to produce gods and men as its noblest creations.[3] Is it Zeus he was thinking of under this providence? and how far were the two species of creations, gods and men, distinct from one another?

The astronomical poem of Manilius, who wrote towards the close of the reign of Augustus, preached a kind of fatalistic pantheism, borrowed probably from Stoic sources. To him the

---

[1] Diod. i. 1, p. 2. [2] Polyb. vi. 54; Dionys. ii. 13; Strabo, i. p. 19.
[3] Strabo. xvii. p. 810.

world itself is God, and he explains himself thus,—that "the spirit infused into the world," the world-soul, is God; who has preferred man alone of all creatures, has descended into him and striven to become conscious of himself in him.[1] Who could form an idea of God for himself, without being at the same time a portion of the deity? Therefore Reason can neither deceive nor be deceived.[2] But the destiny and life of man nature has made dependent on the stars,[3] so that nothing can be withdrawn from the empire of the supreme intelligence; and for the prevailing corruption, for the fears that torment us, the blind desire and the everlasting anxiety, we have no other consolation proffered than that "the fates steer the world's course, and each must bear his own destiny."

Virgil and Ovid, contemporaries of Manilius, make use of the entire Græco-Roman system of gods and mythology in their works. That this is but matter of poetical and theatrical effect, and of acquiescence in the current ideas, on their part, is transparent from passages in the works of both. There is a soul, says Virgil, in the centre of the universe filling and moving the huge body. Heaven, earth, sea, sun, moon, beast, and even man himself, are penetrated with it. It is the divine fire, bestowing and sustaining universal life. As soon as the particle of the world-soul assigned to each has broken its earthly bonds, down it descends into the lower world, where it encounters a just judgment. A new body is assigned to it to animate; and if at last, after long migrations, its stains are wiped away, it returns like purified ether back again to its fount.[4]

This ether-god, with the pythagorising doctrine of souls, is also Ovid's favourite notion. The formation of the world out of chaos is with him the work of nature herself.[5] For the etherial fire, or holy ether, the igneous power of the heavens, has chosen itself a dwelling-place on the heights of Olympus. The ether, therefore, is Zeus, the hurler of lightning. A spark of this divine ether, descending into the womb of the earth, only just formed, gave being to man.[6] Further on Ovid puts his views into the mouth of Pythagoras,[7] who has received the doctrine from

---

[1] Manil. Astron. ii. 104-107, "seque ipse requirit."
[2] Manil. ii. 128-131.   [3] Ibid. iii. 58.
[4] Æn. vi. 727-751.   [5] "Deus et melior natura," Metam. i. 21.
[6] Ibid. i. 26, 27, 254, &c.   [7] Ibid. xv. 153-175.

the gods; and it is no other than that of the eternal and universal metamorphosis of Apollonius. As concerns the gods, he says elsewhere quite openly, "It is useful there should be gods; and as it is so, we should therefore hold that they do exist."[1] But Virgil esteems the man as blest "who has been enabled to fathom the causes of things, and has trampled under foot all fears, and destiny the inexorable, and the din of greedy Acheron."[2]

Horace is, in practice, the disciple of the Epicureans, whom he ridiculed in his poems. It is impossible to get any where a clear grasp of his sentiments, so changeful is he in his varying sharply-contrasted colours. True to his often-quoted maxim, that the shortness of life admits but of the enjoyment of its sweets,[3] he seems to have kept all serious thought and inquisitive reflection at a distance. At one time he confesses his unbelief, and his hostility to the worship of the gods, and talks of the Manes as fables;[4] at another he would turn his back upon the human wisdom which has led him astray with its delusions, and return to the old gods; warning the Romans to rebuild the decayed temples, and discovering in impiety the cause of public calamities and corruption of morals.[5]

We must look for the sentiments of the more serious Romans upon religious points in the elder Pliny, and in Tacitus. First and foremost, in Pliny we find the universe explained pantheistically to be a divine being, and in it again the sun to be the supreme deity in nature, as being the spirit of the whole.[6] Man, however, weak and circumscribed, has divided the whole into parts, so that every one might worship the one of which he stood most in need. It is folly to believe in countless gods, and to convert even the vices and virtues of men into them. Nevertheless the number of the inhabitants of heaven has become greater than that of earth; while every one adopts his own favourites, and coins Junos and Genii at will. To the mortal, he is God who is of use to the mortal, and this is the road to undying fame; and the names of the gods, Pliny thought, have usually originated in the very ancient practice of deifying those to whom man's gratitude was due. That undefined supreme being does not trouble himself about human things; and it is difficult to decide whether it were more pious on the part of the human race not to worship

---

[1] De Arte Amandi, i. 397. [2] Georg. ii. 490. [3] Hor. Carm. i. 9.
[4] Hor. Carm. i. 34. 1. [5] Ibid. iii. 6. 1 sqq. [6] Plin. H. N. ii. 6.

this deity at all, than offer him a service at which man must needs blush nowadays. This is therefore hylozoistic pantheism; and Pliny thought the number of gods had been increased in some measure by the deification of certain parts of nature, as also by the apotheosis of men. He concludes with the expression, "The imperfection of human nature supplies a special consolation in the thought that even to the deity not every thing is possible, inasmuch as in itself it is nothing but the power of nature." Whether this nature-power be intelligent in the sense of the Stoics, or not, he leaves undecided.

The confessions of Tacitus, the greatest of the Roman historians, are much less explicit. He has let fall no hint about the being of God. In one passage he denies, with bitter irony,[1] there being any appearance of a retributive justice in human affairs; and the concluding sentence of the Germania, that "the Fenni were secure against the gods by their poverty and want of civilisation," is conceived in the same spirit. In fact, he seems to have imagined the gods to be, if not utterly hostile to man, at least enemies of the Romans. He speaks distinctly and repeatedly, to this effect, of the anger of the gods weighing heavily on the Romans since the times of Sylla and Marius, and of its fruit being always new impieties and vices amongst them.[2] He has no belief in the conduct of events by a divine providence; only he is not certain "whether human affairs are set a-going by destiny and immutable necessity, or by hazard;"[3] adding, "the generality have not their minds made up as to whether their future is decided for all, immediately on their birth; but there is much that happens otherwise than is foretold by the impostures of lying seers; who thereby throw discredit upon a science to which past and present have born undeniable testimony." Undoubtedly when he wrote thus, he was himself a sharer in the fatalistic principles of the generality of mankind.

---

3. Notions of a Future State.

If the belief in God and the belief in a personal existence are most intimately connected together, and if the denial, or mistaken

[1] Ann. xvi. 33. [2] Ibid. iv. 1. 1; xvi. 16; Hist. i. 3. 2, 38.
[3] Ann. vi. 22.

views, of a free personality in God also lead logically to the acceptance of the destruction of a man's personality after death, then we must be prepared to find the ideas entertained by philosophers and educated people generally of man's future state beyond the grave, presenting the same picture of uncertainty, doubt, confusion, and contradiction as their religious ideas have, during the period between Sylla and the Antonines. Unquestionably the greatest influence upon the entire moral world of this age was exercised by the Stoic school; and we must accordingly consider whether the later Stoics, who departed in some weighty particulars from the old Stoa, allowed themselves any license in this matter, or remained faithful to the old dogma.

As has been already mentioned, the older Stoics taught that souls, being substantially an evaporation of blood, penetrated with ethereal fire from the world-soul, continued to exist a certain time after death in a separate state of being, especially in the case of wise men, but that no souls could exist longer than till the general conflagration of the world, when they would be absorbed in it, and return into the primal fire. Epictetus, however, seems to have believed that this refusion of the human soul into the world-soul took place immediately on its separation from the body. Death to him is a joyful return to, and union of man with, kindred elements; whatever was igneous in his composition reverted to the element of fire, and so on; and there was no Hades, Acheron, or Cocytus.[1]

If, as Numenius reports, some Stoics taught that only the world-soul was eternal, but that all other souls would be mingled and blended with it immediately after death, Seneca, on the contrary, speaking at least for himself and such as himself, favours its continuance till the next periodical conflagration.[2] When the whole of matter, he says, is on fire, all that now shines systematically will burn in one mass of fire; and if it please the deity to grant a new beginning to that whole, then shall we, blest spirits, we who have attained to the eternal, in the general ruin, ourselves a small addition to the huge waste and desolation, be metamorphosed into the old elements."[3] Seneca, therefore, must have looked upon the whole question of a state after death as something very uncertain, and have varied

---

[1] Epict. Diss. iii. 13, 1. [2] Ap. Euseb. Præp. Ev. xv. 20.
[3] Consol. ad Marc. 26.

in his views about it. At times the last day of the present life is a birthday to an eternal.¹ He talks much about a happier state after the spirit has been delivered from the bondage of life, and received into the region of the departed. But doubt is ever recurring; he has only believed what he has advanced on the word of great men, who promise more than they prove.² In other passages, again, he has nothing to console himself and others with but a state of insensibility, the loss of all consciousness, and therefore also the impossibility of any condition of discomfort. Death, he says expressly, has already preceded our present existence, we have experienced nothing disagreeable before birth, nor shall we after death.³ Here, then, he agreed with Torquatus the Epicurean, in Cicero.⁴ Marcus Aurelius betrays a like hesitation. He, too, is uncertain whether the dissolution and refusion of the soul is immediately consequent on death or only on the conflagration of the world, yet he inclines to the former opinion. He has no doubt on the principal point, the soul's sooner or later disappearing, or being blended and absorbed into the world-soul, which comprises the germs of all being.⁵ Every part of me, he says, will on my dissolution re-enter into its corresponding portion of the universe, and this again will be changed into another portion of the universe, and so on to all eternity.

Thus Cicero was the only Roman undertaking to rest a real and individual existence of souls after death on philosophical grounds. He did so as a Platonist; but philosophy had made no progress with this question since Plato's time. Dicæarchus and Aristoxenus, the Peripatetics, had denied in a general way that there were souls. The Stoic Panætius had only lately, while renouncing the doctrine of his school touching the periodical conflagration of the world, rejected as well the temporary duration of souls, its corollary;⁶ and with all his respect for Plato, had pronounced his doctrine of immortality untenable. Now Cicero in his Tusculan Disputations accepted the reasoning of Plato in essentials. Whatever the soul is, it is a being that feels, thinks, lives, and is active, and must consequently be of a

---

[1] Ep. 102, ad. Lucil.   [2] Consol. ad Polyb. 28; ad Marc. 25; Ep. 76, 63.
[3] Epist. 55; Consol. ad Polyb. 27; ad Marc. 19.   [4] De Fin. i. 15.
[5] Antonin. Meditat. iv. 21: εἰς τὸν τῶν ὅλων σπερματικὸν λόγον.
[6] Cic. Tusc. i. 32.

heavenly and divine original, and eternal in principle. God and the human soul must be of the same spiritual texture, and therefore after death we ourselves shall be also either gods or at least their associates.[1]

As Cicero, then, while accepting from Plato the eternal duration of the soul, thought himself obliged to its eternal pre-existence along with it; he also took advantage of the Platonic proof derived from the spontaneity of the soul's motion. But as he drew out this proof, starting from the position that the soul had the principle of its own movement within itself, he was driven to regard man's soul as a being existing independently from eternity, and subsisting by its own strength, which it was impossible to distinguish in substance from the deity. Thus he was bound to take the soul for an emanation from the divine spirit;[2] and though he could not go the whole length of Euripides and say it was God, he still thought and called it divine; God, as he thought, being either air or fire, the spirit of man should be of the same consistence.[3] With a rapturous eloquence he resigns himself to the confident expectation of the glorious day on which he was to join the divine society and communion of souls, and be delivered from this bustle and turmoil here, adding, "If I err in holding the souls of men to be immortal, I do so gladly; nor while life lasts will I suffer this error, in which I delight, to be torn from me. If we are not immortal, then it is desirable for man that he should be extinguished at his hour of departure." The doubt betrayed in these words came out more clearly in his letters, where, to console himself and others, he does not rely on immortality, but insensibility;[4] "if there is nothing good in death, at least there is no evil."[5] He himself both felt and said that his arguments, invariably drawn from the subtle, airy, fiery, or ethereal nature of the soul, produced but a certain amount of probability. He was a total stranger to all moral grounds. Neither a divine providence, nor a retributive justice in God, seemed to him to further the cause of immortality; the latter the less, as he denied expressly avenging justice in the deity. Herein, he said, agree all philosophers, not only those who maintain that

---

[1] Tusc. i. 27, 31.
[2] Tusc. v. 13; cf. de Divin. i. 49.   [3] Tusc. i. 26.
[4] Ad L. Mescin. Epp. v. 21; ad Toran. vi. 21; cf. de Amicit. c. 4; Epp. vi. 2.
[5] Tusc. Disp. i. 38.

God neither troubles himself or others, but such as allow God to be ever active and energising, that he is never angry, nor ever punishes." Nevertheless, his view of the preëxistence of souls led him on to the idea of their existence here being in a general way a state of punishment and penance for sins committed in a previous life. He threw this out in his "Hortensius" and in his "Consolation," written after the death of his daughter Tullia, coupling it with an observation, also borrowed from the Greek, " Not to have been born were best ; the earliest possible death the next best."[1] In the same essay he made a formal confession of Euhemerism ; men and women after death had been raised to be gods, and therefore he would have his daughter exalted to the same honour, as having deserved it best, and he would dedicate a temple to her.[2] And yet, as far as we know, in all these questions he never got beyond conjecture, and a state of doubt and vacillation.

The greater proportion of his contemporaries, and the Romans of the subsequent period, were far from imitating Cicero in this half-hopeful, half-doubting tone. Cæsar and Cato, in the senate's hearing, were agreed there was an end of all things after death, and neither joy nor sorrow found place beyond the grave.[3] Cicero, too, in one of his orations against Catiline, speaks of the doctrine of punishment after death as but an old fancy, cherished by the ancients. Virgil, Ovid, and Horace, sought protection against the comfortless thought of an inevitable descent into the gloomy night of the nether world and into an eternal sleep, in the enjoyment of the present moment, in the pleasures of the table, wine, women's love, and cheerful intercourse with friends of like mind.[4] They encouraged themselves and their friends not to waste the fleet but precious hour, on which was to supervene a weary night and an eternity of exile, when we shall be but dust and ashes. "Let us live and love," cried Catullus to his Lesbia; "for when the short day is past and gone, the sleep of eternal night awaits us both." "Even children no longer dream of there being any truth in the Manes and a subterranean realm," is Juvenal's expression.[5] "There is

---

[1] Lact. iii. 18, 19 ; Aug. contra Julian. iv. 15.   [2] Lact. i. 15.
[3] Sall. Catil. 5.
[4] Æn. vi. 390 ; Hor. Od. i. 4. 15 sqq. ; ii. 3. 27 ; iv. 9. 28, 7. 7.
[5] Sat. ii. 149.

nothing after death, and death itself is nothing; you will then be with the unborn," says the tragic poet who bears the name of Seneca. Lastly, Pliny, in his short and dry style, declared the idea of existence after death to be an invention of childish folly, and of the insatiable desire of mortals not to come to an end. To him it is sheer vanity to dream of the immortality of the soul; and yet his contemporary Tacitus hoped that a few distinguished souls would be allowed an existence beyond the tomb.[1]

The notions of the nature of the soul, as then current, had a great deal to do with this general unbelief. Philosophers utterly failed in grasping the idea of personality. Hemmed in by their material horizon, they understood by the soul a kind of secretion or evaporation of brain, blood, or heart, or a sort of respiration.[2] They described it as a subtle, aerial, or fiery substance; or conceived it to be a mere quality, like the harmony of a musical instrument, which was lost in the dissolution of the body.[3] Hence the alternative of either admitting the soul to be extinct along with the body, or of explaining it to be a portion and emanation of the divine world-soul. In the latter case, it was open to one to speak in high-flown language, along with philosophers, of the heavenly origin of the soul, of its having descended from the bosom of the Deity to this life, and its return after death to its home, without meaning more than the Epicureans (Lucretius, for instance) expressed, when speaking of the heavenly seed from which we all are sprung.[4] The return was only a refusion into the whole of the part, temporarily separated or severed from it, accompanied by the extinction of individual consciousness. The relation was conceived to be like that of an ocean, in which were floating a number of bottles filled with water; break one of these, and then the hitherto severed portion of sea-water is again united with its whole.[5]

But the ideas of man's annihilation or existence after death are also further influenced by those of the origin of the human race. Such, then, as would not be satisfied with the myths of Prometheus and Deucalion had to choose between two theories;

---

[1] Agric. 46. [2] Cic. Tusc. i. 9, 10, 11.
[3] Stob. Ecl. Phys. 80; Seneca Ep. 88; Pseudo-Plut. de Plac. Philos. iv. 23.
[4] Lucr. ii. 990.
[5] Comp. the observation of Gassendi, Animadv. in Diog. Laert. x. 550.

the one, maintained by Peripatetics and Pythagoreans, that the human race had no more a beginning than the world had, but that both existed from all eternity, through an infinite series of successive generations; the other admitted a beginning of the race, not, however, through a conceivable act of divine creation. Man was a product of the earth; and, like other animals, first crept in pairs out of the slime of the earth, impregnated either by the sun or spontaneously. The question was raised, where this teeming of the earth with a human progeny originated; and Attica, Arcadia, and Egypt, all asserted their claims to the distinction.[1] The two theories led to an annihilation of individuality. The first made the history of the human race a great circle as it were of perpetual birth and death, without any abiding personality. The second was forced to the adoption of a material soul, consisting of finer matter, and then to leave it to the destiny of all that was thus generated of earth or slime.

Plutarch tells us what the later Greeks thought of the state of souls after death. "The idea of annihilation was," he says, "intolerable to the Greek mind. If they had no choice left them between entire extinction and an eternity of torment in Hades, they would have chosen the latter; almost all, men and women both, would have surrendered themselves to the teeth of Cerberus, or the buckets of the Danaïdæ, rather than to nonentity." But there were but few believers in, and tremblers at, punishment in Hades. The generality looked on the accounts as old women's tales; while such as feared secured themselves by initiations and purifyings, and then had no doubt but that they would spend a pleasant life of playing and dancing in Hades.[2] His own opinion was, that it was useless to inquire what rewards or punishments awaited the soul in its state of loneliness or severance from the body; it was beyond us, and, indeed, it was hidden from us. Yet Plutarch expressly defended the immortality of the soul itself; a divine providence, he said, and the immortality of the soul, are truths which stand or fall together. It was absurd to imagine souls were made only to bloom for a day in a delicate body of flesh, and then to be for ever annihilated on the most trivial occasion. The Dionysic mysteries are in his eyes a special warrant and a mainstay of

---

[1] Censorinus de Die Nat. c. 4; Theodoret. Therap. 5.
[2] Plut. Non pos. suav. viv. sec. Epic. pp. 1104, 1105.

this belief of his.¹ He certainly treats the fear of things after death as the workings of superstition; and speaks once of the hope of immortality being founded on mythic representations;² yet, though rejecting such myths, and agreeing with other philosophers that there could be nothing to fear after death,³ he still clings firmly to the dogma in question,—the immortality of the soul; and, in the story of Thespesius, probably an invention of his own, has left us a view of the state of the departed. The souls of the dead, ascending through the air, and, in part, reaching the highest heaven, are either luminous and transparent, or dark and spotted on account of sins adhering to them, and some have even scars upon them. The soul of man, he says elsewhere, comes from the moon, his "nous" from the sun; the separation of the two is only completely effected slowly after death. The soul wanders awhile between the moon and earth for purposes of punishment, or, if it be good, of purification, until it rises to the moon, where the nous leaves it, and returns to its home, the sun, while the soul is buried in the moon.⁴

Lucian, on the other hand, whose writings for the most part are a pretty faithful mirror of the notions in vogue among his contemporaries, bears testimony to the continuance of the old traditions of the good reaching the Elysian fields, and the great transgressors finding themselves given up to the Erinyes in a place of torment, where they are torn by vultures, crushed on the wheel, or otherwise tormented; while such as are neither heavy sinners nor distinguished by their virtues, stray about in the meadows as bodiless shadows, and are fed on the libations and mortuary sacrifices offered at their sepulchres. An obolus for Charon was still placed in the mouth of every dead body.⁵

There is as little trace in the Greek literature of the day as in the Roman of any very strong hope. In the epigrams of the Anthology, the dead is content with asking passers-by to strew flowers on his grave, or bewailing his early death. The transitoriness of every thing human is frequently alluded to, but always for the sole purpose of enforcing the moral, that as much enjoyment as possible should be won, and as it were pressed out, of the fleeting moments. "Let us drink and be merry; for we

---

¹ Consol. ad Uxor. p. 611.
² Ἡ περὶ τὸ μυθῶδες τῆς ἀϊδιότητος ἐλπίς. Non poss. suav. viv. sec. Epic. p. 1104.
³ De Ser. Num. Vind. pp. 563-567. ⁴ De fac. in orb. Lun. pp. 942-945.
⁵ Lucian. de Luct. 7-9.

shall have no more of kissing and dancing in the kingdom of Proserpine: soon shall we fall asleep to wake no more." Such is the ordinary burden of poem and discourse.[1] In harmony with this the prevailing current of thought is the common custom remarked upon by Crito, in Plato's Phaedo, of allowing criminals condemned to death to spend the last day of their life in eating and drinking, and other and worse excesses.[2]

A similar strain of thought occurs in many of the inscriptions on Roman sepulchral monuments of that period. Such as, "What I have eaten and drunk, that I take with me; what I have left behind me, that have I forfeited."[3] "Reader, enjoy thy life; for after death there is neither laughter nor play, nor any kind of enjoyment."[4] "Friend, I advise, mix thee a goblet of wine, and drink, crowning thy head with flowers. Earth and fire consume all that remains after death."[5] Another assures us on his gravestone, that as he believed in life, so has he found it in death. "Pilgrim, stay thee, listen and learn. In Hades there is no ferryboat, nor ferryman Charon; no Æacus or Cerberus;—once dead, and we are all alike."[6] A third is concise: "I have lived, and believed in naught but life;" or, "Hold all a mockery, reader; nothing is our own."[7]

Cornelius Fronto, rhetorician and senator, master and friend of Marcus Aurelius, is a striking proof of the utter helplessness of the men of that day, if it happened (as in his case, one of losing a beloved grandchild) that a heavy domestic calamity fell like a thunder-bolt, and made them sensible of the comfortless night of an existence without hope and without belief. How Fronto beats about to find a single solace! what efforts to catch at every straw of hope, and how each and all evade him in the grasp! "Is it the gods," he cries, "who have struck me this blow? Is it cold, dead destiny? Is there a divine justice, a providence? Is death really better than life, so that the earlier one dies, one is to be esteemed the more blest?" He preferred to believe this rather than that the world is swayed by no providence at all, or only an unjust one.[8]

[1] Asclep. Epigr. 9, Anthol. i. 145. cf. p. 148; Alex. ap. Athen. xi. 9.
[2] Phaed. pp. 401, 402. [3] Ap. Murat. Thes. Inscr. p. 1677, n. 2.
[4] Novelle Fiorent. i. 27, p. 362. [5] Fabretti, Inscr. Ant. expl. c. 5, n. 387.
[6] Murat. p. 1321, n. 10. [7] Nov. Fior. xxxiii. p. 38.
[8] Front. Reliq. ed. Niebuhr, p. 117 sqq.

On the whole, the tone of literature and philosophy towards religion from the beginning of the Empire was more guarded and respectful in countries where Greek was spoken than in Rome. Since the middle of the first century after Christ, a growing prominence was observable in the return to a more believing disposition. One feels that a great change has taken place in the intellectual atmosphere when one compares Polybius, Strabo, Diodorus, and Dionysius, with Plutarch, Aristides, Maximus of Tyre, and Dio Chrysostom; and the difference between Greek and Roman is discernible when expressions of such men are contrasted with those of Seneca, Pliny, or Tacitus.

The Greek spirit was too elastic, whilst keeping in the track of the Stoic and the Epicurean schools, to allow itself to be crushed under the burden of the fatalism which was necessarily the offspring of the identification of the deity with nature. The consciousness of the personal and supernatural powers which swayed nature revived vigorously among them; and for this reason the Platonic philosophy recommended itself afresh, with its rich mines of speculation and images, and its capacity for assimilating new and foreign ideas, borrowed, in fact, from the religions of the East. Far from the exclusive stiffness of physico-mechanic systems, Platonism offered the advantage, so important to all people who feel the need of religion, of having conceived a supreme deity really and purely intellectual, and independent of matter.

The development of the Neo-Pythagorean school took place also about the same time, in the first century. What was Pythagorean in this school was the doctrine of a metempsychosis, and its consecutives, abstinence from animal food, with the rejection of bloody sacrifices. Its metaphysics were Platonic, with a mixture of Peripatetic and Stoic ideas. So also was the doctrine of a world-creating God, though one identical with the world itself, being acknowledged as the intelligent soul dwelling in material nature. The popular gods were accepted as protecting genii of the various parts and powers of this world; the immortality of the soul, because divine and unbegotten; the present life as a punishment and imprisoning of the soul within the body, from which it is freed by the true philosophy: whosoever has a particularly active consciousness of a previous existence partakes in a proportionately higher degree of the divine being, to which each individual human life is essentially akin. Man is even allowed to become actual God by means of this enduring reminiscence, and the virtue and wisdom which are its necessary results. For in principle it is the one divine spirit who, ever one and the same, individualises himself in the different souls of men.

Such is the groundwork of the doctrine which Philostratus represents as taught by Apollonius, in the life he has written of him. There is evidence elsewhere, too, of its being the common confession of the school, then and in the succeeding period, propagated from the old Orphico-Pythagorean sect. The two Pythagoreans, Nicomachus and Moderatus of Gades,—the latter a contemporary of Apollonius, the former of a somewhat later date,—both laid down the dualism of God and matter. The "numbers" of Pythagoras, identified with the Platonic "ideas," are the principles and types of all things preëxisting in the divine reason, the real and eternal, yet completely immaterial substance.[1] Apollonius himself, in a fragment still preserved of his work upon sacrifice, taught that man ought not to sacrifice to the one supreme God, for there was nothing in all nature pure enough to be offered to him; nay, every single product of nature, vegetable or animal, not even excepting the air itself, was infected with a miasma, by virtue of the antitheistic principle of matter already abiding in it. Omitting, then, every external and symbolical action, man should do homage to God by that which is distinctive of what is noblest in him, his nous,—by thought, and elevation of mind, without words.[2] On the other hand, there is no doubt Apollonius approved of making unbloody offerings to the gods of the lower order.

This proves that Platonists and Pythagoreans at this time were agreed in many and important points. Above all, they had a common platform in religious sentiment, and in the endeavour to indoctrinate heathendom, and to effect what none of the earlier philosophical systems were able or willing to do,—the conciliation of philosophy with the existing and popular state religions. To this object they were helped by their distinction of the one supreme God, between whom and the gods of the upper

---

[1] Nicomach. Arithm. i. 6; Moderat. ap. Simplic. Phys. 50.
[2] Ap. Euseb. Præp. Evang. iv. 13.

and lower worlds they interposed a deep gulf, and whose residence they fixed far from all worldly contact, and on a height only attainable to philosophic speculation. Here they could make Zeus pass either for this distant god, or as one of the lower gods, in which case he would more and more assume the signification of a sun-god. All the rest of the people's gods found their place in the two classes of intermediate beings adopted by the two schools, namely, the souls of the stars, and the genii of the different provinces of nature and the demons. It was, however, only the few who drew an accurate line of demarcation between gods and demons; these were confounded by the generality.

To represent this system, there are three individuals of the second century, almost contemporaries,—Maximus of Tyre, Apuleius, and Celsus; all three, the two last especially, hot partisans of polytheistic religion, and devoted to Plato. Maximus conceived his one supreme God as also maker of the world out of matter, and that matter the source of all evil.[1] Celsus and Apuleius, on the contrary, discovered in God a being exalted above all activity, the maker of nothing that was mortal, and with whom the souls of men originate.[2] The gods of the lower sphere are God's sons, says Maximus, not a mere thirty thousand, as Hesiod thought, but innumerable; some of them stars, some demons of the ether, and therefore in part visible, in part invisible; some of them, so to speak, intimate friends of and sharers of house and table with the great king, others their servants and helpmates, and others of a lower grade again.[3] These lower gods or demons dwell between heaven and earth; their power is less than that of gods and greater than that of men; they are mediators of the communion of gods and men; they appear, and reveal themselves to the latter, affording them that support which mortals require of the deity, healing their sicknesses, and making known to them the future. To individuals they are united as guardian spirits; and the multiplicity of their natures is equal to that among men.[4] Maximus himself asserts positively that Æsculapius and Hercules had appeared to him, not in his dreams, but when wide awake; and the Dioscuri too, whom he had seen on shipboard, as luminous stars,

---

[1] Diss. xli. 4. [2] Apul. de Deo Socrat. 3; Celsus, ap. Orig. iv. 52.
[3] Diss. xvii. 12. [4] Diss. xiv. 8.

harbingers of safety in a storm.¹ He too deems the human soul eternal and divine: so long as it dwells in the prison of the body, it has but a dreamy consciousness, without a clear remembrance, of its real existence; but the moment it is free by death, it attains to the society of the gods, and is incorporated in the heavenly host under its leader, Zeus.²

The teaching of Apuleius is somewhat different. He also divides the gods into visible or the stars, and invisible, amongst whom he reckons the twelve Olympic gods, offshoots of the supreme Spirit, eternal and blest. Most men worship these gods, but in a wrong manner; all fear them, indeed, simply from ignorance, and only a few deny them.³ Demons enjoy immortality in common with the gods, and partake of the passions of man; they are accessible to anger and pity, and let themselves be won by gifts. They are properly the objects of god-worship. Their nature accounts for the great variety in the ritual and worship of popular religions, the Egyptian gods delighting in lamentation, the Greeks in the dance, and those of the Barbarians in the din of trumpets, timbrels, and flutes.⁴

The supreme God, Celsus teaches, is absolutely immutable. Hence he cannot condescend to men, else he would submit himself to change, in other words, of a good being become an evil one. But between him and men are the spirits presiding over the world, God's vicegerents, and controllers of all things in heaven and earth. It is a duty to believe in these spirits, to do sacrifice to them as the laws of the land prescribe, and to invoke them to be gracious: we have all come into the world under this obligation. Whatever we enjoy, the water even, and the air we breathe, all is the gift of these spirits placed over nature. Whoso serves them, by his act includes the supreme God; he honours a something that pertains to him, beings whom he recognises as his own. If the Sun or Pallas be praised, the honour done to the Supreme at the same time is the greater. For all these beings, gods, demons, heroes, are only carrying out his law given once for all; he has once established the world immutably, and it has no further need of his immediate supervision and government. Evil is only a necessary result of this arrangement

---

[1] Diss. xv. 7.   [2] Diss. xvi. 3 sqq. 9.
[3] De Deo Socr. pp. 668, 669; Theol. Plat. p. 584.
[4] De Deo Socr. pp. 684, 685.

of the world, according to which all remains in a groove of eternal sameness, past, present, and future, all perfectly alike, with the same proportion of evil always in the world.[1]

This was the way these Platonists and Pythagoreans, clearly as they saw the practical corruption in existing heathendom, effected a compromise with the polytheistic forms of worship, and befriended them. Astral deities were generally adopted; for hardly any one doubted but that stars were intelligent beings, with a will and power extremely great. Seneca himself proves that we owe to sun and moon a homage of thankfulness, as they benefit us willingly and knowingly;[2] and Apollonius went into India to obtain better information concerning the gods there than any where else, as the men of that country were nearer to the fount of life-giving heat, and therefore to the deity.[3] But apart from the heavenly bodies, the popular gods were open to an interpretation inserting them in the cosmical theory of philosophers. Thus the Platonists, not without a glimmer of truth enabling them to a deeper insight into the essence of God, represented Athene coming in full armour out of the head of Zeus, as the being through whom the hidden and supreme God made the first manifestation of himself. She remains, they said, with the Father, as grown with his growth. She breathes back her being into him again.[4] She only is alone with him as his assessor and counsellor. Zeus begot her by withdrawing himself into himself.[5] The Ephesian Artemis was nature, as universal nursing mother,[6] Hestia, the central fire or world-soul; and, if the earth were distinguished into a Psyche and a nous or intelligence, then Hestia was the latter, and Demeter the soul of the earth.[7] How clever Plutarch was in laying all he could on the goddess Isis and her Osiris, filling up many a gap in his theory therewith, in which no Hellenic deity would stand! To him she is the mediatrix between the first or supreme God (Osiris) and earthly and transitory things, and the female side of nature as well, to whom all generation is attributable, who carries implanted within her the love for the first and highest of all beings that is identical with the good.[8] Apuleius, too, makes

[1] Ap. Orig. adv. Cels. viii. 55 sqq.
[2] De Benef. vi. 23.
[3] Philostr. Vit. Apul. i. 31; ii. 38; vii. 10.
[4] Ἀναπνεῖ εἰς αὐτόν.
[5] Aristid. Or. i. pp. 12 sqq., Dindorf.
[6] Nicomach. Arithm. p. 24.
[7] So Plotin. Enn. iv. 4, p. 779, ed. Oxon.
[8] De Isid. 53.

almost all the female deities run off into Isis; and she is nature, mother of all things, mistress of all the elements, the beginning of all times, the supremest among the gods, queen of departed souls, ruling over heaven, ocean, and the lower world, Phrygian mother of the gods, Pallas at Athens, Urania at Cyprus, the Artemis of the Cretans, Persephone too, Demeter, Juno, Hecate, Bellona, and Rhamnusia.[1] But Maximus makes the easiest work. "You have only to change denominations, and you find philosophers saying exactly the same of the gods as the poets. Call Zeus the all-supreme intelligence, which is the primal cause and ruler of all things. Let Pallas be styled prudence in action and life; in Apollo's stead put the sun, in Poseidon's the motive and sustaining power that pervades earth and ocean."[2] With such notions as these, an accommodation with the religion of the state and people surely could appear nothing else than irony and a silly mockery.

We have already seen what a close connection there was between the defective knowledge which the old philosophy had of human freedom and of the nature of evil, with the relation in which the Deity stood to both. These thinkers were wanting in an insight into the nature and conditions of the personality of God, as well as of men; and therefore looked upon evil as partly resulting from mere defectiveness or infirmity of means of knowledge, they set it down to ignorance, and thought accordingly there was no other or higher remedy than philosophy. And partly from not distinguishing between the physical evil and the moral bad, they charged matter and its natural repugnance to the intellectual with being the source of the bad. Hence, the idea of sin was in fact strange to them; they had no perception how a free act of evil done by the creature bore upon divine holiness and justice. In fine, the Stoics had further obscured this important question by their theory that evil was as absolutely necessary in the order of the world as the shadow is to the light, and that all evil was equal. They raised man above all responsibility and account, and represented him as without freedom, the irresistibly determined tool of destiny. Even the emperor Marcus Aurelius, with his mild temperament, found a complete justification herein for the greatest criminal. A man of a certain nature can do nothing else but act viciously.

[1] Metam. xi. p. 241.   [2] Diss. x. 8.

To make him responsible for his actions, would be on a par with punishing another for having bad breath, or bidding a fig-tree bear any thing besides figs.[1] It was utterly impossible for vicious men to act otherwise than we see them act, and to demand impossibilities is folly.

This view of evil was expressly combated by Platonists like Plutarch. Evil had not come into the world like an episode, pleasant and acceptable to the Deity; it filled every human thing; the whole of life, equally stained from its opening to its concluding scene, was a mass of error and misfortune, and in no part pure and blameless.[2] Later on he said, "No one is sober enough for virtue; but we all of us are in unseemly and unblest confusion." This severe notion of evil, its universality in the life of man, and the deep roots it had struck in his nature, is a characteristic of thinkers of this period. We meet with similar expressions in Seneca, to the effect that not a man will be found who does not sin, has not sinned, and will not continue sinning till his dying hour.[3] Galen, a physician, and at the same time one of the acutest of the philosophers of this latter time, went further still. He declared the dispositions of children to evil to be in excess, and thought that only by little and little the disposition to good got the upper-hand, the more the intelligent soul attained the mastery over the two others—for he adopted with Plato a threefold division of the soul.[4]

The solution of the problem of the origin of evil appeared all the more difficult now. All did not accept the comfortable expedient of Platonists like Celsus, of its having sprung from matter in existence from eternity; or, like Plutarch, who accepted an evil and eternal world-soul, and an unintelligent element of essential evil in the soul of man. Maximus of Tyre, therefore, thought that Alexander, instead of consulting the oracle of Ammon about the sources of the Nile, should rather have put a question of importance to humanity generally, namely that of the origin of evil. He then made an attempt of his own at a solution, which only ended again in placing the seat and fount of all evil in matter.[5]

---

[1] Medit. ix. 1; x. 30; viii. 14; v. 28.
[2] Adv. Stoic. 14. [3] De Clem. i. 6.
[4] Compare Daremberg, Fragmens du Commentaire de Galein sur le Timée, Paris, 1848, pp. 18, 19. [5] Diss. xli. p. 487 sqq.

DURATION AND INFLUENCE OF THE SCHOOLS OF PHILOSOPHY:
THEIR DISSOLUTION.

EVEN after the creative power and productiveness of Greek philosophy had died out, to be, and to be called, a philosopher continued a title to honour and reputation. Those who were partisans of one or other existing school made a livelihood upon the rich inheritance of ideas and glory which the golden age of the Greek mind had left them in survivance. The splendour of great names, like Pythagoras, Socrates, Plato, and Aristotle, shed still a partial lustre on their successors, little as they understood the management of the intellectual patrimony that had devolved upon them. To belong to the herd of Epicurus was nowhere, it is true, matter of credit or respectability; the members of that school had only to pride themselves on their unity and obstinacy in adhering to the unbroken tradition of their founder. The Stoics, Platonists, and Peripatetics, stood higher in public estimation, on the whole. The latter had fallen out of notice, and became extinct, after descending, as they had long done, to be mere interpreters of the works of Aristotle. The majority of Cynics were despised, in literature as well as in society, on the score of their ostentatious disregard of propriety, and animosity towards religion. Coarse fellows, and proud as beggars, throwing the Cynic mantle over disgusting vices, they thronged greedily to the tables of the rich, and were flatterers and blusterers in turn. Lucian's testimony is, that it was they who degraded philosophy in the eyes of the people. In Nero's time, however, they still had a man esteemed as a model of a philosopher, Demetrius. The Platonists enjoyed a better reputation, being already favoured by the general diffusion of the works of Plato, which were really read a great deal at that time; but as far as concerned seriousness and depth of thought, they were far below a master whom they did not always understand. The Stoics knew how to inspire esteem by the rigorism of their ethical principles, which, in fact, frequently degenerated into an ill-founded conceit of, and idle talk about, virtue (*aretology*). The ideal life held up for a pattern in their schools was never realised in the individual life of their philosophers; and, after Marcus Aurelius, no distinguished man bore the designation of

Stoic. The Pythagoreans meanwhile had shot up again into an influential sect, still in the ascendant.

In all parts of the empire the priesthood was dumb, without doctrine or tradition, a mere liturgical executive; and through this the philosophers attained to so considerable an influence upon the people. They, and they only, were in possession of a doctrine; and from out the circle of their ideas they could counsel, warn, and interpret, speaking to the heart of practical life in its confusion and errors. Had a priest attempted to do so on the strength of his office, he would have been regarded as arrogant and absurd, so little did people connect the idea of teaching and the care of souls with that of a priest of the gods. This entire social province, ever indispensable to civilised people, thus fell to the share of the philosophers; and hence we are told, when a misfortune befell a man, the death, for instance, of a beloved object, he would have a philosopher summoned to impart consolation to him.[1]

This favourable situation, notwithstanding the credit of philosophers, began gradually to be on the wane from the close of the first century after Christ. As numbers of them wore the beard, cloak, and stick, by which they were recognised at first sight, it was the more perceptible that the ranks were swelled with a medley of insignificant, and often disreputable, persons; and after Marcus Aurelius established the payment of a salary to them, it was observed that the care of a magnificent beard was, with many, the only occupation to justify the drawing of their pension.[2] Without method in philosophising, as without a fixed tradition, they extracted at will a few isolated and paradoxical maxims from the teaching and works of their great masters, and made account of their example to excuse their own vanity and presumption. The extremest disapprobation is universally expressed by their contemporaries of the character of the philosophers at the end of the first, and during the second and third centuries. The picture drawn by Lucian of their hypocrisy, vanity, avarice, and immorality, is surpassed by the one which Aristides has left behind him. "Their greediness," he says, "is insatiable; their pillage of others' property they call community of goods; their envy is nicknamed philosophy; their

---

[1] Dio. Chrysost. Or. xxvii. p. 529; cf. Plut. de Superst. 7.
[2] Tatian. Apol. 32.

beggary, contempt of money. Haughty to all others, they creep before the rich, nay before the very cooks and bakers of the rich. Their strength lies in impudence in asking, in abuse, and in calumny."[1] Quintilian is no less severe upon them. "In our days most people hide the grossest vices under those names (old philosophers); a long face, gloominess, and a demeanour entirely different from that of other men, are used as a cloak for the worst morality."[2]

The influence and respectability of the schools suffered much with the people from this rabble of philosophers, but more from the contests which the different sects had with one another, the weapons used in them, and the means by which they won and retained their disciples. As all the schools occupied a distinct position, friendly or not, towards the popular religion, some declining, others attempting eclectic reforms in it, so they had assumed towards one another quite the aspect of a variety of religious parties engaged in a hostile struggle. The war was conducted with all the passionate bitterness of religious discord, and presented to the eyes of lookers-on a spectacle of irreconcilable contradictions, and a deep-rooted division upon the first and most important questions. The age was by no means sceptically inclined; on the contrary, it had a strong drawing to philosophic and religious knowledge, a deep avidity for belief and for authority that could be relied on. But the teachers and disciples of the several philosophical schools destroyed the confidence which thousands would have willingly reposed in their teaching. They were themselves far too evidently the slaves of an authority arbitrarily constituted and internally valueless, wanting in capacity as well as inclination for steady and conscientious sifting of truth. "Before they themselves were able," says Cicero, "to discern what was best, they were bound down to a system, and then, at the very weakest period of their life, either from some deference to a friend, or caught by a display of the first speaker whom they ever listened to, they form a judgment on points which they are utterly ignorant of, and to whatever school the wind, no matter from what quarter, drives them, there they squat as on a sand-bank. They have hardly heard a thing, and they are ready with their judgment; and the authority of a single individual is enough to determine them."[3]

[1] Opp. ed. Jebb, xi. 307-11.   [2] Inst. Or. i. pro. 15.   [3] Acad. Qu. ii. 3.

Lucian, in his Hermotimus, describes in a lively and agreeable manner the situation of a person going to decide upon one or other of the philosophical schools or sects, and the principles guiding him in his choice. Hermotimus is giving an account to his friend Lycinus for his selection of the Stoic sect; and first he tells him he had been directed in choosing the true philosophy by the number of its adherents, confessing at the same time he does not really know if the Stoics are more numerous than other schools or not. As a farther ground he assigns his having heard it generally said, that the Epicureans lived for pleasure merely, that Peripatetics loved money, the Platonists were puffed up with empty conceit; but the Stoics were persevering and wise withal, and their disciples the only perfect men. He is obliged, however, to allow that all his information is really derived from the ignorant and uneducated. Therefore, he tried another ground, the one that decided him, that is, he had observed the Stoics were orderly and serious in their deportment, decently clad, and with their heads closely shaven. On this Lycinus makes him sensible of the worthlessness of all these grounds, and compares philosophy to a city, the road to which a man is seeking. There are a number of roads running in the most opposite directions; many guides present themselves, each one, affirming he alone knows the right way, abuses the other guides. The upshot of the debate is, that one would need the life of a phœnix, in addition to the qualities of acuteness, unwearied assiduity, and perfect impartiality, in order to make a fair trial of all the sects; that possibly all may be error, and the truth not yet discovered; that if a man were minded to give himself up to another as teacher and guide, he would first require the warrant of a third person for his chosen teacher's capacity, and then a security for this, and so on *ad infinitum*.

The Stoics, therefore, were the most popular and respectable sect up to the second century; they defended the religion of the people, and asked, with some few exceptions, for no radical changes in it; though, indeed, the grounds on which they took religion under their protection were, to one who had a knowledge of their system, highly transparent, and often not much better than the grand conclusion, the sheet-anchor of the Stoic Timocles in Lucian,—" If there are altars, there must be gods; now altars there are, therefore gods there must be."¹ The school had not even a solid answer to make to the question what God really was. For while Zeno and the generality of Stoics replied the ether, or the subtle fire, penetrating the whole world, Cleanthes maintained the sun was the god who ruled the world. Touching this point, Cicero says, "In such difference of opinion amongst the wise, we are in no position to know our lords and masters, as, in fact, we are uncertain whether we are subjects of the sun or the ether."² And how many, on nearer inspection of the esoterical part of Stoic doctrine, might have affirmed Plutarch's reproach, "That it was spreading an abominable and impious doctrine to make the gods into mere personifications of physical things, as the Stoics did, and, like Cleanthes, to call Persephone the breath sighing and dying away among the fruits of the field."³

Thus all the schools died a natural death, while Paganism was still in full swing, and, to all appearance, in unbounded reputation. Indeed, the historian Dio Cassius praises the emperor Marcus for the measure by which he granted a considerable pension to the occupiers of philosophical chairs at Athens, and so had not only honoured Athens, but in Athens had supplied the whole world with teachers.⁴ In the more important towns, at least after Antoninus, there were professors of philosophy, well paid, and often with money made up in part from the imperial treasury. In Rome, Severus and Caracalla declared philosophers exempt from taxes, whether with or without salary. There was no want then of external encouragement. Longinus assures us that in his youth (about 230 A.D.) many philosophers were living, with all of whom he became acquainted, and he mentions by name several Platonists, three Peripatetics, and four Stoics, who exerted their influence in Rome, Athens, and Alexandria, partly by writing, and partly by giving oral instruction. He seems to have passed over the Epicureans through contempt, as he would not hear of their being called philosophers. These philosophers, however, as Longinus himself observes, were only able to comment upon the labours of their predecessors. And after a few years, the symptoms of decay were so evident, with the entire cessation of all after-growth, that Longinus himself added, "But now (about the year 270) there is an incredible want of them."⁵

¹ Luc. Jup. trag. 51. ² Academ. ii. 41. ³ Plut. de Isid. 66.
⁴ Dio. Cass. lxxi. 31. ⁵ Ap. Porphyr. Vit. Plotini, c. 20.

Thus the chairs of philosophy became empty. Master and pupil disappeared together; the bands of studious youth gathered more eagerly round the rhetoricians, who taught how to put words in the place of thoughts, and hid their deficiency in exact knowledge under their flowers of speech. At last, on the ruins of the collective schools of the elder philosophy, there remained but one as universal inheritress to Greek speculation, that of Ammonius Saccas and Plotinus, founded in the third century. This school, combining a groundwork of Platonism with Pythagorean principles of life, attempted a reunion of philosophy and religion by means of ecstasis, and to impart fresh youth and a new form to the pagan worship of the gods.

II. STATE OF RELIGION.

1. IDEA OF AN IMPERIAL RELIGION—RELIGIOUS TOLERANCE AND PERSECUTION.

AFTER the Roman religion had adapted itself to the Grecian, and people in Rome as well as in Greece indulged in the innocent belief of identity of the gods of both, it appeared to the Romans that the deities of other people whom they had subdued showed a strong affinity to their own; the names, as they thought, only differed, but they were in principle and essence the same forms in different localities. As they became acquainted with the gods of oriental nations, of Syria, Asia Minor, and Egypt, chiefly through a Grecian medium and under the Greek names already given them, they found every where confirmations of their previous judgment, and came into contact with them with a settled resolution to find well-known forms under the images of stranger gods. No sooner had Cæsar set foot in Gaul than he was certain the Gauls had pretty nearly the same notions about the gods that other people had. He overlooked, or ignored, the peculiarities of the Gallic deities. To him they must be Mercury, Jupiter, Mars, and Minerva. Tacitus, and those who preceded him, took precisely the same line about the German deity system; and so it was in Spain and Illyria. As deities of nature, of course they all had certain traits in common, and where a god failed to correspond with a Græco-Roman deity, the difficulty was easily got over by understanding the god to be a mere "genius loci." The natives of the different countries were, on their side, quite content that their gods, those of the vanquished and the subject, should turn out identical with those of their victors and rulers. Accordingly, temples were speedily raised in the provinces, in which Roman and barbarous deities exchanged names and attributes with one another, little claim as they had to personify the same thought originally. In this way throughout Gaul Jupiter was worshiped in company with Hesus, Mercury with Teutates, Mars with Camul, Hercules with Ogmius, and Apollo with Belen.

Thus there grew up in the minds of Roman statesmen and dynasts the idea of a universal religion of the Roman empire, in which, notwithstanding all the variety of forms of cultus and names, the same gods were every where worshiped. The doctrine of the Stoa, under whose influence many Roman politicians stood, came in aid of this theory of political fusion of gods and of empire-religion. From it the Romans learnt that the significance of the gods of all nations was equally little or equally great; that as many might be conceived and adored as there were manifestations of divine power in nature; that every god, or name of a god, was always a way of terming an incorporation of the god identical with primal matter; and thus that nothing could prevent the admission of ten, a hundred, or, with Hesiod, of thousands of gods along with the one God, or the ether omnipresent as the world-soul, nor, in fact, could forbid the claim of the wildest produce of the imagination to a cultus.

The Platonists, on their part, took a point of view which admitted of all these pagan systems being considered as nearly related, as so many distinct forms representing one single fundamental idea. "Great," said Maximus of Tyre, "as is the want of unity, and the variance and contradiction amongst men, concerning religion, yet will you find universally upon the face of the earth one maxim and one speech, namely, that one God is the king and father of all, and that there are many gods who are his sons and sharers in his rule. Greek and barbarian agree in this."[1] Yet this theory is evidently based upon a very super-

[1] Diss. xvii. 5, ed. Davis.

ficial induction, and did not apply, in fact, to any one of the religions of the day; still it squared all the better with Roman policy.

In the worship of Augustus and other deified emperors, Rome already found a religious bond to link together every part of the empire. Rome herself was a microcosm, in which as well all people as all the various divine rites in the empire met together, settled down quietly side by side, and, willingly or not, submitted to the despotic mind of the great imperial pontiff; nay, the priesthood itself, which presented the strongest organisation combined with the strictest exclusiveness, the Egyptian, submitted to the supremacy of a Roman arch-priest. Thus Roman potentates had reason to hope that the process of religious fusion would progress steadily on a par with the already successfully-established identity in administration and language. There were religions, however, which shrunk from and withstood this process; some, as being under the conduct of a well-organised priesthood, having a tradition to maintain, and preserving strictly a religious difference between things pure and impure; others again, because knowing and adoring but one God, they held themselves in an attitude of exclusiveness and abhorrence towards all other pretensions to deity.

On these principles the Roman state regulated its relations towards non-Roman and strange religions. In general there was a sufficent tolerance, or, properly speaking, contemptuous indifference and disregard in respect of doctrines and opinions started in the province of religion. Stoic or Epicurean, Platonist or Pythagorean, all were left alone in peace. Scornful criticism, even of the whole existing religious system, was indulgently endured; and when a persecution of philosophers broke out, as it did under Domitian, it was by no means because of their religious views. Such toleration or indifference, however, found its own limits at once whenever the doctrine taught had a practical bearing on society, interfered with the worship of the state-gods, or confronted their worship with one of its own; as well as when a strange god and cultus assumed a hostile attitude towards Roman gods, could be brought into no affinity or corporate relation with them, and would not bend to the supremacy of Jupiter Capitolinus. Hence, as a rule, the religion of conquered nations remained unassailed; in other countries of the empire all could honour the gods of their own native land after their own fashion; in Rome itself peregrini were allowed to set up the gods, altars, and shrines which they had brought with them, and to assemble for religious purposes. But the religion of Egypt, though it had free play at home, soon became intolerable at Rome. It was too demure and whimsical; and it was only after a long time, and with much reluctance, that those in power at Rome gave in to the irresistible hankering of their people after the Isis worship. True, the rite was banished from the Pomœrium, the suburb of the city; still it maintained its ground in the vicinity, and also slunk into the outlying quarters of the city, where the charm of mystery gave it a greater impulse. A decree of the senate under Tiberius shows with what rigour and cruelty a religion could be suppressed that was not acceptable. Four thousand freedmen, tainted with Jewish and Egyptian superstitions, were ordered out to Sardinia against the banditti there, in case they did not renounce the profane rite within a specified time. This was equivalent, in a climate so fatal, to condemning half the number to be executed. After resorting to various expedients of alternate violence and mercy, both emperor and senate had at last to give in, and the Egyptian worship became formally domiciled.

So long as the Druidical priesthood stood its ground with its well-knit organisation and its traditionary creed, the religion of the Gauls also stoutly resisted fusion with the Roman. The Romans accordingly threw all their energy into the scale to crush and extirpate Druidism, not merely on account of its human sacrifices, which they had suppressed elsewhere, in Africa for instance, without attacking the actual religions there, but because the resolution had been come to of annihilating the whole Druidical system wherever the Roman power extended. The practice even of the unbloody rites of that worship was accordingly punished with death. That Gallic knight who wore a supposed serpent's egg on his person had to pay the forfeit of his life; and Suetonius boasts of the emperor Claudius having completely annihilated Druidism.[1] Such was at least the intention. Along with these violent measures against their territorial religion, the cultus of their deified emperor was also pressed on the inhabitants by force. The Gauls had made a feint of cheerful ac-

---

[1] Suet. Claud. 25.

ceptance of the imperial deity, and sixty Gallic clans had raised a temple to Augustus at Lyons by common contributions; but the spirit of their British neighbours was not yet so broken. According to Tacitus,[1] the temple of Divus Claudius, erected by the Romans at Camulodunum, was a religious fortress-prison for the British people, the priests of the temple practising the most frightful pillage under the cloak of religion. A great insurrection took place in consequence, followed by a bloody war. In other cases it happened that it was mere cupidity that incited the Romans to attack religious belief in their provinces; at least there seems to have been no other motive in the destruction of the sanctuary of the god Men-Arcæus at Antioch in Pisidia with its numerous hieroduli and large landed property.[2]

The ancients therefore, whether Romans or Greeks, knew nothing in the main of religious tolerance proper. The conduct of Antiochus Epiphanes, king of Syria, towards the Jews was a formal religious persecution. Every means, inclusive of the most sanguinary cruelty, were to be put in force to compel them to deny their God and his law, and to worship the Hellenic gods. This indeed was not purely out of religious zeal for Zeus and Apollo; the king had political reasons of his own. So long as the Jewish religion existed, a complete fusion of the people with Greeks and Syrians was impracticable; they continued always behind their own strong lines of demarcation, paid their tribute, but could never be brought to the condition of subjects, nor form a part of a compact united state. That people would be persecuted for opinions only in Greece even, Anaxagoras had early experience; then Diagoras and many others; still later, the philosopher Stilpo, and a good many Epicureans. No more cases of the kind occurred under Roman rule, as the cities of Greece no longer possessed power for the purpose; while the Romans themselves refrained, not at all from any principle of religious tolerance, but simply because all depended on the external act, the rite prescribed, and by no means on the interior sentiment. This was a general rule in pagan religions, and particularly suited Roman notions. As for any one having refused on the ground of his opinions, for conscience-sake, to take part in the worship of state-gods, such a case never occurred. No philosopher ever

---

[1] "Arx (or Ara) æternæ dominationis." Ann. xiv. 31.
[2] Strabo, xii. 577.

had the boldness to practise such an act of religious isolation himself, or to advise it in others. Romans and Greeks had their first experience of an actual resistance to the state-religion, on the grounds of doctrine and conviction, from Jew and Christian. If an opinion unfavourable to the apotheosis of any member of the imperial dynasty happened to be dropped, it was dangerous in itself as falling within the purview of the law of high-treason; and so it fell out in the case of Thrasea Pætus, who refused to believe in the deification of Poppæa.[1]

In other respects religious crimes were very numerous according to Roman ideas. It might easily happen to believers, and vigilant ones, to incur a charge of disrespect to the gods or their shrines. Thus, in the year 104 B.C., Æmilius Scaurus was indicted because the service of the Penates at Lavinium was not properly conducted through his fault.[2] We may see how easy it was to trump up an accusation, by the haruspices declaring in answer to the senate, that the gods were angry because "holy places had been desecrated." There were numberless such, and a man had only to build on a spot once occupied by a holy place to incur a charge of profanation. One of Cicero's speeches[3] shows us that a considerable number of people were exposed to danger of a condemnation on like grounds. Clodius used to boast of no less than two hundred decrees of the senate having issued against him for offences against religion.[4] Pretexts were multiplied under the emperors, as negligence or mistake in the service of the deified emperors was so easy.

2. Apotheosis.

In investigating the peculiarities of the later system of pagan religion throughout the Roman empire, if we would characterise it more accurately and in detail, the first striking point will be the worship of new gods, to wit, the emperors, living and dead. Already in the title of "Augustus," as Dio Cassius has observed, men's minds were being directed to a something superhuman. And in later times it was said that on the assumption of the title of Augustus, the emperor was to be worshiped as a deity present

---

[1] Tac. Annal. xvi. 22.
[2] Asc. in Cic. pro Scauro, p. 21.
[3] De Harusp. resp. 14.
[4] Cicero, l. c. c. 5.

in the body.[1] If it is undeniable that the predominant calculation in the imperial minds with regard to Apotheosis was one of consolidation of power and name, we have on the other side the fact that, since Augustus, these divine honours were rather forced upon, than sought, by them. The provinces soon began a race of emulation in dedicating temples and altars to the living and dead Augustus; and there is an appearance as if a presentiment of a divine Redeemer of the world having appeared among men had then touched their minds; a presentiment, however, that had missed its right object, and had transferred their homage and adoration to the ruler of the world in Rome. And yet that ruler, if he did not break the yoke of error and sin, still freed them from the chaos of civil war, and the tyranny of proconsuls.

Octavian had tolerated in Pergamus and Nicomedia the dedication of an altar and temple to him in common with the deified city of Rome, the services of which were to be directed by Greek and not Roman citizens; at Nicæa and Ephesus even Roman citizens were allowed to worship not him, but the goddess Roma and the Cæsar. This example was now followed by other cities. After his death, the worship of the new god was introduced into Rome and Italy, where it had not been tolerated during his life. The senator, Numerius Atticus, made oath to having seen Augustus ascending to heaven; and his assertion procured him a valuable present of money from Livia, while an indictment on the charge of having profaned the deity of Augustus by perjury cost Rubrius his life. By the time of Tiberius it had become a crime to testify an indisposition to worship the imperial god; and for it the city of Cyzicus forfeited its freedom.[2] Under the same emperor eleven Asiatic cities contended for the honour of being allowed to build a temple to the Cæsar on the throne. Smyrna was the successful candidate, on the ground of having been the first to erect a temple, as early as after the second Punic war, to the goddess Roma.[3] Yet Tiberius pretended afterwards to repent of having granted this permission. Cities now began to covet the distinction and privilege of styling themselves Neocori, servants of the temple of the Cæsar-god, and inserted the title on their coins.[4] They had to obtain this

---

[1] Lydus de Mens. iv. 72. Veget. 25: "tanquam præsenti et corporali Deo fidelis est præstanda devotio."

[2] Tac. Ann. iv. 36.   [3] Ib. iv. 56.   [4] Mionnet, Suppl. vi. 162, n. 518.

privilege from the senate at Rome. Then there were periodical games in honour of the emperor connected with this Neocoria; and on the election of a new one, the office was granted two or three times over. Thus Ephesus, under Caracalla and Heliogabalus, reached a fourth neocoria, and did not fail to inscribe this singular distinction on its coins. Though the whole city or all its citizens were avowedly considered as bearing the title inclusively, particular priests were of course appointed for the service. Every temple had a statue of the Cæsar to whom it was dedicated, which was held more sacred than any images of the other gods.[1]

It was a principle in Rome, till the time of Caius Caligula, to follow the general analogy of the Manes, and not to raise the Cæsar to divine honours till after his death, and then by special decree of the senate and his successor. Caius desired to be acknowledged and worshiped throughout the whole empire equally as visible god. A decree of the senate had conceded him one temple in Rome; he erected another to himself, and had priests and priestesses of his own, amongst them his uncle Claudius, and the Cæsonia who was subsequently his wife. This ministry was bought at enormous prices. Only rare and costly animals, pheasants, peacocks, and the like, were allowed to be sacrificed. He himself ordained a temple to be built to him at Miletus, for all Asia, and wanted to have one of those belonging to Apollo there to be appropriated for the purpose. Not content with having a simple chapel in the sanctuary of Jupiter Capitolinus, he must have a public worship in a temple of his own on the Palatine Hill. The theatrical display which he made of his godhead and worship might have seemed ridiculous, and a proof of pride that had run over into madness, had not the Cæsar-god met with such spontaneous devotion and homage from the whole extent of the empire, with the single exception of the Jews.[2]

And now princesses of the imperial family came to be deified. Caius had the same divine honours as were paid to Augustus decreed to his sister Drusilla, with whom he had lived in incestuous intercourse. Claudius raised his grandmother Livia to the same dignity, and made the vestal virgins conduct her sacrifices, and women swear by her name. He would not accept for

---

[1] Philostr. Vit. Apoll. i. 15.
[2] Dio. Cass. lix. 28; Suet. Caius, 21. 22.

himself the divine honours of genuflection and sacrifice, though he had a temple in Britain.¹ So matters went on. Nero had his father Domitian, and Poppæa his wife, exalted into deities after death. Vitellius possessed a chapel, where he even adored the freedmen Narcissus and Pallas, favourites of his uncle Claudius.² Domitian followed the example of Caius. He styled himself in documents "Lord and God," and no one dared afterwards to address him otherwise. The roads to the Capitol, Pliny tells us, were filled with flocks and herds, that were being driven to be sacrificed before his image.³ The same Pliny praises Trajan for having inserted his predecessor Nerva among the gods, not with any view to his own exaltation, but from a real conviction of his being a god.

But the greatest extravagance on this head was reserved for Hadrian's time. Diviners had warned the emperor of his being exposed to great danger in case a creature that was dear to him should not offer himself as a voluntary sacrifice for him. Antinous, a young Bithynian, living in the shameful relations with the emperor that were common in that day, devoted himself and threw himself into the Nile. The priests, after an inspection of his entrails, declared that Hadrian had fully satisfied the decree of the gods. The emperor wept like a woman for him, built the city Antinopolis to his honour on the spot where he died, erected temples to him, and had games celebrated at Mantinea and elsewhere, and statues of him raised all over the empire. Antinous received priests and prophets, who interpreted his oracles, the composition, it is ordinarily supposed, of Hadrian himself. Coins are still found with his likeness, as the new Iacchus, in Asia, Greece, Syria, and Egypt; and astrologers were not long in discovering a new star in which Antinous was recognised to be shining, as Cæsar had been in a similar one before. This affair by no means ended with Hadrian's death, and therefore was not the effect of mere fawning and flattery, exhibited towards a freak of the then emperor. The worship lasted for centuries more, particularly in Egypt, where the god worked a succession of miracles in the city erected to his honour; and, as Origen says, men, tormented by their own weak and stricken consciences, fancied the god Antinous chastised and punished

---

¹ Dio. C. lx. 5; Tac. Ann. xiv. 31.   ² Suet. Vitell. 3.
³ Suet. Dom. 13; Oros. vii. 10; Plin. Paneg. 11.

them.¹ An inscription on the Isis temple at Rome actually gives him the title of "the temple associate of the Egyptian gods."²

Between the first deification of Cæsar and the apotheosis of Diocletian fifty-three of these solemn canonisations may be reckoned, fifteen of which were of ladies belonging to the imperial family. The difference between the deification of the living, and apotheosis of the dead, may be stated thus: the latter swelled the numbers of the heathen Pantheon as new gods; while the former were usually venerated as incarnations of a god already generally worshiped, and mostly of that particular one for whom they had a special predilection. That this was so, we find from the coins of Greek cities in particular. The Empress Sabina, Hadrian's wife, was invoked as the new Demeter.³ Faustina, the wife of M. Aurelius, was represented on coins as Cybele, with the attributes of the Mother of the gods; and there is discovered, as far away as the town of Jotapa in Cilicia, a high priestess of the goddess Faustina.⁴

Every one who possessed the means to give the matter a certain degree of consequence and *éclat* was, in reality, free to deify his deceased relations and to treat them as heroes, with the worship of an established sacrifice. Thus Herodes Atticus inserted his wife Regilla in this class, and erected a monument to her at Athens in the form of a temple.⁵ In Smyrna Asclepiades, the physician of Augustus, was honoured after death as a hero. Engraved on stone, and to be found at Verona, is a will of the Spartan Epicteta, instituting the worship of her deceased husband Phœnix and her sons, to be solemnised in a temple which she had built and consecrated to the Muses, and also to serve as a sanctuary for an Heroüm. She appoints her grandson Andragoras priest. The relations were to meet every year, in the month Delphinium, at the sanctuary, to offer sacrifice, on the nineteenth to the Muses, on the twentieth to the hero Phœnix and heroine Epicteta, and on the twenty-first to their two sons.⁶ Here we see the testatrix decreeing herself divine honours by anticipation, to be paid her after her death. There was nothing extraordi-

---

[1] Dio. Cass. lxix. 10; Spartian. Hadr. 14; Plin. H. N. 219; Pausan. viii. 9. 4; Tatian. c. Græc. 26; Orig. c. Cels. iii. 36.

[2] Ap. Gruter. lxxxvi. 1.

[3] Inscription at Megara; Letronne, Inscr. Egypt. i. 102.

[4] Corp. Inscr. Gr. n. 4411.

[5] Zoëga de Obelisc. p. 369. [6] Maffei, Mus. Veron. p. 11 sqq.

nary, therefore, in Cicero's intention of converting the sepulchre of his daughter Tullia into a temple;[1] and it is a feature of the time adopted by Apuleius, who makes his widow have her deceased husband, for whose loss she is inconsolable, represented as Liber the god, and paying the image a worship of its own, with the ordinary testimonials of divine honour.[2]

---

3. The Element of Superstition.

In this later age of heathendom, the complaint of the spread of superstition is frequently repeated. Nothing, however, is more vague, indistinct, or capricious than the "deisidaimonia" of Greeks, and the "superstitio" of Romans. No one drew or was capable of drawing the line between this erroneous excess of religious sentiment and real religiousness. The Romans of the early period had certainly a simple criterion. A religious man they deemed one who adhered to the legal traditions of his country in his relations to the gods; one who gave himself up to strange gods and rites, a superstitious one.[3] But this distinction was no longer available in the earlier times of the Cæsars; when there were, on the one side, hardly any persons to take up the cause of the entire hereditary cultus, with its endless confusion of gods, or, on the other, to reject every outlandish worship and god merely because of their foreign original. Still less was this distinction available to those who spoke Greek; for with such the old internal connection of religion with the state had ceased on the fall of the latter, or had utterly lost its importance. So the attempt was made to fix the relative position of religion and superstition by other criteria. This was Varro's notion;[4] he thought the superstitious were those who feared the gods as enemies; the religious, those who honoured them as fathers. Maximus of Tyre explained the religious man as the friend, the superstitious as the flatterer, of the deity. Both are interpretations pointing to a particular feature in superstition, and yet in reality quite inadequate to form a canon of religious manifestations in life by. In the Greek idea of superstition, the notion of dread was predominant, as is evident

---

[1] Ep. ad Att. xii. 35. [2] Apul. Metam. i. 527, Oud.
[3] So the definition in Festus, s. v. "Superstitio." [4] Ap. Aug. C. D. vi. 9.

from the meaning of the word; accordingly Theophrastus explained superstition as nothing else but a cowardly fear of any deity;[1] and Plutarch's whole treatment of it hinges on the sentiment of anxiety, and terror of the wrath of the gods and the punishments of the world below, as evidenced by those whom it haunted. It is true, the sensation of religious fear in Greek and Roman was usually expressed as a distortion, often betrayed under the most monstrous and absurd forms; all here turning on the conception, entirely external and mechanical as it was, of the nature of defilement, of ritual omissions and errors, or the jealousy of one deity aroused by recourse being had to other powers. The idea of the divine holiness, if we except a few philosophers, was quite unknown to the ancients in practical life and in intercourse with the gods; and therefore they were equally ignorant of the true fear, grounded precisely upon this sanctity of God, and of which fear theirs was but a caricature, an anxious trembling before the power of capricious tyrants, whose smiles could neither be won nor retained, except by continual sacrifices, and the most painful observance of ceremonies; and could be forfeited again, and converted into wrath, by an infinite number of possible mistakes and omissions. Now philosophers, while they rejected all such ideas of the deity, and discovered the essence of perverted religion or deisidaimonia in them, fell into the assertion of the contrary view, that the deity need not be the object of fear at all, but only required to be loved and honoured, love and fear being incompatibles; such, for instance, was Seneca's ground.[2] They had no perception of fear being inseparable from the true love of an all-holy God.

Hence nothing was so vague or subjective as the reproach of superstition. In principle every one regarded his neighbour as superstitious if he worshiped different gods, or the same in a different manner; or if he performed the same function, but more frequently than seemed necessary to the party passing the sentence. Theophrastus includes the frequent lustration of houses among superstitions, though this was a traditionary usage, either performed, or that ought to have been performed, by every Roman. Washing the hands on coming out of a temple, he considers religious; but the sprinkling of oneself with blest water, superstitious. To a Polybius the whole Roman system of religion

[1] Charact. 16. [2] Epist. 47.

appeared in reality a deisidaimonia, but calculated on a basis of prudence and policy. On the other hand, philosophically educated Greeks of this later period must have looked upon as genuinely religious and commendable just what the patriotic Roman rejected and persecuted as superstition,—for instance, the worship of strange and outlandish gods, Isis and Osiris, and others. The piety, the Greek would say, which extended itself to every thing was the most perfect.[1] All the honours paid to the gods, Hellenic as well as Asiatic and Egyptian, terminate in the glorification of a supreme God, and all acts of disrespect in the same manner fall back upon him. But how dangerous it was, on the contrary, to intend to serve this one supreme God only! "Be, above all things, on thy guard," said the judge Rogatian to a Christian, "lest in thy acknowledgment of one God only, thou draw upon thyself the anger of many to thy ruin."[2]

But as in theory superstition could not be distinguished from religion, so in life and in practice religiousness ordinarily assumed the appearance of superstition. Three of the most prominent characters in ancient history may be quoted as examples of this,—Sylla, Augustus, and Alexander. The dictator Sylla, distinguished by his good fortune as well as his vices, and those the bestial ones of excess and unnatural lust, esteemed himself a special favourite of the gods; his confidence, however, was principally placed upon a certain little image of Apollo from Delphi, which he carried about with him in war, and used to embrace in the presence of his troops, beseeching it for victory.[3] No one gave more thorough credit to Chaldeans, oracles, dreams, and signs than he. He even had his dying wife carried into another house, that his own might not be polluted by the corpse.[4] The same Augustus who, in the provinces of the empire, allowed himself to be invoked as a living god, observed every sign with the most minute care. It was a presage of an evil if in the morning he had the left shoe brought him instead of the right. He had faith in days, never undertaking any thing important on the nones, and never setting out on a journey on the day after the nundinæ.[5] He, the supreme pontiff, the restorer of Roman

---

[1] So, for example, Celsus, ap. Orig. c. Cels. 8.
[2] Ruinart, Acta MM. sinc. p. 281.
[3] Val. Max. i. 2. 2; Front. Strat. i. 11; Plut. Sylla, 26.
[4] Plut. 35.   [5] Sueton. Octav. 90-92.

religion, punished the god Neptune because he lost a fleet in a storm, by forbidding his image to be carried in the procession of the next Circensian games; and in a public oration against the prevalent celibacy of the day, he recommended marriage to the Roman grandees as a desirable state, because it was the practice of the gods themselves to marry. The treatment of Neptune by Augustus reminds one of Alexander the Great, who first set out by giving an example of religious expansiveness on a large scale, sacrificing to Achilles and Priam at Troy, doing homage to Apis in Memphis, in Tyre to Melkarth, and to Bel in Babylon. Besides, his palace swarmed with soothsayers, who had to sacrifice and perform ceremonies of purification for him; and in every unusual event he recognised a sign of warning from the gods; and yet, on the death of his favourite Hephæstion, he had the altars and images of the gods overthrown, and wreaked his vengeance on Æsculapius in particular, whose temple he ordered to be burnt. When he had the misfortune to kill his friend Clitus in a fit of frenzy, he fancied, or allowed his diviners to persuade him, that Dionysos had instigated him to the fatal act in requital for his having neglected him in a sacrifice.[1] Such outbreaks of passion against particular gods as have been mentioned in the instance of Augustus and Alexander were not unfrequent even amongst the most jealous servants of the gods. Thus, when the emperor Julian, in the Parthian war, intended to sacrifice ten choice and beautiful bulls to Mars the Avenger, nine of them sullenly lay down as they were being led to the altar, and the tenth broke his bands; whereupon the infuriated Cæsar swore, by Jupiter, he would offer no more sacrifice to Mars.[2]

4. Fall of the old Religion of Rome.

STRANGE GODS AND THEIR RITES—FEMALE PIETY—TAUROBOLIA—INCLINATION TO JUDAISM—THEOLEPSY—THEOREA AND WORSHIP OF IMAGES—INTERCOURSE OF MAN WITH THE DEITY—PRAYER.

The old Roman religion pure had, in fact, already come to an end by the time of the Cæsars, even though the worship of Janus

---

[1] Plut. Alex. 13; Curt. viii. 2, 6; Arriani Exp. Al. iv p. 261.
[2] Amm. Marc. xxiv. 6.

and a few other ancient Latin and Sabine deities were continued, as ancestral rites, and offered by the state; but the popular confidence had been transferred to other gods, Greek, Asiatic, and Egyptian. As early as the close of the Punic wars, the desire of the people for a more lively type of deity, and one richer in mystic lore, and the influence of Sibylline books, with their collegiate interpreters, the quindecemviri, had contributed in the first instance to place the entire Grecian system of gods immediately at the side of the old Roman; and then, by degrees, it grew up along with the other, by a transfer of its mythology and its individual stamp of deity to the Roman gods, with the exception of a few who were too unhellenic to undergo transformation. Thus it came to pass that many religious ceremonies, formerly of great importance, disappeared utterly. In the early periods, in great calamities and perils of the commonwealth, when all other resources had failed, or seemed unequal to the pressing nature of the danger, it was the custom to choose a dictator for the sole purpose of driving a nail into the temple-wall of Jupiter. Later on, after the time of Scipio, no reliance whatever seems to have been placed on the virtue of this nail, and the matter was no more mentioned. Lectisternia and supplications, the holding of the Latine feriæ, vows of costly offerings, or the introduction of a new worship, became the remedies resorted to in misfortunes and danger.

Strange rites ever grew and multiplied in Rome, and encroached grievously upon the old ones. And now, after a long struggle, the worship of Isis had taken its place with those of Æsculapius and Cybele. From the times of the Mithridatic war the Romans had become acquainted with Ma, a goddess of Comana, as to whom the Greeks could not be certain whether she was their war-goddess, Enyo, or a moon-goddess, or their own Athene;[1] the Romans blended her with their own old Italic goddess, Bellona, or Duellona, who already occupied a temple in the vicinity of the city, erected a new sanctuary for her, and gave the administration of her worship to the Bellonarii, a college consisting of Cappadocian priests and priestesses.[2] These "fanatici," clothed in black, made their progress through the city on festivals of the goddess, using the same means as the priests of Cybele to throw themselves into an ecstatic state of frenzy, during

[1] Plut. Sylla, 9.   [2] Orelli, Inscr. 2316, 2317; Acron. ad Hor. Ser. ii. 3, 223.

which their bodies were without sensation; they prophesied, gashed themselves with a double-headed axe on the arms and other parts of their bodies. The blood that flowed was caught in a small shield, and given to such as desired to consecrate themselves to the goddess, as an initiating drink.¹ The trick was to cut themselves so as to let the blood flow without the wound being dangerous, and therefore Commodus ordered the Bellonarii to make a deeper incision into the flesh.²

So powerful was the charm exercised by all that was dark, sombre, and mysterious in the gods, that the very ignorance of the nature of this goddess seems to have been her best recommendation to the Romans. Every rite, indeed, pursued under the veil of secrecy was held to be more salutary and effective than public and official rites of religion; an error partaken in by the greatest and worthiest of the ancients. Even his Stoic philosophy proved no preservative against the attraction to Marcus Aurelius. In the war against the Marcomanni, he ordered priests from all countries to come to him at Rome, and spent so long a time over the rites of strange gods, as to keep his army waiting for him. Sacrifices were commanded on so large a scale on the occasion, that it was jestingly hinted the white oxen had written to him thus: "If thou art victorious, we are all lost."³ At the bidding of an oracle, interpreted to him by the wizard Alexander, he had two lions, with an abundance of aromatic herbs, and the most precious offerings, thrown into the Danube; the lions, however, escaped by swimming, and instead of a victory, the Romans suffered an overwhelming defeat, leaving twenty thousand men on the field of battle.⁴ Thereupon the emperor betook himself to an Egyptian priest, Arnuphis, and was fully convinced that he was indebted to his incantations and skill in magic for the timely rain which helped him and his army to victory.⁵ From this date he seems to have become a devoted worshiper of Egyptian deities. On Roman inscriptions he avowed himself an adorer of Serapis; and in the journey which he shortly afterwards undertook to Egypt he is said to have behaved like an Egyptian citizen and philosopher in all the temples and sacred groves.

---

¹ Tibull. i. 6, 43; Tert. Apol. 9; Lact. i. 21; Juven. vi. 511.
² Lamprid. Commod. 9.   ³ Amm. Marc. 25.
⁴ Lucian. Pseudomant. 48; comp. Jablonskii Opusc., ed. Te Water, iv. 20 sq.
⁵ Dio. Cass. ii. 1183, ed. Reimar; Suid. s. v. Ἰουλιανός.

So, in the time of Domitian, the cities of the Hellespont were alarmed by an earthquake. Their public and private resources were drained to offer in common a very special and secret sacrifice to Poseidon and the Earth, through Egyptian and Chaldean priests, who demanded no less than ten talents for their services. Of course, in case of earthquakes, the danger was great of making a mistake in the invocations and sacrifices, and of going to the wrong god altogether, in lieu of the real author of the mischief.[1] Every where we see how the religious bias of the period was, not to be satisfied with the old deities of the country. The ground of confidence in them was cut away since the time these deities were unable to maintain the independence of their worshipers against the superior power of Rome; and the foundations of their worship were shaken after the political framework of the several states was broken up. And as soon as men felt themselves to be members of a vast empire, embracing an immense number of nationalities and rites, the infinitesimal division of the divine nature, and medley host of gods and goddesses became disgusting to them, from the exorbitance of their pretensions, and the painful uncertainty about them and their worship. Hence a powerful revulsion towards, and longing after, a one deity, to surrender oneself entirely to, and be a stay and resource in all situations and difficulties, without the disquiet and doubt arising from the necessity of flying first to this and then to that god. The sharp-cut features and speciality of Hellenic gods, further limited by their belonging to a numerous divine society, had no such fitness for the purpose of filling the void as the Egyptian gods had, from their being far less individualised, and far more enveloped in the attractive cloud of mystery,—Isis and Serapis, for instance, or the sun-gods of the Orientals.

The Isis worship took the lead of the rest; and since the time of Alexander had begun to spread over all the countries where Greek was spoken. We find a strong evidence of the great attraction to the service of this goddess in the fact that, in Rome, where before it was not tolerated, the emperors in person, Otho, Domitian, Commodus, Caracalla, and Alexander, now became its zealous partisans. The priests of the goddess announced that she cured diseases of every kind; and it was these miracles

[1] Amm. Marc. xvii. 7.

of healing, Diodorus says, by which her name was acknowledged throughout the whole world.[1] The Greeks, by grecising her myth, had quite domiciled her amongst them; while the Orphic minstrels exalted her into the omnipotent queen of nature and of the rest of the world of gods. She often stepped into the place of Demeter, Persephone, Artemis, and Hecate, and became dispensatrix of food, mistress of the lower world and of the sea, and goddess of navigation. She was also metamorphosed into Fortune; and the philosophico-physical view discovered in her the sum of female passive nature and matter in opposition to the male sun-power, as also the humid universal mother of life. Thus she became identical with the Phrygian mother of the gods, with Rhea, and the Syrian goddess of Hierapolis; and her being grew daily more comprehensive and formless, till it reached the extreme and last conception—that chaotic primal night, from out of which the universe was evolved,[2]—with it, of course, all her personality was lost, and the imagination, in search of an universal god, rested, in fine, upon a mere hollow, ghostlike abstraction. In inscriptions she was now styled pantheistically, "the one, who is all."[3] This, however, was no popular view, nor ever became so. The people worshiped her principally as Isis Salutaris (a title often found in inscriptions), the inventress of remedies, and revealer in dreams of cures for diseases. She was distinguished for restoring sight to the blind. Hence it was that the incubatio took place in her temples, and the walls were covered with votive tablets.[4]

Wherever the Isis worship existed as a standing institute, or was only performed by priests errant, there Anubis with his dog's head was sure to be found, represented by a priest in the train of the goddess; as also the entire drama of the search after, and discovery of, Osiris, with its cries of lamentation and joy to boot. For nine days and nights the actresses in the play fasted, and, to merit the favour of the goddess, abstained from sexual intercourse, after the pattern set them by herself in her grief. The silver serpent, borne by the image of the deity in her left hand, gave notice of errors committed by shaking its

[1] Diod. i. 25.
[2] Plut. de Isid. 56; Iamblich. Myst. Æg. viii. 5; Simplic. in Aristot. Phys. ausc. iv. p. 150.
[3] Orelli. Inscr. n. 1871; Mommsen, Inscr. R. Neap. n. 3580.
[4] Tibull. i. 3. 27.

head, and they were atoned for by gifts of geese and cakes to the priests.¹

Serapis too, about whose true character much obscurity prevailed even in Egypt itself, gradually rose into a god of universal importance from the beginning of the second century after Christ, and was much worshiped. He himself was said to have answered a client of his, Nicocreon, king of Cyprus, with an oracular response to the effect that the heaven was his head, the sea his body, and the earth his feet, his ears being in the ether. He was frequently given out as the sun-god, or identical with Zeus. Aristides, in an oration of his, describes him as a god who rules the winds, makes the sea-water drinkable, awakes the dead, and displays the light of the sun to mankind. The whole of human life, from the cradle to the grave, is committed to his charge, and he is the bestower of wisdom as well as riches.² But he, too, was eminently a god of healing, who reveals to the sick, or rather the priests for them, the proper remedies for their restoration to health, by the process of incubatio in his temples. The verse of Julian indicates how Serapis absorbed other deities, or blended with them: "Serapis is a Zeus, a Hades, a Helios;" and Mithras, Attis, Jupiter Ammon, and Adonis were all regarded as his counterparts.³

The worship of the Idean mother of the gods constantly maintained an undiminished, or rather an increasing, reputation. It certainly contributed to the lasting credit of this rite that the Galli went about, in their voluntary effeminacy, speaking testimonies to the might of the goddess; for what other explanation could be given of the ecstatic state in which the painful operation was consummated by them on themselves, than the overpowering influence of the goddess, before which both Athens and Rome had long since bowed? so much so, that the Galli were fully acknowledged in the Roman state by the laws of the twelve tables.⁴ Juvenal depicts the crude superstitions of this rite in its most pitiable aspect; how the plump Archigallus, his voice predominant amid the hoarse din of his subordinates, and the drums of his herd of followers, terrified the credulous women with the threatened dangers of September, and the south wind that brings autumnal fever; and then how these

¹ Juven. vi. 533-541. ² Aristid. Or. in Serap. p. 82 sqq. Dind.
³ Mart. Cap. p. 233, Kopp; Jul. Or. iv. p. 136. ⁴ Cic. de Legg. ii. 9.

women redeemed themselves with hundreds of eggs, and cast-off clothes, into which the Galli exorcised the fatal miasmas of the season.[1]

A more serious matter still was the rite of Taurobolium and Criobolium, attached to the worship of the Idean mother, and one of the most solemn, and, as was thought, the most effective, religious functions of later paganism. The old and ordinary rites of purifying and lustration, common to Greek and Roman, no longer sufficed, though they still continued steadily in use. People were still purifying houses, temples, property, whole cities, by carrying water about and sprinkling it for expiatory purposes.[2] Living animals, oxen, sheep, and swine, cats and dogs, were led, or carried, round about; persons and things were asperged with the blood of the victims, and their ashes were also used; the purgamenta (or different articles employed in the ceremony) were then thrown away with averted face into a stream or the crossways. Ovid paints to the life Roman tradespeople sprinkling themselves and their wares with water drawn from the Mercury-spring at the Porta Capena, in order to clear off the guilt incurred by their lies and cheating and false oaths.[3] Both Ovid and Tertullian allude to the notion of the general efficacy of bathing in running water, or washing, for the removal of the stain of any crime, murder inclusive, as an idea and a practice of an earlier time; the poet crying, "O fool of heart, that thinkest to remove from thee the irremediable guilt of murder in the running stream!"[4] On the other hand, the notion remained of blood, the seat of vital power, being the most effectual means of atonement and purification, particularly at the very moment of its gushing in a warm stream of life from the victim consecrated to the deity. Whoever was completely bathed in this blood, and thoroughly well saturated with it, became radically pure from all guilt and defilement, and supplied with a fund of sanctity for many years to come. Such was the origin of the taurobolia and criobolia. A roomy grave was covered with pierced boards. The victim, a bull or ram, was brought and sacrificed on these, so that the blood dropped through the holes like rain, and was caught by the man below on his whole body, who took especial care that cheeks, ears,

---

[1] Juv. vi. 511-521.
[2] Tertull. de Bapt. c. 5.
[3] Fasti. v. 673-690.
[4] Fasti, v. 2-45.

lips, eyes, nose, and tongue, should be wetted.¹ He then came out of the hole, dropping with blood, and exhibited himself to the people, who greeted him reverentially as a being perfectly pure and hallowed, and threw themselves on their knees before him. He continued to wear his bloody clothes till they were in tatters.² A taurobolium such as this purified him who submitted to it, and rendered him pleasing to the gods, during a space of twenty years, at the expiration of which he again put himself under a similar shower of blood. A certain Sextilius, however, was found to affirm of himself that he had been regenerated for an eternity by the application of the taurobolium as well as the criobolium.³

The taurobolium was resorted to not only for individual purification, but also for the welfare of others, particularly the emperor and the imperial family; and this, too, frequently at the express instance of the Mother of the gods, communicated by herself through the mouth of her priest.⁴ Whole cities or provinces would undertake a taurobolium for this object; and in this case it was usually women who had themselves consecrated by the rain of blood. The solemnity with which the function was performed is shown by the priests from Valence, Orange, and Viviers, all appearing at the celebration of one at Die;⁵ while at another, offered by the city of Lyons for the well-being of the emperor Antoninus, on the Vatican hill at Rome, Æmilius Carpus, who was the recipient of the expiatory blood on the occasion, carried the frontal bone of the bull sacrificed, with the horns gilded, to Lyons, where it was buried with religious ceremony.

The first instance of a taurobolium, as far as is known at present, occurred in the year A.D. 133. This we learn from an inscription.⁶ The act then must have been esteemed one of great importance and effect, for the remembrance of it to have been preserved on a monument, even if it only regarded the purification of a private individual. The sacrifice of A.D. 133,

---

¹ Prudent. Peristeph. x. 101 sqq.; Firm. Mat. de err. prof. rel. c. 27.
² See the verses edited by Salmasius in Van Dale, Diss. ix. Amst. 1743, p. 48.
³ Ap. Van Dale, l. c. p. 127.
⁴ e. g. It is said in an inscription found at Jein on the Rhone, "ex vaticinatione Pasonii Juliani Archigalli." Colonia, Hist. Litt. de Lyon, p. 206. In others, "ex imperio Matris Deûm."
⁵ Colonia, l. c. p. 223. ⁶ Mommsen, Inscr. R. Neap. n. 2602.

however, was not offered to the Phrygian Mother of the gods, as all the others were, but to the Carthaginian Cœlestis, who was, in fact, identical with Cybele by this time. The common opinion that the taurobolic atonement of blood originated in an imitation of Christian baptism, is certainly erroneous, for one reason, because the origin of the rite falls in a period when the attention of the heathen had never been directed to the imitation of Christian rites; and the mouthpieces of the age, Plutarch, Pliny, Dio Chrysostom, Aristides, and Pausanias, were some of them unacquainted with Christians, while the rest treated them with silent contempt, as unworthy of notice. A second reason is, because the heathens had long had a substitute for Christian baptism in ablutions and bathing in running water. But in the fourth century, when the taurobolia were become general and frequent, and the most distinguished officers of religion and state submitted to the disgusting rite, the need of a sacrament on which implicit reliance could be placed, equal to that of the Christians in their baptism and communion, may possibly have contributed to their multiplication.

It might seem strange that in this confused medley of rites, each overbidding the other in its promises, the Jewish religion should have found a place so early as Augustus,—for a worship, devoid of image or sacrifice, and at a distance from its temple, poverty-stricken in point of ceremonial, necessarily formed the most striking contrast with heathen worships. But the very aspirations after the one omniscient and omnipotent God, which the heathen conscience (lacerated, as it was, by the multitude and the pretensions of its deities) could nowhere else satisfy, explain how the God of the Old Testament drew to Himself vast numbers of proselytes from paganism in Rome herself, and wherever a Jewish synagogue happened to be built. Precisely because He alone was not one amongst many, and endured not another by his side, and because no myths were attached to his name, the imagination of many a Gentile, wearied with the search after a higher and less anthropomorphic being, was won over; while the observance of the Sabbath, prayer, and the law of abstinence from meats, laid a yoke on him, borne by no means unwillingly; for man finds repose the easiest and most cherished in the consciousness of a worship precisely formularised and strictly enjoined.

To the generality, indeed, in those times, the Jewish God was so strange and unintelligible a being, that Juvenal imagined the Jews prayed to nothing but the clouds and empty heaven.¹ Accurate observer as Strabo was, he thought the God of Moses was naught else but what we call the heaven, or world, or nature of the universe.² Celsus, too, insisted that the Jews prayed to the heaven.³ Notwithstanding these mistakes, and the combined hatred and contempt shown to the Jews more than any other people, the number of those inclined to Jewish rites kept continually increasing; and Seneca, by his time, could lament the wide extent of the influence which the customs of this degraded people had gained, their having already made their way into all lands; and that, though conquered, they had given laws to their conquerors. The observance of the Sabbath seemed to him only one of the many forms of superstition in which man wasted the seventh part of his life in doing nothing, and much harm resulted from one's not acting just at the proper moment.⁴

Heathendom presented another almost invariable feature in the wide-spread and contagious tendency to produce a state of violent excitation of body and soul, mounting up to Bacchanal frenzy, spectators as well as actors holding the effect to be an operation of the deity and a part of his worship. This took place not merely in the case of members of certain colleges of priests, like the Bellonarii before mentioned, for with them it was part of their vocation; there were numbers of others gadding about as god-possessed people. They were called Fanatici, because they stayed in the temples or their vicinity, and were supposed to inhale the "numen," the divine spirit, along with the exhalations of the sacrifices which they diligently attended.⁵ These theoleptics were dirty and of bewildered aspect, with long matted hair. Violent agitations of the head, and distortions of limbs, accompanied the broken phrases which they jerked out, as if they had a difficulty in delivering their breasts of the message of the god which they were intrusted to announce to men.⁶ The variety of expressions in use among the Greeks for this condition is already a proof of its frequency; and the dry Roman jurists put the question whether it were a defect making the

---

¹ Sat. xiv. 96 sqq. ² Str. xvi. p. 760.
³ Orig. c. Cels. i. p. 18, v. p. 241.   ⁴ Ap. Aug. C. D. vi. 11.
⁵ Tertull. Apol. 23.   ⁶ Firmic. Mathes. iii. 7 ; Minuc. Octav. 27.

sale of a slave null, if, after it, he proved to have been one of these fanatical prophets who jerked his head about.[1]

Thus, then, the gods had in reality a vast number of instruments through which to make known their will; and those of the greatest variety, from the Delphic oracle downwards to the slave shaking from inspiration as from the chill of a fever. And yet, in this wealth of divine manifestation, the souls of men were hungry and starving; not as if there was any lack of believers, nay, rather, any one who came forward in the name of his deity, and as inspired by him, provided he played his own part decently, was sure to gather round him crowds of followers. "If a man shakes a sistrum" (an Isis priest), Seneca says, "and lies as he is bid; if a master in the art of slashing" (a Bellona priest) "with upraised hand makes arms and shoulders drip blood; if one creeps in the public way on his knees, howling; or if a grizzled fellow, clothed in a white vestment" (an Egyptian priest), "crowned with laurel, and carrying a torch in full daylight, shouts at the top of his voice, 'Some one of the gods is angry,'—then run ye together in crowds and cry, 'The man's inspired.'"[2]

Such states of possession, real or fictitious, were, one may imagine, much more frequent among men than women; at least, there is but little mention of the latter. Still, the yoke of heathen superstition pressed with double weight on the female sex. The constant demand, though always theoretical, of Roman and Greek, Cato and Plutarch, was that wives should have and worship no other deities than their husbands; but if the men had long ago broken through the limitations of earlier times, the women were still less able to be satisfied with the ancient gods and the simpler rites and sacrifices. Fear and hope stir them stronger; swayed by sentiment and imagination, and torn by their passions; at once more helpless and dependent on another's will; incapacitated, besides, by a more susceptible organisation for the endurance of doubt or uncertainty, and to suspend their judgment until after patiently investigating, they threw themselves headlong into any worship which a chance slave-juggler or greedy priest enticed them to by vaunting its superior efficaciousness. It was said of the Greek women of the period, that they worshiped gods whose very names were unknown to their husbands; while Juvenal speaks of the Roman women as quite

[1] Digest. xxi. 1, 1. 9.   [2] De Vitâ beatâ, 27.

prepared, at the bidding of a priest of Isis, to stand naked in the Tiber in the early morning, and afterwards to creep on bare knees from the end of the Campus Martius as far as the Isis temple.[1] Moreover, the established mystery-rites of the Thesmophoria and Bona Dea, performed by women only, were fully calculated to goad them on to the lust of other worships, promising a more plenary satisfaction of their passions.

One may well fancy in what the religious practices of women consisted, when the Roman men served their gods at the Capitol in the way which Seneca describes. "One," he says, "sets a rival deity by the side of another god; another shows Jupiter the time of day; this one acts the beadle, the other the anointer, pretending by gesture to rub in the ointment. A number of coiffeurs attend upon Juno and Minerva, and make pretence of curling with their fingers, not only at a distance from their images, but in the actual temple. Some hold the looking-glass to them; some solicit the gods to stand security for them; while others display briefs before them, and instruct them in their law cases. Artistes, in fact, of every kind spend their time in the temples, and offer their services to the immortal gods." These were men's proceedings. Seneca continues, "Women, too, take their seats at the Capitol, pretending that Jupiter is enamoured of them, and not allowing themselves to be intimidated by Juno's presence."[2]

Theopœa was the art of inducting the gods into their statues, and of compelling them by mysterious hymns and ceremonies to take up their abode in the new places prepared for them, and was constantly practised, particularly by Egyptian and Greek priests and wizards. It was pronounced the most sacred and effective kind of worship;[3] and writings are extant in which Hermes instructs his son Asclepios that it is in man's power to animate images by means of the secret art, handed down amongst them, and to compel the gods to a union with them, similar to that of soul with body.[4] Notwithstanding, the gods not unfrequently took themselves off, and quitted temple and image, to the no small alarm of the people. They did not do this unobserved, but left indications of their departure: for instance, the images fell down from their pedestals, or, as most fre-

---

[1] Sat. vi. 522.
[2] Ap. Aug. C. D. vi. 2.
[3] Orig. c. Cels. vii.
[4] Ap. Aug. C. D. viii. 1, 2.

quently happened, the temple-gates opened of their own accord at night-time. The Roman historians repeatedly observe, on the occurrence of great catastrophes, that traces of the withdrawal of the gods had been discovered in Capitol or Forum.[1]

Lucian, who drew so impartial a picture of the religious system of his times, and represented it as he found it in the mass of mankind, always asserts that the worship of the people was paid directly to the metal or stone images of the gods; that they saw, in these representations, the earthly residences of their heavenly forms, the bodies inhabited by the deity as by a soul. He makes his Cyniscus (little Cynic) say to Zeus, "Many of you, if of gold and silver, had to suffer being melted down when Destiny so decreed."[2] Of the far-famed statue of Zeus, at Olympia, he observes, "All who entered the temple believed they beheld, not the gold and ivory of the image, but the son of Cronos and Rhea *in propriâ personâ*, transferred to this earth by the hands of Phidias."[3] In an amusing scene of his "Tragic Zeus," Hermes has to show the gods to their seats in the assembly according to their value; the consequence is, that Bendis and Anubis, Attis, Mithras, and Lunus, the gods of the barbarians, all occupy the first places, as being of gold, taking precedence of the Hellenic deities, who are generally of stone or brass, only in a few instances of ivory.

Lucian's banter is borne out by the more serious complaint of Plutarch, as to the fatal error to which the Greeks gave firm hold, by calling gods the image-work of brass or stone, or even pictures, and then saying that Lachesis had stripped Athene, Dionysius shorn Apollo of his golden locks, and that the Capitoline Zeus had been burnt and destroyed in the civil war;[4] and yet Stilpo was punished with banishment from Athens for maintaining that the statue of Athene by Phidias was no deity.[5]

Seneca charged the Romans with this same sin of idolatry in the strictest sense of the word. "People pray," he says, "to these images of the gods, implore them on bended knee, sit or stand days long before them, throw them a piece of money, and sacrifice beasts to them, and in so treating them with deep respect, despise meanwhile the men who made them."[6] "I my-

---

[1] See the passages in Ansaldi, De Diis Romam evocatis, Brix. 1743, p. 19.
[2] Jup. Confut. 8. [3] De Sacrif. 11. [4] De Iside, 11.
[5] Diog. Laert. ii. 116. [6] Ap. Lact. ii. 2.

self," says one, by no means of the lowest grade, but on a level with the educated persons of his time (the close of the third century), — "I myself, not so long ago, worshiped gods just taken out of the furnace, fresh from the hammer and anvil of the smith, ivory, paintings, old trees swathed in fascias; and if I happened to cast my eyes on a polished stone smeared with olive-oil, I made reverence to it, as if a power were present therein, and addressed myself in supplication for blessings from the senseless block, doing grievous despite to the very gods in whose existence I believed, while implying they were wood, or stone, or ivory, or to be found in any such material."[1]

It is worthy of notice, that the worship of mere stones, here alluded to by Arnobius, should have maintained itself in such favour with Greek as well as Roman. Theophrastus beforetime had mentioned it as one feature of deisidaimonia, that people could not pass a holy anointed stone at the cross-roads without pouring oil upon it, genuflecting, and showing it reverence. Lucian remarks the same of one Rutilian, a noble Roman.[2] Every one, it appears, took care to have stones of the kind on his property; for Apuleius stigmatises Æmilian, one of his adversaries, because no such thing as an anointed stone, or garlanded branch, to say nothing of a holy grove, was to be found on his premises.[3]

If we attempt to dive deeper into the springs of religious action peculiar to the period, and to answer the question, what was really the motivum of a worship, so active, often toilsome, and always claiming so large a proportion of time, as was then offered to the gods, it cannot but strike us most convincingly that the higher powers of the soul, and the moral requirements of man, had little or no share therein. A few words suffice to indicate the void. There was wanting there the conviction of divine holiness, and the need of human sanctification. The state of his soul was never laid open to the deity in prayer. The thoughts of man, or the direction of his will, never approximated to the deity, nor were troubled thereupon about them; many even imagined that the gods knew nothing of them. Nay, the very notion of a god really omniscient had something in it frightful to many. It was intolerable to them to be unable to be alone with their own thoughts and wishes, to acknowledge an

[1] Arnob. i. 39.   [2] Pseudomant. 30.   [3] Apul. p. 349.

overseer above them, who saw through their most inward inclinations and desires. "A god," says the heathen Cæcilius,[1] "who carefully notes the ways and acts of all, ay, and their words too and most secret thoughts, must needs be a troublesome, restless, and shamelessly inquisitive being; who, as he wanders about every where, is incapacitated from helping individuals, divided as he is among all together, nor yet can satisfy that corporate whole, as being occupied with individuals." The philosophy of the time was in keeping with this fundamentally. "The human race," says Seneca, "is assuredly under the providence of the gods; still it is only at times they trouble themselves about individuals."[2] Plutarch accepted the axiom of Euripides, that the deity was only concerned about the most weighty matters, leaving the more trivial to accident.[3] Cotta in Cicero designates this as the ordinary teaching of the Stoics;[4] and the Platonists, besides, were of opinion that it was not generally becoming the dignity of the celestials to enter into, and interest themselves about, things happening on the earth below.[5] It was pretty generally believed, however, that certain sudden instincts, passions, and resolves were kindled in the soul of man by a god; people were always ready to set down to the account of a deity acts which they were ashamed of or rued. "It was the god who tempted me to it," is the excuse of the seducer of a maid to his father in a play of Plautus.[6]

The examination of one's own interior state, the sifting of the conscience before God, therefore, formed no part of heathen prayer. The idea of reconciling the two things, and bringing them into an intimate connection, would have seemed not only strange but absurd to men of those days. They had no apprehension of the duty of any such return into oneself; and hence, in spite of the good counsel given on the point by the Stoic philosophy, there was a universal deficiency of self-knowledge:

"Yet not one of us strives, not one, to sift himself to the bottom;
All eyes as we are to discern the burden on shoulders before us."[7]

So, people prayed for wealth, the comforts of life, good for-

---

[1] Minuc. Oct. 10.   [2] Epist. 95.
[3] Præcepta ger. Rep. xv. p. 811.   [4] Cic. Nat. D. iii. 36-39.
[5] Apul. de Deo Socr. p. 669 sq. "neque enim pro majestate Deûm cœlestium fuerit hæc curare."
[6] Aulul. iv. 6, 11.   [7] Pers. Sat. iii. 23 sq.

tune, and success in undertakings; but no one ever thought of asking moral good of the deity. "Let Jupiter bestow life and riches on me," says Horace, "I'll be indebted to myself for a quiet and contented mind."[1] Epictetus and Marcus Aurelius made an exception here; but Seneca himself teaches, "Man must make himself fortunate: it were a shame to burden the gods with applications of the kind. By virtue, man's own gift to himself, he begins to be a companion meet for the gods, and leaves off being a suppliant."[2] Maximus of Tyre devoted a whole treatise to prove it were better for man to omit prayer altogether. All human affairs were, he thought, subject in part to a divine providence, immutable in its decrees; partly ordained beforehand by a firmly fixed destiny, and in part depending upon accident: in any case, therefore, prayer is useless and absurd.[3]

Taking one's point of view from another religion, one might expect in the masses, involved as they were in the greatest moral corruption, an entire cessation from prayer. This effect, however, was not in consonance with the spirit of paganism. It is not on the score of abandonment of prayer and sacrifice that contemporary writers deplore the moral state of their age, but it is the frightful exposition which they make of the objects of prayer. They prayed for the speedy demise of a rich uncle; that they might find a treasure; for success in forging an alteration in a will; for an opportunity of gratifying unnatural lust.[4] Married women prayed for the welfare and success of dancers or actors with whom they carried on adulterous intrigues.[5] To sanctify these prayers, as Persius says, people plunge over head in the Tiber three times a morning. Nothing indeed could be expected from the gods gratis. When the object was important, or the favour great, the promise of a corresponding return was looked for. The senate set the example; and in cases of emergency, used to vow a thousand pounds of gold together for a votive offering to the temple of Jupiter Capitolinus.[6] Luckily for the less rich, there were often ceremonies, formulæ of prayer,

---

[1] Epist. i. 18, ad fin.
[2] Ep. xxxi. 11. If Seneca once bids a friend ask, "bonam mentem bonam valetudinem" (Ep. 11), he does not mean thereby the moral but physical health of the mind, which is not in man's power, and therefore the opposite of craziness, &c. &c.
[3] Diss. xi. p. 155 sq. [4] Pers. Sat. ii. 3 sq.; Petron. lxxxviii. 7 sq., lxxxv. 5.
[5] Juven. vi. 366-378.   [6] Petron. ut supra.

exorcisms or sacrifices, appointed to secure a hearing to prayer; only it was very easy, and at the time dangerous, to make some mistake or other in the names or the ceremonies; and if a god was addressed wrongly, his anger might be roused, and the imprudence unpleasantly requited.[1]

The sources of acquaintance with the Greek life of this period are only scanty, and therefore but few features bearing on the point are traceable. We recognise one of the prevailing sentiments in a remark of Artemidorus, that persons who fell into any great misfortune never failed to renounce religion.[2] In the letters of Aristænetus, an adulteress prays the gods to show her the way to the embraces of her paramour;[3] and in the epigrams of the Anthology they are besought to be propitious to that hideous vice so inseparably connected with the Greek name.[4] Theocritus actually represents the death of a youth struck by lightning, before an image of Eros, as a punishment from the gods for having a short time previously rejected a shameful proposition.[5]

When prayers and vows did not attain their object, the tone towards the gods often changed right round, and indignation was vented in blasphemies, or ill-treatment of the images, instances of which have been mentioned before. Germanicus, Titus, and Servian who was executed by Hadrian, are reported as having charged the gods with injustice, or loaded them with execrations at the time of their death. The same angry feeling comes out even in inscriptions on the graves of relatives snatched away by an early death. Take, for instance, one on a child who died at five years of age. "To the unrighteous gods, who robbed me of my life." Or another, on the monument of a maiden of twenty, called Procope, "I lift my hand against the god who has deprived me of my innocent existence."[6]

There is another trait not to be passed over, namely, that it was no easy matter to get a friend to promise to pray for you, or no one was anxious, or made it an object, to gain the intercession of another. On the other hand, it was quite a common practice to offer sacrifices for another, and, so far as prayer entered into that function, it may well be said that intercession

---

[1] Arnob. iii. 43. [2] Oneirocr. ii. 133. p. 199.
[3] Epist. ii. 15. [4] Meleag. Epigr. xxii. 5; Automed. Epigr. 2.
[5] Idyll. 23. [6] Mabillon, Iter Ital. p. 77.

was of frequent use in heathendom. The dread of execration was all the stronger and more universal according to Pliny's observation.[1] A greater influence was attributed to a man's hate than to his love; and a prayer for vengeance was believed to find a readier hearing from the gods than one of blessing.

---

5. CONTINUED ATTACHMENT TO THE OLD GODS AND RITES—WORSHIP OF APHRODITE—MYTHS: THEIR INFLUENCE, AND HOW REPRESENTED BY MIME AND PICTURE—IMPURITY IN THE TEMPLES—RELIGIOUS IMPOSTURE AND WIZARDRY.

ON the whole, and taking a large view, the period from Augustus to the Antonines is by no means to be looked upon as one of wide-spread unbelief. With the exception of the greater cities, the masses continued to cling fast to the old gods of the country, whom they had inherited from their fathers. In the time of Pausanias there were hamlets in Greece where a firm faith in the sagas of god and hero, with the memories of the days when gods and mortal men shared a common roof and table, still survived among the natives, male and female. The fable of Cronos and his dethronement was actually believed by many still, as Sextus Empiricus tells us.[2] The ashes of the funeral piles of Niobe's children, the stones of Amphion, and the cypresses of Alcmæon were still pointed out.[3] In Phocis the belief still existed that larks laid no eggs there for the sin of Tereus; and Delphi possessed the stone which Rhea gave to Cronos to devour. Plutarch speaks of the modellers in clay and wax, and the statuaries of his time, as not doubting that the gods had assumed human forms, and fashioning some for themselves accordingly, and praying to their own creations in contempt of philosophers and statesmen, and of all their demonstrations to prove that the majesty of the deity is united to goodness, benevolence, generosity, and providence.[4] Even the ridicule of religious belief and worship in Lucian shows this belief still prevalent in the masses, and among the educated too: man of pregnant wit as he was, he would never have brought a whole

---

[1] H. N. xxviii. 2.   [2] Pyrrh. Hyp. i. 147.
[3] Paus. ix. 17. 1.   [4] De Superst. 6.

armoury of sarcasm into play upon a subject already thrown aside and out of date. Up to and after the second century, evidence may be found every where to corroborate an earlier observation of Dionysius, that the people took the myths in their grossest and most obvious sense, and therefore either treated the gods with contempt, or fortified themselves in the commission of the most shameless crimes by their example.

There were, it is true, gods and shrines forgotten and neglected, and temples in ruins;[1] but others were visited all the more eagerly: new temples were constantly being built, new feasts established, new gods introduced into cities from the stranger by popular decree. Nowhere did any reform movement show itself, nor was any effort made to purge worship of what was particularly offensive to morality, or to replace antiquated absurdities, or morally noxious rites, by more rational and pure ones. The image of Hermes Dolios (the cheat) was still standing, up to the time of Pausanias, on the road to Pellene, and the god was said to be always ready to listen to the prayers of his worshipers.[2] The people of Chios sacrificed to their hero from gratitude for his having made known the artifices and knavery of their slaves; the slaves on their part offered him the first-fruits of their pilferings.[3] At Altis, the statue of Ganymede was seen by the side of Zeus.[4] Young maidens of Trœzene dedicated their girdles to Athene Apaturia, the deceiver, as she was called for having wilily betrayed Æthra into the hands of Neptune, the island where it happened being styled the holy island.[5] On festivals of Bacchus prizes were given to the deepest drinkers; and festivals were kept at times with still greater license and debauch, and even cruelty, than ever: for some of the more opulent, not finding further scope for their ambition in political activity, tried to earn popular favour by multiplying shows and games on solemnities, and by the most lavish expenditure. They exhibited fights of gladiators, had hecatombs slain, feasted a whole populace luxuriously, and then the grateful cities immortalised them in monumental inscriptions.[6]

Pausanias was a spectator of the cruel sacrifice to Artemis at

---

[1] Joseph. c. Apion. ii. 35, p. 1287, Oberth.
[2] Paus. vii. 27. 1.
[3] Nymphod. ap. Athen. vi. 90.
[4] Paus. v. 24. 1.
[5] Paus. i. 33. 1.
[6] See the inscriptions in the Corp. Inscr. Gr. ii., particularly those of Galatia.

Patræ, where a number of animals were burnt alive; and also of the bloody scourging at the altar of Artemis Orthia in Sparta, though Spartan discipline had long since come to an end with the state.[1] Unbridled mockery and shameless ridicule were invariably practised as religious acts, even at the most solemn festivals, such as that of Demeter at Eleusis; for there were gods whom the law, as Aristotle said, ordered to be honoured by buffoonery;[2] that of Apollo Ægletes at Anapha was of this kind; and the Attic feasts of Pan, and those of Anna Perenna at Rome,[3] were so celebrated; and Lucian specifies a filthy panegyric of pæderastia as the kind of thing one fell in with only on a holy day.[4] In all countries speaking Greek, and at Rome as well, the worship of Aphrodite was characterised by a shameless impurity, and a studied excitement of gross lust, surpassing all that earlier times had seen up to Alexander. The old cosmical signification of Aphrodite Ourania was forgotten; and though the distinction between Ourania and Pandemos was retained, both were honoured with the same sensual and lustful rites. Lucian's women of pleasure make their vows of she-goats and heifers to one as well as the other for success;[5] and in an epigram of Dioscorides it is to Urania that Parmenis consecrates a fan purchased by the earnings of her prostitution.[6] The solemnities of the Aphrodisia, usually kept up three days and nights consecutively, were celebrated often in groves or gardens, with banquets and song and frantic whirls of the dance, accompanied by prayers to the goddess, amid a tumult of inebriety and lust. This was the Pannychis or Pervigilium of Venus. Whatever was done, was done in honour of the goddess, and as a means, consecrated by herself, to assure her favour. Plautus may be consulted for the petitions addressed to her on such occasions, not by loose women merely, but modest maidens.[7] On those days, too, pimps plied their trade actively, under the protection of the gods, in buying and letting out maidens for prostitution; and one of them, in Plautus, laments over his ill luck in having already sacrificed six lambs to the goddess without results.[8] Famous courtesans now maintained shrines under the different titles of Aphrodite at their

[1] Paus. vii. 18. 7. [2] Polit. vii. 15.
[3] Conon. 49; Lucian, Bis accus. c. 11; Ov. Fast. iii. 675.
[4] Amor. 53. [5] Dial. Meretr. vii. 5.
[6] Diosc. Epigr. 12; Anthol. i. 247. [7] Pœn. i. 2. 120, iv. 2. 27, v. 3. 13 sq.
[8] Pœn. ii. 6; comp. iv. 2. 25 sq.

own cost. Such were those of Aphrodite-Lamia and Pythionike at Athens and Babylon, the Leæna Ctelesylla in Ceos, and Aphrodite-Stratonikis at Smyrna.[1] In Rome there was now a Venus Drusilla in the temple of Venus Genitrix.

Here was the worship of a goddess proving an ever-open school of vice, and a gulf of corruption yawning for successive generations of youths and maidens. But we must not pass over the additional evil of the myths. These sagas of the gods, possessing wholly the imagination and conscience of men who fed on them from youth upwards, exercised a most pernicious influence on their morale; gods were taken as patterns of behaviour, and their example pleaded in excuse for all misdeeds. No one had recourse to the physical explanations of the myths which the Stoic school attempted to put in circulation, nor was any acceptance found among the people for the theories of Platonists, like Plutarch, that instead of the gods, inferior beings and demons should be considered as the actors in myths dishonourable to the deity. Neither the already-quoted testimony of Dionysius, nor the well-known scene of Terence, shall be reproduced here. The serious Seneca, the true mirror of the condition of his age, observes in regard to the myth of Zeus and Alcmene: "What else is this appeal to the precedent of the gods for, but to inflame our lusts, and to furnish a free license and excuse for the corrupt act under shelter of its divine prototype?"[2] In another treatise he waxes warm against the poets for representing Zeus as an adulterer, ravisher, and corrupter of youth, of his own kith and kin too, as unnatural towards his own father, and so on. "This," he adds, "has led to no other result than to deprive sin of its shame in man's eyes, when he saw the gods were no better than himself."[3] What notions the Romans had of their gods by the time of the second Punic war may be better judged from a single feature in the year 216 B.C. than from a whole treatise. After the defeat at Cannæ, the belief was that the anger of Juno had brought this disaster on the Roman arms. Her anger or her jealousy had been aroused, because Varro, who had the command on the fatal day, had once, when ædile, placed a beautiful youth in the car by Jupiter's side in the procession of the Circensian games. Some

---

[1] Athen. xiii. 595; Anton. Liberal. c. i.   [2] De vitâ brevi, 16.
[3] De vitâ beatâ, 26.

years afterwards an expiatory sacrifice was offered to the goddess, in sober earnest, on this very ground.[1]

Lucian, too, makes the Cynic Menippus tell how, in his youthful years, he had read much in Homer and Hesiod of the wars and quarrels of the gods, their adulterous gallantries, and acts of violence and robbery, all of which had seemed to him praiseworthy, and proved no little spur to him to attempt the like. But when he reached manhood, and found the laws forbidding such things, his embarrassment and doubt were great whether he should obey gods or lawgivers.[2] Ovid dwells on the strain, that women would do well to shun the temples of the gods, in order never to be reminded of Jupiter's doings or the adventures of the goddesses, and so be led into temptation.[3]

But it was not only in Homer and Hesiod people read these myths; it was not only in the nursery that they listened to them;—they were represented to the life in public spectacles, and the most voluptuous ones the most frequently. Already by the time of Socrates it was usual to give representations from the mystic history of the gods, to enliven the guests at a banquet. In the Symposium of Xenophon[4] there is a description of the mime of the loves of Dionysos and Ariadne, their courtship and union, being played before Socrates and his friends for the delight of the spectators. Afterwards, this art attained a high degree of perfection in the theatre. The Greeks invented a number of names for the different species of these mimic dances. The loves of Aphrodite with Mars and Adonis, the adventures of Ganymede, Danae, Leda, and others, were the subjects most in favour. These mimic entertainments had become so frequent in Rome by the time of the emperors, that the whole year was filled up with them, except the winter months: they were given as interludes, together with the drama proper, and proved the darling pastime of the populace; for their sensual attractions were excellently calculated as food for lustful eyes to dwell on. Such fables about the gods as related to the intercourse of the sexes, were represented by dancing men and women in expressive pantomime with a flute accompaniment. They wore a close-fitting dress, which showed the forms and motions of the whole body as completely as a state of nudity.

[1] Val. Max. i. 1, 16; Lact. ii. 16. [2] Luc. Menipp. 3.
[3] Trist. 2. [4] Symp. ix. 1, 5.

Juvenal paints vividly the effects produced upon the impressible spectators of both sexes;[1] and it was no exaggeration in Zosimus, after him, to find one of the principal causes of the decay of the Roman empire in these pantomimes.[2]

"The sacerdotal colleges and authorities," says Arnobius, "flamens, and augurs, and chaste vestals, all have seats at these public amusements. There are seated the collective people and senate, consuls and consulars, while Venus, the mother of the Roman race, is danced to the life, and in shameless mimicry is represented as revelling through all the phases of meretricious lust. The great mother, too, is danced; the Dindymene of Pessinus, in spite of her age, surrendering herself to disgusting passion in the embraces of a cowherd. The supreme ruler of the world is himself brought in, without respect to his name or majesty, to play the part of an adulterer, masking himself in order to deceive chaste wives, and take the place of their husbands in the nuptial bed." He then describes how the whole assembly rises, and makes the vast space of the theatre echo with a tumult of applause, when the gods themselves are bespattered with all the ridicule and contempt of these comedies:[3] and thus, says Augustine, the very gods were laughed to scorn in the theatres, who were worshiped in the temples.[4]

Now these games themselves were regarded and conducted as religious acts. They formed part of the festal solemnity, and were vowed to obtain a favour of the gods, as well as exhibited in expiation, when opportunity presented itself of appeasing and averting divine indignation manifested by natural phenomena. People really thought the gods themselves commanded these shows, or extorted them as if by threats. The very same assembly that assisted at them one morning, on the same or following day would glut themselves with the carnage of a gladiatorial fight. There again they all are reseated, priests and senators, ministers of state and their wives, and the vestal virgins and people of all ranks and classes, to drink in and dwell on the sweet draughts of human blood flowing in streams, and to feast their eyes on the gaping wounds and convulsive throes of dying men. Banishing mercy, they call to the champion to make an end of his fallen adversary, that none might escape by a feigned death. They lose all patience with the combatant if

---

[1] Sat. vi. 67 sqq. [2] Hist. i. 6.
[3] Arnob. iv. 34, 35. [4] De Civ. Dei, vi. 8.

one does not speedily breathe his last. And then fresh pairs must enter the arena at their call, so that no time be lost in satiating their eyes with blood. Thus the inhabitant of the vast city went round the cycle of his year in devilish alternations of lust and blood, and all to the greater glory of the gods.[1] He could vaunt that his entire life and his every enjoyment were one sustained act of divine worship.

What mimic art produced in the theatre, was reproduced in paintings on the walls of temples and houses. It is known full well what abundant material for obscene pictures mythology supplied. Religious-minded men, like Aristides, indeed, complained "of revolting and impious images being introduced into the very temples." Aristotle had recommended the authorities not to tolerate any obscene statues or images, but had nevertheless allowed of their use in the temples of those gods in whose worship the law connived at banter and buffoonery. At every step which a Greek or Roman took, he was surrounded by images of his gods and memorials of their mythic history. Not the temples only, but streets and public squares, house-walls, domestic implements and drinking-vessels, were all covered and incrusted with ornaments of the kind. His eye could rest nowhere, not a piece of money could he take into his hand, without confronting a god. And in this way, through the magical omnipresence of plastic art, the memory of his gods had sunk into his soul indelibly, grown up with every operation of his intellect, and inseparably blended with every picture of his imagination. There were, besides, it is true, representations not unworthy of the divine majesty, such as the Zeus of Phidias, which produced a profound impression, and elevated the thought to the deity. They were, however, but comparatively few. How many there must have been who never in their whole life fell in with such an image! How many, on the other hand, in whom the Ganymede, standing close by, awoke an opposite current of thought! And there was far too great a profusion of these lascivious and impure images. The youth of both sexes grew up constantly in sight of them; their first ideas of the gods were irretrievably coloured by them, and their imagination polluted. A Propertius[2] even allows a complaint to escape from him that modest virgins should be made acquainted far too early, through the house-images, with things that would otherwise have been

[1] Compare the life-like description in Lactantius, vi. 20.   [2] Eleg. ii. 5. 19-26.

hidden from them. And if he only looks at one side of the question, on the injury done to female modesty, Clement, a later writer, takes up the matter energetically in a religious point of view.¹ The naked Aphrodite, caught in the net with Ares, Leda and the swan, and the like, were, we learn from him, the favourite pictorial decorations of wall and ceiling. It was thus a show of religiousness was thrown round what was in principle only calculated to supply fuel to impure passions. According to Clement's expression, men treated with religious reverence these records of their shamelessness, because they were images of the gods at the same time.

As impurity formed a part of religion, people had no scruple in using the temple and its adjoining buildings for the satisfaction of their lust. The construction of many of the temples and the prevalent gloom favoured this. "It is a matter of general notoriety," Tertullian says, "that the temples are the very places where adulteries are arranged, and procuresses pursue their victims between the altars."² In the chambers of the priests and ministers of the temple, impurity was committed amid clouds of incense; and this, Minucius adds, more frequently than in the privileged haunts of this sin.³ The sanctuaries and priests of Isis at Rome were specially notorious in this respect. "As this Isis was the concubine of Jove herself, she also makes prostitutes of others," Ovid said.⁴ Still more shameful sin was practised in the temples of the Pessinuntine mother of the gods, where men prostituted themselves, and made a boast of their shame afterwards.⁵

It is well known what a bloody vengeance Tiberius took for a crime committed by Isis priests in Rome. Under the pretence that the god was enamoured of her, they had betrayed a Roman lady to the passion of a young Roman in the temple. A case of the kind happened in Alexandria afterwards. Tyrannus, a priest of Saturn, announced the orders of his god that certain beautiful women should spend the night in his temple. Their husbands trusted him; and the priest, who had concealed himself in the hollow image of the god, contrived to extinguish the lamps by drawing some strings, and then became the god's substitute.⁶

---

¹ Cohort. p. 53, Potter. ² Apol. c. 15.
³ Octav. c. 25. ⁴ Art. Am. i. 77; cf. iii. 393 sqq.
⁵ Firmicus is to be understood as speaking of these alone, when he uses the expression "in ipsis templis," without entering into further detail. De Err. Prof. Rel. iv. p. 64, Œhler. ⁶ Rufin. H. E. xii. 24.

Alexander of Abonotichos is a flagrant example of the excess to which credulity in marvels was carried in those times, and of what a practised impostor could cheat men into without fear of being unmasked. Alexander lived under Antoninus and Marcus Aurelius. In the Apollo temple at Chalcedon he buried tablets of brass bearing an inscription to the effect that Æsculapius would soon be coming to Abonotichos with his father Apollo. The tablets were laid where they could easily be found, and produced the effect, foreseen by Alexander, of intense expectation. An oracle, composed and circulated by himself, promising the advent of a divine prophet, with no obscure allusion to himself, assisted his enterprise. In the foundations of a new temple at Abonotichos, he hid an egg containing a young serpent. The next day he sprung, as if inspired, upon an altar in the market-place, and proclaimed to the people the immediate appearance of Æsculapius. He then extracted the egg from its hiding-place and broke it before the Paphlagonians, who exulted in the presence of their god among them in serpent form. The fame of the portent attracted multitudes to the spot. A few days afterwards, Alexander, who gave himself out to be a son of Podalirius, and therefore a grandson of Æsculapius, exhibited himself under the guise of a prophet, in a half-darkened room, with a huge tame serpent brought from Macedonia, which wreathing itself round his body, displayed a human head and black tongue; and this was the serpent-god Glycon, soon grown to his strength—the last epiphany of Æsculapius. The new god had his worship and oracle, and was represented in silver and bronze; and not only the whole of Paphlagonia, but Bithynia, Galatia, and Thrace streamed thither. Questions were transmitted to the prophet in sealed writing tablets, who knew how to open them unobserved by a secret legerdemain, and returned oracular responses in metre. Even Severian, the Præfect of Cappadocia, who was intending an expedition against the Parthian king, was fool enough to consult the oracle. In Rome too Alexander met with a warm reception; and Rubilian, a noble Roman, married his daughter, the fruit, as he pretended, of an amour with the goddess of the moon. He ransacked the entire of Asia and Europe, and was able to maintain in his temple a whole host of well-paid retainers, emissaries, scouts, composers of oracles, sealers, and interpreters. He also invented a new mystery festival, to last three days, in which were represented the bringing to bed of Latona, the birth of Apollo, of Æsculapius, and the new god Glycon, not forgetting his own love-intrigue with the goddess Luna. The towns of Pontus and Paphlagonia were required to furnish him the most beautiful youths for the service of his oracle, and for chanting the hymns, and these he shamefully abused. Many married women boasted of having children by him, and their husbands considered it a distinguished honour.[1]

An extraordinary combination of intellectual and bodily gifts were requisite to play the part which Alexander played with brilliant success for so many years, up to his death at an advanced age. His history may supply us with the data for calculating the vast numbers of religious impositions carried on by priest and wizard on a smaller scale in so fertile a soil. We are acquainted with a few of the numerous expedients most frequently employed in making gods, demons, and the dead, who had to be conjured up, appear. The believer was bid to look into a stone basin, filled with water, which had a glass bottom, and stood over an opening in the floor. The imaginary god was found below. Or a figure was traced on the wall, which was smeared over with a combustible composition. During the evocatio a lamp was imperceptibly brought close to the wall so as to set fire to the material, and a fiery demon was exhibited to the astonished believer.[2]

The apparition of Hecate was specially efficacious. Believers were told to throw themselves prostrate on the ground at the first sight of fire. The goddess of the crossways and roads, the Gorgo or Mormo wandering among the graves at night, was then invoked in verse, after which a heron or vulture was let loose, with lighted tow attached to the feet, the flame of which frightening the bird, it flew wildly about the room, and as the fire flashed here and there, the prostrate suppliants were convinced they were eye-witnesses of a great prodigy. Similar artifices were employed to make the moon and stars appear on the ceiling of a room, and to produce the effects of an earthquake. To make an inscription show itself on the liver of a victim, the haruspex wrote the words previously with sympathetic ink on the palm of his hand, which he kept pressed on the liver long enough to leave the impression behind. And so

[1] Lucian, Pseudomantis, 10-51. [2] Hippol. Philosophum, pp. 70-73.

the neo-Platonists contrived to cheat the emperor Julian when Maximus conducted him into the subterranean vaults of a temple of Hecate, and caused him to see an apparition of fire. By means of a grain of incense purified, and the low soft melody of a hymn, the same Maximus made the statue of Hecate smile, and torches light of themselves.[1]

The "Pneumatica" of Heron, who lived at Alexandria about the middle of the second century B.C., abound in this kind of lore. Here you have instructions how to build a temple so that, on the kindling of the fire on the altar, the doors open spontaneously, shutting again in the same way when it is extinguished; as also how, by lighting a fire on an altar, to contrive that two figures at the side of it should pour a libation on the flame, a serpent being heard to hiss at the same time. Plans are given for the construction of a vessel of sacrifice, the throwing of a piece of money into which makes water flow; as also how to manage that, on opening the door of a temple, the clang of a trumpet should be heard; and to build an altar, on which, while the sacrificial fire is burning above, dancing figures are shown in its under-part, which is transparent.[2] We see the variety of artifices with which the priests were conversant; and if any one is tempted to think that such transparent impostures could not fail of being detected, and of drawing down public disgrace, or what was still worse, on their contrivers, he has only to recur to the adventures of Alexander of Abonotichos, and a great deal that is similar, even among the phenomena of more modern times.

These impostures and juggleries are not to be estimated by a later and Christian standard, for it was an acknowledged principle, that it was both lawful and expedient to impose upon the people, to conceal the truth from them, and to confirm them in their errors by public speeches and state ceremonial. Accordingly, the pontifex Maximus Scævola declared it to be unadvisable to rectify popular religious notions as, for instance, to the deification of Hercules, Æsculapius, and Castor and Pollux, who were but mortal men; or as to the sexual distinction of the gods,

---

[1] Theodoret, H. E. iii. 3; Greg. Naz. Or. iv. 1. 1014; Eunap. Vita Max. p. 62, ed. Boisson.

[2] The Pneumatics of Heron, translated by B. Woodcroft, London, 1851, pp. 35, 37, 57, 83.

and holding their images in the temples to be truthful representations.¹ Varro, in the same spirit, would have a great deal of truth withheld from the people, and that the public weal required their continuance in their false notions.² With such principles religious impositions need not be thought of any great importance, as long as no one was hurt by them, and they really contributed to the maintenance of a trust in the power of the gods. The authorities never troubled themselves to investigate and to compromise the priests, and there were many instances of a neighbourhood or city suffering detriment when the reputation of its local sanctuary was diminished by a discovery of the kind. In the time of Pausanias the Eleans were still proud of Dionysos having visited them in person. Three empty cauldrons were placed in a cellar, and sealed up by priests in the presence of citizens and strangers; the next day they were found filled with wine by the god's own hand, a prodigy confirmed on oath by all present. At Andros too, every year, on the festival of Dionysos, wine flowed from the temple, as Pausanias was told, though Pliny only says the spring-water had a flavour of wine on the day.³ Servius mentions the temple of the mother of the gods being opened, not by the hand, but by prayer.⁴ Pausanias was eye-witness to smoke issuing of its own accord from the tomb of the Heraclid Pionis in Pioniæ every time a mortuary offering was made to it.⁵ These sacerdotal impostures seem to have been practised most frequently in the temples of Æsculapius and the Serapæa. The object was to support the credit of these places of healing, the priests on the spot taking care to hire poor people to feign suffering and disease of all kinds, and to pretend to be cured by a miracle wrought in one or other of these temples, or by an oracle therein communicated.⁶

One need not be astonished, then, that people appealed so confidently to these theophania, or various appearances of the gods, manifesting themselves to individuals; instances of which were rife, according to Celsus; whilst Origen tells us that Æsculapius still appeared to different persons.⁷ Maximus of Tyre speaks positively to having seen gods more than once. When educated people allowed themselves to be so imposed upon,

¹ Ap. Aug. C. D. iv. 27. ² Ibid. iv. 31. ³ Plin. H. N. ii. 106.
⁴ Æn. vi. 52. ⁵ Paus. ix. 18. 3.
⁶ Clementin. Homil. ix. 18. p. 691. ⁷ Contr. Cels. iii. 3.

we may conceive how easily in outlying country places counterfeits were produced of the visit of Paul and Barnabas to Lystra in Paphlagonia, where the cure of a palsied man by the former induced the inhabitants to adore them as Zeus and Hermes.

---

6. Oracles—Media of Divination—Dreams—Astrology.

An irresistible desire to pry into the future, and a belief that the will of the gods was made known through signs and prodigies, possessed the souls of men of these times. The old and scientific augural school of the Romans had indeed fallen into decay and discredit, and in the imperial period not much notice was taken of fowls eating or birds flying, or how the lightning fell; the Italian sortes, or divinations by tablets with inscriptions, which a boy mixed and then drew, as once practised at Caere, Falerii, Patavium, and Praeneste, had gone out, with the exception of those of the last-mentioned town. Cicero some time ago had explained them away as a patent imposture, which no officer of state or educated person would employ.[1] Afterwards, however, these sortes were again in greater demand.

The extinction of so many Greek oracles was a particularly striking feature in the last times of the republic and under the first emperors, and partially indeed before. In Bœotia, once so rich in oracles, that of Trophonius at Lebadea was alone in existence in Plutarch's days: the others were either silenced, or their sites completely desolate; and so the generality of those in Greece and Asia Anterior, as well as that of Ammon in Libya, were either defunct actually, or had sunk into contempt. This lasted till the time of Hadrian and the Antonines, when the pagan religion every where gave signs of returning vigour, and a more cordial coöperation in its votaries. Many oracles then revived, and became again places of resort and consultation. In particular we find that Delphi had been able to maintain an uninterrupted tradition, though with inferior pretensions, and a single Pythia instead of the three of better days. The oracles next in reputation to the Delphic were that of Claros near Colophon, which was only interrupted for a short time, for Germani-

[1] De Div. ii. 41.

cus, the nephew of Tiberius, consulted it,[1] and the oracle of the Branchidae at Didymi near Miletus. The responses here continued to be made in verse; and we learn from inscriptions, besides a prophetés, it had a poet of its own,[2] whose business it was to clothe the language of the prophetés in poetry; and still at times the answers were made in Homeric verse.[3] The prophetess at Didymi had, up to the later age of heathendom, to prepare herself by a strict fast of three days, by baths and solitary retirement in the sanctuary, so as to be already in an exhilarated state of ecstasy before she entered the oracular chamber or set her foot in the vapour of the spring. The case was the same at Claros, where the prophetés who returned the oracles was of the male sex. He too submitted to a lengthy preparation for the act, the ceremonies lasting some nights. He observed a strict seclusion, fasted a day and a night, and abstained from every dissipating occupation. On drinking of the spring he fell into a state of unconsciousness, in which he gave the responses without being seen by the consultants, and only came to himself by degrees, and without any remembrance of what he had said.[4]

The cave of Trophonius retained throughout its ancient power of showing visions. The oracle of Apollo at Argos was still standing in the time of Pausanias, where the priestess threw herself into an ecstatic state by drinking the blood of a lamb sacrificed.[5] After the middle of the first century B.C. Apollo also had an oracle in the island of Delos, where the answer was given in words, while that of Dodona employed only the sounds of vessels of brass for communication. In the East, besides the Cilician oracle of Mopsus, that of the sun-god at Heliopolis in Syria was of considerable repute. There the image of the god was borne on the shoulders of the priests, gave an answer in the affirmative by a forward motion of the bearers, and a negative by the contrary.[6] In Alexandria, Serapis not only revealed remedies in dreams, but at times gave responses in words. Both Æsculapius and Isis had numbers of places where incubation was practised; and that of Amphiaraus, at Oropus, of the same kind, where people slept on the fleece of a ram of sacrifice, and

[1] Tacit. Ann. ii. 54. [2] Inscr. Gr. 2895.
[3] Sozom. H. Eccl. i. 7. [4] Jambl. Myst. Æg. iii. 11, p. 73.
[5] Paus. ii. 24. 1. [6] Luc. de Deâ Syr. 36.

dreamt the cures of their diseases, was always reckoned one of the most frequented.[1]

The history of the oracle established by Alexander at Abonotichos is a proof of the insatiable credulity of the people of the second century, and of the strength of their passion for oracles. It cannot be matter of astonishment, then, that many of the decayed oracles revived, *i. e.* that persons were to be found to spread the report that the god, who had long kept silence, was now again graciously minded towards men, and wished to be consulted; and they took care accordingly that answers were given to such as applied. This was all the easier, as the questions usually put were only about ordinary matters of private life, and the god was no longer called upon to arbitrate upon political relations between rival states.

Nevertheless, the disappearance of many oracles, and the protracted silence of others, has still to be accounted for. There were oracles too, the Delphic, for instance, that were never interrupted, but which no longer maintained their old reputation for veracity, and more frequently took people in. Thus evasion had to be attempted before Cicero's time to account for the fact of the spot from whence the exhalation issued that inspired the Pythia having long lost its virtue. The Roman sarcastically replied, "This is as if one spoke of wine or salted fish which lose their flavour by time, whereas the question is of a divine, and therefore eternal and incorruptible, power."[2] There was, he thought, a simple solution of the problem, in people having become less credulous than of old. Plutarch, who had the credit of the oracles profoundly at heart, when as yet there were no appearances of their revival, attempted to frame a more acceptable and better-grounded explanation. Writing on "extinct oracles," he maintained that the inspiriting vapour which threw the prophetess into frenzy was by no means possessed of a virtue eternal and unalterable, but the contrary, and therefore that it might easily be dissolved by violent rain, or absorbed by lightning, or put an end to by an earthquake filling the chasm up. The oracle of Teiresias, at Orchomenos, had thus entirely ceased on account of a pestilence there.[3] He brought to his aid, as analogous, his favourite Platonic theory of intermediate beings, mortal demons; these, as presiding over particular localities,

[1] Paus. i. 35, 3. [2] De Div. ii. 27. [3] De def. Orac. 44.

might die, and the virtue of the oracle disappear simultaneously; and he quoted, as a case in point, the pilot of a ship in the time of Tiberius being hailed from one of the islands off the Ætolian coast, and being told to announce, on his arrival at a certain place, that the great Pan was dead, and that the message was given and received with a general lamentation.

But there were individuals who set themselves against all such apologies for the oracular system, and subjected them to a severe critical inquiry, while explaining the whole as imposture and jugglery. Chrysippus had done this before, in one of his works; and in the second century, a Cynic, Œnomaus of Gadara, in Syria, wrote an "Unmasking of the Jugglers,"[1] in which, in a popular style and tone, at times of irritation, at others of humour, he aimed at showing that these oracles had exercised a destructive influence so long as the Greek republics put themselves under their guidance, and in particular under that of Delphi; that they were often guilty of causing war and bloodshed, and that by ambiguous answers and inexplicable enigmas requiring another oracle to interpret them, they had imposed upon and befooled mankind. His own experience embittered him. Partaking himself, as he said, in the reigning folly, he had consulted the Clarian oracle about the true wisdom, and received an answer capable of application to any thing, the burden of which was a garden of Heracles always in full bloom. A bystander swore he had heard the identical response made to a merchant of Pontus who had consulted the god about his trade. Œnomaus then assailed a canonisation by oracle of a certain Cleomedes of Astypalæa, a common prize-fighter, and the flatteries and homage paid by them even to sanguinary despots, not forgetting the injunction laid upon the Methymnæans to worship a log, which the sea had cast up, as Bacchus.

Withering as this exposure might have been, still it seems to have had but little effect; for the publication of the book corresponds exactly in date with the new impulse which the oracles received. Maximus, a contemporary, speaks with respect of the oracles; and a historical work of Phlegon, a freedman of the emperor Hadrian, was stocked with answers of oracles fulfilled to the letter. The longing after divine revelations was far too powerful; and even though many responses had been proved to

---

[1] φωρὰ γοήτων. The fragments are in Eusebius, Præp. Evang. v. 19 sqq.

be false and base impostures, was that any reason for the rejection of all? and was pure gold to be thrown away as adulterated because found among coins of base metal? A number of oracles, brilliantly confirmed by the event, were in general circulation, all attempts to explain which, in a natural way, must be a failure; and the very persons who had been taken in by the oracles, attempted to satisfy their thirst of inquiry into the future by one of the numerous other media of divination then in fashion.

That some of these media at least, if not all, really performed what they pretended, few people then were inclined to doubt. Men will never make up their minds to believe in the worthlessness of that which they passionately desire and covet, and the aid of which seems indispensable to them. And this was the case with divination. Heathendom was utterly without religious teaching and teachers: no authority any where, only traditional ceremonies and myths. The gods were bound to speak, if men were not to despair; and as they did not do so through a doctrine revealed by a firmly-organised body of teachers, they necessarily did so by oracles and birds, liver or spleen of animal victims, by dreams and stars, and any thing at all capable of being moulded into a sign to which a meaning could be attached, and by which hope or fear could be fed.

Plutarch and Sextus Empiricus, though so opposed in other respects, both agree in their testimony that divination was universally honoured as a divine and infallible science.[1] To recommend and corroborate this view of divination, Celsus adds that it was borrowed from the beasts, which, as being endowed with a higher intelligence, had a foreknowledge of the future, and were more pleasing to the deity, with whom they stood in closer relations than man.[2] That sober investigator of nature, Galen, was himself an apologist for the possibility of predictions from the position of stars, the flight of birds, and the like.[3] In fact, the dominance of this error was a general yoke pressing on the men of that day, from which but very few were ever able to escape, and which formed a main support of the religion and worship of the gods. Cicero eloquently describes this thraldom.

---

[1] Plut. de Fato, p. 574; Sext. Emp. c. Mathem. ix. 132.
[2] Ap. Orig. c. Cels. iv. 88, p. 569, Delarue.
[3] In the treatise περὶ δυνάμεων φυσικῶν, i. 12.

"Wherever we turn, superstition follows us; be it soothsayer thou hearkenest to, or omen (that crosses thy path), suppose thou seest a sign in the victim, or the flight of a bird, thou must betake thyself to a Chaldean, or an *inspector of entrails;* the same if it lightens, or thunders, or a bolt fall, or any kind of prodigy is born or happens, all things, one or other of which must always be happening; so that man nowhere can be tranquil of heart, not even in sleep, for the greatest number of anxieties and alarms spring from dreams."[1]

The primitive belief, in fact, was, that dreams were sent men from the gods for their instruction, warning, and encouragement; and the whole history of antiquity is full of dreams, attaching to the weightiest and most decisive events. The same Chrysippus, who tore the veil of imposture off the oracles, took the trouble to make a collection of prophetical dreams in order to show their meaning. Neither Hippocrates[2] nor Galen[3] doubted of dreams being god-sends, or of there being men who understood the art of interpreting them; and Macrobius distinguished five kinds of dreams, two of which were exceptionable, and three prophetic.[4] With the Greeks the interpretation of dreams formed a complete literature of itself. Artemidorus, whose treatise on the subject is extant, assures us he compiled it at the express bidding of Apollo; and that the science of interpretation of dreams occupied him day and night.[5] Merely with the view of collecting dreams, he took long journeys into Asia, Greece, and Italy; and he furnishes precise instructions for the method of soliciting the grace of a prophetic dream from the gods.[6]

It was a dream that determined the emperor Augustus to appear one day every year in the streets of Rome as a beggar. Galba took the precaution to have expiation made for a dream that disturbed him. This, too, was deemed necessary to avert ill consequences that might result from menacing dreams, to resort to certain deities called the Averrunci, and offer them incense and salted cakes of meal.[7] Purifications were also submitted to, and the Greeks employed women for the purpose. When harassed by a dream, people bathed in the sea, remained sitting a whole day on the ground, wallowed in filth or besmeared themselves

[1] De Divin. ii. 72.   [2] Opp. ed. Van der Linden, p. 633.
[3] Opp. ed. Paris, 1679, t. vi. c. i. 3, 4, 5.   [4] In Somn. Scip. i. 3.
[5] Oneirocrit. ii. 70.   [6] Ibid. iv. 2.   [7] Tibull. i. 5.

with it.[1] Numerous records and inscriptions of these later times testify to the frequent apparitions of gods to their votaries in dreams, and expressing a desire for something or other, commonly a sacrifice. A nocturnal visit from Isis seems to have been the commonest of these inflictions.[2]

Astrology, one of the most clinging and obstinate diseases of the human spirit, was greatly in esteem from the influence of the star-gazers, the Chaldeans who came into contact with the West after Alexander's conquest, and of the Stoic philosophy playing into their hands. Starting from the principle of the unity of essence in God and nature, Stoicism had got so far as to consider the stars as eminently divine, and to place the divine government of the world in the unalterable determination of the course of the heavenly bodies. The heaven and its stars, the planets especially, passed with them for a book in which the events of earth and human destinies were written in a hand intelligible to the initiated; and the skill of the Chaldeans in deciphering these characters was the less doubted, as they professed to have studied them four hundred and seventy-three thousand years, up to Alexander's time. After him the Mathematici and Genethliaci, astrologers of the Chaldean and Egypto-Alexandrine schools, were dispersed over Asia, Hellas, and Italy. They agreed in teaching[3] that a secret virtue streamed incessantly from heaven to earth, and that a connection and sympathy existed between planets, in the heavenly bodies, and earth with its creatures; that human affairs entirely depend upon the stars, the planets especially being the rulers of their destinies: it is they whose operation is decisive in the birth, death, and actions of man; some of them, as Jupiter and Venus, are essentially benevolent; others, as Mars and Saturn, noxious; others again, like Mercury, of an undecided character, alternately doing good and harm. Their peculiarities are shared by the constellations which they inhabit, so that a cycle of action and reaction takes place among them, and their properties are modified and altered according to their mutual positions and aspects. The result of this is, that

---

[1] Plut. de Superst. 3.

[2] Comp. the Inscriptions collected in Marquard, in the continuation of Becker's Röm. Alterth. iv. 109, 110.

[3] Clem. Alex. vi. p. 813; Chaerem. ap. Eus. Praep. Ev. iii. 4; Sext. Emp. adv. Mathem. v. p. 338; Tetrabibl. ed. Norimberg, 1535, pp. 2 sqq. This work was long ascribed to Ptolemy, but is in any case older than that of Firmicus.

mixture of good and evil streaming from them upon earth, and the possibility of increasing the good, and averting the evil, by prayer and worship addressed to them. For in their dwellings, that is, within their distinct sphere of operation, the planets have greater powers than out of them, and they can be influenced accordingly by homage and vows of prayer. Hence particular astrological formulæ of prayer were composed and used in favour of certain emperors; for instance, Antoninus.

In the same spirit, people believed that by the horoscope or exact position of a star, taken at the moment of birth, the whole destiny of a man's life and his character itself could be calculated; little as there was to answer the adverse argument, as to those born under the same constellations exhibiting the most striking differences in character as well as fortunes. They were Greeks chiefly who practised this, as well as every other lucrative art. By the year A.U.C. 615, an edict of the Roman prætor P. Lænas was issued against them, bidding them quit Italy within ten days; but, thanks to the support of the Roman nobility, they were soon back again. To Pompey, Crassus, and Cæsar, they promised a long life of repose, and a late death in peace. Cicero expresses his astonishment that their numerous followers were not undeceived by the palpable falsity of their predictions. But confidence in them was still in the ascendant. People were convinced that they possessed in astrology a science in earnest, based on profound calculations and scientific and systematic combinations. The former edict of banishment was followed by another from Agrippa, in 721, without effect. Augustus, who forbade their speaking of life and death in their predictions, consulted the mathematician Theogenes before he ascended the throne. Tiberius and Otho had their private astrologers, though the former ordered one of his to be thrown down the Tarpeian rock, and another to be scourged and beheaded, "in conformity with ancient custom."[1] They retaliated on Vitellius, who had ordered them to leave Rome and Italy before the tenth of October, by predicting he would not himself see that day. Justly did Tacitus reflect on his countrymen, when he asserted that this kind of people, whom the great could not rely upon, and who deceived the hopeful, would always be found in the capital, in the face of all the edicts against them.[2] The perniciousness of their influence was most

---

[1] Tac. Ann. ii. 32. [2] Hist. i. 22.

sensible under **Domitian**, whose cruelty they stimulated through their artifices, at the same time showing him his victims, and how to strike the blow. Their predictions that he would be murdered filled him with the gloomiest suspicion, which cost a multitude of victims. He had the horoscope of many men of high rank cast, and ordered to execution all of whom he seemed to gather that they were born to greatness. At last Alexander Severus, notwithstanding the number of decrees against the astrologers, allowed them to open public schools in Rome.

7. MAGIC—NECROMANCY AND THEURGY.

Of a higher grade than astrology, magic occupied a position in closest relation with the pagan religion, and necessarily and infallibly developed out of it, in the most varied forms and ramifications. We cannot here undertake to give a complete account of all the experiments and practices forming the basis of magic, nor to distinguish how much, in this boundless field, was mere deceit and jugglery; nor again how far an abuse of mysterious powers of nature, which have not even yet been satisfactorily explored, or a formal worship of demons, was mixed up with it. Our task here is only to exhibit in some of its features the connection between magic and the heathen creed, and the collective moral and religious aspect of the period.

The Greek and Roman states, in addition to their public worship, had also sacrifices and ceremonies of secret observance, to which the special power was attributed of making the gods subservient to the will of man. This barrier betwixt the religion of state and magic proper being partially removed, we discover the magic character in particular rites and ceremonies, as, for instance, the Roman rites of the dead, in the formulæ of prayer, a matter which the Romans were so thoroughly conversant with, that the perceptible difference between a prayer and a charm was rather formal than essential. The Roman evocation of the gods falls entirely within the province of magic. We have already seen what an important position the magic element occupied in the Persian religion of Zoroaster by means of its dualism, its doctrine of Ahriman and his demons, and the operation of the herb Omomi. The same is true of the Egyptian religion, with its threatenings of the gods, its star worship, and the thoroughly magical character of its system of therapeutics. The same again is true of the Chaldeans, who were not satisfied with merely forecasting destiny by the constellations, but undertook to fix it by sacrifice and ceremony, and through these media to react upon the stars, avert foreseen calamities, or direct them upon others. Thus, from Persia, Babylonia, and Egypt, a tide of magic arts and usages set in towards the west, and mingled with the kindred rites and ceremonies which had been long previously in existence there.

The influence of philosophy contributed to this result. It is true the Stoic teaching, with its comprehensive and binding fatalism of a mere concatenation of physical causes, was not favourable to the development of magic art; but the Pythagorean system, on the other hand, was all the better suited for and disposed to it: in it was a supreme first cause, anterior to all quantity, though virtually comprising it, by means of which it was supposed possible for man, provided he knew how to put himself *en rapport* with them, to sway the laws and conditions of the physical world. Hence among the younger Pythagoreans, magic was quite identical with the genuine worship of the gods in its higher and purer forms; to their minds it consisted in the science and art of using certain means,—sacrifice, formulæ, and ceremonies,—so that the gods being carried away in the current of events, and implicated in the chain of physical causes, in accordance with man's desires and wants, changed that current in our favour: and not only gods, but demons, heroes, and souls of men, endowed with greater or less power over nature, in the different quarters of the universe which they were distributed amongst, could thus be made man's subjects, upon the Pythagorean principle that all beings with souls are homogeneous.[1] By reason of this homogeneity and affinity the spirit of man can act directly on higher natures, and attract them into the circle of its existence and its requirements; but as he has a double soul, that is, besides that which has emanated from the deity, a natural one, in affinity with other natural beings, so he is enabled, on the strength of this other soul, to exercise a magic power on nature.

[1] Porph. Vita Pythag. p. 13.

To this may be added the doctrine of demons, a favourite one of the later Platonists. Plato himself had referred mantic inspiration and magical effects to these higher beings of a mediate character.[1] The notion was, that they inhabited the region of air near the earth, having passions in common with men, so as "to be moved," in the words of Apuleius, "by anger or pity, enticed by presents and appeased by prayers, exasperated by insult and influenced by demonstrations of respect."[2] Plato's idea of demons was a higher one, nearer the Christian angel, perfectly good and loving men, yet accessible to sorrow and joy.[3] Xenocrates had been the first, as far as we know, to assert the existence of evil demons by the side of the good, spirits of gloom and hostile to man: and this too was the Stoic view. The result of this acknowledgment of it by religion and philosophy opened a wider field for magic. According to the object in view, white or black magic might be used, and good or malicious demons be addressed.

Magic in Greece was not an appendix to the worship of the Olympic gods, but in part to that of deities of foreign origination, in part to that of the subterranean ones, in whose train these demons were supposed to follow as ministering spirits. Foremost was Hecate, the genuine goddess of witchcraft, invoked by men in the preparation of charms to infuse irresistible virtue into them.[4] Further, the whole worship of the Phrygian mother of the gods was stamped with a magic impress; and the Metragyrtæ were among the most energetic, though the lowest and most mountebank adepts in witchcraft, and adroit enough to insinuate themselves every where.

Magical means were employed in striking others with disease or madness. Cicero mentions loss of memory as caused by them.[5] The craziness of Caligula was attributed to a potion he had been induced to swallow, which was intended to work as a philter.[6] Caracalla's frenzy, too, was considered to be the consequence of magical adjuration.[7] Love-potions were in great request at Rome, and were prepared with magical practices from the so-called hippomanes, a humour flowing from mares; wax-

---

[1] Conviv. p. 1191; Phædr. p. 1220.
[2] Apul. de Deo Socr. pp. 132, 147, Oud.
[3] Epinom. i. 984 sqq.
[4] Hor. Epod. v. 57; Sat. i. 8.
[5] Brut. 60.
[6] Juven. vi. 615.
[7] Dio Cass. lxxvii. 15.

images, too, for melting in the fire, and a vast variety of other charms, are on record, with an infinity of amulets and talismans for protection, engraved with mystical characters. Among formulæ of the kind, the Ephesian and Milesian words and names enjoyed the reputation of greatest efficacy. The former were characters engraved on the pedestal, girdle, and crown of the Ephesian Artemis, meaning "Darkness, Light, Earth, Year, Sun, True Sounds," and were worn engraved on a stone or ring as amulets.[1]

Necromancy had been domesticated in Asia as well as in Greece from primitive times, and was most intimately connected with the magical worship of demons. The Greeks early had their own oracles of the dead; for instance, the one consulted by Periander in Thesprotia, where secret arts were employed to compel the soul of a deceased person to appear and answer.[2] There was one of this kind in Italy at Misenum, on the lake Avernus. Their use was not only investigation of the future or hidden things, but also in appeasing the angry manes of such as had died a violent death. Maximus says[3] of the Italian one, that on the victim being slain, the libation poured forth, and the dead invoked, a form appeared, though dim and not easy of recognition, which, however, spoke, and disappeared on answer given. Besides these institutions, there were also a number of necromants, or psychagogues, who practised the art of adjuring the dead. Apion, the grammarian of Pliny's time, assures us he consulted Homer about his native land, but has suppressed the reply.[4] Appius, a contemporary of Cicero, gave himself up to these wizard arts of evocation;[5] and of the emperors, Nero[6] and Caracalla[7] practised them, the former on the score of his murdered mother, the latter to appease the spirits of his father and brother, all according to the rites once used by Thessalian psychagogues for the Lacedæmonians, in laying the ghost of Pausanias, whom they had put to death.

There is a proof of the great spread of this art of magic in the fact that people might publicly and avowedly practise it, provided they had no object of injuring others. Thus, Tibullus confesses to having resigned himself into a witch's hands in order to secure himself the love of his Delia. The hag purified him,

---

[1] Clem. Alex. Strom. p. 568; Hesych. s. v.   [2] Herod. v. 92.
[3] Diss. xiv. 2.   [4] Plin. H. N. 32.   [5] Tusc. i. 16.
[6] Suet. Ner. 34.   [7] Herodian. iv. 12. 3.

and made him sacrifice a black lamb by torch-light.[1] It was chiefly women, as was naturally to be expected, on the score of their more passionate temperament and deeper sense of their own weakness, from whom the countless tribe of wizards, male and female, drew their most credulous votaries. Thus the old man in Plautus enumerates amongst the disadvantages of marriage the constant calls of the wife for supplies of money to pay witches and interpreters of dreams, and people of that cast.[2] Magic was also resorted to for murdering others. The whole empire believed that Tiberius had thus caused the death of Germanicus. Parts of exhumed corpses were found on the floor of his house, charms and curses, tablets of lead inscribed with his name, bloody bones half scorched, and all the apparatus by which souls were devoted to the infernal deities.[3]

Wherever human sacrifice was offered, it was always either in direct connection with magic, or magical usages were coupled with it. Thus Pliny remarks the generality of the art in Gaul and Britain, and connects it with the Druidical human sacrifices; he even speaks of cannibalism among them. The Romans had children sacrificed principally with this object of witchcraft. The decree of the Senate in the year 97 B.C., forbidding human sacrifice, was probably meant to include boys and children; but the existing system of slavery made it impossible to carry it out to the letter. Cicero could cast into the teeth of Vatinius, " It is thy wont to evoke by adjuration the spirits of the dead, and to offer the bowels of slaughtered boys to the gods of the lower world."[4] Pliny said of Nero that there was no lack of human blood in the magical incantations to which he had given himself up for a time.[5] Catiline and the emperors Didius Julianus and Heliogabalus are all accused of child-sacrifice, Julian's object being to appease thereby the hate of the populace towards him. The emperor Valerian was prevailed upon by an Egyptian magician " to sacrifice the children of unhappy fathers, to disembowel new-born babes, and mangle God's creatures."[6] The same expressions are used by Juvenal of the haruspex of Commagene, who promised the lustful wife a lover or a rich inheritance :[7]

---

[1] Eleg. i. 2. 40-64. [2] Mil. Glor. iii. 1. v. 95-100.
[3] Tac. Ann. ii. 69 ; Dio Cass. lvii. 18. [4] Cic. in Vatin. c. 6.
[5] H. N. xxx. 2. [6] Dionys. Alex. ap. Eus. H. E. vii. 10.
[7] Sat. vi. 550.

" Pullets' breasts he ponders o'er, and the entrails of a whelp,
 And now and then a boy's."

There was a still more revolting custom, that of cutting the embryo child out of a living woman's womb, as did the tribune Pollentianus in order to conjure up the spirits whom he was curious to consult as to the successor of Valens.[1] Maxentius did the same at Rome.[2] After the death of the emperor Julian, a woman was found suspended by the hair and her body cut open in a temple at Carræ, which he had devoted to mysterious rites.[3] He was suspected of having committed the crime himself, but the priests of the place might have done it without his bidding. The custom itself was already described by Lucan.[4]

People of philosophical education used to speak with contempt of those magicians and wizards who were chiefly natives of Egypt, or had been schooled there, because their whole science was exposed for sale in the market-places for a few oboli; they pretended to expel demons from the possessed, to blow diseases away, to summon the souls of heroes, and made tables appear spread with sumptuous repasts, and figures of animals move as if animated.[5] But, with the exception of the Epicureans, it was not easy to find people who rejected magic *in toto* and in all its forms, or looked upon it as a mere imposture. Pliny seems to have regarded the greater part of it as worthless. He thought Nero had experienced the deceitfulness of these things, he having thrown himself with a passionate curiosity on the black arts of theurgy, and it being an easy matter for him to furnish all that the magicians gave out as necessary for the success of their experiments, human sacrifices, and sheep perfectly black, &c.[6] Artemidorus begins with the Pythagoreans, and goes through a long list of proficients in the mantic science, whose predictions he conceived should be considered as a cheat, for not one of the professors understood any thing of the true mantic art; while people were bound, on the other hand, to rely upon and accept the art, and the declarations of priests sacrificing, of the observers of birds, of interpreters of stars and dreams, and inspectors of livers. As to the mathematicians and genesialogists (horoscopists), he suspends his judgment, nor does he pronounce upon or enumerate the different species of true magic.[1]

The highest and most difficult part of magic was theurgy, the secret science so lauded by neo-Pythagoreans and Platonists, by which a man did not communicate with the lower and mediate beings or demons, but was enabled to enter into the presence of the very gods, and make them subservient to certain of his purposes. This was done by a purification of the lower soul, which was put through a severe discipline, cut off from the external world, and thrown back upon itself. An exact knowledge, under the strictest secrecy, of the right names of the gods, sacrifices, and forms of prayer, was requisite for success in theurgy. An acquaintance with the names adequately representing the properties of the gods was imparted by themselves to the theurgi of the time of Marcus Aurelius, Proclus assures us, and that in return for the use of these appellatives, the accomplishment of one's own desire was received from them.[2] Further, there were forms which served equally as passports for souls, and had, besides, such powerful influence upon the middle class of beings (demons) dwelling in the mid regions of the air, as to oblige them to give free passage through their demesne to souls winging their way through to heaven.[3] The magician philosophers of this discipline had their mysteries, into which their pupils were to be initiated step by step till they reached the contemplation of the gods manifesting themselves in a variety of forms, chiefly human, but not unfrequently too in formless light only.[4] Probably this did not mean a mere scenic phantasmagoria, but an artificial state, akin to magnetic clairvoyance, in which people found themselves surrounded with light, like that of the Byzantine navel-inspectors of the fourth century. It was not seldom these pretentious theurgic operations failed of effect, in consequence of some mistake or other having been made; and then, instead of the god invoked, beings of another kind, demonic, of grosser material and called Antithei, appeared to mock the ignorant with lying and illusive phantasms.[5]

[1] Oneirocrit. ii. 69.
[2] Procl. in Cratyl. p. 77.
[3] Arnob. ii. 62.
[4] Procl. in Polit. p. 379.
[5] Arnob. iv. 12; Iambl. Myst. iii. 31.

BOOK IX.

SOCIAL AND MORAL STATE OF GREECE, ROME, AND THE ROMAN EMPIRE.

I. THE GREEKS.

1. Citizenship—Greek versus Barbarian—Political Liberty—Idleness and Industry—Condition of the Rich—Slavery—Education.

The Greek was a political being in the strictest sense of the term. Citizenship and political freedom, consisting in a participation in the supreme power of the state, was his highest good. A complete dependence on the state, and the absolute surrender of the individual member to the body, was the sentiment that had grown with his growth, and formed the groundwork of his moral being. The sum of his duties was to merge his personality in the state, and to have no will of his own distinct from that of the state. What position an individual was to occupy in the community was not left to his good pleasure, but was traced out beforehand for him. And, properly speaking, there was no department within which a Greek could be justified, according to his judgment, in free action merely as a man; and wherever the good of the individual clashed, or seemed to clash, with the welfare of the whole, in that case he must yield and fall a sacrifice; he and his rights were trampled underfoot. Hence ostracism in Athens, Megara, Miletus, and Argos, and petalism in Syracuse.

The Greek idea of justice, then, may be summed up in this,

that all was right and just that benefited the state. Morality and virtue consisted in the conformity of one's own will with that of the community, in capacity for its service and for advancing the public weal in the highest degree. The religiousness of the Greek partook of the same political character; the worship of the gods was accurately prescribed and enjoined on each member of the state, itself of divine constitution; and its precepts were fulfilled for the sake of the community, and as a political duty.

There was no such thing, however, as a Greek confederation, but only small and separate states, generally with a single city and a limited territory. All the Greeks felt themselves united by their common language and customs, and an identity of religion and national character, in opposition to the barbarians, *i.e.* all non-Hellenic nations. They had an instinctive feeling of their intellectual superiority to all these people, many of whom had never attained to a regular social life, while others lived in shameful and degraded servitude. Even the Egyptians, whose ancient traditions and sacerdotal wisdom they held in a high esteem; the Carthaginians, whose constitution an Aristotle condescended to panegyrise and thought worthy of comparison with the Greek;[1] Phœnicians, Etruscans, Macedonians, and Romans, —were all stigmatised by the Greeks as barbarians. They believed themselves in possession of all the qualities combined, but one of which at most distinguished the above-mentioned nations. Though there was much they had received secondhand from other nations, they claimed the glory of having always perfected what they received, and inserted it, as a well-fitting member, into the organism of a civilisation that embraced the whole of man. Hence, Maximus of Tyre compared a soul delivered from the body and transferred to a higher region to a man who had passed from a barbarian land into the Hellenic soil;[2] and Socrates gave expression to the general feeling in his countrymen when he thanked the gods daily for being man and not beast, male and not female, Greek and not barbarian.

The hostility of the Hellenes and barbarians was natural and necessary.[3] The Greek, at least his orators and poets told him so, was fitted by nature and appointed by the gods to be

---

[1] Pol. v. 10.   [2] Diss. xv. 6.
[3] Plat. Rep. v. 170; Demosth. adv. Mid. 40.

lord over the barbarian. As to the expressions of individual philosophers, Democritus, Socrates, and Plato, that the contrast between Greek and barbarian was by no means so decisive, and that there was a cosmopolitan view, fully borne out by fact, which regarded humanity as an organic whole,—they were not recognised by the Greeks in general, to whom the word "humanity" was a stranger. In the letters ascribed to Apollonius of Tyana, and probably written under Christian influences, we first meet with the expression that it is of obligation to regard the whole world as one's fatherland, and all men as brothers and friends, bound together by community of descent.[1]

There was therefore no question about the barrier of an international law with reference to barbarians; the inviolate character of ambassadors is perhaps the only exception, and that was not acknowledged as a principle, and was often, in fact, infringed. But besides, there were no recognised equitable relations between the several Greek states, and in their intercourse with one another, "might makes right" was the real order of the day; and no circumlocution was needed to envelop the plain maxim, that man's real mission was the subjugation of his fellow-man to prevent his own;[2] or, as Pericles put it to the Athenians, that one may confidently despise the hatred of others only when one is dreaded by them.[3] The gods themselves, as the Athenians said to the Melians, had given men the example of the stronger turning his power to account in keeping down the weaker.[4] Yet in the second century, the rhetorician Aristides gave the name of sophists and pedants to those who pretended to doubt this law of nature, that the strong man should use his power to trample on his inferior.[5] Now the Greeks in their international dealings carried out this law, the only one that they knew and acknowledged, with a hardness of heart and mercilessness sufficient to make one who is acquainted with their history ask the question, if deceit and cruelty were not deeply-graven traits of the Greek national character? Wholesale executions, the exterminating of entire populations, the sale of women and children as slaves, were all practised by Greek on Greek, not in the transient madness kindled in combat, but in cold-blooded deliberation after victory, and on a calculation carefully made beforehand; and de-

[1] Ap. Philostr. p. 395; Ep. 44.   [2] Thuc. i. 76, 77.   [3] Ibid. iii. 37-40.
[4] Thuc. v. 105.   [5] Aristid. Panathen. 1288, Dind. cf. Or. xliv. 1. 835.

mocracies and aristocracies, Athens and Sparta, rivalled one another therein. And as the selfish love of domination and gain did not only arm state against state, but also introduced the spirit of division and party-faction into the several states, so the absorption of individuality which we have delineated above was far the most frequently exhibited under the form of an envenomed hatred between democrat and aristocrat, in which but few succeeded in extricating themselves from taking a side. Fortunate it was for the worsted faction when it was only exiled and plundered, but escaped death, for only a few instances occurred of this. The selfishness of party quenching all spirit of community soon aroused an individual selfishness fatal to every nobler aspiration; and hence, as Aristotle records, the oath by which the oligarchs bound themselves in their clubs to a perpetual hostility to the demos, and to do it all the harm they could.[1] Isocrates complains of there being more banished and proscribed people from a single state than from the whole Peloponnese in older times.[2] And thus Greece swarmed with homeless outlaws, collecting in troops of banditti to plunder and waste, and serving any chance master as mercenaries. The freedom and independence of states, and along with them the whole groundwork of Greek morality, were utterly and irrecoverably lost. "All," said Aristotle, "desire justice to be done themselves, but in their relations to others the question of justice is unheeded."[3]

In antiquity, and among the Greeks in particular, the idea of freedom differed *toto cœlo* from that of later Christian nations. In antiquity either not a notion of a conscience appears, or one very unlike the Christian one, and therefore the freedom, which was coveted and realised, was quite a different thing. Christendom has blended the moral and religious consciousness of man into an indissoluble whole; and this moral principle in him, informed and regulated by religion,—this consciousness of the most scrupulous responsibility, in regard of every action, to an omniscient Creator,—is called his conscience, and is fundamentally, or ought to be, the sole ruler and lawgiver in practical conduct. Through this, and over against the power of the state, which, being independent for itself, cannot possibly be the rule of his conscience, there is within man's bosom an indestructible ne-

[1] Pol. v. 7, 19.   [2] Archidam. 68.   [3] Pol. vii. 2, 8.

cessity for, and effort after, autonomic action and comprehensive self-determination. He then understands by liberty the greatest admissible enlargement of those spheres in which, according to his light, and following simply the voice of his conscience, he can exercise command untrammelled by political or official tutelage. He requires to manage his own affairs personally, or in corporate union with men of like mind and will; to maintain and pursue his own interests; while he regards as the state's proper function to keep its distance from, and respect, this province of his own free self-determination, and to protect him and it, without interference or tutelage, through the forms of administrative justice and the shield of power.

Quite different was the Greek's case. First and foremost he felt himself to be a member of a small corporate body, with a horizon easily commanded, and interests patent to the eyes of all, the welfare of which was most intimately bound up with his own. His moral convictions were influenced by religion in but a few points. The greater part of his moral conduct, when he had given the gods their own in regard of their traditional sacrifices and ceremonies, had little to do with them. Morality and goodness to him were limited to what was expedient to the well-being of the state, and also to the well-understood interest of the individual at the same time. Any other canon, such as might consist only in a conscience guided, even in minutiæ, by faith, there was none, properly speaking. The end, the state's good, sanctified the means; and in matters to which this general good could in any way be extended, the desire of being free, and of following a subjective and selfish direction, was like a contradiction to a Greek mind, and bore every appearance of an egoistic intention and one hostile to the state. Thus there was no sphere of life in which the individual wished to be, or knew himself, completely extricated from the grasp of the state. He felt not the prescription of the state as an oppressive yoke, for he had his own share in the creation of the law by which it was governed; he was joint sovereign. The succession might happen to include him, to take his own part, as magistrate, in carrying the law into effect: there was no distinct order of state officers, acting on views and interests of their own. In antiquity, therefore, freedom was synonymous with participation in the power of the state, together with a conviction of being a subject, in common with others, of the laws that proceeded from the votes of a majority, however deep those laws might penetrate into private life. The will of the state, of the majority that is, was the will of the individual; the laws themselves being so many contracts by which all were mutually obliged of their own accord to one certain mode of action. The minorities, in case of being out-voted,— the rich, for instance, if a law was carried in the interests of poor and less substantial members,—had no resource left, no freedom more. They had got the worst of it, and were obliged to submit to the law of the conqueror in its full measure. Protection there was to be had in a Greek state for individual as against individual, but there was none as against the state or the majority.

It is well enough known to what lengths state tutelage and restrictions on the whole of social life were carried in Sparta. Speaking in the strict modern acceptation of the word, and according to our own feelings, the Spartan was the being of all the world furthest from freedom conceivable, though he indeed was quite of another mind. The laws of Zaleucus and Charondas subjected ordinary intercourse with bad citizens to a penalty;[1] and the use of unmixed wine without the leave of a physician was visited actually with death.[2] Athenian law had decided how often a month a husband should sleep with his wife;[3] and hence, too, self-murder, regarded as a robbery of the state, had the penalty of atimia (public disgrace) imposed upon it, and at Athens, for example, was punished with the cutting off of the right hand.[4]

Consistently with this view, the state enjoyed an indefinite right to the property of its members. The lawgiver in Plato declared, "Ye yourselves are not your own, still less is your property your own: you belong collectively to your whole family, and still more does your collective family appertain to the state."[5] On this principle the Spartan constitution was founded, and went so far in the limitation of ways of gain as to forbid the possession of silver under the pain of death, and no trade or commerce could be pursued. There, then, the *far niente*, the exclusively national education for war, and the perpetual community life among the men, admitted of no manner of

---

[1] One could indict another for κακομιλία, Diod. xii. 12.
[2] Athen. x. 33.
[3] Plut. Sol. 27; Amator. p. 769.
[4] Aristot. Eth. Nic. v. 11.
[5] Legg. xi. p. 923.

earning money by business. The fall of the Spartan republic was, all the more inevitably, the consequence of impoverishment —in the year 240 B.C. their whole landed property being found in the hands of one hundred individuals—and the exhaustion of the male population.

In Athens, where the conduct of the state was wholly in the hands of the popular assembly, the poorer class by its majority of votes had completely the upper hand of the rich, and threw all the government expenses upon them, causing themselves to be maintained, and entertained with gorgeous festivals, processions, and dramatic shows, at the cost of the state, *i.e.* of the rich and of their allies. Athens was a paradise to the poorer citizens. They received pay for attending the Ecclesia; and as Heliasts shared in largesses of corn, and were pampered with sacrificial and festal banquets. The demos understood the squeezing of the rich like sponges by means of liturgies, choragic, gymnasiarch, archithcoric, and trierarchic, the last of which, especially the equipment and maintenance of ships at sea, was the chief cause of the ruin of many great fortunes. Another, and still more ruinous, expense was brought on the rich by the administration of justice being in the hands of the poor, as it were a sword suspended over the heads of men of property by a hair, which the others had only to cut. Exclusive of the Areopagus, there were at least ten tribunals in existence, in which the poor, always a majority, were judges, and where they feasted their eyes upon the misery of the defendants in trembling expectation of their sentence, and scarcely protected by juridical forms.

The Greeks had neither jurisprudence nor jurisprudents. All the law they had was subject to manifold change, from the changing minds or humour of the majority making the law, and it was therefore unfitted for scientific treatment; by far less stress was laid on the strict observation of protective forms with them than with the Romans. The judges, of course, were all the more at ease, and the use they made of their judicial power was all the less considerate, influenced often by jealousy, hatred, selfishness, and party interest.[1] The orators, as might be expected, frequently omitted to appeal to the sense of justice in

---

[1] Cf., e.g., Isoc. c. Lochit. Or. Att. ii. 475; Demosthenes also in his speech against Midias. The same is frequently met with in Isæus, e. g. Orat. Att. iii. 52.

the judges, and addressed themselves directly to their interest and passions. The legal obligation on every citizen to bring any one to trial who seemed to them to have inflicted an injury on the state, opened a wide door to the disorders caused by sycophants, those bloodhounds of the democracy, who, while they frowned on the demos, drove at the same time a thriving trade by prosecutions. Matter for such could not fail to be found in the vague term of the "welfare of the state." The accused, it often happened, was not once admitted to speak in his own defence.[1] Sometimes the fines were paid to the judges themselves,[2] though they generally fell to the state, and thus they returned, at least indirectly, into the hands of the judges. The rich were therefore driven to buy themselves off from the sycophants' threats of prosecution, and conceal their wealth, and keep the demos in good humour by gross flattery and lavish expenditure. Men, generally speaking, whom predominance of personal character or fortune exposed to the jealousy and cupidity of their neighbours, had no security nor any tolerable existence in a city where a despotic democracy acknowledged no law above itself, and a precarious majority of votes passed decrees, involving the life and property of citizens. Men therefore of that class drew off and lived out of the way, only showing themselves now and then, after long intervals, in their native city. This was particularly observable during the last years of the Peloponnesian war, and the period subsequent to it, down to the extinction of the independence of Athens.

Aversion to work, and propensity to idleness, is a characteristic trait of the ancients. Mechanical trades and industrial occupations were held in special contempt. "The Germans," says Tacitus, "cannot endure repose, and yet are fond of inactivity. They consider it *lâche* and dishonourable to earn by the sweat of their brow what they can win by the sword. They hand over the care of house and field to women and old and infirm people, sleep and the banquet forming their own pastimes."[3] The Gauls too looked down upon every kind of labour, agricultural included.[4] The people of Tartessus, in Spain, appealed to a law of their first lawgiver, Hatis, by which manual labour of any kind

---

[1] Isocrat. de Antid. Oratt. Att. ii. 351.
[2] Demosth. c. Aristogit. 1; Or. Att. v. 92.　　[3] Germ. xiv. 15.
[4] Cic. de Rep. iii. 6.

was forbidden to citizens, and reserved for slaves.¹ The Lusitanians and Cantabrians intrusted all works of necessity to their women and slaves, and preferred living themselves by plunder.²

Herodotus, speaking of the Greeks, says he does not know whether they borrowed the contempt with which they regarded work from the Egyptians, as he found the same to be the case amongst Thracians, Scythians, Persians, and Lydians, and that by the larger proportion of barbarians the learners of mechanical arts, and their children too, were looked down upon as the lowest order of the state. All Greeks, the Lacedemonians especially, were educated in this idea.³ It was not, of course, the mere handiwork of itself that brought this stigma upon trades, but the notion of the pay they are recompensed by, rendering the workmen dependent on the buyer or orderer.⁴ In many states, and Sparta especially, manual labourers were excluded from offices and political privileges; and a citizen of Thebes must have given up handicraft at least ten years to enable him to take part in the government.⁵ People thought the pursuit of manual labour only fitted for slaves and non-citizens; and the free labourer was already degraded in the eyes of others by having slaves for competitors. Sedentary occupations, keeping aloof from the agora and the gymnasia, and defective education, combined to render the idea of the banausos and banausia in the highest degree distasteful in Greek eyes, and every paid work of the hand vulgar and mean.⁶ Such folk could not be reckoned good men and true as passed their life not in the open air, but sitting still in close shops.⁷ The Corinthians alone formed a remarkable exception, as Herodotus already remarks. Hence, in Athens, commerce and trade were pursued by strangers, or carried on by wealthy people through their slaves, or hired operatives almost on the level of slaves. There was no real middle class. The first thought of the poorest Athenian citizen was to be free, *i. e.* idle, and to trouble himself only with business of state, and to be supported by the state. The day was spent in the agora, in the assemblies of the people, the courts of law, the gymnasia, and theatres. Of twenty thousand Athenians, Demosthenes tells us every one spent his time in the agora, and was occupied there

---

[1] Justin, xliv. 4.   [2] Ib. xliv. 3.   [3] Herod. ii. 167.
[4] Aristot. Pol. iii. 2, 8.   [5] Ib. iii. 3, 4; vi. 4, 5.
[6] Ib. viii. 2; Plat. Rep. vi. 495, ix. 590.   [7] Xen. Œc. iv. 2.

either with public or private business.[1] The democracy had abrogated the earlier laws, restraining idleness as an attack upon their independence. It was not till sunset a man repaired to his house, which was used but as a shelter for the night.

Trade, then, and commerce on a small scale, were left in the hands either of slaves or of domiciled settlers, called metœci, who, though Hellenes (non-Hellenes being always reckoned as barbarians), had no rights, could acquire no landed property, and therefore were excluded from all privileges attaching to such property, were not allowed to intermarry with citizen families, and always required the protection and mediation of a native patron to obtain justice. Every Greek was a stranger from the moment he set foot without the walls of his town or the territory of his petty state.[2] So a special contract was needed merely to enable the two inhabitants of different Cretan towns to intermarry.[3] In modern states, naturalisation places the stranger on an equality with the citizen, and a second generation usually makes the fusion complete; in antiquity disadvantages and exclusions continued to be visited on the descendants of immigrators. But, in fact, the condition of a stranger in Hellas was far better than in the East, where—in Egypt and Persia for instance—he was held to be impure, religiously speaking, and his society defilement; besides, hospitality, as practised towards travellers, and in the mutual relations of states, was held sacred by the Hellenes, and contributed to soften down many asperities in the law regarding strangers; least, however, in Sparta, where the law of xenelasia entirely prevented the settlement of strangers, and frequently too mere visits.[1]

Slavery was the foundation on which the whole social and political life of the Greeks was based. Doubt as to the equity and advantage of such an arrangement never entered into a Greek mind; it was a self-evident case; the idea of another state of things was impossible to conceive; and what would have become of Greek civilisation, Greek power and independence, if slave-labour had to be suppressed, and men to work themselves, or let themselves out to hire for others? There is no perfect

---

[1] Demosth. Aristog. i. 51.

[2] Böckh's Public Economy of Athens, i. 151; on the authority of Demosth. pro Phorm. 6.

[3] Sainte Croix, Législ. de la Crète, p. 358.   [4] Plut. Lycurg. 27.

household state, according to Aristotle, that does not consist of slaves and freemen, the slave being but an animated instrument, as an instrument is a slave without a soul.[1]

The Stagirite has, in fact, left us a complete theory of slavery, as an institution founded on the nature of social order. Slavery, according to him, is necessary, as a true household could not exist without slaves; and it is equitable, as corresponding to a natural law,—the greater part of the human race, the barbarians to wit, being born slaves, whom it beseems only to be governed and to obey, and who, being in reality minors, were furnished with but just wit enough to comprehend orders. Slaves and domestic animals supply our requirements with their bodies, with but a slight shade of difference. And as the master stands towards his slave in the relation of an artist to his tools, and as the soul to the body,[2] he cannot have much more love for him than for his horse or his ox, for there is nothing in common, and no equity between the parties. Still Aristotle remembers that a slave is also a human being; and overlooking the contradiction in this compulsory distinction, is of opinion that the master may feel friendship for his slave in so far as he is man.

The number of slaves was considerably greater than that of the freemen. The census of Demetrius Phalereus showed a sum total of 20,000 citizens, 10,000 metics, and 400,000 slaves, in Attica;[3] this not including female slaves, who were, however, much fewer than the male. In Sparta there were 36,000 citizens, 244,000 helots, and 120,000 periœci, whose condition only differed from the helots' in their masters not having power of life and death over them, or selling them off the land. There were 460,000 at Corinth, and, at one time at least, 470,000 in Ægina. Of these, the great proportion were employed in agriculture, in mines, and manufactures. They were in part descendants of the ancient inhabitants of the land, who had been conquered, and in part were purchased in the slave-market, a regular appendage to every town of importance. Others were slaves born in the house, children of its master by a slave-woman or of slave-marriages, which, though generally no formal unions took place between slaves of both sexes, were sometimes allowed as a favour by the master,[4] yet were not legally acknowledged or pro-

[1] Polit. i. 3; Eth. Nic. viii. 13.   [2] Eth. viii. 13.
[3] Athen. vi. p. 272.   [4] Xen. Œc. ix. 5.

tected, it being always open to the master to sever the tie, if the slave could not. It was generally found more economical to purchase able-bodied adults than to educate them from childhood; the more so, as these house-born slaves, or œcotribes, were looked down upon as of little use. Those purchased were exposed for sale, naked, in the market; of whom some were prisoners of war, not unfrequently Greeks; others had fallen into this condition from piracy or kidnapping. In most cases, however, prisoners of war, being Greeks, could ransom themselves: perhaps a tenth of the slaves may have been Greeks, reduced by war to servitude; and these were either without the means of redeeming themselves, or an embittered feeling denied it them. Metics, not paying their taxes or without a patron, suppositious children, and strangers who had usurped the rights of citizens, all equally passed under the hammer. The large proportion of slaves constantly purchased were barbarians, Carians, Phrygians, Thracians, and Cappadocians. The principal slave-markets at Chios, Samos, Cyprus, Ephesus, and Athens supplied the whole of Greece. The Cilician pirates, in Strabo's time, disposed of myriads of slaves at Delos in a day.[1] The poorest Greek, if not utterly destitute, kept his one or two slaves; and was invariably attended by one, or if of better condition by several, when he went out of doors.[2] It was not the custom for women to leave the house without several female slaves.[3] Plato takes it for a general rule,[4] that every wealthy man at Athens possessed more than fifty slaves; such a man could say with Democritus, "I treat my slaves as members of my body, and put each one to a different use."[5]

On the whole, the condition of the Greek slave was not so bad as that of the Roman: it was best at Athens,[6] where the constitution guaranteed him many privileges, only reserved for freemen elsewhere.[7] The beating of foreign slaves was forbidden there; and in dress and external appearance, their hair inclusive, they were not distinguishable from their masters. The master could not put his slave to death, but he could ill-

---

[1] Strabo, vii. 467. [2] Athen. vi. 88. [3] Ibid. xiii. p. 582.
[4] Rep. ix. p. 578. [5] Stob. Floril. lxii. 45.
[6] And worst at Sparta (Plut. Lyc. 28); the best place to be a freeman, the worst to be a slave. (Th.)
[7] Xen. de Rep. Ath. i. 12.

treat him if he chose. Many thousands worked in the mines in chains.[1] When severely treated, the slave could take refuge at an asylum, like the Theseum, or at an altar, and excite the people to take compassion on him, and procure his being sold to another master.[2] Runaway slaves were frequently branded on the forehead.

The situation of the serfs of the state differed in many respects. These consisted, for the most part, of the older conquered and subjugated inhabitants of the soil,—the Penestæ, for example, in Thessaly, the Bithynian Mariandyni in Heraclea of Pontus, and particularly the Helots in Laconia. The state gave private persons the use of the latter, but they could neither be sold nor emancipated. They had families and a dwelling of their own, but were compulsory servants to their masters, whom they had to supply with agricultural produce to a fixed amount. All the ancients agree in describing their lot as a frightfully hard one. Whether the particulars entered into by many of them—for instance, the historian Myron[3]—are correct, and detail a permanent condition or not, is extremely doubtful. If it was really the custom to scourge them once a year for no offence, but only to remind them they were slaves, and to oblige them to wear a degrading dress, it is hard to understand how the Spartans could employ them on expeditions as soldiers so frequently. It is certain that the cryptia were not formally intended as sanguinary raids upon the helots; yet it would appear that many of those who were surprised in the streets, in spite of the notice given, were put to death in the barbarous chase. It is a fact, however, that the helots, and the penestæ in Thessaly, were always ready to take advantage of any calamity occurring; while the Spartans, on their side, were ever on the alert, watching their helots as dangerous foes, and sometimes trying to weaken them by a massacre. In the Peloponnesian War two thousand of the bravest of these helots were declared free, but all were afterwards quietly put out of the way by assassination. This is why the hatred of the helots and all the other slaves rose against their masters to such a degree, that, according to the testimony and expression of an eye-witness in 397 B.C., they would gladly have torn every Spartan in pieces, and eaten him alive.[4]

[1] Athen. vi. p. 272.
[2] Plut. Thes. 36; Poll. vii. 13.
[3] Ap. Athen. xi. p. 657.
[4] Xen. Hell. iii. 3. 6.

When a slave had to give testimony before a court of justice, his deposition was always accompanied by torture; a custom quoted with approbation by all the Attic orators, Lysias, Antiphon, Isæus, Isocrates, Demosthenes, and Lycurgus. What the oath was to the freeman, torture was to the slave; except that the latter was generally regarded as the more reliable expedient of the two.[1] Very little confidence was placed in the oath of a witness at Athens. Dependence was placed only on the evidence of a slave given under torture, and that whether it concerned the public or private citizens.[2] Demosthenes was always for resorting to this expedient; it was the last and most effectual resource, which, when he had exhausted his other stock of proofs, he reserved for the end as decisive.[3] The accused offered his slaves for torture, and the accuser demanded it, pretty much in the same way as an oath is tendered to the opposite party nowadays. To elude the demand was dangerous. When Andocides refused to submit one of his slaves to this proof, all the world held him convicted of the crime on which he was charged.[4] Female slaves were equally exposed to this barbarous treatment with the males, sometimes even more, when the question was one of domestic misdemeanour, the details of which they were supposed to be more likely to know. If the slave came out of the torture maimed, or otherwise in bad plight, at the most a pecuniary recompense was made to his master.[5]

The prevailing notion was, that every slave's soul was fundamentally corrupt, and that no one in his senses could trust a slave.[6] Philosophers, such as Plato, were against keeping many slaves of the same country and language; they were to be dealt with rigorously and chastised sedulously; remonstrance was only employed to spoil them; simple words of command should be used to address them.[7] Plato, too, regarded it as one of the marks of an educated man, that he despised his slaves.[8] The state of the poor slave was all too well adapted for making this contemptible being of him. As a general rule, he was furnished with but two springs of action, fear and sensuality; and the employment of his life was to carry out the latter in all its branches,

---

[1] Antiph. p. 778. [2] Isocr. Trapezit. 27; Isæus de Nared. Ciron. p. 202.
[3] Demosth. contra Aphob., Oratt. Att. v. 136.
[4] Plut. Vit. x.; Orat. Andoc. iii. p. 384. [5] Demosth. c. Near. p. 1387.
[6] Plat. Legg. vi. p. 777. [7] Ibid. p. 778. [8] Rep. viii. 549.

and revel in every form of vice, gluttony, drunkenness, and wantonness, cheating and robbing his master, and yet so as to avert vengeance from his own head. The moral disadvantages of this relation were equally prejudicial to the master as to the slave. The Greek knew right well that all unlimited and irresponsible power over others was the moral ruin of a man, the certain development of the vices which it fed and fanned, arrogance, perpetual suspicion, anger to infuriation, and lust: these effects they painted in their tyrants in strong relief. And yet they could not see that every slave-owner was a petty tyrant, though they had abundant evidence of the worst of despotism every day before their eyes in slavery and its consequents. If it was the master's pleasure to debauch his male or female slave, resistance was naturally impossible to conceive. Tired of his slave-concubine, he would make her over to the Pornæum,[1] let her out for hire, or sell her to a brothel-keeper. It was no uncommon thing for female flute-players to be sold during a drinking-bout, and even to pass through several hands.[2] It was considered a duty of hospitality to provide the stranger-guest a female house-slave to pass the night with;[3] and even when she obtained her freedom, no other resource, generally speaking, was left her than to stay where she was, or to embrace prostitution.

The education of youth was one of the domestic relations in which the prejudicial operation of slavery made itself sensibly felt. The education of the child during its first years of life was the business of the mother and the female slaves of the house. From boyhood upwards to his seventeenth year, the father gave his son a pedagogue, who was a slave, who attended the youth every where, took him to school and to the palestra, and particularly had to guard him against the corruptions of paidcrastia. For this purpose a slave was frequently selected whose bodily infirmities and advanced age rendered him incapable for other duties; and thus Pericles himself assigned as pedagogue to his ward Alcibiades the gray-headed Zopyrus, the most useless of his slaves.

School education was general even in the villages; but the state did not meddle with masters and schools, which were treated as matters of private concern. There was no public instruction in the modern form. Every one who liked could keep

---

[1] Antiph. p. 611. [2] Athen. xiii. p. 607. [3] Plaut. Merc. i. 1. 101.

a school; slaves seem to have been used by their masters for the purpose; and it was an occupation looked down upon, as all paid ones were. This made Plato propose to intrust all the education in his republic to salaried strangers.[1] The instruction given was the same every where, with the exception of Sparta. Grammar, including reading, writing, and arithmetic, music and gymnastics, were the subjects generally in requisition for the education of a Greek. His gymnastic exercises began as early as his seventh year, or still earlier, according to the demands of Plato and Aristotle.[2] The paidotribe, in his palestra, imparted the first instruction in the practice of running, throwing, brandishing, and wrestling. Besides these private schools for bodily training, there were also gymnasia, institutions of state, where the Greek youth amused themselves under the eye of the gymnasiarch, though just as they chose, and without compulsion, in darting the spear, pugilism, and the pentathlon. Music was cultivated from the thirteenth year, ordinarily, as Aristotle remarks, as an accomplishment of taste befitting an idle hour, but also with a view to religious choir-singing: in Athens the lyre and singing, in Thebes the flute. The reading of the national poets, Homer and Hesiod, formed a main ingredient in school instruction. Homer especially was the real and only schoolbook. In vain did Xenophanes of Colyphon, and Heraclitus, demand the expulsion of the two poets from schools, on the score of their mythological contents. Homer maintained his ground as the universal educator of the Greek intellect and of the national spirit, the religious book of boys, youths, and men, to supply for deficiencies in instruction, along with the sight of the divine images and ceremonies. To an Athenian, however, dramatic poetry, with its different aspects and nobler forms of deification, made a counterpoise in some degree.

In Sparta, where no effort was spared to form the boy into a brave, hardy, and implicitly-obedient member of a military and conquering state, intellectual training went to the wall. According to Socrates, not even the elements of science were taught among the Spartans; and Aristotle reproaches them for educating their children to be as wild as the beasts.[3] The gymnasia and sword-exercise were, it was said, their only anxiety; if they

---

[1] Legg. vii. p. 804. [2] Ibid. vii. 794; Arist. Pol. vii. 17.
[3] Pol. viii. 4.

happened to want music, poetry, or a physician, they would call in strangers to their aid.[1] Besides them, the Bœotians come second in reputation as the most ignorant of men.[2] For youths of intellectual enterprise, from and after Plato's time, philosophy had become a study accessible to the educated classes; and philosophy with rhetoric furnished worthy subject-matter for employment upon. In the Roman period, though the general obligation to gymnastic training had ceased, every city still had its own gymnasium, frequented by its ephebi. Nevertheless, the growing impoverishment of Greece deprived most young people of much leisure for training in these athletic arts and exercises.

---

2. WOMAN AMONGST THE GREEKS—MARRIAGE—HETAIRAI—PAIDERASTIA—EXPOSITION OF CHILDREN—DECREASE OF POPULATION.

ARISTOTLE boasts, with justice, of its being a capital distinction and immense advantage of Greek society over oriental and barbaric, that woman amongst them had been raised to be the real helpmate of man, and not degraded to the level of the slave.[3] The Greeks had a healthy and well-organised political existence only through their adherence to a real domestic life, founded on monogamy. Plurality of wives was unknown among them, bigamy occurring but rarely, and polygamy only coming in with the Macedonian monarchy, along with other oriental habits then introduced. Hence their women were not kept under lock and key, and watched by eunuchs, as in a harem; but their position was rather one to which law and custom multiplied securities, and maintained with acknowledged rights. In the interior of the household they exercised authority over slaves and children.

In reality, however, woman amongst the Greeks was regarded but as a means to an end, as an evil indispensable for the order of the household and procreation of children. It is true, the custom of the Lydians and Etruscans did not extend to the Greeks, of the maiden's dower being composed of the earnings of her prostitution; but the carelessness in which the Greeks left their daughters intended for marriage to grow up, without true

---

[1] Ælian. V. H. xii. 50.   [2] Dio. Chrys. Or. x. p. 306, Reisk.
[3] Polit. i. 1. 5.

education or instruction, is a convincing proof of the low estimation of women amongst them. Their education was limited to the performance of the most necessary household duties, and a little dancing and singing, to enable them to take part in certain religious festivals. The virtues of the wife were reduced to the maintenance of good order in her household, and obedience to her husband.[1] There was a general notion of the woman being more naturally vicious and inclined to evil than the man; of her being more addicted to envy, discontent, evil-speaking, and wantonness; and of her being equally ready to deceive as to be deceived. Hence in Athens the wife was treated, all her life long, as a minor, the mother falling to the guardianship of her son when he attained his majority. The law invalidated whatever a husband did by the counsel, or at the request, of his wife: the wife, on her part, could transact no business of importance in her own favour, nor by will could she dispose of more than the value of a bushel of barley.[2] Cases of marriage of mutual inclination between the parties could occur but seldom, as marriage was concluded often without their having seen one another beforehand, the father disposing of his daughter as he liked, and the brother after the father's death. No stranger was allowed to enter the women's apartment; the wife being allowed but scant intercourse with her nearest relations, and, indeed, with her own husband, as they lived in separate parts of the house: thus the principal society she had was that of her slaves. If the husband entertained a guest, her presence was not allowed.[3] Hence Plato designates women as a sex habituated to a life of seclusion and darkness; and it occurred to him that syssitia, or common meals, might be established amongst them.

Greek history accordingly, and, if we except Euripides, Greek literature, is not distinguished by noble specimens of the sex. We hear or see but little of the beneficial influence of mother or wife on the actions or character of son or husband. Marriage was of obligation, the gods requiring an ample succession of worshipers, the state one of citizens and warriors, and the human species of posterity. The principal object of marriage being perfect citizens, bachelors were looked down upon as men who

---

[1] Aristot. H. A. ix. 1. cf. Polit. i. 5; Magn. Mor. i. 34; Plat. Legg. vi. p. 781; Democr. ap. Stob. i. 73. 62.
[2] Isaeus de Arist. Hær. p. 259.   [3] Herod. v. 18.

did not fulfil their duties as such, and were quite set aside in many cases, an Athenian law decreeing that only a married man should be an orator or a general;[1] nay, further, Plato and Plutarch both say expressly, that marriage was a matter legally compulsory in Athens. Nevertheless the number of voluntary bachelors went on increasing; which was all the worse for the women, as voluntary virginity could not occur in the entire deficiency of a religious motive, or of a tolerable position in society, while involuntary virginity was contemplated as the height of misfortune.[2] What confidence could a Greek have in daughter or sister when intemperance was considered the ordinary failing of the sex?[3] Plato says quite commonly that marriage and the procreation of children were acquiesced in, not naturally and spontaneously, but by the compulsion of the law.[4]

Spartan legislators, regarding marriage entirely as an institution for the supply of healthy and robust children, regulated the relations of husbands and wives accordingly. Their maidens, obliged to the gymnastic exercises of the palestra in a state bordering on nudity, and in the presence of men young and old, including frequently strangers, were educated in a reckless freedom and a hardihood ill becoming their sex;[5] their very dances are represented as of a license degraded to indecency. The idea of conjugal fidelity being of sacred obligation, was in reality never dreamt of. Marriage was, in their eyes, but a form, having its object attained in the produce of sturdy soldiers for the state, whose paternity was matter of perfect indifference; for, as Plutarch observes, citizens should not be jealous and exclusive about the possession of their wives, but rather should readily share them with others,—an oldish man ought to give up his wife to a younger for a time, in order to have children of her: and so it was accounted a proper thing, as Polybius tells us[6] (and it was of frequent occurrence), for a husband who had already several children by his wife to lend her to a friend of his. Therefore, in Sparta, if a man was desirous of children,

---

[1] Dinarch. in Demosth. p. 51.
[2] Soph. Œd. Tyr. 1492 sq.; Eurip. Hel. 291.
[3] Anthol. Pal. xi. 298; Aristoph. Thesm. 735, Eccl. 218; Athen. x. 57.
[4] Sympos. p. 192.
[5] Plut. Lyc. xiv. 15; Athen. xiii. 20. On the island of Chios young men and maidens were actually allowed to wrestle together in public.
[6] Hist. xii. 6.

without burdening himself with a wife, he would borrow his neighbour's wife for a period;[1] and this promiscuousness was carried so far, according to Polybius, that three, and sometimes four, Spartans had one woman for a wife in common.[2]

If, then, the assertion of a Spartan is quoted, to the effect that adultery never happened in his state, the meaning only could be, that the relation called marriage in Sparta was in fact never broken by what was elsewhere looked upon as adultery, the state not acknowledging such a crime; on the contrary, it was a kind of legalised ordinary occurrence of every day. Already in the time of Socrates, the wives of Sparta had reached the height of disrepute for their wantonness throughout the whole of Greece:[3] Aristotle says they lived in unbridled licentiousness;[4] and, indeed, it is a distinctive feature in the female character there, that publicly and shamelessly they would speed a well-known seducer of a woman of rank by wishing him success, and charging him to think only of endowing Sparta with brave boys.[5]

Such a state of things was offensive to the other Greeks, and especially the Ionians; nor had female licentiousness of the kind any attractiveness in Athens; but this was compensated, and more, by the room given to the capricious humours of the husband, who might put away his wife at will, and take another fairer and younger and richer. It was pretended, on the agreement of the two parties, the marriage might be dissolved thenceforth, without the observance of any formality beyond a single attestation in writing before the archon; but the wife's consent was in most cases illusory, as she was entirely in her husband's power, and dared not refuse. She had to allow things to take their course, and to be but a chattel, transferable and marketable to others, and a subject of testamentary disposition. Besides, the husband's will alone seems to have been adequate to dissolve a marriage. Only the dower, which belonged neither to the husband nor to the wife properly speaking, but to the guardians of the latter (who had given her in marriage), and which was only for the usufruct of the husband, acted in some slight degree as a protection when it was inconvenient to the husband

---

[1] Xen. de Rep. Lac. i. 8.
[2] Fragm. in Scr. Vet. Nov. Coll. ed. Mav. ii. 384.
[3] Plat. Legg. I.   [4] Aristot. Polit. ii. 5.
[5] Plut. Pyrrh. 28. cf. Parth. Narr. 23.

to restore it.[1] Marriage without a dower bore, in fact, a considerable resemblance to concubinage.

Demosthenes declares before the Athenian people, "We have Hetairai for our pleasure, concubines for the ordinary requirements of the body, and wives for the procreation of lawful issue and as confidential domestic guardians."[2] The relation of concubinage was often the subject of contract, and under the protection of the law. The influence of hetairai was still greater, and more corrupting. If retirement, restraint, ignorance of the world, and legalised respect, were the portion of married women; freedom, education, and the homage of men, ending in contempt, fell to the lot of the hetairai. Young women destined for this pursuit received a careful education, such as was denied daughters intended for the marriage state. Hence the hetaira was connected with the arts, the literature, and even the religion of her country, and this gave her a kind of historical importance. As regards her religious aspect, it has only to be remembered that the Aphrodite Anadyomene of Apelles, and the Cnidian goddess of Praxiteles, were both statues of the far-famed Phryne;[3] that the courtesans of Athens raised an image to their goddess at Samos from their gains;[4] and that those of Corinth were for reasons of state under the obligation of assisting at the sacrifices offered to Aphrodite in public dangers or misfortunes.[5] It was held to be no profanation of the national sanctuary at Delphi that an image of Phryne should be placed there.[6] After Aspasia and Pericles had refined, if not ennobled, this condition and relation in the eyes of the Greeks, it never occurred to any one to disapprove of the intercourse even of married men with hetairai. Hence a dispute for the possession of one of these courtesans between two rivals was decided in court of law by assigning her to both for a day each in succession.[7] Considering the precautions which Socrates recommended to his disciples in their intercourse with women, and his own visits in their company to the courtesan Theodota, and the counsels

---

[1] Examples: Demosth. c. Eubulid., Oratt. Att. v. 514, 515; pro Phorm., ib. p. 218; c. Aphob. pp. 103, 104.
[2] Dem. c. Near., Or. Att. v. 578. cf. Athen. xiii. 31.
[3] Ath. xiii. 59.   [4] Alexis of Athen. xiii. 31.
[5] Athen. xiii. 32; Strab. p. 581.
[6] Plut. Amat. p. 753; de Pyth. Orac. p. 400.   [7] Demosth. c. Near.

which he gave her as to the mode of winning and retaining her lovers;[1] and further, that this is all contained in a book written with the avowed object of defending Socrates from the charge, among others, of being a corrupter of youth,—we are sufficiently furnished with the means of estimating the prevalent opinions of the day as to this connection. Every time it was publicly mentioned in legal processes or on other occasions, it was always in the light of a thing indifferent or of course. Artists, poets, philosophers, orators, and statesmen, set the fashion by connecting themselves with hetairai. The names of Pericles, Demades, Lysias, Demosthenes, Isocrates, Aristotle, Speusippus, Aristippus, and Epicurus, are but a few in the long list of their protectors. Areopagites, even, were met at the table of Phryne. Many of these courtesans were treated as queens, and public statues were erected to a great number.

A closer insight into the relations of paiderastia among the Greeks will be indispensable here, as it bore most closely on the marriage state and domestic life generally among them. The vice itself, it may be truly said, was shared by the Greeks in common with most of the nations of antiquity, but with this one distinguishing feature, that the inclination of a man of ripe age for a youth hardly out of boyhood assumed, with them first, an aspect at once educational and political, and æsthetically philosophical. Reference to the heat of the climate and the refinement of civilisation explains nothing. Against the former it is enough to set the fact, that people dwelling in a far warmer climate—Egyptians, Jews, and Arabians—kept themselves in great measure free from this sin; whilst, on the other side, the Celts of the north were deeply tainted with it. As to civilisation, one glance at the people with whom the vice was domesticated suffices to indicate that the degree of civilisation a people had attained to might qualify the form, but not affect the substance of the matter. The descendants of those hordes who conquered central and northern Asia under Genghis Khan and Timour, the Usbeck Khans, had plunged so deep into it as to consider it a bad sign and a weakness for one to keep himself free from this universal habit.[2]

With the Greeks this phenomenon exhibited all the symp-

---

[1] Xen. Mem. Socr. iii. 13.

[2] Sylv. de Sacy, in the Journal des Savans, juin 1829, p. 331.

toms of a great national disease, a kind of moral pestilence. It showed itself like a passion stronger and more vehement, wilder and more irregular than the love of women among other nations. Infuriate jealousy, unconditional self-sacrifice, hot lust, tender toying, night-long vigils at the door of the beloved one,—all that makes a caricature of the natural love of the female sex was to be found here. The strictest moralists in pronouncing upon this relation were excessively indulgent, nay, worse than indulgent, for they often treated it with mere ridicule, tolerating even the society of the guilty. In the whole of the literature of the anti-Christian period there is hardly a writer to be met with who has expressed himself decidedly in hostile terms as to it. In very truth, the whole of society was infected with it, and people inhaled the pestilence with the air they breathed. It was glorified by poetry in all its forms. The erotic sayings or discourses of philosophers contributed to fan the evil flame. The tragic drama made it the turning-point of many of its creations; while the comic indicated, openly and by name, generals, statesmen, and leading citizens engaged in this commerce of love; thereby impressing thousands with the conviction, that if they entered the same boat they would find themselves in goodly company. The Greeks, we know, generally chose to attribute their darling sins and vices to their gods, and to represent them plastically in myths: hence the sagas of Ganymede, and of the rape of Pelops by Poseidon, necessarily assumed the form of the reigning vice, and Apollo and Heracles were turned into paiderasts. Hence, too, it came to pass that in countless passages,—poets, orators, and philosophers,—where the subject is love, woman's love is not thought of; and in a court of justice a case of "criminal conversation" with a boy would be dealt with as publicly, and with the same shamelessness, as one with a courtesan.[1]

In the Doric states, Crete and Sparta, the love of the male was favoured as a means of education, which the law itself acknowledged. The assertion of Aristotle, that Cretan legislation had in view to check the growth of population by such provision, perhaps does not touch the real root of the matter, though showing what a baneful influence was at work in the island, and how the Cretan character was affected. In Sparta, according to Xenophon, the connection between the elder lover

[1] Lysias, Apol. c. Simon, Oratt. Att. i, 191, 192.

and the young beloved was just as pure as that between parent and child. Exile and disgrace were the punishments of a child's violation; but the reprobatory sentence of Plato is evidence that the law was frequently set at naught in society.[1] Plutarch describes the violent effort at self-mastery it cost Agesilaus to keep under his passion for the youthful Megabates; and while his friends ridiculed his refusing even the kiss of the youth, it was the opinion of Maximus of Tyre that Agesilaus deserved greater praise for so doing than Leonidas for the exploit at Thermopylæ.[2] Socrates himself, who in other respects took a far higher ground, removed from the follies, weaknesses, and vice of his countrymen, could not forbear feeling like a Greek on this point. Plato makes him give expression, in the Charmides, to the strong emotion which he experienced in happening to see a beautiful youth half-naked. He confesses on the occasion he could not, for his part, remember any time he had not been enamoured of some one or other,[3] and that he always was smitten with the beauty of boyhood.[4] He was himself certainly free from acts of vice; his intention was rather to ennoble a propensity which had enslaved the whole of Greece, not excepting himself, and to make use of it as a means of beneficial action on the part of the lover to the object of his affection. Still, the question is, whether, in lending the sanction of his honoured name to it, he did not in reality inflict a greater injury on succeeding generations than on his immediate contemporaries. So strong was the influence of the prevalent epidemic on Plato, that he had lost all sense of the love of women, and, in his descriptions of Eros, divine as well as human, his thoughts were centred only on this boy-passion. The result in Greece confessedly was, that the inclination for a woman was looked upon as low and dishonourable, while that for a youth was the only one worthy of a man of education. Ideally as Plato has pictured this unnatural passion in the Phædrus and Symposium, yet he adds, that in an unguarded hour, or in the excesses of inebriety, "the two wild horses meet together," meaning, that at times also in the nobler erotic intercourse between men and youths, something may happen that "passes with the multitude

---

[1] Legg. viii. p. 836.
[2] Plut. Ages. xi. cf. Lacon. Apophth. p. 209; Max. Diss. xxv. p. 307.
[3] Xen. Mem. viii. 2. [4] Plut. Amator. 138.

for the height of enjoyment." In his last work, however, on Laws, when age and experience had doubtless taught him better, he has expressly rebuked and condemned a relation, the ruinousness of which he fully recognised.[1]

The general opinion that Athens was the head-quarters of this impurity, and that it was worse there than elsewhere in Greece, is already untenable on Plato's evidence. He says expressly that a special law was necessary to prevent his fellow-citizens from being corrupted by the rest of Greece and most of the barbarians, exposed as they were to seeing and hearing of the progress of this abominable vice amongst them, and the fearful mastery it was gaining every where.[2] Our acquaintance with other Greek cities and their interior state can only be drawn from the fertile sources which we possess in Athenian literature. Most of these cities had no law against the vice.[3] It was in the time of the emperors first, when Athens and Corinth were the only two flourishing cities of Greece much frequented by strangers, that the former town was characterised by Lucian[4] as being the head-quarters of paiderastia, as the other, Corinth, was the metropolis of the association of hetairai. Bœotia and Elis had the reputation of the vice being practised throughout them shamelessly and with a kind of public approval;[5] while at Athens it was looked on as discreditable, according to Xenophon, or the author of the Symposium bearing his name. But this passage can only be meant of the pathics at Athens, who prostituted themselves; as it is patent on the face of all their literature, in Aristophanes, Plato, and the Orators, that the attempt to possess himself of the person of a youth reflected no actual discredit on the aggressor; and the Athenian law only included two cases, inflicting the punishment of atimia, of infamy and incapacitation for public offices, on the citizen who sold himself for money to this shameful vice, and a fine upon the violation of a boy a minor. In order to protect youth from corruption, an older law had forbidden grown-up people to enter schools, gymnasia, and the palæstræ; but this law had fallen into general desuetude from the time of Socrates, a period with which we are better acquainted. The legislation of Solon, in forbidding

---

[1] Legg. p. 837.
[2] μέγιστον δυναμένην, Legg. p. 840.
[3] Xen. Rep. Lac. ii. 14.
[4] Am. 51, and the Scholia.
[5] Xen. Sympos. viii. 34.

this impure attachment to slaves, seems to have regarded it as a privilege to be allowed to free persons only.[1] On the other hand, young slaves were driven by their masters to public prostitution, as houses were appropriated there to male impurity.[2] Thus Phædo, the founder of the Socratic-Elean school, had been publicly subjected to this treatment as a prisoner at Athens; and Agathocles, the tyrant of Syracuse, is said to have been in his youth a victim of the same class.[3]

The example of the renowned tyrannicides, Harmodius and Aristogeiton, whose infamous connection gave occasion to the murder of Hipparchus, was always quoted in Athens with special approbation in excuse of the dominant vice, which in the time of Aristophanes had reached such a height, that, notwithstanding the law, many young people made a traffic of their persons for money, or, what was considered more respectable, the present of a horse, or sporting dog, or a valuable suit of clothes.[4] Formal contracts were actually drawn up for the purpose; and yet this vice left an indelible mark on those who practised it, and a proverb was current, which said it was easier to hide five elephants under one's arm than one pathic.[5] But the state made profit of the numerous subjects of this wretched trade, imposing a prostitution tax, which was annually leased out by the senate of five hundred, and had to be paid to the lessees.[6] Hence there was no very great shame attaching to young persons who came before the court to claim the reward of their prostitution from such as refused the payment:[7] and Æschines, in one of his court speeches, while he designates with strict accuracy the citizen who hired Timarchus, and always kept some young people in his house with the same object, adds, " he mentions him by name not in order to damage him in public estimation, but only that it may be known whom he had in his eye."[8]

In such a state of things, producing exactly the same scenes, fighting, trials, and bankruptcies, as are common in connections with courtesans, one may conceive fathers and pedagogues never once allowing young people to enter into conversation with a

---

[1] Plut. Sol. 1; Æsch. cont. Timarch., Or. Att. iii. 295.
[2] Æsch. cont. Tim. p. 274.   [3] Suid. s. v.
[4] Aristoph. Plut. 153 sq.; Av. 701 sq.; Æl. ap. Suid. v. Μέλητος.
[5] Lucian. adv. indoct. 23.   [6] Æsch. c. Tim., Or. Att. iii. 289.
[7] Æsch. l. c. p. 301.   [8] Ibid. p. 263.

stranger, unless before witnesses.[1] This extended even to philosophers, who were fond of attracting beautiful youths, and enticing them into such relations. Hence their reputation generally was so bad in this respect, that, as Plutarch observes,[2] parents commonly would not tolerate their children having any acquaintance with philosophers. Parmenides, Eudoxus, Xenocrates, Aristotle, Polemo, Crantor, and Arcesilaus, are all specially pointed out as paidcrasts, and the names of the youths they were enamoured of are recorded. According to the statement of Sextus,[3] the Cynics and the heads of the Stoic sect treated the love of boys as a thing indifferent. Even Zeno, the founder of the Stoa, speaks with a Cynic hardness, as if it were exactly the same, an adiaphoron, whether a man lived in impurity with a boy, or contented himself with the natural intercourse with the other sex;[4] nay, it is told of him that he never had connection with women, but always with beautiful youths.[5] Cicero ridiculed the excuse, that this love of philosophers for children and boys was not of a coarse and sensual kind. "Why, then," he cries, "how does it happen that no one falls in love with an ugly youth, or a handsome old man?" And he justifies Epicurus for having spoken out as to the thoroughly carnal character of this affection.[6] Lucian expressed himself to the same effect. "It was not souls, as philosophers pretended sometimes, but bodies that were the objects of their tenderness;" and at last he concludes with this distinction, that the marriage-bond was made for all other men, but that philosophers might be indulged in their passion for boys.[7] "It is the beginning of vice to bare the body among citizens."[8] Such are the words in which Ennius had, betimes, pointed to the practice of nudity in the gymnasia and palæstræ, as the main source of the Greek vice we are speaking of. Long before him, Plato himself had declared,[9] that the perversion of the sexual instinct was a burden incurred by all states in which the public exercises, with their indispensable nudity, were in practice.[10] In many gymnasia and palæstræ an altar was erected to Eros, which was the ordinary resort of

[1] Plato, Sympos. p. 183.   [2] De educ. puer. 15.
[3] Pyrrh. Hypot. iii. 24.   [4] Ap. Sext. Emp. adv. Ethic. 190.
[5] Athen. p. 563.   [6] Tusc. iv. 33.
[7] Amor. 51. t. v. p. 315, ed. Bip.   [8] Tusc. iv. 34.   [9] Legg. i. p. 636.
[10] It is inconceivable how, in the face of such evidence, Otfr. Müller (Dorians, ii. 294) and Höck (Creta, iii. 118) can deny these facts.

the paiderasts, and there his wings grew so large, to use Plutarch's expression, that there was no longer any containing him.[1] So when Polycrates would not endure these connections, he began with closing the gymnasia and palæstræ.[2]

Further, as a second main cause of the evil, we may add the displacement of the relative position of the sexes, the degradation of the woman, and the exclusion of the uninitiated part of them from men's society. Wherever such a state of things exists, the sensual instincts of the male are sure to deviate towards the younger and fairer portion of his own sex, and the deviation once made will infallibly increase. Socrates, speaking of Critobulus, takes for granted that there was no one he spoke less to than his wife, evidently only because such were the general habits, and he (Critobulus) confirms this.[3] Men and striplings, on the other hand, lived perpetually together at the agora, in the syssitia, and hetairiai. The effect then must have been such as we know it to have been among a people so susceptible and sensual, and at the same time so excitable and imaginative, as the Greeks. The careful tending and strengthening of the body, with the continual use of rich meats and strong wines, joined to idleness, the privilege of the free Hellene, who would never consent to be a base mechanic, all contributed their modicum to the evil. And from this unnatural passion again there resulted a disinclination and aversion to the marriage state, which was now generally considered a burden. Plato and Plutarch both remark this feature of the times. The former says, "It is not naturally, but only by the compulsion of the law, that a man whose inclinations have been to youth enters into the bonds of matrimony."[4] But so soon as legal compulsion, and the motive of patriotism, the procreation of citizens and soldiers for the state, disappeared with the dissolution of the Greek republics, the evil of celibacy must have developed to a terrible degree; and one might be quite justified in attributing the subsequent and lasting depopulation of Greece, at least in part, to the baneful effects of this national vice.[5]

A variety of causes, however, were coöperating to bring about a gradual decrease in the population. The larger propor-

---

[1] Amator, p. 751.   [2] Athen. xiii. 78.
[3] Xen. Œcon. 12.   [4] Plato, Sympos. 192; Plut. Amator, p. 751.
[5] Zumpt on the State of Population in Antiquity, p. 14.

tion of the inhabitants of Hellas consisted, as we have before mentioned, of slaves. The agricultural serfs were, indeed, married, but not so the workers in the mines and manufactories. As for house-slaves, they seem to have been allowed to marry in Attica only, and there but partially. As the number of female slaves in the towns was very hmuc the minority, and of these again a considerable proportion were reserved for the pleasure of freemen,—some in houses of prostitution, and some as flute-players and concubines,—celibacy became a necessity for most of the male slaves, inasmuch as there were no wives to be found for them, even if their masters had allowed them to marry. The medium price of a grown slave, able to work in field or mine, was somewhere about two hundred florins;[1] and as the expense of rearing a slave child was much more considerable than that of purchasing an able-bodied slave, the interests of the master became an additional hindrance to the propagation of the slave species.

Putting together, then, the mode of conducting warfare, the incessant ravaging of countries, the destruction of fruit-trees, and the consequent deterioration of the soil, the wide-spread distaste for marriage, paiderastia, the condition of slaves, and the means hereafter to be mentioned that were taken to diminish the full number of children in families, one cannot forbear coming to the conclusion that no people in history laboured more obstinately than the Greeks at their own obliteration and extinction.

It is striking how few examples we find of a numerous family among the Greeks, at least in the times succeeding to the Peloponnesian war. We hear of two, sometimes three, brothers and sisters,—seldom more. Some of the older legislations had indeed prohibited abortion by the mothers;[2] yet the matter was of such ordinary occurrence, that philosophers like Plato and Aristotle formally approved and recommended it. "If perchance the custom of the place," says the latter, "is against the exposition of newly-born children,[3] abortion previous to the embryo

---

[1] Dureau de la Malle, in the Mém. de l'Acad. des Inscr., nouv. sér. xiv. 319.

[2] Stob. Serm. lxxiv. lxi. and lxxv. 15.

[3] Aristotle uses ἀποτίθεσθαι.—exposition in an out-of-the-way or unfrequented spot, to allow of the child's perishing,—in distinction from ἔκθεσις, or the putting out of a child to any one who would take it.

receiving life and sensation must be resorted to, to prevent the births being too numerous."[1] It would seem that the ancients were acquainted with means of obtaining such a result without endangering the mother's life.[2] And Hippocrates accordingly tells us, with the utmost simplicity, of his having thus relieved a woman to whom pregnancy had become burdensome.

The exposition of children had been always permitted in Greece, and was termed "chytrism,"[3] because an earthen vessel was often used for the purpose. It was most ordinarily practised in cases of weak and deformed children. In Sparta it was under the superintendence of the state; the elders of the family inspected the newly-born babe, and if it did not please them it was carried into the chasms of Taygetus.[4] In Athens, Solon is said to have allowed the parents of the child to put it to death.[5] The frequent mention of exposition in plays shows that it was not of rare occurrence. According to Ælian, Thebes formed the only exception, and there the child whom its father refused to bring up was sold by the magistrate to the highest bidder, whose slave it then became. Plato adopted the prevailing custom in his Utopian republic. "Children born to wicked men, misshapen, illegitimate, and of parents advanced in years, shall be exposed, that the state be not burdened with them."[6]

Now for the evidence of a statesman like Polybius as to the effects produced in Greece by this custom. "It is," he says, "the unanimous opinion of all, that Greece now (in the first period of the Roman rule, after the taking of Corinth) enjoys the greatest prosperity; yet there is such a scarcity of population, and the cities are so desolate, that the soil begins to lose its fertility from want of hands to cultivate it. The reason is, that men, even when they live in the married state, will not bring their children up, and this because of their effeminacy, love of comfort, and idleness; at best they will only rear one or two out of many, in order to leave them a good inheritance. Hence the evil has been becoming gradually greater; for when war or sickness has snatched away the only child, the family

---

[1] Ar. Pol. vii. 14. 10.
[2] Barth. St. Hilaire makes this observation on the passage of Aristotle, p. 110.
[3] Mœris Attic. p. 138; Hesych. s. v.   [4] Plut. Lyc. 16.
[5] Sext. Emp. Hypotyp. p. 3, 24; Hermogen. de Inv. i. 1.
[6] Rep. v. p. 460.

dies out, of course. This state of things," he says, "is not to be remedied by recourse to gods or oracles; men are able to help themselves, and ameliorate it by adopting another practice, and where they will not, the law should define that all children who are born shall be brought up."[1] The Greek mind, however, did not change in this respect: no law was passed, and a couple of centuries later, even after a long period of repose and peace, we have the pen of Plutarch to record what the results were.

In the times following the Peloponnesian war, the dark side of the Greek character came out in stronger and clearer colours. Cunning and cold ferocity in war, and interior political conflicts, unrestrained sensuality and lust, greediness after gain in all shapes,—these were the features that struck even a Greek in his own nation, as also the Romans, their conquerors. Venality had become so ingrained amongst them, according to Polybius,[2] that no one would do any thing gratis. King Philip, betimes, directed with his gold the politics of the Greek states at his own will, and to their own destruction. Scarce a man was to be found who had not cheated and plundered the state when opportunity presented itself.[3] For long the evidence of a slave, wrung from him by torture, had more weight assigned to it with the people than the testimony upon oath of a freeman.[4] No one trusted his neighbour in a matter of money or gain: witnesses, hand-writing, nothing was binding enough.[5] Greek honour, Greek cupidity and lying, had become proverbial. Even the excess of intemperance and wanton debauchery was nicknamed "grecising" by the Romans.[6] Pliny, in fine, designates the Greeks as the inventors of every vice.[7]

---

[1] Polyb. Exc. Vatic. ed. Geel, Lugd. Bat. 1829, p. 105 sq.
[2] Polyb. xviii. 17.   [3] Ibid. vi. 56.
[4] Demosth. pro Phano, 21; Anaxim. Rhetor. xvi. 1.
[5] Polyb. vi. 56; Cic. pro Flacco, c. 4.
[6] Cic. Verr. ii. 1. 26; Hor. Sat. ii. 2. 11.   [7] Hist. Nat. xv. 5.

II. THE SOCIAL AND MORAL STATE OF THE ROMANS.

1. Character of Roman Nationality—Roman Jus Privatum—Strangers—Power of the Father of a Family.

We encounter here a nationality of power so intensive, and of energy so overwhelming, as to absorb and convert into its own substance all the foreign material of people which it admitted within its circle. In league with this energetic national system, there appears a gigantic selfishness, to which nothing was wanting on the score of readiness for self-sacrifice and self-mastery in the pursuit of the great object of world-empire. The Romans mastered all other peoples, because they were always masters of themselves first, and always preferred the final success and aggrandisement of the whole body, the state, to their own private advantage, the pleasure, and the convenience of the individual.

Rome, as a military republic, excellently organised for the purpose of sustained wars of conquest, was a school of citizens habituated to strict discipline, obedience, and the privations of a prolonged military service, and taught to look on all as light and easy, for the sake of the one object, victory and conquest. Thus the Roman national character developed in its profound egotism, valuing each thing according to its fitness to the one end with an obduracy as of steel, a patience never to be tired out, a steadfastness in misfortune, and a sober practical sound sense.

The Romans were not, in reality, possessed by one simple idea, for the propagation or realising of which they strained every sinew; it was not the universal acknowledgment and worship of the gods which they strove to spread. Far from surrendering themselves to these gods of theirs as their property and their instruments, they rather looked upon them as, by quasi contract, their ministers, under obligation to point them the way to dominion and the means of securing victory to their side. For five hundred years they persisted in their labour of world-conquest, with no other higher motive in view, with only the instinct of being called to rule all nations, and thereby to fulfil the destiny provided them by the gods and by fate. Their whole history and action is exhausted in the two problems of legal and political equality at home, and of world empire abroad. The first of these, however, was never pursued at the expense of the latter, and the exuberant fulness of vigour which filled the veins of this people would assuredly have long before been suicidally turned upon themselves and their own state, had not the continual wars served as a diversion and safety-valve. Accordingly one Roman was mostly the facsimile of the other. All their distinguished men were of the same stamp. Individuality was merged; and the rich profusion of original characters which Hellas had to exhibit, while they are all Greek every inch of them, had no counterpart in Rome, nor was it till the last times of the republic that there was any change in this respect.

Avarice and rapacity, however, early showed themselves to be features of the Roman character. War was not conducted only for honour's sake and the glory of conquest, but served besides as a main source of gain for those who took part in it. While there was a greater simplicity of manners and a stricter frugality in private life, there were still always landed properties as prizes for the increasing numbers of citizens to win. It was indeed only at a later period that the genuine insatiate, all-absorbing greediness developed when fed by thoughtless profusion; but in order to recognise this feature in its original symptoms, one has only to cast a glance at the merciless iron laws against debtors of the olden time, when almost every patrician house was at the same time a prison, where poor plebeians, victims of usurious interest and patrician cupidity, pursued their slavish toil, the law "for their protection" allowing their chains not to weigh more than fifteen pounds each,[1] and authorising the creditor to sell his insolvent debtor for a slave on the other side of the Tiber.

Setting aside its wars and conquests, the Roman people only accomplished one great enduring work,—a work, sooth to say, of imperishable value and effect, namely, the creation of its Jus privatum (or civil law of individuals),—a huge edifice that took twelve hundred years to build, yet a work of one casting, unsurpassed for temperate reasonableness, sharp-cut details of general design, and logical consequence calculated with a mathematical precision. Its foundations were laid in the keenest appreciation of meum and tuum, the perfect grasp of the absolute and exclu-

[1] Gall. xx. 1.

sive notion of personal property; while its starting-point was that of "taking with the hand," or mancipatio, *i. e.* strength of arm appropriating its booty. "What Romans take from their enemies," says Gaius, "that they hold, before all things, to be their own property."[1] Such possession only gives a right, does not involve an obligation: one may do what one likes with one's own plunder; the dominion over one's own is unlimited, requiring no account to be given of the use made of it, so long as there is no infringement on the property of others of equal right with your own. Hence there was but one duty accompanying this unconditional right, and that merely a negative one, "Injure no one." Whoever only does not interfere, against the consent of others, in the province of their rights, is safe from external assault: it is no matter how he uses his power, and how he treats things or persons subjected to him, whether morally or immorally. This was the spirit and principle of the Roman law; this sovereign action of the possessor might be softened in its application to particular cases, by usage or the prevalent public tone, and by the institution of the censorship, subservient to both.

The Roman commonwealth in its aspect of individual right thus became a vast institute for the security of private property. This absolute and exclusive possession, this unlimited dominion over property, dead as well as living, things as well as persons, without reciprocity between property and proprietor, master and servant, or father and children, formed the basis and soul of Roman legislation.

The citizen, the active participant in state matters, and lord and master of himself, enjoyed a far larger share of freedom in Rome than in the Greek republics. That tight hold which the Greek state laid on the whole life of its citizen, including even his domestic relations, and that omnipotence of state, as Plato himself has attempted to spiritualise it in his model republic, was natural to the Greek; the Roman was unacquainted with, and would not have endured it. The foundation of personal liberty, in the sense of a right and title to regulate oneself and one's actions according to one's own standard within the limits set down by law, is contained in the Roman law,[2] though it did

---

[1] Gaius, iv. 16.

[2] According to the definition, L. 3 pr. D. de statu hominum.

not receive its full extension till towards the close of the republic. As the Roman citizen shared in the government of the state, shared in the powers of legislating and of judicial punishment, and had a voice in the election of officers, and even in the management of the police, it follows that the limitations imposed by particular laws, which in certain cases and relations circumscribed his freedom, were self-imposed laws. Legislation, as practised by the assembled citizens (and the practice was preserved, at least in theory, under the emperors) required no submission to another's will. Thus the Romans were actually the first among whom the citizen (and he alone) gained the greatest latitude for his own caprice, with a complete independence of rights as regarded his person and his goods; but to this autocracy of self-will, acknowledging no duties collateral to and curtailing his rights, or any reciprocity of action, was due that selfish hardness in his character, which the Roman and his law exercised against the vanquished, the debtor, and the poor. A people with such law, and such liberty, was like a powerful crushing machine, pursuing the ceaseless toil it was so thoroughly fitted for, of imposing an iron yoke of domination on all the other nations of the world.

Agreeably with the Roman view, or rather that of antiquity generally, those who did not belong to the same state considered one another as "hostes," a name given to strangers by the Romans from the earliest times. Hence the law of the stronger was the only one in existence between Romans and non-Romans, where no special league or covenant of amity intervened: the one party was entitled to subjugate the other, plunder its possessions, and make its members into slaves.[1] Accordingly "peregrini," for so strangers were called afterwards, had no claim in Rome to legal protection, except in the case of a Roman patron taking up the matter and making it his own, or of support from a member of a Roman family with whom the stranger's house had relations of hospitality. After the first Carthaginian war, however, when the confluence of strangers to Rome became greater, and it was her pride as well as her interest to become one of the centres of the world's resort, matters were changed. A new magistracy was created, that of the prætor peregrinus, whose tribunal was exclusively for strangers, and a Jus gentium

[1] L. v. 2. D. xlix. 15.

formed to regulate the intercourse of peregrini one with the other, and with the Romans. Yet they always remained, whether provincials or barbari, subject to great restrictions and disadvantages; were repeatedly banished the city; were allowed neither connubium nor commercium, and were therefore incapable of being testators or inheriting, or contracting a marriage with the ordinary civil consequences. They were exposed to the disgraceful punishment of scourging; and were excluded from participation in Roman sacrifices, to many of which they were not even admitted as spectators.[1]

Only as father of a family and master of a household the Roman citizen became entitled to all the power which the legislation conferred upon individuals,—a power that converted his will into an absolute law for all the members of his household. There was no difference, as far as law went, between the paternal power over the children, that of the "manus" over the wife, the master over the slave, and the dominion over movable property. In his own house the Roman was despotic lord, neither constrained nor restrained by any thing beyond his own inclination, and a regard to custom and public opinion. As father, he had right of life and death over his children, and the cases of fathers having their sons put to death are by no means of rare occurrence; yet custom seems to have required that a family council should be called before the act was perpetrated:[2] several parents exempted themselves from this restriction, and judged their children without assessors. Alexander Severus was the first to ordain that a father should take his son before a magistrate to be tried, and not put him to death without a hearing.[3] A father could also sell his children, and the law of the twelve tables decreed that a child should not be exempted from the paternal authority till after the third sale, that is, after the first or second manumission by a purchaser he fell again into his father's power.[4] A married son, however, could not be sold, according to a law attributed to Numa.[5] In the earliest period probably the sale of children was of frequent occurrence, but at a later date custom and regard to public opinion considerably modified this exercise of parental power.

[1] Paul Dinc. v. Exesto, p. 82.
[2] Val. Max. v. 8; Plin. H. N. xxxiv. 4.
[3] Cod. viii. 47. 3.
[4] Ulp. x. 1; Gaius, i. 132; iv. 79.
[5] Plut. Numa, 17.

2. Women in Rome: Marriage—Aversion to and Divorce from it.

The Romans, like the Greeks, regarded marriage as a contract entered into for the sake of procreating, and for the education of, children. Yet with them it was not devoid of a kind of sacredness; it was a covenant embracing the duration of the life of the parties to it, and a community of joy and sorrow, together with the mutual cares of education. The husband reserved nothing to himself exclusively; on the contrary, the wife enjoyed her full share in all her husband's possessions and rights, the religious ones of sacrifice inclusive. Monogamy was expressly secured. Every second marriage during the life of the parties to the first was null, entailed infamy and the punishment of adultery through the decree of the prætor.

The position of the mother of a family by her husband's side was an honourable and respected one; she conducted the affairs of the house, and had free access to her relations; but in the case of the full and strict marriage, that contracted by the "hand," she was entirely dependent on her husband, and was under his "hand," in other words, completely in his power: for in the earlier times the will of the father of the household ruled the family with despotic authority, and with the right of life and death. He could put his wife to death on the spot when surprised in the act of adultery, and even when he caught her having drunk wine; and Egnatius Mecenius actually put his wife to death for this reason, without having to answer for the act.[1] The husband alone had the property; all the family earnings were his. There were two safeguards with which the wife was provided against the abuse of this power: one consisted in the censorship, the office of which in old Rome was to preserve the ancient customs, thus forming a salutary refuge for marriage, and the position of the wife; the other, in the husband being bound by public opinion to exercise his authority over his wife with the concurrence of her relations, at least in a matter involving life and death.

There was also in existence from ancient times yet another

---

[1] Serv. .En. i. 737; Plin. xiv. 13.

form of marriage, of less strictness, a marriage "without hand," in which the wife, if withdrawn from the domestic tyranny of her husband, remained under her father's power or the guardianship of her relations, and in possession of all her property, dower excepted. But she was not any the freer in reality, for she continued under the strict surveillance of her father or agnates; and a father could either demand the wife back from her husband or divorce her from him. Yet the husband retained his right of chastising his wife, in this kind of marriage too, which, by the beginning of the empire, had already become the more common form, and by degrees completely excluded the other.

Full marriage "with the hand" took place either by "coemption," where the husband acquired his wife by an imaginary sale, or by "usus," on her having remained a full year uninterruptedly with him. In case she spent three consecutive nights of this time away from her husband's house, the father retained his rights over his daughter, and the privilege of redemanding her. The true old way, consecrated by religious solemnity, of contracting a full marriage was "confarreation." This genuine patrician nuptial rite, as giving a title to the priesthood, required the presence of the pontifex maximus, the flamen dialis, and ten citizens as witnesses: what was, essentially, a kind of communion took place: the bride and bridegroom, after sacrifice offered, being seated on the fleece of the victim, had the sacrificial cake divided between them, and ate it with the accompaniment of a solemn form of words.[1] By the formula used for the occasion, the espoused parties were united in the presence of the gods, and their union placed under their protection. But this religious sealing of marriage became in time very inconvenient, partly because a mistake might easily be made in the ceremonies, which would oblige the repetition of the whole, and partly because women generally became more and more disinclined to the strict form of marriage. Thus it came to pass, under Tiberius, that there remained but three patricians to be found who were issues of a marriage of confarreation, and who could as such be eligible to the sacerdotal dignity of flamen dialis.

If the account of Dionysius be literally correct,[2] that not a single divorce had taken place in Rome during a space of five

---

[1] Ov. Fasti, i. 319; Tac. Ann. iv. 16; Caj. i. 112; Serv. Æn. iv. 374.
[2] Dion. ii. 25.

hundred and twenty years, Carvilius Ruga being the first to furnish a precedent for it, the Romans must be accorded the meed of estimating the sacredness of the conjugal tie beyond all the nations of antiquity. Still we must remember that as early as 422 A.U.C., and therefore a century previous to this divorce of Carvilius, a number of wives entered into a conspiracy against their husbands, the most distinguished of whom died by poison; whereupon twenty married women were compelled to partake of the poison which they had prepared, and died at the moment. On further inquisition made, one hundred and seventy others were discovered to have been implicated in the like guilt, and were all sentenced to death. Also, fifty years after the divorce, a number of wives, all of high rank, were involved in the abominations of the bacchanalia. These facts, betraying so profound a corruption among the female sex and in the heart of domestic life, make such a state of innocence, as could furnish no example of divorce, both incomprehensible and incredible. In the year 447 there also occurs a case of repudiation on frivolous grounds, which was punished by the censors;[1] and according to the old laws, the husband was allowed four grounds of divorce from his wife,—poisoning, adultery, drinking, and the substitution of a spurious child. But as such crimes were ordinarily punished with death, under the sentence of the husband, conjointly with the kindred of the wife, as assessors, it might easily happen that at that time a formal divorce was of rare occurrence.[2] The wife, besides, had no right to sue for a divorce. We are justified, then, in maintaining, on these grounds, that, till the period of the second Punic war, the popular voice and current of moral feeling were against divorces as a general rule; that they were limited through censorial supervision; and that the husband who arbitrarily repudiated his wife was punished in his property and possessions. We must not, however, overlook the further fact that a husband at all times was free to make what use he chose of his female slaves. A marriage of confarreation was dissolved by the ceremony of "diffarreatio;" for as man may not of himself, and of his own authority, separate what the gods have joined together, a solemn act of religion was requisite to obtain their consent, and to make atonement for the rupture of a bond religiously entered into. Diffareation was

[1] Val. Max. ii. 9. 2.   [2] Plin. xiv. 13; Plut. Num. comp. 3.

performed by a priest, and was accompanied by lugubrious rites and maledictions, that were probably meant to fall upon the guilty party. The marriage of the flamen dialis was indissoluble, until Domitian allowed him too free right of divorce. To marry again, or live in second marriage, was generally considered as an unfavourable omen, at least in earlier times, which accounts for the pontifex maximus and the sacrificial king not being permitted to take a second wife;[1] and therefore, too, it was discreditable to a woman to take a second husband, only those who had been but once married being allowed as pronuba, and admitted to the worship of Pudicitia, Fortuna Muliebris, and Mater Matuta.[2]

The case was different with the freer kind of marriage without hand. Here the tie was always dissoluble at the option of the wife's father, and, as was natural, of the husband too, and also by mutual consent of both parties; with the exception that, in the old time, the censors animadverted upon frivolous divorces, even in this instance, by fine or in other ways. After the second Punic war the series of divorces was multiplied, and facilitated, in rapid progression. The most trifling reasons were adequate to the purpose, or served as a pretext. C. Sulpicius divorced his wife because she had gone into the street without a veil; and Q. Antistius Vetus his, for speaking confidentially in public to one of his freedmen. P. Sempronius Sophus repudiated his wife for going to the theatre without his knowledge;[3] and Paulus Æmilius, the conqueror of Perseus, put away his without assigning a reason of any kind. And how stood matters with Cicero's contemporaries? He himself separated from his first wife in order to take a wealthier; and from this second because she was not sufficiently sorry for his daughter's death. The stern moralist Cato divorced his first wife, Atitia, who had borne him two children, and gave up his second, Marcia, with her father's consent, to his friend Hortensius, and wedded her again after his death.[4] Pompey put away Antistia in order to connect himself with Sylla, whose stepdaughter, Æmilice, he espoused, and she had first to be separated from her husband Glabrio, by whom she was pregnant at the time. After her death he took Mucia to

---

[1] Tertull. de Exh. ad Cast. 13; de Monog. 17; ad Uxor. i. 7.
[2] Plut. Quæst. Rom. 105; Tac. Ann. ii. 86; Propert. v. 11. 36.
[3] Val. Max. vi. 3. 10-12.   [4] Plut. Cato Min. vii. 57.

wife, whom he divorced in like manner to enable him to marry Cæsar's daughter, Julia. Wives, on their part also, took to getting divorced from their husbands, on no ground whatever but their own fancy, though custom required of the wife to tolerate her husband's debaucheries;[1] and the sin of adultery in Rome, as among other nations in general, was only laid upon the wife: the only exception being when a husband seduced the wife of another, in which case the man was regarded as the adulterer.

The disorders of nuptial and domestic life now increased enormously. A kind of rivalry in impurity grew up between the two sexes, and there were more seducers than seduced of the female sex.[2] At the Gallic triumph of Cæsar, the cry of the soldiers to the Roman citizens was, "Citizens, see to your wives; we are bringing you the bald gallant."[3] Augustus, censor for life, as Cæsar was, not only debauched other people's wives for reasons of policy, as his friends said, to worm their husbands' secrets out of the wives, but also despatched covered litters to the houses of Romans of quality, to bring their wives to him in his palace.[4] His daughter, whom he exiled to an island for her incorrigible debaucheries, used to spend the whole night drinking in the public squares.[5]

And yet Augustus conceived the intention of arresting by legal enactments the corruptions which had already assailed the foundations of the state, and of restoring at least the semblance of order in domestic life. If, on the one side, divorce and adultery were the order of the day in Rome, on the other, celibacy was making alarming advances, and through this every kind of impurity and licentiousness was being multiplied in either sex alike. The men dreaded to ally themselves and their fate to such furies and insatiable prodigals as the women were, or soon became; the unfettered life of celibacy was far more to their mind. Even in the better times of old, marriage had been regarded as a necessary evil; and, in the year 602, the censor Metellus had gone so far as to say in public, "Could we but exist as citizens without wives, we should all be glad to get rid of such a burden;"[6] and now that all sense of patriotism had disappeared along with the old constitution, the generality of Romans were

---

[1] Plaut. Merc. iv. 6, 1 sqq. [2] Drumann, Gesch. Roms, cxi. 741.
[3] Suet. Cæs. li. [4] Dio. Cass. lvi. 43.
[5] Dio. Cass. lv. 10. [6] Gell. N. A. i. 6; Liv. Epit. 59.

very far removed from the notion of sacrificing their own comfort to the public good.

When, in the year 736 (b.c. 18), Augustus struck his first legislative blow against celibacy, he encountered a strenuous opposition; and as the lavish expenditure and moral degeneracy of the sex were pleaded as causes leading to the dislike of marriage, he attempted first to reduce these evils. Female expenditure was limited, women of rank were forbidden the stage, and adultery was punished with deportation to an island and heavy fines; but the husband was deprived of the right of taking self-satisfaction on the adulterer or his paramour, by putting them to death.[1] At last, he overcame the resistance made to his law of marriage, the Lex Julia and Papia Poppæa, after being obliged to soften it down considerably, and to allow its coming into operation to be frequently deferred. The law had for its basis the principle, that all Romans, men or women, at maturity, were under obligation to marry, and procreate children, males till sixty, and women till fifty years old. The penalties were directed against both celibates and childless couples (against the former the heaviest of the two), and were sorely oppressive in a financial point of view. On the other hand, married men with at least three children, provided they had not married wives of damaged reputation, were rewarded with many privileges, and exempted from many burdens.[2] Augustus also made an attempt to reduce the frequency and facility of divorces by the introduction of an established procedure, and the infliction of a pecuniary mulct upon the guilty parties.

These laws, however, did not attain their object, or at least had but a transient effect. Augustus indeed stood firm against all demands made by whole classes for the repeal of the law, and, even so, could not help frequently overlooking its evasion; and it was just as often mollified by himself and his successors conceding to childless or even unmarried persons the "rights of those who had three children." The advantages of celibacy and barrenness outweighed the legal disadvantages. Instead of prodigal sons, anxiously awaiting their father's decease, an unmarried man had his devoted adherents, and was loaded with adulations and presents from all who hoped for a share in his succession.

---

[1] Dio. liv. 2.

[2] Ulpian, xvi. 1; Juven. ix. 86; Tac. Ann. iii. 28, ii. 51, xv. 19; Dio. liii. 13.

"In our state," says Seneca, "the being without children brings more of favour with it than it destroys, advancing old people to power, so that many fall out with their children, repudiate them, and make themselves out childless."[1] Pliny gives utterance to the same remark, that many felt their children to be a burden, while the advantages of being without them were so great.[2]

Equally ineffectual were the attempts to impede and diminish divorces, the remedies resorted to being, in fact, thoroughly inadequate. By enacting that the husband should restore his injured wife's dower, or that the guilty wife should forfeit the eighth, or sixth, part of it, but few could be induced to continue in a relation that had become either burdensome or intolerable. "There is not a woman left," says Seneca, "who is ashamed of being divorced, now that most of the high and distinguished ladies count their years, not by the consular fasti, but by the number of husbands, and are divorced in order to marry, and marry in order to be divorced."[3]

3. SLAVERY IN ROME.

THE slave in Rome was a chattel and a possession, had no individuality or "caput;" whatever he earned belonged to his master, and he might be made a present of, lent, pawned, or exchanged. His union with a wife was no marriage, that is, was devoid of all its privileges and effects, and only a contubernium, or cohabitation. A master might torture or kill his slave at will; there was no one to prevent his doing so, or to bring him to account. The modes of torture and punishment were various and cruel, and the ordinary punishment of death was crucifixion. Every thing was allowable and privileged as against a slave. There was nothing a master could not do, and a great deal that any freeman could. Insult, ill-treatment, and violence, gave even the master of the slave who had been subjected to them no action or remedy against the free oppressor.

The numerous female slaves in personal attendance on their mistresses were often obliged to perform their various services with shoulders and bosom bare, that their nudity might intensify

---

[1] Consol. ad Marc. c. 19.   [2] Epist. iv. 15; cf. ii. 20.
[3] De Benef. iii. 16.

their feelings of pain.[1] One cruel infliction, and not unfrequently resorted to, was chaining to a block of wood, which served the poor sufferer for a seat, and which she had to drag about with her day and night. This was the ordinary meed of such as had provoked the jealousy of their mistress.[2]

Slaves in the country, who had to till the ground, were chained by the foot, and kept at night in an ergastulum, or underground room.[3] Terrible was the fate of such as endeavoured to escape ill-treatment, either in city or country, by flight. The tracking and recapture of runaway slaves formed a trade of its own, that of the fugitivarii.[4] Recovered slaves were branded on the forehead, and their sum of ill-treatment and labour doubled; or, in case the master was indifferent to the life of his slave, he was thrown to the wild-beasts in the amphitheatre.[5] In order to escape the cruelty of their masters, many offered themselves in their despair to fight in the arena with the beasts, or as gladiators, and yet were restored to their masters afterwards.[6].

The conduct of the elder Cato, that brilliant example of Roman virtue, may supply us with groundwork for a picture of the merciless treatment dealt out to these "souled instruments." To him there was no difference between the beast and the slave, except that the latter as a reasoning being was held accountable. That his view was the genuine Roman one is proved by the old Roman legislation, which inflicted the punishment of death for killing a plough-ox, while the murderer of a slave was called to no account whatever.[7] Cato, too, was in the habit of selling his slaves, or expelling them the house, when old age rendered them useless. He had them trained like dog or horse, and allowed them to couple in order that they might breed. To prevent their mutinying, he sowed dissension and enmities amongst them; their least transgressions were visited with an ample return of chastisement, and no sparing of executions; and his credit stood so low for merciful dealing, that a slave hung

---

[1] Juv. vi. 475 sqq.; Martial, ii. 60; Ovid. de Art. Am. 235-243; Amores, i. 14, 13-18.

[2] Juv. ii. 57.

[3] Colum. i. 8. 16; Seneca de Ira, iii. 32; Plin. H. N. xviii. 3.

[4] There was no asylum in Rome where a slave could take refuge, as at Athens; so he was almost sure to be caught again, sooner or later.

[5] Gell. v. 14.   [6] Dig. xi. 4. 5.

[7] Colum. vi. præf. 7.

himself who had not done what he was bid by him.¹ The same Cato made a traffic of his fellow-men under a disguised name. His slaves were ordered to buy and train boys, whom he sold again.

The proverb, "As many slaves a man has, so many are his enemies," was a universal one. "They are not our enemies," Seneca replied, "but we make them such;" and he describes the mode. "The unhappy slave (in his master's presence) is not free to move his lips, even for speaking. Whispering is silenced with the rod: even accidental acts, like coughing, sneezing, or hiccuping, meet with the same retribution. Every sound to break the silence has a heavy penance attached to it: they have to continue the whole night through fasting and dumb;—we abuse them, in fact, not as if they were men, but beasts of burden."

As it seldom happened any crime was committed without the aid or privity of slaves, their masters had often urgent grounds for putting such dangerous witnesses out of the way, or making them incapable of doing harm. Cicero mentions the case of a slave being crucified, but not till he had had his tongue cut out to prevent his betraying his mistress.² Martial records a similar case of a master cutting his slave's tongue out, and alleging it had been done by others.³ If a slave murdered the master of the house, all his fellows under the same roof were doomed to die. Thus, when Pedanius Secundus was assassinated under Nero, four hundred slaves were executed for not preventing the murder.⁴ There were instances of masters having their slaves' hands cut off, or ordering them to be thrown to feed the murænæ in the fish-pond, for breaking a vase. Augustus, who had himself saved a slave of Vedius Pollio from this punishment, ordered Eros, his steward,⁵ to be crucified on the mast of his ship, for having roasted and eaten a quail of his that had been trained for the quail-pit, and had won many mains.

The slave-merchant made his purchases from armies after battle, pirates, or even in the slave's own country and home. He then exposed them for sale in the cities upon a wooden scaffold. They all had tablets round their necks, stating the particulars of their health and freedom from blemishes. The fairest and finest

---

¹ Plut. Cat. M. x. 21; Plin. H. N. xviii. 8. 3.
² Cic. pro Cluent. 66.   ³ Epig. ii. 82.
⁴ Tac. xiv. 42-45.   ⁵ Plut. Apophth. vi. 778, Reisk.

slaves were to be found at the taberna of the merchant, where they had to strip themselves at the request of purchasers.[1] Asia was the great supplier of slaves: Syrians, Lydians, Carians, Mysians, Phrygians, and, above all, the vigorous, large-limbed Cappadocians, were purchased in troops at Rome. Accident has furnished us with a notion of the way in which these people became slaves. When Marius, at the command of the senate, required Nicomedes, king of Bithynia, to supply his contingent of auxiliary troops, the king replied he had no subjects fit for service, for nearly all his able-bodied men had been carried off by Roman collectors of customs, converted into slaves, and dispersed among the different provinces.[2] Slaves from Gaul and Germany were chiefly employed in field-labour. All the issue of female slaves, besides, were slaves-born, and belonged to the master of the mother, whoever the father might be. Thus it must have frequently happened that a brother was the slave of his brother.

The rich employed one slave only in one office, and the same duty was often performed by several. There were atrienses for the hall; cubicularii for the sleeping apartments; secretarii for letters; lectors, introductors, nomenclators, dispensators or stewards, bath-attendants, cooks, tasters, letter-carriers or tabellarii, litter-bearers, grooms, &c. The porters were chained, like watch-dogs. The mistress of the house had her own suite of slaves of both sexes; and as for city slaves, no less than 120 different officials and duties were reckoned up. Many of them never saw their master at all, or had any acquaintance with him;[3] and many masters must have had a slave for the sole purpose of telling him the names of his slaves at need. There were also silentiarii, to maintain silence and order among the throng.[4] Some rich people possessed as many as 20,000 slaves, the majority of whom, as might be expected, were field-labourers.[5] Crassus had so many, that his company of architects and carpenters alone exceeded 500 head. Scaurus was master of more than 4000 urban slaves, and as many country ones. In the time of Augustus, a freedman died, leaving 4116 slaves, and that after suffering considerable losses in the civil wars. When the wife

---

[1] Suet. Octav. 69; Pers. vi. 77 sqq.; Mart. ix. 60.
[2] Diod. Fragm. xxxvi. 3, 1. [3] Petron. 37.
[4] Sen. Ep. 47; Fabretti, Inscr. p. 206; Salvian de Gub. iv. 3.
[5] Sen. de Vitâ beatâ, 17; Plin. H. N. xxxiii. 1.

of Apuleius left the smaller portion of her country villa to her son, 400 slaves were found upon it. A number of slaves was a principal evidence of wealth in the possessor: hence they formed part of a bride's dower. A law of Augustus, to limit testamentary emancipation, forbade a master to set free more than a fifth of his slaves, and fixed one hundred males as a maximum to manumission at one time, which proves that 500 male slaves was not an unusual number in a household. Horace seems to have accounted ten as the lowest number admissible to be kept by a person of means, and will not tolerate the prætor Tullius coming into Rome from his country house with but five slaves.[1] Many slaves, however, of the higher class had slaves of their own, or had deputies called vicarii.

In Rome, as well as in Greece, the deposition of a slave was not admissible in a court of justice except after torture; only in Rome no slave could lay information, or give evidence, against his master, a few cases excepted. Yet slaves were tortured, to get a favourable testimony out of them for a master on his trial; and the same was done to stranger slaves, to obtain evidence from them against an accused person, whose property they were not.[2] If it were the case of misdemeanour, a crime committed by a slave himself, torture was ordinarily in requisition.[3] In the time of the emperors, however, slaves were frequently tortured for evidence against their masters.[4]

It is in vain one looks for any thing like common human feeling in the Roman slave-law of republican times and that of the earlier empire. The breaking-up of slave families was entirely in the hands of the merchant or the owner; husband might be separated from wife, and mother from children, all dispersed and sold off into the houses of strangers and foreign towns. Slavery is equivalent to death in the eye of the civil law, which does not admit the existence of the slave;[5] which entirely avoids and annuls the contract of a master with his slave;[6] gives the slave no action at law against him;[7] admits not of adultery being committed by or with one of them;[8] makes over all a slave's earnings to his

---

[1] Sat. i. 3, 12, 6. 107 sqq.
[2] Tac. Ann. iii. 67; Paull. v. 16. 2 sqq.   [3] Paull. v. 16. 1; Cod. h. t. 15.
[4] Abundant testimony on all these points is to be found in Wasserschleben de Quaest. per Torment. ap. Rom. (Berlin, 1837), pp. 18 sqq., 35, 78 sqq.
[5] Dig. xxxv. 1. 50.   [6] Ibid. l. 17. 32.
[7] Cod. ii. 14. 13.   [8] Dig. xlviii. 5. 6.

master; and compels female slaves to surrender themselves to their master's lust against their will:[1]—such were the dominant principles of the Roman slave-law. Even in the imperial time, the sick or infirm slave, who had become useless or burdensome to his master, was exposed on an island in the Tiber to pine away there,—an abuse afterwards prohibited. The emperor Claudius allowed his freedom to an infirm slave[2] dismissed by his master; an ordinance indeed which proved in most cases of no benefit at all to the unlucky wretch; for what could he gain, ill and helpless as he was, from the boon of freedom? Hospitals there were none. Vegetius too observes, such used-up slaves as masters were in a hurry to get rid of, were sold for a ridiculously small sum, not equal to that of a beast of burden. Almost the only trace of protection afforded to slaves occurs in the earlier times, when the censorship was in activity as a guardian of public morals; and then the master who treated his slaves with excessive cruelty, or suffered them to die of hunger, was visited with censorial penalties.[3]

In the imperial time, the lot of the slave was in one respect aggravated, as torture was more frequently resorted to then than before, in order to induce the slave to compromise his master by his admissions. But in another respect there were considerable alleviations introduced. As long as the Romans framed their own laws, they had no thought of curtailing despotic dealings of the owner with his slaves;[4] but when obliged to accept them from imperial masters, the Lex Petronia made its appearance, interdicting the sale of slaves for the combat with beasts without approbation from competent authority.[5] This prohibition was extended by degrees to putting a slave to death, or making a eunuch of him, at will.[6] The prætor urbanus could interfere in cases of savage treatment, or starving a slave to death through the avarice of the master.[7] And then asylums for slaves were introduced; and one who had taken refuge there from the cruelty of his master might be sold by the magistrate to another. Augustus and Tiberius had previously ordered visitations of the ergastula, into which it sometimes happened freemen had been

---

[1] Sen. Controv. v. 33.
[2] Suet. Cl. 25.
[3] Dionys. Fragm. xx. 1, ed. Maii.
[4] Dig. l. 17. 32.
[5] Dig. xlviii. 8. 11.
[6] Spart. Hadr. 18; Suet. Domit. 7.
[7] Sen. de Benef. iii. 22.

thrust, and compelled to hard labour.¹ Hadrian, who did the most of all the emperors for the general alleviation of slavery, suppressed these subterranean dungeons entirely;² and yet they still continued to exist in many places.

Slavery was spread over the whole face of heathendom, and found in Gaul and Germany as well as in Rome; but the institution of gladiators was peculiar to the latter, nor was there any exhibition of the kind elsewhere. Compulsory combats of these unfortunates were first established by private persons, as mortuary games; but in the last century of the republic became public amusements, forming part of the state expenditure, and therefore under the care of the ædiles, which made their celebration periodical and fixed. Rich and distinguished individuals still indeed kept them up in honour of their dead at their private charges, but principally with a view to win popular favour. The number of combatants went on increasing. A lucrative trade was pursued by the lanistæ, who had the training of the slaves as gladiators, let them out to hire, and otherwise trafficked with them. Most of the powerful Romans maintained troops of gladiators, who at the same time served them as a body-guard in several instances. The fashion set by Rome now grew contagious. Schools (ludi) for gladiators arose in many places, and a passion for the sanguinary scenes of the arena possessed the inhabitants of all the cities of importance. Perseus had introduced them betimes into Macedonia;³ and Herod Agrippa, in Judæa, made seven hundred couple fight in one day.⁴ The people of Pollentia, in Liguria, would not allow the body of a centurion to be buried until his heirs paid down a certain sum for a combat of gladiators.⁵ In Greece, too, the same exhibitions were given, at Athens and Corinth, and in Thasos.⁶ Amphitheatres were built every where. Emperors were zealous in procuring themselves and the people these gratifications; for which the day no longer sufficed, the combat being prolonged by torchlight. Cæsar once brought 320 pair of gladiators into the arena;⁷ but Trajan on one occasion had 10,000 slaves engaged together, and prolonged the massacre 123 days.⁸ For a change, the Roman people

---

¹ Suet. Oct. 32; Tib. 8. ² Spart. Hadr. 18.
³ Liv. xli. 21. ⁴ Joseph. Ant. Jud. 15. 8, xix. 5.
⁵ Suet. Tib. 37. ⁶ Luc. Demon. 57; Orelli, Inscr. 2564.
⁷ Suet. Dom. 4. ⁸ Dio. Cass. lxviii. 15.

enjoyed the baiting of wild-beasts, in which the bestiarii, for the most part condemned slaves, engaged lions, leopards, tigers, and other animals, which they had to face naked and weaponless, and sometimes actually chained together.[1] Or there were naval combats (naumachiæ), for which great reservoirs had to be excavated, and in these thousands were killed, or perished in the water, at a time, in one sham fight. Gladiators were selected from the strongest prisoners or slaves, Thracians, Gauls, Germans, or Sarmatians. At the leading schools of Ravenna, and in Campania, they were practised in different modes of fighting, and by that, as well as by variety of armour, a kind of relief to the monotony of carnage was obtained. In return for the abundant food which the lanista provided them with, they swore to suffer themselves to be burnt, fettered, and killed by the sword;[2] and after living months and years in daily intercourse,[3] they were necessitated to murder one another, like mortal foes, to please the spectators.

Conspiracies, risings, and executions *en masse* of slaves, draw one continuous track of blood through the later Roman history. Under Eunus in Sicily, and Spartacus in Lower Italy, slave armies were formed of enormous magnitude; Cleon and Eunus having 200,000 fighting men under their orders at a time. They all at last fell, to a man. The struggle was murderous beyond all precedent, and the revenge such as was to be expected from Romans. Crassus, the conqueror of Spartacus, had crosses erected the whole length of the route from Capua to Rome, on which 10,000 slaves were executed.[4] In the civil wars both parties strengthened themselves by arming their slaves; and Augustus lauded himself, on the Ancyran monument, for having delivered to their masters for execution (in violation of his parole) 30,000 slaves who had fought for Sextus Pompeius.

Only a kind of approximation can of course be made to the relative numbers of slaves and freemen; the provinces of the empire certainly varied considerably in this point. For example, there were probably many fewer slaves in Egypt than in Gaul. Wherever Roman colonies were planted, their numbers were always peculiarly large. In Rome herself the proportion of slaves was at the largest; but the calculations differ widely.

---

[1] Cic. pro Sest. 64; Ep. ad Quin. fr. ii. 6.
[2] Sen. Ep. 37.   [3] Sen. de Irâ, ii. 8.
[4] Plin. Ep. x. 38, 39.

Blair[1] supposes the number of freemen and slaves to have been nearly equal, between the expulsion of the kings and the destruction of Carthage; but that from the fall of Corinth to Alexander Severus (146 B.C. to 222 A.D.), the slaves were three to one. On the other hand, Dureau de la Malle[2] maintains the proportion of slaves to free men to have been as one to twenty-five in 476 B.C., and in 225 B.C. to have been as twenty-two to twenty-seven, counting in peregrini. Zumpt holds Bunsen's numbers to be far too low, when he puts the slave population of Rome in the year 5 B.C. at 650,000, and would himself count two slaves for one freeman.[3] With greater certainty it may be affirmed, that male slaves exceeded female four to one; and as no slave could intermarry with a free citizen, it is evident that to at least four-fifths of the males a contubernium even with a female slave was rendered an impossibility. It is not necessary to enlarge upon the depth of the abyss of destruction we gain a glimpse of from this one relation.

---

4. Effects of Slavery on the Free Population—Poverty—Exposition of Children—Decreasing numbers of them—Paiderastia—Courtesans—Corruption of the Female Sex.

Slavery in Rome, as well as in Greece, was one of the main causes of the prevailing moral corruption, and of progressive decay. The Roman law, by its distinction between a novice and a veteran slave, furnishes a test of the operation of servitude on the slaves themselves in Rome. A slave who had been in service a year or more was a veterator, and an experienced hand, and therefore of proportionately less value; for, says the code, it is a very hard task to mend one who has been in use, and to fit him for the service of a fresh master. For this reason, the slave-merchant would often pass off a veterator as a novetius. Thus we see one year of slavery was enough to corrupt a man, so as to lower his value considerably, like any other second-hand article.[4]

---

[1] Inquiry into the State of Slavery among the Romans, Edin. 1830, pp. 10, 15.
[2] Econom. polit. des Romains, i. 270 sqq.
[3] Ueber den Stand der Bevölkerung, p. 60.   [4] Dig. xxxix. 4. 16, § 3.

If the masters ruined their slaves, the slaves, on their part, were the most influential agents in the moral corruption of their masters. As a consequence of this reciprocity of evil, Rome, and all the towns, were thronged with people devoid of all motives of morality, and whose only duty was unconditional obedience to their owners. They were mostly influenced by one fear, that of corporal punishment; and while accustomed to see themselves employed in all that was shameful and degrading to a human being, they nevertheless came frequently into contact with the mistress of the house and children of the family, as also with freemen out of the house. Being composed of every variety of nations, eastern and western, they formed a company to which each member contributed, as it were, the failings and vices of his own country and race, as to a huge capital of human depravity, each imparting to the other the species of debauchery to which he was as yet a stranger. The frequency of manumission enabled these fellows, who had often grown gray in the school of every vice common to slaves, to mix without restraint among free people, and to swell the complement of the half-extinct citizen body. They brought with them for their portion, from their former class to their new one, an ingrained propensity to lying and deceit, that had become a second nature to them; and renouncing every spring and rule of moral action, they became mere blind tools of others' wills, or rushed as blindly to the satisfaction of their own lusts, living like parasites upon the rich, and as indolent consumers of the public exchequer. It was the lucky and wealthy adventurers of their body who supplanted the patrician families, decayed in fortune through their vices and the civil wars. Tacitus puts into the mouth of a speaker in the time of Claudius the confession that the greater part of the knights, and very many senators, derived their descent from freedmen;[1] while, by the time of Nero, these liberti formed the main stock of tribe, curia, and cohort.

Already, by the time of the Gracchi, we find slavery exercising a baneful influence on the free population of Italy outside the towns, who were capable of bearing arms. Great people, with their swarms of agricultural slaves, exempted from military service, oppressed the small landed proprietors and free labourers: from this arose that vast agglomeration of property called

---

[1] Ann. xiii. 27.

the latifundia, and nothing but slaves were to be met with for large tracts of country. The free population disappeared. The plebeian, as possessor, found himself driven out of his patrimonial acres, and as tenant from the lands of the state, and, at last, excluded from all agricultural pursuits whatsoever.[1] By degrees people found it more comfortable and profitable to change plough-land into pasture; and then on the spot where an industrious and free race of tillers of the soil had settled, and formed the training-school of Roman legions, there wandered a bondsman or two watching his flocks and herds. Thus was obliterated the Italic peasant, the stoutest prop of the gigantic empire of Rome. Where once Cincinnatus ploughed, there were now gangs of chained and branded slaves to be seen, and ergastula cumbered the ground once occupied by populous hamlets: the soil, according to the expression of Columella, was handed over to the refuse of the Roman slaves as to a hangman.[2] Italy became sterile, and dependant on foreign lands; and Africa and Sicily had to contribute their corn-harvests, Cos and Chios, Spain and the Gauls their vintage.[3]

The population, expelled the country, streamed into the towns, principally into Rome, whither the charm of public largesses of corn and money attracted them,[4] and where every one could traffic with his vote. The oligarchy of the wealthy grew more and more contracted; till a consul, Lucius Philippus, could say, in an harangue to the people, there were not two thousand citizens in Rome who possessed means of their own.[5] In fact, there was no class of free artisans well-to-do in Rome; for trade was looked down upon there too, though the repugnance to, and disrepute of, handicraft was not so great as it was in Greece. Still the Romans did not acknowledge any other manual employment than agriculture as respectable: Cicero pronounced all mercenary trades to be sordid and degrading, where the remuneration was paid for the labour and not the art. According to him, all mechanics pursued an illiberal craft, as a workshop could never be beseeming a freeman's dignity. Hence all petty retail trades were classed by him in the same category: only

---

[1] Hor. Od. ii. 18. 23 sqq.; Sall. Jug. 41; Sen. Ep. xc. 38; Quintil. Declam. 13.
[2] Colum. i. præf. 3.
[3] Varro de R. R. ii. præf. 3; Colum. i. præf. 20; Tac. Ann. iii. 54.
[4] App. Bell. Civ. ii. 120.   [5] Cic. de Off. ii. 21.

architecture, medicine, commerce on a large scale, and teaching, could respectably be pursued by certain classes of men.[1]

Hence the confluence of slaves must have contributed further to the freeman's aversion to labour. Wealthy people, from the number of slaves they had working for the house, could dispense almost entirely with free labour and free products. The larger slave-masters, besides, found it advantageous to buy up young slaves and have them educated to a trade, on which they might employ themselves on their master's account, or as hired servants. It was thus the sturdy, industrious, middle class was lost to Rome; the free population consisted of proletarii, living in republican times by the sale of their votes, and under the emperors upon the public distributions of money and corn; degraded and demoralised, they were despised by the rich, and assimilated more and more to slavery. Their rulers attempted to remedy the evil. Cæsar compelled twenty thousand families to leave the city and devote themselves to tillage. Eighty thousand men he sent from Rome over sea to distant colonies, and thus reduced the number of applicants for largesses from three hundred and twenty thousand to one hundred and fifty thousand.[2] Augustus and the best of his successors took pains to induce the free to return to labour in the city as well as the country; and yet Augustus was obliged to admit two hundred thousand citizens to share in the sportula.[3] The Roman people was, through slavery, diminished, depraved, and utterly changed in its heart's core. The genuine plebeian stock had in reality ceased to exist. Already, by 150 B.C., Scipio Æmilianus had taunted the grumbling populace with the assurance that he should never tremble before those whom he had himself brought in chains to Rome.[4] It was not the latifundia, as Pliny thought, but slavery that had ruined Italy: had the latifundia been peopled by free tenants, the consequences would have been different. But the slaves on the estates drove the free people into the towns, where, instead of founding families, they mostly died out in a short time, for the inclination to celibacy went on increasing, till, under Augustus, the number of unmarried

---

[1] De Off. i. 42. The opposition is between sordidi quæstus, sordidæ artes, and ingenuæ.

[2] Suet. Cæs. xli. 42; Dio. Cass. xliii. 21.

[3] Dio. Cass. lv. 10.   [4] Val. Max. vi. 11.

citizens in Rome far exceeded that of the married.¹ And this, indeed, was the case with the slaves too, who were still more speedily made away with by bad treatment, inferior food, unwholesome dwellings, and severe labour; but they were easily replaced by continual reinforcements from all quarters of the globe.

Besides the prevailing disgust for marriage, there was yet another impediment to the growth of population, namely, the frequent exposition of new-born children. It was quite at the father's option whether he would educate his offspring, or cast it away and leave it to perish. The old Romulean code only allowed of the exposition or murder of the infant in the case of malformation, and then under the inspection of neighbours; a law holding as to all males and to the first-born daughter.² How long this law continued in observance is uncertain; in later times it was quite effete. Paulus the jurist, under the emperors, admits the right of the father to put his children to death immediately on their birth without limitation; and, in fact, exposition was the ordinary practice of the day. Thus Suetonius records that the day of the death of Germanicus was signalised by exposition of children born upon it, as one of the proofs of the general sorrow.³ Tacitus quotes, with a side-blow at the malpractice of the Romans, the Jews and Germans as considering it a crime with them not to rear all their children.⁴ Even Augustus, who made such marked efforts against the causes tending to diminish population, not only did nothing to check so shameful and immoral a custom, but actually sanctioned it by his own example, when he ordered the child born to his granddaughter Julia after her banishment to be exposed.⁵

Tertullian expresses himself strongly and freely upon this vice. "How many"—(he is speaking to the Roman people)— " how many are there among you, and they, too, in the magistracy, who put an end to your children (by exposition)? You deprive them of the breath of life in water, or you suffer them to die of cold or hunger, or to be eaten by dogs." And in another work, "The laws, indeed, forbid your taking the lives of your newly-born children, but never was law so little heeded, or set

---

¹ Dio. Cass. lvi. 1.   ² Dionys. ii. 15.
³ Calig. 5.   ⁴ Hist. v. 5; Germ. 19.
⁵ Suet. Oct. 65.

aside with such indifference."¹ This also happened not unfrequently, as Tertullian himself observes, under the hope that a passer-by would pick the child up and educate it. The lanistæ were in fact allowed to appropriate the males whom they found exposed, and to bring them up as gladiators. The female children, however, were the most frequent victims; and there were women every where on the look-out for the poor creatures to make a profit of them, when grown up, by their prostitution. Justin remarks, "This was not only practised in the case of female children, but that men, eager for gain, reared males, whom they found exposed, in order to their future prostitution." Thus, then, it came about, as Minucius expresses it, that father or mother unwittingly fell into incestuous commerce with their own children.² Not unfrequently these infants fell into the hands of men who disfigured and maimed them, with a view to associate them with themselves in the vocation of mendicants.³

Exposition was by no means so common amongst the higher classes. These, like the Greeks, made use of ascertained means of abortion in the womb, which were compression of the embryo, or medicaments; and there were women, as Juvenal expressly tells us, who committed child-murder for hire,⁴ *i. e.* made a trade of procuring abortions. And this was so frequent, that the same poet asserts there were hardly any women of rank who were brought to bed. Not seldom was the crime committed out of mere weakness and coquetry, the women being afraid of the pains of child-birth, and the detriment to their figure and complexion. The children so lost were readily supplied by foundlings, of whom there was no scarcity.⁵ Matters must have been carried to a great length, if Seneca could claim as a special distinction for his mother, Helvia, that she had never destroyed the hopes of motherhood in her womb, after the fashion of other vain women.⁶ It is true, a woman could have been banished, according to the law, for causing her child's death by abortion against the father's will;⁷ but it is well known how easy it was for wives, with the help of their female attendants, to deceive their husbands on this score. The average number of children,

---

¹ Tert. Apol. 9, ad nationes, 15. Here he is alluding to the above-mentioned law of the twelve tables.
² Octav. xxx. 31.   ³ Sen. Controv. x. 4.   ⁴ Sat. vi. 592 sqq.
⁵ Juv. vi. 602.   ⁶ Consol. ad Helv. 16.   ⁷ Dig. xlviii. 8. 8.

issues of Roman marriages, is a sufficient test of the state of a family, and of the means that must have been resorted to. Among Christian people the average issue of a marriage is four or five; but in Rome the law granted to the father of three living children exemption from all the personal burdens of state, while the six children of Germanicus passed for an extraordinary instance of fecundity. Five children to a marriage was considered an exceptional case among the higher ranks. Not one of the Roman emperors left a numerous family, and many died childless. It has been observed before this,[1] that the authors of the early imperial times, though living a married life in obedience to the lex Papia Poppæa, yet remained without issue: thus Ovid, Lucan, Statius, Silius Italicus, Seneca, the two Plinys, Suetonius, Tacitus. Martial, in one of his epigrams, sues Domitian for the jus trium liberorum in his own favour, and, in the succeeding one, takes leave of his wife, as having no more use for her.[2]

We are obliged here to revert again to the vice of paiderastia; for though the spread of it was not so great, nor its effects ruinous in such a wide circle as among the Greeks, yet it had no small share in the accumulative destruction of society, as having struck deep root into the Roman empire, and tainted every social relation with its poison.

In the earlier centuries of the republic cases of this vice were few and isolated. In the fifth, Titus Veturius, the son of a Roman general, who had fallen into the hands of C. Plotius as a slave for debt, was punished in servile fashion by the latter, as his master, for refusing to prostitute himself;[3] an act at the same time evincing the consequences of the nexum, that disgrace to the Roman patriciate. From this date, in spite of the heavy penalties imposed for the prostitution of a freeman, instances of such prostitution became more numerous; a centurion, Lætorius Mergus, extricated himself by suicide from the punishment of death incurred by that crime. At the close of the sixth century the evil had become so general, that Polybius tells us of many Romans paying a talent for the possession of a beautiful youth.[4] The abuse of slaves and freedmen had always passed as an admitted license. Caius Gracchus actually claimed in public

[1] Zumpt, über den Stand der Bevölkerung, p. 97.

the merit of uncommon self-restraint for never having coveted the slave of another for such purposes.[1] The Scatinian law, imposing a pecuniary mulct on those who committed the sin with a free person, soon fell into desuetude.[2] It was dormant under the empire; only Domitian once had some senators sentenced upon its provisions:[3] and generally the emperors themselves, even the best of them, such as Antoninus and Trajan, set the example of violating it. By the time the last days of the free republic were reached, the vice had attained a fearful degree among the Romans. On a political trial, beautiful youths, the sons of senators, and they too of the first Roman families, were offered to the judges, thus serving to buy the votes of such as were inaccessible by money.[4]

With the exception of Ovid, all the poets of the Augustan age have left behind them in their works traces of their paiderastic propensities, frequently, as in the case of Catullus, with a shamelessness beyond belief: and as regards Ovid, the reasons which he assigns for his contenting himself with women, are worthy of the man and of the age. On the whole, this vice exhibits a grosser aspect among the Romans than among the Greeks; with the latter it had often a dash of spiritualism mixed up with it; the sin, so to speak, was crowned and veiled with the flowers of sentiment, and of a devotion amounting to sacrifice. But in the Romans it came out in its naked filth, so common and so grossly disgusting as to defy and reject all excuse. We are forced to conclude, from the number of examples, that alternate commerce of impurity with women as well as boys and youths was the general fashion. The shameful connection of Cæsar with the Bithynian king, Nicomedes, furnished the theme for the satirical songs of the soldiers in his Gallic triumph.[5]

Horrors such as only the most depraved imagination could conceive were made possible through slavery. The Romans now came to have harems of males, euphemistically styled paidagogia. Here the unfortunate victims destined for the lust of the possessor, and called exoleti, were first made eunuchs of, in order to expose them to abuse the longer,[6] and these were given

---

[1] Gell. xv. 12.   [2] Christii Hist. Legis Scatiniæ, Halæ, 1727, pp. 7, 9.
[3] Suet. Dom. 8.   [4] Cic. ad Att. i. 16.   [5] Suet. Cæs. 49.
[6] "Exoletos suos, ut ad longiorem patientiam impudicitiæ idonei sint, on putant." Sen. exc. Controv. x. 4.

a certain kind of educational polish to render them more effectually objects of desire; while all artifices were resorted to to delay the development of the child into the youth, and the youth into the man. "Decked out like a woman," as Seneca says of one of these, "he wrestles and fights with his years. He must not pass beyond his age of boyhood. He is kept back perforce; and, though robust as a soldier, he retains his smooth chin; his hair is all shaved off, or removed by the roots."[1] These epicenes were sometimes classed together by nations and colour, so that all were equally smooth, and their hair all of one tint.[2] That they might keep a fresh complexion longer, they were obliged, when on a journey with their master, to cover their faces with a mask.[3] It was thus Clodius on his travels took also his exoleti about with him as well as his women of pleasure.[4] Tiberius, at Caprea, and even Trajan, kept such boys in droves; and in those days formal marriages between man and man were introduced with all the solemnities of ordinary nuptials.[5] On one of these occasions Nero made the Romans exhibit the tokens of a public rejoicing, and treat his elect, Sporus, with all the honours of an empress.[6]

The cause, however, of the wide spread of celibacy, that was sapping the foundations of the state, is not to be looked for so much in this unnatural vice, as in the general facility of intercourse with women of pleasure. Multitudes of female slaves, manumitted along with their daughters, afforded a free choice. The law of Augustus, imposing penalties on adultery, and intercourse with free-born maidens out of marriage, was for the most part impracticable, and its only effect was to drive the Romans to attach themselves still more to foreign women, who had been emancipated, and who were thoroughly experienced in all the artifices of wantonness and luxury. In order to escape the punishments inflicted by the Julian law on adultery, in the time of Tiberius, married women, and even those of illustrious family, had themselves enrolled as public prostitutes on the lists of the ædiles, renouncing utterly their rank and position as honoured wives. Every free-born woman could do this; and when Tibe-

---

[1] Epist. 47.   [2] Ibid. 95.   [3] Ibid. 123.
[4] Cic. pro Mil. 21; Julian. Cæs. ed. 1796, p. 6; Spart. Hadr. 4.
[5] Juv. ii. 117 sqq.; Mart. xii. 42.
[6] Suet. Ner. xxviii. 29; Dio. Cass. lxii. 23. lxiii. 13; Tac. Ann. xv. 37.

rius wanted to except from this category wives whose husbands or brothers were senators or knights, he met with resistance.[1]

These relations were all the more seductive to the male sex, young and old, as no feeling of shame, or apprehension of public opinion, could find place to disturb them. A young man would be told how Cato, the strict censor of morals, meeting a youth coming out of a house of ill fame, expressed his satisfaction thereat: and Cicero declares, in one of his public speeches, that intercourse with prostitutes had, at all times, been looked upon at Rome as a thing permitted and uncensured.[2] Hence, too, there were some twenty temples and shrines of Venus there, some of them to Venus Volupia, or Lubentina.

In times when and countries where religion still preserved a salutary ascendant, and extended protection to the female sex, the case might occur of the males being plunged into the grossest moral corruption, while the females kept clear of being carried away in the vortex, and on the whole retained possession of a higher degree of purity. In Rome, where such kind of religious influence was not to be dreamt of, the women were necessarily deprived of all moral support, and became just what the men made them, and so sank, with them, incessantly deeper and deeper. The generality of marriages became mere temporary connections, with a virtual though tacit agreement on both sides to break off the relations as soon as they became a burden to one or both. "No woman," says Seneca, "is to be found so contemptible or so mean as to be contented with a couple of gallants, without having laid out her hours one after the other, the day being otherwise too short to go the circuit of all."[3] And thus the law of Augustus against adultery became completely obsolete within ten years of its enactment. The higher-minded emperors, indeed, took some pains to put an end to the immoral practice of men and women bathing together. Trajan, Hadrian, and Marcus Aurelius, all launched edicts against it, but to no purpose; Alexander Severus made a fresh attempt at an interdiction.[4] The custom had now been introduced of wearing fine stuffs of texture quite transparent, that made clothes incapable

---

[1] Tac. Ann. ii. 85; Suet. Tiber. 35.
[2] Pro Cælio, c. 15.   [3] De Benef. iii. 16.
[4] Plin. H. N. xxxiii. 54, 3; Spart. Hadr. 18; Capitolin. M. Ant. Phil. 23; Lamprid. Alex. Sev. 24.

of hiding the body or its shame, and such as, when put on, a woman could not swear with a good conscience she was not naked.¹

In the debauchery, which the Romans carried out to a greater extent than any other people, the women would not be in arrear of the men. The same witness observes upon their having forfeited the ancient privilege of the sex, to be exempt from certain complaints; and baldness and gout had become common amongst them.² As wives of proconsuls and other foreign officials, these degraded creatures turned into scourges of entire provinces. In all indictments for extortion, it was always the wives against whom the loudest and most general cry was raised: it was on them the rapacious rabble of the provinces depended, and on their account Cæcina, in the time of Tiberius, brought forward an unsuccessful motion in the senate, forbidding the functionaries appointed to the provinces to take their wives along with them.

---

5. Treatment of the Poor—Education—Public Spectacles.

The view has frequently been taken, that it was slavery which prevented the extension of education to the poor and the proletarii in the ancient states; but this was to overlook the fact that the existence of slaves was a source of poverty, and a cutting-off of their means of subsistence to the lower classes. There can be no mistake about the numbers of the entirely needy and destitute, at any time, under the imperial sway, having been very considerable, and always on the increase. To the question now asked, What the position of the rich and wealthy was towards the poor, and how the poor were circumstanced? the answer must be, that mercy and kindness to poverty did not, as a general rule, belong to the Roman character at all. "A Roman never gives any one any thing ungrudgingly," Polybius informs us. The case, however, was different when such immense fortunes were accumulated in the hands of a few. It was then the interest of the possessors to bethink themselves of the ways and means of expenditure, and how to gather a following round them

¹ De Benef. vii. 9: cf. ad Helv. 16. ² Ep. 95: cf. Juven. vi. 250.

from the poorer citizens and clients. Not a few of these latter owed their entire subsistence to the largesses of the sportula from their wealthy patrons. At the same time the state had 200,000 poor citizens to provide for, besides their wives, sisters, and daughters; and further, there were crowds of poor excluded from these bounties, and who found their only shelter in the public halls and the colonnades of the temples; and, moreover, the collective peregrini, who had no claim at all. These swarms of proletarii and beggars were further increased by the manumission of slaves, after it had become a custom among the greatest to present a number of their slaves with freedom by their wills; a practice which Augustus was obliged to limit. As for other cities, where there were no such regular distributions of money and corn, the number of helpless poor must have been still larger.

There were thus herds of beggars. Seneca often mentions them, and observes that most men fling an alms to a beggar with repugnance, and carefully avoid all contact with him.[1] To the ancients it was of evil omen only to meet a mendicant.[2] "Could you possibly let yourself down so low as not to repel a poor man from you with scorn?" was said by a rhetorician of the imperial times to a rich man.[3] The extremest concession which Roman morality admitted of towards the indigent, was to give a stranger what you could bear the loss of without any further prejudice to yourself.[4] "What is the use, too," says a popular poet, "of giving a beggar any thing? One loses what one gives away, and only prolongs the miserable existence of the receiver."[5] On this point the Stoic philosophy came in aid of the rich with its maxim, that there was no real evil in any human wretchedness, necessity, or poverty; and therefore bidding the wise man be on the watch against giving way to any active compassion for misery.[6] It is characteristic, too, how Virgil, in his beautiful passage describing the peace and repose of the wise

---

[1] De Clem. v. 6.

[2] Hermogen. περὶ στάσεων, cap. περὶ στοχασμοῦ (ap. Walz. Rhett. Gr. t. iii. p. 25), makes one of them say he had begged at night and not by day, ὅτι οὐ βούλεται δυσοιώνιστὸς εἶναι.

[3] Quintil. Decl. 301, iii. 17.   [4] Cic. de Off. i. 16.

[5] Plaut. Trinumm. i. 2. 58, 59. The passage afterwards excited much displeasure. Lactantius called it "detestanda sententia," Inst. vi. 11.

[6] Epist. Enchir. c. 22.

man, introduces as one of the features his being exempted from feeling pity for a necessitous person.[1] No one, then, of the thousands of rich men settled at Rome ever conceived the notion of founding an hospital for the poor, or hospital for the sick. Julian was the first to be struck with the aspect of Christian institutions of this kind, and to view them as a standing reproof to heathen selfishness.

And now, if we cast a final glance at the question of education, we shall find but little to say of it, as far as regards the period before Cicero. In the republican times the state did not trouble itself about the training of youth: a few prohibitory regulations were laid down, and the rest left to private individuals.[2] Thus no public instruction was given; public schools there were, but only as private undertakings for the sake of the children of the rich. All depended on the father; his personal character and the care taken by the mother in education decided the development of the child's disposition. Books there were none; and therefore they could not be put into the hands of children. A few rugged hymns, such as those of the Salii and Arval brothers, with the songs in Fescennine verse, sung on festivals and at banquets, formed the poetical literature. A child would hear, besides, the dirges or memorial verses, composed by women in honour of the dead, and sometimes, too, the public panegyrics pronounced on their departed relatives, a distinction accorded to women also from the time of Camillus. Whatever was taught a boy by father or mother, or acquired externally to the house, was calculated to make the Roman "virtus" appear in his eyes the highest aim of his ambition; the term including self-mastery, an unbending firmness of will, with patience, and an iron tenacity of purpose in carrying through whatever was once acknowledged to be right.

The Greek palestra and its naked combatants always seemed strange and offensive to Roman eyes. In the republican times the exercises of the gymnasium were but little in fashion;[3] though riding, swimming, and other warlike exercises were industriously practised, as preparations for the campaign. The slave pædagogus, assigned to young people to take charge of them, had a higher position with the Romans than the Greeks; and was not allowed to let his pupils out of his sight till their

[1] Georg. ii. 449.   [2] Cic. de Rep. iv. 3.   [3] Cic. Legg. ii. 15.

twentieth year. The Latin Odyssey of Livius Andronicus was the school-book first in use; and this and Ennius were the only two works to create and foster a literary taste before the destruction of Carthage. The freedman Sp. Carvilius was the first to open a school for higher education. After this the Greek language and literature came into the circle of studies, and in consequence of the wars in Sicily, Macedon, and Asia, families of distinction kept slaves who knew Greek. Teachers quickly multiplied, and were either liberti, or their descendants. No freeborn Roman would consent to be a paid teacher, for that was held to be a degradation.

The Greek language remained throughout the classical one for Romans: they even made their children begin with Homer. As, by the seventh century of the republic, Ennius, Plautus, Pacuvius, and Terence, had already become old poets, dictations were given to scholars from their writings. The interpretation of Virgil began under Augustus,[1] and by this time the younger Romans were resorting to Athens, Rhodes, Apollonia, and Mitylene, in order to make progress in Greek rhetoric and philosophy. As Roman notions were based entirely on the practical and the useful, music was neglected as a part of education; while, as a contrast, boys were compelled to learn the laws of the twelve tables by heart. Cicero, who had gone through this discipline with other boys of his time, complains of the practice having begun to be set aside; and Scipio Æmilianus deplored, as an evil omen of degeneracy, the sending of boys and girls to the academies of actors, where they learnt dancing and singing, in company with young women of pleasure. In one of these schools were to be found as many as five hundred young persons, all being instructed in postures and motions of the most abandoned kind.[2] This taste of the Romans for the dance grew into a very passion afterwards, under the influence of the mimic dances of the theatres. It is of course natural to man that he should practise himself, or have at his home, what he sees and admires out of it: and so Horace describes the enjoyment young women had in being taught the soft and voluptuous movements composing the Ionic dance.[3] On the other hand, the gymnastic exercises, which had once served the young men as a training for war, fell into disuse, having naturally become objectless and burdensome, now that, under Augustus, no more Roman citizens chose to enlist in the legions.[1]

Still slavery was, and continued to be, the foremost cause of the depravation of youth, and of an evil education. The dwellings of the rich and noble had no sooner become hot-beds of all vice, and schools for propagating corruption, through the conflux of slaves of both sexes, and of every imaginable nation, than morals were poisoned at the root through them, and children from the earliest age fell into the worst of hands. It was no longer the mothers who educated their own children: they had neither inclination nor capacity for such duty, for mothers of the stamp of Cornelia had disappeared. Immediately on its birth, the child was intrusted to a Greek female slave, with some male slave, often of the worst description, to help her.[2] Young maidens were frequently committed to a pædagogus; and thus it was that Fannius Saturninus killed his own daughter and the slave who had debauched her.[3] The young Roman was not educated in the constant companionship of youths of his own age, under equal discipline: surrounded by his father's slaves and parasites, and always accompanied by a slave when he went out, he hardly received any other impressions than such as were calculated to foster conceit, insolence, and pride in him. He knew he was, one day or other, to become master of his teacher and pædagogus, who, on his part, lost no opportunity of winning and keeping favour and influence with his young master, taking care to aid and abet him in the satisfaction of passions that were all too early roused, or to lead him on to pleasures and vices of which he had as yet no experience. The theatre and circus formed the complement to the education which the slave had begun and conducted.[4]

Thus the consideration of this state of things brings us necessarily back again to the public spectacles, which formed one-half of the existence of rich as well as poor. "Bread and the circus games!" Now that the Romans had renounced the political life, contemporaneously with the fall of the free republic, the games only were equal to rousing them from their lethargy and indolence. The circus, the theatre, and the arena, were the places

---

[1] Suet. Oct. 24; Tib. 8.
[2] Tacit. de Causis Corr. Eloq. c. 29.   [3] Val. Max. vi. 1. 3.
[4] Compare the scene in Plautus, Bacchid. ii. 1. 16, iii. 3. 405.

where public life concentred, and where the people still felt itself in its strength. People roused themselves, and formed parties in behalf of the pantomime or the chariot-driver. An armed force was not always able to put down the fights of the theatre factions: imprisonment and exile were the only processes available against the impetuosity of partisans of the different actors.[1] No popular festival or pleasure-party was complete unless a gladiatorial combat, or a fight of wild-beasts, or a naval engagement, formed part of the entertainment. Titus gave on one and the same day a naval engagement and a fight of gladiators, with a battue of wild-beasts, in which five thousand were destroyed. So universal was the passion, and so exciting, that patricians, knights, and women rushed down into the arena, and of their own accord joined in the fray with the gladiators. In one of these combats there fell twenty-six Roman knights, who, after squandering away all their fortune, were quite willing to sacrifice their lives as well.[2] In Nero's time, men of knightly and senatorial rank came out as charioteers in the circus, and as gladiators and fighters with beasts in the amphitheatre. Others, including women too of the highest families, appeared on the boards as players, singers, and dancers.[3]

By the side of such violent emotions as gladiatorial fights, in which women and maidens, by a motion of the hand, surrendered the wounded combatant, in the act of imploring mercy, to the fatal blow, the ordinary tragedies, with their cut-and-dried catastrophes, proved insipid, and the sentiments they called forth all too feeble and void of charm. Here also living realities were in demand; and accordingly the actor who played the robber-chief, Laureolus, was actually nailed on the cross, before the spectators' eyes, and torn in pieces besides by a bear.[4] The emasculation of Atys, and burning of Hercules on the pile on Mount Œta, were realised in the persons of condemned criminals.[5] Plutarch speaks of boys at the theatre full of admiration for, and regarding as the happiest of mortals, the players whom they saw coming on the stage in gilded vestments with purple mantles and crowns, till they perished before their eyes by the sword or the scourge, while the fire consumed their fine clothes.[6]

[1] Tac. Ann. i. 77, ii. 13, xiii. 28. [2] Dio. Cass. lix. 9.
[3] Ibid. lxi. 17. [4] Martial, Lib. de Spect. Ep. 7.
[5] Tertull. Apol. 15; ad Nat. i. 10. [6] De Ser. Num. Vind. 9.

The theatres consequently were schools of barbarous cruelty and voluptuousness, places to dull the edge of every finer feeling in man, and to rouse and foster every animal principle in him. Seneca says, "There is nothing so destructive of morality as being a spectator at the plays, where vice insinuates itself into us the easier under the veil of pleasure; and I return from thence all the greedier, and more ambitious, more sensual, more savage and inhuman, because I have been amongst men." He then proceeds to mention his having gone to the theatre at mid-day, and there lit upon, by way of interlude, a combat of gladiators, all fighting exposed without armour, so that it was a mere butchery; they were driven back with clubs into the bath of blood to receive the strokes with their naked breasts. "The morning's amusement," he adds, "is exposing men to lions and bears, and again at mid-day to their spectators. The only end for all engaged can be but death: they go to work with fire and sword, and there is no respite till the arena is empty of combatants."[1]

Life became a mere drug in the market. People saw numbers put to death every day for mere pastime, dying courageously in cold blood, uttering no prayer or cry to avert the final blow. Life, on the other side, had no more to offer to thousands who had emptied the intoxicating cup of pleasure to the very dregs. Amid the facility with which the Roman could procure and exhaust every enjoyment, no charm any longer attached to difficulties and dangers to be overcome; and thus the existence that had become a burden was thrown away right willingly. It was not only under the yoke of despotic emperors, but even under better government, that contempt of life and suicide were the order of the day in Rome; and the Stoic creed contributed to the general inclination by setting up a theory of suicide, and enumerating a variety of cases in which a man should and ought to make away with his life, with honour to himself and the approbation of the wise and good. Life, according to this view, was one of the indifferent things; if it became a burden, it might be thrown aside unhesitatingly, like a cast-off garment. Seneca was astonished that a greater number of slaves did not make use of this simple means of emancipating themselves. Freedom is so close at hand, he exclaims, and yet there are slaves. He quotes the expression of a distinguished

[1] Ep. 7.

Stoic, in which are strikingly blended contempt of slaves and of life: "There is nothing great in living; all slaves live, and all beasts too."[1] Then Marcus Aurelius also recommended "retiring from life," if a man did not feel himself strong enough to maintain a certain moral elevation. Cato's example acted on the Romans who succeeded him for long. Many ran to death instinctively, in a kind of frenzy, as the younger Pliny expresses it; but he took it to be the act of a great soul to give itself the *coup-de-grace* after a calm and thoughtful survey of the grounds.[2]

6. GENERAL SURVEY—AUGURIES OF THE FUTURE.

IT is the state of things in Rome with which we are principally acquainted; very fragmentary notices of life and doings in the provinces and the other cities of the empire are furnished us. Yet the Roman military roads ran eastward from the forum of the world's metropolis as far as the Thebaïs and the borders of Arabia, and to the west right up to Caledonia; Roman rulers lorded it every where; the law and language and manners of Rome prevailed throughout. Rome carried its own moral corruption into all lands, and they again poured back their own into Rome, as into a vast reservoir. One can see from the accounts of Tacitus how every spot occupied by the Roman executive became a school of demoralisation, where insatiable rapacity and luxury indulged in every caprice.[3] The great historian confesses the Romans had more power over their subjects by exciting and gratifying their sensual tastes than by their arms.[4] The luxury of their baths and the splendour of their entertainments, which were styled ways of civilising men and ennobling their minds, were in reality but means of subjugation;[5] and even barbarians, as he tells us, allowed themselves to be won over by the insinuating vices of their Roman conquerors.[6]

And thus, to use the words of a Roman poet, corruption had attained its full tide at the commencement of the second century.[7] Vices gnawed at the marrow of nations, and, above all,

---

[1] Epist. 77.   [2] Plin. Epp. iii. 7.
[3] Ann. xiii. 31, xvi. 23, iv. 72, xii. 33; Agr. 38.

of the Romans: their national existence was more than menaced; the moral sickness had become a physical one in its effects,—a subtle poison penetrating into the vitals of the state; and as before in the sanguinary civil wars, so now the lords of the world seemed minded to destroy themselves by their vices. True, the marvellous fortune of the Roman empire still clung steadily to her, and had not passed away; but those who saw deeper beneath the surface could not blink the truth, that the alternative was either a moral revolution and regeneration, or an entire dissolution and ruin. Men were denuded of all that was really good, and, surrounded on all sides by the thick clouds of a blinded conscience, they caught with wild eagerness at the grossest sensual enjoyments, in the wild tumult of which they plunged to intoxication.

The number of such as kept themselves free from the general contamination and brutality, or at least endeavoured to do so, was but small; and of them the disciples of the Stoic school were the most prominent. In the senate, a few Stoics, amid universal deterioration and mean-spiritedness, were the only ones to preserve the dignity of independent men, by their speeches or an expressive silence;—and many of them had to pay, by exile or death, for the declaration, or for being suspected, of Stoicism. The Stoics of the imperial time ranked high as moralists, their intellectual horizon had a wider and freer expansion, and the notion of man as a great interdependent whole had developed itself among them. Marcus Aurelius already speaks of a universal republic, where Roman and barbarian, slave and infirm, were all to have the rights of citizens, and equality was to be dominant.[1] Just as physicians acquire most knowledge in times of great pestilence, the Stoics sharpened their moral vision amid the general corruption of morals. Strict censors they were, and telling advice they could give upon the methods of moral reforms and amelioration. How trenchant, lively, and brilliant, how full of profound acquaintance with the human heart, its weaknesses and malice, is Seneca! how solemn, how sorrowfully pathetic, Marcus Aurelius! How confidently and irresistibly do Epictetus and his interpreter Arrian carry away the reader, when they preach patience and self-denial, and bring him to the point of desiring nothing passionately, and,

[1] Marc. Aur. iv. 5.

while he always keeps a steadfast eye on his own intellectual freedom, of being in dread of nothing in the path of virtue! And yet their influence was, on the whole, more inconsiderable, and their schools sooner extinct, than one would have expected. Their system was intrinsically beset with internal contradictions amounting to actual annihilation, and men felt no comfort, no moral strength, from this ostentation of virtue enamoured with herself, that would be indebted to nothing but itself, and, while she put herself on a par with the Deity, advanced her pretensions as far as a divine security and steadfastness in the midst of human frailty.[1] Quite a different lever was requisite to lift mankind generally from their fallen state. No one, says Seneca, is in a position to help himself; he needs another's hand to raise him up;[2]—and this hand of help and rescue was never and nowhere to be seen.

There were but a few to flatter themselves with the hope of finding an answer to their questions, repose to their spirit and their conscience, and full relief of their necessities, in a system of philosophy. As the product of the human mind left to its own resources, philosophy had travelled through, and exhausted, every conceivable system, at an astonishing outlay of acuteness and speculative power; and still there was no appearance any where of a site upon which to found, or a creative spirit and fertile imagination with which to construct, the new edifice. Individual schools had run through and consumed their patrimony; none had been able to maintain themselves, all were approaching dissolution. Men became more and more conscious of their own deepening aspirations after a God who was absolutely elevated above every thing earthly and mundane. A God they must have and they coveted, whom they could in all sincerity address in prayer, who, as all-ruling lord and judge, would be the object of dread and fear, and, as all holy and merciful, the cynosure of homage and love, satisfying every want of the troubled and longing heart. But the Stoics, though still the highest in repute among philosophers, had nothing to tender to men in this need of God, but their nature-power, bound up in matter, and only manifesting itself in the development of the universe, much as they laboured to attribute intelligence and bliss to this world's soul of theirs, that contained every vital principle in it-

---

[1] Sen. Ep. 53.   [2] Ibid. 52.

self, this god of the ether, ruling in the world with the arm of necessity. And then, as regarded conscience, they could do nothing but refer man, who had God within himself, was himself divine, and yet was wearied and woe-begone of his own godship, back to himself again and his own dignity. He was to pass judgment on his own actions, and to be summoned to answer for them, not before God's tribunal, but his own; to blush for himself and to himself, and to look on the moral law as one given by himself to himself alone. But a self-imposed law not being absolutely inviolable and holy; the question of the transgression of it would always revert, in the last instance, to the court of a man's own judgment, who would acknowledge no higher authority, and no lawgiver external to and above himself; and this process might perhaps engender in him a confounding consciousness of his own malice and infirmity, but never that of sin.

Besides, there were many now who no longer found any contentment in the hereditary worship of state or popular deities. With what eagerness did the Roman world hurry to invoke the deified Augustus! And in this rivalry, common to cities and individuals, there was not merely *lâche* flattery involved, but also the desire of having in heaven a mediator and protector for the Empire, a god who had been himself man, and had, but a short time before, been in visible converse with man: he was, like Dionysos of old, the youngest of those who had become deities; the world, in its decrepitude, had once again produced a god; and his worship was, in principle, the only one spread throughout the whole empire, and really a universal one. But when all his successors and their wives had trod the same imperial road of apotheosis (and what despicable beings, what monsters of moral iniquity the most of them were!), this resource was worked out too, and the god Augustus fell into the same disrepute as the others. Numbers followed the example of the emperor Hadrian, and went the round of all religions, practised every worship, and were initiated as often as they could, to finish their career, helpless and perplexed, at the gates of eternity, or to sit themselves down on the sandbank of a vague and comfortless hylozoic pantheism. All these popular religions exhibited but the produce of an exclusive nationality, morally powerless, and presenting the grossest contradictions. The gods were made-up creatures, stamped with the indelible characters of those to whom they owed their origination, its partialities and vices; and were exalted by their makers over their own heads more to minister to their lusts, and to be tools of their selfishness, than to be really their lords and masters. And now that the consciousness of a unity in the human race was aroused, men were logically led further to seek and inquire for a God raised high above all nationalities, and common to all. There were so many people now externally united to one great empire, and the sword of Roman dominion had so beaten down all the bulwarks under the shelter of which the nations had hitherto reposed in their exclusiveness, and fancied themselves secure, that there was but one single thing left to sustain the old separation, namely, the opposition of god to god, worship to worship. Two languages had gained the day, to the exclusion of all others, and now served alone for every purpose of communication of thought; and yet these organs, forming as they did a kind of intellectual chain between all people, were wanting in the capacity for ideas, principles, and doctrines, of a genuine universalism that would embrace every nationality, every order of intellect, and people of all ranks. The vessel was ready, and waited for the wine of the new doctrine which it was destined to receive.

And the men in Rome who were above their age—men like Tacitus, for instance—were oppressed with a profound sentiment of disheartenment and sorrow. Recognising the futility of the resistance to the tide of corruption, and the impotence of law, they were unable to discern any where the germ of a new life, of a great moral and political regeneration. Tacitus was fully persuaded that Rome and the state lay under the lash of divine displeasure;[1] and thus they were driven to the conclusion that every thing of this world was void and empty, and human life a huge imposture.[2] Cicero in his time had characterised a contempt for all human things as a sign of greatness of mind;[3] under the Empire, when individual men generally were denied any political activity, this view of the emptiness of existence became more frequent, and all relation to a higher and better life beyond the grave was utterly wanting. This contempt of earthly

---

[1] Ann. iv. 1, xvi. 16; Hist. iii. 72.

[2] Ann. iii. 18,—" Ludibria rerum humanarum cunctis in negotiis,"—and frequently.

[3] De Off. i. 4, 18.

things and of life could only be properly adjusted, and value be again attached to life, when mankind should recognise Him who unites as with a golden chain this transitory existence to an eternal one, for which it is to be the preparation, and who therewith imparts to life its true scope and its highest significance.

The Stoic creed had seen itself forced to declare, that the truly wise man, the ideal of virtue and moral heroism, had not yet appeared on this earth, though Cicero had already described the delight that men would experience if they were ever so fortunate as to see perfect virtue alive and in the flesh.[1] And thus on all sides there was a diffusion of this sentiment of moral and intellectual wants unsatisfied. As the better kind of people longed for the light of a visible exemplar of human virtue by which continually to steer their moral conscience, they had also aspirations after a steadfast divine doctrine, to extricate them from the labyrinth of opinion, conjecture, and doubt as to the real end of their being, and the state of man after death. They sighed for a rule of life and discipline, which, leaving no choice to the fluctuating caprice of self-will, would lend consistency and confidence to their moral conduct; and the sight of the Roman empire might well kindle a presentiment of another, which uniting the people of the earth in free and spontaneous obedience, would have the promise of permanence, and which would not, like the Roman, have an avenging God threatening it with destruction. And such hopes and aspirations were not, in fact, without their foundation. In the Erythræan collection of Sibylline prophecies, as known in Rome, there was one promising the birth of a divine child; and on his descent from heaven and appearing upon earth, a new period of the world, a new order of things, a better and golden age, was to begin.[2] The Romans expected the dawn of this halcyon age after the horrors of the civil wars. If flattery led Virgil into the mistake of referring the fulfilment of this expectation to a son of Pollio, as others, somewhat later, interpreted of Vespasian the prophecy about a ruler of the world, who was at that time to arise in the East, there were certainly not a few above such weakness, or at a sufficient distance from those in power, who had a presentiment of the fulfilment of a purer hope, and the contentment of a deeper-rooted necessity.

It was on the 19th of December in the year of grace 69,

[1] De Fin. v. 24. 69.   [2] Virg. Ecl. 4.

during the civil war between the Vitellianists and the Vespasianists, that the Capitol, including the Temple of Jupiter and the sanctuaries of Juno and Minerva, were consumed by a fire kindled by Roman hands. Tacitus calls this event the saddest and most shameful blow which the Roman state had met with since the foundation of the city;[1] and he could only explain its being permitted to take place by the anger of the gods against sinful Rome. Eight months afterwards, on the 10th of August A.D. 70, a Roman soldier threw a brand into the Temple of Jerusalem, which reduced it to ashes. And thus within a few months the national sanctuary of Rome and religious centre of the empire, as well as the temple of the true God, the two most important places of worship in the old world, owed their destruction to Roman soldiers, thoughtless instruments of the decrees and judgment of a higher Power. Ground was to be cleared for the worship of God in spirit and in truth. The heirs of the two temples, the Capitoline and that of Jerusalem,—a handful of artisans, beggars, slaves, and women,—were dwelling at the time in some of the obscure lanes and alleys of Rome; and only two years ago, when for the first time they had drawn the public attention on themselves, a number of them were sentenced to be burnt alive in the imperial gardens, and others to be torn in pieces by wild-beasts.

[1] Hist. iii. 72.

PART II.

THE JEW.

Book X.

Sed obtusi sunt sensus corum . . . . sed usque in hodiernum diem, cum legitur Moyses, velamen positum est super cor corum.

2 Ep. ad Corinth. c. 3.

BOOK X.

HISTORICAL DEVELOPMENT.

1. Until the Elevation of the Asmonean Dynasty.

Far off, in the south-eastern corner of the Roman empire, dwelt a people, not only the most widely-spread among all the nations then subjected to the Roman sceptre, but also the most thoroughly hated. This people sprang from the single family of the Abramidæ, who went into Egypt barely seventy in number, but multiplied exceedingly in the space of 430 years, the latter portion of which period was spent in oppression and slavery. Up to this time, the Israelites had dwelt in Egypt as strangers, united together only by the bond of family and race, yet without any national existence; the man elected to be their deliverer was also, as their lawgiver, to give them the form and organisation of a people and a state. This task Moses completed during the forty years' wandering in the country between Egypt and south Canaan. By the strict discipline of this long sojourn in the desert, he strengthened and purified his people, who had been enervated by their Egyptian bondage. The basis of the legislation which Moses gave in God's name was, His having chosen the people from amongst all the nations of the earth to be His own as a priestly kingdom, and to be a people[1] consecrated to Himself. The fundamental law of this kingdom was, the belief in one God, the creator of heaven and earth and all men, and the father and guide of all nations, — no national god, in the sense entertained by others, but one to whom the

---

[1] Exod. xix. 5, 6; cf. Deuteron. vii. 6-14.

Israelites stood in a relation in which no other people were to be found. For they were fashioned by Himself, to be the instruments of His decrees, their whole existence and history was to bear witness of Him, while the barrier of His law was to cut them off completely from all polytheistic nations. Without this barrier, the people would have soon given entire way to their inclination to heathenism, for long so powerful.

The land of Canaan was conquered under Josue; but the Canaanite nations there domiciled, and who were sunk in a horrible religion of child-sacrifice and impurity, though subdued, were not completely extirpated. The Israelites even lived along with them in some of the towns, and thus began to intermarry with them, and hence their frequent relapses into idolatry. It was a fundamental point of the Mosaic law, that God was the real lord and owner of the land given to the Jews, they themselves being only as stewards, having a temporary usufruct of the soil. No one, as was said in the law, can sell his field in perpetuity, because he is not the proprietor thereof.

For four hundred and fifty years the Israelites formed a theocratic republic of no very strict sort, and ruled by judges. This period was preparatory to their erection into a kingdom. The judges were individual men, raised up by God, and only appearing at certain intervals, and in times of necessity. The tabernacle and the ark of the covenant formed their centre and rallying-point, and were generally stationed at Silo. The nation solicited Samuel, their last judge, to erect them into a kingdom, as the only means of preserving their integrity, and saving them from the imminent danger of subjugation to the heathen. In the year 1099 B.C. they received their first king in the person of Saul, a member of the tribe of Benjamin. His successor, David, of the tribe of Judah, set in order and consolidated the kingdom. He first conquered Jerusalem, and then converted it into the seat of power and capital of the state. Thither he brought the ark of the covenant, and by successful wars extended his kingdom as far out as the Euphrates and the borders of Egypt. Under Solomon, the builder of the temple, the kingdom reached its highest political prosperity, as far as inward strength, extent, and consideration in the eyes of the neighbouring states went. But from this time it began to decline; for Solomon, by forming polygamous alliances with the daughters of heathen princes his neighbours, was led astray into the nature-worship of the Syro-Phœnician nations: he exhausted his people by compulsory labour, and tributes; and the succession of his son Rehoboam (975 B.C.) was followed by the division of the but recently united kingdom. Solomon's son only retained dominion over the tribe to which he belonged, and that of Benjamin; the remaining ten, who were settled in the parts of the country more remote from Jerusalem, united themselves into the kingdom of Israel, or Ephraim, and chose Jeroboam for their king; and thus was consummated their severance both from the temple at Jerusalem and the Levitical priesthood. A new cultus with an Egyptian idolatry was established in the new kingdom; priests were made who were not of the tribe of Levi, and soon the worship of Baal crept in. Samaria became afterwards the capital of the kingdom, and the greater number of its princes died violent deaths, so that nine different dynasties soon followed each other. In spite of the sanguinary reaction against Baal-worship under Jehu, heathenism gained the upper hand in the religion and morals of the Israelites, and after 253 years this monarchy fell. Salmanasar, king of Assyria, conquered Samaria 722 B.C., carried the Israelitish king Osee and his people into exile, and planted in their stead Assyrian colonists. Ten members were cut off from the parent stock of the chosen people.

And Judah, the smaller moiety of the nation, where the house of David remained in possession of the throne, in consequence of the marriages contracted by its royal family with the princes of Tyre, fell more and more into Phœnician idolatry, the licentious rites of which suited the tastes of the court, although Ezechias and Josias restored the true belief and worship as well as they were able. On occasion of some temple-repairs in the time of Josias, the forgotten, and till then mislaid, law of Moses was discovered and read aloud to the people. Placed between the more powerful kingdoms of Babylon and Egypt, and by turns dependent on, or conquered by, one or other, the kingdom of Judah was at length brought to an end in the year 588 B.C., 134 years after the fall of Israel. Nabuchodonosor, king of Babylon, destroyed Jerusalem, with the temple, all the holy vessels of which he carried off to Babylon, while the kernel of the nation was transported to Chaldæa.

Thus it appeared as if the career of the Jewish people were

closed, and their part in history played out. On coming forth from Egyptian bondage, it had commenced its existence as a state and nation, and now again, externally broken up, and rent as it were into pieces, it was found in bondage among strange nations. This was but so in appearance, however; Israel, indeed, was for ever annihilated as a state and nation; the measure of its iniquity had been filled to the brim; idolatry had completely loosened its naturally licentious people from all ties of shame and restraint, and with it lusts of every kind made their appearance without disguise. The ten tribes had actually surrendered their nationality in spirit, before they were carried away. Without law and sacrifice, or a Levitical priesthood, they were thoroughly leavened with pagan customs, and they lacked in exile the institutions and ordinances which would have supported and strengthened their religion and nationality. They therefore dissolved, and were all but entirely lost among the heathen inhabitants of Assyria, Media, and Mesopotamia. And yet in later centuries numerous Jewish colonies were to be found in the Medo-Babylonish provinces, of which the descendants of the ten tribes may have been the founders. On the other hand, only a portion of the population of the kingdom of Judah, consisting of the principal families with the kingly house, were carried to Babylon and the banks of the Chaboras. Others had taken refuge in Egypt. The country people remained in their homes, and Jerusalem, though in ruins, still continued throughout their religious centre; but those sons of captivity had the priesthood and the book of the law with them as their rule of life, and on the whole remained true to their belief. They were held together by this bond of religion, and prophets rose up among them who promised them the restoration of their kingdom.

In the year 536 B.C., after the fall of the Babylonian empire, Cyrus, king of Persia, granted the exiles permission to return; and 43,360 souls, of whom 4280 were priests, together with 7000 slaves, set out on their journey back. Being almost all of them of the tribes of Judah and Benjamin, the name of Israel was gradually lost sight of, and the resuscitated people were called after Judah, the leading tribe. The greater portion remained behind, scattered through the provinces of the great Persian empire. The leaders of those who returned home were

Zorobabel, a descendant of the house of David, and Josue the high-priest; and at their instance the rebuilding of the temple on the old site was commenced, and completed in 516 B.C. The rule of the Persians over the Jews was a very mild one, and placed no hindrances in the way of their religious or national development, the religion appearing to them to bear an affinity to their own, and the God of Judah to be their own Ormuzd.

To the north of the country lived a mixed people, the Samaritans, sprung from the remnants of the Israelites who were left behind when the ten tribes were carried away, and from the heathen colonists settled in the towns. Their religion was a medley, like themselves. They prayed to Jehovah, but to heathen gods also, Phœnician and others, brought with them from home. They were therefore repulsed by Zorobabel and Josue when they offered to share in the building of the temple. From that time there was enmity between them and the Jews, who no longer acknowledged any relationship with them, and would only consider them as heathen. Later on, either in 410, or perhaps not till 332,[1] the Samaritans had their own temple dedicated to Jehovah on Mount Gerizim, near Sichem, when Manasses, the grandson of a Jewish high-priest, rejected by his own people, on account of his marriage with the daughter of the Samaritan viceroy Sanballat, undertook the office of high-priest to the Samaritans.

The Jews returned home sobered and improved by their sufferings in exile, and entirely cured of their early hankering after idolatry. Having no political independence, and living under a governor, they devoted themselves all the more to religion, the only source and support of their nationality, and became zealots for the law, and for a devout carrying out of all its precepts as far as practicable. All, indeed, could not be again restored. The most holy of the new temple was empty, for it was without the lost and irreplaceable ark of the covenant; the oracular ornaments of the high-priest had disappeared. As Jerusalem was now, far more than formerly, the head and heart of the nation, the high-priesthood, continuing hereditary in the house of the before-named Josue, was the authority to which the nation willingly submitted; it served as the representative and pillar of unity, and the sons of David were forgotten. Another of the

---

[1] Joseph. Antiq. xii. 1. 1.

abiding consequences of their exile was, the altered mode of life which the nation led. At first they had been exclusively devoted to agriculture; but after mixing with strangers they learnt to engage in trade, and this inclination went on always increasing; it contributed essentially to their being spread far beyond the borders of Palestine, and to their multiplying their settlements in foreign lands.

In consequence of the breaking-up of the Persian empire, Judea, situated between the kingdoms of Syria and Egypt, was forced to submit at times to the Egyptian Ptolemys, and at others to the Seleucidæ in Syria, and formed the battle-field on which both powers contended against each other. At length it became an integral portion of the Syrian empire, under Seleucus Philopator and Antiochus (180-167). These kings promoted the settlement of Greeks and Syrians in Palestine, so that it was by degrees all covered with cities and towns of Grecian nomenclature. The narrow territory of Judea alone kept free of them, but was surrounded with settlers whose speech, customs, and creed were Greek. On the other hand, the Jews went on spreading in lands where Greek was spoken. A good many of these were planted in Egypt, in the newly-founded capital Antioch, in Lydia and Phrygia.[1] Led on by their love of trade, they soon became numerous in the commercial cities of western Asia, Ephesus, Pergamus, Miletus, Sardis, &c. From Egypt and Alexandria, in which city, at a later period, they formed two-fifths of the inhabitants, they drew along the coast of Africa to Cyrene and the towns of the Pentapolis, and from Asia Anterior to the Macedonian and Greek marts; for the national love of commerce became more and more developed, till it absorbed all other occupations, and to this certainly the general inclination for commercial intercourse, prevalent at that period, greatly contributed. Thus it happened that two movements, identical in their operation, crossed each other, viz. an influx of Greek, or of Asiatic but hellenised, settlers into Palestine, and an outpouring of Jews and Samaritans into the cities speaking the Greek tongue.

In olden times, while the Israelites still possessed a national kingdom, they felt their isolation from other people as a burden. It was as an oppressive yoke to them, which they bore

[1] Joseph. Antiq. iii. 1-4.

impatiently, and were always trying to shake off. They wanted to live like other nations, to eat, drink, and intermarry with them, and, together with their own God, to honour the gods of the stranger also; for many raw and carnally-minded Jews only looked upon the one special God and protector of their nation as one god amongst many. But now there was a complete change in this respect. The Jews every where lived and acted upon the fundamental principle, that between them and all other nations there was an insurmountable barrier; they shut themselves off, and formed in every town separate corporations, with officers of their own; while at the same time they kept up a constant connexion with the sanctuary at Jerusalem. They paid a tribute to the temple there, which was carefully collected every where, and from time to time conveyed in solemn procession to Jerusalem. There alone, too, could the sacrifices and gifts which were demanded by the law be offered. In this wise they preserved a centre and a metropolis.

And yet there followed from all this an event, which in its consequences was one of the most important in history, namely, the hellenising of the Jews who were living out of Judea, and even, in a degree, of those who remained in their own land. They were a people too gifted intellectually to resist the magnetic power by which the Hellenistic tongue and modes of thought and action worked even upon such as were disposed to resist them on principle. The Jews in the commercial towns readily acquired the Greek, and soon forgot their mother tongue; and as the younger generation already in their domestic circle were not taught Greek by natives, as might be supposed, this Jewish Greek grew into a peculiar idiom, the Hellenistic. During the reign of the second Ptolemy, 284-247 B.C., the law of Moses was translated at Alexandria into Greek, probably more to meet the religious wants of the Jews of the dispersion than to gratify the desire of the king. The necessity of a knowledge of Hebrew for the use of the holy Scriptures was thereby done away with, and Greek language and customs became more and more prevalent. Individuals began to join this or that school of philosophy, according to predilection and intellectual bias. The Platonic philosophy had necessarily most attractions for the disciples of Moses.

The intrusion of Hellenism into Judea itself met with a much more considerable resistance from the old believing and conservative Jews. Those of the heathen dispersion were obliged to be satisfied with mere prayer, Bible readings and expositions, in their proseuchæ and synagogues, and to do without the solemn worship and sacrifices of the temple; but in Jerusalem the temple-worship was carried out with all its ancient usages and symbols. There presided the Sopherim, the Scribes or skilled expounders of the law, a title first appropriated to Esdras (about 450 B.C.). He was one of the founders of the new arrangements in the restored state, and was a priest, and at the same time a judge appointed by the king of Persia. He made it the object of his life to investigate the law and to act as its expositor, and from the time of his appointment was the model of a priest learned in the Scriptures. He and his scholars and successors attained a powerful and abiding influence over the spirit and character of the people. They preached and set forth the unconditional authority of the law as a rule for every relation and circumstance of daily life. From that time forth dependence on the law, pride in its possession as the pledge of divine election, and the careful custody of this wall of partition, sank deep into the character of the nation, and became the source of many advantages as well as of serious faults. This zeal for the law, however, was the main bulwark under which the nation was strengthened into freshness and individuality of life.

The later Jewish tradition makes much mention of the great synagogue believed to have existed already in the time of Esdras, or to have been founded by him. It is supposed to have mustered 120 members, and, under the presidency of the high-priest, was to be the guardian of the law and doctrine. One of its last rulers was Simon the Just, who was high-priest, and the most distinguished doctor of his time (that of the first Ptolemys). Afterwards this threefold dignity or function of high-priest, scribe or rabbi, and of Nasi or prince of the synagogue, were never united in one person. There is no doubt that a tribunal with definitive jurisdiction, watching over doctrine and morals, existed in the Persian and early Grecian period, which appears to have turned by degrees into a merely judicial and governing body, while authoritative exposition of the law passed into the hands of some Scribes of distinction, and of the schools which they founded. A leading maxim of the great synagogue, given as a precept to the people, was, "Make ye a hedge about the law," wherein the principle is expressed, that, in order to be sure to avoid every injury to or unfulfilment of the letter of the law, it was necessary to do more than this letter demanded. The consequence of this necessarily was, that new principles, new decisions, and extensions of the old, were always being produced, laws were heaped upon laws, and the original purpose of the law was overlooked, as either indifferent or not certainly known; while, on the other hand, the outward adherence to its smallest and most trivial letter was regarded as the climax of religious observance.

On this growing bias to extension and glorification of maxims, the increasing respect paid to the Sopherim, the teachers of the law, or "Scribes," acted both as cause and effect. The Levites specially belonged to them, but so also did any one of the lower orders whose zeal led him to choose the study of the law and its exposition as his vocation or favourite pursuit. With this period originated the rabbinical axiom, that the crown of the kingdom was deposited in Judah, and the crown of the priesthood in the seed of Aaron, but the crown of the law was common to all Israel. The high-priesthood fell into contempt, the more it served foreign rulers as the venal instrument of their caprice; but the Scribes flourished as being the preservers of all theological and juridical knowledge, and were supported by the respect and confidence of the people. They had their tradition, that is to say, certain precepts and maxims, founded partly on the decisions of celebrated teachers, partly on scientific exposition of the Scriptures, which was gradually established, and the precepts accumulating by degrees to form a hedge about the law. The consideration paid to the Levites now also abated, and the Sopherim became the object of all the national veneration which they had formerly enjoyed. This ascendency of the Scribes caused a division among the Levites into two parts; the one class joined the Scribes, and now enjoyed respect and influence, not as members of the tribe of Levi, but of the learned body of the legal professors; the others were merely ecclesiastical ministers and performers of ceremonies.

By the year 170 B.C., Hellenism had undoubtedly made such progress among the Jews, in Palestine even, that the Assyrian king, Antiochus Epiphanes, was able to plan the extirpation of the Jewish religion, and the conversion of the temple at Jerusalem into a temple of Jupiter Olympius. The richer and nobler among them had made acquaintance with Greek manners and Greek luxuries of art and life in the courts of Antioch and Alexandria. The law, with its developments and restraints, probably was anyhow a heavy yoke in their eyes, and the proud rule of the Scribes a hateful tyranny. In face of the refinement of the Greeks and their ridicule, they grew ashamed of their "barbarous" law, which denied them all participation in the pleasures of the Grecian symposia; they would gladly have had gymnasia, theatres, and the contests of the arena in Jerusalem itself. But the two ends of emancipation from the yoke of the law and of hellenising Jewish life could only be compassed for them through the powerful aid of the Syrian sovereign, for the people rejected them with horror as "apostates from the holy covenant, lawless and godless men."[1]

It was Jesus, or Jason (the Hellenistic form of name that he adopted), brother of the high-priest, Onias III., who bought the office of high-priest from the king, and who began the work by setting up a gymnasium on the Greek model. There were so many of the same way of thinking, that even priests deserted the temple service, and many Jews assumed an artificial foreskin, so as to appear naked at the arena, without exhibiting to the Greeks a characteristic token of their creed. Jason already sent ambassadors (theoroi) to the feasts of Hercules at Tyre, with sacrificial presents; he was outbid, however, in zeal for Hellenism and in bribes at court, by Menelaus, who was named high-priest by the king; and then Jerusalem was converted into a regular heathen city, out of which the faithful and strict observers of the law fled. Royal edicts soon appeared, forbidding, throughout Judea, circumcision, the keeping of the Sabbath, and the use of the book of the law. The sacrifices of the temple ceased, and a smaller altar was built over the large altar of sacrifice, on which thenceforth sacrifice was offered to Jupiter Olympius, and swine were actually slain in scorn of the Jewish law. A party of apostates supported him. Thus were the words of Daniel fulfilled—the sanctuary profaned, the daily sacrifice done away with, and the abomination of desolation set up.

In the midst of the bloody persecution raised against the

[1] 1 Macc. i. 12, vii. 5.

faithful, Mattathias, of the priestly family of the Asmoneans, gave the signal for a rising. His son, Judas Maccabeus (the hammer), gloriously continued the fight, after the death of his father; he went up to Jerusalem, purified the temple in the year 164 B.C., notwithstanding the Syrian garrison on Mount Zion, and restored the true worship. These successes, however, were but transitory. Judas fell on the field of battle; Jerusalem again passed into the hands of the Syrians, whose Jewish adherents recognised Alcimus as high-priest, on the institution of king Demetrius. This man was of the family of Aaron, and came forward as the head of the Græco-heathen party. As he was planning to pull down even the wall of the temple which separated the heathen court from the Israelites, he died suddenly, B.C. 159. Meanwhile Jonathan, and after him Simon, brothers of the deceased Judas, managed to maintain themselves at the head of a small band of patriots and believers. The Syrian power soon afterwards became weakened and divided by contentions for the throne; till Simon succeeded in taking the Zion fort in Jerusalem, B.C. 141, upon which the grateful people made over to him and his family the highest spiritual and temporal power, the hereditary dignity of prince and high-priest, till God should send them a "true prophet,"[1] for Simon was neither of the family of David nor of Aaron. From this time the Hellenistic party ceased to exist.

2. The Chasidim — Sadducees — Pharisees — Essenes — Therapeutæ.

During the wars of the Maccabees, there was a school or party among the Jews called the Chasidim, the pious or fearers of God, who were not essentially different from the Sopherim or Scribes, but were remarkable for their excessive strictness in the observance of the law and all that was included therein. They had joined in the revolt of Mattathias on the occasion of the Syrian general Bacchides executing sixty of their number, but afterwards they supported the traitor high-priest Alcimus, on account of his descent. They play no further part in public events under Jonathan and Simon.

[1] 1 Macc. xiv. 41.

The antipodes of these Chasidim were the Sadducees. According to one tradition, this party was originated by Sadoc, a disciple of the celebrated teacher of the law, Antigonus of Socho (291-260 B.C.). Their rise is undoubtedly to be traced to the influences which the Greeks exercised on Judaism philosophically, as well as morally and socially. At the time when we first meet with them in history, that is to say, under Jonathan the Asmonean (159-144), they were, though in a modified form, the heirs and successors of the Hellenists, who had now for long been in existence; they were far removed from actual apostasy; nor did they endeavour, like the earlier Hellenists, to manifest their Greek spirit by an imitation of foreign customs. Hellenism was conquered under the Asmoneans, and beaten out of the field, and a new gush of Jewish patriotism and zeal for the law had taken its place. The Sadducees, who from the first appear as a school suited for the times, including the rich and educated statesmen, adopted the prevailing tone among the people. They took part in the services and sacrifices of the temple, practised circumcision, observed the Sabbath, and so professed to be real Jews and followers of the law, but the law rightly understood, and restored to its simple text and literal sense. They repudiated, they said, the authority of the new teachers of the law (now the Pharisees), and of the body of tradition with which they had encircled the law. In this tradition they of course included all that was burdensome to themselves. With the letter of the law, the few principal points of circumcision, the Sabbath, and sacrifice excepted, it was easier to deal; and the Sadducees knew how to lighten its yoke and to simplify and keep it within its narrowest limits. The way that they appeal to the Thora alone has been interpreted as if they rejected all the other sacred books in the prophetical collection, and only recognised the five books of Moses as Scripture; but evidence and fact testify the contrary, especially the assertion of Josephus, that the twenty-two books of the Old Testament were received by all Jews without exception as the divine word.[1] It is plain, however, that the Thora, as being the law, was of higher estimation among them than the prophetical scriptures and hagiographa.

The peculiar doctrines of the Sadducees obviously arose from

[1] Contra Apion. i. 8.

the workings of the Epicurean philosophy, which had found special acceptance in Syria. They admitted indeed the creation, as it seems, but denied all continuous operation of God in the world. He, it is true, had given the law to His people, once for all, but then had withdrawn Himself, and had left the people and every individual person entire freedom, so that good and evil depended only on the free will of man. They said, there was no such thing as destiny, for that must be a thing established by God, whereas He takes no part in earthly matters; man is master and author of his own destiny, and the evil affecting him he has brought on himself, without the participation of God.[1]

The Sadducees proved they were real followers of Epicurus, by denying the life of the soul after death. The soul, they said, passes away with the body. They consequently denied the resurrection.[2] Furthermore, they disbelieved in the existence of angels. We know not how they interpreted the frequent mention of them in the Pentateuch. The peculiarly negative character of the Sadducee school made it easy for persons of very different views to join it;—as all were interested in common to extricate themselves from a double yoke, that of the more complete body of doctrine as imposed by the dominant teaching body of the law-learned, which hampered the free will of individuals, and of those stricter and more extended requirements of the law to be found in the explanations of the Sopherim, or in the ordinances of later times. It happened, however, that the Sadducee principle of carrying out the dry letter of the written law, led sometimes to great harshness, as, for instance, in the case of punishments for bodily injuries; "an eye for an eye, a tooth for a tooth;" while the Pharisees, following a milder and traditional interpretation, allowed the guilty person to buy himself off by a pecuniary compensation.

The mass of the people stood aloof from the Sadducees, whom they regarded with mistrust and aversion. Since Hellenism had brought such incalculable evil on the nation, and exposed the faithful to so bloody a persecution, zeal for the law, and a stringent severance from all that was heathen or foreign, was the prevailing feeling of the Jews, or at any rate the only one by which a school or party could recommend itself to the people. Hence the Sadducees, as a rule, only accepted public offices un-

[1] Jos. Bell. Jud. ii. 8, 14; Antiq. xiii. 5, 9.   [2] Antiq. xviii. 1-4.

willingly, partly from love of ease, when there was more trouble than profit attached to them; partly because the popular feeling forced them to administer the law according to the principles and custom of the Pharisees.[1] Josephus remarked that they were rude and unkind, not only to those who disagreed with them, but even towards each other. Every thing tends to show they did not form in reality a compact and organised sect, nor had they probably any established body of teachers of their own; rather it was the loose bond of a mode of thought, that harmonised in denying more than in affirming, which allowed of their being designated as a united school. To be specially active in making proselytes, or expanding the circle of their opinions, was no concern of theirs. No Sadducee writings probably ever existed which laid down a system or set up a confession. It did not occur to them, even when it was in their power, to indoctrinate, to perplex the people in their belief and life according to the law. They were the enlightened and cultivated of their day and nation, who made religion easy to themselves, and only held to as much as was needful for appearance-sake, and to maintain their position as Jewish citizens; about as much, in fact, as any enlightened Greek, who never withdrew himself from the participation in the religious festivities and sacrifices of his people, would have deemed necessary. As a political party they were averse to all democratic and republican tendencies, and were friends and supporters of the sovereign authority, both under the later Asmoneans and under the Romans.

It is the custom to contrast the Pharisees with the Sadducees, as if they were two opposite sects, existing in the midst of the Jewish nation, and separated from the body of the Jews. But neither the Sadducees nor the Pharisees were sects in the common acceptation of the word, least of all the latter. Taken at bottom, the nation were for the most part pharisaically minded; in other words, the Pharisees were only the more important and religiously inclined men of the nation, who gave the most decided expression to the prevailing belief, and strove to establish and enforce it by a definite system of teaching and interpretation of the sacred books. All the priests, who were not mere blunt senseless instruments, clung to the pharisaical belief. All the Sopherim, or Scribes, were at the same time Pharisees, and, when

[1] Jos. Antiq. xviii. 1-4.

they are spoken of side by side as two different classes, by the latter must be understood those who, without belonging by calling or position to the body of the learned, yet were zealous in setting forth its principles, teaching, and practices, and surpassed others in the example they gave of the most exact observance of the law. Thus Josephus could speak on one occasion of more than 6000 Pharisees in Herod's time. This numerical calculation is only arrived at, however, from the fact of there being 6000 who refused to swear fidelity to the king and the Romans, and were fined in consequence.[1] And when he speaks of three heresies, or philosophies, among the Jews, it is only, as usual with him, an accommodation to Greek ideas. Neither the Greeks nor Romans had ever met with any thing like the Pharisees in all their history, to wit, such a union of religious zeal, national pride, and patriotic sentiment. Hence they could only be supplied with an approximate idea of the peculiar position and character of the Pharisees by a comparison of them with the Grecian philosophical schools of the Pythagoreans, or perhaps Stoics. Besides, the Sadducees had the strongest interest to designate their most determined adversaries as a mere party, and to invent a party name for them, in order to disguise the fact that these men in reality only followed the common traditional belief and religious practice of the nation. This, in fine, was coupled with a political and religious opposition against all foreign sovereignty or dominion exercised by rulers of foreign descent, unavoidable among the Jews in Judea, unless they were Hellenists, or indifferent to religion. For the people of God had an imprescriptible right to be free from all foreign rule; any thing of the sort was but a passing punishment for their national sins and breaches of the law. And now that the nation had taken a religious bias, and strove so earnestly after an observance of the law to its fullest extent, the continued duresse of a foreign yoke appeared to the Jews a kind of injustice and an inexplicable misfortune, which they bore with angry impatience, resolved to seize the first opportunity of shaking it off. The Pharisees were obliged to take the initiative in this too, on account of their consideration with the people, and when allegiance to God or the law seemed to require the example of opposition to the government: and thus they were generally the first victims of kingly vengeance.[2]

[1] Jos. Antiq. xvii. 2. 4.   [2] Ibid. xvii. 24.

The Pharisees accordingly were in the eyes of the nation a guard set over all the spiritual goods of Israel, over purity of doctrine and maxims, faithfulness in conduct to the law, and national dignity and freedom; and to this post some were summoned by their vocation, some offered themselves of their own free will. They were spokesmen and representatives of the people whenever any question connected with religion arose; and with the Jews, whose whole public and private life was overspread by the law as by a mighty net, every thing that occurred assumed at once a religious signification. On the one hand, they were as a faithful mirror reflecting the inclinations and views astir among the people; on the other, their authority reacted on the people, and gave the direction to their minds. The light as well as the dark side of the national character, and the prevalent mode of thought, were potentially represented in them. The aristocracy of Jewish blood was to be found amongst them, such as had kept free from the taint of Greek and Syrian infusion, the Hebrews of the Hebrews, who gloried in being true-born issue of the Covenant.

If the term "Pharisees" was undoubtedly derived from a word signifying "separation" or "exclusion," it certainly does not imply, as has frequently been asserted, that they received this name because they separated themselves from the people as claimants to a devotion of a special character; for such a severance from the mass, as if impure, and as if intercourse with them was contaminating, could never have been suggested to the Pharisees by the spirit or letter of the law, and would assuredly have brought down on them the hatred and aversion of the people, instead of the confidence which they possessed in so high a degree. They acquired the name, because at the time of its origination the great battle with Hellenism and its disturbing influences had to be carried on, and the pious, or Chasidim, now practised and preached a careful avoidance of all that was Hellenistic. This name, therefore, was perhaps first given them by their adversaries, the Hellenists, while they received it willingly as a title of honour: and thus the Jewish tradition is historically probable that the origin of the Pharisees may date as far back as Antigonus of Socho, for he is named as the first to maintain that the "gader," or hedge of the law, was a part, and as binding as the rest, of the divine law itself; and his disciples and followers would acquire the name of Pharisees, because they strove to separate themselves from all strangers, heathen, and contaminating folk, by this "hedge of the law." It was natural, in the great danger from Hellenism, which was insinuating itself through a vast variety of channels, corrupting the Jews by every kind of allurement, and enticing them more and more from their belief and their law, that they should have felt the inadequacy of their old ordinances. These statutes were given several centuries back, under a far simpler state of things, and for persons living in very different circumstances; and therefore, when appeal was made to the complications which had arisen in later days and the very different situation, they might easily be evaded, or be rendered impracticable for present needs, by interpretation: many cases which were daily occurring were unprovided for altogether. A reference to the spirit and object of the law would of course be useless when the mass of people were longing for Hellenistic enjoyments. Thus amplifications and sometimes also limitations of the law had to be introduced, and its prescriptions extended, by an interpretation, often artificial and arbitrary, to things and actions which now seemed dangerous or to be rejected; and to these "hedges" drawn around the law, the same binding power had, as they fancied, to be attributed as to its written letter. Now, it was not easy to stop in such a course when once entered on: and hence a species of legal casuistry arose, whereby small matters of no moment were weighed with a painful scrupulousness, and raised to the same level and importance as the first duties of life.

Since the times of Esdras, Hebrew had become a dead language to the mass of the people:[1] the holy books were therefore incomprehensible to the generality, though detached portions were read in the synagogues in Hebrew, and expounded. The learned alone, who from their youth had been regularly instructed in the law, and made it their study, were able to explain and apply it. The Scribes, *i. e.* the Pharisees, were accordingly the guardians of the people, and preservers of an indispensable science and tra-

---

[1] Esdras and Nehemias were zealous in trying to preserve the Hebrew tongue in its purity, 2 Esd. viii. 13, xiii. 1 and 23 sqq.; but the Maccabee princes having coins struck in the second century with Hebrew legends proves no more, as regards its national use, than the Latin inscriptions on our coins prove that the people are familiar with Latin.

dition, as well as the living exemplars and mirrors, in which the true mode of a life according to the law was represented. They were, in short, counsellors in doubtful cases. A peculiar doctrine they neither had nor could have, as they formed no particular school, still less a sect, but were spread throughout the land as the ruling and teaching body of the nation, "who sat in the seat of Moses;" so that even the Sadducees had to conform to them in word and deed, when once chosen to fill public offices connected with religion. Nothing but the opposition between them and the Sadducees could have led to the idea that the Pharisees, too, were a distinct school or "heresy."

The Pharisaical explanation of the law was a traditionary one; and if the Sadducees rejected the tradition of the Scribes, and pretended to hold only to the letter of Biblical prescript, they rejected at the same time not only the various additions and new ordinances of the Pharisaical school tradition, but also the whole current interpretation of the law, leaving this to the private opinion of each man, who in this matter (they said) was bound by no authority. It was with them a mere matter of ceremonial and civil law; the "Deuteroseis," or glosses on the law, for which Christ reproached the Pharisees, saying that by such human traditions they rendered the law of no avail, and weakened and injured its true sense,[1] belonged chiefly to this category. Their anxiety was about such things as washing of hands before meals,[2] and bathing the body when on their return from market they believed themselves made unclean by contact with a variety of unclean things or persons; the washing of dishes, flagons, and pots, as well as of the couches on which they reposed when at table; if, for instance, a dead fly fell into an earthen pitcher, it had to be broken. Further, these traditions involved a troublesome extension of, and severity in regard to, the law of the Sabbath. No one was allowed to go more than a thousand steps from home on that day: all marketing, carrying of burdens, plucking ears of corn, or healing the sick, was called Sabbath-breaking. In the Deuteroseis, or Mishna, thirty-nine occupations were enumerated, to which are to be added many other things of a similar kind, all equally forbidden on the Sabbath. Besides, the Sabbath was lengthened, as it was made to begin before sunset, on the "hedge" principle of insuring no

---

[1] Matt. xv. 3; Mark vii. 9.   [2] Matt. xv. 1 sq.; Mark vii. 2 sq.; Luke xi. 38.

desecration of the holy time. The law of tithes was in like manner extended. In the Mosaic law they were not to be taken from every kind of produce, but the Pharisees paid a tithe of mint, anise, and cummin.[1] Later on, the Pharisaical priests and Levites gave, it appears, an additional tenth upon the tithe paid. As most insects belonged to the class of unclean creatures, and, in drinking, a gnat might easily be swallowed, the zealots used to strain what they drank, and this is what our Lord referred to in speaking of "straining at gnats." In addition to the fast prescribed by Moses for the day of atonement, other fasting times were added to commemorate national misfortunes, such as the taking of Jerusalem by the Chaldees. Many fasted twice a-week in memory of Moses ascending Mount Sinai. A Pharisee was easily recognised by his loud prayers in public places, ostentatious almsgiving, large fringes on his clothes, broad phylacteries,—or pieces of parchment with the commandments written on them, and tied on the forehead and left hand.

Josephus, a Pharisee himself, reveals what the Pharisees thought of themselves: "in their own idea, they are the flower of the nation, and the most accurate observers and expounders of the law." That mutual love and concord which according to him is a distinction of the nation, and one marvelled at and envied by the heathens, he accords as a special characteristic to the Pharisees.[2] "Through their intercourse with God, many of them possess the gift of prophecy."[3] "They are proud of their literal and strict exposition of the law, and convinced of their being the prime favourites of God."

By his method of adapting what he said to the Grecian mode of expression, Josephus has given ground for the assertion, that not only among the Essenes, but, in a degree at least, among the Pharisees, a fatalistic theory of the world prevailed. The Essenes, he says, viewed destiny as all-dominating, so that nothing happens to man which is not decreed to him by fate. The Pharisees, it is true, also maintained that every thing came to pass through destiny, but still that man had free will to do good or evil, and hence a mixture of freedom and fatalism results. In most cases it is in the power of man to act rightly or wrongly, but destiny coöperates in every thing.[4] It is obvious

---

[1] Matt. xxiii. 23.   [2] Bell. Jud. ii. 8. 14; cf. adv. Apion, ii. 19 sqq.
[3] Antiq. xvii. 24.   [4] Ibid. xviii. 1. 3.

here that, in the sense of the Essenes and Pharisees as well, divine providence, or predestination, ought to be substituted for destiny. The Essenes taught that all is in the hands of God; whatever man does or meets with, that he does and meets with through the will of God. In contradiction to this doctrine, destructive of human freedom, and also to the opposite extreme of the Sadducee view, making God withdraw himself entirely from human life, and all will and deed to rest with man alone, the Pharisee taught that man's freedom and God's providence and guidance are so interwoven that generally both factors are to be conceived as working together, yet without disparagement to human power of choice; and that, on the whole, divine government of the world attains its end in the long-run, undisturbed by the exercise of man's freedom. According to later accounts, many of the Pharisees were engaged in astrology, and thus were led to adopt a sort of fatalism[1] dependent on the course of the stars. Philo says that many Jews, from the time of the Babylonian captivity, believed in the influence of the stars, interpreting the seven higher angels of the Presence as the spirits of the seven planets, and that they occupied themselves with astrology.[2]

The Hellenistic predilections of Josephus have also led to a misunderstanding on the belief of the Pharisees regarding the state after death. He shrank from speaking of a subject so offensive to the Greek mind as the resurrection of the body, and therefore said that the souls of the just passed into another body,[3] or that, in the revolution of the cosmical periods, they received again pure bodies to dwell in. His words are, I think, purposely so chosen that the Greek might gather the doctrine of a metempsychosis from them, and the Jew his well-known one of the resurrection, which made so sharp a distinction between the Pharisees and Sadducees. That a belief in the transmigration of souls did exist among the Jews from the times of the Maccabees, and in consequence of Greek and Oriental influences, there is abundant proof; but it was not the dominant belief, nor was it a doctrine of the Pharisees.

The sect of the Essenes arose during the troublous times shortly before the first Asmoneans, when Hellenism obtruded

---

[1] Epiph. Hær. xvi. 2.   [2] De Migr. Abr. p. 415.
[3] Antiq. xviii. 2. 3; Bell. Jud. ii. 7. 14, iii. 8. 5 and 7.

itself on Judaism in such force, with intellectual and material weapons, and caused such a ferment of spirits amongst the Jews. The school of the Sadducees appeared at this crisis, and that of the Essenes seems to have formed simultaneously; for Josephus mentions the three parties of Pharisees, Sadducees, and Essenes for the first time in the days of Jonathan (161-143), and afterwards informs us that Judas, an old Essene, prophesied the murder of Antigonus by Aristobulus (107 B.C.).[1] Their numbers in Palestine amounted to four thousand in the time of Josephus. Some part of them were dispersed about in the towns, carrying on trades; others were united together in communities in the country, where they were employed in agriculture. Pliny says that in his time they dwelt on the western side of the Dead Sea; if so, they must have gone there first in consequence of the catastrophe which befell Judea in the great Roman war. They themselves appear to have laid claim to a high antiquity, and to have attributed the foundation of their community to Moses: hence Philo's expression, that the lawgiver himself urged an immense number of his most trusted followers to form a community, which was called that of the Essenes.[2]

The Essenes were a body of ascetics, but their asceticism rested more on Greek (Orphico-Pythagorean) views than on purely Jewish ones. They did not spring out of the Chasidim, or from Nazaritism, nor could any one say that an Essene was nothing but a Nazarite for life.[3] For the very points which were distinctive of a Nazarite — viz. abstinence from wine and all intoxicating drinks, and the letting the hair grow — are not spoken of as being Essene; while no Nazarite ever led such an un-Jewish life as that of the Essenes was. In a general way, it is quite clear that the Essenes could not have developed out of Judaism spontaneously, and without the help of external influences (as, for instance, has been recently maintained),[4] through their effort to realise the character of the sacerdotal monarchy, and on the basis of the general rights of Israel to the priesthood to form a sacerdotal community. On such an hypo-

---

[1] Antiq. xiii. 2; Bell. Jud. i. 3. 5.   [2] Fragm. ed. Mangey, ii. 635.

[3] As Grätz mentions in his "History of the Jews from the Death of Judas Maccabeus," Leip. 1856, p. 97.

[4] Ritschl, in Zeller's Theol. Jahrbüchern, 1855, p. 315.

thesis, there would be no satisfactory explanation of the heterogeneous un-Jewish asceticism, nor of the rejection of animal sacrifices, nor of the election of particular priests. Finally, the Essenes could not be a product of the Jewish Alexandrian religious philosophy,[1] for in it Platonism predominated, while we find nothing of the sort in the Essenes, but, on the contrary, a large infusion of Orphic Pythagoreanism. The numerous sallies and jests occurring in the comic poets of the Alexandrine period show that the ethical doctrine of the followers of Orpheus and Pythagoras, and the mode of life corresponding thereto, still lasted in the form of an order or free community without speculative activity in the time of Alexander, even though the philosophical schools of the Pythagoreans were extinct as early as the middle of the fourth century B.C. In this school or sect we find specifically the rejection of animal sacrifice, and the abstinence from flesh-meat, which had been already noted by Plato in the Orphici;[2] the worship of God in white linen vestments; and the like. It was natural that these Orphic Pythagoreans should spread into Syria, and come into contact with the Jews when Palestine became hellenised.

In spite, therefore, of this admixture of Jewish and heathen elements to be found in the Essenes (without injury, however, to their strict monotheism), they were unquestionably real disciples of Moses in their own estimation, and, indeed, the only genuine ones; and they were zealots for the law, as they understood and explained it. Their veneration for the great lawgiver went so far, according to Josephus, that they revered his name next to that of God, and punished any disrespect towards it with death. They rivalled the Pharisees in their strict interpretation and amplification of some points of the law, and carried the burdensome observance of the Sabbath even further, not only preparing their food the day before, to avoid lighting a fire on the Sabbath, but not even allowing any vessel to be moved from its place, or any of their own natural wants to be satisfied.[3] How they could reconcile such zeal for a portion of the law with the setting aside of another, very weighty and comprehensive,—viz.

---

[1] Dähne (article 'Essäen' in der Halle'schen Encyklop. no. xxxviii. p. 183) lays this down as quite indisputable.

[2] Legg. vi. 782.

[3] Jos. Bell. Jud. ii. 8. 9; Porphyr. de Abst. iv. 13, p. 341.

that of animal sacrifice, thereby excluding themselves from the Temple worship, and from religious communion with the whole nation,—would be incomprehensible, unless the Græco-Pythagorean leaven had exercised an overpowering influence upon them in this matter. They must have either taken some deprecatory expressions of the later prophets as a formal abrogation of the animal sacrifices before ordained, or, by a most arbitrary and strained allegorical interpretation, have volatilised the clear commands of the law.

Ideas about the purity or impurity of material things swayed the whole life of the Essenes, to a degree seldom equalled by any other creed, and rendered their intercourse with others far more difficult than that of the Jews with the heathens. Mere contact with one who was not an Essene, or with even one of their own people of a lower grade, was considered contaminating, and required ceremonies of purification. Oil was also held to be defiling; so if any one had been anointed against his will, he had to wash his body immediately. Meals in common were looked upon quite as religious actions: every one washed his whole body beforehand, and put on a clean linen garment, which he took off again as soon as the meal was ended. The baker placed the bread before each guest, and the cook in like manner a plate with one mess; the priest blessed the victuals, and no one dared to taste any thing before the prayer was said.[1] Thus we see each meal was a sacrificial one; and it is of these sacrifices that Josephus speaks when he says that, although excluded from the common sanctuary of the Jews, the Essenes nevertheless performed the same sacrifices in their own domestic circle.[2]

The Essenes had a complete theory of demons or angels. One of the solemn obligations undertaken by a person entering

[1] Here Ritschl is right in what he maintains against Zeller, that ἱερεῖς διὰ ποίησιν σίτου τε καὶ βρωμάτων means, "priests (are chosen) for the offerings of bread and victuals;" not, as Zeller (Jahrbücher, 1856, p. 414) thinks, "for the preparation of bread and victuals;" for it would have been strange, and little in keeping with the general character of the Essenes, if they had chosen priests merely to turn them into bakers and cooks: and moreover Josephus expressly distinguishes, in the description of their meal-times, the σιτοποιός, who portions out the bread, from the μάγειρος, who brings the plates with the meats, and the ἱερεύς, who says the prayer. In order to attend carefully to the requisite purity in preparing the food, it was not necessary to have any priest, every Essene of the highest class being competent for that, as perfectly clean.

[2] Jos. Antiq. xviii. 1. 15.

their order was that of keeping secret the name of the angel then communicated to him. Apparently this is connected with the veneration which they showed to the sun. They durst not utter a word on profane matters before sunrise, but addressed certain prayers to the sun, which had descended to them from their fathers, calling on him to arise. In their estimation, as well as in that of Philo, the sun was a living intelligent being, and without doubt had a name to be kept secret. One feature of the worship consisted in keeping out of sight whatever would be offensive to the sun, as the private parts of the person and all evacuations of the body. Accordingly, every Essene was presented, on his reception, with a hatchet to be used as a spade, and with which he dug a hole a foot deep every day. There he satisfied the necessities of nature, taking care to cover himself with his garment, so as not to desecrate the rays of the deity; the hole was filled up with the earth afterwards. He had also an apron given him, with orders not to perform an ablution without it, so that the sun should not be deprived of due respect.

A community of goods existed among the Essenes. All profit from labour was thrown into a common chest, under the supervision of certain stewards chosen for the purpose; and no individual possessed any thing of his own. He handed over to the community whatever he had before his entrance: thus there was neither buying nor selling amongst them. Marriage was forbidden; hence Pliny calls them the "everlasting" people, amongst whom no one was born.[1] They limited themselves to bare necessaries in food and clothing, and they were not allowed to change their clothes or shoes until quite worn out. Their sick who were unable to work, as also the stranger and traveller belonging to the sect, were liberally provided for out of their funds. The aged were honoured as fathers. They would not tolerate slavery, nor allow arms or warlike implements to be made by their workmen. The duty of obedience was carefully observed. No Essene did any thing without the command of his superior. Only two things, Josephus says, were left to their free will, viz. helping their neighbours and mercy. They were forbidden to take an oath. A solemn repose reigned during their assemblies and meals, such as gave those not yet associated the impression of the society being possessed of some

[1] Plin. H. N. v. 15; Philo, Fragm. vol. ii. p. 633.

awful mystery. In judicial decisions, a congregation of at least a hundred was requisite.

The Essenes only received persons of mature age, and these not till after a year of probation. The admission was a gradual one. After the expiration of the year, the novice was only admitted to the holy purifications by water, but not to the meals. Then followed a further period of trial two years long, during which, if they evinced sufficient proofs of strength of character and endurance, the complete reception ensued, upon which they took a solemn oath, the last permitted to them. The oath enjoined, besides the rules of strict morality, secrecy as to all the concerns of the society, even if they were tortured to death for it. The fate of those expelled from their body for any offence was pitiable: being bound by their vows, they could not receive any food from others, and were therefore obliged to eat nothing but herbs till they slowly wasted away, and were only readmitted from compassion, when at the last extremity, to save their dying of starvation. The Essenes were divided into four classes, according to the date of their admission; and an Essene of a higher class was obliged to purify himself if touched by a brother of inferior rank. They were thoroughly Pythagorean in teaching that the soul, which emanated from the finest ether, was girt by the chain of the body, into which it was plunged by some natural power of attraction: when once freed from this bodily chain, as out of a long captivity, it would rejoice and take flight to heaven. Yet they taught besides an earthly paradise for the good, a country beyond the ocean, where the weather was always genial; while the wicked dwelt in a cold and gloomy place, and there were tormented.

The Essenes, as Philo remarks,[1] quite set aside logic and physics, and devoted themselves to ethics, which with them abounded in asceticism, and were directed to the mortification of sensuality. They abhorred pleasure as sin; temperance was their first and highest virtue, and the foundation of all the others; and through it they generally lived to an advanced age, often above a hundred years. Their constancy in enduring torture was wonderful. Many were supposed to have the gift of prophecy. One branch of them differed from the main body in permitting marriage. The men put their betrothed through a

[1] Quod omnis prob. lib., p. 458, Mang.

probation of three years, and married them only after three menstrual purgations, as a proof of their ability to bear children.

Thus a strange compound of heathenism was exhibited in this remarkable body, in union with an apparently exaggerated Pharisaism in some of its observances of the law. The worship which they paid the sun was borrowed from heathendom, and is a feature proving their Pythagorean colouring, with which they assuredly did not imagine that they did prejudice to the monotheism of the Mosaic law. That, indeed, expressly prohibited the worship of the sun;[1] but the exegesis which set aside animal sacrifice came to their aid here too; many expressions of the Bible concerning the sun and its relation to God were interpreted in apparent proof that, if an inferior, it was still a godlike being, somewhat in the same relation that the Persian creed indicated as existing between it and Ormuzd. The Jews of that period must have rejected them as a foreign growth, and refused religious communion with them, although the Essenes sent their gifts to the Temple in due course. After the fall of the Temple, indeed, their rejection of animal sacrifices lost its immediate practical import, while their extraordinary constancy and adherence to the law during the Jewish wars won them the hearts of many of the orthodox; and this explains how Josephus came to speak of them with such evident partiality.

Whilst the Essenes led an active and laborious life, without absolutely separating themselves from the other Jews, the Therapeutæ devoted themselves to one of contemplation, and kept apart from towns in the neighbourhood of Alexandria. They lived isolated in small mean buildings, following no trade, and occupied only in reading the Scriptures (which they interpreted allegorically) and in holy meditation; each house had its holy place, called the semneon, or monasterion, where, according to Philo, they carried out the mysteries of their holy life in complete seclusion. They only met together in one common sanctuary on the Sabbath; here the men and women were placed in two divisions, and listened while an elder discoursed. On this day they allowed themselves a more generous diet, but during the week they observed a strict regimen and constant fasts. Meat and wine were entirely prohibited. They met every seven weeks at a solemn meal, dressed in white, when they had prayer, religious dis-

[1] Deut. iv. 19; xvii. 3.

courses, and hymns. On this followed the holy night solemnity, in which men and women, at first in two choirs apart, commenced dances, accompanied by singing, during which the two choirs mingled together. The dance was kept up all night until daybreak.[1]

There is no evidence to prove that the Egyptian Therapeutæ were allied to the Essenes in Palestine. The latter were an heretical sect. Philo, who is the only authority on the matter, says nothing to imply that the Therapeutæ were cut off from religious communion with the other Jews, while it may be gathered from his silence, and from the custom of religious dances, that they did not join the Essenes in their exalted notions about what was clean and what unclean. The Orphico-Pythagorean doctrines and customs, which strike us in the Essenes, are not mentioned as existing among the Therapeutæ, *e. g.* the rejection of animal sacrifice, the worship of the sun, the doctrine of the etherial soul in its prison, and the prohibition of oaths. There is no reason at all to imagine that the Therapeutæ were under the influence of Greek philosophy, because of their habit of interpreting the Bible allegorically. They were nothing more than a body of Jewish ascetics, who neither wished to separate themselves from religious communion with the rest of their brethren, nor were expelled by them from its pale.

---

3. The Times of the Asmoneans, and Family of Herod— The Roman Government.

Simon was treacherously murdered 135 B.C., and was succeeded by John Hyrcanus, the Asmonean. The thirty years' rule of this able and aspiring prince, prudent as he was warlike, and who always wore a coat of mail under his priestly habit, was outwardly brilliant and victorious.

The Samaritan temple on Mount Gerizim was destroyed. The Idumeans, those ancient step-brothers, next, faithless subjects and constant enemies of Judah, were conquered, and compelled to adopt circumcision and the Jewish religion, and incorporated into the Jewish state. Hyrcanus had no presentiment

[1] Quod omnis prob. lib., p. 458 sqq., Mang.

that an Idumean family would bring destruction on his house and supplant it. In the mean while, the sea-coasts too were conquered, and the Jews in Palestine gave themselves up to commerce with an undiminishing ardour, and in this their brethren of the Dispersion had anticipated them. At the same time they also sought to form a closer alliance with the mighty and protecting power of Rome.

The interior intellectual disruption already began in the bosom of the nation to assume an alarming aspect, and the Jews had to learn, at the price of their ruin, what it was to tolerate a party like the Sadducees in the midst of them, and that just in the highest and most influential positions. A Pharisee, Eleazar, had exacted of Hyrcanus to resign the priesthood, on the pretext of his mother having once been a captive, and to content himself with the princely dignity. The other Pharisees had assigned the calumnious offender too mild a punishment in the eyes of the exasperated prince. He therefore turned from them, who had hitherto been the firmest supporters of the Asmonean house, deposed them from high offices, and filled up their places with partisans of the Sadducees.[1] The people were for the first time constrained to acknowledge these men, who were estranged from them and their most precious privileges, and who would gladly have made Judea as like as possible to the heathen and Hellenistic states, as the representatives and expounders of their law.

The horrors of the Asmonean dynasty now began. Aristobulus, the eldest son of Hyrcanus, was not contented with the dignity of high-priest, but was the first of his house to assume the kingly title. He made his mother perish of hunger in prison, executed his brother, and died in torments of remorse of conscience after a year. Under his brother and successor, Alexander Jannæus, the Pharisees, favoured by the princess, appear to have been restored for a time to considerable influence; for Jewish traditions say that Simon-ben-Schetach, the Scribe, succeeded in expelling the Sadducees by degrees from the Sanhedrim, and making it once more the absolute organ of the teaching of the Pharisees; so much so, that the day on which the supreme council was entirely purged of Sadducee members (about B.C. 100) was raised into an annual memorial day.[2]

[1] Jos. Antiq. xiii. 10. 6. [2] Grätz, pp. 134-471.

But Jannæus was soon incited by his favourite, Diogenes, to join the Sadducees; as high-priest, he treated the Pharisaical rite with such contempt, during the Feast of the Tabernacles, that the people pelted him with lemons in the Temple, and insulted him by calling him the son of a slave; whereupon he charged them with his body-guard, and 6000 men were killed (B.C. 95). The Pharisee party excited a civil war, which in six years cost the lives of 50,000 men. Jannæus was at length victorious, and caused 800 Pharisee prisoners to be crucified, and their wives and children to be massacred before their eyes, while he gave a great entertainment to his concubines. The same night, more than 8000 Pharisees fled abroad, some to Syria, and some to Egypt. After such a deed, Jannæus dared to enter the Holy of Holies as high-priest, and, with hands dripping with the blood of his people, to offer sacrifice for his own sins and those of the nation. Nevertheless, on his death-bed, he recommended his wife, whom he appointed to be regent, to give herself up entirely to the counsels and guidance of the Pharisees, perceiving that the Sadducees were too much hated by the people to be a secure support for a dynasty. Thus the succession to power of Salome Alexandra was a complete victory of the returned Pharisees over the Sadducees; and according to Jewish accounts, this was the epoch at which, with the two heads of the Sanhedrim, Juda-ben-Tabbai and Simon-ben-Schetach, began the administration of legal Judaism in the Pharisaical sense. They were, therefore, designated as the restorers, who had brought back the "crown" (of the law) to its former splendour. Memorial days were afterwards fixed for the annual celebration of the victory then gained, of the abolition of the penal code of the Sadducees, and the introduction of Pharisaical decrees of rites,[1] and a heavy vengeance befel several of the Sadducees.

On the death of Queen Salome Alexandra, in the year 70 B.C., the bloody conflict broke out between the brothers Hyrcanus II. and Aristobulus, her sons. Both parties called in the aid of the Romans, and from that time the freedom and independence of Judea was at an end. Pompey made himself master of Jerusalem and the Temple in the year 63, when 12,000 Jews were killed. He entered with his staff into the interior of the Temple, where no heathen hitherto had been able to set foot; and to the

[1] Grätz, pp. 143-412.

profound grief of the Jews at the unheard-of desecration, he even penetrated into the Holy of Holies, where he was astonished to find no image of a deity. In the year of the birth of Augustus the Maccabean kingdom ended, after the independence of the nation had lasted a century.

A double yoke was now laid on a nation which, above all others, bore a foreign sway impatiently, as an aggression on their religion. Antipater, an Idumean, through the weakness of Hyrcanus, who required leading, and by his prudence in obtaining and using Roman favour, paved the way for his own elevation and that of his son Herod to the kingdom. The real rulers, however, were the Romans. Before them the two Idumeans cringed, and to them Herod sacrificed the wealth of the people by constant and costly presents, procured by heavy general exactions of money contributions. If Judea had become a Roman province at once upon its subjugation by Pompey, its condition, at least from the time of Augustus, would have been more tolerable, and under a well-regulated though strict government it would have been able, like other provinces, to regain some measure of prosperity. But the intermediate state of a dependent kingdom, a prey alike to the despotic cruelty of a Herod and the cupidity and arbitrariness of Roman rulers, proved an almost unbearable accumulation of misery. The last descendant of the Asmonean house perished either in a futile attempt to obtain possession of the crown of Judah, or by assassination at Herod's command. For a short period only, Antigonus, the son of Aristobulus, under Parthian protection, was enabled to play the king; and he had the ears of his uncle Hyrcanus cut off, who was weak to imbecility, to render him unfit for the high-priesthood. Meanwhile, however, Herod the Idumean was named and crowned as king of Judea at Rome, where he had arrived an almost despairing fugitive but eight days before. He was brought back by Roman legions; and for the second time, and on the same day on which, twenty-seven years before, Pompey conquered the city, Jerusalem fell, after a siege of five months, into the power of a Roman army exasperated by the long resistance. The inhabitants were murdered in the streets and houses; and Herod, who had no desire to reign amid ruins, only succeeded in preventing the town from being burnt to ashes by lavishing large sums of money upon individual soldiers. Antigonus, the last of the eight princely high-priests of the Asmonean family, was beheaded at the instigation of Herod and the command of Antony.

As monarch of a kingdom now considerably extended through favour of Rome and by his own conquests, the productive resources and taxes of which he indeed stretched to the uttermost, Herod was enabled to display a pomp and sumptuousness that must have astonished even the Romans. By the nation he was deeply hated as an Idumean and usurper, the murderer of the Asmonean house, and the executioner of so many thousands, including the best and most zealous observers of the law amongst the Jews. They beheld with the deepest sorrow the national kingdom polluted by this blood-stained tyrant of foreign origin, who bent subserviently before each successive Roman general and potentate, and the profanation of the high-priesthood, the bearers of which dignity he invested and deprived of it according to his fancy, and converted into mere tools of his caprice or his interest. But the people were tired and exhausted by the preceding thirty years of confusion and civil war, and their power of resistance was broken down. There were, indeed, plenty of conspiracies and desperate attempts; but the good fortune and prudence of Herod weathered all dangers, and each time he took a terrible revenge, so that the hatred of him was coupled with an equal proportion of fear and desponding belief in his lucky star. Accordingly they now put up with many heathen innovations which had kindled the desperate struggle of the Maccabees a century and a half ago, and this although the Hellenistic party amongst the people had much decreased, and the unanimous sentiment of abhorrence for every thing heathen had grown far more strong and general throughout the nation than it was then.

Herod went great lengths in this direction; he built theatres and gymnasia, and solemnised heathen games in honour of the emperors. He even had the Olympic games celebrated with Jewish money, and rich presents went to foreign pagan cities, temples, and worships. At an enormous outlay he finished the city of Cæsarea (Strato's tower), intended as a harbour for Judea, quite like a pagan town. This city, which was in reality the capital of Judea, arose with threatening aspect against Jerusalem; and the Jews must have felt that the polytheistic Cæsarea and the monotheistic Jerusalem were like the two buckets of a well, of which one must sink while the other rises. And every where now Judaism seemed flooded over with paganism; the whole thirty-seven years' reign of Herod was calculated to make the people feel that it only existed to do compulsory service for heathen masters and their semi-heathen adherents, and to suffer extortion.

Herod may have remembered that his forefathers had only adopted the Jewish religion on compulsion, and seen in Jehovah a national God, whose worship was quite compatible with the service of other gods; this at least might explain his rebuilding the Pythian temple at Rhodes (which had been burnt down) at his own expense (that is to say, with Jewish money), and the many occasions of his manifesting a predilection for heathen observances and foreign customs, inexplicable in a Jew. In fact, he probably remained a Jew, only because he was wise enough to see that if he openly declared himself a heathen, every Jewish member of his family would have been more welcome and tolerable to the people, and, in the end, to the Romans also, than himself. But Herod manifested zeal for the Jewish religion too in his own way; for he rebuilt the temple of Zerubabel, now 500 years old, and small and unsightly, on a much larger and more magnificent scale, in which, in accordance with the demands of the Scribes, he caused the materials collected and prepared to be put together by a thousand priests clad in priestly vestments, instructed in building, so that the whole seemed to be erected by consecrated hands. The temple was consecrated with much rejoicing after eight years, and by degrees the large outer courts and colonnades, and the countless cells and chambers around the temple, were also finished.

Meanwhile Herod waxed furious against his own family; he had allied himself to the Asmonean house by his marriage with Mariamne, the granddaughter of Hyrcanus, yet he caused her father and grandfather to be executed, and her brother to be drowned in a bath. After that, she and her mother Alexandra fell victims to his suspicions, as well as the two sons he had by her. Finally, when he was on the brink of the grave, and his body was becoming putrid while yet alive, he caused his eldest son Antipater, the prime mover in all these horrors, to be executed. Up to his dying breath he continued to persecute every symptom of resistance, founded on religious motives, with implacable cruelty. In homage to the Roman supremacy, he caused a golden Roman eagle to be set up over the principal entrance to the temple. This eagle seemed to the Jews in mockery of the prohibition of images, so they threw it down. Upon this Herod caused Matthias the Scribe, and his friends, who had either instigated or done the deed, to be burned alive.

A frightful incubus, which had oppressed the nation for thirty-seven years, seemed to be removed by his death: people dared to breathe again; many dreamed already the national freedom might be restored, and revolts and insurrections arose throughout the whole country. With a judicious estimate of their position, a large embassy was deputed from Jerusalem to Augustus, which was supported by the 8000 Jews then dwelling in Rome, to petition the emperor to deliver them from the family of Herod, and to declare Judea to be a Roman province united with Syria. But in vain: Augustus divided the kingdom of Herod amongst his sons. Archelaus ruled over Judea, Samaria, and Idumea, with the title of ethnarch, not of king. Antipas received Galilee. After ten years of misrule, however, the Jews at length obtained their wish. Archelaus, who walked in the footsteps of his father, was banished by Augustus to Vienne in Gaul, on fresh complaints made against him by his subjects. The country was now united to Syria, and governed by a Roman procurator, who lived in Cæsarea, and only came to Jerusalem to the great feasts. This order of things was interrupted for a short time when Claudius made Herod Agrippa, the grandson of the old Herod, king over all Palestine, A.D. 41. On his death, in the year 44, the government by procurators was resumed.

Thus Romans and Jews, the two proudest nations of the earth, met together in immediate contact, both convinced that they were the favoured children of the Deity. For 500 years indeed the Jews had had to learn to serve foreign masters, with all their consciousness of their own high privileges and destiny; but they now had a ruler who was not contented with such marks and forms of servitude as had formerly satisfied their Persian lords and most of their Syrian ones. The Romans would suffer no distinction among the subjected nations; all were alike obliged to bend beneath their iron sway; the Jews were exempted from no one mark of bondage, and Roman cohorts were quartered in their country. How any attempt at resistance would be treated was shown to them by Varus, when, shortly after the death of Herod, he set Sabinus free from beleaguerment in Jerusalem, and caused two thousand Jews to be nailed to the cross. Still the Jews were deeply impressed with a sense of their dignity and privileges as the only people of the true God, and of a special call to rule over all other people, and receive tribute from them. They were convinced that the promised one, who was to deliver them, and raise them by victory on victory to the summit of earthly power and glory, could not tarry long ere he appeared. They fancied that at no period of their history had they been so faithful to the law, and zealous for the service and honour of Jehovah, as just now. In the old prophets they met on nearly every page with pictures of relapses into idolatry; their forefathers had been ever contemptuously trampling under foot their own crown, and dallying with the heathens and their idols. Hence the chastisement of the Assyrian and Babylonish captivity was merited and explicable. But in what way had they now—they, the far better descendants of those guilty ancestors—deserved such a fate as to fall under the power of Rome, that beast with great iron teeth, devouring and breaking in pieces, and treading down all that was left?[1] And how far below the Jews stood the Roman, the unclean being whose very touch was contaminating! Were he even a proselyte, the real Jew thought lightly of him, and he could not put himself at all on a level with a born Israelite. How readily, therefore, was any one listened to, who told the people that the children of Abraham ought not to serve strangers and worshipers of false gods, and that the moment had come to shake off the yoke, and that God would bless their arms. Even when this did not happen, and when the Jews remained tranquil from a sense of their weakness, as in the dispersion, they did not conceal their haughty spirit. In the midst of the heathen world, the Jew was the Ismael of the desert; his hand was against every man, and every man's hand was against him; he was looked upon as an enemy to mankind, despising every one, and hated by all. Thousands waited eagerly for the first opportunity of falling upon the Jews, and washing out the long-cherished enmity in their blood. Thus the Jews were every where standing

---

[1] Dan. vii. 7.

as if on a mine of gunpowder, that only required a spark to ignite it.

The procurator was now inheritor of the kingly power in Judea. The Sanhedrim was at liberty as before to discuss and decide upon religious matters, but the ratification of the sentence of death rested with the Roman governor; even the sacred vestments which the high-priest wore on the three great festivals of the year and on the annual fast were in his custody, and only given out by him for use on these occasions, after which they were again locked up: this already put the high-priesthood in his power, and he could compel any high-priest to resign who displeased him.

As the Romans had all their subjects registered and their property valued for purposes of taxation, their direct dominion was made in the most painful way perceptible to every Jew throughout the land. Under the Herod family, there was still a semblance of a national rule, exercised by believing worshipers of Jehovah. But now, the fact of their serving and paying heathen masters, and that the holy land had become the property of idolaters, met the sight of an Israelite in all its repulsive nakedness. The law only acknowledged taxes for the use of the sanctuary, and thus, to the mind of a zealot, it was an exaction injurious to their holy law that they should now pay tax to heathen potentates. And to whom were these imposts to be paid? To the emperor? while the law bid them to set over themselves a king from amongst their brethren, not a stranger who was not of their brethren.[1] Hence arose a party and a doctrine which Josephus calls the fourth philosophy of the Jews,[2] as if they had formed a special faction alongside of the Pharisees, Sadducees, and Essenes. Judas the Gaulonite, and Sadoc the Pharisee, were at the head of these zealots. "Be zealous for the law, and give your life for it," were the words of the dying Mattathias, the father of the Asmonean dynasty, to his own family; and such zealots the founders and adherents of the new religious republican party meant to be. God alone should be the lord of the holy people; and the Jewish theocracy ought to admit no other constitution than that of the law of Moses. Hence they were to fight against the Roman usurpation, sacrificing possessions, family, life, and all; and as the theory and

[1] Deut. xvii. 15.   [2] Antiq. xviii. 1. 1.

practice of this party soon developed, the lives of others were as little to be spared as their own to obtain the one great object.

The levies made upon them were in truth heavy, and loud complaints about them were carried to Rome from Syria and Judea. Those who coöperated in this infliction as farmers of these taxes, or publicans, were hated by the people as bloodsuckers, and despised as functionaries of a heathen government; people shunned them, and would not allow them to be witnesses in courts of justice. The Romans were aware of this state of feeling, but it did not alarm them. A couple of legions, in their opinion, was equal to crush any attempt at rebellion thoroughly and for ever. But, in spite of all the weakness and interior divisions of the nation, which made any grand effort impossible, the Jews had one characteristic which rendered them terrible even to the Romans, *i.e.* their daring contempt of death when religion was concerned, and their unflinching fortitude in the endurance of torture. Every outrage now assumed the colour of religious zeal; all open disturbances and rebellion sprang from a religious motive, or sought to pass for a venture undertaken in the name of God and the law. The nature of the country, and the multitude of hiding-places, favoured the assemblage of large bands of brigands, who now professed to be patriots and champions of Jewish national independence against heathen oppression. Every rising ended, usually after a short struggle, in the defeat of the rebels; but so great was their contempt for death, and so ardent their enthusiasm for the law and for freedom, that thousands were always ready to rush in turn to certain destruction.

Mere trifles sufficed to kindle the blind rage of a people full of profound hatred. A soldier of the procurator Cumanus, on guard at the temple, by an unseemly gesture insulted the Jews as they were entering for the Paschal feast: at once a tumult arose. The cry was for the soldier's head; and in the *mêlée* which ensued, ten thousand men were killed or squeezed to death. Shortly after this a soldier tore up and burnt a copy of the Pentateuch which had fallen into his hands. The exasperated Jews fiercely demanded the execution of the soldier from Cumanus. He consented, but with the intention to take his revenge; and soon afterwards an attack of the Jews on the Samaritans gave him the welcome opportunity to massacre them.

A gloomy conviction prevailed amongst the people that under

the iron sway of the Romans, which absorbed and levelled gradually all national peculiarities, their religion, and their nationality conditional on it, could not be secured. Events had already occurred which must have appeared to the Jews as forecasts of projects entertained by the Romans against all that they valued most. In spite of their most urgent solicitations, Pilate wanted some shields dedicated to Tiberius as a god, to be hung up in the temple at Jerusalem. They were forced to send ambassadors to Rome on the matter, who so far succeeded that the shields were, by order of the emperor, placed in a temple dedicated to him at Cæsarea. It was a more serious matter still when Caligula ordered a whole army to be set in motion to erect his statue in the temple, thereby turning the national sanctuary into an idolatrous temple. Nothing but his death prevented his injunction from being carried into effect, which would have inevitably resulted in a civil war, and one probably that would have been undertaken with greater national unanimity than the one afterwards under Nero and Vespasian.

It was precisely the dignity of the high-priesthood, which in earlier times had served the nation and commonwealth as a living point of union, and had often turned the scale in difficult positions; this had now for a long time been enfeebled and dishonoured, partly through the guilt of the later Asmoneans, and partly through the arbitrariness of the Herod dynasty, and now of the Romans; and the confidence of the people in their highpriests was thereby destroyed, or at least much shaken. During many centuries the Jewish church only witnessed the deposition of one single high-priest: now, since the conquest of Jerusalem by Herod till its destruction under Titus, a period of 108 years, twenty-eight high-priests had been nominated,—so that each could have been in possession of the dignity about four years only on an average, and depositions had become the order of the day. No respect was any longer paid to descent or personal merit. Herod Agrippa, and his nephew Agrippa Second, the last descendant of the Asmonean line and that of Herod, had obtained powers from the emperor Claudius to nominate the highpriest, and they preferred Sadducees, as submitting more readily to the demands of the Romans. So in the year 52, Ananias, and in 61, his son Ananus, both Sadducees, were raised to the highest spiritual dignity. At length open discord broke out between the high-priests and the other members of the priesthood on the question of the appropriation of tithes; as the high-priests claimed them for themselves (by reason of the frequency of depositions there were several of them), the inferior clergy were thus exposed to the risk of starvation, and many of the priests and Levites put an end to their lives in despair. Both sides surrounded themselves with armed adherents, and it came to open fight between them in the streets. Shortly after this, and before the breaking out of the Roman war, a regular battle for the high-priesthood took place in Jerusalem between the three candidates, Josua the son of Damnæus, Josua the son of Gamaliel (both nominees of Agrippa the Second), and the old Ananias, who all strove to obtain the dignity, each supporting his own pretensions by hired troops.

One great hope, however, filled the hearts of all the nation, and that was the expectation of the Messias, in whom their fathers had believed, and whose coming the prophets had announced in manifold ways, and in terms of progressive clearness. But this hope was coloured by the fancies and passions which the mass of people were filled with; the past and present state of the nation were reflected in their representations of the Messias. As to the present, it was their sense of the intolerable oppression with which the Roman dominion weighed upon them, and the degradation which they experienced in this bondage; the thought that, considering their moral and religious worth, they ought to take a very different place amongst nations, and were called to rule and not to serve, which gave form and tone to these ideas about the Messias. They longed for an avenger, who, with a strong arm, would make an ample retaliation for all the vexations and indignities that they had been daily subjected to by the presumptuous heathen. The Jews were bitter enemies to all who lived within their territory or on its borders; with the Samaritan on the north, the Arabian to the south, the Greeks and Syrians in the cities: even the powerful arm of the Romans was unable to control the bloody outbursts of this reciprocal hatred, and the heavy punishments consequent on them were equally unavailing. The Messias was, therefore, above all, to enable his people to triumph over these their nearest enemies.

Looking back to the earlier history of his people, the Jew exulted in pictures of a glorious past of national greatness and independence, which the expected Messias would again restore. He was to be a son of David; the father had been the most powerful king whom the Jews ever had, and had conquered the Syrians and Ammonites: could the son do less? A new Elias was to go before him to prepare his way. The Jew dreamed of a vigorous and terrible prophet of wrath, who, like the first, should strike the priests of Baal with the edge of the sword, and openly announce to the potentates their sentence of death. So long as this Elias did not appear accompanied by palpable punishments of all sorts against idolatry, no one could be believed to be the Messias. And if the Messias really came, how else could he enter on his high office than by breaking the Roman yoke asunder? Above all, an end must be put to this state of compulsion, and this continual profanation of the law, the people of God serving heathen rulers and paying taxes; to the national sanctuary being in the hands of the Romans, and also the sons of such a people being pressed into the legions, and forced as soldiers into daily breaches of the law, defilements, and participations in heathen enormities. The Messias must restore the true kingdom, the throne of his father David, and, ruling over the nations afar, establish a new world-empire in which the sons of Abraham would be the dominant class. He who did not present himself as a mighty conqueror, at the head of a victorious army, could not be the true Messias of the promise, for in the prophets it was said that his kingdom should extend from sea to sea. Abraham had received the promise of all the nations of the earth being blessed in his seed. How, then, could this blessing be fulfilled but by the nations being previously conquered and placed under the sway of the Jews, delivered from idolatry, and led by their Jewish masters to the knowledge and worship of the true God? Was it not Jerusalem that was so clearly designated as the seat and capital of the new kingdom of the Messias, where his throne was to be erected, and whither the costly offerings of all nations, their silver and gold, were to flow together?[1] Had not the greatest of their prophets promised that they should eat the good things of the Gentiles, and pride themselves on their glory;[2] that they should suck the milk of the Gentiles, and be nursed with the breasts of kings;[3] that strangers should build up their walls, and that their kings should minister unto them?[4]

[1] Isaias lx. 9. [2] Ib. lxi. 6. [3] Ib. lx. 16. [4] Ib. lx. 10.

"Bowing down," Isaias says, "shall they come to thee that afflicted thee, and all that slandered thee shall worship the steps of thy feet."[1] Nay further, the house of Israel were to hold in captivity those who had held them in bondage; they were to rule over their taskmasters, and to possess the strangers in the land of the Lord as servants and bondmaids. And was not a time foretold wherein ten men of different languages of the Gentiles should take hold of the skirt of one man that was a Jew, saying, "We will go with you, for we have heard that God is with you"?[2] And their teachers taught the people that all this was to be fulfilled to the letter.

Greedily did they swallow the sweet and intoxicating drink of such promises, only attending to whatever flattered their own wishes and gratified their national prejudices, overlooking the conditions to which their fulfilment was attached. All that was required on their side as a condition of the appearance of the Messias and the erection of his kingdom was, their teachers daily told them, scrupulous observance of the law; and that they were not wanting therein was a testimony, they were convinced, which they dared to give for themselves. This national fidelity was a merit which, they thought, gave them a formal claim to the favour of God, and, above all, to the greatest fulfilment of the promises regarding the Messias; and besides, there were the inherited merits of the patriarchs.

Hence the Jewish logic: whoever declares himself to be the Messias, by this declares himself to be the king of the Jews; but whoever does this puts himself in opposition to the dominion of the emperor, and whoever acknowledges such a one as the Messias already, becomes guilty of high treason.[3] It was no use for the accused to draw a distinction between the kingdom of the Messias and an earthly kingdom, and expressly to decline all claim to the latter. The Jews had once for all settled the question, and the nation was unanimous that no one could be their Messias who was not also their king, and would not overthrow the dominion of the Romans. Had he entered Jerusalem at the head of an army, and a victor over a few Roman legions, those very priests and Pharisees, who now desired that he might be crucified, would have joyfully thrown themselves down in the dust before him.

[1] lx. 14.   [2] Zach. viii. 23.   [3] St. John xix. 12; Acts xvii. 7.

All, at the same time, who were zealous for the law, and they then included nine-tenths of the nation, were resolved to recognise no one as the true Messias unless he equalled and surpassed themselves in its observance with all its definitions, and in all its minutiæ, and with the whole "hedge" of interpretation around it, setting a bright example of faultless fidelity to the law in keeping the Sabbath of rest, and carefully shunning all contact with unclean people and things. If he healed a sick man on the Sabbath, or allowed publicans to associate with him, it was clear that he could not be the promised Messias. If they remarked that he had also a mission to the heathen, except it were a command of submission to the chosen people, he must necessarily be destroyed.[1] If he appeared as a sharp censurer, accusing the whole nation, and especially the flower and intelligence of the people, the Scribes and Pharisees, of heavy guilt, he must rather be a Samaritan in disguise than a genuine Jew; for at no time had the law been so carefully observed by the nation as a whole, had the sanctuary been more visited, or the sacrificial services so accurately directed. And now it was the time to inspire the people with courage and boldness, not to humble and fill them with images of penance and compunction.

Many thought that if the sword were but once drawn, the nation engaged in a warfare of life and death with the Romans, and the holy city and temple menaced, the Messias would infallibly appear as a deliverer and avenger. Even during the siege they confidently expected this aid;[2] and when all hope from man was at an end, this delusion nerved their arms and caused them to fight with admirable bravery. We may imagine how carnal the expectations in Palestine were, when we hear those which, in spite of all his Platonism, a Philo cherished in Alexandria but a few years before the great war broke out. "The war shall not extend to the territories of the godly (the Jews); and even if their enemies were mad enough to meet in battle array against them, five of them shall chase a hundred, and a hundred put to flight ten thousand, and they who came by one way shall be scattered asunder through many. For there is a prophecy that a man shall arise who will fight against and conquer great and powerful nations; for God will send his saints the help needed, and he

---

[1] Acts xxii. 22.   [2] Jos. Bell. Jud. iii. 27, vi. 35, vii. 4.

shall be the head over all the children of men."[1] Philo indeed attached to these hopes concerning the Messias the condition that the Jews should subdue their passions; but he also expects that his people, who had met with nothing but misfortune for long, would live to be triumphant, and that their adversaries would give up their own laws and customs, and adopt those of the Jews.[2] By means of this law he believed all true happiness would accrue to mankind: heretofore this had been but a barren wish; but he was now convinced that it would be realised so soon as perfect virtue should, by God's aid, be manifested: "and if we should not live to see it," he adds, "yet we have felt an ardent longing for it from childhood."[3]

Fidelity to the law, and steadfastness in the knowledge and service of Jehovah, was at this time the strength of the Jewish people, their noblest feature, and the source of all that was good in them. When Pilate set up the Roman eagles, with the images of the emperor in Jerusalem, the Jews crowded to Cæsarea, and remained for six days in supplication before the prætorium; on the seventh day the procurator surrounded them with his troops, and threatened to mow them all down; but they threw themselves on the ground, bared their necks, and called on him to kill them rather than impose on them a breach of their law.[4] Such traits of heroic fidelity the Roman must needs have admired, however much he might be tempted to look down on this people, otherwise so incomprehensible to him.

On the other hand, however, this tenacious adherence to the law in its distortion acted as a heavy curse on the nation, and rendered them obtuse to, and unsusceptible of, all higher spirituality, or any thing beyond the narrow boundary of their nationality and ritual maxims. For, after all, it was in fact but the skeleton of a law, adapted for the most part to other circumstances and a different sort of men, to which the Jew clung so tightly. The Scribes had done their work with it, and all life and spirit had deserted the skeleton. Wherever the strict legal point of view wins the day, a narrow system of interpretation also gains ascendency, whose aim is to lower all that is high, and to compress it into the limits of a maxim easy of application; while, on the other hand, it exalts trifles, and laboriously distorts them into

---

[1] De Præm. et Pœn. p. 924 sq., Paris, 1640.   [2] De Vitâ Mos. p. 660.
[3] Ibid. p. 929; cf. Vit. Mos. p. 696.   [4] Jos. Antiq. xviii. 3. 1.

a network of entanglement for daily life. Thus, under the hands of the Pharisees legal traditions thickened at length into a shell, through the incrustations of which the true inner kernel of the original law was no longer discernible. The Jew had reached the point, only to use distinct and palpable commands and prohibitions as rules and springs of conduct. His conscience was dumb, if no such concrete command was to be found, or in cases to which the casuistry of the Scribes had not expressly applied the law. He was not guided and controlled by a moral conscientiousness, resting on general principles, but by the letter of an isolated statute; and the principle of obedience was rather dulled than sharpened in him through the burden and multitude of the precepts.

No thought was so unbearable to this legal people as that of the heathens ever being on a par with themselves in religious matters. If a pagan submitted himself to circumcision and the whole burden of the law, and became a proselyte of justice, a gulf always separated him from the noble Israelitic stock, and he remained as a mere citizen in the earthly kingdom of grace. No heathen could ever become a true son of Abraham, or a participator in his full privileges. Zealous as the Pharisees were in making proselytes, they did not wish their sacred law to be accessible to the heathen, or that the doctrines it contained should be spread abroad by translation into other languages. A legitimate conviction also did certainly actuate them in this respect, viz. that the holy Book, if severed from the living commentary furnished by the Jewish people themselves in their rites and customs and traditional belief, would inevitably be misunderstood; and that in general a religion was not to be propagated by the dead letter of a book, but by the living word of an ordained teaching class; but at the same time the jealousy regarding the possessions and privileges of the nation discovers itself in the notion that what had been confided to themselves alone should not be imparted to others. In this sense the Jewish legends designated the day of the Alexandrian translation as an evil day, like that whereon the golden calf was made, from which to the third day darkness overspread the world.[1] Even Josephus, who wrote his history chiefly for Romans and Greeks, mentions, like a true Pharisee, how Jehovah had punished Theo-

---

[1] Tract. Sopher. 1; Meg. Taquith, f. 50, c. 2.

pompus the historian, and Theodectes the tragedian. The former had given an account of the Jewish belief in his work, and in consequence lost his senses for thirty days. On being warned in a dream of the cause of his malady, viz. that he had dared to spread the knowledge of divine things among profane men, he destroyed what he had written, and was restored to the use of reason. Theodectes was struck blind for having interwoven some passages of the holy Scriptures in a tragedy of his; and on becoming sensible of the reason why, he made atonement to Jehovah for his offence, and his sight was restored.[1]

During this very time of Roman oppression there lived two celebrated teachers of the law in Jerusalem, Hillel and Shammai, founders of two schools which had a marked effect on the later developments of Judaism. Hillel migrated to Jerusalem from Babylon, and became so highly thought of, that he was looked upon, next to Esdras, as the chief restorer of the law, that had heretofore fallen into decay. This condition of it, however, must be only understood as referring to doctrine, in which there were still many disputable points and arbitrary and contradictory decisions; for in practice there was greater zeal for the law then than ever. The merits of Hillel, therefore, consisted in introducing greater solidity and uniformity into the construction of statutes, and also in facilitating their observance by tempering the interpretation. He is said to have brought many a tradition with him from Babylon.[2] Hillel's antagonist Shammai, on the contrary, enforced the strictness of the law and the duty of literal obedience. Characteristic anecdotes have been related of him: he wanted to make his son, though but a little boy, observe the laws of fasting on the day of atonement, so that his friends had to compel him to spare the health of the child; once also, when his daughter-in-law happened to be confined on the feast of tabernacles, he broke through the ceiling of the room where she was, that his new-born grandson might also comply with the precept of the law. His school, however, had the merit of counteracting the corrupt doctrines of the Hillelites, which opposed the most important moral duties. This school went so far as to justify in principle the adulterous degeneracy of the Jews, who then rivalled the Romans in the facility of divorce; they inter-

[1] Antiq. xii. 2, 13.
[2] Grätz, p. 210; Biesenthal, im Lit. B. C. des Orients, 1848, § 683.

preting that "the shameful act" for which the Mosaic law permitted a man to tender his wife a letter of divorce was to be understood of all that might displease a man in a woman, so that he could put away his wife because she had burnt the victuals in cooking, or, as Akiba added, if he found another more handsome. The school of Shammai, on the other hand, taught that he could only send her away if he had discovered any real unchastity in her.[1] But the rigorism of this school by no means suited the later Jews. A bath-kol, or voice from on high, the Rabbis assert, settled the controversy between the two parties in favour of the Hillelites; the disciples of the two schools having often gone so far as to testify their opposition to each other by bloody combats. But it seems that it was not until later, after the destruction of Jerusalem, that this became the prevalent view. During the commotions before the final catastrophe, the Shammaite party was the more popular one, their hatred against the Romans, and their severe interpretations of all maxims regarding the uncircumcised, being better adapted to the dominant feeling.

II. THE LAW.

1. THE MORAL AND SOCIAL CONDITION OF THE JEWISH NATION ACCORDING TO THE LAW.

HOLINESS was designed as the highest scope of the entire law. Israel was to be holy, as and because Jehovah is holy. In this sanctity of Jehovah he was to be able to see the exemplar of his own life, and therefore to strive that his whole conduct, in state and family, should be a mirror for strange nations in which to perceive the sublimity and holiness of the God whom Israel adored. For to this people the high destiny was reserved of being a blessing to all the nations of the earth; and hence holiness was an essential; and this an Israelite only attained when he comprehended the "inner side," so graphically brought out in the last part of the Thora,[2] the spirit of the law, and strove to fulfil it in the fear as well as in the love of God. Hence the high requirement of loving God with his whole heart and all his

---

[1] Biesenthal, p. 726.   [2] Deut. vi.

strength was the compendium of the entire law, being the condition by which Israel might become in reality a priestly kingdom, the highest and noblest of people, and model of all others. As the priest is the guardian and propagator of religious truth, and a mediator of atonement with God, so Israel, amid the nations in its loneliness and isolation, kept at a distance from the distracting and seductive tumult of the world, was to be the priestly people, the sheltering ark, in which the pledge intrusted to it of the true knowledge of God was deposited and preserved, and wherein the seed was sustained and propagated from which the high-priest and saviour of all nations was to be born. The fulfilment of this high destiny demanded the closest union of Israel with God, a union of devoted love. Comprehended and carried out in this spirit of the love of God, the law was, as is so beautifully expressed at the close of the legislation, neither at a distance from them, nor dark, nor hard to be understood; it had not to be fetched from heaven above, nor from beyond the sea, but was very nigh unto them, on their lips, and in their hearts.[1] This precept of the love of God was to be inculcated on their children, and spoken of always and on all occasions. Every where the letter thereof, at least, was to be before the eyes of the Israelite: he was to bind it upon his hand, and to write it on the door-post of his house and the gates of his city.[2] If at a later period the mass of the people fell into a mechanical routine way of caring only for the exterior part of the law, and setting at naught purity and sanctification of the heart, that was not the fault of the law.

From the theocratic nature of the Hebrew state, legislation necessarily pervaded the whole of life in all its details,—family and marriage, personal habits, care of the body, property, police, and international law. All relations of life had to be viewed in their religious aspect, and all main actions and centres of human conduct to be sanctified in the service of Jehovah. The first-fruits of the field, the first-born of each animal, the fairest parcel of land, the beginning of a season, great occurrences and decisive turning-points in the history of the race and people acknowledged as being specially directed by providence, were religiously consecrated. The state was also to be a church; the people, as a national and political body, were destined to be at

---

[1] Deut. xxx. 11 sq. [2] Ibid. vi. 7-9.

the same time a holy possession to the Lord, a priestly kingdom.

Law and morality were not definitively severed from each other in this legislation. Precepts regarding food, the externals of religion, public and private life, were mixed up with laws upon the most important moral questions. Beneficence often appears as a political duty. All, even to the relations of men to nature, to the animal and vegetable kingdom, was accurately marked out. Whilst the law took notice of a number of apparently trifling and indifferent matters, it is surprising that the political constitution should have been so slightly defined legally. Israel might be made a monarchy or a republic without detriment to the law, and could place itself under judges, kings, or a supreme council. It cannot, however, be denied that a kingly government was less adapted, on the whole, to the necessities and peculiar circumstances of a theocratic state, founded on such a comprehensive and stringent law; and so it was that the numerous bad kings of the Hebrews wrought more of evil and ruin than their few good ones did of blessing. Hence also when the people demanded a king from Samuel, it is said, "they have not rejected thee, but me, that I should not reign over them."[1] A kingdom had indeed become necessary on account of the prevalent anarchy; but this itself was only a consequence of the sins of the people, and their rebellion against Jehovah.

A veneration for kings, as habitual in other oriental nations, was impossible on religious grounds to the Jews. Their kings also never obtained the sovereign majesty in its plenitude: they indeed represented the people in its relations to other nations; they concluded peace and waged war, and they exercised the judicial power as a court of last instance, but were without the highest and most important attributes of sovereignty; they could not originate any law; they only wore the sword to protect the law. Legislation had been concluded once for all; even the prophets never took upon themselves to proclaim new laws in the name of God. God reigned in Israel through the law, and its exposition did not rest with the kings, but with the priesthood, and in later days with the Sanhedrim.

For, at a later period, there was a high court of justice, spiritual and temporal, at Jerusalem, consisting of seventy-one

[1] 1 Kings viii. 7.

members, chosen from among the priests, elders, and scribes. This was the Sanhedrim, usually presided over by the high-priest. It has been attributed to Moses, but the seventy assistants named by him in the desert were only of temporary institution. The earlier history of the people contains nothing as regards the existence of such a body. The Sanhedrim is first mentioned in the time of Antipater and Herod,[1] and may have arisen during the time of the Syrian dynasty. In a letter addressed to Ptolemy, king Antiochus already promises the "Senate" of Jerusalem,[2] the priests, and scribes of the temple, exemption from imposts. The members of the tribunal were consecrated to their office by an imposition of hands, and assembled daily to decide all weighty or difficult questions, religious or legal. They judged in trials for religious offences, such as blasphemy or false prophecy, and decided matters touching a whole tribe or the high-priesthood. According to Josephus,[3] even the kings were bound by the decisions of the Sanhedrim, the jurisdiction of which extended beyond the borders of Palestine.[4] By it sentence of death was passed according to the law; but when Judea was governed by Roman procurators, the sentence had to be confirmed and its execution carried out by the procurator.[5]

The family pedigree was of a special importance among the Jews, as well on account of the peculiar law of inheritance, as also because of their constitution. The groups of families formed tribes with special rights; tribes constituted the state, and the government of the state was a government of tribes. The whole glory of an Israelite lay in his pedigree; and as the childless were struck out of the genealogical tree of their tribe, it was every thing to them to have a numerous offspring, and thus to perpetuate their names in the register of their family. In the genealogies, however, only the male children as a rule were entered; any heiresses who succeeded to the family property were included, as were also individual women of any special importance to the family.

The custom of paying a regular price for a wife was frequent amongst the Hebrews as well as amongst other nations. In early times a dowry is seldom found given with brides; at a

---

[1] Joseph. Antiq. xiv. 9. 4. [2] Γερουσία, Antiq. xii. 3. 3.
[3] Antiq. iv. 8. 17. [4] Ibid. xx. 9. 1. [5] Acts ix. 2.

later period this became general. The Mosaic law settled nothing regarding either it or the rites to be observed at the conclusion of the marriage; and the marriage contract was usually arranged between the parents. The principle of monogamy, as a spiritual and corporal unity of man and wife, a connexion making of two persons one flesh, is so expressly declared in Genesis, that we should have expected to find in the Mosaic law also a prohibition against plurality of wives, which is positively opposed to the true spirit of the Old-Testament religion. But it is silent on the subject; and so polygamy was tolerated, and propounded as permitted by the law.[1] The example of the patriarchs may have contributed to this; yet Isaac had but one wife; and Abraham only took Hagar as his concubine at the wish of Sarah; and Jacob became the husband of two sisters merely because of the deceit of Laban. It was the "hardness of heart" and ill-restrained sensuality of the people, manifested in their passion for the licentious idolatry of the Syrians, that determined the lawgiver to permit polygamy or the keeping of concubines as the lesser evil. The latter were chiefly taken because of the sterility of the lawful wife, and from amongst the prisoners of war or domestic slaves. Yet it must not be forgotten that the Jews are spoken of in their sacred books as a stiffnecked, obstinate, carnal, and haughty people.[2] Had monogamy been strictly enjoined, the yoke of the law would have been still oftener set aside; attraction to the entire freedom of heathenism would have become yet stronger, and many times the life even of a wife who was childless, or no longer pleasing to her husband, would have been endangered. Besides, it was chiefly the example of the kings, who had complete harems, full of wives and concubines, which reacted so injuriously on the people, and yet the law of kings expressly forbade them a plurality of wives.[3] After their return from exile, when the people were more earnest and religious, monogamy prevailed over polygamy, and the Jews of later days appear to have kept free from such plurality.

The Mosaic law retained divorce, which had come to be customary, on account of the people's hardness of heart, as we learn from the highest authority. It consisted in the formality of

---

[1] Deut. xxi. 15.   [2] Ibid. ix. 7, 24; 1 Kings xii.; Isaias i. 3, 4.
[3] Deut. xvii. 17.

putting a letter of repudiation into the hands of the wife, and her being ordered out of the house. The grounds on which such severance was permitted were contained in the expression, admitting a variety of interpretations, of "something shameful" that the husband observed in his wife. The law specially prohibited the husband from taking back a divorced wife after the death of her second husband, or her subsequent repudiation by him; because by her second marriage she had become defiled in the eyes of her first husband.[1] Women were not allowed to give a letter of divorce to, or to demand a divorce from, their husbands. The progress made in facilitating divorce, at least afterwards, has been previously mentioned in speaking of the Hillelite glosses, and is further shown in the instance of Josephus, who, being a priest, repudiated his first wife only because her ways displeased him, and then proceeded to marry a second, and even a third.[2]

Jewish marriage-legislation distinguished itself from the moral and legal code of other people by a distinct and detailed prohibition of marriage between near relations, thereby providing for an increased population, as well as for the morality of families. Marriage was forbidden not only between blood relations of the first degree, but also with step-mother, mother-in-law, aunt, widow of a brother, daughters-in-law and sisters-in-law, as well as with daughters and sisters by marriage. Such unions were partly threatened with the judicial punishment of death, and partly with the divine and physical one of barrenness. There was a peculiar ordinance established by ancient custom as to the marriage of the brother of a deceased husband: if a man died childless, his brother or the next of blood was bound to marry his widow, and she was allowed by law to insult him on his refusal of this obligation. This prescription aimed at raising up seed to the dead, the eldest son of such marriage inheriting the property and name of the departed, and transmitting it down.

Adultery with the actual or espoused wife of a stranger was punished with the death of both the guilty parties; yet it depended on the husband whether he would denounce the offenders judicially, or give his wife a bill of divorce out of compassion. If the sin was committed in the fields, where the wife could not

---

[1] Deut. xxiv. 1-4.   [2] Vit. 75, 76.

cry for help, the adulterer alone incurred the penalty. Where there was strong ground for suspicion of adultery, the husband took his wife before the priest, who gave her to drink the water of cursing as a kind of divine ordeal. Whoever violated a free and unespoused maiden was forced to marry her, and could never put her away;[1] if she were a slave, he offered a ram as an atonement. A master was to take as wife or emancipate a slave of Hebrew parents.

On the whole, the social status of the woman was a lower one than among the Germans, and a higher one than among the Greeks. The Hebrew maiden, even in her father's house, stood in the position of a servant:[2] her father could sell her if a minor; he, and after his death his son, disposed of daughter or sister in marriage at their own will and pleasure. As a rule, the daughter inherited nothing. The succession came to her only in the case of there being no sons *in esse*, and of her thus being deprived of the support of a brother. Not the adulteress only, but the espoused virgin also, having fallen into sin before her espousal, was punished with death,[3] while in the latter instance the seducer escaped with a light sentence. The mother of a female child remained unclean twice as long as she did for a male.[4]

Women were occupied in the house with preparation of stuffs and clothing, and the cooking and baking, without being burdened, as among barbarous nations, even the Germans, with the harder kind of labour appropriated to men. They were also visible to strangers, and not excluded from the society of men; they took their meals with them. They contributed to the celebration of festivals by singing and dancing to timbrels; and the history of Israel records names of such as the heroic Deborah and the prophetess Hulda. It is remarkable that the female sex had no proper duties assigned to them as their share in religious acts; all were confined to men only; men only were bound to visit the temple, or make offerings there on festivals; women could offer no sacrifice in their own person, *i.e.* could not lay their hand on it. An exception, however, was made in the case of the Nazarene woman, and those who were suspected of adultery. The value and consequence of the female sex was

---

[1] Deut. xxii. 28, 29.
[2] Numbers xxx. 17.
[3] Deut. xxii. 20.
[4] Levit. xii. 1-5.

wholly in marriage and maternity, there being no place proper in the old covenant for the higher importance and dignity of voluntary virginity; and yet there were women who willingly devoted themselves to the service of the sanctuary, the tabernacle first, and doubtless to that of the temple afterwards;[1] they seem to have done manual labour, such as women do for the use of the holy places. If servants of the sanctuary formed a community, young maidens might be educated there: and thence the old tradition of Mary, the mother of Jesus, having been brought up in the temple might derive confirmation.[2]

Child-murder and abortion were punishable with death according to the law. A woman causing herself to miscarry was, as Josephus tells us, considered doubly guilty, as causing her child's death and impairing the family;[3] and yet it was allowable to destroy it if the life of the mother was endangered in confinement and the head of the child was not yet visible.[4] Abortion and the exposition of infants were acts utterly at variance with the popular ways of thinking and with the law, and were of very rare occurrence.

The law sought in various ways to bring itself to bear by way of restraint upon sexual connexion. Every act of nuptial intercourse made both parties unclean till the evening;[5] and if it took place during the woman's menstrual discharge, both incurred the forfeit of their lives,—an ordinance in its nature indicating no more than the gravity of the transgression in conscience, a juridical conviction being almost always impossible.[6] Prostitutes there were not to be in Israel; prostitution at least was interdicted to the Israelite women under severe penalties, and the dread of the contagion of Syro-Phenician abominations produced a like special denunciation against male prostitution. The priests were forbidden to receive the wages of sin, *i. e.* the piece of money or kid offered by prostitutes at heathen sanctuaries to sanctify their wanton trade.[7] Immorality, however, was stronger than the law, as might be expected in a people so sensual as the Hebrews; and there were always prostitutes among them; but a marriage with one of them was contrary to

---

[1] Exod. xxxiii. 8; 1 Kings ii. 22. [2] Greg. Nyss. in Nat. Ch. Opp. iii. 546.
[3] Adv. Apion. ii. 24. [4] Tertull. de Anim. 25.
[5] Levit. xv. 16-18; Joseph. contra Ap. ii. 24. [6] Levit. xx. 18.
[7] Deut. xxiii. 18.

law,[1] and the sons of such women were denied for ever the political and religious privileges of a citizen of the state.[2]

The slaves, who were generally aliens, although compelled to receive circumcision, were partly captured in war, partly purchased in peace, or born as such in the house. An Israelite only became a bondsman when he sold himself from poverty, or when he had committed a theft which he was unable to replace, and was sold in compensation.[3] A father, indeed, could sell his children and himself; but, on account of the high value attached to the possession of children, this only happened in cases of extreme distress. He who was reduced to slavery through poverty was always capable of redemption; and if he found no relation or friend to set him free, he and his children with him became so without fail in the jubilee year. According to the law, an Israelite who was in a state of bondage was not treated as a slave, but as a hired servant and guest.[4] The soil, in fact, being so tied up and exclusively divided, such transient bond-service was the mildest form under which the pauper and his offspring could be preserved from utter misery; and, on the other hand, the agrarian arrangement of the country precluding all free disposition of labour, slavery was indispensable. If a Jew became enslaved to a stranger, the law urgently recommended the repurchase of his liberty.[5] There was a possibility of a hard-hearted creditor making an insolvent debtor into a slave, but this was not legal.

The lot of the slaves was, on the whole, better than among other nations, and their existence and dignity as men was more secured. The runaway slave was not to be delivered up, but to be protected from the revenge of his master.[6] The repose of the Sabbath was a boon to the slave; he shared in the solemn feast of sacrifice with the rest of the family.[7] If the master had struck out the eye or the tooth of his slave, or otherwise injured him, he was obliged to set him free; if the slave died under punishment, his master was punished judicially.[8] Suppose the master gave the slave a wife, she and her children remained in his possession after the husband was released.[9] A female slave

---

[1] Jos. Antiq. iv. 28, 23. [2] Deut. xxiii. 2.
[3] Levit. xxv. 39; Exodus xxii. 3. [4] Levit. xxv. 35, 39, 40.
[5] Ibid. xxv. 47-55. [6] Deut. xxiii. 15, 16.
[7] Ibid. xii. 12, 18. [8] Exodus xxi. 20. [9] Ibid. xxi. 4.

whom her master had given for wife to his son stept into the rights of a daughter. It also happened that slaves married their masters' daughters[1] when the masters had no sons.[2] If a slave declined taking advantage of the legal manumission of the seventh year, and preferred always remaining in the house of his master, he was received through the symbolic action of piercing one of his ears.[3]

In the prevalent disgraceful practice of the East, to make use of eunuchs at court and in harems, so that there were even eunuch-markets in various places, the Mosaic enactment forbidding such mutilation of man or beast was a veritable boon;[4] and so every injury inflicted on the body given a man by his Maker, was regarded as a sin. If eunuchs were kept at the courts of several of the Jewish kings, they were brought into the country from abroad.

"Love thy neighbour as thyself" is a command of the law following one that forbids all hatred and revenge. "Thou shalt not be revengeful nor spiteful against the sons of thy people;" a duty this which was mentioned in connexion with the administration of justice, to warn the Israelite that, though he might appear as a complainant before the judgment-seat, he was to bear no malice or hatred against the offender.[5] Under the title "neighbour" who should be loved, only those of their own people are to be understood according to the context. Besides this, strangers who took shelter with the Israelites were included in this love of neighbour. The command in itself could not, in the then condition of the Jews, be extended to those of strange and idolatrous nations, who appear throughout the law too thoroughly enemies of Jehovah and his people for this. The precept of universal love of mankind was reserved for a higher development of religion.[6]

No legislation of ancient times had so well guarded against the pauperism of part of the nation, and the rise of a proletarian class, as that of the Hebrews. There were no real beggars in Judea, and no Hebrew word for begging. After the conquest of the country, its acreage was equally divided amongst the Israelites, and the land then assigned was intended to remain in the possession of the descendants of the first possessor for ever; the

---

[1] Exodus xxi. 9.   [2] 1 Paralip. ii. 35.   [3] Exodus xxi. 6.
[4] Levit. xxii. 24; Deut. xxiii. 1.   [5] Levit. xix. 18.   [6] Matt. v. 43 sq.

year of jubilee making provision for the ultimate reversion of property to the original owner, even when he had sold it outright. Thus continual and hopeless beggary in whole families was prevented. During harvest-time the poorer people were allowed to glean what was left in the fields and olive- and vineyards; a reservation which required that the owner should not gather up his harvest too closely.[1] Besides this, they were at liberty to appropriate all that grew of itself in the sabbatical year, and were to be invited to the entertainments provided on the feasts of the second tithes, with a view to supply which feasts in the temple this special tithe was enjoined. Even personal slavery was to many, no doubt, a much-coveted refuge, as, for a child of the soil, it could never last longer than a few years.

Thus the law could truly say, "There shall be no poor man among you, if you only hearken to God's voice and keep all his commandments."[2] The law afforded every possible security against unmerited misfortune, but, naturally enough, it was impossible that it should come within the scope of any lawgiver to provide for the prosperity of the individual, if he frustrated what was done for him by his own moral depravity, or to guard against the consequences of a great apostasy or general degeneracy and neglect of the law in the nation. The poor were also greatly aided by the manner in which the law inculcated the equality of high and low in the sight of Jehovah, and their union as brethren, and the duty of brotherly love, warning them of the "baseness" of heart that would turn them aside from the poor.[3]

The law willed that the Israelite should be ready to help his necessitous brother by a loan, and to take interest thereon was forbidden. "Lend without usury, that the Lord thy God may bless thee in all thy works."[4] It was also forbidden to enhance the price of natural products lent; but it was allowable to take pledges under certain restrictions. On the other hand, the law expressly permitted interest to be taken from strangers; as was but natural under their circumstances,—loans without interest would imply closer and more intimate relations than could exist between a Jew and a stranger. It is well known, however,

---

[1] Levit. xix. 9; Deut. xxiv. 19 sq. [2] Deut. xv. 4, 5.
[3] Ibid. xv. 7-11. [4] Ibid. xxiii. 20.

what interpretation was in process of time put by the Jews upon this distinction between the stranger and the Israelite, and how they thought usury, even to the most shameful extent, allowable from all who were not Jews. In olden times, when the Jews lived apart as a nation, and held but little intercourse with their neighbours, this disgraceful trait in their character was not yet brought to light.

Although the law aimed at cutting off or hindering any close union between Israel and other nations, it offered full protection to the stranger dwelling in the land. We may say the Jewish legislation was more favourable to strangers than that of all other nations. "There shall be one law," it is written, "for the stranger that dwells and those that are born in the land;"[1] and yet further, "the stranger shall be unto thee as one of thy own people, and thou shalt love him as thyself, for ye also were strangers in Egypt."[2] Strangers were therefore permitted to partake in the festival and tithe feastings, in the gleanings of fields and vineyards, and the harvest of the year of jubilee. They were to be on an equality with the Israelites in matters of justice; only they were compelled to conformity with the laws of the land so far as to avoid what was an abomination to the Israelites, and therefore all open acts of heathen worship. Gifts and sacrifices, sent by heathens dwelling without the land, were received in the temple; they were not permitted to enter the courts of the temple of the Israelites, but might offer up prayer to Jehovah in the outermost court, called the "court of the Gentiles."

The law was specially careful about the welfare of animals; they were to be treated with compassion and kindness. Domestic animals were to be well fed, and to enjoy the rest of the Sabbath. "Thou shalt not muzzle the ox that treadeth out the corn." They were to help to lift up the ass which had fallen beneath its burden, and to bring back the beast that had gone astray.[3] The harnessing of animals of different species, or yoking them to the plough, was prohibited. The young was not to be taken from its mother before the seventh day; it was not to be killed on the same day with its mother, or seethed in its mother's milk. From these and similar ordinances,—such,

---

[1] Numbers xv. 15. [2] Deut. x. 19.
[3] Exodus xxiii. 5, 12; Deut. xxv. 4.

for instance, as about the least painful method of killing animals,—it is plain that the law tried to subdue that coarse turn of mind and unfeeling cruelty which are engendered by the maltreatment of animals.

In the punishments enjoined by the law, the principle of equality of indemnification (and sometimes more than indemnification) is chiefly visible. Bodily injuries, if wilful, were to be repaid by the like infliction on the corresponding member. It seems, however, this punishment was seldom really carried out; the judges were almost always satisfied with compensation in money. The penalty of death, "the being cut off from among the people," was of frequent occurrence, for various religious offences, by the sword or by stoning;[1] and herein the full severity of a law of fear came prominently forth. He who struck or cursed his parents, or was guilty of sodomy, of kidnapping bodies, or of selling souls, forfeited his life equally with the murderer. But, on the whole, the penal code was a mild one. Bodily chastisements were carefully and strictly limited, with compassionate regard to the health of the victim; of ignominious punishments there were none. The only penalty for theft was the restitution of more than the amount stolen.[2]

Judicial proceedings in criminal cases were humane and considerate. Two witnesses were requisite for sentence to pass; in default, the deponent was put on oath. The use of torture was unknown to the Israelites and their laws, and was first introduced under the Herods.[3] The judges were the "Elders," representatives of the community, who discussed and regulated matters concerning the city and country; and then the kings, who also constituted the final court of appeal, but often pronounced arbitrary and unjust sentences. The holy Scriptures of later date contain strong and frequent complaints of the venality of the judges, and of the repeated employment of false witnesses.

The vengeance of blood, an older custom, peculiar to all races not yet fully developed into a complete polity, was recognised by the Mosaic law, though with restrictions in conformity with the spirit of the whole. The rooting out of the offender from amidst the people was the necessary punishment for a

---

[1] Lightfoot, Horæ Hebr. p. 282. [2] Exodus xxii. 1 sq.
[3] Jos. Bell. Jud. i. 30, 3.

grievous crime committed on one made in the likeness of God, and against God himself, the Creator and Lord of human life; it was a religious duty, and for the nearest relations of the murdered man it was also a family duty; but it was only commanded for intentional murder. To protect such as had inadvertently or accidentally killed a man, six cities were appointed, to any of which the man-slayer could flee from the avenger of blood, and there he had to remain until the death of the high-priest in whose time the homicide took place.[1] After the Captivity, and even before, the avenging of blood was extinct as a custom.

---

2. Religious Life — Circumcision — The Sabbath — The Priesthood and Prophecy — The Temple — Images — Proselytes — Sacrifice — Prayers and Festivals — The Clean and Unclean.

The Jews had circumcision in common with the Egyptians; and it is easy to believe that it was first introduced into the land of the Nile, and from thence found its way into Palestine through the patriarchs of the people of Israel. Herodotus at least maintains, that the inhabitants of Palestine themselves attributed the origin of the rite to Egypt. But it was not of general usage there, being confined to the sacerdotal order and military caste, while it was a mark of nationality with the Jews. From Palestine it passed over to the Edomites, Moabites, and Ammonites, doubtless through their relationship of race to the Israelites, and by the same way it reached Arabia. Thus we can only adopt the assertion of Josephus with considerable reserve, that the lawgiver intended to separate the Israelites by this sign from all the other nations of the earth. According to Herodotus, the Colchians, an Egyptian colony, and the Ethiopians, also had this rite. The physical and medical reasons by which its origin has been explained, that it was an assistance to being cleanly and prolific, and prevented particular maladies common in the East, are not satisfactory. Probably its first signification was that of a sacrifice of the human person, and intended to counteract, at least in Syria and Palestine, the sacri-

---

[1] Exodus xxi. 13; Numbers xxxv. sq.; Deut. xix. 1 sq.

fice of children, in use there. If we consider how the earlier human sacrifices both in Rome and Gaul were replaced by a slight wound, a simple scratch on the head, with the loss of a few drops of blood, it is quite conceivable that circumcision too was a similar substitutive sacrificial rite, standing in the same relation to the Jewish usage as the pagan lustrations did to baptism. And then afterwards was annexed the idea of sanctifying the membrum virile and the act of propagation of the human species.

According to the statement of the later Jews, circumcised children were called the espoused of blood (*i.e.* by God);[1] a child thus was specially consecrated to God by circumcision, and then admitted into the community which was to form "a priestly kingdom and a holy nation."[2] Circumcision had been discontinued during the wanderings in the desert; Josue, however, entirely restored it, and from that time it was a disgrace to be uncircumcised;[3] and the notion of an unclean and profane person, contact with whom should be avoided, was implied in it. Any Israelite might perform the rite, but it was generally done by the father of the family on his son the eighth day after his birth. Even servants, not of the posterity of Abraham, were to be circumcised. Every one was threatened with being cut off from among the people who remained uncircumcised, for "he destroyed the covenant with God."

One of the institutions quite peculiar to the Hebrews is the observance of the Sabbath introduced by Moses. This day, on which God completed the work of creation, belonged to Him in a special manner, and was to be sanctified principally by entire repose, not only on the part of men but also of beast, from all work. On this day the Israelite was to participate in the rest of God, and give a visible token of his veneration for the Creator and Lord of the world; it was the day of covenant, and its observance was to be a perpetual sign of the covenant still in existence between God and Israel.[4] On the Sabbath no fire was to be lighted even for cooking; cold meats were eaten, and the evening meal was prepared after sunset (between five and seven). Beyond this, the law exacted no positive obligations from the Israelites in regard to the Sabbath; no form of religious worship

---

[1] Cf. Exod. iv. 26. [2] Ibid. xix. 6.
[3] Ezech. xxxii. 19, 21. [4] Exod. xxxi. 13-17; Ezech. xx. 20-22.

was prescribed; complete rest sufficed to satisfy the precept. The ordinances regarding the sacrifice of the Sabbath and the change of the showbread only concerned the priests in the temple.

It was not till later times that all that was to be left undone on the Sabbath was accurately laid down. Travelling was prohibited on this day, and the length of the distance which a man might journey (2000 furlongs) was settled. The Sabbath rest extended, Philo tells us, even to the vegetable creation. No sprout or twig could be pruned on that day, nor fruit be plucked. Josephus is the first to remark that it was considered a duty, or at least advisable, to devote the Sabbath to religious employments.[1] In the days of our Lord, the Sabbath was celebrated in the synagogues with prayer, reading, and exposition of the Scriptures. People put on their holiday clothes and assembled at social meals, and there was no fasting on this day.

As religion had sanctified the relations between an Israelite and the land promised and given him by God, it also had its corresponding Sabbath and its share in the rest of God.[2] Every seventh year the fields were not sown, nor the vineyards pruned; what the ground brought forth of itself was not to be reaped, nor were the grapes to be gathered. The produce of the year belonged to all the living; and therefore, too, no debts were to be demanded. Thus the sabbatical year answered the double purpose of a fallowing to increase the productions of the fields, and of a longer time of repose to man and beast. The landowners lost the produce of a year, while the people, as a whole, especially the poor, were gainers, and the loss of the proprietor was made up by the richer growth of the six following years.

A similar sabbatical year, but of far more extended operation, was held every seven times seven years, or fiftieth year. In this year of jubilee, field-work ceased in like manner. All slaves of Jewish descent were set free. Each one reëntered on his old property. Sales of property, therefore, were, properly speaking, only departures with the right to the usufruct thereof, and were made under the condition of reversion to the owner; and therefore the purchase-money was but a rent, varying considerably in amount according as the year of jubilee was further

---

[1] Antiq. xvi. 2. 4.
[2] Exodus xxiii. 11; Levit. xxv. 2-8; Jos. Antiq. iii. 12. 3.

off or nearer at hand. This regulation, unique of its kind, aimed at producing a constant social regeneration, and restoring the old conditions of property. Those excessive inequalities caused by the otherwise unavoidable accumulation of real property in the hands of a few, the eviction of the poor by the rich, or their degrading into mere tenants or hirelings, were thus avoided.

The Levites, in fact, took the place of the first-born in Israel, for according to the law these were to be holy unto the Lord; and Jewish tradition asserts that, in the beginning, all the first-born sons of all the tribes of Israel were called to sacrificial service. From the time of the vocation of the sons of Levi, the first-born of the other tribes were only carried up to the temple a month after their birth, and redeemed by paying a tax according to the valuation of the priests, which, however, was not to exceed five shekels.[1] The Levites were now specially the possession of the Lord, and he was their inheritance.[2] When they were separated for the first time from the rest of the Israelites, and placed before Aaron and his sons, the children of Israel, that is to say, the elders as their representatives, put their hands on the heads of the Levites,[3] as a gift consecrated to God from the whole nation, and they were like the first sacrifice of the people.

The tribe of Levi had no territorial possessions, and therefore the tithes belonged to them. But they thereby forfeited the basis of any considerable power or influential position. Their dwelling-places were scattered among the whole nation, and consisted of forty-eight cities, with allotments round them for their cattle and other necessaries of life. They were divided into four classes, consisting of servants of the priest (hierodouloi), who were 24,000 before the Exile; door-keepers, 4,000; singers and musicians, 4,000; and judges and officials, 6,000.[4] The singers and musicians were subdivided again into twenty-four classes, who were on duty successively a week each. The Levitical period of service extended from the thirtieth until their fiftieth year; but in consequence of a decree of David they began to serve from their twentieth year. The occupations of the Levites in the temple consisted of opening, shutting, and cleaning it, and

---

[1] Exodus xiii. 13. [2] Josue xiii. 33.
[3] Numbers viii. 5 sq. [4] 1 Paralip. xxiii. 4, 5.

the custody of its treasures and provisions; they had also to collect the tithes and firstlings, and to provide all that was required in the way of libations, incense, sacrifices, and feasts. They had to assist the priests in the killing and flaying of the victim, but could not approach the altar. The most menial offices of the temple, that of the hewers of wood and drawers of water,[1] was not performed by the Levites, but by temple slaves, who were the descendants of conquered races. In fine, the Levites wore no particular dress, and were free from military service and taxation even under foreign rulers; the administration of justice and municipal duties did not exclusively belong to them, but from the time of David they filled such posts repeatedly.

As the whole people were holy, and elected by Jehovah to be a priestly people peculiar to himself, so the priestly office, attached to the descendants of the one family of Aaron, formed the part of the nation in which the religious dignity and obligations of the whole came out most prominently as dominant over the rest, or as the means used for realising that position. The priest was the representative of and substitute for the people before God, considered as a moral personality. This fact of selection was intended to be particularly prominent through its hereditary nature, in its being confined to one certain priestly family selected by God. The priesthood, requiring no particular mental culture or special accomplishments, was to be no matter of free choice, but a vocation manifested through birth, and therefore by a higher power. Whoever exercised priestly offices without belonging to the priesthood was threatened with death. The isolation of the Jewish priesthood, however, was not the strict severance of a caste; the priests were at liberty to marry women of other tribes.

The priests called to approach the Holy One, and to go up to the altar, were obliged to be free from bodily defects; a blemish did not, indeed, lessen his maintenance, but necessitated his keeping at a distance from the altar, for his exterior was not, as it ought to be by its faultlessness, a reflexion of the perfections of the Godhead and the holiness of the service.[2] For the same reason, he was forbidden to marry a concubine, or one who had been put away by her husband; and if the daughter of a priest fell into impurity, she was to be burnt, for having dishonoured

---

[1] Jos. ix. 23; 1 Esdras ii. 58, viii. 20.   [2] Levit. xxi. 22.

the sacerdotal dignity of her father. No priest was permitted to perform ritual observances till his twentieth year. As in the latter times, after the Captivity, a priest was obliged to make good his claim to the priesthood by proving his descent, the family registers[1] had to be kept with great exactness. Their chief duty was that of sacrifice; hence also their consecration was a sort of sacrificial act, completely interwoven with the sacrifice. The person to be consecrated was first freed from sin by the offering of a bull as an atonement; for sins, as causing a perpetual division between God and man, must be first removed from one who would be entirely devoted to the service of God. Then followed the burnt-offering of one ram, while with the blood of a second the ears, thumbs, and big toes of the postulant were anointed, thus consecrating hearing, hands, and feet to the service of the altar.[2] The remaining blood was poured forth around the altar, and at the same time the person of the consecrated and his vestments were sprinkled with a mixture of it and the oil of unction. The quarters of the ram, with some cakes of unleavened bread, were placed in the hands of the new priest, and then consumed on the altar. In this consecration all the three kinds of sacrifice were thus made use of,—the sin-offering, the burnt and peace offering, and the thank and meal offering.

The priests alone could minister at the altar; they kept up the perpetual fire on the altar of sacrifice; they laid the sacrifice on the altar; undertook the various sprinklings of blood; set fire to what was to be burnt; entered the holy place; took care of the lights on the golden candlestick, and performed the public devotions. They were appointed to set forth the law to the people,[3] especially on the three great feasts, and to expound it judicially in all private matters. King Josaphat appointed a regular court of justice in Jerusalem formed of priests and Levites.[4] The priests even went to battle with the rest, and received their share of the spoil, and the priesthood was compatible with military appointments; thus, Benaias, the priest, was commander of the bodyguard of king Solomon and general of his army. Sadoc and Joiada, both descendants of Aaron, belonged to the staff of

---

[1] 1 Esdras ii. 62; 2 Esdras vii. 64; Joseph. contra Apion. i. 7.

[2] Exodus xxix. 15-20.   [3] Deut. xvii. 8 sq., xix. 17, xxi. 5; 2 Paral. xvii. 9.

[4] 2 Paral. xix. 8; Joseph. contr. Apion. ii. 21.

David's army. It is well known that the Maccabees were of the priestly race.

The maintenance of the priests was provided for by the firstlings—which were offered three times a year—of the corn, bread, fruits, and animals; by the showbread, and the gifts or heave-offering, and the ransom-money of the first-born. The remains of the sin-offerings, the breast and right shoulder of the peace-offerings, also belonged to the priests, and the right of partaking in the sacrificial repast extended to the members of their family. This participation in the meats of sacrifice was coupled with the condition that all ritual uncleanness was to be most carefully avoided. Hence they could not approach a corpse unless that of a very near relative; and whilst they were serving in the temple they had to abstain from all intoxicating drinks[1] and conjugal intercourse. Before they approached the tabernacle of the testimony, or altar of incense, they had to wash their hands and feet.[2]

Like the Levites, the priests had several cities, thirteen in all, for their especial residence; they were situated near Jerusalem, and in the territory of the tribes of Judah, Benjamin, and Simeon. It was not till after the Captivity that some of the priestly families lived in Jerusalem itself. Whilst they were in attendance at the temple, they inhabited rooms within its precincts. The priests received a tenth from the tithes of the Levites. They formed a closely united body, occupying in some degree the position of an aristocracy, and were on the whole much respected by the people. They wore the ordinary national dress when not in the temple, and when there a white linen one; but they only stepped barefoot on the holy places. They were divided into twenty-four classes, and took the services of the temple in rotation: constantly recurring celebrations were apportioned to individuals by lot. The custody and exposition of the book of the law, committed to them or to all the elders of the people, also formed part of their office; but the knowledge of the law was indispensable for all who had a right to administer justice, and every king received a copy when he commenced his reign. A female priesthood was impossible amongst the Hebrews, as they not only had no worship of nature, but their religion was expressly calculated to exclude and suppress any attempt or disposition to develop its cultus.

[1] Levit. x. 8-11.   [2] Exodus xxx. 19 sq.

The high-priest formed the apex of the whole priesthood. In his person the nation was collectively, as a priestly people, consecrated to God. He was the mediator between Jehovah and the people, and supreme head of the Jewish church. Hence the greatest purity and holiness (in the Old-Testament sense of the words) was demanded of him as befitting one who had to appear before Jehovah in the name of the people, to bring the unholy people into his presence, and whose holiness was to overflow upon others so as in a certain sense to supply the want of purity in the mass. But it was also well known to all that this their sacerdotal head and representative before God was but a sinful man, himself requiring the atonement and purification of the blood of sacrifice, and indeed through the very same oblation as that offered up for the whole people. Yet stricter ritual purity was required of him; only a pure virgin could be his wife; every sign of mourning was forbidden to him, and he durst not even touch the corpses of his parents. He had to absent himself from his own house seven days before the day of atonement, that the purity demanded by the sacrifice of this day might not be sullied by approaching his wife.

The dress of the high-priest was exquisitely splendid and significant: Moses had consecrated the first high-priest, by vesting him therein and anointing him before the assembled congregation.[1] The close-fitting ephod, or short tunic, was fastened on the shoulder by onyx-stones, on which were engraved the names of the twelve tribes. Over the ephod on the breast was the square Rational of judgment, of the same material, with twelve stones, each bearing one of the names of the twelve tribes. On this square-shaped breastplate, open at top, was placed the holy oracle, the Urim and Thummim (that is to say, 'light and salvation;' or, according to Philo, 'manifestation and truth'). It is matter of dispute in what the oracle consisted. The testimony of Josephus, however, is clear and decisive, and in nowise contradicts the assertions of Philo. From the greater or less, entire or partial, illumination in the stones and play of colour thereon, the high-priest prophesied; in order to bring out this light he made use of the urim and thummim, for that these were distinct from the stones in the breastplate is evident from the words, "Put the urim on the breastplate," &c. It is plain something

[1] Levit. viii. 1-12.

must have taken place when the oracle was consulted, to make the stones change their ordinary condition into an extraordinary one, and to produce any effect out of them. Now it is clear, from the expression of the law,[1] that the urim and thummim was a different object from the twelve stones, and was laid or fastened in the breastplate. According to Philo, the "logion" or "oracle" was double; that is to say, it consisted of two tissues, so that the stones were separated from the urim by a covering placed between.[2] If the oracle had to be consulted, this covering or tissue had to be removed, and the urim playing on the gems brought a light out of them. There was something, however, out of the common way in this matter, as is shown by the statement of Josephus, that for two hundred years the light of the breastplate had ceased, by reason of God's anger on account of the transgressions of the law. Thus it was not a matter dependent on human volition; for had it been so, its duration would have been undoubtedly secured, as there was nothing similar to take the place of the oracle.

What the urim really was, is, nevertheless, quite uncertain. According to Jewish tradition, it consisted of two stones with the two sacred names of God, which produced an illuminating effect on the gems. The account given by the rabbis, that the high-priest, from the particular way in which the letters forming the names of the different tribes shone, was able to read the divine will, or to prophesy, is probably an illustration of later days. The Greek fathers, St. Cyril, for instance, are undecided whether the urim and thummim was a golden tablet, or if it was formed by two stones, one of which was called urim and the other thummim, or on which these two words were engraved.[3] So much is certain, that it was not a mere symbol in the sentences flowing solely from the inspiration of the high-priest,[4] and that it was not a purely internal inspiration that took place,

---

[1] Exod. xxviii. 30.

[2] One time he says (Vit. Mos. 3. ii. 152), τὸ λόγιον τετράγωνον διπλοῦν κατεσκευάζετο; at another (Monarch. q. ii. 226), ἐπὶ τοῦ λογείου διττὰ ὑφάσματα καταποικίλλει. Here one passage explains the other, and confirms Josephus, who does not say that the twelve precious stones were the λόγιον, but rather distinguishes between the two (Antiq. viii. 3. 8), σὺν ποδήρεσιν ἐπωμίσι καὶ λογίῳ καὶ λίθοις; and (ib. iii. 8, 9) he says the breastplate was called λόγιον, just as Philo does.

[3] See the passages collated in Bernard's long note to Josephus (ed. Havercamp, i. 165).   [4] As Bähr thinks, Symb. des Mos. Cult. ii. 136 sqq.

as in the case of the prophets.[1] The high-priest may have found himself in a state of spiritual excitement, the effect perhaps of a special ascetic preparation; but he was bound by what he perceived on the stones of the breastplate. Had it not been so, Josephus, who must unquestionably have been well informed on this point, as he was of priestly descent, would have said, for two hundred years the prophetical inspiration of the high-priest was extinct, as prophecy generally was. Instead of this, he says the light of the stones has ceased; not only that of the twelve stones on the breastplate, but also that of the onyx-stones on the shoulder.

The high-priest wore a mitre on his head, which had a golden plate on the front, bearing the inscription, "Holy unto the Lord." He was consecrated by the pouring of the anointing oil on his head, symbol of the imparting of the Holy Spirit; after which act, according to Jewish tradition, a cross was made on his forehead, in the form of that of St. Andrew; he thus was styled emphatically the anointed priest. The Jews say this anointing continued up to the time of Josias; from which period, as the holy anointing oil was lost, the high-priest was only consecrated by investment.

In his highest function on the great day of atonement, when he entered the holy of holies as representative of the repentant people, the high-priest only wore a simple vesture of white linen.[2] The whole sacrificial rite was specially his, "the ministry of Aaron."[3] The other priests acted in it as his deputies; yet he only offered up sacrifice himself on the sabbaths, especially on the great festivals.[4] Of course the supervision of the divine worship and temple treasures devolved wholly on him. Without doubt the dignity was from the first given for life, and the eldest son was to follow him in it. There were eighty-three high-priests in all; thirteen from Aaron to Solomon, eighteen during the continuance of the temple of Solomon, and fifty-two under the second temple.[5] Up to Eli the dignity remained in the line of Eleazar, one of the sons of Aaron. With Eli it entered the

---

[1] So Bellerman, Urim and Thummim, the most Ancient Gems, p. 22. It is a modern idea to say, as Ewald (Alterthümer Isr. p. 339) and others do, that the two stones were shaken in a purse, and one taken out; and it contradicts the clear and consistent testimony of older writers.

[2] Levit. xvi. 4.   [3] Ecclesiasticus xlv. 16.
[4] Joseph. Jud. v. 5, 7.   [5] Joseph. Antiq. xx. 10.

family of Ithamar, another of the sons of Aaron. When Abiathar was deposed by Solomon, the priesthood recurred to Sadoc, of the race of Eleazar. During the Syrian rule, from 160 till 153 B.C., the succession of the high-priesthood was interrupted. With Jonathan, son of Mattathias, began the line of Asmonean high-priests, who were descended from Eleazar. The period of the Herods we have seen was one of the deepest degradation, during which the high-priesthood was the puppet of foreign potentates, and at last of the mob.

If there was no king or judge in Israel, the high-priest alone possessed and exercised the supreme authority. Thus Heli, the high-priest, judged Israel forty years; and so it was also under the Asmoneans. The relation and division of power as between high-priest and earthly head of the people (king or judge), was not legally defined. The king certainly had no right to interfere in the legitimate exercise of the sacerdotal power, independent in its own sphere and derived from God, not from him; and if Solomon deposed the high-priest Abiathar (the only instance of the kind before the Captivity), who, as the king looked at it, had deserved death, on the other hand, Athaliah the queen, after a reign of six years, was deposed by the high-priest Joiada (who had secretly anointed her grandson king), and executed as an idolatress and seducer of the people at his order; and Joiada himself reigned for a long time in the name of his youthful protégé Joas.

Parallel to the priesthood were the Nazarites, who were the Old-Testament ascetics or religious. There were Israelites of both sexes specially "set apart" and consecrated to God. They observed the general commands as to purifications with extreme rigour; above all, they avoided defilement by corpses, and abstained particularly from wine, all intoxicating beverages, and all that came from the vine plant, as grapes and raisins.[1] The Nazarite also let his hair grow. "No scissors were to come near his head." This seems to have been so, partly because wearing long thick hair in hot weather was a great penance, and partly

---

[1] This shows that Bähr is quite incorrect in thinking this abstinence was merely a means to an end, viz. that of being always in a state to discriminate that which was clean and unclean (Sym. ii. 432). In Palestine it was certainly a greater act of self-denial to abstain from grapes than from wine. Celibacy was apparently not binding on the Nazarites in earlier times.

because, as in circumcision the organ of generation, so in the Nazarite vow the hair, was the part of the body specially consecrated to God. Accordingly when the vow was at an end, the hair was cut off and burnt as a sort of sacrificial offering. There were Nazarites who were consecrated to God for life by their parents even before their birth, as Samson, Samuel, and St. John the Baptist. Generally, however, the dedication took place for a certain time only, and in order to the attainment of a special end, *e. g.* the granting of a prayer, and such like. At the expiration of the time vowed, the Nazarite brought a lamb as a burnt-offering, a sheep as a sin-offering, and a ram as a thank-offering, as well as a basket of unleavened oil-cakes. If he had defiled himself during the time of his Nazariteship by coming in contact with a corpse, he began the time afresh, after bringing the triple sacrifice. In the time of Josephus many persons were in the habit of vowing, especially in sickness and other distresses, that they would abstain from wine for thirty days before offering a sacrifice, and would pray and cut their hair.[1] This was not a Nazarite vow proper, for in that, on the contrary, they promised to let the hair grow.

As the Hebrew nation were to be a standing mirror, a warning and a sign to other nations, so were the prophets to the people. Times when the prophets did not appear were times of corruption or death. If the words of the seer were not obeyed, it was a proof of an unhappy lethargy, and of a heavy chastisement weighing on Israel. There were examples of prophetical agency before Samuel in Ehud and Deborah. Just before he arose, coincidently with the general public degeneracy, the gift of prophecy seemed to have ceased. But with him, 400 years after the Exodus, and about 1100 years B.C., began that series of prophets who continued with but few interruptions till the days of Malachias, a period of nearly 700 years.

Samuel founded real schools of the prophets, of which later on there were several to be found in Rama, Bethel, Jericho, and Gilgal. In these schools lived together young men called the "sons of the prophets," who were under the guidance and instruction of their elders and masters. Not indeed that prophetic inspiration could be taught or artificially acquired, but young men could be prepared beforehand by strict discipline, an ascetic

---

[1] Bell. Jud. ii. 15.

mode of life, and continual occupation with the Thora, and penetrating into the spirit of the sacred text, nay even by religious music and dancing, so as to stand ready like vessels at hand, fit for the outpouring of the prophetic spirit when vouchsafed. We find that in these schools a sort of ecstatic condition was kept up by artificial means, probably in the same manner as among the therapeutæ of later ages, so that strangers coming suddenly upon a company of these sons of the prophets were seized with a similar enthusiasm, and carried away to like gestures and acts.[1] The schools of Samuel were an attempt to realise the wish which Moses once had cherished and expressed, that all the people might prophesy, and to prepare a body of men, in the hope that such an extensive outpouring of the prophetic spirit, as Jael had foreseen in the far future, might arise in the succeeding generation.

How long these schools of the prophets subsisted cannot be precisely determined; they appear to have decayed after the days of Elias; the last traces of them are to be found in Amos. But the weight of the prophetic office, an institution quite unique and not comparable with any thing to be met with of the kind in history, from this time forth exercised a deep and powerful influence upon the destiny of the nation and the course of the development of the theocratic kingdom. Without any legal power or credentials the prophets arose from amidst the people, now priests or Levites, and at other times simple Israelites of other tribes, independent of family and position, and often impelled by an uncontrollable pressure in despite of all the revoltings of nature against their mission. A prophet, in consciousness of and with the authority of his immediate vocation, was at once the "mouthpiece" or messenger of God, and the personified conscience of the nation, who held up to all the reflection of their transgressions. He was a demagogue and patriot in the noblest sense, who at great and decisive moments came forth to face people, potentate, and king, as preacher of penance, warner or consoler, guardian of the law, and expounder of the ancient promises of the covenant. Within the bounds of the law, which the true prophet never overstepped, he exercised unlimited freedom of speech, often attended with peril and sacrifice of life. The law itself had foreseen his position, and decreed that a true prophet should

[1] 1 Kings x. 10-12, xix. 20-24.

be at liberty to speak in the assembly or elsewhere to the people, and that he should be unassailable, and accountable to God alone.[1] False prophets who spake in the name of strange gods, or seduced the people to break the law, or to fall away from Jehovah, were to be stoned to death.[2]

The prophets opposed and combated chiefly the prevailing and fundamental sin of idolatry, and they raised their voice in warning and denunciation against the immoralities which reciprocated with the popular pagan inclinations and practices; they also set forth the fall into a mere mechanical holiness of works, the degeneracy of the priests, and the venality of the judges. They announced the divine vengeance; but they also raised up the broken-down people when dragged into captivity. Their theme was not limited to the exaltation or depression of their own people; their prophecies often extended to the fate of other, even distant, nations. And as the prophets in their moments of ecstatic elevation only beheld that which every Israelite possessed in his creed, though more obscurely and vaguely pictured, they clothed even their visions in images whose form and colour were borrowed from ordinary life, and from the individual experience of the seer, his own immediate horizon.

The prophets directed their admonitions, and not unfrequently their sharp reproofs, against kings themselves, entering fearlessly into palaces and denouncing the false policy of theirs that formed destructive alliances with foreign powers, and placed confidence in the powerful heathen states. The kings also consulted them in their distresses; when, however, they joined with the people in idolatry, the prophets were persecuted to blood. In the kingdom of the ten tribes they were almost annihilated as early as the days of Ahab;[3] at a later period (in the time of Amos) they were forbidden to speak publicly to the people.[4] In the kingdom of Juda, Manasses caused the warning prophets to be killed. "Your sword hath devoured your prophets as a ravaging lion," said Jeremiah;[5] at that time Isaias too is said to have fallen a sacrifice to a king's vengeance. Under Joas and Joachim two more prophets were slain for their frankness of speech.[6] It was a characteristic of Jerusalem, that it had killed the prophets and

---

[1] Numbers xii. 6. [2] Deut. xiii. 1 sq.
[3] 3 Kings xviii. [4] Amos vii. 10 sq.
[5] Jeremias ii. 30. [6] 2 Paral. xxiv. 20, 21; Jerem. xxvi. 20-23.

stoned them that were sent unto it.¹ Afterwards, indeed, people of Judea were zealous in searching for their graves and adorning them.²

The mission appointed to the Israelites, and the position which they occupied in the midst of heathen nations, made it necessary to have but one holy place for the whole nation. As the unity of the God of the Israelites was in contrast to the multiplicity of the heathen deities, so his temple, the only one in the nation, and, in a certain sense, in the world, stood opposed to the multitude of heathen places of worship. If the heathen could pray to and serve his idol gods, not in temples only, but in chapels, groves, on heights, or under trees, for the Israelite there was but one city where God could be lawfully honoured, and where every temptation to and danger of the idolatrous worship of nature was cut off.

The temple was to be the dwelling of God amidst his people, and a place of assembly; but the people only appeared before the Lord in the holy of holies by their substitutes, the priests. The temple-house itself, therefore, was not particularly large, nor to be compared to many Christian churches. It consisted of three parts: an outer court, the holy place, and the holy of holies. It was surrounded by three tiers of rooms, intended and used as treasure and provision chambers. The holy place was lighted by lamps; the windows only served to let out the smoke of the incense and for ventilation. The holy of holies (quite empty in the second temple) was separated from the holy place by a door with a curtain. Next came the priests' court, entirely surrounding the temple; on the eastern side there were two other courts, those of the men and women, which were separated from each other by a wall. The outermost enclosure was the court of the heathen. It went all round the temple, as did the priests' court, and was divided from the others by stone grating, with inscriptions prohibiting under pain of death non-Israelites from entering the inner parts of the temple, and especially the sanctuary.

In the sanctuary stood the golden seven-branched candlestick, with its lights always burning; the altar of incense, on which the daily incense-offering was burnt; and the table with the showbread, and the vessels filled with wine, the daily offering

---

¹ Matt. xxiii. 37.   ² Ib. ver. 29.

of bread and wine of the people. In the court attached was the altar of burnt-offerings, often simply called the altar, for it was the only one for all the animal sacrifices of the whole of Israel. A perpetual fire burnt upon it, in token that the sacrifice as a symbol of an offering of self to God, daily renewed on the part of the people and each individual, ought to be an unbroken one. A pipe at the side of the altar conveyed the blood of the sacrifices by a subterranean channel into the brook Cedron. There was a cavity under the altar into which the drink-offerings flowed.

The people were forbidden to enter either the holy place or the holy of holies; they could only see the priests in the sanctuary performing their daily ministrations through the curtain, which was drawn back. The most holy was closed for ever against the foot and gaze of even the priests; and when the high-priest entered on the day of atonement, no one was allowed to remain in the holy place.[1] The high-priest, however, had to enter at least twice on that day; once with the blood of the bull slain for his own sins, and the other time with that of the ram sacrificed for the sins of the people. On both occasions he had to dip his finger in the blood and sprinkle the top of the ark of the covenant with it seven times. According to Jewish tradition he went in twice more, first to incense the holy place, and then to bring out the pan of coals and the incense-burner.[2] Whoever had dared to enter the holy place either alone, or with the high-priest, would have been punished with death, as would the high-priest himself had he ventured in on any other day of the year.[3]

In contrast with heathenism, which always reduced the Deity to a level with nature, investing it with a body, and blending it with nature, the Jehovah of the Hebrews was ever to be adored and known as the Unseen, having no tangible form accessible to the senses, and infinitely removed from the world of matter. Hence the strict prohibition against making any "likeness" of him, or honouring him by any pictorial or symbolic representation. To their heathen neighbours an image or picture was not only a memorial or intimation of the Godhead, but an independent divine being and power. They were real

---

[1] Lev. xvi. 17.
[2] Mischnah, tr. Jomah, v. 1 sq., vii. 4; cf. Maimonid. de fest. exp. 4.
[3] Phil. Leg. ad. Laic. xxxix. p. 1035.

idols, dead and powerless gods, as the law calls them,[1]—wood and stone, the work of their own hands, which the idolaters and apostate Israelites worshiped with a cultus directed to the image itself. Hence all representations of human or animal forms were forbidden to the servant of Jehovah. In contradistinction to the heathen divinisation of nature, he was bound to leave nature at her wide distance from the Creator, without an attempt at approximation: thus, no grove was to surround the temple; neither monuments nor statues were to be erected;[2] the altar was only to consist of earth or rough stones, as the tool of the carver would have desecrated it.[3] For in the weak and diseased sense of the people, heathen representations and rites clambered and clung with a rank exuberance round all these objects. Art had to be quite excluded from religious things, and it was therefore certainly better for the Hebrews to have no plastic art at all than to have one entirely stripped of religious sentiment.

The interdiction of images went yet further, for every graven thing in stone, wood, or metal, in the likeness of any object in heaven above, or in the earth beneath, or of those things that are in the waters under the earth, was forbidden;[4] even pictures, which were not formally mentioned in the law, were included. The worship of false gods and images were so indissolubly connected, the one being only the manifestation and realisation of the other, that the entire renouncement of all outward representations of men and beasts was necessary to withdraw from the Israelites every possible aliment of their deeply-rooted inclination to heathenism. There is proof of this in the keeping of teraphim,—a custom so hard to uproot. These were a sort of household god in a human form, probably an inheritance from their Aramean forefathers, which were consulted as domestic oracles,[5] and which were to be found in private houses until the reform of religion under Josias. The representation of animals was also obliged to be interdicted, for the Israelites on Mount Sinai worshiped the Godhead under the form of a calf in Egyptian fashion, and afterwards Jeroboam regularly set up the worship of calves in the kingdom of Israel, in the two border towns of Bethel and Dan.[6]

An exception was made to this universal and unconditional

---

[1] Deut. xxxii. 37, 38.   [2] Deut. xvi. 21, 22.   [3] Exodus xx. 24, 25.
[4] Exodus xx. 4.   [5] Judges xviii. 14 sq.   [6] 3 Kings xii. 28 sq.

prohibition against images, and that even in the time of Moses. In the most holy both of the tabernacle and temple, at either end of the ark of the covenant, were two winged cherubim. These, it is true, however, were in a place where no Israelite, except the high-priest, ever looked. The so-called brazen sea, which was a large vessel for water in the outer court, was supported by twelve colossal cast bulls; but these were offensive even to the stronger-minded Jews, as we perceive by the decided dislike of Josephus, who saw in them a breach of the law.[1] For the Jews really understood the law to forbid absolutely every representation of a living being: so that, according to Philo and Origen, no painter or sculptor could live amongst them. Philo, to whom the plastic arts appear to have seemed especially pernicious, remarks that no picture was tolerated either.[2] The Jews would not put up with the image of the emperor on the standards of the Roman legions, and even thought it a breach of the law and a profanation to have them carried through their country. One of the palaces which Herod the tetrarch built in Tiberias was burnt by order of the Sanhedrim because it was ornamented with figures of animals, and this contrary to the law.[3]

It is manifest, we must distinctly remember, it was not the mere abstaining from all service of false gods, but positive enmity to and abhorrence of idolatry that was a fundamental part of Judaism. For to the Jew, any honour paid to false gods was a felony and rebellion against the one only Ruler and King of his people and kingdom. Individual offenders were punished with stoning for the crime; the nation, as a whole, with dispersion and extermination. Every prophet who prophesied in the name of a strange god, perverted or led others astray to serve him, was to be stoned to death; any reticence or lenity in this matter was criminal, even on the part of nearest relatives. The Israelites were to destroy the idolatrous statues generally in their campaigns, and not to suffer any idolaters to remain in the land.[4] Yet Israel had no mission or injunction to carry the knowledge and worship of Jehovah beyond the bounds of his own country by force of arms: on the contrary, they were not to be a conquering people; it was only within the limits of the terri-

[1] Antiq. viii. 7. 5.   [2] Opp. Mangey. i. 496; ii. 91, 205, 215.
[3] Joseph. Vit. 12.   [4] Exodus xxiii. 24-34.

tory allotted to them that they had to suppress every species of idolatry with the utmost rigour. It is well known that this was not fully accomplished, but rather that a great part of the nation yielded for centuries to the attractions which the nature-worship of their heathen neighbours had for them, that Baal or Moloch, Astarte, Chamos and Thammuz, with all the abominations of their worship, were adored, and not unfrequently by Israelites appointed for the purpose by the kings themselves. Therefore the law forbad still more stringently all that was of heathen original, the choice of certain days, the respect to the flight and cries of birds, charms, and the evocation of the dead.

Those Gentiles who desired to be fully received into the Jewish church, the "proselytes of justice," had to submit to be circumcised, to which ceremony, in post-Christian times, an ablution was added. Whether this washing or baptism existed as early as the times of the Herods or not, is a much-contested point; neither Josephus nor Philo mention it. As the neophyte also brought a sacrifice, and it was a universal custom amongst the Jews to purify themselves by water before offering sacrifice, this may have been the origin of the baptism of proselytes. Women more frequently became such proselytes than men, as a sacrifice was necessarily all that was required for their reception. A proselyte of justice was treated as one newly born. Accordingly, he broke all ties of parents and relatives, and his obligations towards them were at an end.[1] The number of "proselytes of the gate" was much greater. Their name was probably derived from their being only allowed to come as far as the gate of the temple porch. In earlier times these were heathen strangers, who, on the condition of becoming such proselytes, were allowed to domicile themselves amongst the Israelites in Palestine. They were only enjoined to give up the worship of idols, and to observe the seven precepts of Noah,—to wit, to renounce blasphemy, worship of the stars, incest (including paiderastia), murder, theft, rebellion against the Jewish authorities, and the eating gobbets of raw meat with the blood in them.

Sacrifice, that relation which brings man close to the Deity, forms the kernel and marrow of all true religion: all that he desires to obtain from God of gifts and blessings are conveyed to him through it. No religion, however, had a system of

[1] Tac. Hist. v. 5.

sacrifice carried out so far; in none did it so thoroughly penetrate every situation of life, and embrace all human necessities, as in that of the Hebrews. For the principal features of all religious life,—the destruction of sin and effacing the guilt of it, as the partition-wall between God and man, for thanksgiving to God, worship and homage to him, the free sacrifice of self to God, and, in fine, the closest union with him,—for all these wants the law had provided by the sacrifices ordained for sin, —the sacrifices of expiation, the burnt-offering, the meat and drink offerings, and those of thanksgiving. Hence nothing was so important in the eyes of the people as not to be slack in the sacrifices of God, no misfortune was so sad as the compulsory suspension of sacrificial worship, and the consequent impossibility of maintaining the reciprocity of giving and receiving, of supplication and its answer, through the medium of sacrifice.

"Thou shalt not appear before my face empty:"[1] the Israelite was not to present himself to God in the sanctuary empty-handed, but with a gift of the labour of his hands, and of the blessing which Jehovah had bestowed upon it; he was also to bring of the produce of the cattle or of the field, of the flocks and herds, of the goats, of corn, oil, and wine. Only that which was valuable and could be eaten or enjoyed by men, and especially that sort of food which was at once the produce of his toil, and the preparation for and earning of which made his vocation, was fit for the altar of God. All uneatable animals, and all eatable but wild ones, were excluded from sacrifice. Even fruits of trees were not employed in sacrifice proper, although they were offered as first-fruits. The sacrificer, by laying his hand on the head of the animal, testified to and realised the substitutive relation which the animal occupied in his regard. He drew the animal into the circle of humanity, and transferred to it his meaning and purpose: if, for instance, it was a matter of atonement for sin and guilt, he made a transfer of the sin to the animal, which was to die in his stead, and at the same time a practical acknowledgment of his own guiltiness. If he intended through the sacrifice to give himself to God, by imposing his hands on the animal it again became consecrated in his stead, as a recipient and medium of this self-oblation.

The animals were not slain by the priests, but by the sacri-

[1] Exodus xxiii. 15; Deut. xvi. 16.

ficers; the priest himself only killed his own sin-offering. He who had wrought the cause of death, himself wrought the death of the beast, his proxy. The blood of the victim was then collected in a vessel by the priests, and was either sprinkled towards the altar or the horns of the altar were anointed with it. This was in reality the most important act of the sacrifice. "I have given you," says the law, "the blood upon the altar for your soul's expiation, because the life of the flesh is in the blood."[1] The natural soul (nephesh) of the animals, or its vehicle, the blood, typified and took the place here of the soul, the life of man. The nephesh, the soul of the beast, was offered by the effusion of blood for the redemption of that of man, indebted to the justice of God through sin. Accordingly, this portion of the animal was not put in the power of men, and they were bound to abstain from eating blood, because of the exclusive rite of atonement through the blood of sacrifice.

The principal and most common sacrifices was the burnt-offering, for which a male animal was always taken; this, after it was slain, was divided, and the priests laid the pieces, after they had been carefully washed, on the altar, where they were consumed along with strong incense. Such sacrifices could be offered alone, others requiring generally the accompaniment of a burnt-offering. Besides the prescribed occasions, such sacrifices were employed on all great occasions. Even heathens could offer them in the outer court of the temple; and Augustus ordered a daily burnt-offering of two lambs and a ram to be made for him.[2] To the Israelites such an entire sacrifice was a sign and expression of complete resignation to Jehovah, a surrender of the body and all its powers and inclinations. The fire represented the appropriating organ, being a kind of mouth-piece of God, at the same time symbolising his purifying power, by which he can convert the human body into a sacred instrument well-pleasing to himself.

The trespass-offering was a compensative and restorative sacrifice, in which the imposition of hands on the head of the victim did not take place. The idea in this sacrifice was the performance of an expiatory satisfaction, or the making good an injury committed, and the payment of a debt. In the case of a

---

[1] Levit. xvii. 11.
[2] Philo. Opp. vi. 592; Joseph. Bell. Jud. ii. 17. 2; contra Apion. ii. 6.

neighbour any injury had to be made good by restoring more than its amount; to God, however, a ram was to be brought as a trespass-offering.[1] The cleansed leper also brought a trespass-offering in return for his restoration to the rights and privileges of the covenant. The flesh of this sacrifice belonged to the priests, who consumed it in a holy place.

The sin-offering was for the removal and expiation of sin. For sins of rebellion against God, arising from daring presumption, there was neither sacrifice nor atonement: all other sins of premeditation or not, and sins of frailty, could be atoned for through sacrifice by the contrite. Whilst, however, the trespass-offering regarded individuals only, the sin-offering was brought for whole communities and for the people collectively. The guilty obtained the desired reconciliation by the blood which the priest sprinkled. In this case the blood was not merely sprinkled round the altar, as in the other sacrifices, but with part the horns of the altar were anointed, and part was poured out at its foot. On solemn sacrifices of this kind it was sprinkled on the curtain behind which was the ark of the covenant. The fatty parts of the animal were then burnt at the altar; all the rest was consumed without the city if it were a standing sacrifice for the sins of the priests and of the people, or the flesh was given to be eaten by the priests in the court of the sanctuary.[2] The eating of this flesh was no sacrificial meal; the sacrificer and his family had no share in it; even the relatives of the priests might not partake of it with them; the priests alone were to eat the meat burdened with sin, that so they might destroy it. The red heifer belonged to the category of sin-offerings, and was slain by the priest outside the city, and then entirely consumed by fire; after which, he sprinkled the blood towards the most holy. The ashes, mingled with water, were reserved for the aspersion of such as had, through direct or indirect contact with a corpse, become unclean.[3]

If no part of the burnt-offerings was eaten, and if the priests alone partook of the sin-offerings, and then only when the sacrifice was not offered at the same time for their own sins, the peace- or thank-offering, on the contrary, was essentially a communion feast. It was offered, in the name of the people, on

---

[1] Levit. v. 15; Numbers v. 5 sq.   [2] Levit. vi. 25 sq.
[3] Numbers xix. 2 sq.

certain festivals, *e. g.* on the election of a king, or after the happy issue of some undertaking, and also on the feast of Pentecost. Generally speaking it was a spontaneous act on the part of individuals, in gratitude to God for some benefit or fulfilment of a vow. The fat pieces of the animals sacrificed were the only ones consumed by the fire of the altar; the rest were divided between the priests and the sacrificer; a repast was prepared out of it, of which the sacrificer and the friends he had invited partook in joyful conviction of being at peace with God and admitted to the table of the Lord. None of the consecrated meat could be taken home, or otherwise consumed without the sanctuary; all was to be finished the same, or at any rate the following, day, in the fore court of the temple; that which still remained was burnt. Here, then, was a double communion: as the whole sacrifice had become God's property by being consecrated to him in sacrifice, what man partook of was received from his hand; they were guests at the table of Jehovah, or, as was also represented, Jehovah did not disdain to become the guest of man through the priests, the ministers of his sanctuary, who partook of the meal, whilst the guests, by participation in the same food and meal, felt themselves united in a holy communion with the priests and each other. It was only by greater solemnity that the praise-offering differed from the thank-offering. It seems that on such occasions people had hymns sung by singers, as a choir of such was called " Toda," a name also given to the praise-offering.[1]

A law, standing isolated, points to a period when every killing of a domestic quadruped, whether slain for a sacrifice or merely for home consumption, had to take place before the tabernacle of Jehovah, and had to be made into a sacrifice, and a sacrificial meal, by a sacerdotal sprinkling of blood on the altar, and the burning of the fat.[2] Hence the law against blood, destined to serve as a sacrifice of expiation, being employed, or perhaps consumed, contrary to its proper use, became a matter of course. This was, however, only practicable while the Israelites were living together in one camp. Later on, when they had entered Chanaan, the ordinance was revoked; altars were, it seems, erected at different places for this purpose, so that the animals might be slain before them, and the blood poured forth.

---

[1] Nehemias xii. 31-41. [2] Levit. xvii. 4-7.

This probably explains an occurrence in the history of Saul: once when the people were exhausted by pursuing their enemies in war-time, they hastily began to eat the flesh with the blood in it; Saul, however, speedily had an altar erected of a great stone, by which the blood might be legally disposed of.[1] But this also was changed again after the building of the temple, when the altar at Jerusalem became the only rightful one in the land.

To the thank-offering belonged the peculiar ceremony of waving; a symbol of transfer to Jehovah, which the priest performed when he put the breast of the victim on the hands of the sacrificer, placing his hands under them, and thus moved them backwards and forwards with the quarters of the victim upon them.[2] According to rabbinical accounts, it was a cruciform motion towards the four quarters of the world, backwards and forwards, right and left.

Unbloody offerings, "mincha," consisting of gifts of meal or oil-cakes, were, in part, attributions to bloody sacrifices; no burnt- or praise-offering could be made without the addition of meat- and drink-offerings (wine): in the former case a handful of meal was put on the altar and consumed with the incense; to the latter, the praise-offerings, unleavened oil-cakes were added. Leaven and honey were to be avoided in case of vegetable offerings, as causing fermentation, and changing the purity of the original substance; while oil and incense, as typical of prayer, and salt, as a preservative from corruption and putrefaction, and symbolic of the bond between God and man,[3] were never allowed to be omitted.

The daily morning and evening sacrifice was offered in the name of the whole people. In the morning a lamb was slain and burnt, together with meal and wine, as a meat- and drink-offering; the same was repeated in the evening: for this purpose there was a special chamber for lambs in the last temple. The sacrifice was doubled on the Sabbath-day. On the days of the new moon the festival sacrifice consisted of ten animals, with the addition of the meat-offering, besides a sin-offering of a ram for the expiation of the guilt of the community. A standing oblation was the showbread, of which twelve cakes, corresponding to the number of the tribes of Israel, were laid on a low

---

[1] 1 Kings xiv. 33 sq.   [2] Exodus xxix. 24 sq.; Levit. viii. 27 sq.
[3] Levit. ii. 13.

table, overlaid with gold, in the holy place of the temple, close to the veil before the holy of holies; it was renewed every week, on the Sabbath. That which was taken away was eaten by the priests in a sacred place.

The Mosaic law contained no ordinances respecting prayer; only on the payment of tithes to the priests, and the domestic solemnity of the presentation of the firstlings, was there a prescribed formula of prayer and acknowledgment, in which the father of the house, testifying his dependence on God, and his obedience to the law, supplicated the Divine blessing on Israel as a nation, and thus consecrated the religious act.[1] By the law, then, prayer was, on the whole, left to discretion; but certainly custom and tradition settled a great deal precisely that was religiously observed, for the Israelites were, above all nations, a people of prayer. It was in early times a universal custom to turn in prayer towards the place where the temple and holy of holies stood; and without doubt there were traditional formulæ of prayer attached to the sacrifices. The daily morning and evening sacrifice was certainly not unaccompanied by prayer on the part of those present, if only made in silence; and they assisted at the divine worship of prayer and psalmody which began to develop under David and Solomon, sometimes taking part in it through antiphonal response. The courts of the temple were the places where the inhabitants of Jerusalem principally offered up their prayers, which were always said with head covered. In order to be undisturbed, they often said them on the flat roofs of their houses,[2] or in the balconies there; they prayed three times a-day, at nine, twelve, and three o'clock. If the hour of prayer came when they were in the streets or fields, they stood still, and so said it. About the time of the Captivity special prayers were said aloud by the Levites, in which the people joined.[3] People usually stood while they prayed, only occasionally kneeling or throwing themselves prostrate on the ground. The phylacteries, or fringes with prayers inscribed, were already in use in the time of Christ.

Among a people of such religious life as the Hebrews, vows played a prominent part, were of very frequent occurrence, and were manifold in form, and whether of promised performance or

---

[1] Deut. xxvi. 12, 15. [2] Daniel vi. 10; Judith viii. 5; Tobias iii. 10.
[3] 1 Paralip. xxiii. 30.

of imposed abstinence, their fulfilment was considered a most sacred and binding duty. The law inculcated freedom in making vows, as well as their obligation when made.[1] "If thou forbearest to promise, thou shalt be without sin." A vow once taken was binding as an oath, and was to be performed without fail, and to its full extent. But wives and daughters, as not free agents, were not allowed to vow any thing contrary to the wishes of their husbands or fathers.[2] Every thing, however, that was the subject of a vow, persons or landed property, with the exception of animals for sacrifice, could be redeemed for a certain sum, the amount of which was generally settled by the priests. Sometimes persons were dedicated by vow to the service of Jehovah in the sanctuary. Vows of abstinence usually consisted of a fast.

The festivals, with the exception of the Sabbaths, had partly an agrarian, partly an historical, signification, relating to the divine guidance of the nation. There were fifty-nine in all through the year, and they were all accompanied by special public sacrifices: seven of these feast-days were solemnised by abstinence from work, viz. the first and seventh day of unleavened bread, the day of pentecost, the seventh new moon, the day of atonement, and the first and last day of the feast of tabernacles; but the day of atonement alone resembled the Sabbath in the prohibition of every kind of work, while the rest enjoined on the other days did not exclude the more necessary business and employments, such as the preparation of food. On the days intervening between the longer feasts, all kinds of work were allowed. Three feasts, the pasch, pentecost, and the feast of tabernacles, were pilgrimage festivals, when it was incumbent on all the males of the land to repair to the temple.

The birthday of the nation was the pasch or feast of the passover, solemnised in memory of their deliverance out of Egypt, and the sparing of the firstborn of the Hebrews during the last plague the Egyptians were smitten with. On the evening of the fourteenth day of the spring month, the first of the year, the whole nation had to kill the victim for sacrifice, to sprinkle its blood, and to observe the sacrificial meal by eating the lamb which was slain. In this, then, all alike had priestly rights, as already Philo brings out.[3] The lamb was slain in the court of

---

[1] Deut. xxiii. 22.　　[2] Numbers xxx. 4 sq.　　[3] De Vit. Mos. 3.

the sanctuary, and then so consumed by the father of each house and his family, with the addition of unleavened bread and bitter herbs, as that nothing was left. Whatever happened not to be eaten was to be burnt, but no part of the sacrifice ever came on the altar. The blood of the sacrifice was to be sprinkled on the door-posts of every house. In this case, therefore, it was the individual families, who, by each partaking of the lamb (which was not to be divided into pieces), realised communion and religious fellowship among one another and with God, to whom the sacrifice was offered. By all the men in the land being obliged to repair to the temple to slay their lamb, the consciousness of a national unity, compacted through God and his temple, was strengthened, and the brotherly feeling nourished of the hundreds of thousands who all joined in offering the same sacrifice, and in partaking of the same sacrament. The festival was also called that of unleavened bread, because the people ate bread of that sort for seven days, in memory of their former bondage, and the hasty flight, which had prevented their forefathers from leavening the dough.[1]

On the fiftieth day after Easter Sunday the harvest-feast of pentecost was solemnised, for the seven weeks between pasch and pentecost were harvest-time. On that day after the Easter Sabbath, the first ears of corn had been brought; now, after fifty days, the first fruits of the bread itself were offered to God as a thank-offering, together with two lambs and several other beasts of sacrifice. In autumn the feast of tabernacles was held for seven days, in memory of the Israelites having lived in tents in their journey through the Arabian desert, and as a thanksgiving festival for the close of the fruit-harvest. At this time they lived in huts made of green boughs, which were erected on the roofs, in the streets, squares, and courts, and special victims were slain daily in the temple. Those who partook in this festival carried a lemon in one hand, and in the other a palm-branch entwined with sprigs of myrtle and willow. Every morning water from the pool of Siloah, mixed with wine, was poured into two perforated vessels close by the altar. On the eve of the first day of the feast, the large candelabra in the court of the temple were lighted; their brightness illuminated the whole city, and a torch-dance took place before them, with music and singing. This

[1] Exod. xii. 19 sq.

characteristic of the feast caused the Greeks to imagine it was nothing but a Jewish appropriation of their Dionysos feast.[1]

Of all the days consecrated to religion, the great day of atonement was the principal one; and it was also the only fast-day prescribed by the law. The Jews called it simply "the day." It was a day of universal expiation of the great number of those sins of the people, which were either unknown or left unredeemed, for which no special sin-offering had been brought. Thus it was a day of profound sorrow for common guilt and sinfulness, in which all had share, high-priest, priests, and people, and for which all stood in need of expiation. Twice on this day did the high-priest enter the holy of holies, which was at other times closed to him as well as to the people. He was then to take of the blood of the two victims, the bull appointed to be offered for himself, and the he-goat slain for the people, and each time to dip his finger therein and sprinkle it seven times against the mercy-seat, the top of the ark of the covenant. As there was no ark of the covenant in the holy of holies of the second temple, he sprinkled the blood towards the roof and the floor; he also filled the holy place with the smoke of incense. The high-priest laid his hands on the head of a second he-goat, and transferring to it the sins of the people, had it led away to the desert, where it was let loose. The flesh of the sin-offering was burnt without the city.

Among the festivals of later introduction the feast of Purim ranks first; instituted in thankful remembrance of the deliverance from the murderous intentions of Haman, wrought by Esther for the Jews in the kingdom of Persia. Although of universal observance as early as the time of Josephus, it was no temple feast, but was kept in the synagogues by reading the book of Esther, and in the houses by joyous entertainments and almsgivings. The feast of the dedication of the temple, or of "lights," was instituted by Judas Macchabeus, in memory of the purification of the temple by himself, B.C. 164, and of the restoration of divine worship according to the law.[2] It was solemnised for eight days by illuminating the synagogues and houses (in reference to the re-lighting of the temple lights). Then followed some days of mourning, in remembrance of Jerusalem having been taken by the Chaldeans, of the destruction of the

[1] Plut. Sympos. iv. 6, 2. [2] 1 Macc. iv. 59; cf. Joseph. Antiq. xii. 7, 7.

city and of the temple, and of the murder of Gedalia,[1] whereby the flight of the remnant of the Jews to Egypt was brought about, and their utter banishment consummated.

The Mosaic law only enjoined one general and strict fast-day, the great day of atonement. But later on, the days of mourning just mentioned were accompanied by fasting. Extraordinary fasts frequently occur in Hebrew history. On these the people desired to humble themselves before God to testify their penitent spirit, and to avert some misfortune. Public calamities of the country, or defeats in battle, were occasions of such fasts. In case of continued drought, for instance, the Sanhedrim usually appointed a fast. A Jewish fast was commonly observed by total abstinence from food from one evening until the next.

From the time of Esdras, synagogues were to be found in Judea for the reading of the law and prayer in common. By degrees they were erected in all the towns and villages, and the notion became prevalent that it was the duty of every one to visit them regularly. The larger cities had several of them. In Jerusalem each Jewish provincial corporation had its own synagogue, and their number in the city is said to have amounted to 460. People assembled there on the Sabbaths and feast-days. Portions of the Thora, and the prophets, and other holy books (Megilloth), were read aloud and explained. They were dismissed by the blessing of a priest, the congregation answering Amen. As places for instruction and edification, the synagogues were under the superintendence of the Sanhedrim and Scribes. There were also recognised interpreters in the synagogues, who translated what was read out of the holy Scriptures into the vernacular.

If we glance, in conclusion, at the decrees of the law as to what made persons unclean, and the unclean animals and kinds of food, much obscurity will be found, as the causes for such prohibitions and distinctions, based upon reasons of climate or other deep principles of physics, are unknown. It is only certain, that the Zoroastro-Persian view of there being a contending good and evil creation, each with its own author, had no influence on the Mosaic ordinances; for the notion of an Ahriman was quite unknown to the Israelites. The tasting blood, or meat

[1] Jos. Antiq. x. 9. 3-5.

with the blood in it, was forbidden, partly because the blood is the seat of animal life,[1] partly and specially on account of the religious signification which the blood of animals had in sacrifice; for it belonged to Jehovah as an "atonement."[2] On the same grounds, *i. e.* their sacrificial import, certain fat parts of the heifer, goat, and sheep were not eaten. Hares, camels, swine, and all serpents and lizards, aquatic animals not squamous, about twenty sorts of birds, chiefly, of course, birds of prey, were considered unclean, and were prohibited as food. These restrictions were very strictly observed by the Jews. In the time of the Syrian persecution, many of them endured the rack and death rather than eat swine's flesh.[3] Unclean animals were not allowed to be kept in Jerusalem, nor their flesh to be brought there.

Besides these, there were certain legal uncleannesses arising from fluid secretions of the human body, diseases such as the leprosy, or contact with a corpse. Such defilements lasted sometimes all day until the evening, sometimes a whole week, and entailed washing the clothes or bathing in spring water. Certain natural impurities of longer duration required a sacrifice of purification. Thus much is plain, that death was looked upon as the consequence of sin, and that the cadaverousness, the corruption, and decomposition which takes place in diseases like leprosy, as well as all the symptoms of death and dissolution of the human frame, formed the groundwork of these legal uncleannesses.

III. THE RELIGIOUS DOCTRINES OF THE JEWISH PEOPLE.

1. Scripture and Tradition.

The Thora, or five books of Moses, were held in high esteem by all as a divine revelation, the national law-book, and the magna charta of the Jewish state and people. How long before the days of Josephus another and larger collection of holy writings was generally acknowledged, is not known. We are told, however, that Nehemias (about 430 B.C.) formed a library, containing the history of kings and prophets, and letters of the kings

---

[1] Levit. xvii. 11-14; Deut. xii. 23; Jos. Antiq. iii. 11, 2.
[2] Levit. xvii. 11.   [3] 1 Macc. i. 65; 2 Macc. vi. 18, 19.

concerning the temple-gifts. Josephus is the first to speak of a collection of twenty-two books, which all the Jews looked upon as divine admonitions. Among these he reckoned, in addition to the Thora, thirteen books, in which the prophets who lived after Moses wrote what had happened in their day. To these were added four more books (the Psalms, Proverbs, Ecclesiastes, and Canticles), which contained hymns of praise to God, and rules of life for man.[1] *What* books these thirteen of the prophets were, remains in uncertainty.[2] It is certain, however, that at a yet later period the book of Esther was not considered canonical by a great number of the Jews. In the Talmud we find expressions and evidence that still, after the days of Josephus, the place of certain books in the canon, especially Ecclesiastes and the Canticles, was matter of dispute. So the canon of the Hebrew Scriptures was only settled in the schools of the Scribes after the destruction of Jerusalem. In the canon of the Alexandrine Jews were further included the deutero-canonical books of Baruch, Sirach, Wisdom, with Judith, Tobias, and the books of Macchabees, which the Jews in Palestine did not receive into their canon, because they were partly written in Greek, or because the Hebrew or Chaldean originals no longer existed.

The Jewish nation moved in a circle of religious ideas which had found only a partial expression in their sacred writings. Little, in fact, was taught in these books, and that only by descriptions of facts, or representations of events. The Thora, the principal source, contained no directly instructive element, except its historical and legal contents. The other books and collections contained as little direct teaching and definite dogma, if we except, perhaps, the book of Wisdom: they imply and make allusion to doctrine in various places, but convey no teaching proper. Now, from the days of their forefathers the Jews had a body of oral tradition, which in early ages undoubtedly consisted of but a few simple fundamental maxims; yet even these already

---

[1] Contr. Apion, i. 8.

[2] Conf. Movers, Loci quidam Hist. Canon. V. T. illustr. Vratisl. 1842, p. 9 sq. Haneberg, History of the Biblical Revelation, 1850, p. 696. It enumerates the thirteen books of Josephus thus: (1) Josue; (2) Judges; (3) Ruth; (4) 1st Book of Kings; (5) 2d Book of Kings; (6) 3d Book of Kings; (7) 4th Book of Kings; (8) Isaias; (9) Jeremias, with the Lamentations; (10) Ezechiel; (11) The twelve minor Prophets; (12) Job; (13) Daniel. Therefore the two Books of Chronicles, Esdras, Nehemias, and Esther, were not included.

included certain points not taught in the Pentateuch, but which in part were either entirely passed over, we might almost believe on purpose,—for instance, the state after death,—or were partly taken for granted. This tradition was not a dead deposit in the hands of a spiritually stagnant people, but, on the contrary, it possessed strength and inclination to develop itself and to grow organically. It had a lively action, and was reacted on by the religious state of the nation, whose whole history and whose relations with foreigners, whether by way of contrast and antagonism or of affinity to their doctrines, contributed to keep and swell the body of tradition in a continuous stream. People became more and more alive to the consequences to be deduced from their dogmas. Much that is contained in the post-Mosaic books is drawn from tradition, and is only to be understood on this hypothesis. It is obvious, of course, that the tradition was always dependent on the text of the Thora; but how little they adhered to a rule of strict and verbal exposition, and how much they went beyond the biblical text, while founding tradition upon it professedly, is clearly shown by the comments of our Lord and of St. Paul.

In the times after the Babylonish captivity, when religious zeal was revived in Israel, and the schools of the law were sedulously frequented, a corresponding activity was manifested as to dogmatic requirements, and people did not any longer give themselves up exclusively to the study of the ritual and politico-moral law. The struggle with Hellenism and the rise of the Sadducees stirred up spiritual activity; and assuredly every Israelite, with the exception of the Sadducees, would have looked upon any one as a fool or a teacher of error who had professed he would believe nothing but what could be clearly proved from the letter of the Pentateuch or other books of Scripture, and who in the interpretation of the text would only follow his own judgment, and not the traditional exposition of the synagogue.

The mixing of the blood which was used for aspersion at the passover with water, and also the sprinkling of the book of the law with it,[1] were matters of tradition, the Pentateuch saying nothing about either. The duty of visiting the Proseuchæ or synagogues on the Sabbath and on festivals, was purely traditional. The doctrine, so important in regard to the whole eco-

[1] Hebrews ix. 19.

nomy of the Jewish religion, that the law had been given through the interposition of angels, is not to be found in the written records, and is a tradition, but a tradition inserted in the text of the Alexandrine translation of the Scriptures, and which Josephus and the Apostles have confirmed and adopted.[1] From the Jewish tradition of his time St. Paul derived his assertion that the rock which gave forth water accompanied the Israelites in their march through the desert.[2] From the same source he derived his belief about the several regions in heaven.[3] The whole doctrine of rewards, of punishments, of the state after death, the distinction between a gehenna as a place of torment for the bad, and a paradise, as a part of Hades, in which the souls of the just were to abide after death until the resurrection, a doctrine sanctioned by our Lord himself,[4] is founded not on the text of the Old Testament, but solely on oral tradition.

---

2. God and the Angels.

That God cannot be thoroughly known, was a truth deeply felt by the Hebrews: God manifests himself to man by lowering himself to him, but he does not show himself as he is; even the prophets only saw God under a symbol; man could not endure the sight of God: "Man seeth me not and liveth."[5] The Hebrew Scriptures treat atheists simply as fools: not a word of proof of God's Being is there; and it is but practical infidelity, the not recognising of God's justice and his conduct of human affairs, which is before the eyes of their writers.[6]

The two principal names of God, Elohim and Jehovah, are primeval ones, and did not reach the Hebrews from without, appearing at the cradle of the people, so to speak. God himself has declared the signification of the name Jehovah, "I will be that I will be."[7] Here the future time indicates the enduring continuance of this existence. God attributes this name to himself as to a personal self-conscious being, immutably the same in

---

[1] Deut. xxxii. 2, according to the Sept.; Joseph. Antiq. xv. 5. 3; Acts vii. 53; Gal. iii. 19; Heb. ii. 2.

[2] 1 Cor. x. 4; cf. Wetstein, N. T. p. 199, and Schöttgen, p. 623.

[3] 2 Cor. xii. 2.   [4] Luke xvi. 22 sq.; xxiii. 43.   [5] Exod. xxxiii. 20.

[6] Psalm x. 4-14.   [7] Exod. iii. 14.

itself. Afterwards it is said, that it was he who appeared to the three patriarchs, Abraham, Isaac, and Jacob, as the Almighty God[1] (El Shaddai), but by his name Jehovah he did not yet make himself known; that is to say, the meaning of this name was not disclosed to them, until the covenanted promise of giving them the land of Chanaan was about being fulfilled. The Jews were afraid to pronounce "the great and only" name of Jehovah. It was frequently made use of in the earlier books of the Bible, but occurs far less so in the latter ones. The Septuagint always uses "the Lord" in its stead. Josephus declares he is not allowed to speak about the name.[2] Philo, however, asserts that the initiated in the sanctuary might hear and pronounce it.[3] According to Jewish tradition, it was changed after the death of Simon the Just into Adonai, even in the temple. After the destruction of Jerusalem, the Jews lost even the knowledge how to pronounce it. Jehovah is the self-determining One who remains ever like to himself in his ways; who, steadfast through all the vicissitudes of time in his eternal truth, forms the strong foundation of the hope of Israel, who hears the prayers of his people, and manifests himself in the guidance of his covenanted people.[4] The name Elohim was in general used of beings of a præter- or supernatural order, of heathen gods, of the good angels, and even men who had power over others as princes or rulers.[5] The word, in its signification, "strong, mighty spirits," appertains to a period when the people's forefathers still served idols;[6] it grew into the national language; and so, when monotheism prevailed, it retained its plural form, though serving to designate the one God. The term Elohim is mostly employed when the general cosmical activity of God is spoken of, and Jehovah, when his relations to his chosen people are in question.

The grand distinctive fundamental view of Judaism was, the complete severance between God and the world; God, pure spirit and creator, brought forth the world, both as to matter and form, through the almighty power of his will, all nature containing nothing which could be looked upon as his image and likeness. The Hebrew language, however, was too little abstract to furnish the requisite terms for metaphysical expla-

---

[1] Exod. vi. 3.   [2] Antiq. ii. 12. 4.   [3] Vit. Mos. ii. p. 152.
[4] Exod. iii. 13 sq.; vi. 2 sq.; Mal. iii. 6.
[5] Psalm lxxxi. 1; xcvi. 7; cxxxvii. 1.   [6] Jos. xxiv. 2, 14 sq.

nations of the being of God; while the holy Scriptures aim so decidedly at practical ends, that though they speak of all that is calculated to set forth the majesty of God and the lowliness of man, and to awaken the feeling of unbounded dependence on God, they are deficient in more precise and sharp-cut definitions of the divine nature. Of God's eternity it is said, "The heavens, the work of his hands, shall pass away and wax old as a vestment, but of his years there shall be no end."[1] His omnipresence is testified by the expression that he fills heaven and earth,[2] and finds man wherever he may be, so that it is in vain that he seeks to hide himself from him.[3] The idea of the providence and omniscience of God is turned into the consciousness of being completely seen through by God, who observes our thoughts from afar, and is acquainted with all our ways. "Thine eyes saw me in embryo; in thy book were all my days written, that were fixed ere as yet any of them were."[4] Thus the prophet knew that he was in the hand of God even before he was born into the world, for he it is who fashions man in his mother's womb,[5] and takes care his image fulfils its destination.[6] The ideas of accident and fate were foreign to the Israelite; all was referred to the decrees of God; and in every thing that occurred, the wisdom, goodness, justice, and power of God were recognised. Accident with him was God's providence.

That the Hebrew Scriptures very often use anthropomorphic and anthropopathic expressions of God is not wonderful, considering what the relations between Jehovah and Israel were. The active reciprocal intercourse between the two, and the way in which Jehovah was interwoven with the whole history of the nation, brought this about. Such expressions and representations were partly a symbolical veil, easy to see through, of which the sacred books themselves afforded the corrective, as they repudiate any representation of low and human passion in God. God's vengeance is but the sternness of his justice. If he is depicted as sometimes rejoicing, and at other times sorrowing, over the destruction which the guilt of man brings on him, or if repentance is attributed to himself, it is only meant to show that diversity of his dealings with man, which results from the unchangeableness of his being. "He is not a man that he should repent," said Samuel.[7]

---

[1] Ps. ci. 26 sq.   [2] Jer. xxiii. 24.   [3] Amos ix. 2-4.   [4] Ps. cxxxviii. 16.
[5] Ps. cxxxviii. 13; Job x. 8.   [6] Jer. i. 5.   [7] 1 Kings xv. 29; Numb. xxiii. 19.

If the anger of God against evil-doers be so strongly expressed, and if hatred and wrath be ascribed to him, it is but the necessary manifestation of the holiness and justice of God against what is wicked. The light of Israel shall become fire, and its holy one a flame;[1] behind the clouds of wrath the compassion of God and the healing discipline of his mercy were displayed.[2] God punishes, whether the amendment of the sinner follows or not. In the latter event the chastisement is but the working of his holiness, it becomes the "being blotted out from the face of God."[3] Whilst the prophets announced a proximate temporal punishment to fall on Israel, to wit, that of exile, they also pointed to another, which was to terminate the whole course of earthly things, to wit, the general judgment, when Jehovah would judge those who would not accept the salvation of the Messias.[4]

We meet with a theory in the Hebrew Scriptures which is of kin to the Platonic doctrine of ideas, and yet is of an essentially different aspect. It is that of the Chokma, or wisdom, as containing that eternal ideal or archetype which is in God, and according to which he created finite beings and determined their destiny. Wisdom is not a mere attribute of God like the others, but it is the ground-plan and scheme of the world, into which God looks as in a mirror. Thus, in the book of Job it is said that when God gave the rain its laws, and appointed the lightning its path, he looked on Wisdom and revealed her, and assigned to man the fear of God as his allotted portion of wisdom.[5] Wisdom says more distinctly in the Proverbs of herself, that God brought her forth before all creatures, as the beginning of his ways, and anointed her as a queen, that she was co-agent with him in the creation of the world as an apt workwoman, and that she took her delight every day, playing before him at all times.[6] This doctrine is more fully set forth in the Book of Wisdom: there she is described as the breath of God's power, a pure emanation of his glory, the reflection of eternal light, the spotless mirror of his operations, and the image of his goodness.[7] She is instructed in the secrets of God, the counsellor of his works, and the assessor of his throne. The son of Sirac says of Wisdom, "She is shed forth over the world;" so is she here identical with

---

[1] Isaiah x. 17.   [2] Psalm cii. 9; lxxvii. 38; Isaiah x. 25.
[3] Psalm xxvi. 9.   [4] Isaias xxxiv. 1 sq.; lxvi. 15 sq.; Daniel vii. 22 sq.
[5] Job xxviii. 24-28.   [6] Proverbs viii. 22-31.   [7] Wisdom vii. 25 sq.

the "spirit of the Lord," filling or encompassing the world. Finally, God is implored to send her down from his throne, "to stand by me and teach me all, to be my companion and my bride."[1] She is therefore by no means a person in God, or hypostasis, but the personified idea of the mind of God in creation, to which she stands in the relation of a mirror, in which the world and mankind are ever present to him.

The gods of the heathen appear in two different points of view among the Hebrews. At one time they are designated as being naught, "Elilim," having no real godlike being or power,[2] in contradistinction to Jehovah; and then again a kind of reality is ascribed to them, and Jehovah is styled, in reference to them, God of gods, and Lord of lords.[3] We read accordingly of an execution of judgment against the gods of Egypt;[4] and thus see in them not merely semblance and empty nothingness, but real existence, personal beings, though of a very different sort to what they were supposed to be by their adorers. When Jehovah and these gods are contrasted, he is the victor, and they the crushed and vanquished, who will one day be entirely subdued.

Jehovah is the Lord of the heavenly hosts. Angels are frequently mentioned as ministering spirits, beings who stand around his throne, and whom he makes use of in the government of the world. It is nowhere said that they were created; they were in fact taken for granted on tradition. They are highly favoured beings; but there are limits where their wisdom and perfection have an end.[5] They form different orders, in which there is a gradation from lower to higher. They never appear as working independently or for themselves, but are always mere instruments to execute the divine mandates. They stand before God, and hence are called the angels of his presence.[6] It is part of their duty to protect the worshipers of Jehovah. "The angel of the Lord encampeth round about them that fear him, and delivereth them."[7] In Job an angel is spoken of as an interpreter, one of a thousand, standing by the sick man, and listening to his penitent entreaties for forgiveness; interpreting them, that is, bringing them before God, as his intercessor.[8] "To which of the saints (angels) wilt thou turn?" said Eliphaz to Job.[9]

[1] Wisdom ix. 9, 10.   [2] Exod. xx. 20.
[3] Deut. x. 17; Psalm cxxxv. 2, 3; cxxxiv. 5; xcvi. 9.   [4] Exod. xii. 12.
[5] Job. iv. 18.   Isaias lxiii. 9.   [7] Psalm xxxiii. 8.   [8] Job xxxiii. 23.
[9] Job v. 1.

Seven angels, as the highest, surround the throne of God, and lay before him the prayers of the faithful.[1] In the vision of Isaias, God is surrounded by the seraphim, who sing in chorus the hymn of the Trisagion.[2] They were cherubim who kept the entrance to Paradise after Adam was driven out.[3] The placing of the figures of cherubim on the top of the ark of the covenant probably had its ground in the typical relation of the holy of holies in the tabernacle and temple to Paradise. The expressions "man," "son of God," were often used in reference to the angels. The worship which was due to Jehovah alone was not to be shown them: and they themselves rejected it.[4] Nations also had severally their guardian-angel, who mediated for them before God. St. Michael was the special patron of the Jewish nation.

The Hebrew writings speak nowhere distinctly of a fall having occurred in the world of spirits, nor how Satan became what he was on first coming in contact with man. We have here, again, another of those many facts so numerous in the Old Testament, only intelligible from oral tradition. The serpent who seduced the first of the human race into sin is not only an animal, but also a spiritual being. The whole demeanour of the serpent is symbolic, through the veil of which we perceive the action and being of a wily and tempting spirit; and the warfare which the seed of the woman, the whole human race, were to wage against the seed of the serpent, is a warfare of spiritual principles. The book of Wisdom expressly says it was Satan through whose envy death came into the world.[5]

For a long time, then, though perhaps not without design, there is no mention made of Satan. He reappears for the first time in the Chronicles, as inciting David to a sinful act.[6] In the book of Job he dares to appear before the throne of God with the other angels, although then an evil spirit, and author of the misfortunes that had befallen that pious man;[7] but he is throughout represented as an impotent tool of the divine decrees. Every where, as in Zacharias, he is spoken of as the adversary, the accuser, and persecutor of man; especially of the pious and just.[8] He tries to make of no effect the expiatory acts of the highpriest. This evil spirit is never coupled in Hebrew literature

[1] Tobias xii. 15. [2] Isaias vi. 2, 3. [3] Genesis iii. 24.
[4] Judges xiii. 16. [5] Wisdom ii. 24. [6] I Paral. xxi. 1.
[7] Job i. 6; ii. 1. [8] Zach. iii. 1, 2.

with any divinity of the neighbouring nations: it is not said that he who worships Baal or Moloch has in truth done homage to Satan; but of the other evil spirits or demons it is said they are identical with the heathen gods. Accordingly, in the Septuagint the word "demons" is used instead of the Elilim[1] and the Shedim, to whom the apostate Israelites sacrificed their sons and daughters;[2] instead of Gad, to whom they offered a banquet.[3] The opinion of Josephus, who imagined the demons to be the souls of deceased evil-doers, who disquiet the living as tormenting spirits, seems not to have been general amongst the Jews, and to have been derived from heathen sources.[4]

3. Creation—Man and his Fall—God's Requirements of him—Penance—Death, and a Future State.

According to the Hebrew account, God began creation by forming the heavens and the earth of one substance, embracing both in common,—a chaotic and fluid primal element wrapped up in darkness. Out of this originally formless mass, this chaos, still incorporating the matter of all bodies, came the planetary system, dry land and sea, in six degrees (days' works), through the separation of the heaven and the earth. The whole creation was completed by God making use of the lower stages of being, already in existence, as the foundation of the higher.

If all other creatures were called into being by the power of God's word, man, on the contrary, in whose creation the world had its culminating point, and received its lord, was formed by God in person. He, as the proper object of the creative energy of God, and for whom all nature was brought forth, was formed of the dust of the earth, quickened by an immediate inspiration of the breath of divine life, and thus was a being composed of earthly matter and of the breath of God, the seal of his divine relationship. Out of the human substance, made primarily for, and wrought into, the male man, God, who had first elicited in Adam a feeling of loneliness, framed the woman. This first

---

[1] Psalm xcv. 5.   [2] Psalm cv. 37; Deut. xxxii. 17.
[3] Isaias lxv. 11.   [4] Bell. Jud. vii. 6, 3.

human pair virtually comprised the whole human race in itself. Man, viewed in his personality and with his lordship over nature, is God's likeness. His first teacher was God, and even his speech is the echo of that instruction. Before man spoke, God had spoken to him.[1]

Through their not standing firm in the decisive moment of probation, and their transgression of the divine command, men fell under the law of death; banishment out of Eden, the garden that had been given to man to cultivate and keep, and a total change in his relations with God and nature were further consequences. To till the earth in labour and toil became now man's lot, while it was the woman's to people it in pain and sorrow.

Sin is now universal; it is a something innate in the nature of man from his birth: "The thought of man's heart is evil from his youth."[2] The greatest persons, the very heroes and favourites of God, are not represented as free from sin, but as fighting against, and sometimes as falling a prey to it.[3] At the same time, however, individual sin appears the product of human freedom, and man is guilty and responsible for it. That the common sinfulness descends from father to son is shown by the longing aspiration of Job for that which he also describes as an impossibility,—for a pure one to be born of the impure.[4]

The fact that, apart from original guilt, particular and single sins are so frequently transmitted from father to son, gives cause to the threat that God will visit the iniquities of the fathers upon the children.[5] There are sins that are propagated through whole races; and yet the law declares that each one shall only die for his own sin.[6]

What, then, does God require from fallen man, according to Hebrew teaching? Above all, to be holy, because he is holy; to love God with all his heart, and all his strength;[7] that he should turn from evil, and follow good and walk humbly before God.[8] God desires love and not sacrifice, and the knowledge of God more than burnt-offerings.[9] To praise God, and to spread his honour over the whole earth, is the highest of all acts.[10] Such high requirements, united to the strict observance of the law,

---

[1] Genesis ii. 7-25.   [2] Gen. viii. 21.
[3] Ps. xiii. 1-3; cxlii. 2; 3 Kings viii. 46.   [4] Job xiv. 4.
[5] Exod. xx. 5.   [6] Deut. xxiv. 16.   [7] Deut. vi. 5.
[8] Micheas vi. 8.   [9] Osee vi. 6.   [10] Ps. viii. 9.

would only have had a discouraging and depressing effect on the Israelite, conscious of his own moral weakness, if he had not also been in possession of the doctrine of the mercy of God. This, the leading feature of the whole religious system of the Hebrews, made the wide gulf between that and all heathen religions perfectly discernible. Deeply the Israelites felt the great and infinite superiority of their religion and their God, for theirs was a merciful and sin-forgiving God. "Where," says the prophet, "is there a god who forgives sins as thou dost? God will not keep his anger for ever, because he delighteth in mercy. He will spare us again; in his mercy he will trample our iniquities under foot, and will cast all our sins into the depths of the sea."[1] "God will not always be angry, else would the souls which he created pine away before his face."[2]

The conditions of God's forgiving mercy are, however, repentance, penance, and the humble acknowledgment of sin. "The Lord is nigh unto them that are contrite of heart; and helpeth the humble in spirit."[3] He dwells in the man of a broken and abased spirit, and in him he works the work of healing, consolation, and regeneration.[4] The acknowledgment of sin to God is so necessary, that he who does not confess is a hypocrite in his eyes.[5] The further condition of mercy, then, is, a real and interior conversion for the better. God hath no pleasure in the death of the sinner, but rather that he should turn and live.[6] Works of compassion and love are specially required. Penance implies the breaking of bread to the hungry, the clothing of the naked, and the harbouring of the homeless;[7] then shall his healing prosper; by mercy to the poor he shall cast away his own guilt,[8] and by love and faithfulness make atonement for his iniquities.

If the Israelite gave way to the illusion that he could blot out his trespasses against Jehovah by external penances, fasts, rending of his garments, sprinkling his head with ashes, or offering up beasts for sacrifice, he did so in spite of the admonitions of the prophets. In the fiftieth Psalm, the type of genuine penitence, the crushed and sorrowful spirit, is contrasted, as an atonement for sin, with the mere outward sacrifice of beasts;

---

[1] Micheas vii. 18, 19. [2] Isaias lvii. 15, 16. [3] Ps. xxxiii. 19.
[4] Isaias lvii. 18. [5] Ps. xxxi. and l.; Dan. ix. [6] Ezec. xxxiii. 11.
Isaias lviii. 7, 8. [8] Daniel iv. 24; Tob. iv. 7.

and God is supplicated to create a clean heart in man, and to renew his spirit.[1] The restoration of what has been stolen, and the making good an injustice committed, was also demanded.[2] Outward signs of penance were only, however, declared to be useless when the interior feeling and earnest wish for amendment were absent; else, as signs of humiliation before God and man, they were of great value, as in the case of David,[3] Achab,[4] and those who returned from the Captivity. All these strewed ashes on their heads, rent their garments, clothed themselves in sackcloth, went barefoot, prostrated themselves on the ground, and made public confession of their sins.

Sacrifice was especially open to the abuse of a blind impenitent confidence, and a mechanical spirit of ceremony. It was so natural for this hard-hearted people to try and make up for the omission of moral duties by burnt-offerings and sacrifices. Hence the strong expressions of the prophets against animal sacrifice as often practised. God had spoken to their fathers, not of burnt-offerings, but of obedience. He had enough of sacrifice, and no more desire for the blood of oxen and lambs and goats.[5] God abhors the sacrifice of the wicked; but the prayers of the just are well-pleasing to him.[6] The sacrifice he desires is that of a contrite and obedient heart.[7] Where this is wanting, no burnt-offerings can be acceptable to him.[8]

The Hebrew descriptions of Sheol, the common sojourn for departed souls, whether of the just or unjust, somewhat resembled those of the heathen concerning Hades.[9] Sheol is a still, gloomy spot in the bowels of the earth, where souls are indeed at rest from the troubles of the world above, but lead, while there, a dull, inactive, and comfortless existence as "shades." In sheol man can no longer praise God, or remember his loving-kindnesses.[10] The description given in Job of the desolate lethargic sadness of this shadow-realm is singularly strong and striking; where the dead know nothing of those who were dearest to them, and have also ceased to care for them, mourning only over their own condition, with a painful, heavy feeling of their own sufferings.[11] But after this dark and almost despairing pic-

---

[1] Ps. l. 19.   [2] Ezec. xxxiii. 15.   [3] 2 Kings xii. 16.
[4] 3 Kings xxi. 27; Nehem. ix. 2, 3.   [5] Jer. vii. 22, 23; Isaias i. 11-13; lxvi. 3.
[6] Prov. xv. 8.   [7] Ps. l. 19.   [8] Osee vi. 6; Amos v. 22.
[9] Ps. lxxxvii. 11; lxxxviii. 49.   [10] Ps. vi. 6.   [11] Job xiv. 22.

ture, Job turns his glance joyfully and hopefully to the life after death: "I know that my Redeemer (Goel, avenger of blood) liveth; he will stand (as) the last one on the dust (of my grave);" that is to say, Though I sink under my sufferings, and die, and be cast out miserably, my Redeemer will arise victoriously over my grave; and though I be dead, and freed from my flesh, I shall see God. "My eyes shall behold him, and no stranger;" that is to say, Not only shall other persons be witnesses of my justification through God after my death; but I myself, living on after death, in proper personal existence, expect this blissful consummation.[1] Parallel with the faith of Job is the hearty confidence of the Psalmist, to whom his God is the highest in heaven and on earth; and "even if my flesh and my heart pass away, God is my rock and my portion for evermore;" and "though I wander in the valley of the shadow of death, I fear no evil, for thou art with me."[2]

The resurrection of the dead, the just as well as the unjust, is proclaimed quite distinctly and unequivocally in the book of Daniel. "Many that lie and sleep in the dust of the earth shall awake; some to life everlasting, some to everlasting shame."[3] From thenceforward the resurrection became a fundamental point in the religion of the nation, though not without opposition from the Hellenisers and Sadducees. The mother of the Macchabees, and her sons, were put to death with the confession of the resurrection on their lips.[4]

Prayers, also, and sacrifices for the dead were already in use in the Macchabean period. When the Jews after a victory found in the clothes of their soldiers who were slain some gold that had been taken from idols, Judas caused prayers and sacrifices to be offered up in Jerusalem for those who had fallen, that they might be loosed from their sins; for, as the narrator adds, "if he had not believed that the dead would rise again, it would have been superfluous and vain to pray for the dead."[5] It was, therefore, a custom that had then existed some time, though not mentioned in the written law, for prayers and sacrifices to be offered for the dead whose life and death gave ground to hope for forgiveness being secured for them; and sheol was a middle state, in

---

[1] Job xix. 25-27.
[2] Ps. lxxii. 25, 26; xxii. 4.
[3] Dan. xii. 1-3.
[4] 2 Macc. vii. 9, 14, 23.
[5] 2 Macc. xii. 40-45.

which the prayers and offerings of the living took effect in bringing about the purification and forgiveness of such departed souls.

IV. PROPHECIES OF THE MESSIAS.

If the religious feelings of the Jews did not strike out into an egotistic haughtiness, the people must ever have had the thought before them, that they were only the chosen people to enable them to serve in the hands of God as instruments for the salvation of other nations; that their present state was a transient one, and that it was no part of their destiny to remain for ever so isolated from the rest of mankind, collectively and individually, as if in prison. Every Israelite must have looked forward to a time for the partition-wall to tumble; and here came in the doctrine of the great Prophet and Saviour of the nation to be expected, towards which every thing in the end converged, and from which all in law and ritual borrowed its colouring, true position, and importance. Do you hope for a Messias?—whom and what kind of person? On this question hinged the destinies of the nation. Their idea of a Messias was the salt which should have preserved their whole religious life from destruction and decay. If it was true to say of the heathen, "like people, like gods," so might it be said of the Israelites; that whatever the people, in the mass, should be at the great crisis, such the Messias would be whom they longed for and trusted in. He was certain to be the genuine reflection of their own tone of mind. The prophetical writings, indeed, contained many features of the portrait of that man of salvation, through whom the fathers trusted God would have mercy on his people; but these were scattered about here and there, and their poetical obscurity and apparent contradictions, not yet cleared up by their fulfilment, left wide room for arbitrary interpretation. The conceit of the carnally-minded Jew had no difficulty, if he only set aside all that was unpleasant and repulsive to him in detail and intimations, in composing an ideal picture of the Messias to his heart's content out of other passages. We cannot escape this conclusion, if we compare the state of the Jews after Pompey with the ideas and hopes regarding the Messias as developed step by step in the holy Scriptures.

Five times was the promise given to the patriarchs, Abraham and his grandson Jacob, that in their seed all the nations of the earth should be blessed,[1] that the knowledge and possession of God should extend to all nations through their posterity, and that they should wish for no higher happiness than that of belonging to the descendants of Abraham.

In the prophecy to Jacob, the tribe of Judah was first indicated as the chief instrument and helper in the divine economy: "The sceptre shall not be taken away from Judah, nor a ruler cease between his feet, till Shilo (the peace or the rest), *i.e.* the great descendant of Judah, who was to bring the blessings of peace, shall come; to him shall the homage of the people be paid."[2]

From the time that David received the promise that his seed and his kingdom were to endure for ever, it was the house of David on which the prophets hung their hopes and predictions. David's kingdom was to be an everlasting one, and God himself is always with him and his posterity.[3] David himself knew that God had made an everlasting covenant with him.[4] "His name," he says, "shall continue for ever; as long as the sun endureth, it shall flourish and be blest."[5] This eternal Ruler, who rules unto the ends of the earth, was to permit all nations to share in the blessedness of his kingdom: the lot of the lowly, the poor, and the suffering, was to be one of special happiness under him.[6] The priestly and kingly power were to be united in him; but a priesthood of a different kind from that of Aaron was to endure for ever.[7] All nations were to be subject to him, and all kings of the earth to serve him. His name was to endure for ever; and as long as the sun continues, his youth was to be renewed in a succession of generations.[8]

Thus hope was centered in a descendant of David's house, who should found and rule over a prosperous kingdom, bringing all the people of the earth to the knowledge and service of Jehovah, so that all nations should come to Jerusalem with their treasures to do homage to the Lord. Bethlehem, the birthplace of the future Saviour, had been already even mentioned by name.[9]

---

[1] Genesis xii. 2, 3; xviii. 18; xxii. 16-18; xxvi. 4; xxviii. 14.
[2] Ibid. xlix. 10.   [3] Ps. xvii. 51.   [4] 2 Kings xxiii. 5; vii. 12 sq.
[5] Ps. lxxi. 17.   [6] Ibid. xx. lxxi. 1-14.   [7] Ibid. cix. 4.
[8] Ibid. lxxi. 17.   [9] Mich. v. 2.

Zemach, the divinely given "shoot," now became the designation of the expected one; at one time he is described as the invincible conqueror, overcoming all resistance to, and rebellion against, his majesty, and whose empire outlasts and humbles all his enemies, who are also the enemies of God. Then, again, and whilst for the first time is announced the dominion of the Messias over the whole world, "from sea to sea, and from the river to the ends of the earth," his influence appears chiefly a spiritual one, blessing with the mild words of peace.[1] From this period pictures multiply, which awakened in the sons of Abraham representations flattering to their minds, that the kingdom of the Messias was to appear under the form of a Jewish monarchy of the world, wherein they and their king were to rule in never-ending majesty. But as a wholesome counterpoise to these brilliant prospects, and apparently in the most harsh opposition to them, there also appeared pictures of a suffering Messias, overwhelmed with every species of obloquy.

In the Psalms we meet with the just man visited by sore affliction, more than any other mortal; whom his enemies deride as one already lost, as one tormented and suffering in every limb, and entirely rejected by his people.[2] Looking at his dying body, he can count each of his bones, while his enemies surround him and feast on his torments, divide his clothes amongst them, and cast lots for his vesture. And these unexampled sufferings of one man were to bring about the conversion of the heathen, and to cause all the kindreds of the Gentiles to adore the true God.[3]

This portrait of Messias in suffering is far more minutely touched by the hand of Isaias. The servant of God, Immanuel, the offshoot (Zemach), is called by God from his mother's womb;[4] God has given him his spirit,[5] and put his words in his mouth.[6] He was to open the eyes of the blind, to heal the contrite, and to preach release to the captive.[7] He was to be a saviour to such as should turn from their iniquity in Jacob, as well as a light to all nations;[8] to extend the salvation of God to the utmost parts of the earth.[9] This servant of God was to be himself the covenant between God and his people, and the

---

[1] Zach. ix. 9, 10.   [2] Ps. xxi.   [3] Ibid. xxi. 28, 29.
[4] Isaias xlix. 1.   [5] Ibid. xlii. 1.   [6] Ibid. li. 16.
[7] Ibid. lxi. 1-3.   [8] Ibid. lix. 20; xlii. 1, 4, 6.   [9] Ibid. xlix. 6.

mediator between God and them.¹ From him was the new law of the new covenant to proceed. Subsequently the prophet describes the sufferings of this servant: despised, forsaken, laden with grief as he is, his sorrows excite only the aversion of men, who regard them as a punishment for his guilt; while he, the innocent one, of his own free will, bears what we, the guilty ones, have deserved. He bears our infirmities, and carries our sorrows; he is wounded for our iniquities, and by his wounds we are healed. Dumb as a lamb led to the slaughter, he suffers and dies for our sins.² His sufferings and death are a trespass-offering;³ and therefore will God glorify him. He shall lead many by his wisdom to justice, and God will make him a leader to the people.⁴ Thus this servant of Jehovah is at once a king, to whom kings do homage; he passes through shame to glory, through death to life; he conquers by yielding, and completes his work at the moment of his apparent annihilation.

According to the representation of Daniel, the Messias is an envoy of God from heaven, to be monarch of a kingdom to be founded on earth, embracing all nations, and to endure for ever. The succession of the powers of the kingdoms of the world, the Assyrian, Babylonish, Persian, Grecian, and Roman empires, was pointed out; and on their ruins, destroying and indestructible, rises the eternal kingdom of the Son of Man, throned in heaven on a divine throne, a kingdom never to be given to another people.⁵

The prophet Zacharias recurs to the Son of David, the Zemach, to whom the longing gaze of the people was directed. In peaceful union of the twin dignities of priest and king, he builds the temple of the Lord with them that come thereto from afar.⁶ His word extends to heathendom, and his dominion beyond the boundaries of the earth. Then he appears under the semblance of a good shepherd, who gently and tenderly takes pity on the people who have been ill-treated by selfish shepherds; but when scornfully and ungratefully denied by the apostate herd (valued at thirty pieces of silver), mildly breaks his staff, lays down his office of shepherd,⁷ and leaves the people to their interior disunion. And now it appears that the shepherd, rejected

---

[1] Isaias xlii. 6; xlix. 8.   [2] Ibid. liii. 7, 8.   [3] Ibid. liii. 12.
[4] Ibid. lv. 4.   [5] Daniel ii. 44, 45.   [6] Zach. vi. 13-15.
[7] Zach. xi.

by the nation, is the Lord himself; when he pours forth the spirit of mercy and prayer, then the Jews, seized with bitter repentance and deep sorrow on account of him they had pierced, will look up to him longingly. The prophet sees how, after the shepherd is killed, the flock will be dispersed, and only a third part remain, who will be refined as silver and gold in the fire of tribulation, whom the Lord will acknowledge as his true people, while they will joyfully recognise him as their God.[1]

Malachias, the last of the prophets, foresees in the distant future a purified priesthood. These purified children of Levi will then belong to the Lord, and by them a clean oblation will be offered to the Lord in every place; from east to west the heathen, now worshipers of the true God, will come to offer sacrifice.[2] This prophecy was the confirmation and complement of that of Isaias, who had already foretold that God would select priests and Levites for himself, even from the heathen, not for the old legal service, but to offer up a new and clean oblation.[3] Malachias puts the last prophetic touches to the picture of the Messias. He announces the "angel," the messenger sent from God to prepare the way of the Lord; this angel he designates as a second Elias, a preacher and exemplar of penance, uniting old and young together in a new life.

Jeremias had long since uttered those memorable words, which of themselves ought to have opened the eyes of the Jews of later days, and quenched their blind zeal for the law; the time will come when there shall be no thought more of "the ark of the covenant of the Lord," neither shall it be missed nor made again; and that shall be the time when the heathen shall be gathered together to the throne of the Lord and to the new Jerusalem.[4] At the same time, a change of the whole typical and legal service of God was pointed out, together with which the same prophet announced a new covenant which God would make with Israel by writing his law on their heart.[5] Ezechiel had promised in confirmation, that God, in order to be able to forgive his people their sins, would give them a new heart and a new spirit; would take away the heart of stone out of their body, and give them one of flesh.[6] Thus the Israelites had a

---

[1] Zach. xiii. 8, 9.   [2] Mal. iii. 3; i. 11.
[3] Isaias lxvi. 20.   [4] Jer. iii. 16-18.
[5] Jer. xxxi. 33, 34.   [6] Ezech. xi. 19; xxxix. 26; xxxvi. 26.

prophetic mirror, which not only presented them with a picture of the Messias and of his age, but also warned them against that one crowning national sin which led them as a nation to their fall; that spirit which accompanied them even in their banishment, and which turned those who were destined to be a blessing to other people so often into their scourge,—hardness of heart, whose root was in pride.

V. ALEXANDRINE JUDAISM. PHILO.

THE contact of the Jews of Palestine with Grecian life and modes of thought during the time of the Syrian dominion had, as we have seen, brought forth its evil fruit in giving birth to Sadduceism; on the whole, however, the Jews there carefully excluded themselves from a literature and teaching associated to them with the most painful recollections. It was otherwise in Egypt, where the Jews had been drawn into the great movement of the philosophico-religious school of Alexandria; and partly by way of apology, and partly because they really were profoundly impressed with Greek philosophy, they, for the first time, endeavoured to found and carry out a Mosaic theology, wherein the forms of Greek thought were blended with the substance of Jewish belief. One might naturally conclude, as was the case, that Greek philosophical problems exercised a strong and material influence in this fusion, and sometimes imparted not the forms only, but also the body of the doctrine.

The Jews in Egypt were in a comparatively favourable and thriving position. They formed perhaps a seventh part of the population of the country, had quarters of their own in Alexandria, and even a temple as a religious centre. Onias, a son of Onias III., the high-priest who was deposed and murdered in Jerusalem during the time when the temple in Jerusalem was given up to heathen desecration, had obtained permission from Ptolemy Philometor, the benefactor of the Egyptian Jews, to rebuild a ruinous heathen temple at Leontopolis in the Nomos of Heliopolis, and to convert it to Jewish uses as a sanctuary of Jehovah. This took place 152 B.C. It was not intended to erect a temple of similar pretensions to that in Jerusalem, nor in opposition to it, nor to draw away the visitors and sacrificial gifts from there, but only to set up a place of worship to meet the exigency of the true temple being in the hands of enemies, and free access to it precluded. The prophecy of Isaias, that God would bless Egypt, and that he should be served there with sacrifices and oblations, was made use of to justify an undertaking otherwise not very easily reconcilable with the law. This temple was endowed with landed property, and continued up to the time of Vespasian with a regular service, performed by its own priests and Levites. The Jews of Palestine tolerated it; and if they looked on it with no complacence, they did not therefore give up religious communion with their brethren in Egypt.

As early as the first half of the second century before Christ, Aristobulus the Peripatetic was living at Alexandria. He was of a sacerdotal family, and was preceptor to King Ptolemy Philometor. In a Greek work, composed in a very good style, he attempted to prove that the oldest and greatest poets and philosophers of the Greeks were acquainted with the teaching of Moses, and confirmed the truths of the Holy Scriptures by dicta of their own to the like effect; thus Plato, he says, met with the Pentateuch in an old Greek translation, and drew from it. It appears that already, before the time of Aristobulus, well-informed Hellenistic Jews had written much to the same purport; as of the numerous pretended verses from Homer, Hesiod, or Orpheus, which he cites, only one here and there was probably composed by himself; the greater part he found already in existence; and Orphic fragments, as vehicles of novel religious ideas, were frequently composed amongst the Greeks from the days of Onomacritus. Later on, and with the same view, Sibylline oracles were concocted to praise the Jewish people and their belief, and to combat Hellenistic heathenism. Aristobulus accounts for the Mosaico-Judaistic purport of his fragments from the Greek poets by the hypothesis that Orpheus met with Moses in Egypt, and that the latter was identical with Musæus, the Greek sage, and that Pythagoras himself was instructed by the disciples or successors of Jeremias. What is known, however, of the theology of Aristobulus by no means suffices to make him into a predecessor or founder of the school of Philo; all we can say is, that he made use of Greek doctrines without binding himself to any one of the peculiar systems. His aim was to set aside the anthropomorphisms in the expression and amplifications of the Bible, to make way for notions and ideas more consonant with the spiritual nature of God.

The Alexandrian Jew Philo was well advanced in years when he appeared in Rome before Caligula, A.D. 40, at the head of a Jewish embassy; he may therefore be supposed to have been born about 25 B.C. He belonged to one of the principal families of his people, and, with the exception of the apostolic circle, was the man most distinguished for intellectual attainments whom the Jews then possessed. He was a man of rare endowments and high cultivation, from his comprehensive studies and intimate acquaintance with Greek literature; his piety was earnest, and his faith firm. His writings breathe a fiery enthusiasm, and an impetuosity of thought, which, it is true, have often to contend against a deficiency of expression, and at times betray an absence of definite perception and of lucidity of thought.

Convinced that the Jewish religion rested on divine revelation, and at the same time mentally swayed by Greek speculation, and specially following Platonic and Stoic views in leading philosophical questions, Philo candidly started on the idea that every system of philosophy in which he recognised truth was contained in the Hebrew religion, even though it were so in a way that was hidden from the great multitude of men. Not unfrequently he remained unconsciously true to his own Hebrew belief, though himself under the notion that he was following the Greek philosophy. Moses is, with him, the greatest of all philosophers: all philosophy emanates from him, and is identical with the revealed religion; where it did not fully accord with this, it is only the handmaiden of wisdom, that is to say, of the highest knowledge of God, only to be arrived at by the way of ascetic contemplation.[1]

The never-failing instrument Philo made use of to support his biblical and speculative theory was, the allegorical interpretation of the Pentateuch; and he used it with the more freedom as he had already received it in a traditional way from the earlier Alexandrian Jews, and was in the habit of seeing it generally applied by the Greeks as a key to their myths. He appears not

---

[1] De congr. quær. erud. grati, ed. Paris, 1640, p. 435.

have had a doubt but that he was really unfolding the hidden meaning of the lawgiver by his allegorical explanations. In the sacred books, all is of divine inspiration; an inexhaustible treasure of divine thought is contained in the husk of the letter; the obvious and literal meaning of the words is of no importance,—that is often false and deceiving; on the contrary, the kernel of religious truth must be extracted from its shell of history or parable. The rabbis of later days were in the habit of saying that whole mountains of instruction hung on every iota of the Scriptures. Philo gave out these interpretations of his as mysteries not fit for every one, but only for such as were worthy to be initiated into such high things.[1] He goes so far, in a series of writings in which he treats of the lives of the Patriarchs, as to represent each of them as being a type of a peculiar state of soul; and on this every circumstance related of them is brought to bear. As all immediate contact of God with the world ran counter to his ideas of the Divinity, all representations or accounts in the Bible to that effect had to be set aside through allegory. The fact of a boundless field being thus opened to caprice gave him no scruple, as he was often in a state which he describes as a theoleptic one, in which high inspirations were lavished upon him. "The most excellent and perfect," he said, "is that which God himself pours out on the soul. I do not shrink, however, from owning that this is a state which I have myself experienced numbers of times."[2]

Philo lived in a totally different atmosphere from his brother Jews in Palestine, and hence he read the sacred books with other eyes than theirs. Being of Alexandria, and having grown up under the influence of the Greek language, speech, turn of thought, and literature, he interpreted Scripture according to ideas imbibed from the mode of life and tone of mind adopted by all around him. He shared with the other Jews the notion of the inexhaustible many-sidedness of the Scriptures being their highest advantage. He had not to endure opposition from adversaries who might press upon him contradictory interpretations, whether good or bad, yet as justifiable as his own; in his ecstatic states, he was possessed by the same set of ideas as in the sober realities of every-day life; the only difference was, that

---

[1] De Cherub. p. 115.
[2] De Migr. Abr. vii. 395; cf. De Cherub. 9.

these ideas became more lively, more highly coloured, and independent of discursive contemplation; herein, too, he found a fancied security for the truth of his views. Philo repeatedly expressed disapprobation of the admission of myths into Bible history, as they relate only to heathen gods and their genealogies.[1] Yet he says there are things recounted in the Pentateuch which are more incredible than myths; but still they are no myths, but allegories, by which he means, true ideas clothed by the writer in a figurative or historical dress.[2]

The people of Israel, "the men in the true sense of the word," Philo teaches, were chosen by God out of the whole human race, and placed under his special guidance, with the intention that the Jews should serve the rest of mankind as priests and prophets of the pure knowledge of God. God never forsakes this people, although they appear like orphans in their isolation and inability of ever reckoning on the help of other nations; who, being given up to the enjoyment of the senses, feel repelled by the strictness of the Mosaic law. God, however, will reward them in the expected advent of the Messias for their sufferings and steadfastness, by the gathering together and bringing back of the dispersed. Philo honours Moses as the "greatest and most perfect of men in every respect," and the "highest saint." In the Mosaic law he sees the most complete picture of the divine government of the world.

Philo's admiration and love for his people and his creed did not, however, interfere with his acknowledgment of the benefits of Hellenism. Plato is great, and even holy, in his estimation: he speaks of the holy community of the Pythagoreans, and of the holy union of godlike men; of a Parmenides, an Empedocles, a Zeno, and a Cleanthes. In Hellas he sees the cradle of knowledge, and a genuine civilisation of man; but in the background here there is always the idea that the best of their views were derived from a Hebrew source. Thus Heraclitus is referred to Moses;[3] Zeno is a nursling of Jewish wisdom;[4] even in the laws of the Greeks there is much that is Jewish.[5] Philo does not hesitate to coincide with the Greek philosophers in their view of the stars; he, too, believes them to be animate beings,

---

[1] De Monarch. i. 814, 818.   [2] De Mose, iii. 691.
[3] Quis rer. div. hær. p. 510.   [4] Quod omn. prob. lib. p. 873.
[5] De Mose, ii.

and considers these astral souls as pure spirits of a higher order.[1] He unites with Plato in calling them the visible gods, although he uses the expression in an improper sense; nevertheless, they are to him the vicegerents of God, though not to be divinely honoured.

Philo starts from the opposition, the infinite distance between God and the world. God and creatures, even so far as these latter are good or perfect, are at such a distance apart that one is obliged to say, God is better than the good and the beautiful; purer than unity; more primeval than the monad, and more blissful than blessedness.[2] He is without qualities, and therefore no name can properly be attributed to him. We only know that he exists, not what he is: the name of the "I am" (Jehovah) is the only one that expresses his essence.[3] Philo does not, however, carry the doctrine that God is without qualities so far as to deny his personality, and to subtilise him into mere abstract being. On the contrary, he holds firmly to the belief in God's personality. God is the absolutely blessed, and ever operating; to him action is as essential and natural as burning is to fire.[4]

Thus there was an active cause and a passive matter;[5] to wit, the soul, and qualitiless matter, of itself merely immovable, but plastic, which, as long as its portioning out into different forms had not yet ensued, can only be predicated of as the confusion, as dead, as the void and needy, darkness, aye, and the nonentity.[6] Philo thus admits a preëxistence of matter, and no creation out of nothing, although he often designates God as the first cause of all being.[7] Indeed, the idea of a material substratum

---

[1] De Mundi Opif. 6; de Confus. Ling. 345.
[2] Fragm. ap. Eus. Praep. Ev. vii. 15. 2. [3] Quod D. immut. 302.
[4] Leg. Alleg. 41. [5] De Mundi Opif. 2. [6] Ibid. 4.
[7] The passage of Philo de Somn. i. p. 577,—ὡς ὁ ἥλιος τὰ κεκρυμμένα τῶν σωμάτων ἐπιδείκνυται, οὕτω καὶ ὁ θεὸς τὰ πάντα γεννήσας, οὐ μόνον εἰς τοὐμφανὲς ἤγαγεν, ἀλλὰ καὶ ἃ πρότερον οὐκ ἦν ἐποίησεν, οὐ δημιουργὸς μόνον, ἀλλὰ καὶ κτιστὴς αὐτὸς ὤν,—appears at first sight quite clearly to speak of God as the creator of matter; and Keferstein (Philo's *Lehre von den Mittelwesen*, 1846, p. 5) says "δημιουργὸς can only here refer to the fashioner, κτιστής to the creator, of matter. This is also confirmed by the context, where God compares himself to light, and shows his preëminence, as not only bringing things before the eyes of man as the sun does, but also as having given him being, and brought him forth out of the darkness of nothingness, and placed him before the eye of the beholder."

If this were so, one must say, that for once the Jewish conscience of Philo

was indispensable to enable him to account for the deficiencies of that which is finite, and not to be obliged to look upon God as its cause; he considered, however, physical ills, which did not exist before the fall of man, merely as powerful means of discipline in the hand of God, and therefore distinguishes them from such deficiencies. Philo contradicted the idea of the eternity of the world, on the plea that Providence was thus done away with, and the entire inactivity of God asserted. True, he thinks that God is removed from all contest with the world and with matter, if we contemplate him in his proper essence; but he rejects the belief in an unenergising God, as a gross error.[1] The Platonic doctrine of ideas is one of those which was fundamental with Philo, not only because it was so completely in accordance with his own way of thinking, but also because it already prevailed amongst the Alexandrine Jews. He appealed to the Jewish commentators, as having proved this doctrine of ideas from the Scriptures.[2] "The blessed one," says he, " could not touch fermenting matter; he made use of his immaterial powers, ideas, to admit of each species attaining their proper form."[3] Ideas, therefore, moulded matter, and stamped their impress on it. These ideas are devoid of attributes in and for themselves; but when they enter into active relationship to matter, which is also without qualities, they mingle together and give birth to qualities in the latter.[4]

All ideas stand in connexion with, and mould, the intelligible world, which was at first brought into being by God, as a

must have been stronger than the mode of viewing things he had learnt from the Grecian philosophy; for his admission of the preëxistence of matter recurs so often and so clearly, that there can be no doubt of his ordinary opinion on the point. Rightly viewed, however, these words by no means contradict the numerous passages in his writings.

Philo distinguishes two sorts of action in God: the one whereby he fashions things into what they are and before were not (but out of preëxisting matter); the other whereby he makes them manifest, like the sun, for non-matter as such is not perceptible to the senses. When speaking of him with reference to this latter, he calls him demiurge; with reference to the former, he uses the word κτιστής, which does not in itself involve the speculative idea of creation out of nothing.

With regard to the other passages cited by Grossman, *Quæstiones Philoneæ*, i. p. 19, J. G. Müller has already shown that they do not contradict the idea of the preëxistence of matter, in his work entitled *Des Juden Philo Buch von der Weltschöpfung, herausgeg. und erklärt*, 1841, pp. 129, 130.

[1] Legg. Alleg. i. 41.   [2] Quis rer. div. 520.
[3] De Victimas offerentibus, 857.   [4] Ibid. 858.

type of the physical world. Philo, however, with whom this representation of the ideal world is not so much developed as in Plato, considers it to have been produced on the first day of the biblical creation. It has no existence in space, but is only the contemplated draught of the physical creation. Just as the architect projects in his mind a plan of a town, and then produces the real town according to this ideal, so God acted when he created the world, this megalopolis.[1] The author of this ideal world is the divine Logos, although it is itself again nothing else but the Logos.

Ideas are not only, however, the models after which God works, or the seal which he impresses on things; they are, at the same time, also the working causes or ministering powers by which he carried out his plan of creation. These powers, which belong, according to Philo, to a middle state of being, are divine operations or manifestations of God to the world, to which a certain independence attaches.[2] They stand half-way between the Logos and ideas, yet so that the Logos is the concentration or compendium of the powers. God who is, in and for himself, as the abstract, without relations or attributes, that is to say, in whom all virtually repose, and who, from his exceeding exaltation, cannot enter into any immediate contact with the world, acts through these powers, who are his servants, his vicegerents, his ambassadors. They form a radiance which surrounds God, and is imperceptible to mortal eye,[3] and which emanates from God himself; like sunbeams, they go forth from him, and revert to him again. They extend every where by means of their elasticity; or through a self-manifestation of God, an extension outwardly from within, an intervention of God with the world is brought about. Philo styles these powers immortal souls, and looks on them as the angels of the Bible.[4] Personal as he generally makes them, he does not cling firmly to the idea of their hypostasis; and he puts them so near God, actually locating them almost in his very being, that to him their personal subsistence and distinction from God often melt away, as it were, from his grasp. And yet his principle of the impossibility of God's direct dealing with the finite, necessitated his adopting such beings, distinct from God, as his agents.

[1] De Opif. p. 5.
[2] De Abr. 366; Migr. Abr. 416.
[3] De Monarch. i. 817.
[4] Confus. Ling. 324, 315.

The Logos is, with Philo, the divine intelligence, sometimes contemplated as a purely impersonal quality included in the divine Being; but more frequently, and by preference, it appears as emanating through the divine word from the bosom of the godhead, and continuing in a self-subsistence and personal distinction from God. "What God speaks are no words, but works," says Philo.[1] In the Logos, God expresses his being. He is the complete manifestation of God, the oldest of all intelligent beings, comprising all divine powers, attributes, and expressions. He is at the same time the chief mediator between God and the world, the immediate image of the father, the divine world of thought, the band by which all things are held together.

Philo not only calls the Logos the Son of God, but also directly a second God, with the limitation, however, that this is only so said by catachresis; for as a Jew he could not possibly maintain in earnest the idea of two Gods. His whole system drove him to hold fast to the personality of the Logos: he required it; but the difficulty of choosing between the alternative of a lapse into polytheism, or of lowering the Logos into a mere angel, was too much for him; so he wavered repeatedly, and left his Logos to be volatilised either into an impersonal quality, or a mere collection of divine ideas. For we do not find that he made a distinction between a Logos internal and one external to God, and yet he has got hold of the idea of a real personal mediator between God and man, and united it to the Logos; he designates him a high-priest and intercessor for man. The Logos bears, he says, to God the assurance that the human race never quite fell away from him, and also gives the assurance to man that he never will be forsaken by God.[2] He here styles him the archangel, and yet he also says he was neither uncreate, as God is, nor created as man; and he anticipates that relationship between the Logos and the Father, which was afterwards expressed by the idea of generation.

It is accordingly through the Logos that all communication between God and the world is effected; for he, as penetrating all things, conveys the divine essence thither. As the spiritual nature of man is derived from him, he also manifests himself to this nature. "He appears as he is to the immaterial souls who serve him, and speaks to them as one friend does to another;

---

[1] De Decal. 750.   [2] Quis rer. div. hær. 509.

while to such as are yet in the body he appears in the form of an angel, without altering his nature."[1] This is based on the Bible theophany. As far as his action on the soul of man is concerned, the Logos is identical with Sophia, the divine wisdom; and Philo appears here to have put together the descriptions of wisdom in the later books of the Bible. His Logos is at bottom Sophia advanced a step further in personalisation, and transformed into a male being. Philo indeed has once made a distinction between the Logos and the divine wisdom as his mother:[2] he represents her gladly as "mother of the universe," of which God is the father;[3] she has from the seed received from God given birth to the world, his only and beloved Son.[4] But if we put all his expressions together, it is plain enough that the Sophia and the Logos are not essentially different in his mind, but are two ways of indicating the same divine mediate being, which, according to the context, he sometimes represented as the material recipient, and at others as the procreating and active principle. If we also meet with an hypostasis similar to that of the Logos of Philo in the "Memra" of the Targum, the contemporary Chaldean paraphrase of Onkelos and Jonathan Ben Uziel, we must, on the other hand, observe that with them Memra is only a descriptive word used to indicate the subject, as "God, man, angel," and is resorted to by the commentator in passages where in the Hebrew "the name, the spirit, the glory of God," are found.

Philo's platonism comes out most strongly in his doctrine concerning souls; angels, demons, and souls are only different names for one and the same being. They are countless as the stars; their abode is the air, which, as being the best of earthly substances, is also provided with the most perfect organisation of living beings.[5] Some of these souls descend here below and unite themselves to mortal frames, being smitten with desire for the earth and for bodies. Many of these are carried away here by the whirlpool of sensuality, and are swallowed up in it; while others, who by striving after higher knowledge strongly enough to resist the pressure, aim from first to last to die to their earthly being, in order to gain the higher life.[6] These return after death to the heavenly dwelling-place, all the more certainly

---

[1] De Somn. i. 599. [2] De Profug. 466. [3] Alleg. iii. 1096.
[4] De Temul. 244. [5] De Somn. i. p. 585. [6] De Gigant. 284. 285.

as some of them, the souls of the wise, only undertook their wanderings on earth out of thirst for knowledge.[1] The vicious, Philo represents as perishing with the dissolution of their bodies. Some of the returned souls are led by earthly longings to visit earth a second time: other souls, on the contrary, who deem intercourse with earthly things to be unworthy of them, the angels of the Bible, the heroes of the Greeks, who dwell in the ether above the regions of air, are employed by God as his messengers and servants, and guardians of mortal men. According to Philo, also, there are certainly bad angels; but he speaks of them as bad men. Moreover, considering, as he does, all evil to consist in sensuality only, he makes the fall and the degeneracy of the spirits coincident with their yielding to sensuality, their union with bodies, or perhaps to be engendered by this union in the course of time.

In this same class of heavenly souls Philo also places the souls of the stars: the most distinguished are rulers of the world state; those who are under the moon, in the regions of the air, are the servants.[2] It is difficult, however, to state precisely what idea he had of the nature of souls or of angels, or of their relation to God. He calls the human "nous" a portion, but an inseparable one, of the universal soul of God (the Logos),[3] from which nothing is detached, and which only is extended. Every man is related to the divine Logos as regards his understanding, and is a copy, a fragment, a reflection of this blessed being.[4] He discriminates, therefore, the nutritive and sensitive soul in man, which he supposes to arise from the airlike elements of the seed, from the intelligence, the nous, that which is akin to God and imperishable, according to which the man is an image of the divine Logos.[5] Whether this intelligent spirit is only an image, or also a portion of the substance of the Logos, Philo does not distinctly say. Here again we see that there were in Philo, as it were, two souls at work at the same time, one Hellenistic, and the other Jewish, and they not unfrequently came into collision. He moved in a sphere of Platonic and Stoic ideas; but his He-

[1] Confus. Ling. 331.   [2] De Monarch. i. 812.
[3] Ἀπόσπασμα οὐ διαιρετόν. Quod det pot. insid. 172.
[4] De Mundi Opif. 33.
[5] Ibid. 31, 33. Philo also ascribes to the ψυχή similarity to God. Quod Deus immut. 300, he only uses this word in opposition to bodies; elsewhere he also uses πνεῦμα.

brew conscience reacted on them, and that gave birth to a wavering and unsteadiness in him, which is very manifest in the most important questions. Thus he also asserts that the spirit of man is an effluence of that ether or fifth element, out of which the heavens and stars are formed,[1] and to which it will return as to its father, when the spirit is severed from the body; a view which, as he himself observes, is borrowed from the ancients (the Pythagoreans).

Philo assumes a primal or ideal man, who, as yet undivided into the two sexes, was a man-woman.[2] He finds a double meaning in the Bible account of the fall; the obvious and real one being that sin arose through the woman's seducing the man to sexual intercourse; and thus voluptuousness, the beginning of all iniquity and sin, was developed. According to the allegorical meaning, the sense is to be understood under the term woman, and sensuality under the serpent. His fundamental thought, then, is, that voluptuousness is the origin and seat of sin; the woman its originatrix, from the pleasure she first gave and experienced in it. Pleasure in its two offshoots, the love of eating and drinking, and lust, is with Philo the source of all vice, and is in itself evil;[3] and as it is sure to develop itself in a being composed of body and mind, so all men are born in sin, which consists precisely in the dominion of sensual pleasure over the soul.[4] No one ever kept himself, from birth till death, wholly free from sin, although there is a possibility of a godly man remaining spotless.[5] Evil, therefore, comes from the earthly shell, the body, this hateful dungeon of the spirit, out of which it longs to escape, as Israel out of Egypt,[6] to enter on that true life which is only attainable after death.

Philo's ethics required the keeping down and greatest possible restraint of sensual inclinations, of the wants and feelings; and here, as well as in his picture of the true and only free and ruling sage, he leans greatly to the doctrines of the Stoics;[7] but he entirely differs from them, and follows his own biblical course, in the prominence he gives to the divine mercy, its might and necessity, and the moral impotence of man without it.[8] To

---

[1] Quis rer. div. haer. 521.   [2] Quis rer. div. 504; Legg. Alleg. iii. 1089.
[3] Legg. Alleg. ii. 73; cf. 106.   [4] De Mundi Opif. 37; Vita Mosis, iii. 675.
[5] De Pœnit. 716.   [6] Quis rer. div. haer. 518.
[7] Quod omnes probus liber. 867.   [8] Legg. Alleg. i. 48, 55, 101.

plant virtue in the soul belongs to God only,[1] and faith is the true wisdom. Human will and thought must recognise and seek for in God the source of all that is good and true.

Strongly as Philo otherwise descants on the unattainableness and intangibility of God, he also teaches that there is a state or way for man, that of ecstasy, in which his spirit, rising above all sensible things, and transcending even ideas and the Logos, becomes enveloped in the glory of God, and contemplates them in his essence. In this state of externation from self, and of painful yielding to the inward operation of God, " man, as a child without speech or consciousness, seized by a divine frenzy, is moved only by the spirit of God, like the strings of a musical instrument, and from a son of the Logos becomes a son of God, and equal in rank to the Logos, who has hitherto been his guide. This is, indeed," says Philo, "an incomprehensible mystery to the multitude, and to be imparted to the instructed only."[2]

There is a certain analogy between this ecstatic condition of individuals, and Philo's hopes, already referred to above, as to the expected Messias producing a kind of national ecstasy. In the days of the Messias the enemies of the Jews were to be seized with astonishment at their virtues, and filled with shame at ruling over a people so much better than themselves, and thus the dispersed were to have their freedom restored them. Upon this they were to come forth from all lands, and to return to their own.[3] The Jews were then to have three paracletes of reconciliation before God: the mildness and goodness of God himself, ever preferring pardon to punishment; the holiness of their forefathers, which would plead efficaciously in behalf of their children; and the genuine amendment of the penitent. Then would the earth spontaneously bring forth its fruits in abundance, so as to prevent their being hindered by temporal cares from employing themselves in higher things; and a long life, almost approaching immortality, together with a numerous offspring, would be the portion of every one. Such millennary representations did not certainly originate with Philo, but were found ready at hand by him among the circle of his compatriots.

[1] Legg. Alleg. i. 103.
[2] Quis rer. div. haer. 490 sq.; Legg. Alleg. iii. 79, 93; De Somn. 587 sq.
[3] De Execr. 937.

VI. THE LAST DAYS OF THE JEWISH STATE, AND CHURCH POLITY.

THERE were four causes coöperating to that catastrophe by which the state, city, and temple of the Jews were destroyed: the conduct of the Roman governors, the hatred of the heathen, the corruption of the Jews, and their blind confidence in false prophets and in counterfeits of the Messias. The insatiable avarice, and systematic severity and cruelty, of the Roman governors drove the nation to despair. The riches of the temple treasury, which, though often robbed, was always being replenished, and quickly, by yearly contributions from all parts of the world, was an incitement to forcible seizures and arbitrary expenditure; but the exasperation of the people was thereby carried to the highest pitch, as they considered such conduct as sacrilegious, and a crime against their religion. Felix the governor exceeded his predecessors in severity and the shedding of blood; the juster administration of Porcius Festus was succeeded by that of Albinus, who looked on his office only as a source of gain, and even sold the administration of justice to the highest bidder. But all were surpassed by Gessius Florus, Nero's worthy favourite, who treated the unfortunate people as if he were an executioner placed over a multitude of sentenced criminals, and with premeditated malice kindled the flames of anger and revenge.

With the exception of the proselytes, the Jews had no friends amongst the heathen. Hatred and malice were the prevalent feelings towards them all about. The grounds for this bitterness, and the mixture of hatred and contempt with which they were looked upon by the Romans in particular, are revealed in the words of Tacitus. "All that we consider sacred, they look upon as godless; and on the other hand, they are permitted to do whatever seems unclean to us. Their antiquity protects certain customs (such as the Sabbath and the sabbatical year); other preposterous regulations have found value from their odious perversity. For the worst men from all places bring gifts and contributions there, though they neglect the religion of their fathers; thus the strength of the Jews waxes. They always keep their word, and are ready to show mercy, to each other, but to every one else they are full of hostility and hatred; they keep separate from all strangers in eating, sleeping, and matrimonial connexions, while every thing is allowable among themselves. Thus they have introduced circumcision to distinguish them from the rest of the world; they who join them submit to this custom; and the first thing they learn is to despise the gods, to abandon their country, and to disown their parents, children, and brethren."[1]

The strong arm of the Roman dominion alone held back the numberless enemies of the Jews. As soon as their rulers themselves, Caligula, for instance, appeared to partake in the universal antipathy, and to promise immunity for its exercise, the long-felt rage against these "enemies of the human race" broke out fearfully. Thus it was in Alexandria, where the heathen populace, excited by the behaviour of Flaccus the governor, set up idols in the Jewish synagogues, plundered and defiled the dwellings of the Jews, and tortured many of them to death. The death of Caligula gave the sufferers some little relief, and for twenty-five years they were at rest. But what happened under Nero gave occasion for fresh persecutions. Soon afterwards Cæsarea, Damascus, and many other cities containing a mixed population of Jews and Greeks, became the theatre of a warfare which was almost always kindled by trifling provocations, and in which the Jews succumbed to their more numerous enemies, and many thousands were slain.

Immorality, and an infamous tone of feeling, with all their adherence to the skeleton of the law, had mounted to such a height amongst the Jews, that there was no longer any moral counterpoise in the nation able to keep up social order amid the bad government of the Roman rulers. As there was no aristocracy, no distinction of classes, no body of citizens properly so called, the government of the people was in the hands of the Pharisees, and of the priests, who were in league with them. But there was now a split even amongst them: the one part, agreeing in their heart of hearts with the Zealots, were persuaded that the heathen rule and imposts were illegal; the other wished for peace and security, and therefore for submission. The high-priesthood had become purchasable: five families intrigued for it, with every art of bribery and corruption. Every new high-priest, being assured

[1] Hist. v. 5.

of the short duration of his power, strove to make the most he could of it, and as rapidly as possible, for the benefit of himself and his relations. Bands of armed men, levied from the Zealots, went about the country, living by robbery and plunder, who excused their misdeeds by the plea of zeal for the law, and justified their robbing and killing all peaceful subjects of the Roman dominion as adherents of Rome. The worst of all were the Sicarii, who, by concealing short daggers under their clothes, slew their victims even in public places and amid groups of people; and as they were usually undiscovered, the terror they caused was so much the greater.[1] They were afterwards organised by Manahem and Eleazar, the grandsons of Judas the Gaulonite, into bands of Zealots. Murders were of such everyday occurrence, that the Scribes did away with the trespass-offering for blood innocently shed;[2] it was impossible to kill as many animals as there were human victims slain by their fellow-men. A desecration of the temple was thought far more serious than a murder.[3]

The expectation of the promised deliverer and saviour was so universal and overstrained, that the people readily and blindly followed every agitator who professed either to be a prophet, the forerunner of the Messias, or even the Messias himself. Most of these "goetæ" and false prophets were not, properly speaking, impostors; carried away by the general infatuation, they believed themselves called to be the instruments of God, and were the first to put faith in the wonders and signs God would work through them. Thus the well-known Theudas (15 A.D.) persuaded multitudes of people to follow him to the Jordan, which would at his bidding divide and let them pass over dryfoot.[4] In the year 55 A.D., under Nero, a new prophet came out of Egypt, who aimed at overthrowing the Roman dominion, and led the numerous followers he had collected in the desert to the Mount of Olives, from whence they were to see the walls of the capital fall down.[5] In the time of Festus the governor, about 60 A.D., another prophet, whom Josephus calls a deceiver, enticed numerous bodies of men into the desert, by the promise of freeing them from all oppression.[6] Even whilst the temple was burning,

---

[1] Jos. Bell. Jud. ii. 13. 3.
[2] Sota, 17 a.; Grätz, 350.
[3] Joma, 23 a.
[4] Jos. Antiq. xx. 5. 1.
[5] Jos. Bell. Jud. ii. 13. 5.
[6] Antiq. xx. 8. 10.

6000 men followed a prophet of this sort, who promised them deliverance, and led them to a cloister of the temple. The Romans set fire to this passage, and they all perished.

When Eleazar, the commander of the temple-watch, persuaded the priests who were ministering to reject the imperial offerings, and to determine that no stranger should again be admitted to sacrifice in the temple, the signal for war was given, and the revolt was consummated. In most of the cities of Galilee and Judea the greater part of the inhabitants would have preferred peace, and with it the Roman rule, as the lesser evil; but they were without leaders, without organisation, isolated, and more inclined to be quiet and look on. The Zealots, on the other hand, ruled over the open country, drew together all who had nothing to lose, overruled the passive friends of peace by their energy, and carried along with them those who were undecided and lukewarm.

After the repulse and retreat of Gallus, the chief counsellors at Jerusalem succeeded but for a short time in defending themselves from the Zealots, and in ordering and guiding the revolt. But soon the "warriors for Jehovah, law, and freedom" triumphed, and the reign of terror began. The most eminent men were executed as traitors, or as being inclined to treason and subjection to the Roman sway. The rabbinical writings mention a meeting of the Scribes which took place at this time, and which Eleazar, the head of the Zealots, held in his own house. It was there resolved, through the preponderance of the Shammaites over the intimidated Hillelites, that no Jew was in future to buy wine, oil, bread, or any thing eatable from the heathen. No one was any more to learn a heathen language, no faith was to be attached to the testimony of a heathen, no gift for the temple was to be taken from them, and no intercourse with heathen youths or maidens was to be held. Eleazar had surrounded his house with his Zealots, with instructions to let any one in, but no one out. Some of the recusant Hillelites lost their lives, certainly by the sword of the Zealots. According to Josephus, the Jews throughout Syria refused to use heathen oil from this time.[1] The day of these "eighteen resolutions" was afterwards looked upon by the Hillelites as a calamitous

---

[1] Bell. Jud. ii. 21. 2; vii. 3. 1.

day; but they were never revoked, "as having been sealed with blood."[1]

Shammaites and Zealots thus went hand in hand, and the latter carried out the principles of the Shammaites. The Zealots, according to Josephus,[2] were particularly strict in the observance of the Sabbath, although they were far from sharing in the scruples of the Maccabees of earlier times regarding it, for they even originated attacks on the Romans on the Sabbath. Now in this we recognise the fruits of the doctrines of the Shammaites, for they taught that it was unlawful to apportion alms on the Sabbath, even for the dower of an orphan, or to offer a prayer for a sick man's relief. Yet they allowed, and even made it of obligation, to attack in battle on that day, or to besiege a town.[3] It was quite another thing in the time of Pompey, whose successful assault on Jerusalem was facilitated by the Jews abstaining from all resistance on the Sabbath.

The steadfast endurance, resignation, and bravery with which this people undertook and carried on the unequal combat against the mighty power of Rome, cannot fail to call forth admiration. The Jews had nothing approaching to an orderly or disciplined army; they had no treasure to meet a long war, and no experienced leaders and generals; they never hit off any united, firm, and comprehensive plan of action; their best strength was wasted in isolated resistance, and undertakings without object, so that the strongest ally of the Romans was to be found in the disunion of their factions. After the disarming of Galilee, all who were disposed for war had assembled in the capital. The Zealots had deposed the high-priest chosen by Agrippa, and elected by lot in his stead a rough man called Samuel, who was a stonemason. In consequence of this, most sanguinary conflicts took place between the more moderate citizens under the guidance of Ananus, and the Zealots, whose party was strengthened by the Idumeans. Thousands of corpses lay in the streets; the chiefs of the conquered citizen-party were executed or murdered. Four factions from this time began tearing each other to pieces in a frenzy of exasperation; the Jerusalem Zealots under Eleazar, the Galilean Zealots under John of Giscala, the Simonites, together with the Idumean and the Sicarian bandits.

---

[1] Jeruschalmi in Grätz, p. 558.
[2] Bell. Jud. ii. 19. 2.   [3] Grätz. p. 545.

The Romans were otherwise occupied, and prudently left Jerusalem a prey to these different parties for three years, and they meanwhile did the work of the enemy, destroying each other and consuming the stores of provisions.

At length the Romans, under Titus, stormed the town step by step, and a war of extermination began. The assertion of Josephus may be an exaggeration, that the number of those who perished during the siege by hunger and the sword amounted to a million; but it is certain that a great part of the population of Galilee and Judea were destroyed, for just before the blockade they had come up to the capital to celebrate the passover. Of the prisoners, the Zealots were put to death, and the younger captives reserved for the triumph; some were sent to the Egyptian mines, and the rest divided amongst the provinces, where they were employed in the amphitheatres as gladiators or in fighting wild-beasts, and many were sold as slaves. Those who were sold while the war lasted must have amounted to ninety thousand. On one day of the public games at Cæsarea, Titus made two thousand five hundred Jews kill each other. The vessels of the temple, the golden table, the candlestick, and the roll of the law, were also borne in his triumphal procession at Rome.

Jerusalem and the temple lay in ruins; but the desperate strife of the Zealots was not yet at an end. In Palestine, indeed, the drama was concluded by the suicide of the garrison at Masada two years after the taking of Jerusalem; but a number of Sicarii escaped to Egypt, where they endeavoured to stir up another Jewish rebellion. Six hundred of them were delivered up to the Roman cohorts by the Jews themselves, and endured the most frightful torments rather than acknowledge the emperor as their lord.[1] Vespasian then commanded the Onias temple at Heliopolis to be closed, and the Jews thus lost their last religious rallying-point. The offerings belonging to this temple were transferred to the imperial treasury. A revolt was stirred up in the district of Cyrene by Jonathan the Zealot, and it was promised that prodigies should ensue; the only result, however, was a great massacre by the Romans. Jonathan himself was burnt alive in Rome.

Israel was now without "king, princes, sacrifice, altar, ephod,

---

[1] Jos. Bell. Jud. vii. 10. 1-4.

or sanctuary." The performance of sacrificial worship had become an impossibility, so closely was it bound up with the temple and its altar; for, according to the universal teaching of the rabbis, all private sacrifices were for ever illegal, from the time Solomon's temple was dedicated. Later on, too, teachers of note declared that every one who sacrificed without the temple ought to be punished with "cutting off."[1] Even the use of serving roasted meat on the evening of the passover, as a feeble remembrance of the former sacrificial repast on that day, was reprobated by the more scrupulous Jews. Hence they said, as long as it was impossible to offer sacrifice, prayer must take its place; and by degrees the characteristics of sacrifice were transferred to prayer in the Talmud literature; but the study and exposition of the laws of the temple and of sacrifice were the principal compensations, as these laws were speedily to become available again; for the Scribes and the people continued to cling with confidence to the hopes of a speedy and miraculous restoration of the temple. God could not really intend his sanctuary, the only one on earth, to continue in ruins. He had only permitted it to become so, that by its sudden and wonderful restoration his power and glory might be more strikingly manifested, and his true people justified before the heathen. Almost from hour to hour the expectant Jew was anticipating the restoration of the temple. Was it not said in the triumphal canticle of Moses and Miriam, that the temple-mount was the inheritance God had made his habitation, the sanctuary which his hands had prepared?[2] Was this hand not to restore it again? He must do so, the Jews thought; for it was said there immediately afterwards, that "the Lord should be king for ever and ever."

It was therefore decreed that a priest was not to drink wine on the day he would have been on duty at the temple, had its regulations still continued in force;[3] for the miracle of the restoration might take place on that very day, and according to the law the priest ought to be fasting then. Proselytes were to deposit a sum of money, that the legal sacrifice might be bought with it, in case of the restoration of the temple. It was only in later times, when weary of waiting in vain, and in some degree recon-

---

[1] The proofs of this are to be found in the article of Friedmann and Grätz, Theol. Jahrbücher von Baur und Zeller, 1848, p. 344.

[2] Exod. xv. 17.   [3] Friedmann in Orient, 1849, p. 549.

ciled by habit to their situation, that they deferred this miraculous restoration of the temple to a far-off age of the Messias, and then the Scribes allowed those who were of priestly race to drink wine on the day appointed them. There were Jewish ascetics, who, in memory of the sacrificial import of partaking of meat and wine, wholly abstained from both after the destruction of the temple of Jerusalem. "Shall we eat flesh," said they, "which was once offered in the sacrifice that now has ceased? Shall we drink wine, of which drink-offerings used to be prepared, but is now no longer?"[1] Their fasts were also lamentations for the sad condition of the people; because, as proof that the God of the Romans had conquered the God of the Jews, all the Jews were compelled to pay a tribute of two drachms, which they used to pay to the temple, to that of Jupiter Capitolinus in Rome.[2] They were forced to do this with wanton severity; so that Suetonius was eye-witness to an old man of ninety being examined to see if he were circumcised or not.

Palestine was not yet depopulated, however; many of the Jews remained in their homes, as friends of the Romans; others were gradually redeemed from slavery, and returned to the land of their fathers, or else ventured to emerge out of caves, woods, and deserts; great tracts of country, especially to the east of the Jordan, were scarcely affected by the war. Jamnia and Cæsarea on the sea-coast, and Tiberias and Sephoris in Galilee, remained or became schools of Jewish scribe-learning. Jamnia and its school surpassed the rest in renown, and took the place of Jerusalem as a national and religious centre. Here a Sanhedrim again assembled, headed by a rabbi or public doctor, a kind of patriarch in fact. Priests and Levites had become for the most part insignificant; but they clung to the hope of the renewal of the temple, and the restoration of the sacred services in their full splendour; and in individual families there still existed vague traditions of a descent from Aaron. There was no more talk now, however, of a body of priests. Rabbinism, on the contrary, flourished unimpaired, continued on the succession of Pharisaism and the traditions of the old Scribes; and in them were centered all the intellectual and religious aspirations and efforts of the nation. This learned oligarchy was held together by a

---

[1] Friedmann, *ubi supra*, after Batra, 60 b.
[2] Jos. Bell. Jud. vii. 6. 6.

tenacious corporate spirit, by similarity of interests and principles, and consisted of men who, both as theologians and priests, laid claim to the guidance of consciences. They replaced to the people all other institutions now broken up, and carefully preserved the mummy of the now almost impracticable law; regulations about property, the temple-ritual sacrifice, and penal justice, impracticable as they had become, were profoundly discussed, and spun out into an ever-widening web of casuistry. The more mutilated and fragmentary the structure of the law had turned out in relation to the present state of the people, and incapable of a living organisation as heretofore, the more eagerly the rabbis strove to breathe an imaginary life into the dry bones by their interpretations and additions. This skeleton they enveloped in a complete covering of collateral decisions and resolutions to meet all possible cases; and where custom and mode of life had stepped beyond the narrow legal bounds, their school exercised its acuteness in finding out the existence, if only a fictitious one, of a harmony with the letter of the statutes.

The rebellious spirit of the Jews was not yet broken: after a forty years' rest, new and bloody wars followed, under Trajan and Hadrian. The risings of the Jews in the Cyrenaic district, in Egypt, and in Cyprus, must have originated in their bitter hatred against the heathen; for they were not at first nor immediately directed against the Roman government. In Mesopotamia, on the contrary, they only rebelled in order to shake off the yoke which Trajan had laid on them. Perhaps, as many have recently mentioned, a universal and deeply-laid plan was at the bottom, though it is difficult to say what political end it could have had but that of revenge. Dio Cassius says the Jews had risen and banded together every where; many other nations had joined them for the sake of gain; and the whole world was in commotion.[1] He also speaks of fearful cruelties and horrors perpetrated by the Jews on some Greek prisoners. They compelled Greeks and Romans to fight in the circus against each other, and with wild-beasts. They were at length subdued every where; in the last year of Trajan, A.D. 117, they were banished outright from Cyprus, where they had destroyed the town of

---

[1] Dio. Cass. lxviii. 32.

Salamis, and slaughtered great numbers. No Jew was afterwards allowed to enter the island, on pain of death.

The rebellion broke out some years later in Palestine, in the year 131 A.D., when Hadrian prohibited circumcision, and began to build a heathen city on the site of Jerusalem, under the name of Ælia Capitolina, with a temple of Jupiter on Mount Moria.[1] Both measures were calculated to drive the Jews to desperate exertions. The prohibition of circumcision was unquestionably intended to break through the wall of separation between them and the heathen, and to render their amalgamation possible. The establishment of a heathen town, with a foreign name, and the destination of places, which had been the inalienable property of God's people, to the occupation of the stranger, seemed to do away for ever with the possibility of the restoration of the holy city, the Jerusalem of the Jews, and of its temple. Then rang the tidings of the appearance of the long-expected Messias, girt with the sword, as the Jews had longed for him, to break off the Roman yoke. He styled himself, or his compatriots did for him, Bar Cochba, that is, "the son of the star;" for to him related the words of the ancient prophecy, "A star shall rise out of Jacob, and a sceptre shall come forth from Israel, and shall strike the princes of Moab."[2] Rabbi Akiba, the "second Moses," considered the greatest light in Israel of the day (the later rabbis gave him 24,000 disciples), declared before the Sanhedrim publicly, Bar Cochba to be the Messias. The only one who made any opposition was rabbi Jochanan, who said, "Akiba, grass will grow out of thy jaws, and yet the son of David not have come." St. Jerome says of Bar Cochba, that he contrived to spout fire from his mouth by a secret contrivance of lighted tow;[3] he did not require to do this any more after Akiba's declaration. He was crowned and anointed as king in the strong city of Bitther. The whole Jewish population flew to arms, and joined his standard. It seems the Jews actually obtained for a short time possession of Jerusalem, the fortified head-quarters of the Roman garrison, as the Romans were obliged to besiege and retake it A.D. 134, when for the first time it was completely destroyed and levelled with the ground. Bitther, their principal fortress, also fell, after a murderous war

---

[1] Euseb. H. E. iv. 6.   [2] Numbers xxiv. 17-19.
[3] Apol. ii. adv. Rufin.

of three years. We know not what became of Bar Cochba, or Bar Cosiba, the son of lying, as his deceived countrymen now named him. Akiba, an old gray-headed man, was made prisoner and executed. The whole land was laid desolate: about a thousand villages, and fifty fortified towns, with four hundred and eighty synagogues, were destroyed by the Romans. This second war of extermination must have been still more ruinous to the physical condition and culture of the land than the first; in fact Palestine has never recovered from it. The numbers of those who perished on the field of battle were computed at 580,000; the multitudes who perished by hunger, disease, and fire, must have been far greater. Hosts of prisoners were dragged to Terebinthe, near Hebron, and there sold at the great mart for slaves to the neighbouring nations resorting thither. Four men were sold for a few bushels of barley, or one exchanged against a horse. Others were carried to Egypt, and even as far as Spain. The whole people were forced to pay a heavy poll-tax in addition to the tax paid to the Capitoline Jupiter.

The emperor's plan of placing the heathen city of Ælia Capitolina on the site of Jerusalem was now carried out. A theatre was built, as well as public baths, and a temple of Jupiter, in which the statue of the god and that of the emperor stood side by side. The Jews were forbidden to set foot in the new city under pain of death, or even to venture near it.[1] They were at length permitted to enter it once a year, and there to lament their misfortunes, on the anniversary of the second destruction. "On the day of the destruction," says an eye-witness of later days, "one sees a weeping multitude drawing thither, feeble women, and hoary old men, pouring in with rent garments to mourn over the ruins of the temple. The soldiers demand a fee, if they wish to weep longer."[2] Hadrian's successor, Antoninus Pius, allowed them to practise the rite of circumcision again. Even this fourth blow to Jewish nationality, which followed the three catastrophes under Nabuchodonosor, Antiochus, and Titus, was not adequate to break the fast-cemented bond of their community. Only fifty years after the war under Hadrian, Judaism appeared in the form of two firmly-organised corporate bodies: the one under the patriarch at Tiberias, embracing all the Jews in the Roman

---

[1] Justin. Dial. c. Tryph. p. 116; Apol. i. p. 71.
[2] Hieron. in Zephan. c. 2.

empire; the other, to which all the Israelites of the eastern countries belonged, being under the prince of the captivity. The fate of shattered nationalities, that of being absorbed into the dominant population, was one not appointed to the Jews. They were to remain a distinct and unmixed race, for witness to the world, and as an instrument of Providence in the distant future.

INDEX.

ABLUTIONS, religious, among the Greeks, i. 220, 232.
Abortion, common among the Romans, ii. 272; forbidden among the Jews, ii. 342.
Abstinences, practised by the Eleusinian hierophant, i. 192.
Acca Larentia, nurse of Romulus, ii. 56.
Achæans, an Hellenic race, their gods and worship, i. 114.
Adam (Adonis Esmun), Samothracian mystery-god, i. 163.
Adonis (Attes), mystery-god, i. 160; identical with Osiris, Korybas, Zagreus, Adam, and Agdistis, i. 161.
Adultery among the Greeks, ii. 236; the Romans, ii. 253, sq.; the Jews, ii. 340.
Adytum, sanctuary of heathen temple, i. 239.
Æacus, Greek judge of the dead, i. 175.
Ægina, mysteries of, i. 175.
Ælia Capitolina, ii. 418.
Ænesidemus, a sceptic philosopher, i. 368.
Æolians, Greek race, their leading deities, i. 114.
Æolus, Greek god of the winds, i. 98.
Æschylus, his myth of Prometheus, i. 297.
Æsculapius (Asclepios), Greek god, i. 94; impostures practised in his temple, ii. 201.
Aerolites, rough stones fallen from heaven, worshiped, i. 69.
Africa, northern, Roman province of, its principal cities and their flourishing condition, proconsular, i. 24.
Agatho-demon (Hor-Hat), Egyptian deity, i. 448.
Age, golden, a Persian tradition, i. 397.
Agonalia, Roman festival, ii. 93.
Agræ, village near Athens, exhibition of the lesser mysteries there, i. 183, 190.
Agriculture, its importance as an element in the Roman religion, ii. 10.
Ahriman, Persian deity, the principle of evil, i. 386; relation to Ormuzd and Zervan, i. 387; his contest with light, i. 394.
Aidoneus, Greek god of the world below, i. 72.
Albania, in Caucasia, its population, i. 43.
Alcinous, one of the later Platonists, ii. 129.
Alexander, of Macedon, declared son of Jupiter Ammon, i. 485; his superstition, ii. 172.
Alexander, Jannæus, the Asmonee, ii. 318.
Alexander, of Abonoteichos, religious impostor, ii. 198.
Alexandria, later capital of Egypt, its general characteristics, i. 18.

Allat, Arabian goddess, i. 434.
Allegorical, interpretation of heathen popular gods and myths, by philosophers, i. 281; ii. 152, sq.
Altars, Roman, their position and form, ii. 89.
Ammon, Egyptian deity, i. 440; oracle of, in Libya, i. 214.
Amphitrite, Greek goddess, i. 80.
Amschaspands, the seven immortal Persian saints, i. 390.
Anahita or Anaitis, Persian and Armenian goddess of fecundity, i. 418.
Anaxagoras, his dualism, i. 267.
Anaximander, Greek philosopher, i. 250.
Anaximenes, Greek philosopher, i. 251.
Androgyne (see Hermaphrodite).
Angels, according to teaching of Old Testament, ii. 384.
Animals, see Beasts; Mosaic law for their protection, ii. 346; worship of, in Egypt, i. 454; holy kinds, i. 456; wars on account of, ib.; care of them, i. 457.
Anna Perenna, Roman goddess, ii. 54.
Anthropomorphism, the, of the Old Testament, ii. 382.
Antigonus, the Asmonee, ii. 320.
Antinous, the, deified favourite of Hadrian, ii. 168.
Antioch, city of Syria, i. 432; worship of Asiatic and Hellenic gods there, and at Daphne, ib.
Antisthenes, Greek philosopher and founder of the Cynic school, i. 306.
Antithei, demonic beings, ii. 216.
Anubis, Egyptian deity, and judge of the dead, i. 461; genius of mummies, i. 463; in connection with the Osiris worship, ii. 177.
Anuke, Egyptian goddess, i. 451.
Apathy, Stoic, i. 356; Epicurean, i. 363.
Aphrodite, Greek goddess, seat of her worship at Paphos, i. 16; blending of Cyprian and Pelasgian, extent and character of her worship, Urania and Pandemos, goddess of sensual love, i. 88-91; conf. Venus, ii. 50; impurity in her worship, ii. 192.
Apis, the sacred bull of the Egyptians, i. 458, sq.
Apollo, Greek god, his relation to Athene, his surnames and nature, i. 82; special influence through his oracle, i. 83; latterly identified with Helios the sun-god, i. 83; connected with Artemis, i. 84; the Cretan A. distinct from the Achæo-Dorian, with his relation to Dionysos, i. 114; his worship among the Romans, ii. 41.

Apollonius, Neo-Pythagorean philosopher, ii. 143.
Apotheosis, among the Greeks, i. 343; the Egyptians, i. 486; introduction into Rome, ii. 32; of the Roman Emperors, ii. 165, sq.; of women of the imperial family, ii. 167.
Apuleius, the Platonist, his views, ii. 151.
Aquitania, the Roman province of, in Gaul, i. 32.
Aquitani, the, their settlement and character in general, i. 28.
Arabians, their relations with Rome and distinctive character, i. 47; their gods and worships, i. 434.
Arcadia, in the Peloponnese, its principal gods, i. 119.
Arduina, Celtish goddess, i. 112.
Arelate, Arles, i. 131.
Ares, war-god of the Greeks, his character and cultus, i. 88.
Aristippus, Greek philosopher, originator of the Cyrenaic school and Hedonism, i. 304.
Aristophanes, his position towards the popular religion, i. 286.
Aristotle, his relation to Plato, i. 333; doctrine concerning God, and God's relation to the world of Providence, 334; his view of the stars, and link to the popular religion, doctrine of souls, 336; immortality, 338; of freedom and evil, his ethics, 340; theory of slavery, ii. 226.
Armenia, Greater, general description of the land and its population, i. 42.
Armenia, Lesser, Roman province, i. 12.
Armilustrium, a Roman festival, ii. 97.
Arnobius, on the public spectacles of Rome, ii. 195.
Arsaces, founder of the empire of the Arsacidæ, i. 44.
Artemis, Greek goddess, the Icarian, i. 69; the Hellenic joined in worship with Apollo, i. 84; her character and titles, 85; the Ephesian extent of her cultus, her temple at Ephesus, 86.
Arvales, the Arvalian brothers, ii. 11, 69.
Asclepios, god of healing, i. 97.
Asebia, impiety, sin of irreligion, its punishment among the Greeks, i. 243.
Asia Anterior, condition of, as a Roman province, i. 13.
Asia Minor, general features of, i. 11-16.
Asmoneans or Asmonees, the, their rise and times, ii. 300, 317, sq.; their cruelties, ii. 318; their fall, ii. 320.
Assyria, fate of, i. 45; its religious system, i. 420.
Astarte, the Syrian goddess, i. 428; her worship at Carthage, i. 488.
Astrolatry, its origin for the most part Chaldean, i. 422.
Astrology, the Chaldean, its wide spread and doctrines, ii. 423; finds its way into Rome, ii. 208.
Astronomy, the Chaldean, in relation to religion, i. 422.
Ataraxia, the, of the Stoics, i. 357; of Epicurus, i. 363.

Atheism of the Greek sophists, i. 271, sq.
Atheists, Greek, persecuted, i. 273.
Athene, Greek goddess, worshiped by Pelasgi as a beam of wood, i. 69; Pallas A., her character, i. 81; her worship at Athens, i. 116.
Athens, capital of Greece, gods and worships, i. 116; political condition, domination of the poor, ii. 223.
Athrava's Persian priests, i. 403.
Atmu, Egyptian god, i. 440.
Atomism of Epicureans, i. 359.
Atomistic school, its cosmology, psychology, and theology, i. 266, sq.
Atonement by blood, ii. 179; great day of, the Jewish fast, ii. 373, 376.
Attes, Attis, or Adonis, mystery-god, i. 160; his worship in Phrygia, in Bithynia, and Lydia, i. 376.
Augurs, their powers and privileges, ii. 72.
Augury, Roman system of, ii. 102.
Augustales, Roman priests, ii. 69.
Augustalia, Roman festival, ii. 97.
Augustus, Octavianus, sole ruler of the Roman empire, i. 4, sq.; his deification, ii. 32, 165; his high priesthood, ii. 33.
Auspicia, Roman divination by birds, ceremonies in taking, ii. 103, sq.; as instrument of policy, ii. 22; as means of inquiring into the will of the gods, its kinds, ii. 103, sq.; Greek method of, i. 207.
Averrunci, a species of gods, ii. 207.
Axieros, Pelasgian deity, i. 73.
Axiokersos and Axiokersa, Pelasgian deities, i. 73.
Axumitic empire, i. 48.

BAAL, extensive signification of the name, i. 425; the Moloch of the Canaanites, his worship of child-sacrifice, i. 426; identical with the Dionysos Omestes of Chios and Tenedos, i. 156.
Baal-Melkarth, city-god of Tyre, i. 427.
Baalbec (Heliopolis), city of Syria, i. 20.
Babylon, the metropolis of heathendom, i. 421; its destruction, i. 460.
Babylonia, situation of the country and its population, i. 46.
Bacchanalia, origin of among the Greeks, translation of, to Italy, i. 157; their suppression and corrupting influence, ii. 28.
Bacchus-Dionysos, the Roman Liber, ii. 51.
Bactria, country and kingdom, i. 50.
Barbarians, in opposition to Greeks, ii. 218.
Bar Cochba, ii. 418.
Bards, the Gallic, religious minstrels, ii. 109.
Beasts, Mosaic law for protection of, ii. 346; clean and unclean, ii. 376.
Bel, principal god of Babylon, temple of, i. 422.
Belenus, Celtic deity, ii. 112.
Belgians, a race of people, i. 28.
Belgica, the Roman province, its extent and population, i. 32.
Belisana, Gallic goddess, ii. 112.

Bellona, Roman goddess, her fanatical worship, ii. 174.
Bellonarii, priests of Bellona, ii. 174.
Berytus, city of Phœnicia (Beyrout), i. 21.
Birds, for divination, their division, &c. among the Romans, ii. 103; Greek observation of, i. 207.
Bithynia, the Roman province of, i. 11.
Bliss in the next world, teaching of the Eleusinian mysteries, i. 196, sq.; according to Pindar and the Orphici, i. 301; of the Persians, i. 409; Egyptians, i. 465; Cicero, ii. 140, sq.; Plutarch and the later Greeks, ii. 145. (See Soul.)
Blood considered as a means of expiation for sin by the heathen, i. 226, ii. 179; poured about the altar, i. 232; how dealt with by the Jews, ii. 368.
Blood, vengeance of, in the Mosaic law, ii. 347.
Bona Dea, her character and secret worship, ii. 44.
Books, the holy, of the Etruscans, ii. 4; ritual ones of the Romans, ii. 18; spurious ones of Numa, ii. 28; holy ones of the Jews, ii. 377.
Bodies, dead (see Corpses).
Body, the human, only a prison of the soul, according to Plato, i. 315; its resurrection according to Persian belief, i. 411.
Boreas, Greek god, i. 98.
Brahminism, its contest with Buddhism, i. 53.
Brahmins, Indian caste, i. 51.
Branchidæ, oracle of, at Didymi, ii. 203.
Britain, its romanising, towns, population, i. 33-35.
Britons, their character in general, i. 34.
Buddhism, doctrines of, and its relation to Brahminism, i. 53; expulsion of, from India, i. 54; penetrates into China, i. 58.
Bull, the primeval, of the Persians, i. 396; sacrifice of the Osiris-bull, i. 475; an attribute of Mithras, i. 415.
Bulls, the four divine, of the Egyptians, i. 458.
Burnt sacrifice among the Greeks, i. 231; among the Jews, ii. 368.

CABIRI, pre-Hellenic gods of Phœnician origin, i. 73; in the Samothracian mysteries, i. 166; meaning of the name, i. 166; their names, i. 169; Lemnian Cabiri, i. 170.
Cadmilos, Samothracian mystery-god, i. 167; Hermes Cadmilos, i. 73, 167, 169.
Cæsars, the Roman, deification of, ii. 165, sq. (see Emperors).
Cæsar, Julius, conquers Gaul, i. 27; deified at Rome, ii. 32.
Cæsarea, city of Judea, i. 23.
Camullus, Celtic war-god, ii. 112.
Candace, name of the Nubian queens, i. 48.

Capitoline Temple at Rome, building of, ii. 19.
Cappadocia, the Roman province of, inhabitants of cities of, i. 12; its cultus, i. 377.
Captivity, Assyrian and Babylonian, ii. 293; return from, ii. 294.
Caria, Roman province, its cities, i. 14.
Carian idolatry, i. 374.
Carmenta, Roman goddess, ii. 57.
Carmentalia, Roman festival, ii. 93.
Carneades, sceptic philosopher, i. 367.
Carthage, site of old, accursed, i. 24; new, i. 24.
Carthaginian religious system, i. 488.
Castes, Indian division into, i. 51.
Cave of Trophonius, the place of an oracle, i. 215.
Celsus, platonising philosopher, i. 151.
Celtiberians, race of people in Spain, i. 26.
Celts, i. 27.
Cerealia, a Roman festival, ii. 95.
Ceremonial system of the Romans, ii. 15.
Ceres (Demeter), a Roman goddess, ii. 43.
Ceylon (Taprobane), i. 55.
Chaldæans, the, in Babylon, their religious system, i. 421, sq.
Charistia, a Roman festival, ii. 94.
Charites, Greek goddesses, i. 98.
Charræ (Haran), a city of Mesopotamia, said to be the starting-point of Heathenism, i. 45; its idolatrous system, i. 433.
Charun, the Etruscan Charon, ii. 3.
Chasidim, a Jewish faction, ii. 301.
Chem, an Egyptian god, i. 443.
Cherubim, ii. 385.
Chests, the holy, in the mysteries, i. 188.
Child-murder punished with death by the Jews, ii. 342.
Children, exposition of (chytrism), among the Greeks, ii. 246; among the Romans, ii. 271; sacrifice of, as practised by Canaanites and Syrians, i. 426; by Arabians, i. 434; by Carthaginians, i. 488; for magical purposes, ii. 214.
Chiliasm, Persian, i. 410.
China, history and population of, general constitution of the empire, i. 55, sq.; gloomy character of its religion helps the spread of Buddhism, i. 58.
Chresmologoi, interpreters of oracles, i. 218.
Chthonios, a title of Hermes, i. 167, 170; of Dionysos, i. 147.
Chytrism, the exposition of children among the Greeks, ii. 246.
Cicero, as philosopher, ii. 119; his sceptical eclecticism, ii. 120; his doctrine concerning God, ii. 121; his ethics, ii. 122; views upon state religion, ii. 123; and immortality of the soul, ii. 141.
Cimri (or Kymri), their settlements, i. 27, 33.
Cilicia, as a Roman province, i. 15.
Circumcision universal among the Egyptians, i. 473; among the Jews, ii. 349.
Claros, a site of an oracle, ii. 202.

Clean and unclean beasts, according to the law of Moses, i. 376.
Clusius, a surname of Janus, ii. 36.
Cneph, an Egyptian god, i. 441.
Colchis and the Colchians, i. 43.
Communion in the Eleusinian mysteries, i. 188; among the Persians through the Homa, i. 402; through the sacrifice of a child at Haran, i. 434.
Community of wives among the ancient Britons, i. 34; in Sparta, ii. 235.
Compita, the parishes of Rome, ii. 21.
Compitalia, a Roman festival, ii. 21, 98.
Complices, Etruscan gods, ii. 2.
Confarreation, the solemn marriage-form of the Romans, ii. 254.
Cong-fu-tse, or Confucius, suppression of his doctrine and sect, i. 56.
Conscience, absence of the idea of, in Pagan antiquity, ii. 221.
Consecrations (see Mysteries and Theopnea), ii. 184.
Consentes, Etruscan gods, ii. 2.
Consivius, a surname of Janus, ii. 36.
Consualia, a Roman festival, ii. 97.
Consus, a Roman god, ii. 52.
Continence of hierophant, i. 192.
Cora, a Samothracian mystery-goddess, i. 167; an Eleusinian goddess, i. 129.
Corinth, mysteries of the isthmus of, i. 173.
Cornutus, a Roman philosopher, ii. 127.
Corpses, considered as defiling, i. 220, 408, ii. 90; their treatment by the Persians, i. 408; by the Egyptians, i. 463; by the Romans, ii. 89.
Corsica, the Roman province of, i. 11.
Corybas, a Greek mystery-god, i. 161; his mysteries at Lemnos, i. 165; the Corybantes, i. 167.
Cosmogony, doctrine of the creation of the world (which see).
Costi, the girdle of the Persians, i. 405.
Courtesans in Greece, i. 91, ii. 237.
Creation (see World).
Crete, the principal deities of the island of, i. 119; its inhabitants, i. 16.
Criobolium, a bloody rite of atonement, ii. 179.
Critias, a Greek philosopher and statesman, i. 271.
Cronidæ, the, divide the world amongst them, i. 77.
Cronos, a Greek god, i. 76.
Curetes, divine beings of the Greeks, connected with the Cabiri, i. 167.
Curiones, ministers of religion at Rome, ii. 63.
Cybele, a Phrygian goddess, character and seat of her worship, i. 102; her relation to the mysteries of Samothrace, i. 168; her famed symbolical representation at Phlya, i. 176; her worship in Phrygia, i. 374; in Bithynia and Lydia, i. 376; in Lycaonia, i. 377.
Cynics, a Greek philosophical school, i. 306.
Cypra, name of the Etruscan Juno, ii. 3.
Cyprus, its population and principal towns, i. 16; its deities, i. 120.

Cyrenaics, a Greek philosophical school, i. 304.
Cyrene, a city of Africa, i. 24.

Dact, the Dacian race, i. 39.
Dadouchoi, or torch-bearers in the Eleusinian mysteries, i. 177.
Dagon, chief god of the Philistines, i. 432.
Damascus, an ancient city of Cœle-Syria, i. 20.
Dardanos, one of the Cabiri, i. 169.
David, king of the Jews, ii. 292.
Days, lucky or unlucky according to Roman superstition, ii. 92.
Dea-Dia, a Roman goddess, ii. 55.
Dead bodies (see Corpses).
Degrees, or steps in the Mithras mysteries, i. 416.
Deification (see Apotheosis).
Deisidaimonia (see Superstition).
Delphic oracle, i. 210.
Demeter, a Greek goddess, originally one of the lower world, i. 73; goddess of agriculture, i. 91; the Samothracian, i. 168; the Eleusinian, i. 178; her myth represented in the Eleusinian mysteries, i. 185; her worship in the Thesmophoria, i. 200, sq.; her oracle at Patræ, i. 215.
Demigods of the Greeks, i. 106, sq.
Demiurge, the creator of the world in Plato's system, i. 308, 330.
Democritus, a Greek atomist, i. 266.
Demonology of Plato, i. 314; Empedocles, i. 264; the Persians, i. 391, 394; Plutarch, ii. 134; Maximus of Tyre, ii. 150; Apuleius, ii. 151; Celsus, ii. 151; its connection with magic, ii. 210, 212.
Demon, the, of Socrates, i. 278.
Demons, belief and doctrine of the Greeks generally concerning, and the kinds of, i. 103.
Derceto, a Philistine deity, i. 432.
Destiny or fate, according to the views of the Greeks, i. 291; of the Stoics, i. 350; deities of, among Greeks, i. 99; among Romans, ii. 47, 57.
Determinism in Plato, i. 318 (compare Freedom).
Dews, the, evil spirits of the Persians, i. 390.
Diagoras, a Greek philosopher, persecuted as an atheist, i. 273.
Diana, a Roman goddess, ii. 49.
Dicæarchus, a Greek philosopher who denied immortality, i. 346.
Didymi, the seat of a famous oracle, ii. 203.
Diocæsarea, capital of Galilee, i. 23.
Diogenes of Apollonia, Greek philosopher, i. 251; of Sinope, a cynic, i. 306.
Dionysius of Halicarnassus, his judgment upon the Roman religion, ii. 135, 136.
Dionysos, a Greek god, origin and influence of his worship, i. 93, 342; D. Omestes, i. 94, 156; his nature-character in Asia, i. 95; D. Zagreus, a god of the lower world, his cultus in rivalry with that of Orpheus, i. 96, 139;

connected with that of Apollo, i. 142; D. Helios, distinct from the god of wine, i. 143; D. Zagreus, i. 146, sq.; as a centre of the Orphic teaching, i. 158; general view of the forms of the Dionysic worship and festivals in Greece, i. 156; D. one with Adonis, Osiris, Corybas, &c., i. 145, sq.; not to be confused with the Thracian god of wine, i. 180; or with the Theban, i. 181; diffusion of his worship, i. 94.

Dioscuri, Greek heroes, i. 109; their relation with the Cabiri, i. 167; their number and names, i. 169.

Diospolis (Thebes), a city of Egypt, i. 19.

Dis, the Roman god of the lower world, ii. 52.

Divination, i. 206; by oracles, i. 209, sq.; favoured by Stoics, i. 354; media of, among the Romans, ii. 99, sq.; belief in, ii. 204, sq.; among the Jews, by Urim and Thummim, ii. 355.

Divorce, among the Greeks, ii. 236; Romans, ii. 254; Jews, ii. 339.

Dodona, oracle of, i. 214.

Dog, the animal held in greatest veneration by the Persians, i. 398.

Donar or Thunaer, a German god, ii. 115.

Dorians, a Greek race, their principal deities, i. 114.

Dreams, prophetic, belief of antiquity in, ii. 207.

Drink-offerings among the Jews, ii. 371.

Druidesses, priestesses of the Gauls, ii. 109.

Druids, Celtic priests, i. 28, 29; priests of the Britons, i. 34; their dignity and power in Gaul, ii. 108; their doctrine of a future state, ii. 110; their suppression by the Romans, ii. 113.

Dusares, an Arabian god, i. 434.

Ears of corn, a symbol of Adonis and the resurrection, i. 188.

Earth, goddess of, worship paid to her by the Pagans generally, i. 67; by the Persians, i. 393; by the Pelasgians, i. 70; by the Romans, ii. 43; by the Germans (Nerthus), ii. 115.

Eclecticism at the fall of Greek philosophy, i. 372; of Cicero, ii. 120.

Education, methods of, among Greeks, ii. 231; and Romans, ii. 279.

Eëtion, one of the Cabiri, i. 169.

Egeria, the nymph, Numa's counsellor, ii. 57.

Egypt, general features of the country and its inhabitants, i. 17; its system of gods, and the origin of it, i. 437, sq.; particular deities, i. 440; animal worship, i. 454, sq.; doctrine of a future state, i. 460, sq.; festivals, i. 467, sq.; priesthood, i. 470, sq.; sacrificial system, i. 474, sq.; gloomy and exclusive character (of system), i. 476; impression on strangers, i. 177; priestly disciplina arcani, i. 479; fate, destiny, and development of religion, i. 482, sq.; deification of her kings, i. 486.

Eileithuia (or Ilithuia), goddess of birth, i. 117, ii. 450; city of same name in Egypt, ii. 450.

Elagabalus, a Syrian sun-god, i. 431.

Eleats, Greek philosophers, their doctrines, i. 259, sq.

Elements, worship of, among the heathen generally, i. 66; among the Persians, i. 391.

Eleusinian mysteries, their origin and establishment, i. 176; relations with the female Cereal deities, i. 178; with Dionysos, i. 180; order and programme of the solemnity, i. 184, sq.; brilliant scenic representations in, i. 187; mystical symbols and formulæ of, i. 188, sq.; degrees of initiation, and their necessary purifications, i. 191, sq.; exclusion of non-Greeks, i. 194; obligation of silence, i. 194; their charm, i. 196; effects produced by them, i. 197.

Elohim, a name of God, its meaning, ii. 380.

Empedocles, a Greek philosopher, his philosophico-didactic poem, i. 262; pantheistic cosmology, i. 263; migration of souls, i. 264.

Emperors, deification of Roman, ii. 165.

Empiricism of the Epicureans, i. 358.

Ennius, a Roman poet, his attitude towards the Roman religion, ii. 26.

Eos, a Greek goddess, i. 98.

Ephesus, a city of Asia Minor, i. 13; its cultus and temple of Artemis, i. 86.

Epibomius, a minister of the altar at the Eleusinia, i. 177.

Epicharmus, a Greek philosopher, i. 286.

Epictetus, a Roman Stoic philosopher, practical tendency of his philosophy, its echoes in Christianity, ii. 128.

Epicurean, ideal of the wise man, i. 364.

Epicurus, a Greek philosopher, venerated by his disciples, his teaching, canonic, and empirism, i. 358; his physics, i. 359; atomism, his material doctrine of the soul, i. 360; of the gods, i. 360; his ethics and adoption of liberty, i. 362; teaching in regard to bliss, i. 363.

Epimenides, the oldest of the Orphici, i. 151.

Epoptæ, the initiated in the Eleusinia, i. 187.

Epopteia, the third leading division of the Eleusinia, i. 184, 187.

Epulones, Roman priests, ii. 63.

Erinyes, Greek goddesses, i. 99.

Eriunies, title of Hermes, i. 107.

Eros, the orderer of the universe, and god of love, i. 96.

Esmun, a son of Baal, i. 167.

Essenes, their rise, ii. 310; ascetic discipline, ii. 311; zeal for the law, and purity, ii. 312, sq.; worship of the sun, ii. 314; ordinances, ii. 314; their position towards the prevalent Judaism, ii. 316.

Ethics, the, of Socrates, i. 275; of the Cyrenaics, i. 304; of the Cynic and Megarian schools, i. 316; of Plato, i. 322; Aristotle, i. 346; of the Greek Stoics, i. 355; of the Epicureans, i. 362;

of the Persians, i. 404 ; of the Roman Stoics, Seneca, ii. 125 ; Epictetus, ii. 128 ; Cicero, ii. 120.
Ethiopia, its history and general state of civilisation, i. 48.
Etrusci, their gods and religion, ii. 1, sq.
Euclides, a Greek mathematician and philosopher, i. 306.
Eudaimonism, a doctrine of the Cyrenaic school, i. 304.
Euhemerus, the philosopher, his explanation of the origin of the gods, i. 345.
Eumenides, or Erinnyes, i. 100.
Eunuchs at the Jewish court, ii. 344.
Euripides, the Greek poet, his expressions about the gods, i. 287. sq
Evil, Greek views of, i. 294 ; Plato's, i. 321 ; Aristotle's, i. 340 ; Stoical (Greek), i. 351 ; Stoical (Roman), Seneca's, ii. 126 ; Plutarch's, ii. 133 ; the later Platonists', ii. 153 ; doctrine of, in Old Testament, ii. 387.
Exoleti, impure youths among the Romans, ii. 274.
Expiations for sin, extraordinary, by blood, ii. 179.
Exposition of children, in Greece, ii. 246 ; in Rome, ii. 271.
Ezra (Esdras), restorer and legislator of the Jewish state, ii. 298.

FACTIONS (or parties) among the Jews, ii. 325.
Fall, the, as represented by the Greeks, i. 295 ; by the Persians, i. 397 ; by the holy Scripture, ii. 387.
Family gods (Penates) of the Greeks, i. 241 ; of the Etruscans, ii. 3 ; of the Romans, ii. 59.
Family pedigree, importance of among the Jews, ii. 338.
Fanatici, priests and priestesses of Bellona, ii. 174 ; other possessed persons, ii. 182.
Fast, nine days, of the mystæ in the Eleusinia, i. 186 ; in worship of Isis, ii. 177.
Fast-days of the Jews, ii. 376.
Fata Scribunda, a Roman goddess, ii. 57.
Fatalism (see Destiny and Liberty), views of, among Pharisees and Essenes, ii. 309.
Fate (see Destiny).
Fauns, Roman wood-god, and the Fauns, ii. 37.
Feasts or festivals of the Greeks, i. 235 ; of the Persians, i. 402 ; of the Romans, ii. 92 sq. ; of the Jews, ii. 373 ; games at, i. 238.
Februatio, a Roman festival, ii. 94.
Feciales, Roman priests, their functions, ii. 74.
Female sex, its position and occupations among the Greeks, i. 233, sq. ; among the Romans, ii. 253, sq. ; among the Jews, ii. 341 ; its profound debasement, ii. 276.
Feralia, Roman festival of the dead, ii. 90.
Feriæ, Roman festival-times, ii. 92.

Ferwers, a kind of guardian angels in the Persian religion, i. 391.
Fetishes, rude representations of gods among the Pelasgians, i. 69 ; among the Romans, ii. 18 ; among the Germans, ii. 114.
Finnish race, i. 63.
Fire, holy to the Persians, i. 391, sq. ; of Vesta, ii. 45, 71 ; the great fire of purification at the end of the world, i. 412.
Fire-worship of Hestia among the Greeks, i. 72 ; of Vesta among the Romans, ii. 45 ; of the Cabiri, i. 73 ; in Cappadocia, i. 378 ; a leading feature in the Persian religion, i. 392 ; tradition as to its origin, i. 382.
Flamines, Roman priests, peculiar ordinances for, ii. 66.
Flocks and gardens, Roman gods of, ii. 55.
Flora, a Roman goddess, her worship, ii. 55.
Floralia, a Roman festival, ii. 96.
Florus, Gessius, governor of Judea, ii. 409.
Fontus, a Roman god, ii. 36.
Fordicidia, a Roman festival, ii. 95.
Forgiveness of sins, in the Old Testament, ii. 388.
Fornacalia, a Roman festival, ii. 94.
Fortuna, a Roman goddess, her nature and cultus, ii. 47.
Fowls, method of divination from, ii. 105.
Freedmen in Rome, their prevalence there, ii. 268.
Freedom of the individual in regard to the state, according to the Greek idea, ii. 220 ; according to the Roman idea, ii. 251.
Free-will (or liberty), man's, not admitted by Plato, i. 318 ; by Aristotle, i. 340 ; the Stoics, i. 351 (compare pp. 350 and 291, sq.).
Fulguratores, Roman observers of lightning, ii. 102.

GÆOLATRY, worship of the earth, in general, i. 67 (see Earth).
Gaia, Ga, or Ge, i. 70 (see Earth).
Gaion, i. 70.
Galatia, the Roman province of, i. 15.
Galilee, its inhabitants and most important cities, i. 22.
Galli, the, mutilated priests of Cybele, i. 376, ii. 178.
Gallia, Gaul, the Roman province, its mixed population, and their character, division and towns of, i. 27, sq.
Games and public spectacles, their obscenity, religious acts, ii. 195.
Gauls, the, their character, their romanising, i. 29 ; their religion, Druidism, ii. 108.
Genii of the Etruscans, ii. 3, 62 ; of the Romans, ii. 62.
Genius, indefinite nature of the idea of, ii. 61.
German confederations, i. 59 ; character and civilisation, i. 61 ; religious system, ii. 113.

Germans, the, their different races, their settlements in the Roman period, distinct from the Celts, their division into three great branches, i. 59, sq.

Germany, in the time of the Romans, extent, division, and towns of, i. 33.

Gladiatorial games, their connection with human sacrifice, ii. 86; universal among the Romans, ii. 195; their origin and spread, ii. 265.

God, according to the Pythagoreans, i. 255; according to the Mosaic law, ii. 380, sq.; of Socrates, i. 276; of Plato, i. 308; of Aristotle, i. 334; of the Stoics, i. 349.

Gods, mother of the, the Idæan, her worship, ii. 178 (see Cybele).

Gods, the heathen, nature-powers, i. 65, sq.; allegorical interpretations of, by Greek philosophers, i. 281, sq.; by the later Platonists, ii. 152, 3; views of poets and historians upon the popular gods, i. 284; of Aristophanes, i. 286; Euripides, i. 287; Sophocles, i. 290; Euhemerus of Sicily, i. 345; jealousy of gods, i. 291; their position in regard to fate, i. 291; blending of their worship (theocrasy), i. 164, 342; grand distinction of Asiatic and Greek, i. 373; Jewish view of the heathen gods, ii. 384; images of, at first very rude, i. 69, 240; latterly very artistic, i. 240; consecration of, or Theopœa, i. 241, ii. 184; the Penates, i. 241; images prayed to immediately, i. 241; ii. 185; degrading effect of, from their obscenity, ii. 196; images of, their prohibition in the law of Moses, ground and extension of this, ii. 363, sq.

Gods, the Greek, system of polytheism, its origin, i. 74; the Olympic system of, i. 77.

Goetæ, religious impostors, ii. 198, sq.

Golden age, Persian belief in, i. 397.

Gorgias, the Greek sophist, i. 271.

Government of the Romans, its character, i. 41.

Governors, cruelty of Roman, in Judea, ii. 409.

Grace divine, in the Old Testament, ii. 388.

Graces, the Charites, Greek goddesses, i. 98.

Grave, its importance in the eyes of Egyptians, i. 463.

Great goddess (see Cybele).

Greater Armenia (see Armenia).

Greece, fall of, under Roman conquest, i. 7; social and moral state of, ii. 217, sq.; demoralisation of, ii. 247.

Greek citizenship, ii. 217, sq.; party contests in, ii. 220; idea of freedom in Greek state, ii. 220.

Greek international law, ii. 219.

Greek language and civilisation, i. 40; spread and influence of, on India, i. 49; on Egypt, i. 485; on the Jews, ii. 297; on the Romans, particularly on their religious system, ii. 18, 20, 25.

Greek philosophy, i. 247, sq.

Greek religion, its gods and their worship, i. 65-123.

Greeks, their hostility to barbarians, ii. 218; their aversion to work, ii. 224.

Groves, sacred, of the Gauls and Germans, ii. 116.

Guardian spirits of the Greeks, i. 103.

HADES, Greek god of the lower world, i. 72-93; the lower world itself, Greek notions of, ii. 145; Hebrew notions of, ii. 389 (compare Bliss and Soul).

Hapi-Mou, an Egyptian god, i. 449.

Haran, i. 433 (see Charræ).

Har-Horus, an Egyptian god, i. 447.

Harpocrates, an Egyptian god, i. 447.

Haruspices, Roman inspectors of sacrifices for soothsaying purposes, ii. 72, 99, sq.; diviners also from lightning, ii. 102.

Hathor, the Egyptian goddess Aphrodite, i. 451.

Hatred borne by the Heathens to the Jews, ii. 409.

Heathenism, originated in the deification of nature, i. 65; assumes a variety of forms, i. 66; element-worship, astrolatry, i. 66; gœolatry, i. 67.

Heathens, longing of the, for a saviour, ii. 289.

Hebe, a Greek goddess, i. 97.

Hecate, a Greek goddess, signification of her name, i. 101; the principal goddess of the Æginetan mysteries, i. 175; her appearance evoked by religious impostures, ii. 199.

Hecatombs, among the Greeks, i. 230; among the Romans, ii. 80.

Hedge of the law, ii. 299, 331, &c.

Hedonism, the doctrine of the Cyrenaics concerning virtue and happiness, i. 304.

Hegesias, a Greek philosopher, his teaching, i. 305.

Heliopolis, a city of Egypt, i. 19; (Baalbec) a city of Syria, i. 20.

Hellas and Hellenes (see Greece and Greeks).

Hellenism, in the Roman empire, i. 40, ii. 18, 25; in Egypt, i. 485; among the Jews, ii. 297.

Helots, their legal position, ii. 229.

Hephæstos, the Greek god, his worship at Lemnos, i. 73; at Athens, i. 170; his nature, i. 91.

Hera, a Greek goddess, worshiped by the Pelasgi under the form of a log, i. 71; originally a nature-goddess, becomes later the wife of Zeus, i. 79.

Heracles, the Greek national hero, i. 107; the Lydian sun-god, i. 379; the Roman, ii. 58.

Heraclitus, a Greek philosopher, his pantheistic teaching, his contempt for the popular religion, and his school, i. 252, sq.

Herald, the, in his liturgical character at the Eleusinia, i. 177.

Hercules, the Roman demi-god (see Heracles).

Hermæ, their form and origin, i. 71.
Hermaphrodite deities, first conception of, i. 67; how to be accounted for among the Egyptians, i. 440.
Hermes, a Greek god, honoured by the Pelasgi under the form of a phallus, god of fructification, i. 71.
Hermes, Cadmilos, i. 73; the Greek, i. 167, 169; the Egyptian, i. 445, 446, 448; the Roman Mercury, ii. 43.
Herod Agrippa I. becomes king of Palestine, i. 22, ii. 323.
Herodotus, his relation to the Greek religion, i. 285.
Herod the Great, his character, i. 22; his nomination as king of Judea, ii. 320; his heathen innovations, his building of the Temple, and cruelties, ii. 321, sq.
Heroes, demi-gods, their multitude, power, and worship among the Greeks, i. 104; their worship originally unknown to the Romans, ii. 12.
Hero of Alexandria, his instructions how to practise religious impostures, ii. 200.
Hesiod, the Greek poet, his theogony, its relation to the Homeric, i. 75, 76.
Hestia, the Greek fire and hearth goddess, i. 72, 87 (see Vesta, ii. 45).
Hesus, a Gallic deity, ii. 112.
Hetairai, courtesans, at Corinth, i. 91; their position and importance in Greece, ii. 237.
Hierapolis, a Syrian city, famed for its cultus of Atargatis, i. 20.
Hierodouloi, priestesses of the goddess Ma in Cappadocia, i. 377; of Anahita, i. 419; of Ammon, i. 473.
Hierophant, the priest of the Eleusinia, i. 177; bound to perpetual continence, i. 192.
High-priest of the Jews, his vestments, ii. 355; his power, ii. 358; his deposition from office, ii. 327.
High-priesthood, Jewish, its design and importance, i. 355.
Hillel, a Jewish doctor, his school, ii. 334.
Holiness, the scope of the law, an essential in the Jewish people, ii. 335.
Holocausts, burnt sacrifices of the Greeks, i. 231.
Homa, a drink, its effects and meaning, i. 400, sq.; the juice a means of immortality, i. 401; a kind of communion, i. 402.
Homa-sacrifice, the Persian, i. 400.
Homer, his relation to the Greek religion, i. 75, 76.
Honover, the creative word, according to the Persian religion, i. 386.
Horace, his religious views, ii. 138.
Hor-hat, an Egyptian god, i. 447.
Horoscope, idea of, ii. 209.
Horoscopi, Egyptian astrologers, i. 472.
Horus, an Egyptian god, i. 447.
Hours, Greek deities, i. 98.
Household gods (Lares, Penates) of the Greeks, i. 211; their worship, i. 212; of the Romans, ii. 59.

Hubal, an Arabian god, i. 435.
Human race, the origin of, according to Greek myth, i. 296; Persian, i. 396, sq.; Greek and Roman philosophers' notion, ii. 144; to holy Scripture, ii. 386.
Human sacrifice, among the Greeks, in the worship of Dionysos, i. 74; of Poseidon, i. 80; of Artemis, i. 85; its meaning, i. 226, sq.; annual, i. 228; in Arabia, i. 435; at Carthage, i. 488; in the worship of Faunus, Jupiter, &c., ii. 37, 85, 91; afterwards replaced by an unbloody substitute among the Romans, ii. 85; remains of, in later times, ii. 86; among the Gauls, ii. 110; magical, ii. 214.
Hyrcanus, John, the Asmonee, i. 317.

Iacchos (see Dionysos).
Iberia, the modern Georgia, i. 43.
Idæan mother of the gods, her cultus, ii. 178.
Ideas, Plato's doctrine of, ii. 308.
Idolatry of the Greeks and Romans, ii. 185; paid to stones, ii. 186.
Idols (see Gods).
Illyria, the Roman province of, i. 36.
Images (see Gods).
Immortality of the soul (see Soul).
Imperial religion, idea of, ii. 160, sq.; how it grew up, and stood towards others, ii. 162.
Impiety (see Religion).
Imprecations, Greek, i. 224.
Impurity, in association with the heathen worship in the temples, i. 377, 428, 431, 432; ii 197 (see Paiderastia).
Incubation, what, i. 215.
India, division of, and first acquaintance with, i. 49; general characteristics of the people of, i. 52; system of castes, i. 51; Brahminism and Buddhism, i. 51, 53; influence of the Greeks, i. 54.
Indigitamenta, ritual books of the Romans, ii. 15.
Inspection of entrails of victims, or extispicium, Greek, i. 207; Roman, ii. 100.
Instruction, system of, Greek, ii. 232; Roman, ii. 279.
Insurrections of the Jews, ii. 410.
Intercourse, sexual, Jewish legislation concerning, ii. 342.
Interest, Jewish law concerning, ii. 345.
Interpreters of oracles, i. 215; of the Sibylline books, ii. 74.
Iris, a Greek goddess, ii. 98.
Isauria, the Roman province of, i. 15.
Isis, Egyptian goddess, her nature and worship, i. 444; her festivals, i. 467, sq.; her worship in Rome, ii. 174, 176.
Israel, kingdom of, its separation from Judah, its fall, ii. 293.
Isthmian mysteries, i. 173.
Italy, its depopulation, ii. 9; northern favourably distinguished from middle and southern, ii. 10.
Izeds, the Persian genii, i. 390.

INDEX.   429

JAMNIA, Sanhedrim and school there, ii. 416.
Jannæus, the Asmonee, ii. 318.
Janus, an Etruscan god. ii. 3; a Roman, ii. 35; his temple, ii. 37.
Japan, civilised from China, i. 53.
Jasion, one of the Cabiri, i. 169.
Jason, or Jesus, buys the office of high-priest, ii. 300.
Jehovah, a name of God, its meaning, ii. 380.
Jealousy of the gods, i. 285.
Jerusalem in the Roman time, i. 23; destroyed by Nabucodonosor, ii. 293; rebuilt, ii. 295; factions in Jerusalem, and their contests, ii. 412, sq.; conquest of, by Titus, ii. 414.
Jewish law, ii. 335; priesthood, ii. 352, sq.; nazaritism, ii. 358; prophets, ii. 359; sacrifices, ii. 366; festivals, ii. 373; religious doctrines, ii. 377, sq.
Jewish state, its historical development, ii. 291, sq.; parties and sects within it, ii. 301, sq.; the times of the Asmonees, Herodians, and Roman supremacy, ii. 317, sq.; corruption, ii. 410; decline and fall, ii. 439, sq.
Jubilee, Jewish year of, ii. 350.
Judæa, or Palestine, i. 21; under the Roman domination, i. 22; general description of the country, i. 22, 23.
Judah, the kingdom of, short sketch of its history, ii. 291; kings of, their establishment, ii. 292; their position in regard to the law, ii. 337.
Judaism among the pagans, ii. 181.
Judges of the dead, among the Greeks, i. 175; Egyptians, i. 461; Etruscan, ii. 3.
Juno, Etruscan goddess, ii. 2; Roman goddess, ii. 48; her surnames, ii. 49.
Jupiter, Etruscan god, ii. 2; Roman god, ii. 39.
Jurisprudence, Jurisprudents, wanting among the Greeks, ii. 223.
Jus gentium, jus privatum (see Roman law), ii. 251.

KAIOMORTS, the first man according to the Persian myth, i. 396; the first also to rise again, i. 411.
Kings, their apotheosis in Egypt, i. 486.
Kymri (see Cimri).

LABOUR, aversion to, among the nations of antiquity, and the Greeks in particular, ii. 224.
Lagidæ, their relation to Egypt, i. 485; their religion, their deification, i. 487.
Laodicea, a city of Syria, i. 20.
Lares, Etruscan genii, ii. 3; Roman genii distinct from Penates, ii. 60; their different kinds, ii. 61.
Larentalia, a Roman festival, ii. 98.
Latin language, its spread and prevalence, i. 40.
Laureacum, a city of Noricum, i. 35.
Laverna, a Roman goddess, ii. 54.
Law, the Mosaic, the principle of love in it, ii. 335; what it embraces, ii. 336, sq.; right of interpretation, ii. 337;

spirit of fidelity to the, ii. 332; esteem for teachers of, ii. 299.
Lectisternia, banquets of the gods among the Romans, ii. 84.
Legends, the holy, in the mysteries, i. 126.
Lemnian mysteries, i. 170.
Lemures and Lemuria among the Romans, ii. 91.
Lernæan mysteries, i. 173.
Lesbos, the island of, i. 17.
Letts and Lithuanians, i. 63.
Leucippus, a Greek atomist, i. 266.
Levana, a Roman goddess, ii. 53.
Levites, the Jewish, their designation, privileges, and duties, ii. 351.
Liber and Libera, Roman deities, ii. 51.
Liberalia, Roman festival, ii. 91.
Liberty (see Free-will).
Libitina, a Roman goddess of the lower world, ii. 52.
Lightning, a symbol of Zeus, i. 70; according to Etruscan teaching, ii. 6; Roman view of, ii. 105; observers of, ii. 102, 105.
Lithuanians, i. 63.
Liturgical personages of the Eleusinian mysteries, i. 177.
Lua, the wife of Saturn, ii. 38.
Luceres, the, an element of the Roman people, ii. 8.
Lucian on the future state, ii. 146; the schools of philosophy, ii. 153; the immorality of the myths, ii. 185.
Lucretius, his philosophical didactic poem, ii. 119.
Lucumones, the, an Etrurian noble family, ii. 4.
Lugdunensis, the Roman province of, in Gaul; its capital, i. 31.
Lugdunum, Lyons, i. 31.
Luna, Roman goddess of the moon, ii. 41; her temple in Rome, distinct from Diana, ii. 50.
Lupercalia, a Roman feast, ii. 37, 94.
Luperci, the most ancient of the Roman priests, ii. 68.
Lupercus, a title of Faunus, ii. 37.
Lustrations, religious purifications among the Romans, ii. 88.
Lutetia, Paris, i. 32.
Lycia, the Roman province of, its cities, i. 14.
Lydia, the Roman province of, i. 13.
Lydians, their character debased by their worship, i. 378.

MA, the principal goddess in Cappadocia and Pontus, i. 377; her worship by the Romans, ii. 174.
Maccabees, the last, i. 22; their rise, ii. 301.
Macedon, the Roman province of, i. 37.
Magadha, the Indian kingdom of, i. 49.
Magic, its connexion with pagan state-worships, ii. 210; with the Pythagorean and Platonic philosophy, ii. 211; media employed in, ii. 213; human sacrifice in, ii. 214.
Magism, or Magianism, origin, and rela-

tion to Persian dualism, i. 382; combated by Persian kings, i. 384; its power and science, i. 404.

Magnetism, in connexion with the oracles, i. 215.

Mamurus, probably Mars, and the procession of the Mamuralia, ii. 68.

Maia, a Roman goddess of death, ii. 44.

Mana Geneta, a Roman goddess of birth, ii. 57.

Manat, an Arabian god, i. 435.

Mania, a Roman goddess of death, ii. 53.

Manilius, a Roman poet, his pantheistic teaching, ii. 136.

Mannus, god and progenitor of the German race, ii. 115.

Mantic art, the (see Soothsaying).

Mantus, a god of the lower world, ii. 3.

Marcus Aurelius, the Roman emperor and philosopher, ii. 129; his superstition, ii. 175.

Marmarica, the Roman province of in Africa, i. 24.

Mars, Roman god of war, ii. 41.

Massilia, Marseilles, a seat of Greek civilisation, i. 31.

Mater Matuta, a Latin goddess, ii. 54.

Materialism of the Atomists, i. 266; of the Sophists, i. 271; of the Peripatetics, i. 346, 369; of the Stoics, i. 348, 369; of the Epicureans, i. 359.

Mathematical philosophy of the Pythagoreans, i. 254.

Matralia, a Roman festival, ii. 96.

Matrons, Celtic cultus of, ii. 112.

Manubiae, kinds of lightning, ii. 6.

Marriage, its sanctity among the Germans, i. 61; position in the Persian religion, i. 405; how celebrated by Romans, ii. 80, 253; monogamy among the Greeks, ii. 233; and Romans, ii. 253; a duty, ii. 234; forbidden by the Essenes, ii. 314; law of, lex Julia, enacted by Augustus, ii. 258; among Greeks, ii. 234, sq.; among Romans, ii. 253, sq.; among Jews, ii. 339.

Mauritania, the Roman province of, i. 25.

Maximus of Tyre, a Platonic philosopher, ii. 150.

Meat- and drink-offerings among the Jews, ii. 371.

Meditrinalia, a Roman wine-festival, ii. 97.

Megalesia, a Roman festival, ii. 95.

Megarian school of philosophy, i. 306.

Melicertes, a Corinthian mystery-god, i. 173.

Melissus, an Eleatic philosopher, i. 262.

Melkarth, a Tyrian god, i. 427.

Memphis, capital of lower Egypt, i. 438, 439, &c.

Men, a Phrygian deity, i. 160.

Mendes, an Egyptian deity, i. 443.

Mentu, an Egyptian deity, i. 440.

Mercury, his worship, ii. 43.

Meschia and Meschiane, the first human pair according to the Persian myth, i. 396; their resurrection, i. 411.

Mesopotamia, its fate in general, i. 45.

Messenians, their chief deities, i. 121.

Messias, the claims of the Jews upon the, ii. 328; expectation of, by Jews, ii. 328; by Romans, ii. 289; prophecies of, ii. 391, sq.

Metoeci, metics, Greek domiciled settlers, ii. 226, 227.

Michael the archangel, ii. 385.

Mimes, their demoralising influence among the Greeks and Romans, ii. 194.

Minerva, a Roman goddess, her nature and worship, her palladium, ii. 46.

Minos, a judge of the dead, i. 175.

Mistletoe, its high repute and use among the Druids, ii. 111.

Mithra, or Mithras, one of the Persian Izeds, his nature and office, i. 390; as mediator, his relation to Ormuzd, i. 413; as sun-god, i. 413; his mysteries, i. 415; conductor of souls, i. 416; degrees of initiation, for admission to his mysteries, i. 416.

Mnevis, one of the sacred bulls of the Egyptians, i. 458.

Moderatus, a Greek philosopher, ii. 149.

Moesia, the Roman province of, i. 38.

Moloch, his cultus of child-sacrifice among the Syrians, i. 426; at Carthage, i. 433.

Moirai, the Greek goddesses of destiny, i. 99.

Moon, the, worshiped as a male god, Lunus, i. 378.

Moon-goddess (see Luna).

Mother, the great, a Phrygian goddess, i. 374; also a Lydian and Bithynian, i. 376.

Mountain-peaks held sacred to Zeus, i. 70.

Mulciber, a surname of Vulcan, ii. 42.

Mummies, their treatment in Egypt, and guardian-god Anubis, i. 463.

Mundus, a cavity dedicated to the gods of the lower world, ii. 52.

Muses, i. 100.

Musonius, a Roman philosopher, ii. 127.

Mut, an Egyptian goddess, i. 450.

Mutilation, self, of heathen-priests, i. 376; ii. 178, &c.

Mutinus-Tutunus, a Roman phallus-god, ii. 56.

Mylitta, a chief-goddess in Babylon, i. 422.

Mysia, the Roman province of, i. 13.

Mystagogues, their office, i. 127.

Mysteries, nature of, in Greece, i. 125, sq.; how estimated by poets and philosophers, i. 131, sq.; by Christian apologists, i. 136; their effects, i. 195, 197; in Persia, i. 415; in Egypt, i. 480; in Rome, ii. 44.

Mysteriousness in the Greek religious system, i. 127.

Myths, allegorical interpretation of, by Greeks, i. 282; demoralising influence of, i. 283; obstinate clinging of people to, ii. 192, 193; foreign to the original Roman religious system, ii. 11; effect of Greek myths on Roman religion, ii. 12; mimic representations of, ii. 194.

INDEX. 431

NÆNIA, the personified death-wail, ii. 53.
Nanæa, a goddess of war (West Asiatic?), i. 420.
Narbonensis, a Roman province in Gaul, i. 30.
Nature, deification of, origin of heathenism, i. 65.
Nazaritism, the Jewish order of monks, ii. 358.
Neben (Saben?), an Egyptian goddess of births, i. 450.
Necromancy, ii. 213.
Neighbour, love of, in the Mosaic law, i. 344.
Neith, the Egyptian goddess, personified matter, i. 439, 449; her inscription at Lais, i. 439.
Nemesis, a Greek goddess, i. 99.
Neo-Cæsarea, capital of Pontus, i. 12.
Neo-Pythagoreans, school of, ii. 148.
Nephtys, an Egyptian goddess, i. 451.
Neptune, ii. 43.
Nereids, i. 80.
Nereus, i. 80.
Nerthus, German goddess of earth, ii. 115.
New Carthage, i. 24.
Nicomachus, the philosopher, ii. 149.
Nicomedia, capital of Bithynia, i. 12.
Nile-god, i. 449.
Ninive, i. 45.
Nona and Decima, ii. 57.
Nonæ Caprotinæ, a Roman festival, ii. 96.
Noricum, the Roman province of, i. 35.
Novensiles, Etrurian deities, ii. 2.
Nub, a surname of Typhon, i. 452.
Nubia, the kingdom of, i. 48.
Nudipedalia, pilgrimages of Roman matrons, ii. 78.
Numa, the Roman king and founder of religion, ii. 16; his spurious books, ii. 28.
Numbers, doctrine of Pythagorean, ii. 254.
Numenius, the Platonist, ii. 130.
Numidia, the Roman province of, i. 24.

OBSCENE paintings and statues, ii. 196.
Oceanos, i. 80.
Œnomaus against the oracles, ii. 205.
Olympia, plain of, the religious centre of Greece, i. 118.
Olympic games, i. 236; oracle, i. 215; republic of twelve gods, i. 77.
Opalia, a Roman festival, part of Saturnalia, ii. 98.
Opeconsivia, a Roman festival, ii. 97.
Ops, wife of Saturn, ii. 38.
Oracle system of the Greeks, attempts to explain their reputation, i. 209, sq.
Oracles in Asia-Minor, i. 214; revival of several of them, ii. 202; fresh longing after, ii. 205; explanations of their decay, ii. 204; writings against, ii. 205.
Orgies in the cultus of Cybele, i. 375; see the cultus of Dionysos in the Roman mysteries, ii. 23; in the mystery-worship of the Bona Dea, ii. 44; of Bellona at Rome, ii. 174; of Aphrodite, ii. 192.
Ormuzd, god of the Arians, i. 384; his names and nature, i. 385, sq.; his relation to Zervan and Ahriman, i. 387, sq.
Orpheotelests, i. 150, 157.
Orpheus and the Orphic mysteries, i. 138, sq.; the Orpheus of Æschylus, i. 142, 144; Orphic worship of Dionysos, i. 139, sq.; Orphic mystery-school, i. 144, sq.; Orphic mode of life, i. 151; connexion with the Dionysos worship, i. 154; with the Essene rule of life, ii. 311.
Osiris, his relation to the Orphic Dionysos, i. 144, sq.
Osiris, the Egyptian, i. 444, sq.; their judge of the dead, i. 461; his festivals, i. 468.
Osiris-bull, sacrifice of the, i. 474.
Ovid, the Roman poet, his religious ideas, ii. 137.

PAIDERASTIA, a vice common to the Greeks with most of the nations of antiquity, ii. 238; its peculiarly national form and extent among the Greeks, ii. 238; opinions of philosophers upon it, ii. 240; causes and effects of it, ii. 243; a joint cause of the decay of Persia, i. 405; its deep hold on Roman society, ii. 273.
Pales, a Roman god of the flocks, ii. 55.
Palestine, becomes a Roman province, divisions of it, i. 21.
Palilia, Roman festival of Pales, ii. 55, 95.
Palladium, the image of Minerva at Rome, ii. 47.
Pallas (see Athene).
Pamphylia, the Roman province of, i. 14.
Pan, his form and cultus among the Greeks, i. 97; resemblance to the Roman Faunus, ii. 37.
Pannonia, the Roman province of, i. 36.
Pantomimes (see Mimes).
Paphlagonia, the Roman province of, i. 11.
Paphos, old, renowned for its worship of Aphrodite, i. 16.
Paradise, belief of the Persians in, i. 397.
Parcæ, Roman goddesses of destiny, ii. 57.
Parentalia, Roman festival of the dead, ii. 90.
Parmenides, the Eleatic philosopher, his doctrine, i. 260.
Parthia, kingdom of, i. 44.
Parties in Jerusalem, and their contests, ii. 412.
Paschal festival, the Jewish, ii. 373.
Pascht, the Egyptian Artemis, i. 450; her festival at Bubastis, i. 469.
Patricians in Rome, their religious prerogatives, ii. 10.
Patulcius, a surname of Janus, ii. 36.
Pelasgi, their settlements and gods, i. 68.
Penates, Etrurian house-gods (Lares), ii. 2; Roman house-gods, ii. 61.
Penance, in the Old Testament, ii. 388; works of, among the Persians, ii. 407.
Pentapolis, the Roman province in Africa, i. 24.
Pentecost, the Jewish harvest-festival, ii. 374.
Pergamum, a city of Mysia, i. 13.

Peripatetic school, its materialistic bias, i. 346, 369.
Persephone, a Greek goddess, i. 92; original meaning of her name, i. 73.
Persian domination, its attitude towards the Egyptian religion, i. 484.
Persian religion, its founder, Zoroaster, i. 380, sq.; teaching about the gods, i. 385; demonology, i. 390; element-worship, i. 391; notions of world-history, i. 394; anthropology, i. 396; sacrificial system, i. 399; purifications, i. 406; ethics and marriage, i. 404; eschatology, i. 408; myth and worship of Mithras, i. 412, sq.
Phallus, a symbol of Hermes and fructification, i. 69; of Dionysos, i. 95; exhibition of it in the Eleusinia, i. 189; in the festivals of Osiris, its meaning, i. 482; at the Liberalia in Lavinium, ii. 51; a symbol of Priapus, ii. 56.
Pharaohs, Egyptian kings, their rich sacrificial offerings, i. 475; their deification, i. 486.
Pharisees (Scribes), the representatives and doctors of the Jewish nation, ii. 304, sq.; extension of the law by, ii. 308; doctrine of, concerning free-will and providence, ii. 310; their victory over the Sadducees, ii. 319.
Pherecydes of Syros, author of a cosmogony, i. 248.
Philippi, city of, i. 37.
Philo, the Jewish philosopher, ii. 398, sq.; his expectation of a Messias, ii. 331; his relation to pagan philosophy, his view of heathendom, ii. 400; derivation of Greek wisdom from Moses, ii. 400; his doctrine of the Deity, ii. 401; matter, ii. 401; dualism, ii. 401; the Logos, ii. 403, sq.; angels, and the souls of men, state after death, composition of the soul, ii. 405; the Fall, and original sin, ii. 407; his ethics, ii. 407; teaching about grace, ecstasies, his Messianic-chiliastic views, &c. ii. 408.
Philosophers, schools of, their position and influence, their decay, ii. 155-160.
Philosophy, Greek, i. 248, sq.; its rise from Hesiod's theogony, i. 249; its relations to the popular religion, i. 346; decay, i. 347, 370; Roman, ii. 118, sq.; its impotence to check the corruption of morals, ii. 286.
Phlya, the mysteries at, i. 176.
Phoenicia, the Roman province of, general description of the country, i. 21.
Phoenician worship of the gods, i. 432.
Phrygia, Roman province of, its cities and population, i. 14.
Phrygian gods and their cultus, i. 374.
Phthah, chief god at Memphis, i. 441.
Phuphluns, an Etrurian god, ii. 2.
Pindar, a Greek poet, his relations with mythology, i. 284; his distinct notion of a retributive state after death, i. 301.
Pisidia, a Roman province, i. 15.
Planets, astrological doctrine concerning their influence, ii. 208.

Plato, his decision upon the myths, i. 282; passes for a son of Apollo, i. 284; universality of his genius, i. 307; his philosophy, on God, i. 308; on ideas, i. 308; on the world and the world-soul, i. 310, sq.; on the star-gods, i. 313; anthropology of, i. 314; on the preexistence and immortality of the soul, i. 316; his determinism, i. 318; his proofs of immortality, i. 319; his migration of souls, i. 320; on the future state, evil, i. 321; his ethics, their connexion with the doctrine of ideas, i. 322; on death, i. 323; his ideal republic, i. 323; on exposition of children, i. 325; his position towards the popular religion and myths, i. 325; his relation to Christianity, i. 328; on paiderastia, ii. 240.
Platonism, the later, ii. 148; among the Romans, ii. 129; of Plutarch, ii. 131.
Plebs, the Roman, their religious position towards the patricians, ii. 9; their admission to the pontificate and augurate, ii. 23.
Pliny, his pantheistic views of religion, ii. 138.
Plutarch, his philosophy, ii. 131; on the myths, ii. 132; on immortality, ii. 145.
Pluto, god of the lower world, Dis compared to, ii. 52.
Poets, Greek, Homer and Hesiod, founders of the Hellenic religion, i. 75; Roman, their religious views, ii. 119, 136, sq.
Politics, Roman, i. 39.
Polyandria, established by law in Sparta, ii. 235.
Polybius on the Roman religion, ii. 135, 136.
Polygamy among the Jews, ii. 339.
Polytheism, its origin, i. 65.
Pomona, Roman goddess, ii. 56.
Pompey conquers Jerusalem, ii. 319.
Pontifex Maximus, the heathen Roman, ii. 64.
Pontifices, Roman priests, ii. 64; their office, ii. 65.
Pontus, Roman province, its population, i. 12; worship, i. 377.
Poor, their mastery over the rich in Athens, ii. 223; condition among the Jews, ii. 334; treatment by rich in Rome, ii. 277, sq.
Populifugium, a Roman festival, ii. 96.
Portumalia, a Roman festival, ii. 97.
Poseidon, a god of the sea, seat of his worship, i. 80.
Poverty overpowering in Rome, ii. 270.
Preëxistence of the soul according to the Pythagoreans, i. 258; according to Plato, i. 316; according to Cicero, ii. 142, 143.
Priapus, the Greek god, i. 97; the Roman god, ii. 56.
Priesthood, Eleusinian obliged to abstinence, i. 192; the Greek generally, i. 203; Persian, i. 405; Syro-Phoenician, i. 425, sq.; Egyptian, i. 470, sq.; Ro-

man, ii. 63; Gallic, ii. 113; German, ii. 116; Jewish, ii. 352.
Priestesses among the Greeks, i. 204, 205.
Priests, impostures practised by, ii. 198; consecration of, among the Jews, ii. 353; consecration of Jewish high-priest, ii. 357.
Privatum jus, the Roman (civil law of individuals), ii. 249.
Processions in the festivals of Dionysos, i. 155.
Prodicus, of Ceos, on the gods. i. 271; punished with death as an atheist, i. 273.
Prodigies, the means to expiate them taken by the Romans, ii. 99.
Proletariate in Rome, ii. 270.
Prometheus, myth of, in Æschylus, i. 297.
Prophets, the Egyptian priests called, i. 471; the Jewish, their energy and zeal, ii. 361; false, ii. 411.
Proselytes, two classes of, among the Jews, ii. 366.
Proserpine, Roman goddess of the lower world, ii. 52.
Prostitution, in connexion with heathen worship, in Lydia, i. 380; in Armenia, i. 418; in Babylonia, i. 422; in Syria, i. 428; in Egypt, i. 473; in connexion with paiderastia, ii. 238, sq.
Protagoras, the Greek sophist, i. 270; persecuted as an atheist, i. 273.
Proteus, i. 80.
Provinces of the Roman empire, their condition generally, i. 6, sq.
Psychagogues, or necromancers, i. 216.
Psychology (see Souls).
Psychomantein, i. 216.
Ptolemies, their relation to the Egyptian religion, i. 485; their deification, i. 486.
Public spectacles, ii. 281.
Punishment, Jewish system of, ii. 347.
Punishments for religious crimes among the Greeks, i. 243; in a future state, according to Egyptians, ii. 466; to Pindar and the Orphici, i. 301; to Plutarch and the later Greeks, ii. 145, sq.
Purification and purity, religious, in the Eleusinia, i. 191; in the Greek religion, i. 219; in the Persian, i. 406; of the Egyptian priests, i. 473; of the Romans, ii. 82, 88, 179; media of purification to the Persians, i. 404; the Essenes, ii. 313.
Purification, sacrifices of, among Romans, ii 88; among Jews, ii. 349, 375.
Purim, Jewish festival of, ii. 375.
Pyrrho, a sceptic philosopher, i. 365.
Pythagoras, his initiation into the Orphic mysteries, i. 151; his association, i. 254; his metempsychosis, i. 258.
Pythagoreans, their connexion with the Orphici, i. 150; their manner of life, i. 151; their philosophy, i. 254.
Pythagoreans, new, ii. 148;" their connexion with magic, ii. 211; with the Essenes, ii. 316.
Pythia, the Delphic prophetess, i. 210.

QUIETISM of the Buddhists, i. 54.

Quinquatria, a Roman festival, ii. 94.
Quirinus, a surname of Janus, ii. 37.
Quirites, a name of the Romans, ii. 7.

RA, Egyptian sun-god, i. 138.
Rabbinism, ii. 416.
Ram, an attribute of the Egyptian god Amnon, i. 441.
Ramnes, ii. 7.
Religion, imperial, the Roman, ii. 160-162 (see Imperial).
Religion, its relation to philosophy among the Greeks, i. 346, 369, sq.; mixed up with superstition, ii. 170; its decay among the Romans, ii. 174; crimes against, and their punishment, among the Greeks, i. 243; among the Romans, i. 163.
Religious tolerance of the Greeks, ii. 164; of the Romans, ii. 162.
Religiousness of the Greek philosophers and poets, i. 281; of the Roman poets and historians, ii. 135.
Resolutions, the eighteen, drawn up in the house of the Zealot Eleazar, ii. 412.
Resurrection, Persian doctrine of, i. 409, 411; Hebrew doctrine of, ii. 390.
Rhadamanthus, a judge of the dead, i. 175.
Rhætia, Roman province of, i. 35.
Rhea, Samothracian mystery-goddess, i. 167.
Rhodes, island of, its population, i. 16.
Rites, sacrificial, in use among Greeks, i. 232; among Romans, ii. 78.
Robigalia, a Roman festival, ii. 95.
Roman empire, its extent and population, i. 1; army, i. 4; language (Latin) i. 40.
Romanising of different people, i. 39.
Roman law, of the citizen, ii. 249; of the stranger, ii. 251; of families and of marriage, ii. 252.
Roman national character, ii. 248, sq.
Roman philosophy, ii. 118, sq.
Roman religious system, historical development, ii. 7, sq.; the several gods, ii. 35, sq.; the priesthood, ii. 63, sq.; forms of worship, ii. 75, sq.; empire-religion, ii. 160; apotheosis, ii. 165; superstition, ii. 170; decay of, ii. 173, sq.
Roman slavery, ii. 259, sq.
Rome, the city of, its splendour and population, its social and moral state, i. 5; ii. 248, sq.; its influence, and the gentle nature of its rule in the heart of the empire, i. 41.

SABAZIA, private mysteries of the Greeks, i. 201.
Sabazius, his worship in Phrygia, i. 376.
Sabbath, law of Jewish, ii. 349.
Sabbatical year, ii. 350.
Sabines, an element of the Roman people, ii. 7.
Sacæ, kingdom of the, i. 50.
Sacæan festival in Persia, i. 419.
Sacrifices, system of Greek, i. 225, sq.; Persian, i. 399, sq.; Egyptian, i. 474, sq.; Roman, ii. 78, sq.; Gallic, ii. 110;

German, ii. 116; Jewish, ii. 366; rites of Greek, i. 233; Persian, i. 402; Egyptian, i. 474; Roman, ii. 80; Jewish, ii. 367; cessation of Jewish, ii. 415; inspection of victim at Greek, i. 207; at Roman, ii. 100; banquets of, Greek, i. 233; Persian, i. 402; Roman, ii. 84; Jewish, ii. 370; cakes of, Roman, ii. 84; king of, Roman, ii. 63, 66.
Sadducees, origin of, and doctrines, ii. 302; position towards people, ii. 303.
Sais, a city of Egypt, the famous inscription of the goddess Neith at, i. 439.
Salii, Roman priests of Mars, ii. 63.
Samaria, country and city of, i. 23; separation from Judah, and fall of, ii. 293.
Samaritans, their medley religion and enmity against the Jews, i. 23, ii. 295.
Samos, island of, i. 17.
Samothrace, mysteries on the island of, i. 163, sq.
Samuel, prophet and founder of schools of the prophets, ii. 359.
Sancus Fidius, a Roman god, ii. 58.
Sandon, Heracles, sun-god, his worship in Lydia, i. 379.
Sardinia under Roman rule, i. 11.
Sarmatia, Sarmatians and their settlements, i. 62.
Satan, in the Old Testament, ii. 385.
Sate, an Egyptian goddess, i. 452.
Saturn, his nature and cultus, ii. 38.
Saturnalia, a Roman festival, ii. 97.
Saul, king of the Jews, ii. 292.
Schammai, a Jewish teacher, his doctrine and school, ii. 334.
School or Sheol, the under world, ii. 389.
School education among the Greeks, ii. 231; among the Romans, ii. 279.
Schools of philosophy (see Philosophy).
Scribes (see Pharisees).
Scriptures, the holy, of the Jews, ii. 377.
Seb, an Egyptian god, i. 452.
Sebaste, city of, earlier Samaria, i. 23.
Sects, religious, of the Brahmins, i. 51.
Seleucia, its greatness and flourishing condition, i. 47.
Self-mutilation of Galli, i. 375.
Semiramis, i. 424.
Seneca, the Roman philosopher, of Spanish descent, i. 27; his philosophy, ii. 125; on God and the world, on man, ii. 126; on the popular religion, ii. 127.
Sephoris, a city in Galilee, i. 23.
Seraphim, ii. 385.
Serapis, an Egyptian god, introduction of his worship there, i. 485; into Rome, ii. 178.
Scepticism, its aim, ataraxia, i. 365; its definition according to Sextus, i. 366.
Sceptics, i. 365, 369.
Serpent, the, in Paradise, ii. 385.
Serpents, symbolical meaning of, in the mysteries, i. 183; fed by the Vestals, ii. 71; silver ones in the Isis worship, ii. 177.
Serpent's-egg, the so-called, among the Druids, ii. 112.
Sethlans, the Vulcan of the Etruscans, ii. 2.

Sex, double, of heathen deities, i. 70, 71, 400.
Sextius, Quintus, a Roman philosopher, ii. 123.
Sextus, a Greek philosopher, his definition of scepticism, i. 366.
Sibylline books, their appearance, and their use, ii. 106; their interpretation, ii. 23, 74.
Sichem, a city of Samaria, i. 23.
Sicily, condition of the island under the Romans, i. 10.
Sigillaria, a Roman festival, ii. 98.
Silence adjoined on the mystæ, i. 194.
Silvanus, a Roman god (same as Faunus?), ii. 37; god of the woods, ii. 53.
Sin (see Evil).
Sirmium, a city of Pannonia, i. 36.
Slaves and slavery among Greeks, ii. 226; views of, and particularly Aristotle's, ii. 227; their numbers, ii. 227; treatment, ii. 230; morals, 230; disadvantages of slavery, 231; among the Romans, slave-law, ii. 259, sq.; number of slaves, ii. 262; effects of slavery on the free population, ii. 267; their condition among the Jews, ii. 343.
Slaves, dwellings and manner of life of the Slave tribes, i. 62.
Smyrna, i. 13.
Socharis, an Egyptian god, i. 442.
Socrates, i. 273; his personal appearance, [274; ethics, 275; psychology and theology, 276; relation to the popular religion, 277; attraction of his teaching, 278; impeachment, 279; death, 280; views of immortality, 303; bearing towards paiderastia, ii. 240.
Socratic schools, i. 304.
Sol, the Roman god, ii. 40.
Solomon, king of the Jews, ii. 292.
Soothsaying (see Divination).
Somnambulism in connexion with the oracles, i. 216.
Sopherim or Jewish teachers of the law, ii. 209; their relation to the Pharisees, ii. 304.
Sophists, their tendency blamed by Plato, i. 270; their atheism and reaction against, i. 271-73.
Sophocles, his relation to religion, i. 290-293.
Sosiosch, the Persian redeemer and prophet, i. 411.
Sotion, Seneca's master, ii. 123.
Soul, the human, its immortality and state after death, the Pythagoreans, i. 256; the Eleusinia, i. 196; the Orphici and Pindar, i. 301; Herodotus, i. 302; Socrates, i. 303; Plato, i. 304, 318; Aristotle, i. 338; belief of the Persians, i. 409; of the Egyptians, i. 462; of the Druids, ii. 110; of Cicero, ii. 141; of Plutarch, ii. 145; doctrine of its materiality and dissolution, the Atomists, i. 267, 301; Ionians, i. 301; Eleats, i. 302; the elder Stoics, i. 352; the later, ii. 139; the Peripatetics, i. 346; the Epicureans, i. 360; general unbelief, ii. 143; comfortlessness, ii. 146.

Souls, festival of, among the Persians, i. 403.
Spain, Roman province of, i. 25.
Spanish-Roman school, names of its poets and philosophers, i. 27.
Spartan state, its constitution, ii. 222; its legislation on marriage, ii. 235.
Spectacles, public Greek and Roman, ii. 195.
Speusippus, Greek philosopher, i. 330.
Sramins, an Indian sect, i. 51.
Stars, the, divine and having souls, according to the teaching of Plato, i. 313; of the later Platonists and Pythagoreans, ii. 150, sq.; of Aristotle, i. 336; have a purifying influence, according to the Persians, i. 394; their worship generally, i. 66; their worship by the Chaldeans in particular, i. 422.
State, relation of individual to the, among the Greeks, ii. 221; among the Romans, ii. 259; Plato's ideal, i. 323.
Stoicism, Greek, its founder, i. 348; material tendency, i. 348, 369; its doctrines, i. 349; position towards the popular religion, i. 353; ethics, i. 354; errors in morals, self-esteem, i. 356; suicide, i. 357; Roman, ii. 123, sq.; its material pantheism, ii. 124; doctrine of immortality, ii. 140, sq.
Stoics, the later, and Roman moral corruption, ii. 284, sq.
Stolists, an order in the Egyptian priesthood, i. 471.
Stones, worship of, among the Pelasgi, i. 69; among the later Greeks and Romans, ii. 186.
Strabo, his judgment upon the popular religion, ii. 136.
Strato, the natural philosopher, i. 346.
Suevi, their settlements, i. 60.
Suicide, views of Stoics on, i. 357; its prevalence in Rome, ii. 283.
Summanus, god of lightning, ii. 40.
Sun, origin of his worship, i. 67; his worship among the Pelasgi, i. 71; Persians, i. 393; Romans, ii. 40; Essenes, ii. 314.
Sun-god, in Lydia Heracles, or Sandon, i. 379; in Syria Elagabal, i. 431; in Egypt Ra, i. 438.
Superstition, of Greeks and Romans, blended with religiousness, ii. 170, sq.; examples of, Sylla, Augustus, Alexander, ii. 172; Marcus Aurelius, ii. 175.
Suovetaurilia, a peculiar sacrifice of atonement among the Romans, ii. 81.
Sutech, a surname of Typhon, i. 452.
Symbols in the mysteries, i. 183, 188.
Synagogue, the great, its origin and object, ii. 298.
Synagogues, or houses of prayer, ii. 376.
Synedrium, or Sanhedrim, the Jewish court of justice, ii. 337; Sanhedrim and school of Jamnia, ii. 416.
Syria, Roman province of, its Greek character, i. 19; cultus of Baal, i. 425.
Syrian goddess, the, her nature and worship, i. 422.

TACITUS, what he asserts regarding the Germans, i. 61; ii. 113; regarding the Slaves, i. 63; his religious views, ii. 139.
Tages, a genius of the Etruscans, ii. 3.
Tagetic discipline, the, ii. 4.
Taranis, a Gallic deity, ii. 112.
Tarsus, capital of Cilicia, i. 15.
Taurobolia, atonements made by blood, ii. 179.
Toletæ, the first degree of Eleusinian initiation. i. 191.
Tellus, a Roman goddess, her worship, ii. 43.
Terminalia, a Roman festival, ii. 94.
Terminus, Roman god of boundaries, ii. 53.
Temple of Jerusalem and its parts, ii. 362; rebuilt by Herod, ii. 322; destruction of, under Titus, and its consequences, ii. 414; hopes of its restoration, ii. 415; dedication of the, a Jewish festival, ii. 375.
Temple, Capitoline, ii. 19.
Temples, their destination and use among the Greeks, i. 239, sq.; haunts of impurity, ii. 197; of religious imposture, 198, sq.
Temple-scribes, the Egyptian, their office, i. 471.
Terentius Varo, attempts to restore the Roman religion, ii. 34.
Teutates, a god of the Gauls, ii. 112.
Thales, an Ionic philosopher, i. 250.
Thammuz (Adonis), a Syro-Phœnician deity, his worship, i. 431.
Thebes, city of Egypt, i. 19; of Greece, with a secret worship, i. 172.
Themis, a Greek deity, i. 98; her cultus, the thesmophoria, i. 200.
Theocracy, the blending of gods, i. 84, 164, 342, sq.
Theodore of Cyrene, an atheist philosopher, i. 305.
Theogony, the Greek, settled by Homer and Hesiod, i. 75.
Theoleptics (Fanatici), possessed people, ii. 182.
Theology, Egyptian, i. 479.
Theopœa, the consecration of the idols, ii. 184.
Theophany, pretended, of the heathen gods, ii. 201.
Theophrastus the peripatetic, i. 347.
Therapeutæ, Jewish ascetics, their mode of life, ii. 317.
Thesmophoria, a secret rite of Ceres, i. 200.
Thessalian gods, i. 118.
Thessalonica, a city of Macedonia, i. 37.
Thetis, a Greek goddess, i. 80; her temple in Pharsalos, i. 118.
Theurgy, the highest kind of magic, how employed, ii. 215.
Thoth-Hermes, an Egyptian god, a judge of the dead, i. 448.
Thrace, Roman province of, i. 37.
Thracians, i. 38; their share in the religious civilisation of Greece, i. 68.
Threats used to Egyptian gods, i. 481.
Thucydides, his religious belief, i. 285.

Thunaer, a German god, ii. 115.
Tiberias, a city of Galilee, i. 23.
Tinia, the Jupiter of the Etruscans, ii. 2.
Titans, conquered by Zeus, i. 76.
Tities, an element of the Roman people, ii. 7.
Trade, left by Greeks to their slaves and strangers, ii. 224; looked down upon in Rome, ii. 269.
Tradition, Jewish, ii. 378.
Trees, some, considered sacred by Gauls and Germans, ii. 116.
Trinity, a, in the teaching of Plato (?), i. 329.
Triptolemus, a Greek judge of the dead, i. 175.
Triton, a Greek god, i. 80.
Trophonius, cave of, i. 215.
Tschinavad, Persian bridge to heaven, i. 409.
Tuisco, god and progenitor of the German race, ii. 116.
Turan, the Aphrodite of the Etruscans, ii. 3.
Turms, an Etruscan god, ii. 2.
Twelve, the, principal Greek gods, i. 77; their worship in common, i. 120.
Typhæus, one of the giants, i. 76.
Typhon, an Egyptian deity, i. 445; his character, i. 452; introduction of his worship, i. 483.

UNBELIEF of the Greek philosophers (see Scepticism); of the Roman philosophers, ii. 143.
Unmarried state, discountenanced by the Persians, i. 406; Greeks, ii. 235; Augustus, ii. 258.
Uranos or Ouranos, a Greek god, i. 70, 77, 283.
Urim and Thummim, the oracle of the Jews, ii. 355.
Usil, sun-god of the Etruscans, ii. 2.
Usury, Mosaic law of, ii. 345.
Utica, a city in Africa, i. 24.
Uzza, an Arabian god, i. 435.

VARRO, see Terentius, ii. 34.
Vaticanus, a Roman god, ii. 53.
Vedius, an Etruscan judge of the dead, ii. 3.
Veiled gods of the Etruscans, ii. 1.
Vejovis or Vedius, a Roman god, ii. 40.
Venus, her cultus among the Romans, ii. 50.
Vertumnus, an Etrurian god, ii. 2; an old Latin god, ii. 56.
Vesta, Roman goddess, her worship, ii. 45.
Vestalia, a Roman festival, ii. 96.
Vestals, their office and privileges, ii. 69.
Vicramaditya, an Indian king, i. 50.
Viduus, a Roman god of the dead, ii. 53.
Vinalia, Roman festival, ii. 95, 97.
Vindelicia, a Roman province, i. 35.
Vindobona, Vienna, i. 36.
Virgil, his religious belief, ii. 137.
Virginity, considered a misfortune by the Greeks, ii. 235; voluntary among the Jews, i. 342.
Vows, Roman, ii. 77; Jewish, ii. 372.

Vulcan, an Etruscan god, ii. 2; a Roman, ii. 42.
Vulcanalia, the Roman festival of Vulcan, ii. 97.

WATER, blest, in the temples, a means of religious purification, i. 220; held sacred by the Persians, i. 393.
Water-gods of the Greeks, i. 79.
Wisdom, the divine, or Chokma, in the Old Testament, ii. 383.
Wives, community of, among the ancient Britons, i. 34; the Spartans, ii. 235.
Wodan, god of the Germans, ii. 114, 116.
Women in child-birth regarded as causing defilement, i. 220; excessive religiousness of Greek and Roman, ii. 183; their licentiousness in Sparta, ii. 236.
World, doctrine of Pythagoreans concerning, i. 255; of Empedocles, i. 263; Plato, i. 311; of Aristotle, i. 334, sq.; of the Stoics, i. 349; succession of worlds, i. 351; eternity of, according to Aristotle, i. 334; to the book of the world, i. 334; creation of, cosmogony, according to Pherecydes, i. 248; to Thales and Anaximander, i. 250; to Anaximenes and Diogenes, i. 251; to Heraclitus, i. 252; to the Pythagoreans, i. 255; to the Atomists, i. 266; to Plato, i. 10; burning of, Persian, i. 412; burning of, Stoic, i. 351; judgment of, Persian, i. 411.
World-soul, among the Ionians, i. 250, sq.; among the Pythagoreans, i. 256; of Plato, i. 310; of the Stoics, i. 349.
World-year, world-periods, Persian, i. 394.

XENOCRATES, the Platonic philosopher, i. 331.
Xenophanes, the Eleat, his polemics against the popular religion, and his philosophy, i. 259.

YGDRASIL, the Scandinavian ash, i. 250.
Youth, their education and instruction among the Greeks, i. 231; among the Romans, i. 279; ruined by slaves, i. 281.

ZAGREUS DIONYSOS, god of the Cretans, i. 145; centre of the Orphic teaching, i. 153; one with Osiris, Adonis, Corybas, i. 161; his relation to the Eleusinian Dionysos, i. 180; physical interpretation of his myth, i. 199.
Zaratus or Zarades, distinct from Zoroaster, i. 381.
Zealots, a Jewish faction against Roman rule, their reign of terror, ii. 325.
Zendavesta, the Persian holy books, their origin, i. 380.
Zeno, the Eleat, i. 262; the Stoic, i. 348.
Zerinthian grotto, the place of the mysteries of Hecate, i. 170.
Zervan Akarana, a god of the Persians, originally a stranger to them, i. 387; his relation to Ormuzd and Ahriman, i. 138.

Zeus, the Pelasgian primal god and god of heaven, i. 70; his three-eyed image of carved wood, i. 70; the Hellenic, vanquisher of Chronos, i. 76; king of the Olympic gods and ruler of the world, i. 77; his wives, i. 79; his cultus at Athens, i. 116; temple and statue at Olympia, i. 118; Crete, the pretended country of his birth, i. 119; his relation to Prometheus, i. 293; his name in Asia Minor, the specific one of the male deities, i. 374.

Zeus of Sinope, the Egyptian Serapis, i. 486.

Zin, a god of the Germans, ii. 115.

Zoroaster, or Zarathustra, founder of religion, his probable era, he is not to be confounded with Zaratus, i. 380, sq.

THE END.

www.ingramcontent.com/pod-product-compliance
Lightning Source LLC
Chambersburg PA
CBHW030323020526
44117CB00030B/960